THE
ACKERMAN
CHARLES HEIDSIECK
GUIDE

to the best
hotels and restaurants
in Great Britain and Ireland

First published 1994 by Leading Guides Ltd
35 Tadema Road, London SW10 0PZ

© Leading Guides Limited, 1994
35 Tadema Road, London SW10 0PZ

Paintings by Alan Halliday
Charles Heidsieck illustration by Chris Ackerman-Eveleigh
Cover design by Alan Halliday & Chris Ackerman-Eveleigh

Contents

CHAMPAGNE

Charles Heidsieck

REIMS FRANCE

The Taste for Champagne

Joie de vivre

Although champagne has always been synonymous with the Champagne region in France, good living, *joie de vivre*, and particularly love, it is ironic to find that some claimants say that the English (today the largest importers) were the first to make and drink a méthode traditionelle sparkling wine.

After the Restoration in 1660, the great wit and arbiter of taste, the Marquis de St Evremond, exiled from the court of Louis XIV, reintroduced the wines of the Champagne region, the district around Reims, to the north-east of France, to the court of Charles II. These highly-prized wines (described as 'the ordinary drink of kings and princes') had been well-known to the English since the 16th century - both Henry VIII and Cardinal Wolsey received 'shipments of wine from Aÿ'. In 1664, the Earl of Bedford bought three casks of wine from Verzenay that, like the other wines of the Champagne region, was much admired for its *pétillant* (lively) qualities. The wine was decanted into bottles and corked, (there is an entry in the Woburn cellar-book for twelve gross of corks), the secondary fermentation that produces the bubbles took place in the Spring, and so the first 'champaign' was made.

This sparkling wine became very popular in England. In one of many contemporary references, Sir George Etheredge in his *The Man and the Mode* produced in 1676 refers to its beneficial qualities:

> To the Mall and the Park,
> Where we love till 'tis dark,
> Then Sparkling Champaign
> Puts an end to their reign;
> It quickly recovers
> Poor languishing lovers,
> Makes us frolic and gay, and drowns all sorrow;
> But alas we relapse again on the morrow.

Refining the style

The honour of first developing champagne has been attributed to a Benedictine monk, Pierre Pérignon, nearly three decades later. Appointed chief cellarman of the Monastery of Hautvillers in 1668, he spent twenty years experimenting with the natural sparkle in the wines of the region to make a better approximation of the champagne we know and love today. He recognised the three essentials for the making of good champagne - a find blend, a good cork, and a strong bottle. A master blender, he could tell exactly where each batch of grapes came from just by their scent, a gift heightened after he went blind towards the end of his life. With his great skill, he could make a consistently superior *cuvée*, or blend.

The Roman method of sealing bottles and amphora with the bark of the cork tree was lost in France during the 5th century AD, and Brother Pierre found that the 17th century wooden bottle-stoppers wrapped in hemp were useless for retaining the effervescence after secondary fermentation. However, he rediscovered the cork for France, so the story goes, when he saw how the water bottles of two Spanish monks from Santiago de Compostela were sealed. He requested supplies of the bark from Spain from which he developed his superior cork.

Such was the pressure in the bottle during the secondary fermentation (equivalent to the tyre pressure of today's jumbo jet), Brother Pierre used *verre anglais* for his bottles. This superior glass was so called after Admiral Sir Robert Mansell, worried about the future of British shipbuilding through the decimation of the English forests by the charcoal burners, petitioned James I to forbid wood-fired glass furnaces. The glass-makers were forced to use coal which, with the higher temperature, made for much stronger glass. Even with this superior English glass, explosions were common. Cellarmen in the 18th and 19th centuries wore iron masks for protection, and were given the glass shards to sell as compensation. The bottles of the 17th and 18th centuries were 'globe and spike' shape - like an onion with a tapering spout.

The Age of elegance

The development of champagne at the end of the 17th century complemented the new Age of Elegance. Louis XIV loved champagne, but was denied it by his doctor towards the end of his life. The king should have been attended by the other royal doctor, the nonagenarian Du Chesne, who ascribed his longevity to drinking only champagne. Champagne flowed at the court of Phillipe, Duc d'Orléans, Saint-Simon who declared that he drank 'too much champagne to be becoming in a Regent of France'. Vast quantities were drunk at his notorious orgies and candle-lit *petits soupers* at the Palais Royal by *roués* and their mistresses - the term roué comes from the Regent's notion that these men were so wicked that they should be broken 'on the wheel', *la roue*. The famous Duchesse du Berry invariably went to bed drunk on champagne, and even died of a surfeit of it.

Champagne was the favoured drink of Louis XV. When he visited Reims in 1741, four fountains spouted sparkling champagne in his honour. His mistress, the intelligent Madame de Pompadour who made his court one of the most civilised ever, was also a devotee. It was she who declared that 'Champagne gives brilliance to the eyes without flushing the face' and the well-known maxim, that champagne 'is the only wine that leaves a woman beautiful after drinking it' is attributed to her too. Quantities of champagne were drunk during the reign of Louis XVI, but not one bottle more sad than the one he drank on 20 January 1793 when imprisoned in the Temple the night before he went to the guillotine.

While destroying everything else of the *ancien régime*, the French Revolutionaries did, however, share their taste for champagne. Danton bathed in it with his mistress, Camille Desmoulins. They, too, drank champagne *(Aÿ pétillant)* in the tumbril going to the guillotine in the Place de la Concorde singing *'Vive l'Aÿ et la liberté*! In 1848, there was another instance of the iniquitous habit of bathing in champagne with a similar end result. Ibrahim Pasha, eldest son of Mohammed Ali, Vali (ruler) of Egypt, plunged into a silver bath filled with ice-cold champagne after reviewing his troops in the desert. He caught a chill and soon (rightly) died.

Every corner of the globe

Nor was the passion for champagne confined to the French aristocracy, Revolutionaries or later Egyptian commanders. In Russia, champagne was introduced to the court of Peter the Great, although it was his daughter, the Empress Elizabeth who was so enamoured of champagne that it superseded the sweet Hungarian wine Tokay for official toasts. In the 18th century, the English were devotees also when tariffs, trade restrictions, and price allowed. The great London Clubs stocked their cellars with vast quantities of champagne, and it was said that at Crockfords, the London gaming club, the rattle of the dice was masked by the pop of champagne corks. George II was addicted to champagne, as was his Steward of the Household, Lord Chesterfield, probably better remembered for his letters to his son (and lending his name to an overcoat and a sofa), than for his considerable diplomatic career. In reply to a toast he would bellow:

> Give me champagne, and fill it to the brim,
> I'll toast in bumpers (a large glass) ev'ry lovely limb.

In a similar vein, The Connoisseur magazine recorded in 1754 that a group of young aristocrats at Vauxhall Gardens, the famous pleasure grounds in London, were entertaining a celebrated *fille de joie*. One of them removed her shoe, filled it with champagne, toasted her, then drank it in one draught. Carried away by her beauty, he then ordered the shoe to be served up for supper. The chef rose to the occasion and made a *ragoût* of the upper, minced the sole, then chopped the wooden heel up into thin slices which he dipped in batter and served as garnish. History does not record the outcome of the meal nor the result of the gallant toast!

Throughout the centuries, champagne has affected different people in different ways - as Kipling observed, 'If the aunt of the vicar has never touched liquor, look out when she finds the champagne'! Lady Hamilton, wife of Sir William and mistress of Lord Nelson, positively revelled in champagne. In her travel book, *Soujourn among the German Courts*, Mrs St George recorded that at the British residence in Dresden, 'Lady Hamilton drunk more champagne than she thought a lady capable of', then entertained

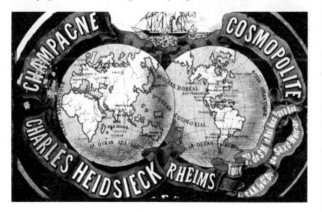

the other guests with her impression of classical statuary. Nelson was delighted and toasted her with more champagne, while Sir William 'lay down on his back, with his arms and legs in the air, and in this position bounded all round the room like a ball, with his stars and ribbons flying around him'. Beau Brummell used the finest champagne for cleaning his boots. Such was the cost of champagne at that time, he complained that his 'blacking was positively ruinous'. Champagne was more appealing to Surtees' lovable huntsman, the fictional Jorrocks who pronounced that it gave him '*werry* gentlemanly ideas'.

Very English tastes

Taste and habits change from country to country and decade to decade, and nowhere is this more apparent than with champagne. Up to the middle of the 19th century, most champagne was artificially sweetened before shipment. In 1848, a London wine merchant tasted a *cuvée* in its natural state and asked for this unsweetened wine to be shipped to England. While the Russians continued to drink their champagne sweet, the Victorians immediately took to the 'dry' champagnes, and the fashion has lasted ever since then. Even the Prime Minister Gladstone was a supporter, as Lord Houghton wrote:

> Trace we the workings of that wondrous brain,
> Warmed by one bottle of our dry Champagne

In England, the sweeter champagne was drunk on its own or with the dessert course of dinner only. Dry champagne could be drunk throughout the meal, so complementing every course. Sales of champagne rocketed throughout the 19th century. It was drunk by everyone, from 'stage door Johnnies' and chorus girls to members of the Royal Family. The Prince of Wales and his Marlborough House Set drank copiously. At that time, champagne was drunk out of an unsatisfactorily shaped glass called a *coupe*, like a bowl on a thin stem, as opposed to a proper flute glass. The 'Marlborough House Glass' had a hollow stem and was named after the group that made it popular. The Prince of Wales preferred pink champagne and had it decanted into a crystal jug so that he could help himself without resorting to what for him would have been the vulgar practice of handling a bottle. It was not uncommon to decant champagne at that time, particularly when served as an aperitif before lunch.

Champagne has been given many nick-names, none pejorative, though many are unworthy sobriquets. Some were personal, like 'the boy' properly used only by those who shot one day with Edward VII. At some Edwardian shoots, it was the practice for a boy to go round the guns after each drive with a wheelbarrow filled with champagne on a bed of ice. On that occasion, it was so hot that the guns continually shouted for 'the boy'. Later the epithet for the lad himself was transferred to the champagne he carried.

The passion for drinking champagne in all parts of the world can, in part, be attributed to the unerring dedication over the last three hundred years of the representatives of the various champagne houses. At the turn of the 18th century, the Marquis de Sillery had gambled away everything but his estate with its fine reputation for producing excellent champagne at Verzenay. The Marquis, a particular favourite at the court of Louis XIV, took a final gamble and gave a sumptuous dinner for all the oenophilist figures of society at Versailles. When the guests were at their most receptive, a bevy of girls dressed as Bacchanals placed before each guest what appeared to be a basket of flowers, but was a bottle of champagne garlanded with flowers. The guests were delighted. The gamble paid off. Champagne became the favoured wine for French society, and so the Sillery fortunes were fully restored.

Charles-Camille Heidsieck

The taste for champagne spread throughout the 18th century, from Russia to America. Champagne houses sprang up to meet the new demand. One such house was that founded by Florens-Louis Heidsieck, the son of a Lutheran pastor from Schleswig-Holstein in 1785. He enjoyed an almost instant success, though the competition between his and the other champagne houses was fierce. During the Napoleonic Wars, representatives of the major champagne houses followed the armies in the hope that their brand would be the one drunk by the victor - it was said that 'wherever French troops were to be found - in Germany, Poland, Moravia - an agent of Heidsieck was never far behind'. Napoleon (who thought that 'champagne banishes etiquette'), held the firm belief that champagne was essential to battle - 'in victory you deserve it, in defeat you need it'.

Childless, Florens-Louis Heidsieck drew on a plentiful supply of German nephews to help him. One of them Charles-Henri Heidsieck, aged just 21, was sent to Russia. Accompanied by his servant and a pack horse laden with samples, he rode a white horse first to Moscow, then to Nijnii-Novgorod on the Volga where traders from all over Russia gathered for the annual fair where furs, leather and tea were exchanged. When Napoleon's army arrived in Moscow the next year, they heard tell of the renowned Charles-Henri and his white horse. Subsequently, he travelled for the firm widely throughout the Balkans before returning to Reims where he married. He died in 1824 leaving a two-year-old son, Charles-Camille.

Charles-Camille Heidsieck founded the present House of Charles Heidsieck in 1851 when he was 29. He had inherited that magic touch of his forebears for making champagne, which indeed characterises the brand today. Not only did he produce the finest champagne, he was also able to combine his highly developed love of adventure and sport (he was one of the best shots in France) with his undoubted skill as a salesman. Much in the pioneer spirit of his father, he often travelled to the United States. His first visit was in 1857, where this 'pistol-packing champagne magnate tickled the fancy of the Americans' who dubbed him 'Champagne Charlie'. A decade later, Charles-Camille Heidsieck was immortalised by George Leybourne in the popular music hall song, 'Champagne Charlie'. The song fitted the age, and swept through London like wildfire. Most people believed that the *jeunesse dorée* had nothing else to do but stop up all night, spend money like water and drink champagne.

Famous moments

There have been (and indeed still are) many loyal supporters of Charles Heidsieck Champagne, not least amongst them Otto von Bismarck - he once boasted that he wanted to drink 5,000 bottles of champagne in his lifetime, a feat he probably achieved after he emptied the Chancery wine cellars on his resignation as Chancellor. Once, when dining with Kaiser Wilhelm I, he was served Sekt, rather than his beloved Charles Heidsieck, 'as a patriotic gesture'. When the Kaiser remonstrated with him for eschewing the German sparkling wine, the Chancellor replied simply, 'Your Majesty, I am extremely sorry. My patriotism stops short of my stomach!'

The Kaiser took the remark badly, but at least it did not cause the diplomatic incident surrounding the launch of his grandson Wilhelm II's yacht, *Meteor*, at a New York shipyard when a bottle of champagne was substituted for the German sparkling wine. When the Kaiser found out, he was so furious that he recalled the German Ambassador from Washington. Another earlier substitution was at the launch of the American four-masted clipper ship, *The Great Republic*, the largest ship of her day. Hoping to curry favour with the powerful temperance lobby of Boston, the builder used Conchituate [sparkling] water instead of champagne for the launch. Within days, the ship caught fire giving rise to obvious speculation. Exactly when it became *de rigueur* for a woman to break a bottle of champagne over the bows at the launch of a ship is unclear, but the origins of such a ceremony must surely lie in mythology, when a virgin called down the blessings of the gods with propitiatory offerings.

The fine traditions of making and selling Charles Heidsieck champagne were carried on through successive generations - since Charles-Camille, all Heidsiecks have 'Charles' in their baptismal names. After the First World War, sales of champagne were universally hit. The old markets, Germany and the former Austro-Hungarian Empire were bankrupt, and Russia was in the hands of the Communists. Before the war, the United States had imported three million bottles of champagne. In 1920, the Prohibition Bill was passed and America was officially 'dry'. For some years the distribution of champagne was in the hands of bootleggers. Cases of champagne were carefully wrapped in oiled cloth in Reims, shipped to within three miles of the coast, and thrown overboard. Often cases were missed by the bootleggers and years later, the winter storms threw up the lost cargo. In the Spring of 1953, a young couple were digging for clams on a beach near Cape Cod when they noticed nine bottles floating in the sea. On opening the bottles they found it to be champagne; though a little brown and syrupy, it was still sparkling. The cork, in perfect condition, read 'Charles Heidsieck, Extra Dry. 1920'!

The cellarmaster's privilege

Today, Charles Heidsieck is drunk and enjoyed all over the world. It embodies the true traditions of manufacture, style and excellence that have evolved over the three centuries. In that time, technique and equipment have vastly improved, but there is no substitute for the skill in blending the wines and in the making of champagne. At Champagne Charles Heidsieck, their cellarmaster, Daniel Thibault, has inherited the mantle of all the great makers of champagne and now produces four champagnes of great harmony and balance - Brut Réserve, Brut Vintage and Rosé Vintage (the current year for both is 1985), and the Blanc des Millénaires, a much lauded blanc de blancs that is made totally from Chardonnay grapes.

Oscar Wilde believed that 'only those who lacked imagination could not find a good reason for drinking champagne'. With Charles Heidsieck, there is no need to find a 'good reason' - to open any of those four beautiful champagnes is reason enough to stimulate even the most vivid of imaginations!

Charles Heidsieck

Introduction
by ROY ACKERMAN

1994 saw a new growth in restaurant openings with some 40 restaurants opening in London during the first six months. This year's Guide shows considerable changes, with 145 new entries, 71 dropped for various reasons and 35 new clover leaf awards.

There have been many changes, but it's good to see the consistency remaining in establishments such as Stephen Bull's restaurants, now numbering three with the Bistro in St John Street, the Restaurant in Blandford Street and now the excellent Fulham Road (name and address!). Another restaurateur who quietly gets on with it is Roger Wren, whose English House, English Garden, Waltons and Lindsay House have their own very special style, as do Christopher Corbin and Jeremy King's Ivy and Caprice, Richard Shepherd's Langans, Odins and Shepherd's and Nick Smallwood and Simon Slater's Kensington and Launceston Places.

There is certainly a range of restaurants in London that rivals that of most capital cities and the restaurant trade looks to be on its way forward again—witness the successful flotation of Chez Gerard and My Kinda Town.

Sadley we lost a few friends in the trade over the last year including the ebullient Graham Needham of Sweetings, Eugène Kaufeler, for many years executive chef at London's Dorchester Hotel, and the irrepressible Bob Payton of My Kinda Town and Stapleford Park.

Restaurant changes have included Nicky Kerman's Scotts going to Chez Gerard, Russell Joffe's Café Flo group going to the Café Flo Group Paris, and the rapid expansion of the Café Rouge chain.

Too late for entry in this year's Guide was the promised return of the legendary Elena Salvoni at L'Etoile in Charlotte Street. The changes at the Savoy Group, including Ramon

Continued on page 14

Continued from page 13

Pajares moving from the Four Seasons to Managing Director, replacing Giles Shepard, and the departures of managers Ron Jones OBE from Claridges, and Stefano Sebastiani from The Berkeley.

Some of this year's more interesting chef appointments include Roger Narbett to the Lygon Arms (from The Dorchester), Richard Corrigan, Fulham Road (Bentleys), Robert Gutteridge, Alfred's (Belgo), and Michael Caines, Gidleigh Park (Robuchon, Paris). Not to be overlooked is the talented Gordon Ramsay of Aubergine, who at the age of 27 celebrated his first year at his restaurant in October 1994.

— Roy Ackerman

I would like to emphasise that there are many more good hotels and restaurants in Great Britain and Ireland – those inluded in this guide are my personal favourites

The Four-Leaf Clover

The four-leaf clover has been chosen because it is a symbol of luck and also a rare find. There is always a degree of luck involved when good ambience, excellent food, wine and service and the response of the customer combine to make a perfect occasion. A White Clover means that in my opinion, this is a very special place for many reasons, and made for a memorable experience. A Black Clover represents excellence in all aspects of food, service and decor, and these are the very best in Great Britain and the Republic of Ireland.With 35 new clovers this year marked [N] and 3 promotions to Black Clover from White Clover marked [P], The Ackerman Charles Heidsieck Guide Clover Leaf Awards for 1995 are given to:

LONDON

Al San Vincenzo, W2 [N]
Alastair Little, W1
Aubergine, SW10 [N]
Belgo, NW1 [N]
The Berkeley, SW1
Bibendum, SW3
Bistrot Bruno, W1
Bistrot 190, SW7
Blakes Hotel, SW7 [P]
Bombay Brasserie, SW7
The Brackenbury, W6 [N]
Café Royal Grill Room, W1
The Canteen, SW10
Cantina del Ponte, SE1
The Capital, SW3
Le Caprice, SW1
Chez Nico at Ninety Park Lane, W1
Churchill Inter-Continental Hotel, W1
Claridge's, W1 [P]
Clarke's, W8
The Connaught, W1
dell'Ugo, W1
The Dorchester, W1
L'Escargot, W1 [N]
Four Seasons Hotel, W1
Frederick's, N1
Fulham Road, SW3 [N]
Le Gavroche, W1
Gay Hussar, W1
Greenhouse, W1
The Halcyon, W11 [N]
The Halkin, SW1
Hilaire, SW7
Hyatt Carlton Tower, SW1

L'Incontro, SW1
Hotel Inter-Continental, W1
The Ivy, WC2
Kalamaras, W2
Kensington Place, W8
The Lanesborough, SW1
Langan's Brasserie, W1
The Langham Hilton, W1 [N]
Leith's, W11
Restaurant Marco Pierre White, SW1 [N]
Le Meridien, W1
Mijanou, SW1
Mon Plaisir, WC2 [N]
Mosimann's Club, SW1
Neal Street Restaurant, WC2
Nico Central, W1 [N]
Odette's, NW1
Odin's Restaurant, W1
Osteria Antica Bologna, SW11
Le Palais du Jardin, WC2 [N]
Pied á Terre, W1
Poissonnerie de l'Avenue, SW3 [N]
Le Pont de la Tour, SE1
Quality Chop House, EC1 [N]
Quincy's, NW2 [N]
Ransome's Dock, SW11
The Ritz, W1
Riva, SW13 [N]
River Café, W6
San Lorenzo, SW3
Les Saveurs, W1 [P]
The Savoy, WC2
Shaw's, SW7 [N]
Shepherd's, SW1 [N]
Simply Nico, SW1
Snows on the Green, W6 [N]

Soho Soho, W1
The Square, SW1
Stephen Bull, W1
Le Suquet, SW3
La Tante Claire, SW3
Turner's, SW3
Waltons, SW3 [N]

ENGLAND

Amberley, Amberley Castle
Aston Clinton, Bell Inn
Aylesbury, Hartwell House
Barnstaple, Lynwood House [N]
Baslow, Fischer's Baslow Hall
Bath, Bath Spa Hotel
Bath, Clos du Roy
Bath, Queensberry Hotel
Bath, Royal Crescent Hotel
Bibury, The Swan
Birmingham, Sloans
Birmingham, Swallow Hotel
Bradford, Restaurant 19
Bradford-on-Avon, Woolley
   Grange
Bray-on-Thames, The
   Waterside Inn
Brimfield, Poppies Restaurant
Bristol, Harveys Restaurant
Bristol, Restaurant Lettonie
Bristol, Swallow Royal Hotel
Broadway, Lygon Arms
Brockenhurst, Le Poussin
Bury, Normandie Hotel
   & Restaurant
Castle Combe, Manor House
Chaddesley Corbett,
   Brockencote Hall [N]
Chagford, Gidleigh Park
Charingworth,
   Charingworth Manor [N]
Cheltenham, Le Champignon
   Sauvage
Cheltenham, Epicurean
Chester, Chester Grosvenor
Colerne, Lucknam Park
Corse Lawn,
   Corse Lawn House
Dartmouth, Carved Angel
Dedham, Le Talbooth
Dorrington, Country Friends [N]

East Grinstead,
   Gravetye Manor
Evershot, Summer Lodge
Faversham, Read's
Fressingfield, Fox and Goose
Gillingham, Stock Hill House
Goring-on-Thames,
   The Leatherne Bottel
Grasmere, Michael's Nook
Great Milton, Le Manoir
   aux Quat'Saisons
Grimston, Congham Hall
Gulworthy, Horn of Plenty
Haslemere, Morel's
Hastings, Roser's
Herstmonceux, Sundial
   Restaurant
Hetton, Angel Inn
Hintlesham, Hintlesham Hall
Hunstrete, Hunstrete House [N]
Huntsham, Huntsham Court [N]
Jersey, Longueville Manor [N]
Langho, Northcote Manor [N]
Leamington Spa,
   Mallory Court [N]
Ledbury, Hope End
Liskeard, Well House [N]
Leeds, Pool Court at The Calls
Longridge, Paul Heathcote's
   Restaurant
Lower Slaughter,
   Lower Slaughter Manor
Malvern, Croque-en-Bouche
Melbourn, Pink Geranium
Moulsford-on-Thames,
   Beetle & Wedge
New Milton, Chewton Glen
Newcastle-upon-Tyne,
   21 Queen Street
Northleach, Old Woolhouse
Norwich, Adlard's
Oakham, Hambleton Hall
Oxford, Gee's Brasserie
Padstow, Seafood Restaurant
Plymouth, Chez Nous
Pulborough, Stane Street
   Hollow
Ridgeway, Old Vicarage
Romsey, Old Manor House
Shinfield, L'Ortolan

South Molton,
  Whitechapel Manor ☘
Speen, The Old Plow Inn at
  Speen ☘
Staddlebridge, McCoy's ☘
Stapleford, Stapleford Park ☘
Ston Easton, Ston Easton Park ☘
Storrington, Manleys ☘
Stroud, Oakes ☘
Stuckton, Three Lions ☘
Taplow, Cliveden ☘
Taunton, Castle Hotel ☘
Thornbury, Thornbury Castle ☘
Thundridge,
  Hanbury Manor [N] ☘
Torquay, Remy's Restaurant
  Française [N] ☘
Tunbridge Wells,
  Thackeray's House ☘
Twickenham, McClements
  Restaurant ☘
Uckfield, Horsted Place ☘
Ullswater, Sharrow Bay ☘
Warminster, Bishopstrow House ☘
Waterhouses, Old Beams ☘
Windermere, Miller Howe ☘
Windermere, Roger's
  Restaurant ☘
Winteringham,
  Winteringham Fields ☘
Witherslack, Old Vicarage [N] ☘
Woburn, Paris House ☘
Woodstock, Feathers Hotel [N] ☘
Worcester, Brown's ☘
York, Melton's ☘
York, Middlethorpe Hall ☘

SCOTLAND

Auchterarder, Gleneagles ☘
Crinan, Crinan Hotel ☘
Edinburgh, Martin's ☘

Fort William, Inverlochy Castle ☘
Glasgow,
  One Devonshire Gardens ☘
Gullane, La Potiniere ☘
Kingussie, The Cross ☘
Linlithgow, Champany Inn ☘
Peat Inn, The Peat Inn ☘
Port Appin, Airds Hotel ☘
Turnberry, Turnberry Hotel ☘
Ullapool, Altnaharrie Inn ☘

WALES

Abergavenny, Walnut Tree Inn ☘
Llandudno, Bodysgallen Hall ☘
Llyswen, Llangoed Hall ☘
Portmeirion, Hotel Portmeirion ☘
Pwllheli, Plas Bodegroes ☘

NORTHERN IRELAND

Belfast, Roscoff ☘
Portrush, Ramore ☘

REPUBLIC OF IRELAND

Adare, Adare Manor ☘
Dingle, Doyle's Seafood Bar
  & Townhouse ☘
Dublin, Le Coq Hardi ☘
Dublin, Patrick Guilbaud ☘
Dublin, Roly's Bistro [N] ☘
Dublin, La Stampa [N] ☘
Kenmare, Park Hotel Kenmare ☘
Mallow, Longueville House ☘
Shanagarry, Ballymaloe House ☘

How to Use this Guide

Main Reviews

Following our established successful formula, the main reviews are set out very simply: London is arranged alphabetically by establishment name. Reviews in England, Scotland, Wales, Northern Ireland and the Republic of Ireland are arranged alphabetically by location, then by establishment name. Some reviews are longer than others. The length of a review does not necessarily indicate the relative importance of an establishment — some have been covered more fully in previous editions of the Guide, which are available from Leading Guides. I have used a small team of reviewers who have worked with me for some years and whose judgement I trust, and who understand what I am seeking in standards of cuisine, atmosphere and service.

Clover Award Winners

The Clover Award Winners are featured on the previous two pages, and Clovers are also indicated alongside the text entries for the winners.

Listings

Where we are unsure about an establishment, or have visited it only once, or where there has been a change of some significance since our last visit, we list it without a full review. These listings appear at their correct geographical point amidst the main reviews.

Vital Statistics

These have been compiled from information supplied to us by the establishments themselves in response to our questionnaires. They have been checked and we have done our best to ensure that all information contained in this book is accurate. However, it is perfectly feasible that a restaurant or hotel may choose to change its last order times, or the days of the week that it is closed. Similarly, an owner, manager or chef may well move on. Even the style of food might be changed. We assume that in most cases you will book before going to a restaurant or hotel, and if you feel that any detail is especially important, we suggest you check it at the time of booking. When we have quoted particular dishes in a review, we cannot guarantee that they will be available on your visit — this is obviously true if you visit in a different season. In most cases, menus will be more comprehensive than the extracts we have chosen.

Price

The price shown is the average cost of dinner for two people, without wine but including coffee, service and VAT. Where possible, we have quoted a set price dinner menu, which in some cases might be four or even five or more courses; otherwise the figure relates to a typical three-course meal.

Vests

As before, I have used the "vested interest" symbol to indicate restaurants in which I have a personal investment:

Cercle des Ambassadeurs

This symbol ✍ indicates that an establishment is host to a member of the Cercle. A full list can be found on page 20.

Academy of Food and Wine Service

This symbol ✢ indicates that an establishment is host to a member of the Academy. More details can be found on page 22.

Telephone numbers

Note that we have printed the new telephone codes, all of which will be effective on Phone Day (April 16, 1995) and most of which were already operative at the time of going to press.

Cercle des Ambassadeurs de l'Excellence

The Cercle des Ambassadeurs de l'Excellence was created by Champagne Charles Heidsieck to celebrate the 140th anniversary of this grande marque champagne. This unique circle has approximately 140 founder members who represent the very best of gastronomic excellence in this country. Listed below are the members and the host restaurant/hotel, applicable at the time of going to press, of the Cercle des Ambassadeurs de l'Excellence. Throughout this Guide, these members are identified by a champagne bottle symbol ⚖ next to their entry.

Member	Hotel/restaurant
LONDON	
Ackerman, Roy OBE	(Leading Guides)
André, Raymond	Le Meridien Hotel
Archer, Vaughan	(Freelance)
Bissell, Frances	(Food writer)
Blech, Neville	Mijanou
Blech, Sonia	Mijanou
Boulding, Doreen	Hotel Conrad
Britten, Philip	Capital Hotel
Broadbent, Malcolm	Cadogan Hotel
Broadbent, Michael	(Christie's)
Bull, Stephen	Stephen Bull Rest.
Carluccio, Antonio	Neal Street Rest.
Cavalier, Susan	L'Escargot
Cavalier, David	L'Escargot
Chambers, David	The London Hilton
Chiandetti, Gian	(Forte plc)
Clarke, Sally	Clarke's
Coaker, Michael	Mayfair Inter-Continental Hotel
Corrick, Philip	(RAC Club)
Cotterill, Brian	(Chefs & Cooks Circle)
Davies, Peter	Le Gavroche
Deblonde, Eric	Four Seasons Hotel
Delteil, Christian	(Freelance)
Dillon, Eoin	(Freelance)
Dorricott, David	(Freelance)
Durantet, Jean-Pierre	(Freelance)
Edelmann, Anton	Savoy Hotel
Forte, Lord	(Forte plc)
Forte, The Hon Rocco	(Forte plc)
Foskett, David	(Ealing College)
Gaume, Bernard	Hyatt Carlton Tower
Gayler, Paul	Lanesborough Hotel
Giraldin, Silvano	Le Gavroche
Goring, George	Goring Hotel
Green, Simone	Odette's
Gwynn-Jones, Patrick	Pomegranates
Hari, Eduard	(Freelance)
Hewitson, Don	Cork & Bottle
Holecz, Lazlo	Gay Hussar
Hollihead, Gary	L'Escargot
Holmes, Terry	(Freelance)
Hopkinson, Simon	Bibendum
Jones, Ronald OBE	Claridges
Kennedy, Kevin	Bistro Bistrot

Member	Hotel/restaurant
Khoo, Eddie	(Freelance)
King, John	Les Ambassadeurs
Koffman, Pierre	La Tante Claire
Kromberg, Peter	Inter-Continental Hotel
Ladenis, Nico	Chez Nico at 90 Park Lane
Lees, Robin CB MBE	(BHRCA)
Leigh, Rowley	Kensington Place
Leith, Prue OBE	Leith's
Lesnik, Marjan	Claridge's
Levin, David	Capital Hotel
Little, Alastair	Alastair Little
Loubet, Bruno	Bistro Bruno
Martin, Pierre	Le Suquet
Mey, Robert	Hyatt Carlton Tower
Mosimann, Anton	Mosimann's
Nadell, Michael	Nadell Patisserie
Obertelli, Ricci	Dorchester Hotel
Pajares, Ramon	Four Seasons Hotel
Picolet, Nicolas	(Freelance)
Podmore, Keith	Boodles
Puxley, Bev	(Westminster Coll.)
Quero, Jean	Le Meridien Hotel
Rhodes, Gary	The Greenhouse
Robinson, Jancis	(Writer/Broadcaster)
Ronay, Egon	(Consultant)
Roux, Albert	Le Gavroche
Rutter, Duncan	(Consultant)
Shepherd, Giles	Savoy Hotel
Shepherd, Richard	Langan's Brasserie
Striessnig, Herbert	Savoy Hotel
Tomasi, Carla	The Peasant
Turner, Brian	Turner's
Webb, Bryan	Hilaire
Webber, Peter	My Kinda Town
White, Marco Pierre	Restaurant Marco Pierre White
Woodward, Dagmar	May Fair Inter-Continental Hotel
Worrall Thompson, Antony MOGB	dell'Ugo
Zago, Paolo	Connaught Hotel
ENGLAND	
Adlard, David	Adlard's, Norwich

Member	Hotel/restaurant
Barrington, Douglas OBE	Lygon Arms, Broadway
Bauer, Willy	Wentworth Club
Blanc, Raymond	Le Manoir, Great Milton
Bregoli, Mauro	Old Manor House, Romsey
Burton-Race, John	L'Ortolan, Shinfield
Cape, Kevin	(Overseas)
Ceserani, Victor	(Consultant)
Chandler, Peter	Paris House, Woburn
Chapman, Kit MBE	Castle Hotel, Taunton
Chevillard, Pierre	Chewton Glen, New Milton
Cole, Christopher	(Consultant)
Coulson, Francis	Sharrow Bay, Ullswater
Desenclos, Alain	Le Manoir, Great Milton
Dicken, John	Dicken's Restaurant
Fretwell, Clive	Le Manoir, Great Milton
Hart, Tim	Hambleton Hall, Oakham
Herbert, Peter	Gravetye Manor, E Grinstead
Hill, Shaun	The Merchant House Hotel
Huber, John	(Thames Vall. Coll)
Hyam, Joe	(Writer)
Johnson, Hugh	(Writer/ Broadcaster)
MacSween, Murdo	Boulter's Lock, Maidenhead
McWhirter, Kathryn	(Wine writer)
Marshall, Sir Colin	(British Airways)
Milsom, Gerald OBE	Le Talbooth, Dedham
Molyneux, Joyce	Carved Angel, Dartmouth
Mouilleron, Guy	(Chef/Consultant)
Murray, Harry	(Freelance)

Member	Hotel/restaurant
Pearn, Martyn	Buckland Manor, Buckland
Perraud, Michel MOGB	(Freelance)
Pitchford, David	Read's, Faversham
Roux, Michel	Waterside Inn, Bray-on-Thames
Sack, Brian	Sharrow Bay, Ullswater
Sinclair, The Hon John	E Sussex National Golf Club, Uckfield
Skan, Martin	Chewton Glen, New Milton
Smedley, Peter	Ston Easton Park, Ston Easton
Slater, Jonathan	Chester Grosvenor, Chester
Smith, Kate	Beetle & Wedge, Moulsford-on-Thames
Smith, Richard	Beetle & Wedge, Moulsford-on-Thames
Stein, Rick	Seafood Restaurant, Padstow
Thompson, Jonathan	Hartwell House, Aylesbury
Waugh, Auberon	(Writer)
Womersley, Michael	Lucknam Park Hotel, Colerne

SCOTLAND

Hill, Alan	Gleneagles Hotel, Auchterarder
Hobbs, Grete	Inverlochy Castle, Ft William
Lederer, Peter MI, FHCIMA	Gleneagles Hotel, Auchterarder
Wilson, David	Peat Inn, Peat Inn

WALES

Taruschio, Franco	Walnut Tree, Abergavenny

The Academy of Food and Wine Service

The Academy of Food & Wine Service was formed six years ago as a joint initiative by the Hotel and Restaurant Industry and the Wine and Spirit Trade.

The objective of the Academy is to increase the level of knowledge, and in particular, service skills, of those waiting staff employed in restaurants throughout the United Kingdom to benefit both the Industry and, more importantly, the Customer, by ensuring that there develops a network of waiting staff throughout the country who have been trained to National Vocational Qualifications Standards, initially at levels One and Two, and ultimately to even higher levels.

The Academy first set about this task by producing an open learning programme for Wine Waiters, which is available as a complete self-study pack, including a skills video, knowledge competence book and work book. This programme has been greeted by the Industry with much enthusiasm and has encouraged the Academy to further pursue research into a similar open learning programme on Food Service.

Development of this new initiative is now completed and the pack is currently available. This edition of The Ackerman Charles Heidsieck Guide to the best Hotels & Restaurants in Great Britain sees another step forward for the Academy.

Readers will notice that certain symbols are marked with the symbol ❖. This denotes that the establishment employs a current member of the Academy or works closely with the organisation and supports its aims and objectives.

You will be able to identify our members by a small uniform lapel badge—green and gold for food service associate members, burgundy and gold for wine service associate members and a combined burgundy, green and gold badge for a full member. Membership is only available to those members of the waiting profession who have been trained and assessed to a National Standard and on whom you should rely for professional service when you are dining out.

Please look out for these badges recognising competence and skills and start to demand that your favourite restaurant employs these dedicated, professional staff.

If you would like to obtain further information on the work of the Academy of Food & Wine Service, or as an employer wish to involve your own staff in the training programmes, please contact the Academy at the address below:

The Academy of Food & Wine Service
Chelsea Chambers
262a Fulham Road
London SW10 9EL
Tel: 071 352 6997
Fax: 071 351 9678

Alan Halliday: a biography

This year, instead of a section of colour photographs, we have commissioned artist Alan Halliday especially to paint a selection of establishments. (See pages 32 to 63).

Our thanks go to all the establishments included for entering into the spirit of things, and for making Alan's job as easy as possible.

Alan Halliday trained at the Courtauld Institute of Art and has an Oxford doctorate. He has exhibited at the International Contemporary Art Fair at the Barbican Centre (1984), at Olympia (1985,1989 and 1990), and Los Angeles (1986 and 1987). He has exhibited at many London galleries and has had nine one-man exhibitions at the Royal Opera House Covent Garden. In 1987 he led the European Artists' Group at the Frankfurt Festival, subsequently transferring to Los Angeles.

Halliday has travelled widely on painting trips to Russia, to America, South America, India, the Middle East and throughout Europe.

As a figure painter he has painted The Royal Ballet, the English National Ballet, the Bolshoi, the Kirov and the Royal Shakespeare Company. In 1990 he was commissioned to go on an extensive tour of Vienna, Prague and Salzburg painting Mozart interiors for an exhibition held at the Barbican Centre in conjunction with the Mozart bicentenary. The exhibition went on a national tour of English country houses and museums before arriving at The Royal Opera House. Following exhibitions at the Royal National Theatre, Halliday worked as artist-in-residence with the Cincinnati Ballet.

In 1992, John Laing Construction sponsored Halliday to paint in the Middle East. And in the autumn of that year he set off on a painting trip in India, the results of which were seen at the Bruton Street Gallery in London, after a showing in Bombay. In 1993, Halliday was a commissioned artist to record the devastation following the London City bomb.

He was also invited by the Caracalla Dance Theatre to paint and exhibit in Montreal, Paris and Beirut and by Béjart in Lausanne. He has recently completed thirty-three large canvases for Orient Lines. Halliday's work is represented in the Victoria & Albert Museum, the London Theatre Museum and the Museum of London.

For further information on the artist and his work contact:
Music Theatre Gallery,
1 Elystan Place,
London
SW3 3LA
Tel: 071-823 9880

London Establishment Reviews

ABBEY COURT   W2

20 Pembridge Gardens, W2 4DU
Tel: 0171-221 7518   *Fax:* 0171-792 0858
Classic, five-storey, Victorian town house with 22 bedrooms, popular with media types, located just off Notting Hill Gate. No restaurant.

L'ACCENTO ITALIANO   W2

16 Garway Road, W2 4NH
Tel: 0171-243 2201   **£50**
Open: lunch & dinner daily (closed Bank Holidays)
Meals served: lunch 12.30-2.30, dinner 6.30-11.30 (Sun to 10.30)

The new conservatory with its sliding roof, converted from the former patio garden, is a big plus at this little Italian restaurant where Andrea Beltramis cooks with skill and confidence. The decor otherwise is fairly minimalist and rustic, like the food, which hails from Northern Italy. A substantial carte offers dishes such as ravioli triangles stuffed with pumpkin, sage butter and parmesan, or risotto of black cuttlefish ink among starters, with main courses such as osso buco with saffron risotto, Ligurian-style seafood stew, and rabbit with Italian sausage braised in mushroom sauce. Classic Italian desserts and cheeses.

ADAM'S CAFÉ   W12

77 Askew Road, W12   *Good couscous—try the*
Tel: 0181-743 0572   *imperial version for two!* **£30**
Open: lunch & dinner Mon-Sat (closed Bank Holidays)
Meals served: lunch English café: 7.15am-6.30pm, Sat 8-2,
    dinner Tunisian restaurant: 7-11

Walk past during the day and you'll see an English café; return at night and it's a Tunisian restaurant, serving a selection of traditional brik starters, the fillings ranging from vegetarian to seafood; followed by couscous in an equal variety of guises, grilled fish and meats, and casseroles. Desserts include traditional Tunisian pastries, plus sorbets, hot lemon pancake and ice-creams.

AL BUSTAN   SW1

27 Motcomb Street, Belgravia, SW1X 8JU
Tel: 0171-235 8277   **£55**
Open: all day daily (closed 25 & 26 Dec)
Meals served: 12-11 (Sun to 10)

Attractive, green-canopied restaurant, serving some of the best Lebanese food in London. Choose from the range of hot or cold hors d'oeuvres—baby aubergines stuffed with pine nuts, spices and garlic; pitta bread toasted and filled with spiced meat; fried chicken livers with pomegranate molasses or lemon juice. Try a main course of lamb or chicken, charcoal-grilled or oven-baked, or for the more adventurous, try one of the raw meat options! Concise, mainly French wine list, with a selection from the Lebanon.

AL SAN VINCENZO   W2

30 Connaught Street, W2 2AF
Tel: 0171-262 9623   **£55**
Open: lunch Mon-Fri, dinner Mon-Sat (closed 2 wks Xmas)
Meals served: lunch 12.30-2, dinner 7-10.15

Elaine and Vincenzo Borgonzolo's tiny little restaurant near Marble Arch is modest in decor but simply excellent in food and service.

Elaine and daughter Angela are delightful at front-of-house, while Vincenzo (pictured, left) slaves away singlehandedly in the kitchen below, exercising innovation and originality on even the most traditionally bourgeois dishes. Minestrone comes with rice, pumpkin, courgettes, peas and parmesan cheese; or for a more unusual starter try octopus casseroled in its own juices, with parsley and white wine sauce. Main courses feature fish of the day, along with dishes such as English grey-legged partridge roasted with grapes and chestnuts, or salt cod and potato stew. Good desserts and fabulous organic Italian farmhouse cheeses.

ALASTAIR LITTLE   W1

49 Frith Street, W1V 5TE
Tel: 0171-734 5183   **£70**
Open: lunch Mon-Fri, dinner Mon-Sat
(closed Bank Holidays, Xmas)
Meals served: lunch 12-3, dinner 6-11.30

Alastair Little caused quite a stir when he opened here in 1985. Ten years on he continues to impress, with even the simplest things done to absolute perfection. The charm of the place, with its '80s minimalist decor and lack of pretension (considering the brilliance of the cooking) both in terms of concept and execution, is what sets the place apart, if not above the rest. Daily-changing à la carte and fixed-price menus offer a fresh and exciting variety of dishes, ranging from a soup of cabbage and bacon served with croutons and sour cream or salad of spicy sausage, to pan-fried scallops with a stir-fry of vegetables with coriander and chili or medallions of beef with polenta and a green sauce. The lunch-time carte is slightly simpler in style, and there are two set lunch menus: one for only £10 served in the bar

Biography

Alastair Little
Alastair's route to becoming a top rated chef include an MA at Cambridge, before waiting and cooking in several fashionable London restaurants – Zanzibar, L'Escargot, Fingal's and 192. His concept of a restaurant is exactly what he's running now, where quality is paramount and extras unnecessary.

downstairs, offering two courses such as chicken liver parfait and toast followed by braised lamb or roast plaice with a parsley crust; the other a no-choice £25 affair of three courses—crostini of herbed tomatoes and chicken livers, followed by fillet of Irish sea trout with grilled vegetables and a butter sauce, and panettone bread-and-butter pudding or cheeses to finish. Friendly, informal service. Reasonably priced wine list.

ALBA   EC1

107 Whitecross Street, EC1Y 8JD
Tel: 0171-588 1798   **£50**
Open: lunch & dinner Mon-Fri (closed Bank Holidays, 1 wk Xmas)
Meals served: lunch 12-3, dinner 6-11

Northern Italian cooking is the name of the game at this friendly restaurant within the shadow of the Barbican Centre. Good, honest flavours come to the fore in familiar favourites and more unusual combinations. Most of the raw materials come either direct from Italy or from local Italian suppliers. The menu is long and varied, starting with insalata di campo—a green salad of wild and interesting lettuces, and moving on through pasta choices such as tagliolini with smoked salmon to trout in walnut sauce, rabbit braised with peppers and served with polenta or fillet steak with Barbera wine and shallot sauce. Desserts from the trolley or Italian cheeses with pear.

ALBERO & GRANA   SW3

Chelsea Cloisters, 39 Sloane Avenue, SW3 3DX
Tel: 0171-225 1048/9   *Fax:* 0171-581 3259   **£60**
Open: lunch Mon-Sat, dinner daily (closed some
    Bank Holidays)   *Busy, interesting*
Meals served: lunch (tapas 12.30-3.30),   *and fun.*
    dinner 7.30-11.30 (tapas 6-12)

Angel Garcia flies the Spanish flag at this spacious corner site where many other restaurants have been and gone before. Choose from a range of tapas in the busy front bar area or take your time over a meal in the splendidly futuristic dining room designed by José Antonio Garcia. One wall is constructed of glass bricks, another is an undulating backcloth—the distinctive colour of the sand in La Maestranza bullring in Seville. The most interesting aspect here though, is the chef's pioneering modern interpretation of Spanish cuisine. Starters such as a gratin of poached eggs and prawns or stuffed griddled squid with black ink sauce are followed by a casserole of duck with figs, baked gilthead in sea salt or marinated pork fillet with roast stuffed apples. The wine list is entirely Spanish and even the bottled water includes a Vichy Catalan.

ALFRED   WC2

Shaftesbury Avenue, WC2
Tel: 0171-240 2566   *Fax:* 0171-497 0672   **£50**
Open: lunch & dinner Mon-Sat (closed 25 & 26 Dec, 1 Jan)
Meals served: lunch 12-3.45, dinner 6-11.45

Fred Taylor's cheerful restaurant, with yellow formica-topped tables,
stained wood floors and painted wood panelling offers good quality
English fare at reasonable prices. Chef Robert Gutteridge comes fresh
from Belgo and exerts the same enthusiasm and contemporary flair on
the menu here. Potted liver paste with toasted rosemary bread and
orange marmalade or toad-in-the-hole are examples of starters, followed by calf's liver, bacon, bubble 'n' squeak or cod in batter, minted
peas and chips. Gingerbread with lavender custard or sticky toffee pudding to finish, if you've got room! Why not enjoy one of the many beers
(draught and bottled) on offer or choose from the concise, medium-
priced wine list. Outside seating on pavement.

L'ALTRO   W11

210 Kensington Park Road, W11
Tel: 0171-792 1066   **£55**
Open: lunch daily, dinner Mon-Sat (closed Bank Holidays)
Meals served: lunch 12-2.30 (Sat to 3.30), dinner 7-11 (Fri & Sat to 11.30)

Fish and shellfish get the modern Italian treatment at this busy, stylish
restaurant around a stage-set Romanesque courtyard complete with
classical statues and trompe-l'oeil stone walls. The cooking is straightforward and simple, allowing flavours to dominate. Daily specials feature dishes such as sautéed broad beans with onions and pancetta,
black tagliolini with assorted seafood, or red mullet wrapped in Parma
ham with rosemary. Regular dishes feature interesting pasta dishes,
gnocchi with asparagus, baked sea bream with fennel or whole sea
bass baked with fresh herbs. One or two meat options, which usually
include lamb, such as baked best end with wild mushrooms and artichokes. The new antipasto bar offers a monthly-changing menu. Sister
restaurant to Cibo, W14, this place has a fun element to it.

ANNA'S PLACE   N1

90 Mildmay Park, Newington Green, N1 4PR
Tel: 0171-249 9379   **£40**
Open: lunch & dinner Tue-Sat (closed 1 wk Xmas,
   1 wk Easter, Aug)   *As popular as ever*
Meals served: lunch 12.15-2.15, dinner 7.15-10.45

Colourful vinyl tablecloths and Swedish posters create an informal,
relaxed atmosphere at Anna Hegarty's long-established restaurant,
renowned for its Swedish cuisine and friendly, welcoming staff. The
food, likewise, is uncomplicated: marinated herrings, gravad lax, diced
marinated beef in mustard, and wholesome meat hotpots in winter. Ice-
cold schnapps, Absolut Vodka or Swedish beer go well with the food.
There are seats for 14 in the small covered courtyard: book the whole
area and go with friends to enjoy a fun evening.

ARCADIA   W8

Kensington Court, 35 Kensington High Street, W8 5EB
Tel: 0171-937 4294   *Fax:* 0171-937 4393   **£50**
Open: lunch Mon-Fri, dinner daily
   (closed 25 & 26 Dec, 2 days Easter)   *Good local*
Meals served: lunch 12-2.30 (Sun to 3), dinner 6.30-11.15 *restaurant*

New owners Stephen and Nicky Barraclough have created a whole
new concept and broken all ties with the past at this long-established
restaurant site, formerly known as the Ark. The menu has become
modern, the decor too, and while the emphasis is on British cooking,
the Mediterranean also gets a look-in. The short, concise carte might
offer baked ricotta with a parmesan and pine nut salad, Caesar salad or
a delicious pea and mint soup served with crème fraîche to start. Main
courses could include roast cod with broad beans and parsley cream,
corn-fed roasted guinea fowl with lemon and lentils or lemon sole béarnaise. Finish with a selection of Coolea, Finn and Stilton cheeses
served with oatmeal biscuits and green tomato chutney. Nicky's stints
at the Carved Angel, Sonny's in Barnes and Clarke's ensure some innovative dishes.

THE ARGYLL   SW3

316 King's Road, SW3 5UH
Tel: 0171-352 0025   **£50**
Open: lunch Tue-Sat, dinner Mon-Sat
   (closed Bank Holidays)
Meals served: lunch 12-2.30, dinner 7-11.15
   (Fri & Sat 6.30-12)

Some very good food and a simple but pleasant setting in this restaurant. The menu is eclectic and modern: from tomato and basil galette,
bang bang chicken and grilled cuttlefish with sauce nero to wild mushroom risotto, bouillabaisse with lobster and saffron rouille and sautéed
guinea fowl with girolle mushrooms. The Bedouin-tented basement bar
serves starters, all priced at under £4. Doors opening onto King's Road,
a young enthusiastic staff and some reasonably priced wines all help to
make an enjoyable evening. Many years ago I was involved with a
restaurant on this site and it's good to see the Argyll proving that the
right restaurant can work here—this is a fashionable, busy place.

THE ARK   W8

122 Palace Gardens Terrace, W8
Tel: 0171-229 4024   £35
Open: lunch daily, dinner Mon-Sat
    (closed lunch Bank Holidays, 4 days Xmas)
Meals served: lunch 12-3, dinner 6.30-11.15

Long-established popular neighbourhood restaurant located just off the
bustling Notting Hill Gate. While the menu remains true to its early
'70s origins—with traditional classics like the Ark steak and kidney pie
and rack of lamb with herbs are still featured—more modern interpretations have also been introduced. The short, concise à la carte offers
around eight choices at each course, and is supplemented by good-
value fixed-price menus at lunch-time, when dishes such as spicy
chicken casserole, Ark fish pie, coq au vin and ox tongue with chick
pea casserole appear.

LES ASSOCIÉS   N8

172 Park Road, N8 8GT
Tel: 0181-348 8944   *Good local*   £55
Open: lunch Wed-Fri & Sun, dinner Tue-Sat   *restaurant*
    (closed 1 wk Xmas, 1 wk Easter, Aug)
Meals served: lunch 12.30-2, dinner 7.30-10

The staff are very French, as is the cooking at this intimate little restaurant run by three partners. The food is essentially bourgeois French,
with a nod towards the modern. Supreme of chicken with orange sauce
and duck liver mousse with onion marmalade might be available as
starters; main courses might feature fillet of pork with morel sauce,
salmon with capers and chives, or magret de canard served with a
honey and lemon sauce.

THE ATHENAEUM   W1

116 Piccadilly, W1V 0BJ
Tel: 0171-499 3464   *Fax:* 0171-493 1860   £50
Open: lunch Sun-Fri, dinner daily
Meals served: lunch 12.30-2.30   ❖
    (Sun brunch 8-3), dinner 6-11.30 (Sun 7-10), (Tea 3-6)

The charming and ebullient James Brown has put his stamp firmly on
this 156-bedroomed hotel overlooking Green Park. Complete refurbishment of the entire hotel and its apartments in Down Street, and the
new luxury health spa in the basement are only half the story. In the
culinary field, the new Bulloch's restaurant offers a lighter, modern
European menu and less formal surroundings than did the previous
main dining room. The emphasis here will be on Mediterranean-
inspired dishes, leaving the Windsor Lounge to focus on the more
traditional dishes. Arrive early to enjoy one of the 56 rare malts on offer
in the famous Malt Whisky Bar. This is a peaceful and luxurious hotel
in a prime location.

AU BOIS ST JEAN NW8

122 St John's High Street, NW8 7SG
Tel: 0171-722 0400
Open: dinner daily (closed 3 days Xmas,
2 days Easter)
Meals served: dinner 7-11.30,
(light meals ground floor Bistro 12-3, 6-11)

Good local restaurant with some reasonably priced wines

£55

This is an excellent local restaurant which has a pianist playing in the evenings. Staff are friendly and professional, serving up a Mediterranean range of dishes such as scallops wrapped in smoked bacon served with sherry sauce, a skewer of monk fish, salmon, sole and prawns oven-baked with pernod sauce, and confit of duck with a cherry sauce. A wine bar-cum-bistro upstairs offers a less formal alternative, but the restaurant itself is small and cosy with much charm.

AU JARDIN DES GOURMETS W1

5 Greek Street, W1V 5LA
Tel: 0171-437 1816   *Fax:* 0171-437 0043
Open: lunch Mon-Fri, dinner Mon-Sat (closed Bank Holidays)
Meals served: lunch 12.15-2.30, dinner 6-11.15

£50

Au Jardin has been around since 1931 and has hosted many a celebrity along the way. Last year there was a change of pace: the ground floor became a brasserie and upstairs a profusion of private dining areas. This year we can report a change of ownership, although Franco Zoia remains front of house, but no further alterations are envisaged. The long menu also remains faithful to classic French origins, with dishes such as sole meunière and beef bordelaise still among favourites. The classic tradition is fringed, however, with modern notes here and there chicken supreme with lime, coriander and turmeric; poached salmon with thinly-sliced beetroot; and a steamed selection of fish cooked in its own juice with spring onions and ginger.

AUBERGINE SW10

11 Park Walk, SW10 0AJ
Tel: 0171-352 3449   *Fax:* 0171-351 6576
Open: lunch Mon-Fri, dinner Mon-Sat
(closed Bank Holidays)
Meals served: lunch 12-2.30, dinner 7-11

The room itself is cool and neutral, but comes to life when full

£70

🏵

Since its opening in late 1993, Aubergine has been under the microscope of gourmets and gastronomes throughout the capital. Chef Gordon Ramsay has done more homework than many, so it was no surprise that the place was rapidly booked up well ahead for dinner. Gordon worked with Marco Pierre White (who backs the project) as well as with Roux Restaurants, the Savoy and Robuchon in Paris, and with Pierre Koffmann too, and experience in this case certainly pays off. Gordon's dishes are well thought out and accomplished, a feast for the senses. The menus change weekly, but you might be fortunate enough to be offered tortellini of lobster with a vinaigrette crustacés or a salad of roasted wood pigeon with wild mushrooms as starters, followed by main courses of red mullet with beignets of sage and aubergine caviar or ribeye of Scotch beef with pomme purée, confit of shallots and red wine sauce. Straightforward but delicious desserts such as pavé chocolate and tarte tatin of pears round off the meal. For once, all the hype surrounding this new venture seems to have been justified—Aubergine looks set to enjoy the scent of success.

L'AVENTURE   NW8

3 Blenheim Terrace, NW8 0EH
Tel: 0171-624 6232   **£60**
Open: lunch Sun-Fri, dinner daily
   (closed 1 wk Xmas, 4 days Easter)
Meals served: lunch 12.30-2.30, dinner 7.30-11 (Sun to 10)

This delightful, local French restaurant owned by Catherine Parisot takes each day as it comes: set menus change at every sitting, lunch and dinner, offering four choices at each stage. The atmosphere is relaxed and friendly, and there's a terrace for alfresco eating should the weather be fine. On the whole, menus are classically based, with main-course options such as roast duck with honey and thyme or blanquette de veau being typical. Starters might include smoked salmon pancakes, a wild mushroom parfait or scallops Florentine.

AVENUE WEST ELEVEN   W11

157 Notting Hill Gate, W11 3LF
Tel: 0171-221 8144   **£50**
Open: lunch & dinner daily (closed Bank Holidays, 4 days Xmas)
Meals served: lunch 12-3.15, dinner 6.30-11.15

An exciting addition to Notting Hill Gate's plethora of eating houses, this one is a sister establishment to the Brasserie du Marché aux Puces. Decor is Notting Hill arty with an almost African ambience—stone floor covered with rugs, wooden tables with brown paper covers. The food has a worldwide mix of flavours: crisp, grilled polenta with poached egg and bagna cauda, Dorset crab with a Chinese style egg custard pancake, shuiitake mushrooms and bean curd and a coconut Thai fry with roast sesame seeds; and main dishes such as open ravioli of rabbit and wild mushrooms in champagne and mustard sauce, noisettes of venison marinated in passion fruit with chocolate tagliatelle show no lack of imagination or courage! It is now becoming fashionable once more to eat savouries rather than puddings, and here you can try devils on horseback (prunes wrapped in bacon), or an interesting variation from the traditional Welsh rarebit—a brioche rarebit with pickled walnuts. Wines are adventurous with house wines at a modest £7.95 and only champagne rising above the £20 barrier.

BASIL STREET HOTEL   SW3

Basil Street, SW3 1AH
Tel: 0171-581 3311   *Fax:* 0171-581 3693   **£45**
Open: lunch Sun-Fri, dinner daily
Meals served: lunch 12.30-2.15, dinner 6.30-10.15

Handy for shopping, (it's situated right between Harrods and Harvey
Nichols), this 93-bedroomed hotel is currently celebrating its 85th
birthday. Built in 1910 in the days of Edwardian elegance, this is a
supremely elegant yet discreet house, which has passed through three
generations of its founding family. Antiques, rich carpets and tapestries, fine paintings and objets d'art abound, yet the overall feeling is
one of relaxed graciousness. This is a much-loved, highly individual
house—a hotel for people who can't bear hotels, according to one
source! Choose between the traditional dining room (English and
Continental classics), carvery and salad bar, wine bar or sandwich
shop. Ladies have a bonus: the Parrot Club, a ladies-only retreat which
serves light snacks and refreshments throughout the day.

BELGO   NW1

72 Chalk Farm Road, NW1 8AN
Tel: 0171-267 01718   **£40**
Open: lunch & dinner daily (closed 25 & 26 Dec, 1 Jan)
Meals served: lunch 12-3, dinner 6-11.30,
    (all day Sat 12-11.30, Sun 12-10.30)   ✤

Denis Blais's popular and unusual restaurant, less than a couple of
years old, has already undergone a transformation: a new wing extension has been added, doubling the seating capacity and so increasing
the number of customers (mostly young and trendy) who can enjoy
Belgian-style cooking at very reasonable prices. Seafood and game still
top the unstructured menu—mussels and beer, in particular, are the
main pull. Moules Mania, served on Monday to Friday at lunchtimes,
offers all the mussels (marinière or provençale) and frites you can eat,
for just £6.95, while Lunch For A Fiver offers mussel platter or smoked
wild boar sausage and Belgian mash, with a bottle of Belgian beer—
there are 32 to choose from. Belgo serves up to two tons of mussels a
week, prepared in ten different ways. Lobster, langoustines and asparagus are other specialities, also prepared in numerous ways. The short
carte offers options such as chicken and vegetable stew, beef braised in
beer and steak and chips. The selection of beers is unparalleled, including organic and specialist, monastery-brewed varieties. Waiters wear
monks' habits. An interesting and alternative place, noisy and fun.

EVEN NON-VINTAGE CHAMPAGNE CHARLES HEIDSIECK CONTAINS THIS MUCH VINTAGE

Traditionally, the best champagne makers always like to include some older, reserve stocks from good years with a non-vintage, to bring the blend a much greater depth and maturity.

Champagne Charles Heidsieck is no exception. Except that, in their case, the proportion included is astoundingly generous.

Nearly 40% in fact.

Brut Réserve

Charles Heidsieck

CHAMPAGNE

FOR THE RARELY IMPRESSED

Bombay Brasserie, SW7

Bombay Brasserie, SW7

Christopher's, WC2

Christopher's, WC2

Conrad Hotel, SW10

IT TAKES 105
VINEYARDS TO
PRODUCE THIS BOTTLE
OF CHAMPAGNE
CHARLES HEIDSIECK.

Every year, up to 105
carefully selected 'crus'
contribute to the
making of Champagne
Charles Heidsieck.
And in an exceptional
year, a champagne will
be made solely from the
grapes of that year.

The declaration of a
vintage year on the label
- such as the excellent
1985 - is your assurance
that only grapes from
that year are used.
A mere 105 vineyards'
worth of them.

Brut Vintage 1985

Charles Heidsieck

C H A M P A G N E

FOR THE RARELY IMPRESSED

The Halkin, SW1

Brut Rosé Vintage

TO PRODUCE AN OUTSTANDING CHAMPAGNE, WE ONLY EVER USE THE FIRST PRESSING

Even the strictest rules of the Champagne region allow grapes to be pressed twice, or even three times, to extract the most from the precious juices.

At Champagne Charles Heidsieck, however, we use the first and finest pressing and no other, having no desire to increase the quantity of our output at even the slightest cost to our quality. Whether the bottle in question is a Brut Réserve or a vintage such as our unique Brut Rosé Vintage.

Charles Heidsieck

CHAMPAGNE

FOR THE RARELY IMPRESSED

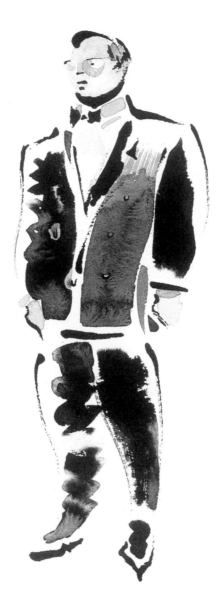

Langan's Brasserie, W1

Langan's Brasserie, W1

Langan's Brasserie, W1

ALL CHAMPAGNE CHARLES HEIDSIECK IS WELL-AGED, IN A CELLAR THAT IS ABSOLUTELY ANCIENT

We have the ancient Romans (or rather their slaves) to thank for digging the deep chalk cellars in which every bottle of Champagne Charles Heidsieck spends at least three years.

The cellars are over 2,000 years old (double 'millénaires') and house many of our greatest treasures, including examples of our pure Chardonnay vintage, Charles Heidsieck Blanc des Millénaires.

Blanc des Millénaires

Charles Heidsieck

CHAMPAGNE

FOR THE RARELY IMPRESSED

Langan's Brasserie, W1

Mimmo d'Ischia, SW1

Mosimann's, SW1

The Faustino Guide to fine Rioja.

Faustino I, a magnificent Gran Reserva Rioja, aged in cask at least 2½ years and another 3 years in bottle. Excellent with all meat dishes as well as fish served with strong sauces.

Faustino V, an elegant Reserva Rioja aged up to 1½ years in cask and almost 2 years in bottle. Its smoothness makes it a perfect partner to pastas, red meats and any smoked meat or fish.

Faustino

FOR THOSE WHO KNOW THEIR RIOJA.

190 Queen's Gate, SW7

190 Queen's Gate, SW7

Poissonnerie de l'Avenue, SW3

COINTREAU ON ICE...

...VOULEZ-VOUS ?

Ransome's Dock SW11

The Savoy, WC2

The Savoy, WC2

The Savoy, WC2

XO SPECIAL
DE
REMY MARTIN

Fine Champagne Cognac comes exclusively from grapes grown in
the two best areas of the Cognac district of France - at least 50% from
the Grande Champagne and the rest from the Petite Champagne.

Rémy Martin XO Spécial is a blend of older Fine Champagne
eaux-de-vie characterised by subtlety, harmony and a warm
lingering aftertaste.

REMY MARTIN
FINE CHAMPAGNE COGNAC

The Savoy, WC2

Thierry's SW3

THE BELVEDERE W8

Holland Park, off Abbotsbury Road, W8 6LU
Tel: 0171-602 1238
Open: lunch daily, dinner Mon-Sat
(closed 25 Dec)
Meals served: lunch 12-3, dinner 7-11 (6-12 summer)

Increasingly popular venue for parties and receptions **£55**

Located in what was originally the summer ballroom of Holland House, this restaurant enjoys a lovely parkland setting, perhaps best enjoyed in summer when the terrace seating comes into its own. The menu offers plenty of choice from an essentially modern English repertoire. Main courses run from traditional English classics like fish and chips to more modern interpretations like crab cakes with lobster sauce; pork and venison sausages with glazed shallots, cranberries, chive and celeriac mash; steamed brill with braised chicory, ginger and honey essence; or char-grilled sirloin steak béarnaise with parsnip chips. Good dessert choice, from soufflés of the day to sticky toffee pudding with caramel sauce.

BENTLEY'S W1

11 Swallow Street, W1R 7HD
Tel: 0171-287 5025
Open: lunch Mon-Fri, dinner Mon-Sat
(closed Bank Holidays, 1 wk Xmas)
Meals served: lunch 12-2.30, dinner 6-10.30

£45

On the ground floor at Bentley's there's an oyster bar, while upstairs there's a comfortable, club-like dining room with walls covered with military prints and traditional oil paintings, with candle-lamps on tables. This renowned seafood restaurant began life back in 1916 and today continues its tradition of classic fish dishes, but now with the addition of more modern interpretations to cater for the more adventurous palate. The all-day set menu (two or three courses) offers good value. The mostly expense-account clientele clearly enjoys the traditional atmosphere.

THE BERKELEY SW1

Wilton Place, SW1X 7RL
Tel: 0171-235 6000   *Fax:* 0171-235 4330
Open: lunch & dinner Sun-Fri
Meals served: lunch 12.30-2.30 (Sun to 2.15),
dinner 6.30-10.45 (Sun 7-10)

£60
☙
❖

One of the Savoy group's impeccably-run hotels with 160 spacious bedrooms, rooftop pool and gym. Fine proportions, panelled ceilings, marble pillars and graceful fireplaces set the scene in the entrance hall and lounges, and the theme is echoed throughout the air-conditioned building. Billed as the hotel's private cinema, the Minema and its café is often visited by people who haven't the remotest idea that it is part of the Berkeley! The main restaurant offers classic French cuisine, while contemporary Italian food is available in the Perroquet. So you can choose délice de sole aux champignons sauvages, tain d'agneau aux tomates séchées au soleil, and soufflé au citron one day; then the next day try rucola e cappesante, costolette di agnello al rosmarino, and zabaglione freddo. An extensive wine list , as you would expect.

BERKSHIRE HOTEL   W1

350 Oxford Street, W1N 0BY
Tel: 0171-629 7474   *Fax:* 0171-629 8156   **£55**
Open: lunch Mon-Fri, dinner daily
Meals served: lunch 12.30-2.30, dinner 5.30-10.30 (Sun to 10)

The spirit of the Edwardian era—a relaxed country house atmosphere—is recreated here in the centre of London at this 147-bedroomed hotel close to Bond Street. The theme is maintained in the restaurant, with country house-style dishes marked as such on the menus, though the overall guiding influences are French and English. Clear chicken consommé with dumplings or Rossmore oysters and scallops in a light pastry case with a cream sauce might be offered as starters. Main courses could run from Barrow-in-Furness winter fish pie and Lancashire hot pot to stuffed fillet of pork with prunes and apple sauce, pot-roasted spring chicken in a rich claret sauce and vegetarian pithiviers set on a tomato and tarragon sauce. Lovely desserts—hot treacle lattice tart, bread-and-butter pudding, or light raspberry mousse encased in sponge served with a blackcurrant coulis.

BERTORELLI'S   WC2

44a Floral Street, WC2E 9DA
Tel: 0171-836 3969   *Fax:* 0171-836 1868   **£50**
Open: lunch & dinner Mon-Sat (closed 26 Dec)
Meals served: lunch 12-3, dinner 5.30-11.30

Virtually opposite the Royal Opera House stage door, Bertorelli's split-level restaurant and basement café is a favourite venue for pre- and post-theatre suppers. Maddalena Bonnino cooks in the modern Italian vein, offering an unusually interesting menu. Antipasti and soups precede fish dishes such as griddled scallops on fennel couscous with saffron dressing. Meat lovers might choose pan-fried medallions of venison with mushroom sauce or grilled calf's liver with a roast onion, pancetta and spinach compote. The less adventurous cossetted by charcoal-grilled Scotch sirloin steak. Pastas feature tomato- and ricotta-filled tortelloni with a ginger and lime sauce, and trofie with pesto and aubergines—none of your usual fare here! Smart and efficient service in relaxed and pleasant surroundings.

BIBENDUM   SW3

81 Fulham Road, SW3 6RD
Tel: 0171-581 5817   *Fax:* 0171-823 7925   *Go there—relax and enjoy!*
Open: lunch & dinner daily   **£75**
  (closed 4 days Xmas, Easter Monday)   ✿
Meals served: lunch 12.30-2.30 (Sat & Sun to 3),   ♫
  dinner 7-11.30 (Sun to 10.30)

Sir Terence Conran's restaurant on the first floor of the fabulous
Michelin building continues to thrive, and is still one of the most fashionable places to eat in the capital. Chef Simon Hopkinson shares the

limelight with Bibendum, the Michelin
Man, who is featured everywhere. Nunc
est bibendum says the motto—now's the
time to drink (eat and be merry, I would
add!)—and make the most of it. This is a
beautiful, light and spacious room, which
changes with the seasons: chairs change
colour throughout the year—a typically
clever Conran design feature. But all this
beauty would be nothing without a talented
chef in the kitchen, so there's no cause for
concern here. Simon's French repertoire
runs from the classical to regional,
Mediterranean and Provence-inspired
dishes. Typical choices might be crab vinaigrette with herbs, risotto primavera and
ravioli of salt pork with sage cream and
crispy pancetta to start; followed by deep-
fried lemon sole with sauce tartare, scallops with salsa and a garlic dressing or
favourites like fillet steak au poivre or
entrecôte béarnaise. At lunchtime, there's a
fixed-price menu option which usually features Simon's rendition of
fish and chips, a favourite. Leave room for the delicious pudding menu.
I wonder when the modern day Michelin Man might fully recognise
Simon Hopkinson's talents? After all, I did some ten years ago when I
persuaded him to join a restaurant I was involved in—Hilaire in Old
Brompton Road.

BIBENDUM OYSTER BAR   SW3

Michelin House, 81 Fulham Road, SW3 6RD
Tel: 0171-581 5817   *Fax:* 0171-823 7925   **£40**
Open: all day daily (closed 25-28 Dec, Easter Monday)
Meals served: 12-10.30 (Sun to 10)

Stylish oyster bar at the entrance to the Michelin building and under
the same regime. The menu offers a selection of Scottish, Irish and
French rock oysters, clams, Sevruga caviar, salads and Mediterranean-
style dishes such as Piedmontese peppers or grilled squid with rocket,
vegetable relish and garlic croutons. Crab, langoustine and prawns
appear au naturel with mayonnaise or in salads. Eat in the small bar
area or at tables in the main foyer of the building and watch the world
go by.

BIG NIGHT OUT   NW1

148 Regent's Park Road, NW1 8XN
Tel: 0171-586 5768   *Fax:* 0171-482 4176   **£45**
Open: lunch Tue-Sun, dinner Mon-Sat
   (closed 25 Dec, 1 Jan)
Meals served: lunch 12-3, dinner 7-11

Choose between the ground-floor dining area, decorated with huge modern Michelango-inspired canvasses or the dark, cosy upstairs room, then relax over a refreshingly short and varied carte or go for the fixed-price menu option. Dishes such as Gruyère soufflé with rocket and red pepper oil, oysters au naturel and quail's egg salad are typical of starters; main courses might include a seared tuna salad with sesame dressing and celeriac chips, breast of Norfolk duckling with turnip and swede gratinée or steak, Guinness and oyster pudding. Popular for Sunday brunch (£10 including drink and coffee), or pop in at lunchtime for two courses—excellent value.

BILLBOARD CAFÉ   NW6

222 Kilburn High Road, NW6 4JP
Tel: 0171-328 1374   **£25**
Open: lunch Sat & Sun, dinner Mon-Sat
   (closed 25 & 26 Dec)
Meals served: lunch 12-3, dinner 6.30-12.30am

Something for everyone at this unpretentious little restaurant close to the Tricycle Theatre. Daily specials supplement the twice-weekly-changing carte which offers a range of salads, interesting pasta dishes and grills, including pounded breast of chicken with cream and mush-room sauce, spicy Italian sausages, steaks and fish of the day. No-choice set menus offer good value in the evening, and weekends see the introduction of a brunch menu (12-3pm)—freshly filled baguettes, omelettes, steak and chips.

BISTROT 190   SW7

190 Queen's Gate, SW7 5EU
Tel: 0171-581 5666   *Fax:* 0171-581 8172   **£45**
Open: all day daily (closed 24-26 Dec)
Meals served: 7am-12.30am
   (Sun to 11.30pm)

Among the capital's trendiest restaurants, Bistrot 190 is a lively, noisy, bustling place in line with the move towards happier, less structured eating. The menu, masterminded by Antony Worrall Thompson, is just as modern—influenced in (now typical) style by the Mediterranean and California above all else. The decor follows suit in bistro-style char-acter—marble tables and bare wooden floor. The repertoire from the kitchen is vast, a feast of choices from morning to night. Wonderful breakfasts offer a lengthy carte alongside a choice of eight set menus—breakfasts from across the world, healthy option and children's choice. The scene throughout the day is similar, with a set lunch menu compli-menting a long and exciting all-day carte. Starters run from country bread with olives and tapenade or warm onion tart to cassoulet of little fishes with chili toast and penne with a shellfish and piquant sauce.

Biography

Born to `theatrical' parents in Stratford-upon-Avon, with eleven `O' levels, four `A' levels and an HND in Hotel and Catering Management to his name, Antony Worrall Thompson's career started in rural Essex before he **Antony** *moved to London where he spent time in a variety of* **Worrall** *establishments including Brinkley's Restaurant, Fulham Road; Dan's Restaurant, Chelsea; and the* **Thompson** *much-publicised Ménage à Trois, Knightsbridge. Another personality of the industry, Antony now masterminds the menus and has interests at a number of leading London establishments (dell'Ugo, Café dell'Ugo, two restaurants at One Ninety Queen's Gate) and consistently remains one step ahead of the rest in predicting and perpetuating food trends.*

Main courses range from light to robust in a selection which might feature salmon fishcakes or risotto alongside three-sausage hot pot, peppered venison steak, and char-grilled halibut or tuna. Desserts show more of a nod towards tradition with rhubarb crumble, chocolate nut fudge cake and lemon tart sharing the space with the likes of the ever-so-mod vanilla croissant pudding with bay custard, or country cheeses served with rocket and Muscat pear. You might be asked to wait in the Club 190 Bar adjacent to the Bistrot, but there are worse places to wait! Bookings can be made only if you are a member of Club 190. (See also Downstairs at 190).

BISTROT BRUNO   W1

63 Frith Street, W1V 5TA
Tel: 0171-734 4545   Fax: 0171-287 1027   **£50**
Open: lunch Mon-Fri, dinner Mon-Sat (closed 3-4 days Xmas)
Meals served: lunch 12.15-2.30, dinner 6.15-11.30

With Bruno Loubet behind the scenes at this Soho restaurant, you can expect a surprise or two. The menu changes monthly and is strongly marked out by gutsy Mediterranean influences and a respect for the culinary traditions of the Midi. It is short, varied and highly imaginative, with dishes such as curry-flavoured crab quiche and chicken liver flan with thyme and bacon sauce preceding main courses like grilled quails with tarragon jus and steamed sea bass with black bean and garlic. For the less adventurous palate, there may be Galway Bay oysters and a home-made soup, followed beef stew niçoise-style, roast guinea fowl on wild mushroom risotto. Bruno likes to break the rules, though, so even familiar-sounding dishes may have the element of surprise. Try shellfish canelloni which comes served in a hot herb broth. Minimal, modernist decor completes the scene.

■ Bruno Loubet biography, page 70

Biography

Bruno Loubet

Bruno Loubet was born in Libourne, and for as long as he can remember he wanted to cook. After catering school he gained experience in a number of top European hotels and restaurants including the Hyatt Regency, Brussels; the Copenhague, Paris; Le Manoir aux Quat'Saisons, Great Milton; Le Petit Blanc, Oxford and the Four Seasons Restaurant at the Inn on the Park in London. Now at Bistrot Bruno and at the top of his profession, he continues to develop his style: flair and innovation.

BLAKES HOTEL   SW7

33 Roland Gardens, SW7 3PF
Tel: 0171-370 6701   *Fax:* 0171-373 0442   **£100**
Open: lunch & dinner daily
Meals served: lunch 12.30-2.30,
     dinner 7.30-11.30   ✿

Blakes was created out of two Victorian mansions by Anouska Hempel and further houses have been added over the years, raising the total number of rooms from the original 28 to 52. Today it's just about the most fashionable place in London for visiting celebrities, from Robert De Niro to fellow designers Armani and Miyake, and many more besides. This is the definitive small luxury hotel, where rooms respect fantasy, not function. Beautifully designed throughout, it is never ostentatious, yet breathtaking. According to Anouska, it is a personal statement about what good design can achieve. When a room needs redecorating, she supervises procedures from start to finish. Colour schemes are daring: black and gold, all lavender, deep reds and a pure, pure white. "I am in the business of making dreams become reality," she says. Nothing if not heroic is the feeling you get, so clearly, she is on the right track. So, too, is the kitchen: classic with some Oriental twists describes the cooking of chef Peter Thornley. It's an eclectic range—this was one of the first restaurants in London to "go eclectic" on one menu—sashimi, soufflé Suissesse, Beluga blinis, tortellini of Landes foie gras to start, followed perhaps by langoustine satay, Szechuan duck with roasted salt and pepper, gyuniku teriyaki with sake, char-grilled baby lamb with rosemary and garlic, and risottos—wild mushroom with thyme beurre blanc or inkfish. Lovely accompaniments, delicious desserts like cinder toffee parfait under barley brittle, and high-roast Chagga coffee. The breakfast menus are quite spectacular in themselves, no surprise here perhaps, but apart from a splendid list of English and Continental offerings, there's also the choice of a Kyoto country breakfast, with miso and ginger soup and fresh fish cooked on lava rock.

This hotel stands the test of time and proves that quality pays. It's expensive, but if you want the best . . .

BLOOM'S   E1

90 Whitechapel High Street, E1 7RA
Tel: 0171-247 6001   **£40**
Open: all day Sun-Thu, lunch Fri (closed Jewish holidays, 25 Dec)
Meals served: 11-9.30 (Fri to 3pm)
Longstanding traditional Jewish restaurant working to strict kosher rules. Salt beef is a speciality. Sister in NW11 (see below).

BLOOM'S   NW11

130 Golders Green Road, NW11 8HB
Tel: 0181-455 1338   **£40**
Open: all day Sun-Thu, lunch Fri, dinner Sat (closed Jewish Hols)
Meals served: 10am-10.30pm (Fri 10am-sunset, Sat sunset-4am, Sun-Thu to 2am)
Kosher Jewish restaurant, sister to the one above, founded in 1920 by Morris Bloom in earlier Brick Lane premises.

BLUE ELEPHANT   SW6

4-6 Fulham Broadway, SW6 1AA
Tel: 0171-385 6595   *Fax:* 0171-386 7665   **£60**
Open: lunch Sun-Fri, dinner daily (closed 24-27 Dec, 1 Jan)
Meals served: lunch 12-2.30, dinner 7-12.30 (Sun to 10.30)

The Blue Elephant is decorated with lush greenery, a waterfall, stream and bridge, all of which create an ideal venue in which to enjoy Thai cooking at its best. For a real treat, enjoy the Thai banquet which offers over six choices at each course.

BLUE PRINT CAFÉ   SE1

Design Museum, Shad Thames, Butlers Wharf, SE1 2YD
Tel: 0171-378 7031   *Fax:* 0171-378 6540   **£45**
Open: lunch daily, dinner Mon-Sat
    (closed Bank Holidays)   *Refreshing decor and food with a*
Meals served: lunch 12-3, dinner 6-11   *young enthusiastic staff*

The Blue Print Café on the mezzanine level of the Design Museum has views towards Tower Bridge and the Thames. The room is bright, with flashes of colour, and the balcony terrace provides a perfect venue for alfresco summer eating. Lucy Crabb's menu of modern European dishes changes daily, offering the likes of cockle and mussel soup, grilled tuna with salsa and guacamole, calf's liver with caramelised onions, spinach and ricotta gnocchi, plaice and chips with sauce tartare, lemon tart with passion fruit sauce and tiramisu.

BOMBAY BRASSERIE   SW7

Courtfield Close, Courtfield Road, SW7 4UH
Tel: 0171-370 4040   *Fax:* 0171-835 1669   **£60**
Open: lunch & dinner daily
  (closed 25 & 26 Dec)
Meals served: lunch 12.30-3, dinner 7.30-12 (Sun to 11.30)

Incredibly successful — expansion planned for 1995

This famous Indian restaurant, with its colonial atmosphere, palms and conservatory room, is the jewel in the crown of Taj International Hotels, and it is without doubt one of the most glamorous and handsome of the capital's Indian restaurants. The lunch-time buffet, offering the chance to sample eight fragrantly spiced dishes from the mildest to the meanest, has been a much-publicised favourite ever since it opened in 1982. Smart, polite staff are more than able to advise on dishes. The kitchen draws its inspiration from all over the Indian sub-continent: colourful puri from Bombay, Moghlai chicken biryani, Goan fish curry, tandooris, and house specialities such as lamb korma and the truly hot lobster peri peri. Good vegetarian options. Popular on Sunday lunchtimes; pianist in the evenings and valet parking after 8pm.

LA BOUCHÉE   SW7

56 Old Brompton Road, SW7 3DY
Tel: 0171-589 1929   *Fax:* 0171-584 8625   **£35**
Open: all day daily (closed 25 & 26 Dec, 1 Jan)
Meals served: 9am-11pm

Tiny, traditional-style French bistro with plain wooden tables, dripping candles and few patio tables in summer. Starters feature oysters, mussels, snails, soups and salads; while main course options range from traditional favourites like steak frites or coq au vin to more sophisticated dishes: calf's kidney with cognac sauce, roasted pheasant, steamed salmon hollandaise or John Dory and roasted pepper with chive sauce. Traditional desserts to finish.

BOYD'S   W8

135 Kensington Church Street, W8 7LP
Tel: 0171-727 5452   *Fax:* 0171-221 0615   **£60**
Open: lunch & dinner Mon-Sat (closed Easter, 2 wks Xmas)
Meals served: lunch 12.30-2.30, dinner 7-11

Boyd Gilmour's pleasant conservatory restaurant complete with glass dome is a good choice along this restaurant-rich stretch of Kensington Church Street. The two-course set lunch menu offers excellent value and an international repertoire, which is fully explored on the evening carte. Starters run from the familiar onion soup with gruyère croûtons, or tagliatelle with wild mushrooms, to marinated tuna and avocado salad with a lime and ginger dressing. Main courses feature fish of the day along with roast lamb, char-grilled chicken with chardonnay sauce or grilled calf's liver with two mustard butters. The quintet of lemon desserts is a refreshing finale, as is the lime and fromage frais sorbet. Some very good half bottles on the extensive wine list. Boyd has adopted a lighter touch over the last year and his cooking continues to grow in stature, to the delight of his loyal, local following.

THE BRACKENBURY   W6

129-131 Brackenbury Road, W6 OBQ
Tel: 0181-748 0107   *A fun, busy and*   **£35**
Open: lunch Tue-Fri & Sun, dinner Mon-Sat   *interesting*
  (closed Bank Holidays, 1 wk Xmas)   *restaurant*
Meals served: lunch 12.30-2.45, dinner 7-10.45

This hugely popular local restaurant is on to a winner with its formula
of sensible pricing and simple modern cooking which encompasses all
the latest culinary fashions. The menu changes at each session, offering around half a dozen choices for each course. Starters might feature
seafood chowder, rocket salad or fritters of lamb's brains and sweetbreads with a ravigote sauce. Main courses include fascinating flavour
combinationas such as salt beef stovey with parsley sauce, or roast
hake with chick peas and chorizo. Homely puds, such as Bramley
crumble and custard or stewed rhubarb with clotted cream ice cream.
Families welcome. The decor is functional, with school benches and
tightly packed tables.

LE BRACONNIER   SW14

467 Upper Richmond Road West, SW14 7PU
Tel: 0181-878 2853   **£40**
Open: lunch Sun in winter, dinner daily
  (closed Bank Holidays, 25-28 Dec, 1 wk Easter, 2 wks Aug)
Meals served: lunch 12.30-2.30, dinner 7-10.45

French regional cooking is the thing at this cosy little restaurant, with
monthly menus which feature a specific region supplementing the regular carte of dishes like cassoulet and rack of lamb. Other favourites
include warm asparagus tart with an onion confit or grilled boar
sausages among starters, and main courses such as entrecôte bordelaise or bourride—trio of monkfish, sole and salmon in a garlic-
flavoured broth. Popular local restaurant.

LA BRASSERIE   SW3

272 Brompton Road, SW3 2AW
Tel: 0171-581 3089   *Fax:* 0171-823 8553   **£40**
Open: all day daily (closed 25 Dec)
Meals served: 8am-midnight
  (Sun & Bank Holidays 10am-11.30pm)

Authentic French brasserie in the Parisian style, complete with French
waiters in long white aprons. The day starts with breakfast and newspa-
pers, moving on mid-morning to baguettes, salads and toasted sandwiches, before the full menu of brasserie classics comes into play from
lunchtime. Dishes such as Toulouse sausages with lentils, goulash,
boeuf bourguignonne, various steaks, casseroles and fish dishes are
supplemented by daily specials. The food has taken an upturn in the
last year and La Brasserie deserves its growing reputation and
popularity.

BRASSERIE DU MARCHÉ AUX PUCES — W10

349 Portobello Road, W10 5SA
Tel: 0181-968 5828 £45
Open: all day Mon-Sat, Sun lunch only
  (closed Bank Holidays)
Meals served: 12 noon-11pm (Sun 12-4)

In perhaps the most colourful of London's famous market streets, this brasserie takes its lead from its bohemian location, with a menu of modern European dishes based as much as possible on local supplies—bread from nearby Ceres; merguez sausages from the Portuguese delicatessen; and local market vegetables. Very much in tune with modern tastes, other dishes might be poached egg with truffles and beurre blanc; crostini with rocket and walnut pesto, served with smoked salmon mousse; roast duck with sage and apple compote; spatchcock chicken with hazelnut, or onion and dolcelatte confit. Delicious puds. Pavement dining in good weather and fruit and flower arrangements on the curved bar add continental authenticity to this French-style brasserie.

BRASSERIE ST QUENTIN — SW3

243 Brompton Road, SW3 2EP
Tel: 0171-581 5131   *Fax:* 0171-584 6064   *Very popular and rightly so*   £45
Open: lunch & dinner daily
Meals served: lunch 12-3, dinner 7-11.30

Previously called simply St Quentin, the name has been altered slightly so as to make a clearer distinction between the brasserie-style operation here and that at the Grill St Quentin (see later). Situated opposite the Brompton Oratory, this place is quintessentially French, in the classic, traditional sense. New chef Nigel Davis came from the Ivy, though his style here is inspired by time spent working in the Midi. His cassoulet comes highly recommended. The menu features many classic dishes, and judging by its popularity, this is what the loyal local clientele like best. Goose pâté, soupe au pistou, fresh foie gras, chicory and Roquefort salad, Dover sole, spicy Toulouse sausages with lentils, beef casserole, pigeon in red wine, rabbit with Agen prunes, confit de canard are what it's all about. Finish with lemon tart or perhaps crème brûlée. French staff are dressed for the part, in formal black and white. Under the direction of Didier Garnier this establishment continues to flourish and has a confident, grown up feel to it.

BROWN'S HOTEL   W1

Albemarle Street, W1A 4SW
Tel: 0171-493 6020   *Fax:* 0171-493 9381   **£50**
Open: lunch & dinner daily
Meals served: lunch 12.15-3 (Sun 12.30-2.30), dinner 6-10
(Sun 6.30-9.30)

A sense of continuity springs to mind when Brown's is mentioned -the
style which made Brown's famous in its early Victorian days has been
carefully preserved. Rich ornate furnishing, traditional elegance and
English charm are the hallmarks of this 118-bedroomed hotel, built by a
retired gentleman's gentleman, James Brown, in 1837. Famous figures
have passed through, from Queen Victoria on a number of occasions, to
Napoleon III and the Roosevelts—for Franklin and his bride Eleanor
this was their honeymoon home. Afternoon tea is an occasion here
(jackets and ties required for gentlemen). The restaurant offers a seasonal menu, though longstanding favourites survive throughout the
year. A typical selection from the carte includes wild mushroom consommé, confit of quail, daube of beef, sausage and mash, and brandade
fish cake with creamed leeks and a light grain mustard sauce. A short
table d'hôte might include the likes of red snapper poached with saffron, carrot and onion, or lamb with a basil and chicken mousse. The
arrival of chef Aidan McCormack has brought a lighter, more modern
approach in the kitchen.

BUBB'S   EC1

329 Central Markets, EC1A 9NB
Tel: 0171-236 2435   **£55**
Open: lunch Mon-Fri (closed Bank Holidays)
Meals served: lunch 12-2.30

French prints, posters, music and staff create an authentic setting for
Francis Bureau's concise lunchtime menu at this attractive little restaurant by Smithfield Market. Good, sound, bourgeois cooking and a carte
which is supplemented by daily specials. Expect to find snails, fish
soup provençale, onion soup and asparagus in season among starters;
main courses might include steak au poivre or béarnaise, duck with
orange, and daily fish specials such as poached salmon hollandaise or
halibut with Dieppoise sauce. Very busy, so best to book.

BUCHAN'S   SW11

62-64 Battersea Bridge Road, SW11 3AG
Tel: 0171-228 0888   *Fax:* 0171-924 1718   **£55**
Open: lunch & dinner daily (closed 25 & 26 Dec)
Meals served: lunch 12-2.45, dinner 6-10.45 (Sun 7-10)

Friendly, local restaurant just south of Battersea Bridge, offering
Scottish and French cooking at reasonable prices. For a quick bite, sit
in the front bar, with polished wooden floor and hand-decorated tables,
and choose from the good range of snacks, salads, soups or sandwiches on offer on the bar menu, or for something a little more substantial, eat in the main restaurant. You might try the likes of haggis
with neeps'n'tatties or mussels with ginger and coriander to start, followed by fillet of red fish with a three-pepper sauce or Scotch fillet
steak either peppered, grilled or flambéed in whisky, finishing with
chocolate truffle cake with brandy butter or spotted dick with custard.
Reasonably-priced wine list with good selections from around the world
and over ten wines by the glass. Warm welcome from owner-manager
Jeremy Bolam.

BUTLERS WHARF CHOP-HOUSE   SE1

Butlers Wharf, SE1 2YE
Tel: 0171-403 3403   *Fax:* 0171-403 3414   **£50**
Open: lunch Sun-Fri, dinner Mon-Sat (closed 4 days Xmas)
Meals served: lunch 12-3, dinner 6-11, (light meals
    Bar: 12-3 (Sat & Sun from 11.30) & 6-11 winter, 12-11 summer)

Riverside Conran restaurant close to Tower Bridge. The bar offers a
light snack menu, with the likes of veal and ham pie, West Cork rock
oysters, steak sandwich and grills; and the main restaurant a selection
of modern dishes. The fixed-price lunch menu and blackboard specials
pull in the crowds with dishes such as salmon and smoked haddock
kedgeree, chop-house sausages and mash, plaice and chips tartare, and
daily roasts and grills. Dinner à la carte runs along similar lines but
there is greater choice. A wide choice of puds runs from Cambridge
burnt cream or trifle to banana fritters with caramel or sticky toffee
pudding. Good wine list with some reasonable buys.

LE CADRE   N8

10 Priory Road, Crouch End, N8 7RD
Tel: 0181-348 0606   **£45**
Open: lunch Mon-Fri, dinner Mon-Sat
    (closed Bank Holidays, 2 wks Aug/Sep)
Meals served: lunch 12-2.30, dinner 7-11

Stylish neighbourhood French restaurant in the shadow of Alexandra
Palace. There is a classically-based repertoire, with around half a dozen
choices at each stage on the short bilingual carte: warm brioche of wild
mushrooms; medallions of monkfish with a champagne and basil sauce
served with saffron rice; rack of New English lamb with Dijon mustard
sauce; Scotch fillet with a foie gras mousse and Madeira sauce; veal
casserole provençale; and game casserole with a crusty pie top. A nod
here and there to modernity, but never moving far from classical traditional interpretations. Reasonably priced wine list.

CAFÉ DELANCEY   NW1

3 Delancey Street, NW1 7NN
Tel: 0171-387 1985   *Fax:* 0171-383 5314   **£40**
Open: all day daily (closed 25 & 26 Dec, 1 Jan)
Meals served: 8am-midnight

Any dish is available at any time of the day at this stylish café-restaurant off Camden High Street. Breakfast, accompanied by papers, starts the day, ranging from Delancey's full-blown English or vegetarian grill to croissants and baguettes. The main menu offers a typical bistro-style choice, ranging from home-made soups or deep-fried Camembert to salads, croques monsieur or madame, steak sandwiches and grills. Relaxed and informal. The full liquor licence here means that you can pop in for a drink during pub hours without eating, if you wish.

CAFÉ DELL'UGO   SE1

56-58 Tooley Street, SE1 2SZ
Tel: 0171-407 6001   *Fax:* 0171-357 8806   *Café dell'Ugo has* **£45**
Open: lunch Mon-Fri, dinner Mon-Sat   *quickly*
  (closed Bank Holidays)   *established itself on*
Meals served: lunch 12-3, dinner 7-11,   *the local scene.*
  (light meals Café/Bar: 10am-11pm)

Its close proximity to the London Dungeon, occupying one of the arches under London Bridge Station, accounts for the cellar-like ambience of this first-floor restaurant with its vaulted brick ceiling and church-candle-lit tables. An Antony Worrall Thompson inspired menu offers exciting, new and unusual combinations—chilled lovage, citrus and grape soup (in summer); spicy sardines on rösti with harissa and yoghurt; rolled soufflé with wilted greens, leeks and cheeses, red pepper sauce and curry oil; a hotchpot of fishes in tomato and fennel bisque with cold lime butter; lamb shank tagine with artichokes, lemon and aubergine; rustic Bramley charlotte with Devon clotted cream; and walnut honey pie. Plenty to choose from—at least ten choices among starters and main courses, slightly fewer among puds. The spacious ground-floor bar also serves a wide choice of snacks.

CAFÉ DES AMIS DU VIN   WC2

11-14 Hanover Place, WC2E 9JP
Tel: 0171-379 3444   *Fax:* 0171-379 9124   **£35**
Open: lunch Mon-Fri, dinner Mon-Sat
Meals served: lunch 12.30-3, dinner 6.11.30
  (light meals in Brasserie 11am-11pm)

Long-established wine bar, brasserie and restaurant (on three floors) where you can get a snack or a full meal, before of after the theatre, and an excellent range of wines by the glass. Traditionally French in most aspects of the operation, and particularly so in the pricing policy where VAT, cover and service are all included. This is the sort of place I wish there were more of in London—full marks to Peter Nottage for maintaining standards here.

CAFÉ DU MARCHÉ   EC1

22 Charterhouse Square, Charterhouse Mews, EC1M 6AH
Tel: 0171-608 1609   **£50**
Open: lunch Mon-Fri, dinner Mon-Sat
   (closed Bank Holidays, Xmas/New Year, Easter)
Meals served: lunch 12-2.30, dinner 6-10

A splendid warehouse setting—exposed brick, wooden floor, cane furniture and large beams—seems appropriate for this restaurant located
near Smithfield Market. Popular with locals and City types, the main
dining room below serves modern French cooking in its relaxed country-style setting, with dishes such as scallop salad with langoustine
sauce, côte de boeuf béarnaise and coffee and walnut tart available on
the short but well-thought-out table d'hôte menu. Needless to say,
given its location, the meat here is of prime fresh quality. Upstairs, the
Grenier (attic room) specialises in grills at lunch-time, and can be used
for private parties in the evening—sounds like fun! All in all this is a
good local restaurant with style, good food and ambience.

CAFÉ FLO   N1

334 Upper Street, N1 8EA
Tel: 0171-226 7916   *Fax:* 0171-704 2965   **£35**
Open: all day daily (closed 25 & 26 Dec)
Meals served: 9-11.30 (Sun to 10.30)

Bustling bistro-cum-café oozing with Gallic charm. One of five in the
London chain (see entries below). This is a perfect place to meet or
grab a quick bite from the multiple choices on offer. Everything from
French onion soup to steak sandwiches and daily specials.

CAFÉ FLO   NW3

205 Haverstock Hill, NW3 4QY   *Right formula, right price,*
Tel: 0171-435 6744   *right time*   **£30**
Open: all day daily (closed 4 days Xmas)
Meals served: 10am-11pm (Sun 10am-10.30pm)

One of over half a dozen London-based Flos
based on the French bistro/brasserie formula.
Pop in for breakfast and linger over the paper, or
rendezvous for a quick and simple lunch. The
choice is extensive, with good-value plats du jour
and a menu rapide to help you along. Soups and
salads, casseroles and steaks, grilled fish and
familiar favourites like Toulouse sausages with
mash or salmon fish cakes are all served in a
relaxed, friendly and unpretentious manner. The
room is adorned with some lovely bric-à-brac
collected during many French trips.

CAFÉ FLO   SW6

676 Fulham Road, SW6 5RS
Tel: 0171-371 9673   *Fax:* 0171-731 5178   **£35**
Open: all day daily (closed 25 & 26 Dec, 1 Jan)
Meals served: 9am-11.30pm (Sun to 10.30)

The Fulhamites' Flo. Pop in for breakfast, a quick bite or full-blown
meal. Good value set menus emulate the Gallic tradition of affordable
all-in meals without any fuss. Good coffee, wine and atmosphere.

CAFÉ FLO   W8

127/129 Kensington Church Street, W8 7LP
Tel: 0171-727 8142   *Fax:* 0171-243 2935   **£35**
Open: all day daily (closed 25 & 26 Dec)
Meals served: 9am-11.30pm

Perfect port of call for sustenance for shoppers in busy High Street
Kensington. Call in for a coffee to take the weight off your feet or sit
down to a meal of daily specials, from soup to plats du jour. The choice
is varied, especially taking account of the regular brasserie carte too.

CAFÉ FLO   WC2

51 St Martins Lane, WC2N 4EA
Tel: 0171-836 8289   *Fax:* 0171-379 0314   **£35**
Open: lunch & dinner daily (closed Bank Holidays, 5 days Xmas)
Meals served: lunch 12-3 (Sat & Sun to 4), dinner
    5.30-11.45 (Sun to 10.30, (light meals 9am-11.30)
(Sun 10-10.30pm)

With its theatreland location, this is the most central of Russell Joffe's
five London Flos. Sound bistro classics keep the young Soho crowd
flocking to this West End brasserie. Stick to regular lunch and dinner
hours to enjoy all that's on offer from the daily specials. Informal and
relaxed like the rest of its siblings across the capital, with plenty of
Gallic spirit and style.

CAFÉ ROYAL   W1

68 Regent Street, W1R 6EL
Tel: 0171-437 9090   *Fax:* 0171-439 7672   **£80**
Open: lunch Mon-Fri, dinner Mon-Sat
    (closed Bank Holidays, 3 days Xmas)
Meals served: lunch 12.30-2.45, dinner 6-10.15

Biography

*After a three-year appren-
ticeship at the Grand Hotel
at Zell-am-See in his native
Austria and work in*

Herbert *Europe,
Herbert*
Berger *Berger came*
*to London and worked in
various establishments
including the Connoisseur;
Keats; the Connaught;
Claridges; the Mirabelle
and Martin's.*

Always one of London's favourite venues, the Café Royal has been given a new lease of life by Herbert Berger's stylish cooking. Choose from the more casual Brasserie or the sumptuous rococo Grill Room. In the brasserie there's a good selection of traditional and contemporary dishes—French onion soup, tartare of salmon with ginger and lime, warm potato salad with paprika sausage or spinach ravioli with peppers, pesto and parmesan are amongst the first courses. Toad in the hole, a braised knuckle of lamb with red beans and cumin, breast of chicken with sun-dried tomatoes and basil or confit of duck with wild mushrooms and herbs are typical main dishes. Over 20 wines are available by the glass. The Grill Room menu matches its refined decor: sautée of scallops with basil, orange peel and tapenade; supreme of turbot with crispy potato crust, braised leeks and beurre rouge, braised calf's sweetbreads with galette of foie gras, sorrel and Sauternes. If you prefer, there are grilled fish or meats and some roast dishes for two such as Bresse chicken, rib of beef and rack of lamb. Extensive wine list.

CAMDEN BRASSERIE   NW1

216 Camden High Street, Camden Town, NW1 8QR
Tel: 0171-482 2114   **£55**
Open: lunch & dinner daily (closed 24-26 & 31 Dec)
Meals served: lunch 12-3 (Sun 12.30-3.30), dinner 6-11.30 (Sun 5-10.30)
Bustling, popular brasserie specialising in char-grilled and fresh pasta dishes. Fillets of lamb and beef, Toulouse sausages and corn-fed chicken are favourites. Very good salads.

CANAL BRASSERIE   **W10**

Canalot Studios, 222 Kensal Road, W10 5BN
Tel: 0181-960 2732   **£35**
Open: lunch Mon-Fri (closed Bank Holidays)
Meals served: lunch 12-3

A former chocolate factory with a canalside location makes an interesting setting for this popular local restaurant which serves the local business community. A glass-covered atrium commands the interior space, which is spacious and modern, with contemporary European artwork providing the necessary colour. A short, simple menu offers imaginative cooking in the modern mode, with dishes such as spicy potato soup followed by soy-glazed leg of duck on beanshoot salad with sweet Chinese sauce, fish cakes with chili tomato salsa or lighter options such as pasta. Puds could include sticky ginger or apple pie. Porthole windows look out on to the canal.

CANNIZARO HOUSE   **SW19**

West Side, Wimbledon Common, SW19 4UF
Tel: 0181-879 1464   *Fax:* 0181-879 7338   **£60**
Open: lunch & dinner daily
Meals served: lunch 12-2, dinner 7-10.30

A country house hotel on the edge of Wimbledon Common may seem an unlikely thought, but this is what Cannizaro is all about. Sweeping lawns and quiet woodland walks, an ornamental lake and formal gardens (the park totals some 40 acres) are among the attractions at this 46-bedroomed Georgian mansion. In its Victorian heyday, the house was owned by the widowed Mrs Schuster who held huge garden parties for the literati and glitterati of the day. Guests included Oscar Wilde, Tennyson, Henry James and royalty. Chef Stephen Wilson now provides a traditional classic repertoire of French and English cuisine to today's discerning guests, completing the picture.

THE CANTEEN   **SW10**

Harbour Yard, Chelsea Harbour, SW10
Tel: 0171-351 7330   *Fax:* 0171-351 6189   **£55**
Open: lunch & dinner daily
Meals served: lunch 12-3 (Sun 12.30-3.30),
    dinner 6.30-12 (Sun 7-11)   ✿

There were changes during 1994 in the kitchen at Marco Pierre White's light and airy Chelsea Harbour restaurant, where conservatory window tables overlook the marina. The menu is seasonal and there is only the one throughout the day. The aim is to offer Marco's style and quality at more affordable prices and it works. Our summer menu featured gazpacho with crab, saffron risotto and roast sea scallops with sauce vierge among the list of a dozen or so starters; main courses included a gratinée of brill with a soft herb crust, pot-roast pork with spices and ginger and roast rump of lamb Niçoise with a jus of olives.

A stylish and well-thought-out formula that deserves continued success

CANTINA DEL PONTE   SE1

Butlers Wharf Building, 36c Shad Thames, Butlers Wharf, SE1 2YE
Tel: 0171-403 5403   *Fax:* 0171-403 0267   **£45**
Open: lunch daily, dinner Mon-Sat
Meals served: lunch 12-3, dinner 6-11

Another in the Conran empire, this one placing the focus firmly on the Mediterranean. The restaurant has a light and airy feel to it, further enhanced by the terrace seating overlooking the Thames in summer. There's plenty of choice from the menu which features pasta, risotto and pizzas alongside the likes of rib-eye steak with porcini, char-grilled squid salad and marinaded spring chicken with courgette and red pepper casserole. Decor is fashionably rustic, sunny and simple—terracotta floor and marble topped tables. Next door to the Pont de la Tour, with outside seating, it shares the same views of the Thames and Tower Bridge.

Deservedly popular, attracting a young, appreciative following

THE CAPITAL   SW3

22-24 Basil Street, SW3 1AT
Tel: 0171-589 5171   *Fax:* 0171-225 0011   **£75**
Open: lunch & dinner daily
Meals served: lunch 12-2.30, dinner 7-11

An unusual, intimate hotel in a superb location, impeccably run by owners David and Margaret Levin. Philip Britten is the chef and he provides a fine variety of dishes that are beautifully presented and perfectly executed. A sauté of scallops, aubergine, courgette and pimento with ginger and coriander or asparagus and foie gras gratin with a Muscadet sabayon, deep-fried lobster beignets with lime and lobster butter sauce or pot-roast squab pigeon on a bed of root vegetables flavoured with cinnamon are typical of his style. For pudding, perhaps a tarte tatin with caramel sauce and Calvados sorbet, a bitter orange parfait with confit of oranges or a gateau of apricots, rice and honey. There are two lovely private dining rooms for receptions, meetings or dinner parties, and for a quick lunch or post-shopping drink there's L'Hotel and Le Metro (see later, within London) just along the road, under the same ownership.

Biography

Philip Britten & **David Levin**

Philip Britten was spotted early at The Dorchester by the legendary chef de cuisine Eugene Kaufeler. After a short time in Switzerland, he then returned to London to work with the likes of Richard Shepherd at Langan's Brasserie and Nico Ladenis at Chez Nico. In 1987 David Levin installed him as chef at The Capital, where he remains an essential part of this well-oiled machine, providing good food in his own, unassuming way. He is now a champion of the drive for excellence of quality, British cooking.

LE CAPRICE   SW1

Arlington House, Arlington Street, SW1A 1RT
Tel: 0171-629 2239   *Fax:* 0171-493 9040   **£60**
Open: lunch & dinner daily   *Go there—but book!*
   (closed 24 Dec-1 Jan, dinner 2 Jan)   🌸
Meals served: lunch 12-3 (Sun to 3.30), dinner 6-12

One of the most famous restaurants in London, Le Caprice is a place
in which to be seen. This highly fashionable, chic restaurant continues
to pull in the glitterati, the young and trendy, and those who simply go
to see what all the fuss is about. Booking is essential, unless you manage to squeeze into a gap at the bar for a quick snack. A modern, international repertoire of dishes is both fashionable and nostalgic. Starters
might offer a straightforward Caesar salad, dressed Cornish crab or
the more exotic Thai-spiced broth. Main courses run from the signature salmon fishcake with sorrel sauce or Lincolnshire sausages with
onion gravy and bubble'n'squeak to steak tartare, grilled yellow-fin
tuna or char-grilled squid with Italian bacon. Good vegetarian choices
include pastas and risotti. The popular Sunday brunch menu includes
more of the same, if on a more casual basis, with dishes like corned
beef hash with fried egg making an appearance. Attention to detail and
the ability to make all the customers feel welcome are what sets Le
Caprice apart.

CASA COMINETTI   SE6

129 Rushey Green, SE6 4AA
Tel: 0181-697 2314   **£40**
Open: lunch Mon-Fri, dinner Mon-Sat (closed 25 & 26 Dec)
Meals served: lunch 12-2.30, dinner 6.30-11

Casa Cominetti has been serving up good Italian home cooking since
1916, which may go some way to explaining the continued absence of
fads and fuss here. The cooking is consistently enjoyable, featuring
specialities such as fillet of beef with olives and sea bass Mareschal.

CASALE FRANCO   N1

134-127 Upper Street, N1 1PQ
Tel: 0171-226 8994   *Fax:* 0171-359 5569   **£45**
Open: lunch Fri-Sun, dinner Tue-Sun (closed Bank Holidays,
   1 wk Aug, 1 wk Xmas)
Meals served: lunch 12.30-2.30, dinner 6.30-11.30 (Sun to 11)

You'll be spoiled for choice at Franco and Gisella Pensa's table. This
family-run Italian restaurant, with modernist designer decor, offers an
extensive carte of familiar favourites. There are at least ten pizzas, ten
pasta dishes and a long list of fish and meat specials, such as spicy
Italian sausages with polenta, whole grilled sea bass, roast veal and fillet steak. (Pizzas are served only in the evening, and not as a single
course meal after 8pm). A fun local restaurant situated on two floors
with some courtyard seating. It is exactly what you might find in an
Italian city, tucked away up an alley way, but this one is marked by a
Citroën garage sign rather than a Fiat one.

CHAPTER 11 — SW10

47 Hollywood Road, SW10 *Good local restaurant*
Tel: 0171-351 1683   **£40**
Open: dinner Mon-Sat (closed Bank Holidays, 4 days Xmas)
Meals served: dinner 7-11.30

This bustling, smart and informal restaurant located just off Fulham Road blends traditional and modern elements on an essentially British menu, though Oriental and Mediterranean influences creep in with dishes like Thai prawn curry and soupe au pistou. Familiar favourites include the likes of asparagus risotto, crab salad, grilled calf's liver with bacon, turbot au beurre blanc and char-grilled chicken with tomato sauce. Traditional puds like bread-and-butter, or lemon tart. The pleasant garden area is a bonus in summer.

CHARLOTTE'S PLACE — W5

16 St Matthew's Road, W5 3JT
Tel: 0181-567 7541   **£45**
Open: lunch Mon-Fri, dinner Mon-Sat (check when booking
     for closures)
Meals served: lunch 12.30-2, dinner 7.30-10

Since its early days as a bistro, Charlotte's Place has 'grown up', earning itself a loyal local following. A family-run restaurant on the edge of Ealing Common, it serves unpretentious French and English dishes which range from the likes of seafood crêpe or snails to individual beef Wellington, lamb cutlets with redcurrant jelly, magret of duck and Scotch salmon hollandaise. Trolley puddings to finish.

THE CHELSEA — SW1

17-25 Sloane Street, SW1X 9NU
Tel: 0171-235 4377   *Fax:* 0171-235 3705   **£50**
Open: lunch & dinner daily
Meals served: lunch 12-2.30, dinner 6-10.30

This modern, 225-bedroomed hotel close to Knightsbridge underground station is an ideal venue for those who come to London to shop. State-of-the-art technology and design have resulted in good facilities and unusual features such as the three-storey, glass-roofed atrium with polished steel spiral staircase which leads up to the bar and restaurant (which offers Mediterranean cuisine). The Pavilion lounge menu operates throughout the day, from 8am to midnight—light meals and afternoon tea, club sandwiches, pizzas, pastas and grills.

CHESTERFIELD HOTEL   W1

35 Charles Street, W1X 8LX
Tel: 0171-491 2622   *Fax:* 0171-491 4793   **£60**
Open: lunch Sun-Fri, dinner daily
Meals served: lunch 12.30-2.30 (Sun to 2),
    dinner 6-10.30 (Sat 5.30-9.30, Sun 7-10)

Fresh red carnations are the hallmark of staff at this
ever-so-English hotel just off Berkeley Square—more
like an exclusive club than a hotel, says the brochure.
Named after the third Earl of Chesterfield for whom
the house was built in the 18th century, the
hotel's 110 bedrooms, including nine sumptuous suites, are furnished in aptly traditional
style. Seasonal menus offer an eclectic range
of dishes, with strong Californian, Italian and
traditional English influences. The bright, elegant
Terrace room offers late breakfasts, light lunches and
suppers; more formal dining in the main restaurant.
Browse through the papers at your ease in the club-
style bar, which has a resident pianist in the
evenings. Afternoon teas are served in the wood-
panelled library.

CHEZ GERARD   W1

8 Charlotte Street, W1P 1HE
Tel: 0171-636 4975   **£40**
Open: lunch Sun-Fri, dinner Mon-Sat (closed Bank Holidays)
Meals served: lunch 12-3, dinner 6-11, (breakfast 8-10.30
    Mon-Fri, wine bar 5.30-8 Mon-Sat)

Located close to theatreland, this popular bistro offers the familiar,
Chez Gerard signature charcoal-grills (see details below) along with
the other regulars, like a fish dish of the day and regional specialities.
The modern decor by Virgile & Stone is a winner, retaining all the
hallmarks of a traditional bistro presented in a modern stylish way.
Like its Chancery Lane sister, Charlotte Street is also open for breakfast and has a wine bar operation, too. Ideal for pre- and post-theatre
suppers.

CHEZ GERARD   W1

31 Dover Street, W1
Tel: 0171-499 8171   **£40**
Open: lunch & dinner Mon-Sat (closed Bank Holidays)
Meals served: lunch 12-3, dinner 6-11.30

As at others in the Groupe Chez Gerard, charcoal grills are the main
feature here, with a range of steaks (from chateaubriand to onglet or
tartare), along with lamb, poultry and fish varieties. These are joined
by a short list of alternatives such as rabbit casserole, sole and spinach
tart, daily fish and regional specials. Traditional bistro-style starters feature pâtés, mussels, snails, rillettes, etc. A simple set menu comes on
line in the evenings from 6pm.

CHEZ GERARD   WC2

119 Chancery Lane, WC2A 1BB
Tel: 0171-405 0290   **£40**
Open: lunch & dinner Mon-Fri (closed Bank Holidays)
Meals served: lunch 12-3, dinner 6-10,
      (breakfast 8-11.30, tea 3-5.30, wine bar 5.30-11)

Old pine panelling, French art and a rustic collection of ceramics provide authentic Gallic charm at the City branch of Chez Gerard. The
upstairs wine bar offers a selection of snacks, from scrambled eggs
with salmon to steak sandwiches or moules marinière. The morning
menu offers both continental and traditional English breakfasts, along
with cereals and fresh fruit. As with all the Chez Gerards, the wine list
is comprehensive, well chosen and reasonably priced.

CHEZ LILINE   N4

101 Stroud Green Road, N4 3PX
Tel: 0171-263 6550   **£55**
Open: lunch & dinner Mon-Sat (closed Bank Holidays)
Meals served: lunch 12.30-2.30, dinner 6.30-10.30

Sister restaurant to La Gaulette in the West End,
offering a robust repertoire dedicated solely to
fish and shellfish. The overriding influence is
Mauritian, the owner's native land, but there are
substantial echoes too of the Mediterranean, with
dishes like provençal fish stew remaining a
favourite. Start perhaps with New Zealand mussels with brandy and garlic, a selection of
smoked fish, or tropical fish served with saffron
and mustard seed sauce. Main courses might
offer parrot fish braised with aubergines, king
prawns chow chow (in a creamy lemon sauce),
grilled salmon or a number of lobster dishes,
from glazed and gratinée, to grilled or maurici-
enne-style. A popular local restaurant which
began life as a café—a large part of its clientele
are longstanding regulars.

CHEZ MAX   SW10

168 Ifield Road, SW10 9AF
Tel: 0171-835 0874   **£55**
Open: lunch Tue-Fri, dinner Mon-Sat
      (closed Bank Holidays except Good Friday)
Meals served: lunch 12-2.30, dinner 7-11

The Renzland brothers, Marc and Max, of Le Petit Max at Hampton
Wick, opened this, their latest venture in the Spring of 1994 in premises
formerly occupied by La Croisette. The basement dining room is
reached down a spiral staircase, with bare wooden tables and vivid
green walls decorated with famous framed menus. Max leads the service, with Bruce Poole at the stove. Menus take a fixed-price format,
with limited choice at lunchtime (three options at each stage). Dishes

range from the unusual (ox cheek bourguignon) to the classical (grilled bavette of beef béarnaise), and modern elements abound in dishes such as herb leaf salad with shallots and shaved parmesan or steamed Cornish cod with artichoke and braised fennel rouille. You can bring your own wine if you wish (corkage £3.50/magnums £7.50). The wine list is otherwise short but well chosen. Puds lean towards the traditional, with crème brûlée, pear tarte tatin and petit pot au chocolat among the favourites. Excellent home-baked, fleur de sel-flavoured bread.

CHEZ MOI   W11

1 Addison Avenue, Holland Park, W11 4QS
Tel: 0171-603 8267   **£50**
Open: lunch Mon-Fri, dinner Mon-Sat
  (closed Bank Holidays, 1 wk Xmas)
Meals served: lunch 12.30-2, dinner 7-11   ❖

One of the longest-established restaurants in the area, Chez Moi has been here for almost 30 years. The menu, previously dedicated more or less to the French classics, has now had its horizons broadened to include dishes like spicy chicken curry or vegetable couscous but on the whole the classic tradition still dominates: tournedos béarnaise, carré d'agneau, salmon quenelles, saddle of hare with a sweet and sour honey-flavoured sauce. Good-value three-course lunches. Good wine list and some reasonable buys. An intimate, good local restaurant that remains popular because of its long history and the way it takes care of its customers.

CHEZ NICO AT NINETY PARK LANE   W1

90 Park Lane, W1A 3AA
Tel: 0171-409 1290   *Fax:* 0171-355 4877   **£125**
Open: lunch Mon-Fri, dinner Mon-Sat
  (closed Bank Holidays, 11 days Xmas, 4 days Easter)   ♣
Meals served: lunch 12-2, dinner 7-11   🍾

Nico Ladenis is a man dedicated to perfection and a meal here is ample proof of that. This supremely talented and artistic chef is not one to rest on his laurels and nor does his team. The dining room is overseen with exemplary professionalism by Jean-Luc Giguel. The menu, with over ten dishes to choose from at each stage, is written in straightforward English, and includes several of Nico's sensational signature dishes, such as his salad of foie gras on toasted brioche with caramelised orange, noisettes of pig's trotter stuffed with morels and sweetbreads and served with leeks; steamed sea bass with fennel and basil purée; warm lobster with artichoke, avocado and mango; or fillet of Scotch beef with truffles and foie gras. To finish, thin apple tart with caramel sauce and vanilla ice cream, or for an unforgettable climax to the meal, why not face the challenge of the grand assortment of mini-desserts—a composition of taster portions which is quite simply dazzling. The lunchtime menu is lighter in design but offers excellent value and variety, in dishes like quail pie with smoked bacon or marinated salmon with sweet pickled ginger and corn pancake. Excellent wine list, with some good half bottles, with prices as you might expect in an establishment of such opulence.

CHINON W14

23 Richmond Way, W14 0AS
Tel: 0171-602 5968 **£65**
Open: lunch Mon-Fri, dinner Mon-Sat
(closed Bank Holidays, 2 wks Aug/Sep, 1 wk Xmas)
Meals served: lunch 12.30-2, dinner 6.30-10.30

This is a pretty, split-level, ground-floor dining room with a large picture window at the rear overlooking a plant-filled terrace, floodlit at night. At the stove is Jonathan Hayes who uses good raw materials to produce a concise carte of mainly French design, with Oriental influences. Jonathan shows a light and careful approach to classical and regional traditions, in dishes such as mussels steamed with ginger and garlic or gateau of fresh crab to start, followed by fillet of beef with Savoy cabbage and potato galette, or sea scallop ravioli served with pak choy greens. Whatever you choose, start with the delicious country bread served with a concasse of tomato and basil.

CHRISTIAN'S W4

Station Parade, Burlington Lane, W4 3HD
Tel: 0181-995 0382 **£50**
Open: lunch Tue-Fri, dinner Tue-Sat
Meals served: lunch 12-2.30, dinner 7-10.30

Christian Gustin's charming restaurant, all regency-striped chairs and smiling staff, offers a short, daily-changing menu of bourgeois classics prepared in a lighter, modern way. Soufflés, such as Christian's English cheese soufflé, are a speciality, arriving beautifully risen, moist and featherlight. Start with one of these, broccoli and walnut soup or rabbit terrine with apricot preserve, before sampling main-course dishes such as roast cod and capers with parsley, char-grilled lamb and rosemary with onion compote or corn-fed chicken sautéed with apple and Calvados. Tempting selections of desserts, which on a recent visit featured smooth chocolate truffle cake and a superb apple flan. This is a charming, really welcoming local restaurant.

CHRISTOPHER'S WC2

18 Wellington Street, WC2E 7DD
Tel: 0171-240 4222   Fax: 0171-240 3357 **£60**
Open: lunch daily, dinner Mon-Sat
(closed Bank Holidays, 1 wk Xmas)
Meals served: lunch 12-2 (Sun to 3), dinner 6-11.30,
(light meals in Bar 11.30-11 Mon-Sat)

Housed in a grand Victorian building, (formerly a casino), the interior of this restaurant is on the grand scale. A sweeping stone staircase leads up to the lofty dining room, decorated in ultra-modern '90s style. The cooking is American, with the emphasis firmly on grills. Starters nod towards the Med and further afield, as shown in dishes such as carpaccio à la Harry's Bar (Venice), lobster guacamole, fettucine Alfredo and Caesar salad. Favourites among the main courses include salmon fish cakes with basil cream, New York strip steak and Christopher's hamburger with fries (all steaks are imported from the US). Great chips. The lunch-time menu is similar, if a little shorter, and the place is popular for Sunday brunch. It's good to see Christopher's—both the bar/café and restaurant—firmly established in a relatively short space of time. Christopher Gilmour's influence on and encouragement of this young and friendly team works wonders.

CHURCHILL INTER-CONTINENTAL HOTEL   W1

30 Seymour Street, Portman Square, W1A 4ZX
Tel: 0171-486 5800   *Fax:* 0171-486 1255   **£70**
Open: lunch Sun-Fri, dinner daily
Meals served: lunch 12-3, dinner 6-11 (Sun from 7.30)   ❖

Idris Caldora cooks at the newly refurbished Churchill, which is a good enough reason in itself to go there. His cheerful menu in Clementine's Restaurant has a great variety of Mediterranean dishes: a warm salad of Portuguese sardines, grilled tuna salad niçoise or Italian plum tomato soup are amongst starters. Char-grilled red mullet is served with catalan romesco sauce, Scottish salmon with balsamic vinegar dressing and Colchester oysters are glazed with champagne sauce. This is stylish cooking in an attractive setting. 448 well-appointed bedrooms come under the overall watchful eye of General Manager Chris Cowdray.

CHUTNEY MARY   SW10

535 King's Road, SW10 0SZ
Tel: 0171-351 3113   *Fax:* 0171-351 7694   **£50**
Open: lunch & dinner daily (closed 26 Dec)
Meals served: lunch 12.30-2.30, dinner 7-11.30

Busy and buzzy, Chutney Mary describes itself as the world's first Anglo-Indian restaurant and certainly the menu is like no other. Likewise the food, both more interesting and miles better than your standard Indian fare. Much of the menu is based on anglicised recipes from the days of the Raj: Memsahib's lacy cutlets (lamb patties); Bangalore bangers and spicy mash; masala roast lamb; scallop kedgeree with lentils. Seafood specialities feature strongly, with dishes like spicy crab cake, crab vindaloo and green salmon curry among favourites. The cooking draws mostly on traditions from the East coast of Madras and the West coast of Kerala, Goa and Bombay. Increasing the vegetarian range of dishes is good news for many. Popular Sunday buffets.

There's really nothing quite like it anywhere else in London

CIBO   W14

3 Russell Gardens, W14 8EZ
Tel: 0171-371 6271   *Fax:* 0171-602 1371
Open: lunch Mon-Fri, dinner Mon-Sat
  (closed Bank Holidays, 4 days Xmas)
Meals served: lunch 12-2.30, dinner 7-11

One of the first modern-Ital style restaurants, Cibo continues to evolve successfully **£60**

Modern Italian restaurant with loads of colour: huge, artistically-designed plates emulate the art-hung walls, creating a splendid presentation for dishes such as lasagnette with scallop and crab sauce, grilled mixed fish and shellfish in aïöli or grilled sliced beef with artichokes, served in its own jus. Interesting starters include pan-fried chicken and duck livers with grapes and balsamic sauce and sautéed wild mushrooms with melted Scamorza smoked cheese. The new antipasto bar offers a good range of light meals from a menu which changes monthly. Well-established restaurant with sister establishment along the same lines (see L'Altro, W11).

CLARIDGE'S   W1

Brook Street, W1A 9JG
Tel: 0171-629 8860   *Fax:* 0171-499 2210
Restaurant: £85
Open: lunch Sun-Fri, dinner daily
Meals served: lunch 12.30-3, dinner 7-11.15
The Causerie: £55
Open: lunch Mon-Sat, dinner Mon-Fri
Meals served: lunch 12-2.30, dinner 5.30-11

Footmen wearing breeches and gold braid have become the hallmark of Claridge's. With all this finery, it's no small wonder than so many foreign heads of state and royalty make it their first choice. The motto is "We strive for excellence" and it's as valid now as it was a century ago when Claridge's was established; and it continues to appeal to anyone who reveres classic elegance and grace. A Hungarian quartet provides background music in the foyer; liveried staff walk to and fro, past the wide sweeping staircase which dominates the hall. Art deco splendour appears at every turn in bedrooms, some of which include precious, original features, though others are furnished in more traditional style. 190 rooms include some splendid suites and apartments with sumptuous, marble bathrooms. Staying at Claridge's is a big event, and eating there no less so, an experience perhaps best savoured over lunch in the Causerie with its Scandinavian influences, or over dinner in the magnificently opulent setting of the main dining room (the art deco theme is based on a 1926 design by Basil Ionides). The new Christopher Ironside mirrored mural is the finishing touch on an elegant room, and maître chef des cuisines, Marjan Lesnik, produces a classically-based French repertoire, with an emphasis on contemporary trends and interpretations. Really, you can't go wrong here.

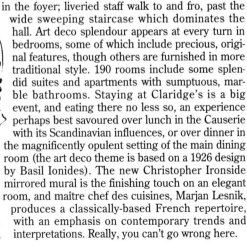

Biography

Marjan Lesnik

Marjan Lesnik was born at Ljutomer, Yugoslavia, where his mother and grandmother were in the service of the Hapsburg Royal Family and his father was a director of one of the famous Ljutomer Riesling vineyards. After a three-year apprenticeship at a local restaurant and some work in Europe, he travelled to the Château Valeuse in the Channel Islands, before moving to London and his stints at the Hilton in Park Lane, and the Connaught. As maître des chef at Claridge's he has truly come into his own: Marjan respects his classical training but desires most to be spontaneous and free, obtaining great satisfaction in finding new combinations of ingredients and flavours.

CLARKE'S   W8

124 Kensington Church Street, W8 4BH
Tel: 0171-221 9225   *Fax:* 0171-229 4564   **£75**
Open: lunch & dinner Mon-Fri (closed Bank Holidays,
    10 days Xmas, 4 days Easter, 2 wks Aug)
Meals served: lunch 12.30-2, dinner 7-10

Sally Clarke and Elizabeth Payne's repertoire is quite astonishing, especially when you consider that the menus change twice daily and are never, it seems, repeated. The range of influences in the kitchen stretches from the Far East to California and back to the Mediterranean, with the char-grill still the mainstay of the kitchen. Great care and thought goes into everything, with marvellous artistic results on the plate. Lunchtime sees a two- or three-course affair while dinner offers a no-choice, four-course menu.  Starters across both menus range from leek and potato soup with black truffles or smoked haddock tart to a vast repertoire of delicious and unusual salads or chicken-filled ravioli in a light broth. Main courses are typified by char-grilled halibut with lemon and rosemary oil and a crostini of black olives and red peppers, or leg of Pyrenean lamb, boned and grilled with beans, roasted fennel and lettuce heart. Cheeses in excellent condition are served with home-made oatmeal biscuits. Desserts are no less inventive—with ginger-baked cream and rhubarb a typical evening offering. Vegetarians should advise on booking. All in all a special place to eat. The specialist food shop next door sells the full range of Clarke's breads, now baked in Sally's own factory, so great has the demand grown.

CONDOTTI   W1

4 Mill Street, W1R 9TE
Tel: 0171-499 1308   **£30**
Open: all day Mon-Sat (closed Bank Holidays)
Meals served: 11.30am-12 midnight

Good-value pizzeria-restaurant open throughout the day. A wide choice
of generous American-style salads, canelloni with ricotta and broccoli
and stacks of pizzas with endless possibilities when it comes to toppings. You can even call in for just a coffee and dessert if you wish.

THE CONNAUGHT   W1

Carlos Place, W1Y 6AL
Tel: 0171-499 7070   *Fax:* 0171-495 3262   **£100**
Open: lunch & dinner daily
       (closed Grill Room: Sat & Sun, Jan-Apr, Bank Holidays)   ✿
Meals served: lunch 12.30-2, dinner 6.30-10.30
       (Grill Room from 6)

Rather more of an institution than a hotel—it's good to know that in
this hectic world, some things don't change. Prices of rooms are
quoted not publicised, but who cares anyway? This is not a hotel for
penny pinchers. Michel Bourdin has now been chef de cuisine at the
Connaught for 20 years and offers similar menus for the Grill Room
and the Restaurant, predominantly in French and in English as appropriate. For lunch you can enjoy grilled sausage and bacon and your
partner could have a coulibiac de saumon d'Ecosse à la russe deux
sauces, then bread-and-butter pudding or a pithiviers aux framboises.
A wonderful mix of Maxim's French and schoolboy English, but executed in grand style. The Connaught is a very special place, and the
majority of customers are third generation regulars.

Biography

Michel Bourdin served his apprenticeship in
Management, Cookery, Service, Food and
Wine at the Ecole Hoteliere Jean Drouant in
Paris, and then gained extensive experience in
some of the top establishments in France
(Hotel Etoile, Paris; Grand Hotel, Brittany;
Restaurant Ledoyen and
Maxim's, Paris; and the
Pavillion Royal, Bois de
Bologne). During his military
service, he was even chef to the
Prime Minister. Now in his rightful culinary
home at the celebrated Connaught, he never
misses an opportunity to motivate others to
share his ideals for the future of his profession
and the art of cooking and service.

Michel

Bourdin

HOTEL CONRAD   SW10

Chelsea Harbour, SW10 0XG
Tel: 0171-823 3000   *Fax:* 0171-351 6525
Open: lunch & dinner daily
Meals served: lunch 12-3, dinner 7-10.30

Outside eating on terrace in summer, overlooking the harbour **£55**

One of London's newer hotels in the attractive waterside setting of Chelsea Harbour. You'll find superb service in the 160 luxurious suites and good food and wines in the brasserie. The hotel will provide a Jaguar to drive you to shop in Knightsbridge, and then you could drive back to tuck into some Cumberland sausages with onion gravy or cod 'n' chips! On the lighter side there's langoustine soup of wild mushroom and parmesan risotto, roasted rabbit fillets with mustard sauce and noodles or supreme of guinea fowl with lentils and cèpes. Dinner sees similar dishes, and there are some good sandwiches, salads and hot dishes available throughout the day in Drake's Bar.

CORK & BOTTLE   WC2

44-46 Cranbourn Street, WC2H 4AN
Tel: 0171-734 7807   *Fax:* 0171-483 2230
Open: all day daily (closed 25 Dec, 1 Jan)
Meals served: 11-midnight, Sun 12-10.30

£35

Look for the blackboard, as there's no formal menu at Don Hewitson's legendary wine bar. Expect the likes of giant grilled Mediterranean prawns with garlic, cassoulets, spicy pork and herb sausages with a tomato and ginger salsa or salmon and monkfish roulade, alongside regular favourites like raised ham and cheese pie or open steak sandwich served with chips and salad. The wine list is extensive with reasonable prices and some helpful comments from those who should and do know a thing or two about wine, including proprietor Don Hewitson.

Treat yourself to a copy of Don's book "The Glory of Champagne." He'll sign it for you and—who knows—maybe buy you a glass!

CORNEY & BARROW   EC2

109 Old Broad Street, EC2N 1AP
Tel: 0171-638 9308   *Fax:* 0171-382 9373
Open: lunch Mon-Fri (closed Bank Holidays)
Meals served: lunch 11.30-3

£60

There's a club-like atmosphere at this, the oldest and smallest (30 seats) in the chain of Corney & Barrows. It was in Old Broad Street where Edward Corney and Robert Barrow opened their shop selling port, sack and claret in 1780. Simple but good food is the aim. The operation is geared toward the City clientele who, not surprisingly, receive a complimentary *Financial Times* to browse through as they eat. Crab and saffron tart, vegetable soup au pistou or a trio of salmon with dill mayonnaise and keta caviar are typical starters, while main courses feature the likes of pan-fried calf's liver with fried onions and bacon; fresh cod and salmon fish cakes with spicy tomato sauce; and sirloin steak served with Café de Paris sauce.

CROWTHERS   SW14

481 Upper Richmond Road West, SW14 7PU
Tel: 0181-876 6372   **£45**
Open: lunch Tue-Fri, dinner Tue-Sat
   (closed Bank Holidays, 1 wk Xmas, 2 wks Aug)
Meals served: lunch 12-2, dinner 7-10.30

Good, reasonably-priced neighbourhood restaurant, run by the Crowthers, offering a concise hand-written carte of modern French and British cooking. Starters range from baked fresh goat's cheese in toasted sesame seeds with tapenade croûtes to smoked mackerel and spring onion fishcakes with hollandaise sauce; main courses might include roast guinea fowl with a marjoram and Madeira sauce, grilled monkfish with mixed peppers and herbs or best end of English lamb with a provençal herb crust and garlic and rosemary sauce. Puds offer the likes of lemon tart, sticky toffee pudding and grilled fruit gratin with Calvados sabayon.

DAN'S   SW3

119 Sydney Street, SW3 6NR
Tel: 0171-352 2718   *Fax:* 0171-352 3265   **£40**
Open: lunch Mon-Fri & Sun, dinner Mon-Sat
   (closed Bank Holidays, 1 wk Xmas)
Meals served: lunch 12.30-2.30, dinner 7.30-10.30

You now pass the bar on the way into Dan Whitehead's revamped bright, informal Chelsea restaurant with its wooden floor and outside view of the first floor kitchen. Dishes are mostly straightforward on the Anglo-French repertoire. Scallops in hazelnut butter, grilled sea bass and escalope of veal with a cider vinegar sauce are among favourites, along with more traditional offerings like entrecôte béarnaise, or crispy Barbary duck with five Chinese spices, and goujons of cod tartare. Traditional puds. Good-value set menu of two or three courses.

DAPHNE'S   SW3

110-112 Draycott Avenue, SW3 3AE
Tel: 0171-589 4257   *Fax:* 0171-581 2232   **£55**
Open: lunch & dinner daily (closed 24 & 25 Dec, 1 Jan)
Meals served: lunch 12-3 (Sun to 4), dinner 7-11.30

The talented Eddie Baines offers a straightforward, modern menu at this trendy restaurant, decorated along the theme of an Italian villa with warm terracotta colours, sliding glass roof in the conservatory room and plenty of plants about the place. The restaurant consists of three linked rooms on different levels. The menu takes its inspiration from Northern Italy. Typical dishes include beef carpaccio with rucola and parmesan shavings, Caesar salad, sea bass with balsamic sauce and herbs, roast breast of chicken with rosemary and caramelised onions, and a good selection of pasta and risotto dishes, such as anolini with zucchini and zucchini flower, lobster ravioli and risotto milanese. A glamorous place. If you want a place in the conservatory in summer months, booking is essential, especially since the name check in Ab Fab: "Quag's or Daff's, darling?" Quite so!

DE CECCO SW6

189 New King's Road, SW6
Tel: 0171-736 1145 **£40**
Open: lunch & dinner Mon-Sat (closed Bank Holidays)
Meals served: lunch 12.30-2.45, dinner 7-11

Bright, bubbly Italian restaurant where the cooking shows care and imagination. Interesting menu of pasta and pizzas, and main courses such as beef in a Calvados and wine sauce served on pappardelle.

DEL BUONGUSTAIO SW15

283 Putney Bridge Road, SW15 2PT
Tel: 0181-780 9361 **£55**
Open: lunch Sun-Fri, dinner Mon-Sat
   (closed Bank Holidays, 2 wks Xmas)
Meals served: lunch 12-3 (Sun 12.30-3.30), dinner 6.30-11.30

The emphasis at this cheerful Italian restaurant is on authentic, classic North Italian cooking, and as such its success is virtually unrivalled (this is the younger sister of Clapham's Osteria Antica Bologna). The decor is simple and attractive, with sand and terracotta colours set against colourful ceramics. The weekly-changing menu offers a truly exciting range of dishes; like its sibling, this is no ordinary Italian restaurant. Starters run from fresh basil, cream and tomato mousse or Piedmontese raw fillet steak with lemon, olive oil, garlic and capers, to Venetian-style fried sardines with onion, pine nuts and sultanas. Pastas might feature fine tagliolini with courgette flower sauce or Sardinian pasta with fresh sausage, ricotta, tomato and chilies. Then there's cuttlefish, large pan-fried oyster mushrooms, fresh tuna in casserole or the likes of oven-baked lamb marinated in fresh herbs and served with fresh asparagus and peppers. Menu degustazione, light fixed-price lunches and seasonal theme menus offer further similar delights. Reasonably priced wine list.

DELL'UGO   W1

56 Frith Street, W1V 5TA
Tel: 0171-734 8300   *Fax:* 0171-734 8717   **£40**
Open: lunch & dinner Mon-Sat (closed lunch Sat
    1st & 2nd floors)
Meals served:
1st Floor: lunch 12-3, dinner 7-12.30
2nd Floor: lunch 12-3, dinner 5.30-11
Ground Floor café: 11am-12.30pm (bar to 11pm)

One of the trendiest places in town: this is European high style on three levels, each with a different pace and style. Downstairs is a bustling Warhol-inspired café, serving snacks, soups and light meals. On the first floor is a lively, mural-painted room with closely-packed tables; and up again is a more sedate club-like room with central viewing to look down on the colourful crowd below. This is an original Antony Worrall Thompson and it's well worth a visit, though without a booking you'll probably find yourself in among the ground floor crowd where it's first come, first served. The menu, typical of Antony's style, is eclectic and full of interesting options. Risotto cake with four cheeses, shallot and spinach; sausages and mash with cassoulet beans and caramelised onion; spicy chicken in yoghurt with cardamon rice; corned beef hash cake; traditional fish and chips with mushy peas; and rump steak frites with field mushrooms, bone marrow and taleggio. Something for everyone. Coffee or "hippy teas" after ginger brûlée tart with a maple and banana compote.

DON PEPE   NW8

99 Frampton Street, NW8 8NA
Tel: 0171-262 3834   **£35**
Open: lunch daily, dinner Mon-Sat (closed 24 & 25 Dec)
Meals served: lunch 12-3, dinner 7-12, (light meals Tapas bar: 12-12)
The first-ever tapas bar in London (opened some 20 years). Sample tapas at the bar or full menu with many traditional classics (paella, Asturian bean stew) in the main dining room. Informal and chatty.

THE DORCHESTER　　　　　　　　**W1**

Park Lane, W1A 2HJ
Tel: 0171-629 8888　*Fax:* 0171-409 0114
Grill Room:　　　　　　　　　　　　　**£95**
Open: lunch & dinner daily
Meals served: lunch 12.30-2.30, dinner 6-11
　　(Sun & Bank Holidays 7-10.30)
Terrace Restaurant:　　　　　　　　　**£95**
Open: dinner Fri & Sat
Meals served: dinner 7-11
Oriental Room:　　　　　　　　　　　**£70**
Open: lunch Mon-Fri, dinner Mon-Sat
Meals served: lunch 12-2.30, dinner 7-11

One of London's grandest of grand hotels, where opulence and luxury abound and service is as service should be. Three dining rooms suit differing moods: the Terrace offers a romantic setting and can also be booked during the week for private parties. Although the Grill Room is decorated in Spanish style, the menu is very English—start with Morecambe Bay potted shrimps, Cornish dressed crab, cock-a-leekie soup or black pudding with warm potato and bacon salad. There's skate wings with brown butter, roast Angus beef with Yorkshire pudding, shepherd's pie, braised oxtails and a good selection of simple grills. In the Oriental Room, chef Simon Yung provides a comprehensive Cantonese menu with some highly original dishes alongside the more traditional ones like hot and sour soup, roast Peking duck and deep-fried crispy chicken together with unusual additions such as jelly fish and mixed seafood marinaded in sesame oil and chili bean sauce, or deep-fried stuffed scallop with shrimp mousses served with herbal salt and chili. At lunchtime you can have dim-sum too. What with tea in the Promenade and an amazing array of sumptuous bedrooms and suites, there's no lack of variety at the Dorchester, all in a opulent setting.

LA DORDOGNE　　　　　　　　　**W4**

5 Devonshire Road, W4 2EU
Tel: 0181-747 1836　*Fax:* 0181-994 9144　　　　**£45**
Open: lunch Mon-Fri, dinner daily (closed Bank Holidays)
Meals served: lunch 12-2.30, dinner 7-11

Thoroughly French, from the menu and wine list to the staff, this local restaurant looks both to the classics and to modern-day trends for its inspiration. Call in to the oyster bar for natives or rocks from Sketrick Island, Co Down and Brittany, or for lobster in a number of ways; or take a table in the restaurant where home-made foie gras, goat's cheese, scallops, mussels and terrines make up the list of starters. Main course include the likes of Dover sole with saffron sauce, steamed turbot with champagne sauce, chicken supreme with tarragon sauce or sliced fillet of lamb cooked with honey and mint. Classic desserts, reasonably priced wine list.

DOWNSTAIRS AT 190   SW7

190 Queen's Gate, SW7 5EU
Tel: 0171-581 5666   *Fax:* 0171-581 8172   **£45**
Open: dinner Mon-Sat (closed Bank Holidays, 1 wk Xmas)
Meals served: dinner 7-12

Situated below the bar and Bistrot 190, this is a busy, primarily fish restaurant, which caters for the modern palate in Antony Worrall Thompson style. The fashionable menu offers a wide choice, with starters both traditional and alternative (fish soup, potted shrimps, soft herring roes on toast with anchovy cream, roasted squash, onion and garlic soup, or razor clams in lime butter). A selection of steamed shellfish, various types of fish cakes (Thai oriental, corn and crab, salt cod, and salmon) and the fish and chips section (fish according to your selection, deep-fried in beer batter and served with chunky chips, mushy peas and tartare sauce) lead the way into a choice of char-grilled or steamed main-course fish and shellfish dishes offered in a number of ways (again, make your choice from the day's selection and match it with your favourite accompaniments). Meat-eaters have their own section from the char-grill and there's always a couple of interesting vegetarian options, such as chicory tarte tatin with salad, or wild mushroom croustade. Lovely puds to finish. There's also a Snacking Food menu, a concise yet exotic repertoire including jumbo shrimp, tempura prawns with spicy dipping sauce, a crostini of fishes, and deep-fried squid with chili mayonnaise.

DOWNTOWN SULEMAN'S   SE1

1 Cathedral Street, SE1
Tel: 0171-407 0337   **£35**
Open: lunch Mon-Fri, dinner Tue-Fri
Meals served: lunch 12-2.45, dinner 6.30-10.30

The entrance to Nadir Suleman's restaurant is actually in Winchester Walk; but once inside you'll be offered a varied but short menu of international dishes—there are influences from the East, North Africa, the Mediterranean and from traditional English country cooking. Smoked haddock with scrambled eggs, satay, tempura prawns and couscous cluster together among starters; and main courses are no less cosmopolitan, with dishes such as Somerset steak and cider pie or fish and chips sharing the limelight with garbanzo and peanut risotto or babi (pork) lombok (an Indonesian-based dish of stir-fried meat with spicy gravy, wrapped in a pancake, then baked in puff pastry—a regular feature here). Jazzy Eats menu in the evening, offering simple hearty fare of similar variety.

DUKES HOTEL   SW1

35 St James's Place, SW1A 1NY
Tel: 0171-491 4840   *Fax:* 0171-493 1264

Traditional values score highly at this oasis of a hotel, tucked away in a picturesque, flower-filled courtyard down a cul-de-sac next to Green Park. An elegant Edwardian building, it is conservatively and tastefully furnished in club-like fashion. There are 66 rooms, a third of which are suites with homely sitting rooms. The restaurant is now open to residents only.

THE EAGLE   EC1

159 Farringdon Road, EC1R 3AL
Tel: 0171-837 1353   **£40**
Open: lunch & dinner Mon-Fri
    (closed Bank Holidays, 2-3 wks Xmas)
Meals served: lunch 12.30-2.30, dinner 6.30-10.30

It's well worth the battle for a table for Mediterranean-style food at this pub in Farringdon Road. Dishes range from gazpacho andaluz to minestra with pesto genovese, Greek salads to proscutto with grilled asparagus and parmesan. There could be robust dishes like fabada or osso bucco milanese, or the lighter baked cod with spinach, olives and garlic or sea bass with fennel, tomatoes and basil. Perhaps the only wine list in London where you can have a glass of any of the 14 listed wines!

ENGLISH GARDEN   SW3

10 Lincoln Street, SW3 2TS
Tel: 0171-584 7272   *Fax:* 0171-581 2848   **£55**
Open: lunch & dinner daily (closed 25 & 26 Dec)
Meals served: lunch 12.30-2.30 (Sun to 2), dinner 7.30-11.30 (Sun to 10)

Another well-designed and elegant menu from Roger Wren. The menu changes with the seasons at this Chelsea restaurant located in a converted terrace of houses. You'll find British cooking which incorporates both traditional and modern in innovative dishes: warm asparagus mousse with lemon butter, salmon tartare with chives and sour cream, grilled Cumberland sausages with bubble-'n'squeak, sirloin of beef with Yorkshire pudding and onion gravy, vegetable kedgeree, and steamed sea bass with fennel show the range. Puds, too, are seasonal, with a recent spring selection offering liquorice ice cream, strawberry roly poly pudding, clementine tart and hot lemon pancakes with spiced sherry and almond butter. The fixed-price luncheon menu is no less varied, though choice is limited to three options at each course. The elegant room also has a Gothic conservatory at the rear.

ENGLISH HOUSE   SW3

3 Milner Street, SW3 2QA
Tel: 0171-584 3002   *Fax:* 0171-581 2848   **£55**
Open: lunch & dinner daily (closed 25 & 26 Dec)
Meals served: lunch 12.30-2.30 (Sun to 2),
    dinner 7.30-11.30 (Sun to 10)

Sister restaurant to the English Garden, with the focus again firmly on
English cooking. The menu, which changes with the seasons, blends
tradition with trends to great success. Typical dishes include the likes
of pan-fried calf's liver with red onion gravy, braised fillet of beef
stuffed with pickled walnuts, grilled salmon with cucumber and
almonds (a spring creation) and individual chicken, lemon and tarragon pies. Starters feature soup of the day, smoked Scotch salmon,
terrines and tarts like wild mushroom. Excellent and varied choice of
desserts, from steamed chocolate sponge with hot chocolate sauce to a
lighter creation such as citrus cheesecake with lemon curd.

ENOTECA   SW15

28 Putney High Street, SW15 1SQ
Tel: 0181-785 4449   **£45**
Open: lunch Mon-Fri, dinner Mon-Sat
    (closed Bank Holidays, 1 wk Xmas)
Meals served: lunch 12.30-3, dinner 7-11.30

This Italian restaurant on a corner site just south of Putney Bridge
offers modern interpretations of many classic traditional dishes.
Bresaola from Valtellina is served with artichokes and shavings of
pecorino cheese, while traditional home-made Sardinian gnocchi
comes with a ragout of duck simmered with white wine and tomato.
The carte is supplemented by daily specials which might feature dishes
such as rabbit agrodolce, baby goat marinated and cooked in milk and
herbs, or mixed grill of fish with Mediterranean grilled vegetables.
Classic Italian desserts include tartufo and torta di ricotta. The recent
addition of good-value fixed-price lunches is worth checking out.

THE ENTERPRISE   SW3

35 Walton Street, SW3
Tel: 0171-584 3148   *Fax:* 0171-584 1060   **£40**
Open: lunch & dinner daily (closed 24-28 Dec)
Meals served: lunch 12.30-2.30, dinner 7-10

This former pub-turned-bar-cum-restaurant specialises in unpretentious, mostly English cooking in a relaxed, informal setting. Pop in for
lunch or dinner, or for just a drink at the friendly, busy bar. The short,
modern menu offers fashionable dishes such as hot goat's cheese salad
with pecans or warm crab tart hollandaise to start; followed by barbecued English entrecôte steak with two-pepper butter, Lincolnshire
sausages and mash with honey-mustard gravy, home-made salmon
fishcakes with tomato remoulade and french fries, or char-grilled lamb
cutlets with rosemary and cassis. Daily blackboard specials, too.

L'ESCARGOT   W1

48 Greek Street, W1V 5LR
Tel: 0171-437 2679   *Fax:* 0171-437 0790
Open: lunch Mon-Fri, dinner Mon-Sat
    (closed Mon 1st Floor, Bank Holidays)
Meals served:
1st Floor: lunch 12.15-2.15, dinner 7-10.45   **£40**
Ground Floor: lunch 12.15-2.15, dinner 6-11.15
Bar: lunch 12-3, dinner 5.30-11.30

Local restaurateur Jimmy Lahoud and friends—talented British chefs Garry Hollihead and David Cavalier—have gone further than might have been expected at this famous Greek Street restaurant, a bastion of the Soho scene. Not only have they saved it (to the joy of many) from extinction, but they have also succeeded in bringing new life and a new identity to this Soho institution, which has been around since the

Biography

David Cavalier

David Cavalier began his catering career when only fifteen, scrubbing pans and cooking crêpes at a family-run restaurant in Amboise, France. He then spent two years studying culinary basics, before coming to London to serve his apprenticeship and working his way through some of the most prestigious kitchens in London, including The Berkeley, The Royal Garden and The Grosvenor House, his training culminated in a stint in The Dorchester under Anton Mosimann. He then ran his own restaurants in Aylesbury and Battersea before appearing in his current double-act.

Garry Hollihead

Garry Hollihead spent most of his culinary career in large hotels with big names - five years at Ninety Park Lane under Anton Edelmann and Vaughan Archer, one year with Louis Outhier at his three-star restaurant L'Oasis, and a year in Florida doing promotional work for The Savoy before returning to London as premier sous chef to Anton Edelmann. He really came to public knowledge, though, in partnership at Soho's Sutherlands, before joining forces with David here.

1920s. The decor is bright and cheery, with abstract modern art on the walls and colourful checked seating which works well, both downstairs against the parquet floor of the ground-floor brasserie, and upstairs in the more intimate, carpeted first-floor restaurant. The brasserie is a great success, with dishes such as provençale fish soup with rouille, roast lobster with tarragon, tuna niçoise and steak béarnaise pulling in the crowds. Upstairs, there's a choice of short, straightforward à la carte or set menus, which are both well-conceived and refreshingly simple: oysters Moscovite, bouillon of rabbit and chicken and sweetbread terrine among starters; with main courses such as roast Aylesbury duck with a leek and foie gras pithiviers, calf's liver with a sage jus or fillet of beef with morel jus. Excellent desserts confirm the talent of these two complementary chefs—raspberry sablé, ginger parfait and pear condé.

EST   W1

54 Frith Street, W1V 5TE
Tel: 0171-437 0666   **£40**
Open: lunch Mon-Fri, dinner Mon-Sat
   (closed Bank Holidays)
Meals served: lunch 12-3, dinner 6-11 (Fri & Sat to 11.30)

Lively Soho bar and restaurant with large, front windows which look out on to the Street. The menu is modern, with a distinct Mediterranean bias which makes much use of the char-grill. Seafood and salads with shavings of Parmesan, lots of garlic and basil and whatever is in season are the mainstay of the menu. This trendy Scandinavian-style restaurant, with its stripped, wood-panelled walls, is packed out with the media crowd at the end of the week.

L'ESTAMINET   WC2

14 Garrick Street, WC2E 9BJ
Tel: 0171-379 1432   **£45**
Open: lunch & dinner Mon-Sat (closed Bank Holidays)
Meals served: lunch 12-2.30, dinner 5.45-11.15

An attractive French brasserie and wine bar off Floral Street in premises once occupied by Inigo Jones. The short, concise, classic brasserie menu runs from French onion soup, mussels and snails to bangers and mash, seafood pancakes, Dover sole, beef bourguignon and grills. Good-value pre-theatre menu, plus daily specials. New World and French wine list.

THE FENJA   SW3

69 Cadogan Gardens, SW3 2RB
Tel: 0171-589 7333   *Fax:* 0171-581 4958
Handsome town house hotel with 12 bedrooms, and access to Cadogan Gardens. No restaurant, but good room service: light meals and breakfast till 2pm for late risers.

FIFTH FLOOR RESTAURANT SW1

Harvey Nichols, Knightsbridge, SW1
Tel: 0171-235 5250   *Fax:* 0171-235 5020   **£55**
Open: lunch & dinner Mon-Sat
    (closed 25 & 26 Dec)
Meals served: lunch 12-3 (Sat to 3.30), dinner 6.30-11.30

An express lift whizzes you up to the new fifth floor at Harvey Nichols, with its food hall, bar, café and restaurant. The menu features some of the trendiest dishes of the day and the atmosphere is informal and relaxed. Hot and sour crab broth, radicchio and red wine risotto, native oysters with grilled spicy sausages, sweetbreads on toast to start; followed by smoked haddock fish cakes with tartare sauce, Bury black pudding with pease pudding, parsley and mustard sauce or chopped lamb steak au poivre typify main courses. Interesting fixed-price lunch menus, which are simpler but no less imaginative in concept. Exotic puds. The busy bar, which has found its own following with the young and beautiful, is adjacent to the restaurant, whilst the café has some outside seating on the terrace. All in all quite a success and looks set to break new ground as its popularity grows.

FLORIANS N8

4 Topsfield Parade, Middle Lane, N8 8RP
Tel: 0181-348 8348   **£50**
Open: lunch & dinner daily (closed Bank Holidays)
Meals served: lunch 12-3, dinner 7-11 (wine bar 12-11)

With a wine bar at the front and a café-style brasserie at the rear, this is noisy, buzzy, popular place. Simple, unfussy Italian food is served up in the lighter, modern style, with dishes such as scallop and monkfish terrine on rocket salad or risotto of the day among starters. Main-course offerings might feature char-grilled swordfish steak with baby spinach salad or escalope of veal wrapped in pancetta and served with a porcini and oyster mushroom stew. Hot ricotta and rum pancake topped with zabaglione to finish perhaps.

FORMULA VENETA SW10

14 Hollywood Road, SW10 9HY
Tel: 0171-352 7612   *Fax:* 0181-295 1503   **£40**
Open: lunch daily, dinner Mon-Sat (closed Bank Holidays)
Meals served: lunch 12.30-2.30, dinner 7-11.15

The food at this typically modern Italian restaurant is simply cooked and well presented, and the alfresco garden setting is a big plus. The emphasis is food from the North, and risotto is a speciality, prepared in a number of ways - al radicchio, di mare and delgiorno. Other dishes might include charcoal-grilled vegetables, thin pasta with thyme and tomato gratinée, noodles with fresh crab and shrimps, cuttlefish with peas and polenta, Venetian-style liver and onions, sole with lime sauce or escalope of veal in dolcelatte sauce.

47 PARK STREET   W1

47 Park Street, W1Y 4EB
Tel: 0171-491 7282   *Fax:* 0171-491 7281

Accommodation in this Edwardian pied-à-terre is in 52 beautifully designed suites which include ensuite kitchen facilities, on the off-chance that you don't wish to take advantage of Albert Roux's world-famous restaurant, Le Gavroche (see entry), downstairs. You do have the option, though of ordering a "take-away"—from Le Gavroche, that is! Round-the-clock concierge and room service are also included, along with other benefits like free entrance to nearby Tramps night-club and the use of a leisure club nearby. All in all, it's quite spectacular, very much in the Roux mould.

FOUR SEASONS HOTEL   W1

Hamilton Place, Park Lane, W1A 1AZ
Tel: 0171-499 0888   *Fax:* 0171-493 1895
Four Seasons Restaurant: **£90**
Open: lunch & dinner daily
Meals served: lunch 12.30-3, dinner 7-10.30,
    (light meals lounge: 9am-2am, Sun 9am-1am)
Lanes Restaurant: **£75**
Open: lunch & dinner daily
Meals served: lunch 12-3, dinner 6-12 (Sun from 6.30)

Ramon Pajares has now been at the helm of this top hotel for two decades and keeps it full of satisfied guests come rain or shine. One of the top hoteliers, his attention to detail and dedication start to explain the hotel's success; his new chef, Jean-Christophe Novelli, is another reason. Complex, well-composed dishes emerge from his kitchen, such as a poached lobster sausage served with couscous with peppers, ginger and cardamom; or oyster ravioli topped with caviar with a cucumber and chervil sauce. Sea bream fillets are filled with tapenade and served with anchovy and olive jus on basmati rice. After the theatre, Lanes Restaurant is open until midnight and has the choice of buffet, grills or daily specials.

FREDERICK'S   N1

Camden Passage, N1 8EG
Tel: 0171-359 2888   *Fax:* 0171-359 5173   **£40**
Open: lunch & dinner Mon-Sat (closed Bank Holidays)
Meals served: lunch 12-2.30, dinner 6-11.30

Classical French food on a fortnightly-changing menu keeps the regulars coming back to Louis Segal's smart conservatory restaurant. The court-yard garden patio offers alfresco eating in summer and early evening opening hours cater for pre-theatre diners. Choose (from either the à la carte or fixed price menus) dishes such as foie gras or char-grilled smoked salmon with sweet peppers and lime to start, followed by fried calf's liver with wild boar bacon and deep-fried capers or grilled sea bass, crispy seaweed and teriyaki sauce. Save some room for dessert such as summer pudding with clotted cream or amaretti and mascapone torte, and take advantage of the suggestions offered on the à la carte for the most appropriate dessert wine to accompany your choice.

FRENCH HOUSE DINING ROOM   W1

49 Dean Street, W1
Tel: 0171-437 2477   *Fax:* 0171-287 9109   **£35**
Open: lunch & dinner daily (closed Bank Holidays)
Meals served: lunch 12.30-3, dinner 6.30-11.30

A deservedly popular first-floor dining room within a legendary Soho pub. The daily-changing menu offers traditional British cuisine, with rarely seen specialities like tripe and onions, roast pork belly and smoked haddock pie. Good British cheeses and Welsh rarebit. The kitchen is supplied with game from Wales and fish direct from the boats in Dorset. A young and confident team is really going places.

FULHAM ROAD   SW3

257 Fulham Road, SW3 6HY
Tel: 0171-351 7823   **£40**
Open: lunch & dinner daily
Meals served: lunch 12.30-2.15 (Sun to 2.30),
    dinner 7-11 (Sun to 10)

With his move from Bentley's to Stephen Bull's new venture here in Fulham Road, young Irish chef Richard Corrigan has made his mark. It's an unusual restaurant, and the decor (pale cream walls, elephant-motifed banquettes and studded dado rail) by Irish designer David Collings has provoked comment. So, too, does the food, not least because offal gets more attention than usual. Lunch-time offers a short hand-written set menu, with two choices at each stage: lamb and cumin sausages with tomato and coriander or warm salad of smoked salmon with aïoli to start; followed by grilled Angus sirloin with pommes mousseline and a truffle jus or roast turbot with lobster and tarragon risotto. Evening sees a change and really brings the offal on line: a lengthier table d'hôte features dishes such as terrine of foie gras and ox tongue with Madeira jelly, followed by pig's head faggots and black pudding with shredded red cabbage and porcini, truffled breast of Bresse chicken with fondant potato and tarragon jus, or sea bass meunière with a mousseline of celery. Great bread and interesting vegetables, including the classic Irish colcannon, reworked in the modern mode with broccoli replacing the root element.

LA GAULETTE   W1

53 Cleveland Street, W1P 5PQ
Tel: 0171-580 7608   *If it's the exotic you're after*   **£55**
Open: lunch Sun-Fri, dinner Mon-Sat   *or simply some*
   (closed Bank Holidays)   *well-cooked fish with*
Meals served: lunch 12-2.30, dinner 6.30-11 *added Mauritian*
                                               zest, look no further

The second of two family-run Mauritian restaurants, the first being
Chez Liline (N4). Simple decor and a relaxed, informal atmosphere are
likewise the hallmarks here. The homely and robust cooking is entirely
devoted to fish, including unusual varieties flown in directly, such as
parrot fish, merou and vacqua. Typical dishes might include
Trinidadian prawns with ginger and spring onions, lobster mauricienne
(with tomatoes and chili), shellfish in a lemon grass sauce, provençal
fish stew and assiette creole. Palates requiring simpler tastes might opt
for asparagus with lemon butter to start, followed by grilled salmon.

LE GAVROCHE   W1

43 Upper Brook Street, W1Y 1PF
Tel: 0171-408 0881   *Fax:* 0171-409 0939   **£150**
Open: lunch & dinner Mon-Fri
   (closed Bank Holidays, 23 Dec-3 Jan)
Meals served: lunch 12-2, dinner 7-11

It was no easy task for Michel Roux Jr to step into the illustrious shoes
of his father, Albert, at what is surely one of England's finest French
restaurant, but he has taken it in his stride and continues to delight the
worldwide clientele. Dishes that have become trademarks during the
restaurant's 20 year history still feature along with
classics and some new ideas. Certain dishes, like
soufflé suissesse have long been a hallmark, but that
isn't to say that there isn't adaptation, development,
evolution. Recently enjoyed dishes have
included gratin de langoustines à l'indienne, petite gelée de rouget à la tapenade, onglet d'Angus aux cèpes et
pommes sautées à l'ail, and eminué de
chevreuil aux airelles et sauce poivrade.
Delicious desserts almost defy description:
the famous omelette Rothschild and the
hardly any less famous tarte des demoiselles tatin
vie for attention alongside soufflé aux épices et
sauce chocolat or poires jumelles pochées et sa
bavaroise. As Michel says, "We have no specialities as such in our menu as we have created the
great majority of our dishes. The few classical
dishes which figure in our menu also have the hallmark of our interpretation." And how! Silvano
Giraldin, the inimitable restaurant manager, is still
in charge and his team provide service that is so
efficient that you will be served with something
before you even realised that you wanted it! Le
Gavroche is truly something rather special.

GAY HUSSAR   W1

2 Greek Street, W1V 6NB
Tel: 0171-437 0973
Open: lunch & dinner Mon-Sat
Meals served: lunch 12.30-2.30,
    dinner 5.30-10.45

£50

Ask someone to name a Hungarian restaurant and they'll come up with
the Gay Hussar, which has been around as long as most of us can
remember. Ask them to recommend some dish, and wild cherry soup
followed by Laszlo Holecz' roast duck are likely candidates. Other
favourites on every Gay Hussar regular's tongue include the
Transylvanian stuffed cabbage, veal goulash, pressed boar's head and
chicken paprikash with egg dumplings. Finish with a sweet cheese
pancake or poppyseed strudel. Happily, little has changed over the
years—plush red seating evokes the atmosphere of a gentlemen's club.
Hungarian charm abounds; expect a warm and friendly welcome from
the manager, Mrs Bela Molnar. Reasonably priced wine list with some
from Hungary and Bulgaria.

Biography

Laszlo Holecz has to be the London
Hungarian chef, for as well as being born
in Hungary, he has been associated with
Laszlo all the Hungarian restaurants
in the capital at one time or
Holecz another, and has been at The
Gay Hussar since 1977. He
finds immense satisfaction in what he
does, is an unashamed champion of old-
fashioned cooking, with a dedicated
following to prove him right.

GEALES   W8

2 Farmer Street, W8 7SN
Tel: 0171-727 7969   *Fax:* 0171-229 8632
Open: lunch & dinner Tue-Sat (closed Bank Holidays
    & following Tue, 2 wks Xmas, 5 days Easter, 2 wks Aug)
Meals served: lunch 12-3, dinner 6-11

£30

Traditional fish'n'chips—the fish cooked in beef dripping, the chips in
vegetable fat—are the main event at this popular Notting Hill Gate
restaurant behind the Gate cinema. And they've been dishing them out
here for 50 years. The fish comes daily from Grimsby, which accounts
for the blackboard-style menu. Home-made soups make a popular
starter, before moving on to the main business: halibut, haddock, cod,
to name but a few. But it's not all plain white fish: clams or parrot fish
are also regular features. It's a busy place which doesn't take bookings,
but you can wait upstairs with a drink for a table. Alfresco eating on
pavement tables in summer.

GILBERT'S   SW7

2 Exhibition Road, SW7 2HF
Tel: 0171-589 8947   **£45**
Open: lunch & dinner Mon-Fri (closed Bank Holidays,
   1 wk Feb, 1 wk Jun)
Meals served: lunch 12-2, dinner 6-10

Julia Chalkley is now at front-of-house but continues to supervise all
the cooking which she now shares with Gina Mahsoudi. There is now
greater emphasis on traditional European cooking and less of the previous New Wave influence. A new business lunch menu concept is proving popular, offering local business people the opportunity to reserve
their menu choice by phone in advance to ensure prompt service, and
the two-course fixed-price lunch continues to offer good value.
Everything is home-made and the menu offers a good balance of light
and more robust, hearty dishes. Traditional English puds to finish.
Excellent walnut and onion or sunflower seed breads. The recent face
lift gives the decor a lighter, more spacious feel.

GLAISTER'S GARDEN BISTRO   SW10

4 Hollywood Road, SW10 9HW
Tel: 0171-352 0352   **£35**
Open: lunch & dinner daily (closed Bank Holidays,
   2 wks Xmas)
Meals served: lunch 12.30-3 (Sat & Sun to 4),
   dinner 7-11.30 (Sun to 10.30)

Bistro-style restaurant-cum-café bar with garden and sliding roof, in a
road opposite the Chelsea and Westminster Hospital. Baked stuffed
aubergine on tomato coulis, fish soup with herb croutons and
Emmenthal, and a choice of salads are typical among starters. Main
courses include popular favourites like salmon fishcakes with parsley
sauce, burgers, and sausages'n'mash, alongside more sophisticated
meat dishes and grills (fillet béarnaise; sautéed calf's liver with sage,
red wine and onions on brioche; rack of lamb with herb crust, served
with honey and port sauce). Sunday lunch for families is made all the
more attractive by a registered crèche service available next door!

THE GORE   SW7

189 Queen's Gate, SW7 5EX
Tel: 0171-584 6601   *Fax:* 0171-589 8127

About as far as you can get from an American corporate hotel, says the
brochure, and indeed such is the case. This is more like the kind of
grand, exclusive, yet relaxed hotel you might find in Paris. Mellow surroundings, rich in mahogany and walnut, with oil paintings and
Oriental rugs, together with intelligent and friendly staff make for a
delightful yet luxurious stay. There are 55 rooms, among them the
dark and atmospheric Tudor room. The hotel houses Bistrot 190 and
Downstairs at 190 (see separate entries).

THE GORING   SW1

17 Beeston Place, Grosvenor Gardens, SW1W 0JW
Tel: 0171-396 9000   *Fax:* 0171-834 4393   **£60**
Open: lunch & dinner daily
Meals served: lunch 12.30-2.30, dinner 6-10

One of the few remaining private luxury hotels in London, a stone's throw
from Buckingham Palace, the Goring
has been in the hands of the Goring
family ever since it was built in 1910.
This was the first hotel in the world,
they say, to have ensuite facilities and
central heating in every bedroom.
During your stay, you are invited to
treat the Goring as home (within reason, no doubt). Each of the 79 rooms,
some with balconies overlooking the
gardens, is luxuriously appointed and
housekeeping is immaculate. Traditional afternoon teas in the elegant
garden lounge are not to be missed.
The restaurant offers a traditional
English repertoire, with the occasional
nod towards modern trends: split pea
soup, warm goat's cheese salad, fish
pie, wing of skate with capers, grilled
lamb cutlets with mint sauce,
Cumberland sausages with onion gravy, steak béarnaise. Managing
Director and Chairman George Goring actually believes the Goring
has "a soul", and who am I to argue?

GRAHAME'S SEAFARE   W1
8 Poland Street, W1V 3DA
Tel: 0171-437 3788   *Fax:* 0181-294 1808   **£30**
Open: lunch & dinner Mon-Sat (closed Bank Holidays,
    Jewish New Year, 2 wks Xmas)
Meals served: lunch 12-2.45, dinner 5.30-9 (Fri & Sat to 8)
A kosher seafood restaurant that offers fish, simply cooked.

GRANITA   N1

127 Upper Street, N1
Tel: 0171-226 3222   **£40**
Open: lunch Wed-Sun, dinner Tue-Sun
    (closed 10 days Xmas, 5 days Easter, 2 wks Aug)
Meals served: lunch 12.30-2.30, dinner 6.30-10.30 (Sun to 10)

A weekly-changing menu of new Med- and Cal-style dishes: this is
healthy eating, without saucing. Broccoli and white bean soup with
pecorino; sorrel and red onion tart; spaghettini with an onion confit,
gorgonzola, red pepper and rocket; char-grilled salmon or roasted
guinea fowl served with mash, sweet garlic, carrots and Savoy cabbage
are the sort of thing you'll find. The decor is simple and modern, with a
zinc bar, wooden floor, and bright, airy feel.

GREEN'S RESTAURANT & OYSTER BAR   SW1

36 Duke Street, St James's, SW1Y 6DF
Tel: 0171-930 4566   *Fax:* 0171-930 1383   **£65**
Open: lunch daily, dinner Mon-Sat (closed 25 & 26 Dec)
Meals served: lunch 11.30-3 (Sun 12-2.30), dinner 5.30-11

Booking is essential at this clubby, wood-panelled, long-established oyster
bar and restaurant off Jermyn Street. The standard à la carte menu offers a
concise range of starters, grills, egg and fish dishes, such as scrambled
eggs with smoked salmon and blini, bangers'n'mash with crispy bacon and
onion gravy, grilled Dover sole and seafood platter. A daily-changing carte
goes up a notch or two in the sophistication stakes, with the likes of scallop
and monkfish risotto, or roast duck breast with swede purée and a sage jus,
but always features a traditional English dish such as shepherd's pie on
Mondays, Irish stew on Thursdays and fish pie on Fridays. Langoustines
and oysters are available across the board. Good range of champagnes and
some reasonably priced wines.

GREENHOUSE   W1

27a Hays Mews, W1X 7RJ
Tel: 0171-499 3331   **£65**
Open: lunch Sun-Fri, dinner daily
    (closed Bank Holidays)
Meals served: lunch 12-2.30 (Sun to 3),
    dinner 7-11 (Sun 6.30-10)

Helped first by Kit Chapman from the Castle at Taunton, then David
Levin, owner of the Capital Hotel and the Greenhouse, Gary Rhodes is
dedicated to putting English food back on the map by virtue of his talent. The menu at this conservatory-style restaurant, with one of the
most attractive approaches in the capital, (complete with leafy courtyard and trellised canopy), is by no means conservative, rather it is
founded on old favourites which Gary then reinterprets. His dishes
include salmon fishcakes, smoked eel on toast, roast loin of lamb with
parsnip crumble, braised oxtail (a favourite), grilled calf's liver with
crispy bacon and onion gravy, and fillet of cod on smoked pecorino
mash with spinach. Desserts are robust and traditional: bread-and-
butter pudding, steamed rhubarb sponge, hot apple fritters.

ALISTAIR GREIG'S GRILL   W1

26 Bruton Place, W1X 7AA
Tel: 0171-629 5613   *Fax:* 0171-495 0411   **£60**
Open: lunch Mon-Fri, dinner Mon-Sat (closed 25 & 26 Dec, 1 Jan)
Meals served: lunch 12.30-2.30, dinner 6.30-11

Good raw ingredients are the mainstay here, but quality does not come
cheap. If it's steak you're after, this is some of the best you will get.
Prime Scotch beefs simply grilled and garnished with tomato, mushroom and watercress, served with a choice of salad, jacket potatoes or
chips has been the speciality here for more than 30 years. The plush
red interior behind a red door is the setting for what is a truly conservative menu. Variations on the institutional theme include baby lamb
cutlets, chicken, veal chop or mixed grill.

GRILL ST QUENTIN   SW3

2 Yeoman's Row, SW3 2AL *Good style, very French, a*
Tel: 0171-581 8377   *Fax:* 0171-584 6064 *favourite restaurant* **£50**
Open: lunch & dinner daily
Meals served: lunch 12-3 (Sun to 3.30), dinner 6.30-11.30

Charcoal-grilled steaks, cutlets and fish served with great chips are the
mainstay of the menu at this spacious restaurant just off Brompton
Road. French staff attend in relaxed, semi-formal style, ensuring your
enjoyment. Plenty of salads, oysters, mussels and langoustines; plus
daily specials and regular favourites like devilled poussin and sausages
with lentils, all served in a modern, French-style brasserie.

GROSVENOR HOUSE   W1

86-90 Park Lane, W1A 3AA   ❖
Tel: 0171-499 6363   *Fax:* 0171-493 3341
Pavilion: **£65**
Open: lunch & dinner daily
Meals served: lunch 12.30-2.30, dinner 6-10 (Sat & Sun to 10.30)
Pasta Vino: **£40**
Open: lunch Mon-Fri, dinner Mon-Sat (closed Bank Holidays)
Meals served: lunch 12.30-2.30, dinner 7.30-11.30

Built in 1929, the façade designed by Sir Edwin Lutyens, Grosvenor
House was the first hotel to open on Park Lane. The magnificent banqueting hall (the largest in a hotel in Europe), began life as an ice-rink
and was used for grand, high-society ice galas, such as the 1930
Halloween Ice Carnival which was attended by the then Prince of
Wales, later Edward VIII, commemorated in a painting which now
hangs in the hotel lobby. Today's banqueting hall, with a capacity of
1500, was created in 1936. The Grosvenor House is not so much a
grand hotel, they say, more a way of life. 454 well-appointed bedrooms,
including 70 suites, are only the beginning. In addition, there are 140
fully-serviced luxury apartments in the specially-designed apartment
block. Facilities are unrivalled. The health club boasts a 65ft pool; the
Park Terrace is a stylish place for afternoon tea; there are various private dining and conference suites, a vast lounge and intimate Japanese-
themed bar. Restaurant facilities include Pasta Vino or the more formal
Pavilion which serves contemporary English cooking in a relaxed and
stylish atmosphere, not to mention Chez Nico at 90 Park Lane.

THE HALCYON   W11

81 Holland Park, W11 3RZ
Tel: 0171-727 7288   *Fax:* 0171-229 8516   *young and enthusiastic staff*
                                                £65
Open: lunch & dinner daily
Meals served: lunch 12-2.30, dinner 7-10.30 (Fri & Sat to 11)

Converted from two Victorian town houses, this elegant 43-bedroomed hotel retains the beautiful proportions of the original houses along with some other lovely architectural features, bringing to life the splendour of the Belle Epoque, enhancing it by fine antique furnishing throughout. No surprise to those who know it, the Los Angeles Times described it as "London's most elegant little hotel, the city's best kept secret". Marlon Brando knew about it though, as did Lauren Bacall - just two of the many celebrities who frequent this exclusive little hotel. However, the true jewel in the crown these days has to be chef Martin Hadden, who arrived in April 1993, full of experience from the kitchens of Nico Ladenis and Shaun Hill. Martin shows a knack for originality and flair in his own right, with dishes like seared calf's sweetbreads with basil-mashed potatoes, Thai-spiced chicken and coconut soup, and pan-fried monkfish with curry-spiced chick peas, cream and coriander sauce, served with rice cake and mango chutney. Good-value, two-course business lunch and separate vegetarian menu. Shades of cream, mirrors and contemporary artwork on the walls provide an elegant setting in which to sit and enjoy the experience. The restaurant leads out through French windows to an ornamental garden patio at the rear where parasols provide shade in fine weather.

THE HALKIN   SW1

5 Halkin Street, SW1X 7DJ
Tel: 0171-333 1000   *Fax:* 0171-333 1100   **£75**
Open: lunch Mon-Fri, dinner daily
   (closed 25 Dec, 1 Jan)
Meals served: lunch 12.30-2.30,
   dinner 7.30-11 (Sun 7-10)   ❖

The neo-Georgian façade of the Belgravia Halkin belies a striking, modern Italianate interior, with marble terrazzo and mosaic lobby floor based on Michelangelo's design for the Campidoglio piazza in Rome. The 41 rooms, including suites, continue the contemporary Italian look, as does the delightful restaurant which overlooks a private garden. The cooking is imaginative, with Stefano Cavallini's menu (Stefano is pictured, left) retaining much of the influence of former head chef Gualtiero Marchesi—roquette gnocchi with lobster, breaded red mullet with black truffles and braised celery, noisettes of venison with blueberries, polenta and broccoli. The Halkin oozes style and has established itself as a very special place to stay and eat.

HAMPSHIRE HOTEL   WC2

31 Leicester Square, WC2 7LH
Tel: 0171-839 9399   *Fax:* 0171-930 8122   **£50**
Open: lunch & dinner daily
Meals served: lunch 12.30-3, dinner 6-11

Retreat from the very heart of London's bustling West End into the
calm and seclusion of the Hampshire. The hotel has 124 rooms, some
of which overlook the square, and the Penthouse Suite, available for
functions, offers panoramic views over Westminster. Diners have a
choice between the elaborate Celebrities restaurant and stylish Oscars
wine bar. Menus offer international cuisine, with a good choice of simple grilled meats and fish alongside the likes of spicy lamb fillet with
okra, basmati and almond rice, or roast lobster with macaroni, mushroom and mustard cocktail.

HILAIRE   SW7

68 Old Brompton Road, SW7 3LQ
Tel: 0171-584 8993   *Fax:* 0171-581 2949   **£60**
Open: lunch Mon-Fri, dinner Mon-Sat
    (closed Bank Holidays, 4 days Easter)
Meals served: lunch 12.30-2.30, dinner 7-11.30

Chef Bryan Webb's unpretentious approach to cooking, coupled with
his undisputed talent in the kitchen, is the key to Hilaire's success.
Drawing on modern European influences, menus offer starters such as
terrine of duck liver with onion chutney and brioche, or griddled scallops with vegetable relish and rocket, while main courses might
include char-grilled swordfish with spinach, chili and pancetta, or
boned coquelet which has been roasted with sweetbreads and morels.
Desserts show the same flair such as stewed rhubarb with mascarpone
and shortbread, or blood orange sorbet. Set menus, at both lunch and
dinner, offer good value and the late supper menu (available upstairs
after 9.30pm or downstairs) is worth noting. Less sophisticated lunch-
time options feature some interesting combinations such as potato pan-

Biography

Bryan always wanted to cook–being a chef
offered an escape from the conventional work
in the Welsh mining village where he grew up.
He trained at the Crown at Whitebrook with
Bryan Sonia Blech, worked with Colin
Pressdee at the Drangway in
Webb Swansea, and after receiving the
William Hopelstein award for
Young Chefs, spent three months in France.
On his return to the UK, he went first to the
Kirroughtree Hotel in Scotland, before moving
down to the Café Rouge (Barbican), and
finally Hilaire, where he cooks simple, good

cake with sautéed foie gras and onion chutney, or roast cod with langoustine sauce. The newly-designed downstairs bar area and extended ground-floor restaurant will increase covers, bringing more fans into the Bryan Webb fold. I take great personal pleasure from Bryan's success at Hilaire, having been involved myself at this site for many years, dating back to its conversion from a burger bar into a restaurant for Simon Hopkinson, now at Bibendum.

HOSPITALITY SUITE   EC3

London Underwriting Centre, 3 Minster Court,
Mincing Lane, EC3R 7DD
Tel: 0171-617 5065   **£60**
Open: lunch Mon-Fri (closed Bank Holidays, 1 wk Xmas)
Meals served: lunch 12-2.30

The setting for this, the latest Roux venture is as haute as the cuisine. Perched on the top of the impressive Minster Court building, with access permitted by a pass issued at a security check at reception, the Hospitality Suite on the seventh floor is a splendid setting for the Roux's classic French cuisine. The dining room, with huge picture windows on two sides, gives uninterrupted views of the Tower of London and the Thames. Mini-boardroom-type tables are well spaced for privacy - where most would seat 70, the Rouxs seat just 28. It's all very plush and private, and the menu is a short, daily-changing table d'hôte affair with four or five choices for each course. Service is aptly polished; the reasonably priced wine list is short and selective. Booking, needless to say, is absolutely essential.

L'HOTEL   SW3

28 Basil Street, SW3 1AT
Tel: 0171-589 6286   *Fax:* 0171-225 0011   **£35**
Open: all day Mon-Sat (closed Xmas)
Meals served: 12-10.30 (coffee & breakfast 7.30am-11am)

A small, unique pension-style hotel just yards from Harrods, under the same professional and friendly management as The Capital Hotel next door. Inside, there's an air of discreet tranquility. Accommodation, in 11 individually-designed twin-bedded rooms (and one suite) in French country style, feels more like a private house than a hotel. The basement houses Le Metro, an all-day bistro-style operation, very busy at lunchtime, and popular with locals and shoppers. Breakfast is served till 11am, then the full, short, French-inspired menu comes into play, with dishes like croque monsieur and salad; seafood fettucini with langoustine sauce; rib-eye steak béarnaise or a warm salad of new potatoes and Toulouse sausage.

THE HOTHOUSE   E1

78-80 Wapping Lane, E1 9NF
Tel: 0171-488 4797   *Fax:* 0171-488 9500   **£45**
Open: lunch & dinner daily (closed some Bank Holidays)
Meals served: lunch 12-4, dinner 6-11 (Sun to 10)

Local restaurant on two floors of a 200-year-old East End spice warehouse, with wooden beams and bare brick walls. Menus are short and
simple, the simpler range being offered on the ground floor. The
Sunday Hothouse Special is popular for its roast beef and all the trim-
mings. Typical dishes (downstairs) include the likes of fishcakes, crab
and coriander risotto, roasts and grills—roast smoked haddock, grilled
sirloin béarnaise, grilled salsicotto sausages with parsley mash. Live
jazz on Wednesday and Friday evenings.

HUDSON'S RESTAURANT   NW1

221b Baker Street, NW1 6XE
Tel: 0171-935 3130   **£55**
Open: lunch & dinner daily
   (closed dinner 25 Dec, Bank Holidays)
Meals served: lunch 12-2.30 (Sun to 3), dinner 6-10.30 (Sun 7-10)

This restaurant is adjacent to the Sherlock Holmes museum and
named after Holmes's housekeeper. The menu, carefully executed by
joint head chefs Andrew Bailey and Mark Stapley, makes the most of
its historic location with dishes which are firmly rooted in the English
tradition. Mrs Hudson's freshly-made soup opens the menu alongside
other starters which run from bubble'n'squeak cake with wild mushrooms or leek and smoked bacon tart to historic salamagundy salad.
Main courses range from home-made venison sausages with Yorkshire
pudding and sage and onion gravy or fillet of Scotch beef with Red
Leicester cheese wrapped in bacon, to smoked haddock fishcakes
served with tomato, white wine and chive sauce. Welsh rarebit or puds;
plus good-value set-price lunches. The atmosphere is that of a Victorian
parlour, far removed from that of its previous life as Martin's.

HYATT CARLTON TOWER   SW1

2 Cadogan Place, SW1X 9PY
Tel: 0171-235 5411   *Fax:* 0171-245 6570   **£80**
Open: lunch & dinner daily
Meals served: lunch 12.30-2.45, dinner 7.30-11 (Sun to 10.30),
   (light meals Rib Room: 12.30-3, 6.30-11.30 (Sun 7-10.30)

Have breakfast in the Chinoiserie, lunch in the Rib Room and dinner in
the Chelsea Room, though not necessarily all in the same day!
Exercise in the fabulous health club on the ground floor and if you just
happen to have won the national lottery, stay in the Presidential Suite,
where the daily rate is £2,000! Mind you, this includes a full-time butler, personal maid and fully stocked bar, and not all rooms are as
expensive. Chef Bernard Gaume's standards are as high as ever, providing excellent food in whichever restaurant you choose. A meal from
the à la carte in the Chelsea room might include a starter of potted
duck with goose liver and truffles, followed by a whole sole baked in a
saffron and almond crust served on tomato coulis, and finishing with
seasonal fruits in a warm sauce and honey ice cream.

HYDE PARK HOTEL   SW1

66 Knightsbridge, SW1Y 7LA
Tel: 0171-235 2000   *Fax:* 0171-235 4552   **£75**
Open: lunch & dinner daily
Meals served: lunch 12.30-2.30, dinner 7.30-10.30 (Sun to 10)

One of London's loveliest hotels stands between the fashionable shops of Knightsbridge and verdant Hyde Park to the rear. Bedrooms are exquisite, with antique furniture and wonderful views; they have hosted royalty and famous names from around the world for nigh on a century. Paolo Biscioni has a formidable team of staff whose aim in all departments is, simply, to serve and to serve well. Whilst the tranquillity of the place has been a little disturbed by the arrival of Marco Pierre White at the Restaurant (see later within London under 'R'), the Park Room continues as ever in its inimitable style. It is one of the best locations in London with views over Rotten Row, and a favourite place for a civilised breakfast.

L'INCONTRO   SW1

87 Pimlico Road, SW1W 8PH
Tel: 0171-730 3663   *Fax:* 0171-730 5062   **£80**
Open: lunch & dinner Mon-Sat (closed 25 & 26 Dec)
Meals served: lunch 12.30-2.30 (Sat to 3),
    dinner 7-11.30 (Sun to 10.30)

Stylish, up-market Italian restaurant located alongside some of the city's most prestigious antique shops, and therefore popular with local art dealers and international jet-setters. The redesign of the exterior and the intimate piano bar has now been completed, and Gino Santin's daughter Charlotte has joined the team this year, full of new ideas. Her One Dish Lunch menu is proving popular, with its half a dozen or so options—pasta dishes, osso bucco, and casseroled squid are typical. The arrival, too, of 23-year-old Venetian Nicola Celmanti in the kitchen is perfectly in keeping with the Gino Santin style: a distinctive Venetian repertoire of simple but honest dishes. Fish mousse with polenta, cuttlefish in ink sauce, tagliatelle with crab sauce, risottos and dishes such as poached sea bass in balsamic vinegar sauce or escalopes of beef with a hint of truffle are the sort of thing to expect. The two- and three-course lunch-time table d'hôte offers lighter, simpler creations.

HOTEL INTER-CONTINENTAL LONDON   W1

1 Hamilton Place, Hyde Park Corner, W1V 1QY
Tel: 0171-409 3131   *Fax:* 0171-409 7460   **£95**
Open: lunch Tue-Fri & Sun, dinner Tue-Sat
   (closed 1 wk Xmas, 2 wks Jan, Aug)
Meals served: lunch 12.30-3, dinner 7-10.30   ❖

It's been a big year for this 467-bedroomed hotel, on prime London property at Hyde Park Corner, with the opening of the new business centre, creation of two spectacular seventh-floor meeting rooms with panoramic views over the city, and transformation of the Grand Ballroom. It's been an even bigger year for executive chef Peter Kromberg following his promotion to chef-patron of Le Soufflé restaurant after 18 years at the helm—Peter joined the Inter-Continental for the hotel's opening in 1975. One of his greatest strengths has always been his commitment to the whole operation, building a strong and inspired team to work to his exacting standards, and this is one of the finest restaurants in the country. Peter's style of cooking, while classically-inspired, is complex, imaginative and informed, always keeping abreast of the times and he has a long list of accolades to show for it. Soufflés, of course, are the signature dish. Have one! Sweet or savoury, it doesn't matter; they're wonderful. Start with lobster soufflé (baked in its shell and served on a bed of lobster with sauce americaine enhanced with tarragon); end with the one made from raspberries, served with a lime-zest-flavoured curd cheese mousse. In between: grilled turbot with champagne and caviar sauce, served with native oysters and tagliatelle of root vegetables; canon of Dorset lamb marinated with garlic and fresh ginger; or perhaps sautéed layers of beef with fresh goose liver served on a base of crisp potato and truffle sauce. Healthy Heart options on the menu denote dishes low in all bad things, high in fibre. A daily gourmet tasting menu offers eight perfectly well-balanced courses but no soufflé component. The dining room is stylish, modern and elegant, with a baby grand piano in the centre, the resident pianist playing popular classics and light classical renditions as you feast. The Coffee House restaurant offers an all-day menu, from breakfast (one of the best in town), to lavish buffets and an international repertoire of light meals and snacks. The hotel is popular with Americans, both from the business and conference and tourist ends of the market. Courtesy luxury airport service provided.

Biography

As a small boy, Peter enjoyed good food, to the point he would even criticise his mother's cooking! At 14 he entered an apprenticeship at a hotel in Buisburg and followed this with stints at various top European establishments. On joining Inter-Continental Hotels, **Peter** he worked first in Bangkok before coming to England, at the Portman **Kromberg** and finally the London Inter-Continental at Hyde Park. Peter's cooking is innovative and creative, based on classical foundations, but developing to current trends. A chef in pursuit of perfection, the continuation of the highest standards gives him the greatest satisfaction.

THE IVY   WC2

1 West Street, WC2H 9NE
Tel: 0171-836 4751   *Fax:* 0171-497 3644   **£60**
Open: lunch & dinner daily (closed lunch Bank Holidays)
Meals served: lunch 12-3 (Sun to 3.30), dinner 6-12

Following in the footsteps of its heyday in the '30s, The Ivy is still a popular haunt for theatrical and arty types. Mirrored wood panelling, stained-glass windows and an abundance of art provide an appropriately indulgent setting for Des McDonald's modern interpretations of classic British and international dishes. The menu opens with a selection of seafood starters—oysters, dressed crab, seared Orkney scallops and Sevruga caviar, before moving on to non-fishy starters such as crispy pork and parsnip salad or sautéed foie gras, and soups. Eggs, pastas and risottos follow, or dishes like corned beef hash with fried egg, fettuccine with two cheeses and wild mushroom risotto. Fish options could include roasted Mediterranean shellfish, daily char-grilled fish, salmon fishcakes, kedgeree and the like. Meat runs from hamburger, Cumberland sausage, Ivy mixed grill and steak frites to confit of duck with truffle mash, tripe and onions, and shepherd's pie. Good accompanying salads and vegetables, and wonderful desserts—bread and butter pudding, cappuccino brûlée, rice pudding with prunes and Armagnac, citrus fruits with a kumquat sorbet. The wine list is a short, no-nonsense affair, with some good drinking under £20. Weekend fixed-price lunches feature roasts such as suckling pig and the likes of deep-fried hake with minted pea purée and chips.

The professional team of Chris Corbin and Jeremy King continue to run the Ivy and its sister restaurant La Caprice with style and dedication.

JAKE'S   SW10

2 Hollywood Road, SW10 9HY
Tel: 0171-352 8692   **£35**
Open: lunch daily, dinner Mon-Sat (closed 25-28 Dec)
Meals served: lunch 12.30-3, dinner 7.30-11.45

A smart, bright, summery restaurant, with an open courtyard at the rear, which serves a straightforward repertoire of English and international dishes. Crispy duck parcels with honey sauce or warm chicken liver salad among starters; followed by a selection of light snacks (polenta, Jake's burger, omelettes) or full-blown main courses typified by chicken Singapore, beef Wellington, noisettes of lamb with herb gravy, sole Walewska, salmon fishcakes and steak, kidney and mushroom pie. Daily specials on the blackboard.

JOE ALLEN   WC2

13 Exeter Street, WC2E 7DT
Tel: 0171-836 0651   *Fax:* 0171-497 2148   **£45**
Open: all day daily (closed 24 & 25 Dec)
Meals served: 12-12.45am (Sun to 11.45)

Trendy American basement restaurant, something of an institution
after all these years. The food is still very much okay, with a menu
which runs from starters such as buffalo chicken wings or black bean
soup to main-course salads and traditional favourites such as chili con
carne (or a vegetarian variety), and numerous grilled or pan-fried
meats and fish, including sirloin steak with frites. Not the sort of place
to go if quiet, relaxed concentration is what you're after, but a reasonably priced wine list and menu make this 150-seater as busy as ever.

JOE'S CAFÉ   SW3

126 Draycott Avenue, SW3 3AH
Tel: 0171-225 2217   **£45**
Open: lunch daily, dinner Mon-Sat (closed 25 & 26 Dec)
Meals served: lunch 12-4 (Sun 11-5), dinner 6-11.15 (Sat at 7)

Chic, fashionable, split-level brasserie-style restaurant offering a menu
of eclectic design. Dishes range from bang bang chicken, steak tartare
and grilled sea bass with salsa verde to grilled lamb chops, Toulouse
sausages'n'mash, eggs'n'bacon and chips, and oxtail stew. A trendy
place to hang out, and many do just that.

JULIE'S   W11

135 Portland Road, W11 4LW
Tel: 0171-229 8331   *Fax:* 0171-229 4050   **£60**
Open: lunch Sun-Fri, dinner daily (closed Xmas, Easter)
Meals served: lunch 12.30-2.45 (Sun to 3),
    dinner 7.30-11 (Sun to 10.30)

At Julie's you have not just a choice of dishes but a choice of rooms too.
Eat in the conservatory, champagne bar, ruby-red Gothic-style or pink
dining rooms. Julie's has served Holland Park since 1969, and is a local
institution. The cooking is essentially British, with a tempting repertoire which incorporates modern interpretations alongside more traditional choices. Starters such as watercress mousse with mint tea jelly
and red pepper coulis or king prawns sautéed with garlic and coriander
are followed by steak au poivre, calf's liver with onion marmalade and
polenta or scallop, prawn and monkfish pie. A delicious range of
desserts: lemon coconut tart with clotted cream, butterscotch crepes
with cream cheese and ginger, or fresh berry pavlova when the season
is right. Return to eat in a different room; they are all delightful. Some
interesting and reasonably priced wines on the list.

*Julie's is a very special sort of place which has a welcoming,
friendly, club-like atmosphere in the bar and restaurant.*

KALAMARAS W2

76-78 Inverness Mews, W2 3JQ
Tel: 0171-727 9122
Open: dinner Mon-Sat (closed Bank Holidays)
Meals served: dinner 6-12

I have a very soft spot for this place **£35**

One of the most authentic Greek restaurants in the capital, Kalamaras is tucked away down a quiet mews which runs parallel to Queensway. A good sign is that plenty of Greeks eat here too. The menu is varied and interesting: spiced Greek sausages, meatballs with mint and shallots, fried salted cod with garlic sauce dip, grilled spliced langoustines, fresh steamed salmon and lamb casseroles show the range. I always leave the choice to Stelios or one of his team and ask for three or four small starters to go with a Greek salad, then some simple grilled lamb with spinach and lemon or one of his fish dishes in season to follow. This is one of the five or six restaurants I always come home to after eating my way around Great Britain and Europe. (Micro Kalamaras is in the same mews at no. 66—take your own wine).

Biography

Stelios Platanos used to help out at his uncle's restaurant in Athens (one of the best in the city) and simply wanted to be like him when he grew up. Knowing that he wanted to have his own restaurant one day, he gained experience in both cooking (Café de Paris, Leicester Square and Les Gourmets, Lyle Street) and front-of-house (White Tower, Percy Street and the Screenwriters' Club, Mayfair). His first restaurant was a French restaurant in Queensway; but when he thought the time was right for an authentic Greek restaurant in London, he opened Kalamaras. The rest, as they say, is history.

Stelios Platanos

KASPIA W1

18/18a Bruton Place, W1X 7AH
Tel: 0171-493 2612
Open: lunch & dinner Mon-Sat (Mon-Fri in Aug)
 (closed 24 Dec-4 Jan)
Meals served: lunch 12-3, dinner 7-11.30

£60

Offshoot of the famous Paris shop and restaurant, Kaspia with its clubby decor creates an appropriate setting for the signature caviar and excellent smoked fish salad. A short list of daily specials introduces the likes of fish soup and beef stroganoff, while the regular carte offers a wide choice of dishes, from blinis and bortsch to gull's eggs, steak tartare and salmon à la Russe with a dill and sour cream sauce. Caviar comes in all its many forms, in keeping with big brother in Paris—salmon, pressed, Sevruga, Osietra and Beluga. Various set menus give the opportunity to taste a little of what you fancy.

KENSINGTON PLACE   **W8**

205 Kensington Church Street, W8 7LX
Tel: 0171-727 3184   *Fax:* 0171-229 2025   **£55**
Open: lunch & dinner daily (closed 24-26 Dec, 1 Jan)
Meals served: lunch 12-3 (Sat & Sun to 3.30),
    dinner 6.30-11.45 (Sun to 10.15)

A lively hot spot, popular since the day it opened (in 1987), much of which is a tribute to the consistently good show from the kitchen under head chef Rowley Leigh, whose modern style of cooking relies on simple techniques without fuss. Starters range from Caesar salad or pumpkin soup to squid and aubergine stew or griddled foie gras with sweetcorn pancakes. Main course offerings include fish dishes like cod with parsley sauce or grilled tuna with salsa verde, alongside meat options typified by roast haunch of venison

with chocolate sauce, featherblade and oyster stew, or calf's liver with capers and lime. Daily specials supplement the carte with dishes such as roast quail with quince chutney and sea bass with spiced pumpkin purée. Good choice of mostly traditional desserts—rhubarb fool, winter fruit compote with mascarpone, lemon tart, tiramisu, pavlovas. The glitzy bar at one end faces a vast mural depicting alfresco eating at the other. Noise volume is high, smiles are plentiful, and so are the customers.

Biography

Rowley Leigh began his career in the most unlikely of places—a hamburger bar, as a grill chef. With no formal cookery education he was taken on by the Roux brothers at Le Gavroche, moving on to the Roux Patisserie, their butchery and then Le
Rowley   Poulbot. At Kensington Place he is able to put into
Leigh   practice everything he learned with the Rouxs, and is honest enough to say that they did indeed teach him everything he knows! He operates with a combination of the basic and the imaginative.

THE LANESBOROUGH   **SW1**

1 Lanesborough Place, Hyde Park Corner, SW1X 7TA
Tel: 0171-259 5599   *Fax:* 0171-259 5606   **£90**
Open: lunch & dinner daily
Meals served: lunch 12.30-2.30 (Sun brunch 11-3), dinner 7-12

A stark Regency façade overlooks Hyde Park Corner belies the comfort and elegance of its interior. Whilst the Royal Suite will set you back £2,500 per day, the other rooms are in line with comparable London hotels. Paul Gayler leads the kitchen and his imaginative cooking won't fail to please. Oriental touches add flair to dishes such as chicken soup with coconut milk and shiitaki, crab spring roll with soy and ginger, or chinese duck cakes with oriental aiöli. European and cajun dishes also combine to give great variety to his menus: cannelloni of ratatouille and ricotta, niçoise salad with grilled tuna and fresh anchovy escabeche, creole glazed rack of lamb or crisp fried cajun seafood salad. A good Sunday brunch menu to follow a brisk walk in Hyde Park.

LANGAN'S BISTRO   W1

26 Devonshire Street, W1N 1RJ   *Good local bistro with a loyal following*
Tel: 0171-935 4531   **£40**
Open: lunch Mon-Fri, dinner Mon-Sat (closed Bank Holidays)
Meals served: lunch 12.30-2.30, dinner 7-11.30

Smaller, younger sister to the famed Mayfair brasserie of the same name. The menu is shorter but the style is very much the same. Start with toasted brioche topped with tomato and mozzarella or a gratin of smoked haddock, before dishes such as spicy lamb couscous, ratatouille-filled pancake, sirloin with a Guinness and onion sauce or grilled fillet of lemon sole with a tomato and basil sauce. Sweets offer Mrs Langan's chocolate pudding alongside date and apple crumble, marbled chocolate pie, ice creams and sorbets. Excellent value –two courses for £13.95, three for £15.95.

LANGAN'S BRASSERIE   W1

Stratton Street, W1X 5FD   *An all-time favourite*
Tel: 0171-491 8822   **£60**
Open: lunch Mon-Fri, dinner Mon-Sat
   (closed Bank Holidays)   ✿
Meals served: lunch 12.30-3,
   dinner 7-11.45 (Sat 8-12.45)   ♪

The legendary, larger-than-life Langan's continues to delight even after a decade and a half in the limelight. An enormous brasserie on two floors, decorated with modern art, it remains the place to see and be seen in. The large but intelligently conceived menu runs the gamut of traditional French and English dishes—Burgundy snails, seafood salad, cod and chips, grilled calf's liver and bacon, bangers and mash with white onion sauce, steak hâché Mexicaine, roast duck with sage and onion stuffing and apple sauce. These and many others sit alongside dishes with a more modern leaning such as griddled venison with gnocchi and a plum sauce, lentil and pea cakes with curried vegetables and grilled swordfish with lime butter sauce. The trendy downstairs area is countered by the more discreet charm of the first-floor Venetian room which features a daily trolley speciality such as roast lamb with Provençal herbs. No less choice amongst desserts, with something in the region of 25 from which to choose. It's hard to get to the top, but staying there is even harder and Richard Shepherd and his team manage just that.

Biography

After an apprenticeship at the Mount Pleasant Hotel, Great Malvern, Richard Shepherd worked first at The Savoy before becoming chef de partie at La Réserve in Beaulieu, France. On his return

Richard Shepherd

to London he worked at The Dorchester and then at The Capital. Richard then joined Langan's Brasserie in Stratton Street, in partnership with Peter Langan and Michael Caine, where he developed an individual style which he calls 'basically English, respecting French tradition'. Richard demands and receives a great deal of loyalty from the staff at all his units and, driven by an innate love of food and flair for cooking, has worked his way to the top of his class and become one of the great personalities in the restaurant industry.

THE LANGHAM HILTON   W1

1c Portland Place, W1N 3AA
Tel: 0171-636 1000   *Fax:* 0171-323 2340   **£75**
Open: lunch & dinner Mon-Sat
Meals served: lunch 12-2.30, dinner 6-10.30,
    (Palm Court Tea: 3-5.30)

The marvel of its age: it was the largest building in the capital when it was built in 1865. Then the legend of the Langham came to an abrupt end in 1940 owing to war damage. It was not until half a century later, in 1987, that work began on reconstructing the hotel and lavishly restoring it to its former days of splendour. The result is a sophisticated modern hotel which retains many of the original features, giving it a certain sense of timelessness. Smart doormen in Tsarist uniforms set the tone for what lies ahead. The floors (strewn with Oriental rugs) and pillars of the lobby are of marble; 379 bedrooms include 50 luxurious suites. There are several venues for eating and drinking. The intimate Palm Court is the place for afternoon tea to the accompaniment of a resident pianist, it's also open for food throughout the day and night. Thirsts and appetites can be quenched at the polo-themed Chukka Bar, or you can sample one of 103 different vodkas with caviar in the Tsar's Bar opposite the Palm Court. The main restaurant, Memories of the Empire, offers a modern French repertoire with Eastern influences. Head chef Anthony Marshall produces dishes such as asparagus and shisho salad with a rose petal dressing, fillet of salmon baked on cherrywood and breast of chicken filled with black trumpet mushrooms. But it's not all sophistication and contrivance. Other alternatives include the more familiar coq au vin and grilled T-bone steaks. A separate area is set aside for children, with drawing sets, board games and video entertainment, during Sunday brunch hours.

LAUNCESTON PLACE   W8

1a Launceston Place, W8 5RL
Tel: 0171-937 6912   *Fax:* 0171-938 2412
Open: lunch Sun-Fri, dinner Mon-Sat
    (closed Bank Holidays)
Meals served: lunch 12.30-2.30 (Sun to 3), dinner 7-11.30

Good local restaurant with style and some good food

£50

Set in a quiet residential street, this comfortable, well-furnished, relaxing restaurant is popular with locals. Cathy Gradwell, ex-Kensington Place (which is owned by same proprietors) offers an adventurous repertoire in the modern British mould, with dishes such as chicken liver pâté with toast and onion marmalade or warm smoked eel with sauté potatoes, crème fraîche and mustard among starters. Main courses range from the likes of wild mushroom cakes with aïöli or fillet steak chasseur to roast wood pigeon with fresh herb risotto or steamed fillet of brill with creamed garlic and parsley. The new late-supper menu (10-11.30pm) offers good value, with simple choices like steak and chips, spinach and herb risotto or cod tartare. Beef and Guinness stew and roast meats are popular on Sundays.

LAURENT   NW2

428 Finchley Road, NW2 2HY
Tel: 0171-794 3603
Open: lunch & dinner Mon-Sat (closed 3 wks Aug)
Meals served: lunch 12-2, dinner 6-11

£30

Laurent Farrugia's simple couscous restaurant is now into its second decade. The North African signature dish comes in five guises: vegetarian, complet (with lamb and merguez), royal (with mixed grill), chicken, or fish (with halibut steak). The sole starter of brique à l'oeuf leaves no choice other than to tackle this rather tricky deep-fried pastry parcel filled with a soft egg, but it's fun, and tasty too. Sweets are likewise sensibly limited, with sorbets and ice creams joined by crème caramel and crepe Suzette. Algerian and Moroccan wines, along with mint tea, kir, cognacs and liqueurs. Take-away service available.

LEITH'S   W11

92 Kensington Park Road, W11 2PN
Tel: 0171-229 4481   **£85**
Open: dinner daily (closed 2 days Aug
    Bank Holidays, 4 days Xmas)
Meals served: dinner 7.30-11.30

The new-look Leith's, following redecoration in shades of yellow with a colourful triptych by Dewe Matthews to celebrate its 25th year in 1994, has been favourably received by customers. And with head chef Alex Floyd in the kitchen, producing new and exciting dishes and novel slants on classic British dishes, all is well at Prue Leith's renowned restaurant between Notting Hill and Ladbroke Grove. A weekly set menu runs alongside the seasonal cartes, one for omnivores, one for vegetarians. Choose from a selection of hors d'oeuvres from the trolley or one of the seasonal specials such as a tartlet of crab and oysters with a ginger and lemon grass dressing. For your main course you can look forward to dishes like navarin of lamb with roasted sweetbreads and tarragon or pan-fried salmon with wild mushrooms, spinach and oxtail broth. Vegetarians may find a casserole of braised vegetables and tarragon with garlic cream or layers of roasted aubergine and goat's cheese served with a ratatouille vinaigrette. Wherever possible, organically-grown produce is supplied by Leith's own farm. For dessert, there's a typically- Leith light selection: rhubarb soufflé with vanilla ice cream; lemon and raspberry crème brûlée; white chocolate truffle torte. Managing Director Nick Tarayan controls the front-of-house and buys the wine.

Biography

Prue Leith

From humble beginnings, Prue Leith has expanded her influence countrywide by her various business enterprises–and her restaurant has enjoyed equal success since the day it opened. Her prime concern has always been to produce stylish, unpretentious, excellent food, be it for a sandwich or a banquet. Her disciples can be found spreading the word all over the place - teaching at the school that still bears her name, supervising parties, testing dishes and wines for commercial companies or other restaurants. Prue Leith is a lady who has had a great influence on both the commercial and domestic cookery scenes in this country over many years.

■ **Pictured: Prue with head chef Alex Floyd**

THE LEXINGTON   W1

45 Lexington Street, W1R 3LG
Tel: 0171-434 3401   *Fax:* 0171-287 2997   **£55**
Open: lunch Mon-Fri, dinner Mon-Sat
   (closed Bank Holidays, Xmas/New Year)
Meals served: lunch 12-3, dinner 5-11

Simple but smart, in the contemporary mould, Martin Saxon's West
End restaurant offers a modern repertoire of light European dishes.
Wild garlic, sorrel and mu ▲ rooms feature strongly, alongside sun-
dried tomatoes, porcini and truffles from Piedmont. The decor changes
twice a year—warm colours for autumn and winter; cool for spring and
summer. Seasonal menus, to match, of course: dishes such as fennel
and lemon risotto, roasted cod with saffron mash and chives, and
poached breast of chicken with lentils and mustard are the type of
thing. Good-value two-course lunch and coffee for just £10.

LINDSAY HOUSE   W1

21 Romilly Street, W1V 5TG
Tel: 0171-439 0450   *Fax:* 0171-581 2848   **£65**
Open: lunch & dinner daily (closed 25 & 26 Dec)   *A very special restaurant,*
Meals served: lunch 12.30-2.30 (Sun to 2),   *imaginatively styled*
   dinner 6-12 (Sun 7-10)

Thoroughly English, like its owner Roger Wren—ring the door bell to
gain entry through the heavy front door of this 17th-century house,
where comfortable sofas and armchairs await you in the lounge, before
heading upstairs to the dining room to sample chef Dean Rogers' work.
Hefty appetites might like to start with the game pie with Cumberland
sauce (a signature dish); alternatives include lobster minestrone, trout
terrine or baked goat's cheese on tomato and tarragon relish. Grills
and roasts aplenty amongst the main courses, along with steamed
monkfish with crab and sorrel sauce or vegetarian aubergine charlotte.
Roast beef with Yorkshire pudding requires a two-person order (except
Sunday lunchtimes) and takes around 30 minutes to prepare, but it's
worth it. Puds continue the English theme, with bread-and-butter pudding and chilled lemon and lime soufflé. The fixed-price Lindsay Lunch
offers three choices at each course, with plenty of variety—salmon
mousse, Huntsman pie, nuggets of lamb in red wine sauce.

LONDON HILTON ON PARK LANE   W1

22 Park Lane, W1Y 4BE
Tel: 0171-493 8000   Fax: 0171-493 4957   **£70**
Open: lunch Sun-Fri, dinner daily
Meals served: lunch 12.30-2.30, dinner 7-11.30 (Fri & Sat to 12.30),
    (light meals Brasserie: 7am-12.45am, Fri & Sat to 1.45am)   ✧

Top-floor bedrooms in London's first skyscraper hotel facing Hyde
Park enjoy panoramic views of the capital. But you can also enjoy them
from the 28th-floor Windows on the World restaurant and bar, which
serves an international repertoire ranging from Cabicou goat's cheese
soufflé on hazelnut salad or flambé of tiger prawns in a kaffir lime
bouillon to grilled Shetland salmon steak. Indeed, you'll have no prob-
lem satisfying a hungry appetite here. A host of facilities includes an
all-day brasserie, the basement Polynesian-style Trader Vic's restaurant
and the rooftop cocktail and champagne bar. An extensive 24-hour
room service menu is also available. Bedrooms vary from luxurious
suites to standard rooms with polished mahogany furniture. Amenities
include sauna, beauty and hair salon, as well as extensive business and
conference facilities.

LOU PESCADOU   SW5

241 Old Brompton Road, SW5 9HP
Tel: 0171-370 1057   **£55**
Open: lunch & dinner daily (closed 10 days Xmas)
Meals served: lunch 12-3, dinner 7-12

Nautical decor makes an appropriate setting for this noisy, informal,
bustling French restaurant specialising in seafood. The menu starts
with fish soup, oysters, mussels and the like, before moving on to
dishes of red mullet, skate or whatever the market has available that
day. There are also good omelettes, pasta, pizza and steaks for those
who can't leave them alone. Quiet at lunchtime but busy in the evening
when it's first come, first served, so get there early (no bookings).

LUC'S RESTAURANT & BRASSERIE   EC3

17-22 Leadenhall Market, EC3V 1LR
Tel: 0171-621 0666   *Fax:* 0171-336 7315   **£45**
Open: lunch Mon-Fri (closed Bank Holidays, 5 days Xmas)
Meals served: lunch 11.30-3

Busy French brasserie in the centre of Leadenhall Market, serving the
City and its brokers and lawyers with a classically-based lunchtime
repertoire. Soups, salads, steaks of various cuts with béarnaise sauce,
and the likes of skewered scallops wrapped in bacon and served with
wild rice. Bearing in mind the market location, you can be assured that
the meat and fish are fresh. Some reasonably priced wines on the list.

*A bustling first-floor restaurant that
deserves continued success*

MAGNO'S BRASSERIE   WC2

65a Long Acre, WC2E 9JH
Tel: 0171-836 6077   *Fax:* 0171-379 6184   **£40**
Open: lunch Mon-Fri, dinner Mon-Sat
  (closed Bank Holidays, 25 Dec)
Meals served: lunch 12-2, dinner 5.30-11.30

The brasserie-style menu is popular with pre- and post-theatre diners at
this Covent Garden haunt—hardly surprising, given its location at the
heart of London's theatreland. Baked Roquefort in puff pastry, mini
lamb moussakas, ravioli of wild mushrooms, coq au vin and grilled
salmon, served with a confit of vegetables and fennel butter sauce
might be available. Various set menus offer choice and the à la carte
includes about ten at each course.

MANZARA   W11

24 Pembridge Road, W11 3HL
Tel: 0171-727 3062   **£30**
Open: all day daily
Meals served: 8am-11.30 (Sun from 10)
Modern, authentic Turkish restaurant with extensive carte. Simple, traditional
favourites and grills on the lunchtime menu. Good mixed mezes. Speciality
coffee menu, plus excellent home-baked pastries to eat in or take away.

MANZI'S   WC2

1-2 Leicester Street, WC2H 7BL
Tel: 0171-734 0224   *Fax:* 0171-437 4864   **£65**
Open: lunch & dinner Mon-Sat (closed 25 & 26 Dec)
Meals served: lunch 12-2.40, dinner 5.30-11.40

The oldest fish and seafood restaurant in town, with distinctive trail-net
decor and a choice of two rooms. Upstairs is the more sedate, while
downstairs is on the buzzy side. The menu is vast, with each element
available in a number of different styles. Everything from deep-fried
crab claws, jellied or stewed eels to lobster, Dover sole, skate, halibut,
sea bass, plaice and turbot. The simpler, the better, in many cases! One
or two steak options are available for those with non-fishy appetites.
Fifteen modest bedrooms.

RESTAURANT MARCO PIERRE WHITE   SW1

66 Knightsbridge, SW1Y 7LA
Tel: 0171-259 5380   *Fax:* 0171-235 4552   **£150**
Open: lunch Mon-Fri, dinner Mon-Sat
  (closed Bank Holidays, 2 wks Aug)
Meals served: lunch 12-2.30, dinner 7-11.30

Quotes from great historical figures provide plenty to mull over while you wait: "To know how to eat well, one must first know how to wait," we are reminded (by Brillat-Savarin) on the inside of the dessert menu at Marco Pierre White's stylish new flagship restaurant occupying part of the ground floor of the Hyde Park Hotel. The room is elegant, with fine art adorning cream-coloured walls, and the cooking is refined and artistic. Marco is a showman who likes to please—nothing is too much trouble to achieve the desired results for both plate and palate. Designer meals at designer prices. The choice on the regular carte is almost overwhelming—a dozen or so starters and around 15 main courses—every dish a bite to treasure. Try a fricassée of girolles with crayfish, terrine of leeks with truffle vinaigrette or red mullet soup with saffron to start; followed by Pierre Koffmann's signature dish perhaps—braised pig's trotter with essence of morels, Bresse pigeon en cocotte or fillet of brill Viennoise, served with spinach, buttered noodles and a grain mustard sabayon. Chef-patissier Thierry Busset will then take over. Typical desserts include a raspberry soufflé, pear sablé with a Poire William sabayon and caramelised apple tart served with ice cream and a caramel sauce. Lunch offers a fixed menu with three choices at each stage. Extensive wine list at prices you would expect on such a starry stage.

Undeniably, this restaurant has established itself in a very short space of time as one of the most important in the country, and with a growing international reputation it has assured success.

MAY FAIR INTER-CONTINENTAL   W1

Stratton Street, W1A 2AN   *Good value and well-thought-out*
Tel: 0171-629 7777   *Fax:* 0171-629 1459   *buffet lunch choice*   **£70**
Open: lunch Sun-Fri, dinner daily
Meals served: lunch 12.30-2.30, dinner 7-11

The perfect location for shoppers (between Oxford Street, Piccadilly and Regent Street), the Mayfair is a large (322 rooms), well-run hotel complete with health club and business centre. Le Château restaurant provides good modern cooking with set price menus at lunch and dinner, with Michael Coaker at the helm.

LE MERIDIEN   W1

Piccadilly, W1V 0BH
Tel: 0171-734 8000   *Fax:* 0171-437 3574
Oak Room Restaurant: £105
Open: lunch Mon-Fri, dinner Mon-Sat
  (closed Bank Holidays, Aug)
Meals served: lunch 12-2, dinner 7-10.30
Terrace Garden Restaurant: £55
Open: all day Mon-Sat (closed Bank Holidays)
Meals served: 7am-11.30pm (Sun 11.30-2.30)

David Chambers has now moved on from the Oak Room after establishing it as one of London's finest dining rooms. However, there is the good news in that Alain Marechal takes over and is well up to the task, having worked in some very commendable restaurants in France; and Michel Lorain still has a strong influence on the style. Cooking is modern but based on French classics, and you choose from fixed menus at various prices or from the carte. One recent fixed menu featured a bisque of green crab with tomato and asparagus topped with a pastry crust, followed by lobster with green and black olives and ratatouille niçoise. The main dish was pan-fried goose liver on a bed or noodles with crayfish and lobster sauce, and passion fruit soufflé for dessert. The wine list has great depth and not surprisingly is predominantly of French origin. Jean Quero's expertise as maitre d'hotel makes the experience of dining here even more enjoyable. The Terrace Room also offers a tempting menu and a great Sunday brunch.

MESON DON FELIPE   SE1

53 The Cut, SE1 8LF
Tel: 0171-928 3237   £35
Open: all day daily
Meals served: 12-11

The first of Philip and Ana Diment's London tapas bars—they are fun, lively and buzzy. The menu is thoroughly traditional—gambas al ajillo, boquerones (fresh marinaded anchovies), tortilla, calamares, chorizo, albondigas (meatballs) and paella are all featured. Eat in authentic style at the bar here, but be prepared: it's popular! Flamenco in the evenings. Fantastic range of Spanish wines, including those from the Diments' own vineyard.

MESON DONA ANA   W11
37 Kensington Park Road, W11 2EU
Tel: 0171 243 0666   £35
Open: all day daily
Meals served: 12-11.30
The second of the Diments' tapas bars (see above), handy if you're in the Portobello road area. Small bar here, so table eating is likely. The same lively fun atmosphere with good range of authentic dishes and bustling, friendly service.

LE MESURIER   EC1

113 Old Street, EC1V 9JR
Tel: 0171-251 8117   *Fax:* 0171-608 3504   **£55**
Open: lunch Mon-Fri, dinner parties only
    (closed Bank Holidays, 10 days Xmas, 3 wks Aug)
Meals served: lunch 12-3, dinner 6-11

The short lunchtime menu at this small, intimate, French restaurant
close to the City changes every fortnight. Expect to find dishes such as
herb brioche filled with chicken livers and bacon or cheese beignet
soufflé to start; followed by delicious breast of duck with plum purée
served with a rich onion and sage sauce or escalopes of halibut with a
courgette and cheese sauce. For dessert, perhaps pancakes with honey
and hazelnuts or banana, butterscotch and walnut crumble. Gillian
Enthoven will open in the evening for private parties, booked in
advance.

MIJANOU   SW1

143 Ebury Street, SW1W 9QN
Tel: 0171-730 4099   *Fax:* 0171-823 6402   **£75**
Open: lunch & dinner Mon-Fri   ✿
    (closed Bank Holidays, 3 wks Aug, 2 wks Xmas,
    10 days Easter)
Meals served: lunch 12-2, dinner 7-10   🍾

Sonia Blech and husband Neville have built up a loyal following since
they opened here in 1980. Rumours of selling up and leaving are no
longer founded, Sonia informs us. With Neville taking charge of wine
and providing recommendations to match each course, and Sonia
remaining in the kitchen, you can be sure of a perfectly satisfying meal
here. Sonia's inspiration is classically-based and French-inspired, but
the end result on the plate is very much her own. Typical dishes are
grilled veal served with a port, red wine and pecan nut sauce, and
quails stuffed with wild rice and glazed with mango chutney and
ginger. Wonderful desserts could feature delicious Caribbean pancakes with banana, pineapple and coconut flamed with Malibu, or the
exotic Arlequinade, which is a medley of sorbets served with fruit.
Lunchtime sees a simpler menu, with dishes such as mussels in spices,
salmon with watercress sauce and lasagne basquaise.

THE MILESTONE   W8

1-2 Kensington Court, W8 5DL
Tel: 0171-917 1000   *Fax:* 0171-917 1010   **£45**
Open: lunch & dinner daily
Meals served: lunch 12.30-2.30, dinner 7.30-11

Restoration work on this late 19th-century town house overlooking the
Royal Palace and Kensington Gardens is carefully observed by English
Heritage. The house boasts many original features, including the
oratory, as well as every modern facility, and offers accommodation in
57 luxury suites, many of which overlook the neighbouring Royal
gardens. The restaurant offers a modern European repertoire, with
speciality dishes such as pan-fried sea bass with fennel and mushroom
duxelle on a dill sauce. Other dishes on the two or three course,
weekly-changing table d'hôte include the likes of wild mushroom and
leek tartlet with a horseradish and chive sauce and navarin of lamb.
State-of-the-art facilities range from a health spa to private fax machines
and satellite TV and video. Valet parking is available.

MIMMO D'ISCHIA   SW1

61 Elizabeth Street, Eaton Square, SW1 9PP
Tel: 0171-730 5406   *Fax:* 0171-730 9439   **£65**
Open: lunch & dinner Mon-Sat (closed Bank Holidays)
Meals served: lunch 12-2.30, dinner 7-11.30

A warm welcome from the ever-present proprietor
at this bustling Italian restaurant, whose walls are
decorated with signed photographs of the many
celebrities who have dined here. Mimmo (pictured) is something of an old favourite, the man and
the restaurant both long-established, continuing to
draw in the loyal following. Spare ribs are the speciality on an otherwise traditional Italian menu
with modern presentation which features all
the classics—gnocchi, spaghetti vongole,
fritto misto, calf's liver and veal
Milanese, alongside the likes of fresh
Scotch salmon, halibut and Scotch fillet
of beef in black pepper sauce. I
inevitably start with a mixed pasta and
follow with grilled sea bass and fresh
spinach. A good selection of medium wines
on the list.

MIRABELLE RESTAURANT   W1
56 Curzon Street, W1Y 8DL
Tel: 0171-499 4636   *Fax:* 0171-499 5449   **£65**
French restaurant closed for re-furbishment, due to re-open in early 1995. Two
teppanyaki rooms still open—phone for details.

MON PLAISIR   WC2

21 Monmouth Street, WC2H 9DD
Tel: 0171-240 3757   *Fax:* 0171-379 0121
Open: lunch Mon-Fri, dinner Mon-Sat
   (closed Bank Holidays, Xmas/New Year)
Meals served: lunch 12-2.15, dinner 5.50-11.15

Loyal and new customers looked after alike

£55

This is the flagship of the group of three French bistros (Mon Petit Plaisir is in Kensington, Mon Plaisir du Nord is in Islington) which has been in existence now for over 50 years but still manages to stay in fashion. The lunch-time and pre-theatre menus offer great value and the all-day carte is well-balanced and competently prepared. Start with gratinée à l'oignon or brioche with snails in parsley sauce, before main courses such as magret de canard, steak tartare, entrecôte béarnaise, grilled sole or meunière, pan-fried scallops or fillet of salmon with a watercress sauce. Good vegetables and salads. Reasonably priced wine list and buzzy, fun ambience. Alain Lhermite has remained faithful to his successful formula, and has never chased fame.

MONKEYS   SW3

1 Cale Street, SW3 3QT
Tel: 0171-352 4711
Open: lunch & dinner Mon-Fri (closed Bank Holidays)
Meals served: lunch 12.30-2.30, dinner 7.30-11

£55

Victorian monkey prints and paintings adorn the walls of this friendly local restaurant where good home-made food without pretension is the appeal. Here the Benhams turn out dishes such as soup du jour or mousse of sea scallops and lobster sauce to start, followed perhaps by grilled cod with herbs and breadcrumbs or sautéed calf's kidneys and madeira sauce.

MOSIMANN'S CLUB   SW1

11b West Halkin Street, SW1X 8JL
Tel: 0171-235 9625   *Fax:* 0171-245 6354
Open: lunch Mon-Fri, dinner Mon-Sat
   (closed Bank Holidays)
Meals served: lunch 12-2.30, dinner 6-11

It's always a pleasure to eat here

£95

As you would expect, the cooking is excellent at this stylish dining club in a former church belfry, built in 1830. Simple lunch and dinner à la carte menus start with dishes such as wild mushroom risotto, gnocchi provençale, seafood sausage with dill sauce or warm Thai chicken salad; main courses might feature Mosimann's fish cakes with lemon grass, peppered rosette of Angus beef, or daily specials such as halibut orientale or chicken picatta with masala sauce and saffron risotto. Full of invention, intuition and imagination, a delightfully inspiring and different menu. These are perhaps the most sought-after private reception rooms in the capital.

■ **Anton Mosimann biography, next page**

Biography

Anton Mosimann

By the time Anton Mosimann was six he knew he wanted to be a chef, and set about achieving that ambition with the single-mindedness that characterises his every move. At fifteen he was invited by the Hotel Baeren in Twann to be an apprentice. The next four years or so were spent in various establishments in Europe and Canada, then after time at the Palace Hotel, Gstaad, he was recruited by The Dorchester in London, where at only twenty-nine, he became the youngest ever maître chef des cuisines. Following his time at The Dorchester, he achieved another ambition—to run his own exclusive private dining club, Mosimann's in Knightsbridge. An honest, practical and dedicated chef with an ever growing world-wide reputation—one of the most influential figures in the culinary world today.

MOTCOMB'S   SW1

26 Motcomb Street, SW1X 8JU
Tel: 0171-235 9170   *Fax:* 0171-245 6351   **£60**
Open: lunch daily, dinner Mon-Sat
    (closed Bank Holiday Mon)
Meals served: lunch 12-3, dinner 7-11.45

Philip Lawless's popular restaurant continues to pull in the crowds, attracted by an extensive wine list (compiled with help from Heyman Brothers Ltd) and a simple, well cooked menu of classic favourites and modern variations (cooked by David Prego). Choose perhaps their famous smoked trout and salmon mousse or consommé madrilène with a julienne of vegetables; crab and shrimp cakes with mild curry sauce or sizzling calf'sliver with soft sage polenta and Maui onion; tiramisu or bread and butter pudding with apricot jam.

LE MUSCADET   W1

25 Paddington Street, W1M 3RF   *Every London village*
Tel: 0171-935 2883   *should have one*   **£50**
Open: lunch Mon-Fri, dinner Mon-Sat *like this*
    (closed Bank Holidays, 3 wks Aug)
Meals served: lunch 12.30-2.45, dinner 7.30-10.45

Classic French bistro dishes chosen from a handwritten menu still pull in the crowds at this popular local spot despite rumours that proprietor, the ever-present François Bessonard, is considering retirement. Snails, fresh foie gras with Madeira sauce, pan-fried scallops, salmon hollandaise and peppered steak show deference to the classical approach. A fun, personally run establishment.

MUSEUM STREET CAFÉ   WC1

47 Museum Street, WC1A 1LY
Tel: 0171-405 3211   **£50**
Open: lunch & dinner Mon-Fri (closed Bank Holidays)
Meals served: lunch 12.30-2.30, dinner 6.30-9.30

After a six-week spell of closure for refurbishment in spring 1994, the Museum Street Café (close to the British Museum) reopened its doors to reveal an upgraded room, offering greater comfort and space. Another important change has been the acquisition of a liquor licence and new open-plan kitchen. These things apart, Mark Nathan and chef/proprietor Gail Koerber continue with their successful partnership in the kitchen. The cooking is simple and straightforward, but executed with skill and care, with a light hand and sound imagination. Short set menus are the style, both at lunchtime and in the evening. Typical dishes include chicken liver crostini, salmon fishcakes with sherry and cayenne mayonnaise or organic beef burger with bruschetta. Good desserts and cheeses from Neal's Yard dairy.

NEAL STREET RESTAURANT   WC2

26 Neal Street, WC2H 9PH
Tel: 0171-836 8368   *Fax:* 0171-497 1361   **£70**
Open: lunch & dinner Mon-Sat
   (closed Bank Holidays, 1 wk Xmas/New Year)
Meals served: lunch 12.30-2.30, dinner 7.30-11

Famous in the gastronomic world for his love of mushrooms, Antonio Carluccio continues to make lunchtime appearances at his longstanding Covent Garden restaurant, where he circulates among new and old friends alike, more often than not talking or tasting mushrooms over a relaxed informal chat. Meanwhile, in the kitchen, Nick Coombes continues the regional Italian tradition with precision and competence. Starters include the likes of mixed sauté of funghi of the day (for those who share Antonio's passion), along with wild mushroom soup or salad of home-smoked shellfish and eel. Pasta dishes offer an exciting range, with some of the best featuring truffle sauce. Fish and meat courses are

Biography

For Antonio Carluccio, Italian cooking is based on the principle of obtaining the best possible end product from the best quality ingredients. Coming from a northern Italian family of six children, he fostered an

Antonio
Carluccio

early interest in learning at his mother's stove, and during wartime shortages, he soon became adept at spotting what might be turned into something special. He is a generous, passionate man—passionate about what he believes in, generous in sharing the knowledge he has acquired. He is an acknowledged expert on mushrooms.

typified by giant prawns with chili and garlic, or baked schiacciata of beef with truffle cheese. Good desserts, with plenty of choice. This is somehow an ageless restaurant, which always looks good, whenever you visit.

Wonderful gastronomic surprises in Carluccio's shop next door.

NEWTON'S   SW4

33-35 Abbeville Road, SW4 9LA
Tel: 0181-673 0977   **£40**
Open: lunch & dinner daily (closed 25 & 26 Dec, 3 days Easter)
Meals served: lunch 12.30-2.30, dinner 7-11.30,
    (light meals Sat & Sun 12.30-11.30)

This is a popular, local bistro, with appropriately simple furnishings and red-brick walls, and a menu which displays strong Oriental and Mediterranean influences in a varied repertoire described by Sebastian Tyson as modern British. Typical main-course dishes run from half-pound hamburger or steak and chips to venison pudding with baby shallots and mushrooms, Thai winter vegetable curry with jasmine rice, and daily specials which might feature paupiettes of sole and asparagus with dill and mussel velouté or char-grilled smoked gammon with pesto sauce. Saturday is children's day, with balloons and a resident clown to entertain. Simpler set lunches provide good value. Good selection of desserts, with gingerbread pudding and chocolate sauce surely a favourite!

NICO CENTRAL   W1

35 Great Portland Street, W1N 5DD
Tel: 0171-436 8846   Fax: 0171-355 4877   **£55**
Open: lunch Mon-Fri, dinner Mon-Sat
    (closed 10 days Xmas, lunch Bank Holidays)
Meals served: lunch 12-2, dinner 7-11

This is the up-market brasserie-style end of Nico's trio of starred London restaurants. The menu, much like that of Simply Nico, offers an alternative Nicoan feast with starters which run from fresh tiger prawns sautéed in garlic butter or thin pasta with button mushrooms and truffle oil, to main courses such as pan-fried guinea fowl with mushrooms and parmesan, griddled salmon steak with sweet pepper oil, ginger and spring onion, or confit of maize-fed chicken with sweetcorn pancake. The setting is smart and brightly lit; walls are hung with modern artwork—Juan Gris, Picasso et al. A stained-glass, art deco, illuminated skylight dominates the centre of the room, with a polished, granite-topped bar counter running along the side.

NIKITA'S   SW10

65 Ifield Road, SW10 9AU
Tel: 0171-352 6326   *Fax:* 0181-993 3680   **£50**
Open: dinner Mon-Sat (closed Bank Holidays, 2 wks Aug)
Meals served: dinner 7.30-11.30

One of the few Russian restaurants in London, Nikita's was established over 20 years ago. This is a snug basement restaurant serving hearty, seasonal and traditional dishes. Zakuski starters—blinis, caviar and smoked fish; plus soups, including borscht. Main courses are divided into two sections headed Classics from the Days of the Tsar and Seasonal Specialities. The range goes from beef stroganoff, chicken kiev and imperial steak tartare, to dishes such as pork kirga—chunks of tender pork marinated in honey and coriander, then flamed in zubrovka vodka and cream. The rare selection of flavoured and liqueur vodkas add authenticity and not a little warmth! Russian gypsy music is played in the evening.

NOSH BROTHERS BAR & RESTAURANT   SW6

773 Fulham Road, SW6 5HA
Tel & Fax: 0171-736 7311   **£45**
Open: dinner Tue-Sat (closed 24-26 Dec)
Meals served: dinner 7-11.30

Nick and Mick share the cooking at this local restaurant where you'll find a relaxed, lived-in, informal setting - white walls, modern art, candlewax drips and dimmed lighting - in which to enjoy the short, concise daily menu. A summer visit offered half a dozen choices at each stage: smoked haddock risotto and a warm salad of chicken livers among starters; with main courses featuring rump steak and chips, and calf's liver with roast garlic mash and shallots. The whipped cream topping on the banoffee pie is not for the faint-hearted. Trendy, informal service.

NOW AND ZEN   WC2
Orion House, 4A Upper St Martin's Lane, WC2
Tel: 0171-497 0376   *Fax:* 0171-497 0378   **£50**
Open: lunch & dinner daily (closed 25 & 26 Dec)
Meals served: lunch 12-3, dinner 6.15-11.30 (Sun to 11)
Stylish, ultra-modern restaurant on three levels. The menu is a mix of modern and classical Cantonese cooking.

O'KEEFE'S   W1

19 Dering Street, off Oxford Street, W1R 9AA
Tel: 0171-495 0878   *Fax:* 0171-629 7082
Open: all day Mon-Sat
    (closed Bank Holidays, 2 days Xmas)
Meals served: 8am-10pm (Sat 10-5)

Good to see Beth Coventry established at the stove here

£40

Bright, airy and fashionable deli-restaurant in a well-proportioned room, with high ceilings, white walls and large windows which open to the pavement. Healthy eating with strong Mediterranean influences is the focus here on the frequently-changing lunch and dinner cartes. Starters could include a ceviche of fresh salmon marinated in lime and chilis served with hot soda bread, bourride, or a light cheese and onion tart. Main courses might feature salmon fishcakes with dill mayonnaise, seared char-grilled tuna with a chili, garlic and lemon grass vinaigrette, and familiar favourites like char-grilled steak with chips, salad and roasted shallots. A fair choice of vegetarian options is always included. Traditional desserts, from school puds and nurseries to marmalade ice cream.

ODETTE'S   NW1

130 Regent's Park Road, NW1 8XL
Tel: 0171-586 5486
Open: lunch Sun-Fri, dinner Mon-Sat
    (closed Bank Holidays, 1 wk Xmas)
Meals served: lunch 12.30-2.30, dinner 7-11

£55

The menu changes daily at Simone Green's smart, attractive restaurant close to the park. Sit in the balcony room overlooking a conservatory to get the most out of the setting and your meal. The repertoire is modern European, offering both originality and familiarity in starters such as creamed salsify and wilted sorrel soup or Irish rock oysters with shallot relish. Main courses might include grilled tuna with lemon and parmesan risotto, confit of duck with vanilla butter beans and roasted Jerusalem artichokes, or roast saddle of new season lamb stuffed with spinach and sweetbreads and served with a garlic potato pie. The separate dessert menu offers a comprehensive range of mouthwatering options such as rhubarb and mascarpone trifle, lemon pancake torte, and lime and basil sorbet. Good choice of wines on the menu, and in the wine bar downstairs.

ODIN'S RESTAURANT W1

27 Devonshire Street, W1N 1RJ
Tel: 0171-935 7296 **£45**
Open: lunch & dinner Mon-Fri (closed Bank Holidays)
Meals served: lunch 12.30-2.30, dinner 7-11.30

Next door to its little sister, Langan's Bistro, Odin's offers a more robust style of cooking, but the place has a similar feel, with its art-crammed walls and buzzy atmosphere. Home-made soups, terrines and salads dominate starters; main courses run from curried vegetable risotto and steak and venison casserole in puff pastry, to pan-fried wing of skate with capers and brown butter or roast rack of English lamb with herb crust. Mrs Langan's chocolate pudding is included among desserts. Good wine list with some reasonable prices. Dieter Schuldt runs a smooth, professional operation here and Odin's has now established itself as <u>the</u> restaurant in this part of town.

OLIVER'S W14

10 Russell Gardens, W14 8EZ
Tel: 0171-603 7645 **£35**
Open: all day daily (closed 25 & 26 Dec)
Meals served: 12-11.30

A friendly restaurant whose bric-a-brac-laden walls provide interest and a relaxed, informal feel. Close to Olympia, so ideal for those post-exhibition blues. The menu is extensive, with some hearty game dishes a regular feature, along with steaks, grilled salmon, salads, soups and seafood: crab soup, giant king prawns, provençal-style squid are typical. A patio at the rear provides seating for sunny days.

OLIVO SW1

21 Eccleston Street, SW1W 9LX
Tel: 0171-730 2505 **£50**
Open: lunch Mon-Fri, dinner Mon-Sat
    (closed Bank Holidays, 3 wks Aug)
Meals served: lunch 12-2.30, dinner 7-11

Lively Italian restaurant with simple, unfussy decor, which specialises in Sardinian cooking. Char-grilled stuffed baby squid with plum tomatoes and spaghetti with grated grey mullet roe sound a contemporary note, with more familiar dishes such as char-grilled brochette of lamb, risotto with artichoke or pappardelle with chicken livers also featured. The set lunch menu offers the option of either two or three courses.

192 W11

192 Kensington Park Road, W11 2JF
Tel: 0171-229 0482 **£45**
Open: lunch & dinner daily (closed Bank Holidays)
Meals served: lunch 12.30-3 (Sun to 3.30),
   dinner 7-11.30 (Sun to 11)

Off-beat colours are in keeping with the smart, modern decor of this lively, informal restaurant, which draws a young and trendy clientele to its door. The weekly-changing menu has a strong Mediterranean bias to it, with well-structured, innovative dishes, strong on flavour. Artichoke and French bean salad with shaved parmesan, asparagus risotto, calf's liver with onions, grilled veal chops with citrus and marjoram and steamed brill with mussels, saffron and leeks are typical of Albert Clark's repertoire. Straightforward, simple desserts, such as banana and pineapple gratin or apple and almond tart. A good wine list with some very reasonable prices.

192 has been a local favourite of mine for many years and with the 1994 change of decor and more room, looks set to remain so for the future

ORSINO W11

119 Portland Road, W11 4LN
Tel: 0171-221 3299 **£45**
Open: all day daily (closed 25 Dec)
Meals served: 12-10.45 (Sun to 9.45)

The baby sister of Covent Garden's Orso, this popular West End setting offers a modern bourgeois Italian menu. The Mediterranean-inspired menu is matched by old black-and-white Italian prints on the walls. The restaurant occupies the ground and first floors, with seating for over 100, but booking is essential. Typical choices on the extensive carte which includes a number of small pizza options might be grilled cuttlefish, leek and ricotta ravioli, swordfish with roasted peppers and herbs and calf's liver with sage and lemon. Traditional desserts, or pecorino and pear make a pleasing finish. All Italian wine list. This restaurant has quickly and deservedly established itself as a firm local favourite.

ORSO WC2

27 Wellington Street, WC2E 7DA
Tel: 0171-240 5269   *Fax:* 0171-497 2148 **£55**
Open: all day daily (closed 24 & 25 Dec)
Meals served: 12-12

Popular basement restaurant with New York-style feel to the place. Arty black and white photos and rustic Tuscan pottery on tables provides a stylish but simple setting for an interesting menu of Italian dishes. Starters include a range of mini pizzas with various toppings, along with the likes of salad of dandelion, tomato, raddicchio and pecorino or grilled baby squid with roasted peppers. Pastas and risotto are followed by various grills such as rabbit with lemon, rosemary and spinach, or escalopes of veal with roasted tomatoes and asparagus. Smart service completes the picture.

OSTERIA ANTICA BOLOGNA   SW11

---

23 Northcote Road, SW11 1NG
Tel: 0171-978 4771   **£50**
Open: lunch & dinner daily (closed 2 wks Xmas)
Meals served: lunch 12-3, dinner 6-11
    (Fri to 11.30), (light meals Sat 12-11.30, Sun 12.30-10.30)

A friendly, unpretentious Italian restaurant in Clapham, not at all like
the rest. This is true to the osteria style, with wood panelling throughout and rustic-inspired menus which feature seasonal assaggi (typical
of Bolognese osterias), offering

around a dozen taster options.
The rest of the carte, which is
extensive, runs from salads or
polenta-based dishes and pastas
to fillet steak wrapped in speck
and rosemary, lamb meatballs
with ricotta, tomato and basil or
the speciality: capretto alla man-
dorle—goat cooked with rich
tomato and almond pesto. A
lighter lunchtime menu (good
value at £7.50 for two courses). Good and unusual home made puds. A
reasonably priced all Italian wine list and friendly service make this a
very good local restaurant.

■ **Pictured: Rochelle Porteous and Aurelio Spagnolo.**

LE P'TIT NORMAND
SW18

185 Merton Road, SW18 5EF
Tel: 0181-871 0233
Open: lunch Sun-Fri, dinner daily
Meals served: lunch 12-2, dinner 7-10.30 (Sun to 10)

Etienne Uzureau from Le Manoir has joined as manager here **£40**

Chef-patron Philippe Herrard hails from Normandy and his short, straightforward, printed menu reflects the culinary traditions of his birthplace. Dishes such as boudin noir aux pommes, moules normandes, côte de veau normande and magret de canard Vallée d'Auge appear as staples, alongside dishes such as prawns in Calvados, pork with honey and peppered entrecôte steak. Fish dishes depend on what the market has to offer and are listed on a daily blackboard, along with the likes of daily specials such as beef bourguignonne.

LE PALAIS DU JARDIN
WC2

136 Long Acre, WC2E 9AD
Tel: 0171-379 5353
Open: all day daily (closed 25 & 26 Dec)
Meals served: 12-12 (from 10 for light snacks,
    Sun to 10.50pm)

£50

Parisian-style brasserie seating around 250 and offering a traditional menu. It's open for breakfast from 10 through to lunchtime, when in fine weather the glass roof towards the rear of the restaurant is pulled back to provide an alfresco-style setting. The menu, typical brasserie fashion, is extensive, with a wide range of starters, from French onion soup to chilled baby scallops with gazpacho sauce and deep-fried mozzarella with onion rings and a tomato and basil sauce. Salads and grills feature strongly among main-course selections, along with a comprehensive choice of fish and seafood dishes, such as lobster and chicken in coriander sauce, whole cold lobster or seafood platter. Familiar favourites such as bangers'n'mash, coq au vin and beef bourguignonne also make an appearance, along with more sophisticated meat dishes like venison with braised red cabbage and a redcurrant cream. An all-day oyster and champagne bar, with large bar area, offers a popular alternative. Expansion during 1994 to both the restaurant and bar is a good indication of how chef Winston Matthews has been pulling in the crowds since the brasserie opened at the end of 1992.

THE PARK LANE HOTEL   W1

Piccadilly, W1Y 8BX
Tel: 0171-499 6321   *Fax:* 0171-499 1965   **£75**
Open: lunch & dinner Mon-Sat (closed Bank Holidays)
Meals served: lunch 12.30-2.30, dinner 7-10.30

Some of the original Art Deco features of this 320-bedroomed hotel have survived from the hotel's start in life, back in 1927. Stained glass decorates the splendid vaulted ceiling of the Palm Court lounge and the ballroom is strictly in keeping with the style. The best rooms (the suites) overlook Green Park; others look out on to an inner courtyard. There are two restaurants, Bracewells and the Brasserie on the Park which specialises in pre- and post-theatre suppers. Bracewells is traditional in outlook and offers a classically-based repertoire interpreted by chef John Tindall. Alternatively, you can get a light snack over a drink in Bracewells Bar, which like the Brasserie has more modern appeal. Good conference facilities for up to 500 include a dedicated business centre.

THE PEASANT   EC1

240 St John Street, EC1V 4PH
Tel: 0171-336 7726   **£45**
Open: lunch Sun-Fri, dinner Mon-Sat
   (closed Bank Holidays, 24 Dec-3 Jan)
Meals served: lunch 12.30-2.30, dinner 6.30-11

It's good to see Carla Tomasi's (ex-Friths, London) settled at The Peasant. Her simple, Mediterranean-style fare is as good as ever. The decor at this former Victorian pub is suitably spartan, with the original, mosaic floor, and plain wooden tables and chairs. This is a lively place during the day, more intimate at night owing to careful lighting. The short eclectic carte might begin with a soup, among a short list of starters featuring the likes of the Peasant antipasto or hot smoked salmon with spicy potatoes. Main courses offer a choice of three dishes, typified by squid in white wine, olive oil, parsley and capers. At least half the regular menu is suitable for vegetarians. A good range of specialist draught beers.

PELHAM HOTEL   SW7

5 Cromwell Place, SW7 2LA
Tel: 0171-589 8288   *Fax:* 0171-589 8444   **£50**
Open: all day daily
Meals served: 7am-10pm

Kit and Tim Kemp's lovely town house hotel has been decorated with much loving care. It's a blend of the classical and the individual, and gives an impression of an English country house right in the heart of London—swags, drapes, abundant floral arrangements and fine antiques all enhance the atmosphere. In Kemps' the cosy basement restaurant, modern cooking is offered, as perfectly in tune with the mood of the times as is the rest of the hotel.

PELICAN   WC2
45 St Martin's Lane, WC2
Tel: 0171-379 0309   *Fax:* 0171-379 0782   £45
Open: all day daily (closed 24-26 Dec)
Meals served: 12-12 (Sun to 11)
Useful all-day brasserie in the heart of theatre, cinema and gallery land. Light
snacks, full meals, coffees and drinks; pavement tables.

PETER'S   NW6

65 Fairfax Road, NW6 4EE
Tel: 0171-624 5804   £30
Open: lunch Mon-Fri & Sun, dinner Mon-Sat
   (closed 26 Dec, 1 Jan)
Meals served: lunch 12-3, dinner 6.30-11.30

The menus lean very much towards the classic and traditional at this
popular local restaurant decorated in 1920s French style, and with live
piano music nightly. Good-value fixed-price and à la carte menus offer
starters such as provençal fish soup, mushrooms à la bourguignonne
and snails in filo pastry. Main courses might include steak béarnaise,
breast of duck with Calvados and ginger or salmon steak served with
champagne sauce. Sweets fit the same mould, with typical examples
being lemon tart and profiteroles.

PHOENICIA   W8
11-13 Abingdon Road, W8 6AH
Tel: 0171-937 0120   £40
Open: all day daily (closed 24 & 25 Dec)
Meals served: 12-12
Lebanese restaurant offering a long list of hot and cold appetisers (mezze), char-
coal-grilled main courses and sticky sweets. Good-value lunchtime buffet.

PIED À TERRE   W1

34 Charlotte Street, W1P 1HJ
Tel: 0171-636 1178   £85
Open: lunch Mon-Fri, dinner Mon-Sat
   (closed Bank Holidays)
Meals served: lunch 12.15-1.30, dinner 7.15-9.30

Chef-patron Richard Neat's background is sterling—he's spent time
under some of the greatest, in Paris at Jamin with Joël Robuchon, in
Great Milton at Le Manoir with Raymond Blanc and in London at
Marco Pierre White's former Harveys. And it shows. This is a talented
chef whose imagination succeeds in some unusual combinations. The
fixed-price lunch menu (two courses) offers simpler dishes and good
value. Try lamb and broad bean soup—a purée of broad beans with
offal of lamb; deep-fried scallops and courgette with smoked salmon
sauce; fillet of John Dory with deep-fried oysters and leeks. Richard has
a liking for offal and is is used in some of his best dishes. The work of
Warhol, Lichtenstein and Richard Hamilton adorns the restaurant
walls, which was recently redecorated, resulting in more discreet lighting and new table settings with colourful rustic hand-painted plates.
Some top wines available on the interesting list. Front of house is in the
capable hands of partner, David Moore.

PJ's Bar & Grill SW3

52 Fulham Road, SW3
Tel: 0171-589 0025 **£45**
Open: lunch & dinner daily (closed 25 & 26 Dec)
Meals served: 12-12 (Sun to 11)

American-style bar and grill. Spicy Creole fishcakes, New Orleans seafood gumbo, smoked barbecue ribs, steaks, salads all served with some style by a young, enthusiastic team. With a busy bar and a few tables on the pavement in summer, this place is inevitably busy and it deserves its success. There are several more of Mr Stein's establishments in and around the capital.

Poissonnerie de l'Avenue SW3

82 Sloane Avenue, SW3 3DZ
Tel: 0171-589 2457   *Fax:* 0171-581 3360 **£65**
Open: lunch & dinner Mon-Sat (closed Bank Holidays,
    24 Dec-3 Jan, 4 days Easter)
Meals served: lunch 12-3, dinner 7-11.45

A classic French fish restaurant and oyster bar which has been around since the early Sixties, and has recently been altered to allow for more table space. It has its own wet fish shop supplying the kitchen with the very freshest of raw materials. The cooking is careful, simple and classic; the atmosphere relaxed and comfortable; and the carte a panoply of piscatorial pride. You name it, it's probably here: fresh anchovies flavoured with cayenne pepper; light spicy fish soup; raviolis stuffed with lobster and langoustine; seafood risotto; bouillabaisse and lobster thermidor; five different types of oyster; monkfish, sea bass, sole, skate... coming to a close with "Non-Fishy" alternatives like poussin with devil sauce, roast lamb and steak. As we went to press a new chef was due to join the team—watch this space! Peter Rosignoli's classic restaurant has seen sterling service in this neck of the woods and he continues to offer professional service to both old and new customers alike.

POMEGRANATES   SW1

94 Grosvenor Road, SW1V 3LE
Tel: 0171-828 6560   *Fax:* 0171-828 2037   **£40**
Open: lunch Mon-Fri, dinner Mon-Sat
   (closed Bank Holidays)
Meals served: lunch 12.30-2, dinner 7-11.15   ❖

Tour the world, gastronomically speaking, at Patrick Gwynn-Jones'
long-standing basement restaurant in Pimlico. Gravad lax, Jamaican
fish tea (a red mullet broth made with rum), gambas al ajillo Spanish-

style, Welsh salt duck, Turkish bureks with
tabouleh and Sudanese pepper sauce, West Indian
curried goat with plantain, Mexican-baked crab
with tequila, Mauritian chili prawns—the message
is loud and clear. And moving closer to home, the
likes of steak, kidney and wild mushroom pie or
braised oxtail and mash. Dessert addicts might
like to try the favourite honey and cognac ice
cream or specials like treacle tart. Bottomless coffee pot and chocolates to finish. Good-value table
d'hôte lunch and dinner menus supplement the
carte.

*Patrick's exuberant personality helps make this
restaurant more like a club, with the man
himself acting as both host and wine butler*

LE PONT DE LA TOUR   SE1

Butlers Wharf Building, 36D Shad Thames,
Butlers Wharf, SE1 2YE
Tel: 0171-403 8403   **£70**
Open: lunch Sun-Fri, dinner daily (closed 3 days Xmas)   ✿
Meals served: lunch 12-3, dinner 6-12 (Sun to 11),
   (light meals Bar & Grill: 12-12 daily, Sun to 11)   ❖

Part of The Gastrodrome, Conran's epicentre of epicurean delight, with
its bar and grill, restaurant, shellfish bar, salon privé, bakery, wine merchant and foodstore. What's more, in true Conran designer style, the
setting is cool, stylish and elegant, on the south bank of the Thames
right by Tower Bridge, with panoramic views across the city and
alfresco riverside terrace. A fixed-price lunch and evening carte offer a
concise selection of dishes in the fashionable European mould—
Ireland, Britain, France and Italy are all featured. Typical dishes from
chef David Burke include crepe Parmentier, lobster salad, tarte tatin,
Baltic herrings à la crème, rare-grilled tuna with mint, chili and lime,
smoked haddock risotto with coriander and parmesan, fillet of red mullet niçoise, and roast leg of new season lamb with marjoram.
Traditional desserts. Well thought out wine list with some reasonable
prices. It's difficult to do justice to this imaginative and beautifully
designed experience in the space available!

Go visit, you won't be disappointed

PORTERS ENGLISH RESTAURANT   WC2

17 Henrietta Street, WC2E 8QH
Tel: 0171-836 6466   *Fax:* 0171-379 4296   **£40**
Open: all day daily (closed 25 Dec)
Meals served: 12 noon to 11.30, Sun to 10.30

You have to admit that Richard, Earl of Bradford has continued over the years to work very hard with his team to improve and further the cause of English food. Famous for its pies, sausages and traditional British fare, Porters is undoubtedly popular with transatlantic visitors and Londoners alike. An extensive carte offers a wide range of choices: steak and mushroom pie, Somerset honeyed pork pie, lamb and apricot pie, bangers'n'mash with a choice of sausages (venison, lamb and mint), beef with herb dumplings, hot pots and casseroles, salmon fish cakes, fish'n'chips, plus salads. Desserts are no less plentiful, ranging from cold options like orange tart or sherry trifle, to hot puddings such as spotted dick or bread-and-butter pudding. The all-inclusive fixed-price menu (£15.95) offers any pie or winter warmer, plus pudding, coffee and half bottle of wine—excellent value.

LA POULE AU POT   SW1

231 Ebury Street, SW1W 8UT
Tel: 0171-730 7763   **£55**
Open: lunch & dinner daily (closed 24-26 Dec)
Meals served: lunch 12.30-2.30, dinner 7-11.15
    (Sun to 10.30)

Young French staff and totally rustic decor create a French country feel which is totally in keeping with what arrives on the plate at this friendly, cosy little restaurant. Khaki walls, wicker baskets and dried flowers, and weeping fig-filled terracotta pots form the backdrop for old favourites such as French onion soup, Gruyère cheese tart, snails, pot-roast chicken, steak béarnaise and cod à la boulangère. The range extends to smoked salmon stuffed with crab, fish stew with coriander, rabbit with mustard sauce and fillet of veal à l'orange. Classic desserts for the finale.

QUAGLINO'S   SW1

16 Bury Street, St James's, SW1Y 6AL
Tel: 0171-930 6767   **£55**
Open: lunch & dinner daily
Meals served: lunch 12-3, dinner 5.30-12 (Fri & Sat to 1.45,
    Sun to 11), (light meals bar: 11.30am-midnight, Sun 12-11)

A noisy, bustling, fashionable restaurant which was the talk of the town
when it opened in 1993. Established on the original 1920s site of yesteryear's Quaglino, in a vast, stylish theatre of a room, the restaurant has

settled down after all the hype and publicity, and is
proving to be yet another winner from the Conran stable. Design features are strong, as one might expect
from Sir Terence, with stairs leading down to an informal antipasto bar area with all-day snacks, and the
main dining area complete with mirrored altar to the
crustacean lifeform, and a computerised skylight
which runs the whole length of the room, providing a
range of imitation "natural" skies. The food is about as
fashionable as it can be: pigeon salad with pancetta
and beans; calf's tongue vinaigrette; caviar and oysters;
grilled mackerel with soy and lime; skate with sauce
gribiche; spiced lamb with roast onions; and lemon
sole with chips. Finish with pavlova with berries, red
plum parfait or lime meringue pie. Live bands in the large bar area
draw in the youngsters on Friday and Saturday nights. Reasonably
priced wine list.

QUALITY CHOP HOUSE   EC1

94 Farringdon Road, EC1R 3EA
Tel: 0171-837 5093   **£45**
Open: lunch Sun-Fri, dinner daily
    (closed lunch Bank Holidays, 25 Dec-2 Jan)
Meals served: lunch 12-3, dinner 6.30-11.30 (Sun from 7)

The menu at this unfussy, good-value chop
house combines traditional English café
favourites and more exotic versions of the
same, alongside classic French dishes. Reopened in 1989 by Charles Fontaine, it now
offers dishes like corned beef hash, Toulouse
sausages with mash and onion gravy, salmon
fishcakes with sorrel, confit of duck, lamb
chops, grilled steaks, calf's liver and bacon.
Starters range from clam chowder and fish
soup with rouille to salads, snails and scrambled eggs with smoked salmon. The chips
are among the best in the capital. Much of
the atmosphere of the original house has
been preserved in the decor, with embossed
wallpaper and high-back mahogany booths.

Charles Fontaine

QUINCY'S NW2

675 Finchley Road, NW2 2JP *Consistent, enduring and charming*
Tel: 0171-794 8499 **£50**
Open: dinner Tue-Sat (closed Xmas)
Meals served: lunch , dinner 7-11

A good, local restaurant, renowned for its friendly service and reasonable prices. The menu of mixed English, French and Mediterranean influences changes monthly. Starters range from sweet peppers with salt cod brandade and parsley fumet to warm salad of game sausage or chicken liver crostini with sage and chutney. Main courses feature a daily fish dish according to what the market has to offer, plus dishes such as tarte tatin of leeks with a mushroom fricassée, roast guinea fowl with lime couscous, coriander and balsamic vinegar, or rack of lamb with rosemary and creamed onions. Save room for a traditional bread-and-butter pudding or more modern dishes such as poached figs with elderberries served with fromage frais sorbet. Vegetarian options always included.

RANSOME'S DOCK SW11

35-37 Parkgate Road, SW11 4NP *Well worth crossing the river for*
Tel: 0171-223 1611   Fax: 0171-924 2614
Open: lunch daily, dinner Mon-Sat (closed 25-27 Dec, **£50**
   lunch Bank Holidays)
Meals served: lunch 12-3.30, dinner 6-11 (Sat to 12)

Ex-L'Escargot chef, Martin Lam, cooks with confidence at this colourful restaurant which occupies part of the modern Battersea dockside development midway between Albert and Battersea Bridges. The short, modern, brasserie-style menu has already proved popular. Starters might be smoked haddock and parsley soup, tagliolini with ceps and crème fraîche or steamed mussels with curry spices and cream. Main courses are eclectic too: Scottish sirloin steak with red wine, shallots and chips; veal and Parmesan meatballs with artichoke and tomato sauce and fettucine. Lovely sweets which include Devonshire Rocombe Farm organic ice cream. Additional daily specials and good-value, two-course set lunch.

Biography

Martin Lam Martin Lam's career in catering began as a fourteen-year-old washing up in a local restaurant in Bristol! He loved food and had a burning desire to cook well - self-taught, but inspired by Elizabeth David, Martin gained practical experience in Bath and Cheltenham, before moving to London. Here he worked in a number of successful establishments (including the English House, Chelsea; Le Caprice and L'Escargot) before setting up home at Ransome's Dock.

RED FORT   W1

77 Dean Street, W1V 5HA
Tel: 0171-437 2115   Fax: 0171-434 0721   **£60**
Open: lunch & dinner daily
Meals served: lunch 12-2.45, dinner 6-11.30

The Red Fort (named after the sandstone fort built by Moghul
Emperor Shah Jahan) offers some fine Indian cuisine. Why not try
Jhinga Sounsia to start—jumbo prawn simmered in milk with fennel
and saffron, coated with rice batter and fried, followed perhaps by
Akbari Raan (for two people)—leg of lamb delicately marinated in the
chef's own secret recipe and then slow baked. There's a choice of
several traditional Indian desserts and a reasonably-priced wine list.

THE REGENT LONDON   NW1

222 Marylebone Road, NW1 6JQ
Tel: 0171-631 8000   *Fax:* 0171-631 8080   **£75**
Open: lunch & dinner daily
Meals served: lunch 12-3 (Sun from 12.30), dinner 7-11

A stunning refurbishment has transformed this jaded Victorian railway
establishment into one of the capital's most elegant and luxurious
hotels, designed around an impressive atrium. Rising above the central
winter gardens are some 300 spacious bedrooms. You can swim in the
indoor pool, exercise in the gym, slim in the sauna or over-indulge in
the dining room, where Italian dishes predominate.

LOS REMOS   W2

38A Southwick Street, W2 1JQ
Tel: 0171-723 5056   **£45**
Open: lunch & dinner Mon-Sat
Meals served: lunch 12-3, dinner 7-12

Traditional Spanish restaurant and bar. Eat a las tapas—the choice is
vast, everything from tortilla to fried whitebait and gambas al ajillo,
grilled meats and fish. Alternatively sit down to a relaxed, informal
meal from the à la carte menu. There's a wide choice of fish, poultry
and meat dishes, many of which are charcoal-grilled, griddled or deep-
fried, in keeping with preferred Spanish methods. Hake fried in butter
or cooked in white wine, lemon and brandy sauce; chicken in garlic;
Scotch salmon poached or griddled; veal escalope Cordon Bleu-style;
or paella (for a minimum of two persons) are the type of thing. Plenty
of choice between simply prepared, unfussy dishes and more sophisticated ones.

THE RITZ   W1

150 Piccadilly, W1V 9DG
Tel: 0171-493 8181   *Fax:* 0171-493 2687   **£105**
Open: lunch & dinner daily   ✿
Meals served: lunch 12.30-2.30, dinner 6.30-11   ❖

After almost a century The Ritz is still one of the best and most fashionable hotels in town. Everything is on a grand scale but the staff create a
comfortable atmosphere in which to relax amongst the sumptuous
decor. Enjoy lunch on the terrace overlooking Green Park, tea in the
legendary Palm Court or a delightful dinner in the beautiful restaurant.
The recent change of ownership to the Hong Kong-based Mandarin
group might bring some interesting developments.

RIVA   SW13

169 Church Road, SW13 9HR
Tel: 0181-748 0434   *Good local restaurant*   **£50**
Open: lunch Sun-Fri, dinner daily   *well worth the drive*
   (closed Bank Holidays, 2 wks Aug)   ✿
Meals served: lunch 12-2.30, dinner 7-11

Minimalist modern decor and new wave Italian cooking go hand-in-
hand at this smart, local restaurant which has already built up a loyal
following since its 1990 opening. Starters include the likes of smoked
goose breast served on chicory with oranges, nuts and scallion oil, or
grilled seasonal vegetables. Pastas and risotto follow, along with pumpkin gnocchi with spinach and sbrinz cheese. Main courses might feature breaded veal cutlet, braised pig's trotters and cotechino sausage,
or marinated sea bream baked in a bag with herbs, lemon and shellfish. A thoroughly modern menu of honest, robust cooking from start
to finish. Inventive desserts like sweet milk gnocchi with honey butter
sauce, maize and almond crumble soaked in vin santo with mascarpone—just a nod here and there to the classics, with the likes of
zabaglione and tiramisu.

RIVER CAFÉ   W6

Thames Wharf Studios, Rainville Road, W6 9HA
Tel: 0171-381 8824   *Fax:* 0171-381 6217   **£75**
Open: lunch daily, dinner Mon-Sat   ✿
   (closed Bank Holidays, 10 days Xmas, 4 days Easter)
Meals served: lunch 12.30-2.30, dinner 7.30-10

This is a trendy Italian restaurant close to, but not actually overlooking,
the river, specialising in good, honest provincial cooking, served up in
a canteen-like setting, with no tablecloths and simple, unfussy table-
ware. It's hugely popullar. Char-grilled meats and fish, Italian breads
and bean soups are staple elements. Dishes show invention and a genuine love of ingredients. The menu is short, offering dishes which
abound in Mediterranean flavours—fresh anchovies marinated with
sun-dried chili, lemon and parsley; sea bass served with a salad of sun-
dried plum and vine tomatoes, pine nuts and basil, with salsa verde.
Local restrictions insist that the premises are cleared by 11pm. The
River Café has acted as a model for many London openings over the
last three years. Literally as we went to press, a major refurbishment of
the restaurant was taking place, increasing capacity.

RSJ   SE1

13a Coin Street, SE1 8YQ
Tel: 0171-928 4554   **£35**
Open: lunch Mon-Fri, dinner Mon-Sat
    (closed Bank Holidays)
Meals served: lunch 12-2, dinner 6-11

Choose between the upstairs restaurant and downstairs brasserie, the menus of which have now been combined with prices that reflect this middle ground. RSJ stands half way along Stamford Street, within walking distance of the South Bank Centre. It's a friendly, relaxing place, busy and lively at lunchtime, and rather more sedate and formal in the evening. The cooking is in the modern British style with influences from across the Channel. Starters such as risotto of tomato, rocket and parmesan; roast provençal vegetables on foccacia; and Mediterranean fish soup; followed by roast rump of lamb with basil mash potato, roast chicken with a fricassée of pleurottes and Camargue rice, and pan-fried salmon with aubergine caviar, spinach and artichoke. Imaginative desserts—white wine tart with a grape confit; hazelnut and chocolate layered pie. The wine list is weighted towards Loire valley wines, a diverse choice with some keen pricing; well worth a try.

RULES   WC2

35 Maiden Lane, WC2E 7LB
Tel: 0171-836 5314   *Fax:* 0171-497 10181   **£55**
Open: all day daily (closed 5 days Xmas)
Meals served: 12-11.45

Rules is the oldest restaurant in London. Established in 1798, it has spanned the reigns of nine monarchs and played host to many literary and artistic figures over the years, from Charles Dickens and H G Wells to Charles Laughton, Laurence Olivier, and many more. During that time it has been owned by only three families, and it still today serves a traditional English cuisine based on classic game, oysters, pies and puddings. Game is supplied from the restaurant's own estate in the Pennines and quality is therefore assured. The menu is vast, the mainstays being prime Aberdeen Angus beef, and furred and feathered game: light casserole of rabbit, wild Highland red deer, wild woodland roe deer and fallow, grouse, pigeon, quail and guinea fowl. There are a couple of vegetarian options. Despite the long traditions associated with the place, Rules has succumbed to state-of-the-art ordering, with dishes keyed into pocket computers. There are three private dining rooms for hire, named after Dickens, Greene and Edward VII.

St James' Court Hotel   SW1

41 Buckingham Gate, SW1E 6AF
Tel: 0171-834 6655   *Fax:* 0171-630 7587
Open: lunch Mon-Fri, dinner Mon-Sat
   (closed Bank Holidays, 2 wks Aug)
Meals served: lunch 12.30-2.30, dinner 7.30-11

I wonder how long the Taj group can resist repeating their unbelievably successful Bombay Brasserie here?   **£70**

Grand Edwardian hotel close to Buckingham Palace. An ornamental courtyard with fountain forms the centre of this palatial 391-bedroomed hotel which includes a self-contained business centre, Olympian health club and three restaurants. L'Oustau de Baumanière-trained staff and the restaurant's chef, Jean-André Charial, determine the shape of things in the main dining room, the Auberge de Provence, where, under the direction of Jean-André, chef Bernard Brique recreates the style of Provence's most famous restaurant with dishes such as soupe au pistou, red mullet au basilic and sirloin steak served with a rich Ventoux red wine sauce. Alternatively, you can go Chinese, with Szechuan-inspired dishes in the Inn of Happiness, or opt for a little sunshine in the Café Mediterranée with its brasserie-style dishes.

Sambuca   SW3

6 Symons Street, SW3
Tel: 0171-730 6571   **£50**
Open: lunch & dinner Mon-Sat (closed Bank Holidays)
Meals served: lunch 12.30-2.30, dinner 7-11.30

Bustling Italian restaurant opposite the rear door of Peter Jones just off Sloane Square. The menu is a long list of established favourites, with new innovations along the way. Zuppa pavese, pasta marinara, grilled baby chicken, veal piccata with lemon juice, mixed fried seafood, Italian-style goulash and fillet steak tartare set the style.

San Frediano   SW3

62 Fulham Road, SW3 6HH
Tel: 0171-584 8375   *Fax:* 0171-589 8860   **£55**
Open: lunch & dinner Mon-Sat, Mothering Sunday
   (closed some Bank Holidays)
Meals served: lunch 12-2.45, dinner 7-11.30

The cooking at this longstanding Italian restaurant is good, honest, and reasonably priced, which may well account for much of the good-natured humour within. It is a bustling, lively place where old-fashioned Italian charm flourishes unchecked. Veal and pasta are the mainstay of the menu, in keeping with tradition.

SAN LORENZO   SW3

22 Beauchamp Place, SW3 1NL
Tel: 0171-584 1074   *Fax:* 0171-584 1142   **£75**
Open: lunch & dinner Mon-Sat
   (closed Bank Holidays, 1 wk Xmas, 4 days Easter)
Meals served: lunch 12.30-3, dinner 7.30-11.30

Every paparazzo in London knows San Lorenzo's. The question is who's eating there and when? This has been the place for the star-studded set, royalty even, for many a year. Plenty of attention from the waiters and a menu with something for everyone: grilled fish and meat, pasta and plenty of people to watch.

Lorenzo and Mara Berni still manage to make all the customers feel very welcome in their own special Italian way

SAN MARTINO   SW3

103-105 Walton Street, SW3 2HP
Tel: 0171-589 3833   **£60**
Open: lunch & dinner daily (closed 25 & 26 Dec, Easter Mon)
Meals served: lunch 12-3, dinner 6.30-11.30

The Martinucci family, headed by Costanzo in the kitchen with son Tommaso, have earned an enviable reputation for themselves at this popular Italian restaurant, said by many to be both the busiest and friendliest Italian restaurant in London. Costanzo prides himself on offering the best mixed salads in the world. He and his wife grow their own herbs, vegetables (possibly one of the largest producers of courgette flowers in the country, he says) and seven different salads. Familiar favourites here include fish soup and spaghetti cooked with seafood in a paper bag. Seasonal game and daily chef's specials supplement the ever-changing carte of mostly Tuscan-inspired dishes.

SANDRINI   SW3

260 Brompton Road, SW3 2AS
Tel: 0171-584 1724   **£55**
Open: lunch & dinner daily
Meals served: lunch 12-3, dinner 7-11.30

Smart, modern Italian restaurant with extensive carte, which incorporates the traditional with more contemporary influences. Hot spicy curried prawns, wind-dried venison with ricotta, and grilled red lettuce with balsamic vinegar represent modern times among the long list of starters. Main courses feature plenty of veal, chicken and seafood, plus grills. Sirloin topped with Barolo wine sauce, plain-grilled lamb cutlets and Dover sole, or liver and onion Venetian-style show the range. The one-course lunch with glass of wine and coffee for £10 is good for those in a rush.

Outside tables are a bonus in summer

SANTINI   SW1

29 Ebury Street, SW1W 0NZ
Tel: 0171-730 4094   *Fax:* 0171-730 0544   **£85**
Open: lunch Mon-Fri, dinner daily
   (closed 25 & 26 Dec)
Meals served: lunch 12.30-2.30, dinner 7-11.30 (Sun to 10.30)

Like its sister establishment L'Incontro, Santini specialises in Venetian cooking in simple, honest fashion, but the setting is considerably more up-market than at other Italian restaurants in the city. Traditional favourites, like pasta with artichoke sauce, grilled swordfish with tomato sauce and lobster Santini, share the menu with newer creations, such as squid in white wine with polenta or escalope of veal with a fresh orange sauce. The two-course set business lunch has proved very popular.

SAS PORTMAN HOTEL   W1

22 Portman Square, W1H 9FL
Tel: 0171-486 5844   *Fax:* 0171-935 0537   **£40**
Open: lunch & dinner daily
Meals served: lunch 12-3.30
   (Sun from 12.30), dinner 7-11 (Sun to 10.30)

A short walk from Oxford Street and Marble Arch, this 272-bedroomed hotel has recently undergone a multi-million-pound refurbishment programme. A new lobby bar and lounge and improved conference and banqueting facilities are some of the benefits. Rooms have every modern convenience, including satellite TV and teletext, and travellers should be well impressed by the four satellite check-in desks which are unique to SAS International Hotels. Many of the rooms have been remodelled to new styles, which include Oriental, Scandinavian and British designs. A variety of catering facilities include the informal, all-day Portman Corner restaurant.

LES SAVEURS   W1

37a Curzon Street, W1Y 8EY
Tel: 0171-491 8919   *Fax:* 0171-491 3658   **£75**
Open: lunch & dinner Mon-Fri   ✿
   (closed 2 wks Xmas/New Year, 2 wks Aug)
Meals served: lunch 12-2.30, dinner 7-10.30   ❖

Chef Joël Antunès's chic French restaurant
next to the Curzon Cinema is well worth a
visit. French classicism and innovation complement one another in boldy conceived,
beautifully presented dishes which are full of
flavour. Try half-cooked salmon with horseradish cream, a nage of mace- and caviar-
flavoured scallops, slivers of duck with
chicory and fig sauce, or the more familiar
loin of roast lamb provençale. Joël's background includes a spell at the Bangkok
Oriental which may account for his more
exotic style, but his approach is ultimately
classical and elaborate. Desserts get equal
attention and can be truly fabulous; try the
hot chocolate madeleines with almond cream
or chocolate tart with hazelnut ice cream.
The menu format is table d'hôte (two or
three courses as you please), supplemented
by set menu options. Formal setting; very
smart, very chic, with the young professional
team under the management of Emmanuel
Menjuzan completing a first- class dining
experience.

■ Joël Antunès

*Good advice available from sommelier Yves Sauboua on the
top-end-of-the-market wine list*

THE SAVOY   WC2

Strand, WC2R 0EU
Tel: 0171-836 4343   *Fax:* 0171-240 6040   **£70**
Open: lunch & dinner daily   ✿
Meals served: lunch 12.30-2.30,
   dinner 6-11.15   ❖

They even manufacture their own mattresses at the Savoy, and in a
total of 200 rooms, the best being the riverside suites, no two are the
same. This is a hotel where quality and tradition reign supreme, under
the capable management of Herbert Striessnig. Built on the site of and
named after the medieval Palace of Savoy, the hotel is situated on a
bend in the River Thames which allows uninterrupted views in both
directions from the grand River Restaurant, from Big Ben to St Paul's
and the Tower of London. The view is spectacular, the food excellent.
With a classic French repertoire, Anton Edelmann follows in the footsteps of Escoffier, who ruled here back in the early days. Alternatively,
there's the much-loved Grill Room under David Sharland's direction,

catering for the nostalgic palate with dishes such as beef Wellington and Norfolk goose. Above the Grill, next to the popular American Bar, is the Upstairs champagne bar where seafood is the speciality. The Savoy has hosted Strauss conducting, Caruso in song and Pavlova in cabaret. The newly restored Savoy Theatre and Fitness Gallery (with rooftop pool, the first in a London hotel) provide further cause for celebration at this most eminent of hotels.

Biography

Anton Edelmann (born in Bugesheim, Germany) had a fairly traditional route to the top of his profession; after an apprenticeship at the Ulm Bundesbahn Hotel near his home town, he came to London and worked as a com-

Anton

Edelmann

mis saucier at The Savoy. He stayed for a year before returning to Europe for work and military service, then returning to London working firstly at The Dorchester, next Grosvenor House then and finally he realised his ambition: he now leads one of the largest kitchens in one of the world's most fabled hotels: The Savoy.

SCALINI   SW3

1-3 Walton Street, SW3 2JD
Tel: 0171-225 2301   **£60**
Open: lunch & dinner daily
   (closed Bank Holidays)
Meals served: lunch 12.30-3, dinner 7-11.30

The staff in this popular Italian restaurant are friendly, helpful and cheerful, a big plus all round. The extensive menu is traditionally-based, with an emphasis on strong flavours. Plenty of seafood and pasta choices, including pennette with tomato, sausage and pesto sauce or pappardelle with chef's special artichoke sauce. There's also an interesting choice of fish dishes: sea bass with lemon, fennel and pernod sauce; scampi sautéed with curry sauce and river trout cooked in butter, pine nuts and fresh grapes. A long list of meat dishes includes many traditional favourites: carpaccio; calf's liver in butter with sage; roast duck with orange sauce; sirloin cooked with onion mushrooms and red wine. The conservatory at the rear comes into its own in summer.

SCOTT'S RESTAURANT   W1
20 Mount Street, W1Y 6HE
Tel: 0171-629 5248   *Fax:* 0171-491 2477   **£65**
Open: lunch Mon-Fri, dinner Mon-Sat
   (closed Bank Holidays, Xmas-New Year)
Meals served: lunch 12.30-2.45, dinner 6-10.45
Ownership has changed to the Groupe Chez Gerard.

SHAW'S   SW7

119 Old Brompton Road, SW7 3RN
Tel: 0171-373 7774   **£60**
Open: lunch & dinner Mon-Sat
   (closed 2 wks Xmas, 2 wks Aug)   🏵
Meals served: lunch 12-2, dinner 7-10

Frances Atkins cooks in the modern mode, with "Light Food" options
highlighted on the menus at this attractive restaurant on the site of the
former Chanterelle. Frances is one of six behind this new venture: husband Bill runs front-of-house; a third was responsible for decor, which
is elegantly contemporary, with nicely laid tables. A short lunchtime
carte gives way to a fixed-price menu in the evening which offers ample
choice. Ravioli of langoustine with carrot and coriander, Shaw's daily
soup or baby spinach leaves with hot vegetable pasta; followed by wild
mushroom and asparagus risotto, char-grilled venison with roasted
onions and purée of swede served with port-scented jus, and daily fresh
fish dishes. Tempting desserts, coffee and petits fours to finish.

*You will recognise Frances Atkins' name from previous entries in
the Guide over the years.*

SHEEKEY'S RESTAURANT   WC2

28-32 St Martins Court, Leicester Square, WC2N 4AL
Tel: 0171-240 2565   *Fax:* 0171-379 1417   **£70**
Open: all day Mon-Sat
Meals served: 12-11.15 (Sat 6-11.15)

Sheekey's has been around since 1896, a fact which may come as no
surprise after perusing the display of celebrity showbiz photos on the
walls—everyone under the sun has been through these doors, it
seems! This is a classic old-style fish restaurant, now under new management.

SHEPHERD'S   SW1

Marsham Court, Marsham Street, SW1P 4LA
Tel: 0171-834 9552   Fax: 0171-233 6047   **£45**
Open: lunch & dinner Mon-Fri (closed Bank Holidays)
Meals served: lunch 12.30-2.45, dinner 6.30-11.30 (bar 5.30-8)   🏵

Good old British favourites are the mainstay of this Westminster
restaurant, the latest joint venture between Richard Shepherd and
Michael Caine which is proving popular with local parliamentarians.
The menu here takes on a much simpler aspect than that of the flagship, Langan's Brasserie. The Mediterranean influence has all but
gone, while the British element comes to the fore: haddock and mussel
stew, Galway Bay oysters, gamekeeper's pie, Cumberland sausage and
mash, steak and kidney pie, and salmon and prawn fishcakes show the
range. Cold dishes are available in the bar area for those in a hurry.
Having run this restaurant in a previous incarnation, I was not at all
confident about its prospects. I am delighted to say, however, that I was
wrong and Richard's formula of reasonable prices for food and wine
and the flair of the dedicated team has resulted in considerable success.

SHERATON PARK TOWER   SW1

101 Knightsbridge, SW1X 7RN
Tel: 0171-235 8050   *Fax:* 0171-235 8231   **£45**
Open: lunch & dinner daily
Meals served: lunch 12-3 (Sun to 4), dinner 6.30-11

Great views over the city can be enjoyed from the upper floors of this
circular high-rise hotel with 300 bedrooms, two minutes away from
Harrods. The new-look Restaurant 101 opened its door again last summer with a new menu to match. The focus is now on international and
contemporary dishes. Try pan-fried goose liver on potato bread, Middle
Eastern mezze with pitta or chicken satay Thai-style to start. Main
course might feature spiced cod with tomato salsa, seared halibut with
orange zest or cheese hash brown with pink grapefruit and endive
salad among vegetarian choices. Traditional elements continue to feature, however, in dishes such as rack of lamb and best Aberdeen fillet
served with chips and a sauce of your choice. Quick Bites like seafood
spaghetti, eggs Benedict and crab cakes with sweetcorn relish are also
available.

SIGNOR SASSI   SW1

14 Knightsbridge Green, SW1X 7QL
Tel: 0171-584 2277   **£60**
Open: lunch & dinner Mon-Sat (closed Bank Holidays)
Meals served: lunch 12-2.30, dinner 7-11.30

There's a straightforward menu of classic dishes at this fashionable,
little Italian restaurant close to Harrods. Lobster features regularly in
pasta dishes; sea bass and lamb are specialities, along with other
dishes like ham-stuffed veal escalope and calf's liver with butter and
sage.

SIMPLY NICO   SW1

48A Rochester Row, SW1P 1JU   *A little gem, constantly busy*
Tel: 0171-630 8061   *and deservedly so*   **£60**
Open: lunch Mon-Fri, dinner Mon-Sat   ⊛
    (closed Bank Holidays, 11 days Xmas, 4 days Easter)
Meals served: lunch 12-2, dinner 7-11

Just off Victoria Street, in a somewhat neglected area, long starved of
decent restaurants, Simply Nico is a haven of gastronomic pleasure.
The fixed-price Nico-inspired lunch and dinner menus prepared by
Andrew Barber show a straightforward, unfussy approach which is altogether successful on the plate. This is modern cooking at its best, with
its roots firmly embedded in classicism. Start with a kir, the house
aperitif. Typical dishes then run from warm foie gras on toasted brioche
with caramelised orange or risotto flavoured with cep among starters to
maize-fed baby chicken wrapped in bacon, escalope of salmon with
tomato hollandaise, charcoal-grilled rib of beef with red wine sauce and
oxtail in red wine. Lemon tart, Armagnac parfait with chestnuts and
chocolate marquise featured among desserts on a recent menu.

SIMPSON'S-IN-THE-STRAND   WC2

100 Strand, WC2R 0EW
Tel: 0171-836 9112   *Fax:* 0171-836 1381   **£60**
Open: lunch & dinner daily (closed Bank Holidays)
Meals served: lunch 12-2.30, dinner 6-11

Established in 1828, this is one of London's best known restaurants, and the concept begun by John Simpson all those years ago has hardly changed. Trolley-carved roast joints, particularly beef, are the order of the day. The same farm in Scotland has supplied the beef for 70 years. Eighty per cent of customers order it and Simpson's gets through an average of 25 sirloins a day! Other stalwarts on the staunchly conservative menu include roast saddle of lamb, roast Aylesbury duck, and steak, kidney and mushroom pie. Starters range from potted shrimps and trout to native oysters, Dublin Bay prawns, hotch potch and lobster soup. Daily weekday lunch-time specials offer traditional winter warmers such as Lancashire hot pot or braised oxtail. Fish dishes include poached fillet of brill with saffron sauce, Dover sole and salmon. Good-value lunch and pre-theatre set menu, traditional puds. Fabulous traditional breakfast menu, served from 7am-noon, with everything you can imagine—from sausages to steak, lamb's kidneys, black pudding, York ham, Welsh rarebit, kedgeree, haddock, kippers and prunes.

SNOWS ON THE GREEN   W6

166 Shepherds Bush Road, W6 7PB
Tel: 0171-603 2142   **£50**
Open: lunch Mon-Fri, dinner Mon-Sat
   (closed Bank Holidays, 1 wk Xmas)   ✿
Meals served: lunch 12-3, dinner 7-11

The modern Mediterranean menu of Sebastian Snow, pictured, is matched by a charming provençal-inspired setting, with bunches of lavender on the tables and huge landscape pictures of more lavender and sunflowers. Unusual combinations are the hallmark of this popular menu: char-grilled focaccia with red onions, rosemary and ham; baked capiscums with brandade and pine kernels, rump of beef with aubergine and anchovy caviar ravioli; cod in a potato crust with lentils, bacon and glazed onions; and lasagne of wild salmon and sorrel are among the choices. Desserts are rather more classical, with lemon tart and crème brûlée offered as alternative to Roquefort cheese with figs or cherry clafoutis. Some reasonably priced wines on the list.

Good local restaurant, reasonable prices ensure that it's full most of the time

SOHO SOHO   W1

11-13 Frith Street, W1
Tel: 0171-494 3491   *Fax:* 0171-437 3091   **£45**
Open: lunch & dinner Mon-Fri (closed Bank Holidays)
Meals served: lunch 12-3, dinner 6-12,
    (light meals Ground Floor: Rotis 12 noon-1am
    Mon-Sat, Wine Bar: 11-11 Mon-Sat)

Here you can pop into the lively, ground-floor café-bar which spills out
on to the pavement in front, for a drink or light snack from a
Mediterranean menu of soups, salads and grills. Alternatively, there's
the more imposing first-floor dining room where chef Laurent Lebeau
continues the Mediterranean theme with some emphasis on provençal
dishes. The carte is supplemented by daily specials. Typical dishes
include duck leg with Puy lentils, sausages and red wine; wild boar in
red wine with noodles and chestnuts; grilled salmon with mustard-
flavoured mashed potato and a tomato vinaigrette; kebab of
Mediterranean prawns with lemon rice and chili sauce; spicy lamb
casserole with lemon zest and olives; and the popular steak frites. Good
wine list with many reasonably priced wines.

Still packing them in and continuing to produce the goods!

SONNY'S   SW13

94 Church Road, SW13 0DQ
Tel: 0181-748 0393   **£40**
Open: lunch daily, dinner Mon-Sat (closed Bank Holidays)
Meals served: lunch 12.30-2.30, dinner 7.30-11

The highly rated Redmond Hayward is now at the stove of Sonny's and
while he has added his own stamp, the menu retains the modern
stance (short and concise) that keeps its loyal local following happy.
Pan-European and Oriental influences are strong, with dishes such as
polenta with buffalo mozzarella and roast peppers, pumpkin ravioli with
parmesan cream sauce, blackened cod with guacamole and tomato
salsa, and char-grilled pork fillet with piperade typical of the range. A
set menu offers limited choice but excellent value. The restaurant is
located on two levels at the rear of the premises, with a café operating
at the front. Roast beef and Yorkshire pudding feature on the Sunday
set menu, and a short carte offers further alternatives. Reasonably
priced wines and a friendly atmosphere make Sonny's a favourite local
restaurant.

Biography

After Ealing College, Redmond gained his experi-
ence in a number of establishments including the
Redmond *Rising Sun, St Mawes; Anna's Place,*
Islington; and Calcot Manor, near
Hayward *Tetbury. He also ran his own restau-*
rant in the Cotswolds before returning
to London. Gutsy and polished is an apt summary of
Redmond's cooking.

THE SQUARE   SW1

32 King Street, St James's, SW1Y 6RJ
Tel: 0171-839 8787
Open: lunch Sun-Fri, dinner daily
   (closed most Bank Holidays)
Meals served: lunch 12-2, dinner 6-11.45

Chic, well presented and captures the mood of the moment. Not cheap but worth paying for **£70** ✿

Don't be deterred by the shop-like façade of this excellent restaurant just off St James's Square. Step inside and you'll find a modern restaurant, redecorated in 1994, with cream-coloured walls and colourful upholstery in minimalist style. Philip Howard's cooking, in the modern British mould, is entirely compatible with the setting and is not likely to disappoint. Dishes on the refreshingly straightforward carte are light and uncomplicated, but combinations show true artistic flair. Start perhaps with red mullet soup and tapenade served with mini oregano pizzas or roast quail with a wild mushroom tart, before main-course selections such as turbot with pea risotto and parmesan or rump of lamb with aubergines and olive oil.

THE STAFFORD   SW1

16 St James's Place, SW1A 1NJ
Tel: 0171-493 0111   *Fax:* 0171-493 7121   **£60**
Open: lunch Sun-Fri, dinner daily
Meals served: lunch 12.30-2.30, dinner 6-11

There is a hushed, sedate atmosphere in this discreet, 74-bedroomed hotel in the heart of London's clubland. Long-serving staff attend to long-loyal clientele in this former gentleman's club. Bedrooms are of a high standard and include a number of suites, the best of which perhaps is the Terrace Garden suite, which as the name implies has its own terrace (with fountain). There are also 12 rooms and suites overlooking a pretty courtyard in the adjoining Carriage House, which was built as stables for the nobility's thoroughbreds in the 1700s. The kitchen under head chef Armando Rodriguez focuses on the traditions of French and English cuisine. Daily roasts and flambéed dishes are a speciality. Charles, the head barman in the colourful American Bar, has been serving guests for over 30 years; the bar leads out on to a cobbled mews terrace which is delightful in summer. The wine cellar dates back 350 years.

STAKIS ST ERMIN'S   SW1

Caxton Street, SW1H 0QW
Tel: 0171-222 7888   *Fax:* 0171-222 6914   **£40**
Open: lunch & dinner daily
Meals served: lunch 12.30-2.30, dinner 6-9.30

Elegant 291-bedroomed hotel in the heart of Westminster with good conference and leisure facilities. The sounding within the hotel of the Parliamentary Division Bell is indicative of the popularity of the place among parliamentarians.

STAR OF INDIA   SW5

154 Old Brompton Road, SW5 0BE
*Te*l: 0171-373 2901   *Fax:* 0171-373 5664   **£60**
Open: lunch & dinner daily (closed Bank Holiday)
Meals served: lunch 12-3, dinner 6-12 (Sun 7.30-11.30)

One of the first Indian restaurants in London, the Star has been shining
since 1958. As well as traditional and familiar dishes, there are also
some more unusual offerings, such as aloo shirazi—highly spiced
potato croquettes, rolled in almonds and fried; dhuhar pasanda—
escalopes of lamb flavoured with cloves and served smoking; jhinga
nizami—king prawns cooked in a paste of sesame seeds, coconut and
peanuts. And although the north Indian tandoor is well used, there are
also plenty of dishes for vegetarians. For pudding, try ksari shahi
tukra—saffron-flavoured bread soaked in reduced milk garnished with
pistachios and almonds. Fun, over-the-top decor is a bonus.

STEPHEN BULL   W1

5-7 Blandford Street, W1H 3AA
Tel: 0171-486 9696   **£65**
Open: lunch Mon-Fri, dinner Mon-Sat   ✿
   (closed Bank Holidays, 1 wk Xmas)
Meals served: lunch 12.15-2.15, dinner 6.30-10.45   ✒

The menu changes daily at this smart,
informal restaurant, where the emphasis
is on innovation. Even the decor, which is
ultra-modern, is in keeping with the culinary policy. After five years, the modern
European repertoire of Stephen Bull has
created dishes of such success that they
have now become regulars by popular
demand. Such is the case for the delicious, much-praised starter of twice-
cooked goat's cheese soufflé; other
choices might be chartreuse of pheasant
with foie gras and Madeira or warm rabbit salad with snails and pancetta. Main
courses might include a croustade of

Biography

*Stephen Bull was an advertising accounts manager until he was twenty-
seven years old, which at least gave him a taste for good food when he
travelled abroad. Having decided on a change of career, he began his
training as a waiter for Peter Langan in Odin's, then*
Stephen *bought a restaurant in far-off North Wales to practise his
new-found skills! He then opened Lichfield's in Richmond,*
Bull *Surrey, where critics applauded him but the public didn't
follow. So a move to central London was made, and this has proved to be
a great success. He now oversees a group of three highly popular establishments.*

salmon, juniper and porcini with herb butter or corn-fed chicken with risotto milanese, roast garlic and tarragon vinegar. As with the previous two courses, there's a choice of around eight dishes on the dessert menu: prune and Armagnac parfait; lime and passion fruit cheesecake; spiced orange and grapefruit tart.

STEPHEN BULL'S BISTRO & BAR   EC1

71 St John Street, EC1M 4AN
Tel: 0171-490 1750   **£45**
Open: lunch Mon-Fri, dinner Mon-Sat
   (closed Bank Holidays, 10 days Xmas)
Meals served: lunch 12-2.30, dinner 6-10.30 (Sat from 7)

Popular, modern-style, City bistro close to Smithfield Market, with contemporary minimalist decor and a concise, daily-changing menu of modern dishes. Typical of starters are cauliflower and Gorgonzola soup, roast pepper and tomato salad with grilled focaccia or tartare of salmon with fromage frais. Main courses might feature grilled brochettes of pork and lamb with coriander and cashew pesto, grilled grey mullet with Sicilian caponata or daily specials such as stuffed artichoke with couscous and harissa sauce. Puds follow the same course—mango and Malibu parfait with raspberry coulis or mocha and pecan torte with Jack Daniels sauce. Good cheeses and reasonably priced wine list.

LE SUQUET   SW3

104 Draycott Avenue, SW3 3AE
Tel: 0171-581 1785   **£60**
Open: lunch & dinner daily
Meals served: lunch 12-2.30, dinner 7-12.30

The shellfish piled up high on a bark trough with plenty of seaweed at this popular, local, French restaurant is a wonderful sight to behold. The menu is dedicated almost entirely to fish, with shellfish especially prominent. Sit at the bar or at one of the closely-packed tables for langoustines, scallops, mussels, oysters, and more, each offered in a number of different guises, or splash out on the hefty plateau de fruits de mer or grilled sea bass. This is a regular, all-year-round menu of traditional treatments, with daily specials like seafood pot au feu or bouillabaisse introducing the main notes of variety. Steaks (four ways) and confit de canard for meat-eaters.

SWEETINGS   EC4

39 Queen Victoria Street, EC4A 4SN
Tel: 0171-248 3062   **£50**
Open: lunch daily (closed between Xmas & New Year)
Meals served: 11.30-3

Possibly the oldest fish and oyster restaurant in London – an institution in the City, even after more than 100 years in its present premises. Sweetings began life back in 1830 with a succession of Very Superior Oyster Rooms, the first of which was in Islington. The excellent sandwich and savoury counter caters for those in a hurry. More fortunate customers can make the most of the carte which makes no apologies for its singlemindedness -if it's meat you want, the choice is strictly limited. This is a feast for lovers of fish and seafood—turtle soup, soused herring, salmon fish cakes, chef's fish pie, and fish cooked to order, be it fried, grilled or poached. The other attraction here is the traditional puddings—bread-and-butter, steamed syrup, mince tart and home-made apple pie. No credit cards.

TALL HOUSE   SE1

134 Southwark Street, SE1 0SW
Tel: 0171-401 2929   *Fax:* 0171-401 3780   **£45**
Open: lunch Mon-Fri (evenings & weekends for private parties)
Meals served: lunch 12am-4pm (light meals from 9am)

A little oasis in an area not blessed with culinary delights, this restaurant is worth remembering for a quick and wholesome lunch. The cooking is good, straightforward and honest. Freshly-made soups, deep-fried Camembert with quince jelly, smoked salmon ravioli with tomato and basil sauce or gnocchi with spinach and three cheeses are typical of starters. Main courses include daily fresh fish specials, char-grilled salmon steak with cucumber and watercress sauce, but why not go the whole hog with a char-grilled rib of beef. Obviously a favourite. Puds are as simple and delicious as they come—lemon cheesecake, chocolate fudge cake, crème brûlée.

LA TANTE CLAIRE   SW3

68 Royal Hospital Road, SW3 4HP
Tel: 0171-352 6045   *Fax:* 0171-352 3257
Open: lunch & dinner Mon-Fri
  (closed Bank Holidays, 1 wk Xmas, 3 wks Aug)
Meals served: lunch 12.30-2, dinner 7-11

You always leave feeling comfortable and rather special **£125** ❧

Pierre Koffmann's restaurant has been a culinary beacon on the London scene for about 16 years now. His signature dish, the stuffed pig's trotters with morels, continues to captivate after years at the top despite competition from other dishes such as coquilles St Jacques à la planche with ink sauce, roast pigeon en cocotte with a thyme jus or pavé of roast sea bass provençale. The well-spaced tables in this attractive dining room offer plenty of privacy and on the surface little changes. Koffmann is a robust classicist who is not one to be governed by fads, but his classicism is only the starting point for his art. If he were a painter, he'd go down in history as someone treading middle ground, somewhere

between the Old Masters and Van Gogh. It's always a delight to eat at this restaurant with its stylish yet unpretentious decor—Paris has many but London still has few that combine top class, honest food in surroundings such as these.

Biography

Pierre Koffmann began his career at 16, not for the love of cooking but in order to do something with his life, but soon realised he had found his vocation. He came from Europe to London and Le Gavroche and

Pierre

Koffmann

remained with the Rouxs, at Le Gamin in the City, leaving only for an 8-month spell with the Cazalets, before rejoining them for the opening of The Waterside Inn. But, with the help of the Roux brothers he set up La Tante Claire, Chelsea, where he has been for almost 20 years. He is fiercely proud of his work, intent on perfection, and his dedication and generosity are reflected in his cooking.

THIERRY'S   SW3

342 King's Road, SW3 5UR
Tel: 0171-352 3365
Open: lunch & dinner daily (closed Xmas)
Meals served: lunch 12.30-2.30
  (Sun to 3), dinner 7.30-10.45 (Sun 7-10.30),
  (light meals 2.30-5.30)

£40

Hervé Salez' bistro is cosy and popular, with checked tablecloths and window booths, Thierry's is a classic French bistro offering all that you might expect, from spicy fish soup with rouille and moules marinières to beef bourguignonne, coq au vin, confit de canard, steak béarnaise or chateaubriand, cassoulet de Toulouse and Dover sole, grilled with lemon or with parsley butter. The lunch-time carte offers less choice but along similar lines. Fixed-price lunch and dinner menus offer good value with choice. The new afternoon snack menu (3-5.30pm) is proving successful. Some outside tables in the summer.

THISTELLS   SE22

65 Lordship Lane, SE22 8EP
Tel: 0181-299 1921
Open: lunch Tue-Sun, dinner Mon-Sat
Meals served: lunch 12-4, dinner 7-10.30

Good local restaurant

£45

This is an unusual place in a former grocer's shop in Dulwich, with a menu which reflects chef-patron Sami Youssef's Egyptian origins. In a pretty, ornately tiled room you are treated to a repertoire of Middle Eastern and French-based dishes, cooked with confidence. Flash-fried lamb's liver with Eastern herbs (a house speciality), falafel with tahini sauce, tabbouleh and couscous, along with modern and traditional French classics such as duck cassoulet, entrecôte of beef with Roquefort sauce or lamb béarnaise; and vegetarian options like barley and mushroom casserole. Sami, who started out in Dulwich almost 20 years ago with a six-year stint as sous-chef in the kitchen of Nico Ladenis, first made a name for himself with a quirky little French restaurant in Forest Hill Road called Auberge. After a road accident which put him out of action for some time, he is now back doing what he loves most. When she's not baking old-fashioned soda bread for the restaurant, his Irish wife, Anne, is at front of house.

LE TIRE BOUCHON   W1
6 Upper James Street, W1R 3HF
Tel: 0171-437 5348
Open: all day Mon-Fri (closed 23 Dec-3 Jan)
Meals served: 12-9.30

£40

Comfortable French restaurant offering classic traditional favourites. Handy for Carnaby Street.

TURNER'S   SW3

87-89 Walton Street, SW3 2HP
Tel: 0171-584 6711   Fax: 0171-584 9337
Open: lunch Sun-Fri, dinner daily
   (closed Bank Holidays, 1 wk Xmas)
Meals served: lunch 12.30-2.30, dinner 7.30-11.15 (Sun to 10)

£95

Those who know Turner's will not be surprised that Yorkshireman Brian Turner continues in winning form at his comfortable restaurant in busy Knightsbridge. The cooking is very good, and Brian also oversees front-of-house with welcoming charm. The two- or three-course set lunch menus, complete with amuse-gueules and petits fours, is a real bargain at this level, at only £9.95 and £13.50 respectively. Dishes might include a light salad of chicken and foie gras mousse followed by fillet of cod with a butter sauce. The main menu (£32 for two courses) offers a style of cooking with British and pan-European influences: poached haddock with quail's eggs and Caesar salad; cream soup of fresh herbs; light stew of monkfish and mussels with morel mushrooms; grilled rib of beef with a bone marrow and garlic sauce; and roast rabbit with wild mushrooms and tarragon sauce. Sunday lunch brings roast beef with Yorkshire pudding, and the likes of pan-fried salmon with a white wine sauce or grilled calf's liver with onion gravy. Excellent desserts—delicious hot puff pastry piled with apples and caramel ice cream or perhaps rich crème caramel with red berries—and cheeses to finish. Good wine list.

■ **Brian Turner biography, next page**

Biography

Brian Turner's early experience was gained by helping his father in the family's transport café. He left Leeds Technical College with a City & Guilds qualification and a College Diploma in Waiting. He applied to The **Brian** Savoy, but had to wait two years for a vacancy, mean-**Turner** while working at Simpson's-in-the-Strand. He then he spent four months with Dieter Sondermann at St Ermin's Hotel, before joining Claridge's as chef tournant. From there he joined Richard Shepherd at The Capital Hotel. After a brief sojourn into teaching, he returned to The Capital, before moving on to open his own restaurant. Brian is a no-non-sense Yorkshireman who likes all types of food but chooses according to his mood. With a well-timed sense of humour to complement his extro-vert tendencies, he is a popular figure both in the trade and with the public, via his numerous TV appearances.

TWENTY TRINITY GARDENS   SW9

20 Trinity Gardens, SW9 8DP
Tel: 0171-733 8838   **£40**
Open: lunch Sun only, dinner daily
    (closed Bank Holidays, 4 days Xmas)
Meals served: lunch 12-4, dinner 7-10.30 (Fri & Sat to 11)

Daughter Jemima Mann-Baha has taken over from mother Jane Mann and the emphasis on the cooking has shifted slightly since the arrival of new chef Paul Churchill, who looks more to the Mediterranean for his inspiration, though not exclusively. The plant-filled conservatory dining room, bright by day, candlelit by night, makes a relaxing setting in which to enjoy starters such as warm carrot and sesame seed tim-bale with fine tomato sauce or fresh tuna carpaccio. Main courses might include pot-roasted Spring chicken Moroccan-style, monkfish and snapper served in a saffron sauce or pavé au jus d'ail, a speciality - a "flagstone" of rump steak marinated in garlic, olive oil and parsley, served with allumette potatoes. If you've room for a pudding, try the tarte of the day, treacle spotted dick or iced lime soufflé. Situated just off Acre Lane, but by car approach via Brighton Terrace.

UNDERGROUND CAFÉ   NW1

214 Camden High Street, NW1   *Some reasonably priced Italian wines*
Tel: 0171-482 0010   **£45**
Open: dinner Mon-Sat (closed 1 wk Xmas)
Meals served: dinner 6-11

Next to the Camden Brasserie and under the same ownership, this budget Italian restaurant offers an imaginative range of pasta dishes, risotto of the day and a varied selection of main-course dishes such as spicy Italian sausages, warm salad of beef fillet, grilled rabbit with rosemary and white wine, and a fish dish of the day. The setting is simple, the plain walls hung with contemporary art, and the menu is brief enough to relax over. Excellent espresso coffee to finish, along with desserts like rich chocolate torte with crushed Amaretti and cream. Well worth a visit.

VERONICA'S   W2

3 Hereford Road, W2 4AB
Tel: 0171-229 5079   *Fax:* 0171-229 1210   **£50**
Open: lunch Mon-Fri, dinner Mon-Sat
   (closed Bank Holidays)
Meals served: lunch 12-3, dinner 7-12

A cosy, pretty restaurant, with striped table cloths and yellow napkins, run by an ex-headmistress and her film-maker husband whose passion for food is in the research which goes into many of the dishes. Early historical and regional English specialities are the result of scouring through a vast collection of manuscripts, from medieval to Victorian times. Themed dinners are a regular feature: A Renaissance Feast, A Georgian Dinner; as are menus: an Eighteenth-Century Kitchen, Irish Farmhouse Food. The monthly-changing menus are descriptive and informative, with explanations about historical dishes and methods. Typical dishes include onion and cheese sausages on minted apple, medieval mushrooms and beans, twice-roasted duck and chicken rosemary with garlic and potato garnish. When it comes to puddings, Veronica seems to have an army of nursery types to call up!

VILLAGE TAVERNA   SW10
196-198 Fulham Road, SW10 9TW
Tel: 0171-352 3799   **£50**
Open: lunch & dinner daily (closed 4 days Xmas)
Meals served: 12 noon-1am
A personal favourite of mine —good value, local and authentic. Have the kleftico.

VILLANDRY DINING ROOM   W1

89 Marylebone High Street, W1M 3DE
Tel: 0171-224 3799   **£45**
Open: lunch Mon-Sat, dinner once a month
   (closed Bank Holidays, 10 days Xmas)
Meals served: lunch 12.30-2.30 (light meals 8.30-5.30,
   Sat from 9.30)

This is an upmarket deli with a small restaurant at the rear, serving
light meals and snacks. The daily-changing menu has a bias towards
French cuisine but the overall choice remains eclectic. Start perhaps
with a plate of charcuterie, home-made soup or a grilled goat's cheese
salad, before opting for one of the more substantial dishes on the short
lunch-time carte: Cumberland sausages with cranberry sauce, braised
cabbage and mash; grilled entrecôte steak with chips; pan-fried halibut
with a light lemon and butter sauce. Delicious sweets and excellent
cheeses. Special dinners once a month.

WAGAMAMA   WC1

4 Streatham Street, WC1
Tel: 0171-323 9223   *Fax:* 0171-323 9224   **£15**
Open: lunch & dinner Mon-Sat
   (closed Bank Holidays, except Good Friday)
Meals served: lunch 12-2.30 (Sat to 3.30), dinner 6-11

A fast-food, Japanese-style, basement noodle bar with a few rice dishes
for those not into noodles. This is simple, healthy food served at communal tables. Here the philosophy is that positive eating leads to positive living. The menu consists of main courses (based around ramen,
pan-fried noodles or rice) and accompaniments; there are no starters.
Orders are taken on radio-based electronic hand-held systems and are
transmitted direct from the table to the the kitchen and bar. It calls
itself a non-destination food station, which basically seems to mean that
this is not a place where you are expected to linger!

THE WALDORF   WC2

Aldwych, WC2B 4DD
Tel: 0171-836 2400   *Fax:* 0171-836 7244   **£55**
Open: lunch Mon-Sat, dinner daily
   (closed Bank Holidays, 4 wks Jul/Aug)
Meals served: lunch 12.30-2.30, dinner 6-11 (Sun 7-10),
   (light meals the dansant: Fri-Sun 3.30-6.30)

The first of Forte's 800 or so hotel acquisitions, the Waldorf recently
celebrated its 85th birthday with a multi-million-pound refit, much of
which was spent on the bedrooms. At the heart of the hotel is the
lovely Palm Court, famous for its weekly tea dances, a tradition which
dates back to 1913. Outwardly, little has changed. Public areas have
been refurbished but none has lost its original character. A choice of
eating venues provides something for every occasion. The restaurant,
with Corinthian columns and French doors opening on to the Palm
Court, serves a mostly traditional menu, and for something a little
lighter you can head for the Aldwych Brasserie, pubby Footlights bar
or the Club Bar, all of which serve a range of salads, light meals and
snacks. Every one of the 292 bedrooms boasts its own entrance lobby,
and furnishing recalls the opulence of Edwardian days.

WALSH'S SEAFOOD & SHELLFISH REST.   W1

5 Charlotte Street, W1P 1HD
Tel: 0171-637 0222   *Fax:* 0171-637 0224   **£60**
Open: lunch Mon-Fri, dinner Mon-Sat
  (closed Bank Holidays)
Meals served: lunch 12-2.30, dinner 6-10.30

If the exterior colours, lettering and even the menu look familiar, all is explained in that Walsh was the name of the family who founded Wheelers. Bernard Walsh's granddaughter Elaine is following in his footsteps with this West End oyster bar and restaurant. The menu offers a traditional range of dishes such as Dover sole, lobster, turbot and plaice prepared in a number of ways. Less classic, more innovative dishes are also available, such as wild salmon on a bed of lentils and bacon, or John Dory braised with wild mushrooms, all skilfully prepared by ex-Odin's chef, Christopher German. Starters feature marinated mackerel in a wine and lemon sauce, lobster ravioli, gratin of Arbroath smokies, and shellfish bisque.

WALTONS OF WALTON STREET   SW3

121 Walton Street, SW3 2PH
Tel: 0171-584 0204   *Fax:* 0171-581 2848   **£80**
Open: lunch & dinner daily (closed 25 & 26 Dec)
Meals served: lunch 12.30-2.30 (Sun to 2),
  dinner 7.30-11.30 (Sun 7-10)   ✿

Waltons takes pride in showing what great food Britain has to offer, and succeeds in that aim, with good-value quality food in luxuriously comfortable surroundings. Chef Paul Hodgson executes his work with style, skill and flair, producing dishes of the highest standards. Terrine of truffled foie gras, seafood sausage, wild mushroom risotto, prime medallions of Scotch beef and saddle of Southdown lamb with wild mushrooms and a thyme and rosemary sauce show the range. Waltons' sticky toffee pudding, two-chocolate terrine or traditional English burnt cream add the finishing touch to what is truly a culinary feast, as much for the palate as for the mind. Sunday lunch is always popular, with roasts, including beef and Yorkshire pudding, sharing the menu with dishes like salmon stuffed with spinach and herbs. Simply Waltons' Lunch and After Theatre Supper menus offer the chance to sample the chef's talents at a more modest price. An extensive wine list matches the quality of both food and service.

Roger Wren is justifiably proud of his restaurant

THE WESTBURY   W1
Conduit Street, W1A 4UH
Tel: 0171-629 7755   *Fax:* 0171-495 1163   **£55**
Open: lunch daily, dinner Mon-Sat (Sun in lounge only)
Meals served: lunch 12.30-3, dinner 6.30-11
On the corner of New Bond Street, 244-bedroomed hotel. Liveried porters establish an air of formality. Ideal for West End shopping and theatres. Polo Lounge now open 24 hours a day.

WHITE TOWER   **W1**
1 Percy Street, W1P 0ET
Tel: 0171-636 8141   £70
Open: lunch Mon-Fri, dinner Mon-Sat (closed 3 wks Aug)
Meals served: lunch 12.30-2.30, dinner 6.30-10.30
As we went to press, a change of ownership was expected here.

WHITTINGTON'S   EC4

21 College Hill, EC4 2RP
Tel: 0171-248 5855   £55
Open: dinner Mon-Fri (closed Bank Holidays)
Meals served: lunch 11.45-2.15

Dick Whittington is said to have owned these 14th-century cellars at some point, though how he acquired them may be of great interest! The menu at this wine bar-cum-restaurant changes every three weeks or so and is supplemented by daily specials. Starters might include home-made soups, salads, terrines and soufflés. Main courses offer a good choice of fish and meat dishes: steamed supreme of halibut on noodles, with sweet tomato sauce; pan-fried calf's liver with bubble'n'squeak and a rich gravy; pork with Stilton and walnut mousse on a chive sauce; or chicken breast filled with avocado served on a sweetcorn and bacon pancake.

WILLOUGHBY'S   N1

26 Penton Street, N1 9PS
Tel: 0171-833 1380   £45
Open: lunch Mon-Fri, dinner Mon-Sat
   (closed Bank Holidays)
Meals served: lunch 12-2.30, dinner 6.30-10.30

Straightforward English cooking from a short à la carte menu which features kedgeree, split-pea soup and Glamorgan vegetarian sausages among starters. Main courses range from beef casseroled in ale to skate with caper sauce or vegetable and butter bean stew. The carte is supplemented by daily-changing blackboard specials. Puddings feature treacle tart, baked bay custard and iced chocolate mousse.

WILTON'S   SW1

55 Jermyn Street, SW1Y 6LX
Tel: 0171-629 9955   Fax: 0171-495 6233   £85
Open: lunch Sun-Fri, dinner daily
   (closed Bank Holidays)
Meals served: lunch 12.30-2.30, dinner 6.30-10.30

250 years of service, even though it has changed location, keeps things firmly in the old school of thought at this famous London restaurant, with its loyal clientele and gentlemen's club atmosphere. The menu is a classic repertoire of mainstream dishes, with oysters, fish and grills the specialities. Grilled, fried, poached – take your pick from Dover sole, plaice, halibut, salmon or turbot. Elsewhere on the menu, you'll find turtle soup, fresh potted shrimps, dressed crab and lobster in a number of different guises. Daily specials might include fish pie or grilled sea bass with spinach and ginger. Straightforward, traditional puds to finish. Old school service for old school customers.

WODKA   W8

12 St Alban's Grove, W8 5PN
Tel: 0171-937 6513   **£45**
Open: lunch Mon-Fri, dinner daily (closed Bank Holidays)
Meals served: lunch 12.30-2.30, dinner 7-11
Polish and East European restaurant with Franglais derivations: veal goulash, venison and boar sausage, blinis and chunky fish cakes are favourites. Vodka by the glass or carafe.

ZIANI   SW3

45/47 Radnor Walk, SW3 4BT   *Colourful, busy and popular local*
Tel: 0171-352 2698   *restaurant*   **£55**
Open: lunch & dinner daily (closed Bank Holidays)
Meals served: lunch 12-2.45 (Sun to 3.15),
     dinner 7-11.30 (Sun to 10.30)

Named after an aristocratic Venetian family which once ruled Venice, Ziani's menu is a grand affair with a varied and interesting selection of dishes focusing on the culinary traditions of that most beautiful city. There's really plenty of everything, from carpaccio, seafood and pasta to grilled fish and meats. A typical meal might consist of deep-fried mozzarella with spicy tomato sauce, followed by seafood risotto, then sea bass baked in foil or veal chop sautéed with ham, rosemary and white wine. Italian cheeses, ice creams or a home-made sweet of the day to finish.

ZOE   W1

St Christopher's Place, W1M 5HH
Tel: 0171-224 1122   *Fax:* 0171-935 5444   **£45**
Open: lunch daily, dinner Mon-Sat
     (closed Bank Holidays)
Meals served: lunch 11.30-2.30, dinner 6.30-11.30

A basement brasserie and ground-floor café, which in fine weather spills out on to the pavement in Continental fashion. You'll find Conrad Melling in the kitchen and Sam Kemp at front-of-house. Two menus, one for fish, the other meat and poultry, offer a wide choice, from crab and wild mushroom cheesecake, mussel and samphire risotto and langoustine ravioli to beef carpaccio, roast saddle of lamb and pan-fried chicken breast filled with chickpea tagine, chorizo and pine nuts. The all-day café adds even greater choice, everything from mushrooms on toast or Mediterranean crostini to sausages and mash, fish and chips and steak frites. Antony Worrall Thompson-inspired with a menu dominated by the modern Mediterranean appeal.

England Establishment Reviews

ABBERLEY   Elms Hotel

Stockton Road, Abberley, Hereford & Worcester, WR6 6AT
Tel: (01299) 896666   *Fax:* (01299) 896804   **£55**
Open: lunch & dinner daily
Meals served: lunch 12.30-2, dinner 7.30-9.30

A majestic Queen Anne mansion house set in ten acres of formal gardens and parkland, dating back to 1710 and built by architect Gilbert White, who was a pupil of Sir Christopher Wren. The reception rooms have antiques and good-quality reproduction furniture. The 25 bedrooms are either traditional—in the main house—or have a lighter feel in the converted coach house. Many have beautiful views of the surrounding countryside. Ideally situated for Shakespeare country and the Cotswolds.

ABINGDON   Thame Lane House

1 Thame Lane, Culham, Abingdon, Oxfordshire, OX14 3DS
Tel: (01235) 524177   **£45**
Open: lunch Tue-Sun, dinner Mon-Sat (closed 1 wk Jan)
Meals served: lunch 12.30-1.15, dinner 7.15-8.45

Set in large secluded gardens rich with trees, this restaurant with three rooms is also the home of Michael and Marie-Claude Beech. The fixed-price menu is French, with starters such as seafood platter and salmon mousse with a creamy leek sauce, followed by noisettes of lamb or roast hare bourguignonne. Typical desserts are gratin of red fruit or chocolate cake with mocha sauce. Around 30 French wines are well chosen to complement the menus. Booking here is essential.

ALDEBURGH   New Regatta

171-173 High Street, Aldeburgh, Suffolk, IP15 5AN
Tel: (01728) 452011   **£45**
Open: lunch & dinner daily (Wed-Sun Oct-Feb)
Meals served: lunch 12-2, dinner 7-10.15

Robert Mabey's second restaurant (see also Mabey's in Sudbury) offers a concise menu that combines local ingredients with modern European and Oriental influences. Half a dozen local Butley oysters are served with red wine and shallot vinegar and good brown bread; chilled pasta, chicken and mangetout salad has a garlic dressing; classic salad niçoise uses fresh tuna from the Seychelles and local new potatoes; crispy deep-fried won-ton parcels are stuffed with crab, fresh ginger and lime; grilled breast of chicken has a light curry and pineapple sauce as well as steamed rice. Delicious puddings range from traditional crème brûlée flavoured with orange, to baked mascarpone tart with gooseberry coulis, to blackcurrant sorbet studded with diced pear, or rich chocolate chip ice cream with fresh mint sauce. A super place, well worth a visit.

ALDERLEY EDGE	Alderley Edge Hotel

Macclesfield Road, Alderley Edge, Cheshire, SK9 7BJ
Tel: (01625) 583033   *Fax:* (01625) 586343 **£55**
Open: lunch & dinner daily
Meals served: lunch 12-2, dinner 7-10

A short stroll from the famous "Edge", with spectacular views over the Cheshire Plain, this 32-bedroomed Victorian hotel is run by a friendly, professional team. A great deal of money and attention has been lavished here to convert the former home of a local, wealthy cotton merchant to its present-day status. The restaurant offers an extensive, classic à la carte menu as well as fixed-price and light lunch offerings. Specialist homemade breads, cakes and pastries, add to the delights of chef Brian Joy's skilful repertoire. Fish and seafood direct from Fleetwood market every morning are another speciality: Dover sole, fresh Cornish lobster or Irish oysters smoked over maple then served with home-made noodles in a light sabayon. You could start with a warm Cheshire cheese soufflé with fresh scallops before moving on to entrecote steak in a rich, red wine sauce infused with thyme, served with a celeriac and carrot mousse. The patissier's hot puddings are his pièces de résistance. Excellent, all-round performance from the kitchen here, and a spectacular wine list with over 200 champagnes and 1000 wines.

ALDERNEY	Georgian House

Victoria Street, St Anne, Alderney
Tel: (01481) 822471 **£45**
Open: lunch daily, dinner Wed-Mon
Meals served: lunch 12-2.30, dinner 7-10

This is a delightful pub with a cosy, traditional feel. Light lunches are served in the restaurant and bar, with daily blackboard specials to supplement the range—mixed grill, bangers'n'mash with onion gravy, beef stroganoff, poached salmon hollandaise. A more sophisticated carte takes over in the evenings, with a plateau de fruits de mer for two which has to be seen to be believed: crab, lobster, shrimps, prawns, mussels and oysters at least! Prime steaks are also available, cooked to your requirements—plain grilled, with garlic, with pepper sauce or flambéed in cream and brandy.

ALDERNEY   Inchalla Hotel

The Val, St Anne, Alderney
Tel: (01481) 823220   *Fax:* (01481) 823551   **£35**
Open: lunch daily, dinner Mon-Sat
  (closed 2 wks Xmas/New Year)
Meals served: lunch 12-2, dinner 7-8.45

Well-maintained accommodation and well-executed unpretentious cooking are offered at Valerie Willis' charming 9-bedroomed hotel, located in quiet secluded gardens on high ground on the edge of this pretty Normandy-style town with cobbled streets and colour-washed houses. The cooking is eclectic, within the confines of European traditions, and seafood and shellfish feature strongly. Themed evenings step further afield with the likes of Thai cooking in the limelight, but from the normal table d'hôte dinner menu or more extensive carte, expect traditional, familiar dishes such as French-style pot-roasted chicken coated with Dijon mustard and herbs, pork stroganoff, pan-fried fillet of brill with watercress butter and straightforward grills.

ALSTON   Lovelady Shield

Nenthead Road, Alston, Cumbria, CA9 3LF
Tel: (01434) 381203   *Fax:* (01434) 381515   **£55**
Open: dinner daily (closed 4 wks Jan/Feb)
Meals served: dinner 7-8.30

Standing in a sheltered, secluded spot on the banks of the River Nent two miles east of Alston, this 12-bedroomed hotel is an oasis of tranquillity for those who need to get away from it all. The house dates back to the early 19th century and has been carefully converted into the present-day hotel which stands in two acres of well-tended garden in the middle of the wild, rolling fells. Take an early morning stroll and return for an informal lunch in the bar, or make the most of the fresh air all day, returning in time for dinner. There's some good, homely English cooking by chef Barrie Garten, who offers a four-course, fixed-price dinner with three choices at each course. You might be offered potted lamb with mint, followed perhaps by pan-fried breast of Barbary duckling glazed with honey and served with an orange and redcurrant jus, or a tarragon-scented casserole of monkfish tail, mussels and asparagus with cream. Puds might include treacle tart, crumble or sponge pudding.

ALTRINCHAM   Francs
2 Goose Green, Altrincham, Cheshire
Tel: 0161-941 3954   **£35**
Open: lunch daily, dinner Mon-Sat (closed Bank Holidays)
Meals served: lunch 12-3, dinner 5-11, (light meals Sun 12-5)
French bistro with plenty of French air about it and classic bistro dishes. Alfresco eating on terrace in fine weather.

ALTRINCHAM The French Brasserie

24 The Downs, Altrincham, Cheshire, WA14 2QD
Tel: (0161) 928 0808   *Fax:* (0161) 941 6154   **£25**
Open: all day daily
Meals served: 12-11.30 (Thu-Sat to 1.30am)

True to its name, The French is everything that a brasserie should be.
The à la carte, featuring a wide choice of traditional favourites—French
onion soup, salads, coq au vin, porc provençal, home-made sausages,
magret de canard—is supplemented by a number of special fixed-price
menus which are excellent value for money. The French family Sunday
lunch is one such example—accompanied children under 10 are
served free. A lively, popular, relaxed place that promises to be fun.
Live jazz from Wednesday to Saturday.

ALTRINCHAM The French Restaurant

25 The Downs, Altrincham, Cheshire, WA14 2QD
Tel: (0161) 941 3355   **£30**
Open: lunch Tue-Fri & Sun, dinner daily
Meals served: lunch 12-3, dinner 6-10.30

Somewhat more formal and refined than its Brasserie sister next door,
this offers predominantly traditional French and English cooking.
Fixed-price menus are good value and the à la carte features a wide
choice of dishes, with starters such as salade champignoise or game
sausage with sauce bordelaise. Poulet à l'estragon, confit de canard,
pavé de boeuf and fresh poached salmon with asparagus typify main-
course selections. Vegetarians will be delighted by their separate
menu, with a choice of four dishes for each course: layers of puff pastry
with a wild mushroom and asparagus ragoût or noodles in a cheese
and walnut sauce are typical examples.

AMBERLEY	Amberley Castle

Amberley, Nr Arundel, West Sussex, BN18 9ND
Tel: (01798) 831992   *Fax:* (01798) 831998   **£60**
Open: lunch & dinner daily
Meals served: lunch 12-2, dinner 7-9.30

The stuff of legends, Amberley Castle dates back as far as the 12th century. Nestling in the lee of the South Downs, the setting is almost as magical and mystical as the castle itself. Inside the ancient oak portcullis, beyond the 14th-century walls, you enter a delightful garden, the work of owner Martin Cummings for whom the transformation from castle to hotel has been the realisation of a personal dream, shared by his wife Joy. Rooms are named after Sussex castles and the restaurant theme completes the medieval revival, as Nigel Boschetti's Castle Cuisine looks to old English recipes, Saxon and Roman influences for much of its inspiration. Typical dishes include jugged hare, Lancashire hot pot, baked seafood sausage with stewed herbs and steak and oyster pie. Elsewhere the menus feature more modern English country dishes such as roast fillet of pork with black pudding, roast shallots and mash; or roast magret of duck breast with lentils and baked garlic. Puds include warm treacle tart, jam roly poly, spicy fruit crumble and Bakewell tart. The Queen's Room dining room is named after Catherine of Braganza, whose visit to the castle in 1685 is commemorated by a mural which depicts her hunting in Arundel Park with King Charles II. A wonderfully romantic hideaway.

AMBLESIDE	Rothay Manor Hotel

Rothay Bridge, Ambleside, Cumbria, LA22 0EH
Tel: (0153 94) 33605   *Fax:* (0153 94) 33607   **£55**
Open: lunch & dinner daily (closed 3 Jan-10 Feb)
Meals served: lunch 12.30-2 (buffet only Mon-Sat)
    (Sun 12.30-1.30), dinner 8-9, (light meals tea 3.30-5.30)

Formerly the home of a prosperous Liverpool merchant, Rothay was built in elegant Regency style in its own grounds at the very heart of the Lake District. Opened as a hotel in 1967 by Bronwen Nixon, it is now in the hands of Bronwen's two sons and their wives. There are 16 bedrooms, including luxury suites in the grounds which offer greater privacy and isolation. Free use of the nearby leisure club's extensive facilities may come in handy if the heavens should choose to open unexpectedly. The restaurant is popular for afternoon teas and its traditional Sunday lunches and there's a cold buffet table at lunchtime and daily-changing set dinner menu. A comprehensive and moderately priced wine list with several lesser known wines completes the picture. The philosophy in the kitchen is apparent on the plate—"if it's worth doing, it's worth doing properly".

AMBLESIDE	Sheila's Cottage

The Slack, Ambleside, Cumbria, LA22 9DQ
Tel: (0153 94) 33079   **£45**
Open: lunch & dinner Mon-Sat (closed Jan)
Meals served: lunch 12-2.30, dinner 7-9.30, (Tea 2.30-5)
Much-praised, 250-year-old-cottage country restaurant run by the Greaves for the last 30 years. Everything is home-baked and the cooking is excellent.

AMBLESIDE — **Wateredge Hotel**

Waterhead Bay, Ambleside, Cumbria, LA22 0EP
Tel: (0153 94) 32332   *Fax:* (0153 94) 32332   **£60**
Open: dinner daily (closed mid Dec-early Feb)
Meals served: dinner 7-8.30

This quiet, relaxing, 23-bedroomed family-run hotel on the edge of Lake Windermere, has been skilfully converted from a row of 17th-century fishermen's cottages. Garden rooms have balconies or patios, and there are two spacious ground-floor suites with private access. The restaurant, situated within the original cottages, is characterful and atmospheric, with its oak-beamed ceilings and warm log fire in winter. All bread, pastries and preserves are home-made; dinner is a fixed-price, six-course affair, and light lunches and afternoon teas are served in the lounge or on the patio in summer. The style of cooking is best described as traditional farmhouse cuisine—cream of leek and potato soup; roast loin of pork with caper gravy and sweetcorn stuffing; golden pecan nut pie. The Lakeland platter for breakfast will keep you sustained throughout the day.

APPLEBY-IN-WESTMORLAND — **Appleby Manor**

Roman Road, Appleby-in-Westmorland, Cumbria, CA16 6JB
Tel: (0176 83) 51571   *Fax:* (0176 83) 52888   **£40**
Open: lunch & dinner daily (closed 3 days Xmas)
Meals served: lunch 12-1.45, dinner 7-9

The sight of half a million acres of some of England's most breathtaking scenery—the Lake District, the North Pennines and the Yorkshire Dales—is enough in itself to justify a visit to Appleby Manor, a friendly, family-run hotel. Thirty rooms, all bright and cheerful, are located in either the main house, coach house annexe or in the modern wing. Take a long walk to work up an appetite for Dave Farrar's robust British cooking, then take your seat in the hotel's elegant, oak-panelled restaurant to enjoy hearty helpings of Cumberland Guinness pancake, beefsteak and oyster pudding or Roman Way red mullet. The menu changes daily, depending on what's available locally. Home-made speciality breads and a stimulating menu of speciality coffees are added bonuses. Good leisure facilities, including swimming pool, with golf and fishing nearby.

APPLEBY-IN-WESTMORLAND — **Tufton Arms**

Market Square, Appleby-in-Westmorland, Cumbria, CA16 6XA
Tel: (0176 83) 51593   *Fax:* (0176 83) 52761   **£35**
Open: lunch & dinner daily
Meals served: lunch 12-2, dinner 7.30-9.30

Once a run-down Victorian pub, the Tufton Arms was restored by the Milsom family using authentic period pieces and prints (the original building dates back to the late 16th century and was extended in 1883). There are 17 bedrooms: those in the main house are decorated in traditional period style; others are in a more modest, modern wing, but are no less comfortable. The area has some of the best salmon and trout fishing in the North of England, and the Eden Valley provides a rich source of raw material for the kitchen. Ideally located for touring the Lakes, Dales and Pennines.

APPLETHWAITE — Underscar Manor

Applethwaite, Keswick, Cumbria, CA12 4PH
Tel: (0176 87) 75000   *Fax:* (0176 87) 74904   **£65**
Open: lunch & dinner daily
Meals served: lunch 12-1.30, dinner 7-8.30

Forty acres of peaceful grounds and woodland walks, complete with stream, red squirrel, deer and views over Derwentwater, is the setting for this 11-bedroomed Italianate house. Run by Pauline and Derek Harrison of the Moss Nook (Manchester), the hotel has been luxuriously furnished, retaining many of the original Victorian features. Home-smoked fish and meat, home-made black pudding and local, gamey Herdwick lamb are specialities of the hotel kitchen which is in the capable hands of Robert Thornton and Stephen Yare, who pay as much attention to presentation as they do to method and flavour. Large, detailed menus offer diversely influenced interpretations of many classic French dishes, but the style then becomes more eclectic with dishes like chicken breast marinated in tandoori spices alongside a trio of duck (breast, leg confit and rissole) with quail's egg, served hot on a Madeira sauce. Typical main courses are crisp Gressingham duck with a celeriac mousse, pineapple and a honey and vinegar sauce. Derek Harrison's love of wine is obvious from the list, which starts with no fewer than 25 champagnes then wanders through France covering most regions, pops in token selections from other countries and then returns to France for the bulk of his fine wine selections.

ASCOT — Royal Berkshire

London Road, Sunninghill, Ascot, Berkshire, SL5 0PP
Tel: (01344) 23322   *Fax:* (01344) 874240   **£65**
Open: lunch & dinner daily
Meals served: lunch 12-2, dinner 7.15-9.30

Between the racecourse and the Polo Club is where you'll find this 63-bedroomed Queen Anne mansion—it was previously occupied by the Churchills, and Colonel (malted drink) Horlicks. It was he who was responsible for much of the development of the 15 acres of beautiful gardens, parkland and woodland which surround the house. Rooms are large and comfortable and there are good leisure facilities, which include indoor pool, sauna, squash and putting. The dining room overlooks the lawns and makes an elegant setting for dinner. The style of cooking, appropriately for this part of the world, is English through and through.

ASENBY — Crab & Lobster

Asenby, North Yorkshire, YO7 3QL
Tel: (01845) 577286   *Fax:* (01845) 577109   **£55**
Open: lunch daily, dinner Mon-Sat (closed 25 Dec)
     11.30-3, 6.30-11
Meals served: lunch 11.30-3, dinner 6.30-11

Pretty, thatched bar and brasserie, surrounded by beautiful country-side and serving good food at reasonable prices. The interior is decorated from floor to ceiling with nick-nacks and the whole place exudes an old-world charm. At the rear there's a large garden with wooden benches where barbecues, and live jazz (summer Sunday lunchtimes) are held, weather permitting! Or why not attend one of the jazz, gourmet or seafood extravaganza evenings, all of which have their own special menus. Otherwise you can choose from the brasserie menu (ordered at the bar) or the restaurant menu, with seafood predominant on both. The restaurant menu might offer starters such as salad of sea bass and scallops; fish soup with aiöli and croutons or feuilleté of livers and foie gras with truffled sauce; followed by monkfish brioche crusted with noodles and tomato butter; rump of lamb with garlic fritters, madeira and thyme; and lemon sole with smoked salmon, spinach and shellfish sauce. Well-chosen wine list with lots of good drinking under £20 – over 20 bottles at around £10.

ASHBOURNE   Callow Hall

Mappleton Road, Ashbourne, Derbyshire, DE6 2AA
Tel: (01335) 343403   *Fax:* (01335) 343624   **£60**
Open: lunch daily, dinner Mon-Sat (closed 25 & 26 Dec)
Meals served: lunch 12-1.30, dinner 7.30-9.30

Father and son take turns at scouring the early-morning market in Birmingham to select the best. The Spencers' family home, a Victorian hillside mansion in 44 acres of grounds, it has its own bakery and butchery on the premises, and a mile of private fishing on nearby Bentley Brook. The kitchen is well supplied, too, from the hotel's own garden with fresh vegetables and herbs, and produces its own home-made sausages, home-cured bacon and smoked salmon (son Anthony's speciality). The house has 16 bedrooms and is elegant furnished in period style with antiques. Family memorabilia about the place add a homely and informal feel. France is the source of most of the wines, supplemented by a few bottles from other countries.

ASHBURTON   Holne Chase Hotel

Ashburton, Devon, TQ13 7NS
Tel: (01364) 631471   *Fax:* (01364) 631453   **£45**
Open: lunch & dinner daily
Meals served: lunch 12.15-1.45, dinner 7.15-9

Three miles north of Ashburton, the Bromage family's 14-bedroomed country house set in 30 acres of grounds within Dartmoor National Park owns a stretch of the River Dart and thus has long been popular with fishermen. The Bromages have run this hotel for over 20 years and in that time have built up a reliable reputation for their friendly hospitality. Sweeping lawns, stunning views and the outstanding location in the wooded folds of the Dart Valley leave little else to be desired, except of course good food, and that's available too. The kitchen uses vegetables from the hotel's own walled garden, meat from local suppliers and fresh fish from Brixham, all of which are combined in daily menus to create a style of cooking which shows flair and imagination. Start perhaps with chilled smoked salmon soufflé or a warm salad of soft roes. Move on to baked pork in pastry, roast rack of Devon lamb, Provençal fish stew, three-offal casserole or rib steak bordelaise—the choice is extensive. Finish with orange and lemon soufflé, gin and lime sorbet or gooseberry franzipane. Well-thought-out fixed-price menus offer three choices for each course. Good breakfasts, and an international wine list with lots of half-bottles.

ASHFORD   Eastwell Manor

Eastwell Park, Boughton Aluph, Ashford, Kent, TN25 4HR
Tel: (01233) 635751   *Fax:* (01233) 635530   **£55**
Open: lunch & dinner daily
Meals served: lunch 12.30-2, dinner 7-9.30
    (Fri & Sat to 10)

Current Mediterranean cooking trends have reached this comfortable and well-furnished 23-bedroomed Jacobean manor house, where chef Ian Mansfield cooks with skill. Look forward to dishes such as ravioli of crab and ginger with a cardamom-scented jus and beef fillet with garlic confit, mushrooms and red wine sauce, alongside the likes of braised spiced shin of veal with fennel and carrots, turbot en feuilleté with champagne sauce or roast monkfish with cumin, aubergine caviar and a red pepper jus. The hotel is set in 62 acres of landscaped gardens and parkland amid the North Kent Downs. The Manor has a history of royal connections: Queen Victoria and Edward VII visited regularly; Prince Alfred and his wife lived here.

ASHINGTON   The Willows

London Road, Ashington, West Sussex, RH20 3JR
Tel: (01903) 892575   **£45**
Open: lunch Tue-Fri & Sun, dinner Tue-Sat
Meals served: lunch 12-2, dinner 7-10

Old black beams and an inglenook fireplace feature in this 15th-century farmhouse, now a 25-seater restaurant run by Julie and Carl Illes. Carl offers an extensive à la carte as well as fixed-price lunch and dinner menus, and his repertoire is eclectic. Home-made cheese and spinach gnocchi, smoked salmon cornets filled with fresh prawns in a Marie Rose sauce, crispy roast duck with sage and onion stuffing and apple sauce, pan-fried calf's liver with grilled bacon, and medallions of monkfish and scallops with fresh noodles and a tomato coulis are all typical. Separate vegetarian menu. Good desserts including a speciality house ice cream—vanilla, caramel and dark chocolate laced with Amaretto, Strega and Galliano, finished with whipped cream and frosted nuts.

ASPLEY GUISE   **Moore Place**

The Square, Aspley Guise, Nr Woburn, Bedfordshire, MK17 8DW
Tel: (01908) 282000   *Fax:* (01908) 281888   **£50**
Open: lunch Sun-Fri, dinner daily
Meals served: lunch 12.30-2.30, dinner 7.30-9.45
A handsome, 54-bedroomed Georgian country house in the village square. Relaxed,
informal, club-like atmosphere.

ASTON CLINTON   Bell Inn

London Road, Aston Clinton, Buckinghamshire, HP22 5HP
Tel: (01296) 630252   *Fax:* (01296) 631250   **£60**
Open: lunch & dinner daily
Meals served: lunch 12.00-1.45 (Sun to 2.15),   🦚
    dinner 7.00-9.45

This 21-bedroomed 17th-century coaching inn has been in the hands of
the Harris family since 1978. It is a homely place, with log fires and
fresh flower arrangements around the house. New chef Giles
Stonehouse has worked in the kitchens of Le Beau Rivage (Nice) and
at Le Moulin des Mougins with Roger Vergé. Start with the seven
Aylesbury duck delicacies—the duck is bred especially for them and is
the house speciality. Other alternatives might include a fricassée of
woodland mushrooms with sorrel and Vermouth sauce or rich duck
consommé with port and foie gras ravioli, followed by steamed turbot
with lemon butter sauce or a dodine of duck with cep mushrooms. The
Bell Bistro offers a wide choice and more informal setting. Wonderful
breakfasts. Fifteen of the rooms are set around a cobbled former brewery courtyard and those on the ground floor have direct access to the
gardens. Conference facilities available in a purpose-built centre just
across the road.

AUSTWICK   The Traddock

Austwick, Nr Settle, North Yorkshire, LA2 8BY
Tel & Fax: (015242) 51224   **£40**
Open: lunch & dinner daily
Meals served: lunch 12-2, dinner 7-9

Eleven-bedroomed Georgian hotel in an unspoilt Dales village. Good,
hearty breakfasts with free-range eggs and local farm sausages and an
extensive bar menu. This is good homely cooking, served in the pretty,
beamed dining room. Who could resist spotted dick with double cream
custard after some good roast lamb served with an unusual minted
pear?

AVEBURY   Stones Restaurant

Avebury, Nr Marlborough, Wiltshire, SN8 1RF
Tel: (0167 23) 514   **£20**
Open: all day daily (closed Xmas, Jan, Mon-Fri Nov-Mar)
Meals served: 10-6 (lunch 12-2.30)

A wide range of home-made vegetarian dishes features in this self-
service restaurant set in a stone farmhouse building, endorsing the
back-to-nature feeling created by the ancient monuments around
Avebury. Home-baked bread is offered along with organic ales and
wines. The Stones' cream tea with Cornish clotted cream shouldn't be
missed.

AYLESBURY   Hartwell House

Oxford Road, Aylesbury, Buckinghamshire, HP17 8NL
Tel: (01296) 747444   *Fax:* (01296) 747450   **£85**
Open: lunch & dinner daily
Meals served: lunch 12.30-2, dinner 7.30-9.45

Louis XVI spent five years in exile at Hartwell and it was here that he signed his accession papers on returning to his rightful throne. One of England's great stately homes, this Grade I listed house is set in splendid landscaped gardens. Architecturally, it is a gold-mine: Baroque-style Great Hall; Rococo morning room; exquisite Doric dining room;

Gothic hall and staircase with Jacobean carved figures leading up to the bedrooms and suites. The gardens and grounds were laid out by a student of Capability Brown and include a trout-stocked lake, picturesque stone bridge, ruined church and many 18th-century sculptures. Some of the rooms in the main house enjoy access to a sheltered roof garden, and there are 47 bedrooms in all. Even the elegant Spa centre has its own bar and buttery! The kitchen, under head chef Alan Maw, pictured, uses Highgrove lamb and beef in an English repertoire. Expect dishes such as a warm salad of sweetbreads with hazelnut vinaigrette, or saffron-flavoured seafood minestrone, followed by whole sea bass en croute with lime and ginger cream sauce, fillet of beef with potato galette and shallot sauce, or poached corn-fed chicken in champagne cream with truffle-flavoured risotto. Lovely puds to finish. Simpler palates can choose the likes of Dover sole or plain-grilled steak. Richard Broyd and Historic House Hotels really deserve much praise for their careful and sensitive conversion of houses such as this.

BAGSHOT   Pennyhill Park

London Road, Bagshot, Surrey, GU19 5ET
Tel: (01276) 471774   *Fax:* (01276) 473217   **£60**
Open: lunch & dinner daily
Meals served: lunch 12-2.30, dinner 7.30-10.30
Beautiful 19th-century house and country club with 76 bedrooms. Golf (9-hole), riding and fishing on hotel's own trout lake. Good leisure and health facilities. British/French cuisine.

BALLASALLA   La Rosette

Main Road, Ballasalla, Isle of Man
Tel: (01624) 822940   **£40**
Open: lunch & dinner Mon-Sat (closed 25 & 26 Dec, 2 wks Jan)
Meals served: lunch 12-3, dinner 7-10

A French-style restaurant five minutes' drive from the airport. Private
rooms and alcoves provide an intimate setting for simple classic cooking, with local seafood and straightforward meat dishes on a continental repertoire. From turbot, brill, halibut, salmon, plaice, sole, scallops,
and lobster the range extends to dishes such as sautéed lamb cutlets
with red wine sauce. The Café Bistro offers similar fare with less
choice on a three-course dinner menu for £16.

BARHAM   Old Coach House

Dover Road, Barham, Nr Canterbury, Kent, CT4 6SA
Tel: (01227) 831218   *Fax:* (01227) 831932   **£35**
Open: dinner Mon-Sat (closed 25 Dec, 1 Jan)
Meals served: dinner 7.30-9.30

Jean-Claude and Angela Rozard run this former coaching inn, set back
off the A2 Canterbury to Dover Road, very much along the lines of a
friendly and informal French auberge. There's a warm welcome, comfortable accommodation in six en-suite bedrooms and good French
home cooking. Local game in season, fresh fish (turbot, sea bass,
Dover sole) and seafood (grilled lobster, cocktail of crab) are regular
features on Jean-Claude's fixed-price dinner menu which is supplemented by daily blackboard specials. His cooking is planned around
traditional and regional classic favourites, including the likes of boned
chicken bordelaise, trout with almonds, steak au poivre and lamb with
herbs of Provence. Lunches by arrangement.

*Far better to stay here en route to France than closer
to the Channel ports*

BARNARD GATE   The Boot Inn

Barnard Gate, Nr Witney, Oxfordshire, OX8 6AE
Tel: 01865 881231   *Fax:* 01865 881834   **£45**
Open: lunch & dinner daily
Meals served: lunch 12-2.30, dinner 6.30-10
   (light meals in bar 11-11)

George Dailey's friendly pub situated between Witney and Eynsham
just off the A40 towards Oxford has quickly built up a reputation for a
good atmosphere and inventive food. Soup of the day comes with
crusty bread, cold poached salmon with lemon mayonnaise, potatoes
and salad, a whole leg of Lunesdale duck is stuffed with a duxelle of
ham, parsley and mushrooms and served with a spicy apricot sauce
and rösti potatoes—no ordinary pub grub, this! Thoughtfully chosen,
concise wine list. Deservedly popular, so booking is advised.

BARNSLEY   Armstrongs

6 Shambles Street, Barnsley, South Yorkshire, S70 2SQ
Tel: (01226) 240113   **£45**
Open: lunch Tue-Fri, dinner Tue-Sat (closed Bank Holidays)
Meals served: lunch 12-2, dinner 7-10

Nicholas Pound's split-level restaurant opposite the Town Hall began
life (as the sign outside says) as a café-bar, but things have certainly
moved on since those early days. Inside, the decor is very simple, the
food slightly less so; Nicholas cooks in confident and highly imaginative fashion but without gimmicks. Dinner offers plenty of choice à la
carte, starting with dishes such as salad of melted cheese and toasted
brioche or fishcakes with a parmesan crust served with a lemon caper
sauce. Main courses might include fillet of beef with a piquant herb
and garlic sauce, or thick cod fillets in oatmeal with parsnip and saffron
broth. Good desserts, well planned and varied. The lunch-time carte
offers more of the same, along with a choice of lighter dishes, such as
omelette with mushrooms and blue cheese sauce. Early evening diners
may take advantage of the set menu available from 7-8pm.

BARNSLEY   Restaurant Peano

102 Dodworth Road, Barnsley, South Yorkshire, S70 6HL
Tel: (01226) 244990   **£35**
Open: lunch Tue-Fri, dinner Tue-Sat (closed 1 wk Jul, 1 wk Jan)
Meals served: lunch 12-1.30, dinner 7-9.30

At this bright, 40-seater restaurant Tracey Peano manages front-of-
house while husband Michael toils away in the kitchen producing
finely executed dishes of French and Italian inspiration. Pan-fried saddle of English lamb topped with a herb crust and served on white
beans with tarragon sauce, or roast guinea fowl breast with a guinea
fowl-pistachio sausage are typical main courses. Desserts continue the
French and Italian theme with dishes like rich lemon tart and crème
brûlée with rum and raisin parfait. The table d'hôte menu offers
slightly simpler dishes.

BARNSTAPLE   Lynwood House

Bishop's Tawton Road, Barnstaple, Devon, EX32 9DZ
Tel: (01271) 43695   *Fax:* (01271) 79340   **£45**
Open: lunch & dinner Mon-Sat   ✿
Meals served: lunch 12-2, dinner 7-10

Lynwood House has been home to the Roberts family for over 20
years, an elegant, spacious Victorian house run more as a restaurant
with rooms than as a hotel. Ruth Roberts and her son Matthew take
charge of the kitchen while husband John and son Christian look after
front of house. Seafood is the speciality, with home-made chunky fish
soup, crab pancakes, grilled Dover sole, fresh local skate and seafood
pot among the offerings. But if meat it must be, then there's the likes of
roast, crispy local duckling or pan-fried steak with tomato, mushrooms
and red wine. The lighter lunchtime menu offers similar fare, if a little
more traditional—coq au vin, loin of pork with apple and cider sauce.
There are five rooms for overnight guests.

*The type of family-run establishment you see often in France, but
sadly, rarely in Britain*

BASINGSTOKE — Audleys Wood

Alton Road, Basingstoke, Hampshire, RG25 2JT
Tel: (01256) 817555   *Fax:* (01256) 817500   **£55**
Open: lunch Sun-Fri, dinner daily (closed Bank Holidays)
Meals served: lunch 12-1.45 (Sun from 12.30),
    dinner 7-9.45 (Sun to 9.15)

Set in seven acres of lightly wooded parkland, this Victorian country house hotel is conveniently located just off the M3 motorway. The main house, with its ornate carved oak features, magnificent fireplaces and minstrels' gallery, provides the setting for the best of the hotel's 71 luxuriously appointed rooms overlooking the estate. Local writers like Jane Austen and Charles Kingsley are commemorated by plaques on doors and bedside books, and a blazing log fire dominates the lounge in winter. The restaurant, in what was originally the palm house and conservatory, is striking, with its unusual vaulted wood ceiling and pretty floral decor. Ex-QE2 chef Terence Greenhouse offers table d'hote and à la carte menus, which include grand-sounding dishes like twice-baked Swiss cheese soufflé and turban of sole with a castle of courgette and scallops, or the more traditional, old-fashioned steak and oyster pudding. Exotic desserts include Hampshire treacle tart set on a thick crème anglaise with sweet maple syrup ice cream. Good French and English cheeses and an extensive, international wine list.

BASLOW — Cavendish Hotel

Baslow, Derbyshire, DE45 1SP
Tel: (01246) 582311   *Fax:* (01246) 582312   **£60**
Open: lunch & dinner daily
Meals served: lunch 12.30-2, dinner 7-10 (light meals 11-11)

Eric Marsh and his team work hard to make your stay pleasant at this 24-bedroomed hotel on the Chatsworth estate in the heart of the Peak District. The hotel's long tradition of hospitality stretches back more than 200 years, though things have moved on apace since then with well-appointed bedrooms boasting antique four-posters and every modern comfort. Dine in style in the restaurant or go for the informal Garden Room with its lovely views: here, informal meals are served throughout the day. Nick Buckingham produces a varied range of imaginative and carefully constructed dishes: soused mackerel with mild chilies, red sea bream and celery, and venison casserole are typical of the table d'hôte, which is supplemented by a carte of classic favourites including the likes of fresh Cornish oysters, local sea scallops and scampi, kiln-smoked tarragon salmon, foie gras, tournedos Rossini, and double-baked asparagus soufflé. Super selection of farmhouse cheeses with a number of award-winning varieties.

BASLOW	Fischer's Baslow Hall

Calver Road, Baslow, Derbyshire, DE4 1RR
Tel: (01246) 583259   *Fax:* (01246) 583818   **£80**
Open: lunch & dinner daily (closed 25 & 26 Dec)
Meals served: lunch 12-2, dinner 7-9.30,
   (light meals Café Max: 10-10, closed D Sun)

Susan and Max Fischer run this impressive Edwardian, Derbyshire-stone manor in the Peak National Park with pride and commitment. The six bedrooms are individually furnished to a high degree of comfort and character. The restaurant, made up of three separate dining rooms, is an ideal setting for Max's superb repertoire of classic French and modern European dishes, with Oriental and Mediterranean influences also playing a part. Favourite fish preparations are tender scallops with saffron or fillet of sea bass with tomato and root ginger. Other specialities include fricassée of rabbit in mustard sauce and pan-fried zander on a bed of lentils, game in autumn/winter and the finest English lamb in spring and summer. Max uses only the very best of fresh produce, much of it local, and the emphasis is on clarity of taste. Outstanding desserts such as a gratin of spring rhubarb with stuffed prunes and vanilla ice cream provide a breathtaking finale to the whole event. The menus change regularly but whenever your visit expect a feast. Excellent service is unobtrusive. Lighter meals and snacks are available in Café Max, where more traditional dishes such as bangers and mash, liver and bacon or Fischer's home-made fishcakes are on offer.

BASSENTHWAITE	Armathwaite Hall

Bassenthwaite Lake, Nr Keswick, Cumbria, CA12 4RE
Tel: (0176 87) 76551   *Fax:* (0176 87) 76220   **£65**
Open: lunch & dinner daily
Meals served: lunch 12.30-1.45, dinner 7.30-9.30

Bassenthwaite Lake and Skiddaw Mountain form a dramatic backdrop to this 42-bedroomed hotel, situated within secluded deer park and woodland on the very shores of the lake. The hall dates back to 1650, and the house, with its stately home feel, remains faithful to those origins. Bedrooms are spacious, whether you're in the main house or in the converted coach house and stable block. There are also great views of the lake from the restaurant—just the job perhaps to soothe those aching muscles after a day's hacking from the hotel's equestrian centre. Good leisure facilities and a new animal farm park make this a popular place for families. Good roasts from the trolley are among the five main courses on the four-course menu.

BASSENTHWAITE LAKE   Pheasant Inn

Bassenthwaite Lake, Nr Cockermouth, Cumbria, CA13 9YE
Tel: (0176 87) 76234   *Fax:* (0176 87) 76002   **£45**
Open: lunch & dinner daily (closed 24 & 25 Dec)   ✣
Meals served: lunch 12.30-2, dinner 7-8.30

You'll not be disappointed if you come here seeking your dream of a
typical English inn. Open fires, beams hung with brasses, old prints
and antique firearms and a cosy snug bar with tobacco-brown walls and
oak settles... this is the Pheasant, a 400-year-old farm which was converted into a roadside inn in the early 19th century. Mr and Mrs
Barrington Wilson have been running it since the late '60s, long
enough to have built up a sound reputation and regular clientele. There
are 20 bedrooms, all light, cheerful and tastefully furnished. There are
no phones or TV in the rooms, nor piped music or fruit machines in the
reception rooms. There are three lounges for residents, two with log
fires, one non-smoking. Excellent light lunches are served in the
lounge (originally the farm kitchen) or in the garden; dinner is a three-
course affair which offers a cold buffet option. This is traditional
English home cooking. Good hearty breakfasts offer everything from
Rice Krispies to Arbroath smokies with poached egg or the full works
with Cumberland sausage, black pudding and plenty more.

BATH   Bath Spa Hotel

Sydney Road, Bath, Avon, BA2 6JF
Tel: (01225) 444424   *Fax:* (01225) 444006   **£80**
Open: lunch Sun, dinner daily
Meals served: lunch 12.30-2, dinner 7-10
   (Sat to 10.30), (light meals Alfresco: 10-10, £45)

A superbly run hotel housed in a splendid Georgian mansion amongst
landscaped gardens with fine views of the city. The hotel offers impeccable rooms and suites and, as you would expect, there's a swimming
pool, gym, sauna, solarium, tennis and just about anything else that you

could wish for. Jonathan Fraser, pictured, offers you
some fine cooking in either the Alfresco Collonade
where you can enjoy styles that incorporate the Far
East, the Mediterranean and Old England—dishes
like tiger prawns and won ton soup, salmon and
pepper rösti cake with coriander and sour cream or
eggs in cocotte Florentine. Main courses might be
crispy duck teriyaki with spring vegetables and rice,
rich man's cod and chips, a balti lamb curry with
cumin and almonds or simple home-made linguini.
Puddings like squidgy toffee pudding, Cadbury's
chocolate burger or hot lemon pudding with clotted
cream explain why the gymnasium was installed! In the Vellore restaurant, mixed influences are again evident: field mushroom and herb
broth, black ravioli of shellfish with herb sauce, wok-fried scallops with
ginger and lime or saddle of venison with mulled pears, celeriac and
almonds. The wine list leaves nothing to be desired, except a friendly
bank manager: '61 Lafite is £565, '76 Yquem £400—but don't panic,
house wines are just £17.50. Vegetarians have a well-balanced menu
and kids will love dishes such as Treasure Island (2 poached eggs on
toast), Turtle Pizzas or Captain Pugwash's Supper (fish and chips).

BATH — Clos du Roy

1 Seven Dials, Saw Close, Bath, Avon, BA1 1EN
Tel: (01225) 444450 **£50**
Open: lunch & dinner
Meals served: lunch 12-2.30, dinner 6-11.30

The new Seven Dials centre next to the Theatre Royal in the heart of Bath provides a stunning setting for master chef Philippe Roy's latest venture, and for his return to the city in which he first gained his excellent reputation. The restaurant is unique: a spacious, curved dining room with elegant, modern decor, opening out on to a balcony. Rooted in the best traditions of French cuisine, Philippe's repertoire has been expanded over the years to include more robust and earthy dishes. Typical starters include smoked haddock and lentil soup, a salad of pigeon breast with a pepper confit and raspberry vinegar sauce, and a timbale of smoked chicken with a walnut dressing. Main courses include such dishes as pot-roast pheasant with a honey and chili sauce, steamed fillet of brill with fennel served with a green peppercorn sauce, and salmon à la nage with Noilly Prat. Make sure you leave room for a dessert though: fresh fruit gratin with a Cointreau sabayon, or iced nougat parfait served with a fresh fruit coulis. Excellent farmhouse cheeses and a commendable choice of wines, with good-value house wines. The aim here is to produce wonderful, imaginative food at dramatically affordable prices—there's never been a better time to sample Philippe Roy's cooking.

■ Philippe and Emma Roy

Watch the team at work through the large window into the kitchen.

Biography

Philippe Roy

Philippe Roy grew up on a farm near Poitiers in France. After catering school in Poitiers he cooked at Le Relais du Médoc in Bordeaux, then at the Hilton Hotel in Stratford-upon-Avon, before returning to France and the Moulin du Vey in Normandy. In 1982 he came back to London to Ménage à Trois, before moving to Bath in 1983. He moved his restaurant outside the city (to Box) and added rooms in the 1980s, but has now returned to the city he regards as a second home where he continues to delight his loyal following.

BATH   Garlands

7 Edgar Buildings, George Street, Bath, Avon, BA1 2EE
Tel: (01225) 442283   **£45**
Open: lunch & dinner Tue-Sun (closed 25 & 26 Dec)
Meals served: lunch 12-2.15, dinner 7-10.30

A relaxed 40-seater restaurant run with dedication by husband-and-wife team Tom and Jo Bridgeman. Tom's French and English-inspired cuisine includes dishes such as ragoût of shellfish with lime and coriander or Cornish fish cakes with béarnaise sauce to start; followed by main-course dishes such as cutlet of Scotch salmon with a Thai-style crust or breast of Gressingham duck with crème de cassis and oranges. Fish specials depend on market availability. Traditional desserts to finish. The café-bar behind the restaurant continues to serve quick and inexpensive meals. Typical items on offer there include kedgeree with fromage frais, rump steak and chips and king prawns with aiöli. Friday night has become a big event, with a five-course gourmet dinner, for just £15—a snip! Some seats in the courtyard for the summer.

BATH   Hole in the Wall

16 George Street, Bath, Avon, BA1 2EN
Tel: (01225) 25242   **£45**
Open: lunch & dinner Mon-Sat (closed Bank Holiday Mon)
Meals served: lunch 12-2.30, dinner 6-11

A venerable eating place in its heyday (the '50s and '60s), the Hole in the Wall is back, though this time the entrance is from an upper pavement level, leading into the main restaurant decked out with banquettes and polished tables. The kitchen has been moved further back, thus creating a second room. New chef Adrian Walton's repertoire is a combination of his, owner Chris Chown's and original owner George Perry-Smith's ideas. Starters (all at £4.50) run from home-made soup to brandade; main courses (at £11) offer plenty of variety too, from skate in black butter or brill baked in a herb crust to cassoulet, ox kidney and stout pudding or char-grilled beef with roast onions. Try barabrith-and-butter pudding with whisky ice cream for dessert (all are £4). The business lunch menu guarantees a service time of 50 minutes.

BATH

CAFE IGUANA

~~The New Moon~~

Seven Dials, Sawclose, Bath, Avon, BA1 1ES
Tel: (01225) 444407 £40
Open: all day daily (closed 25 & 26 Dec, 1 Jan)
Meals served: 9am-11pm (Sun to 10.30pm)

A smart, modern brasserie in the new courtyard development near the
Theatre Royal. The day starts with continental breakfast and moves on
to lunch, with the likes of onion tart, bollito misto, seafood pasta and
Toulouse sausages with shallot and peppercorn sauce on offer. Dinner
brings similar and more sophisticated dishes on line: crostini of grilled
Mediterranean vegetables, rump of lamb on char-grilled polenta with
sautéed shallots and sun-dried tomatoes; grilled salmon with red wine
sauce; fricassée of chicken with fennel, lemon and rosemary. Typical
desserts include rice pudding with vanilla sauce and fruit crumble with
crème fraîche. There are excellent-value set menus: Lunch for a Fiver
and Dinner for a Tenner. Short but varied wine list, or bring your own
except on Friday and Saturday nights.

BATH   Priory Hotel

Weston Road, Bath, Avon, BA1 2XT
Tel: (01225) 331922   *Fax:* (01225) 448276 £75
Open: lunch & dinner daily
Meals served: lunch 12-1.45, dinner 7-9.15

This Bath stone priory near the centre of the beautiful Georgian city is
a most civilised retreat from which to explore local places of interest.
Bedrooms are very comfortable with spacious sitting areas in the
deluxe rooms. Three dining rooms keep chef Michael Collom busy in
producing his stylish French menus, you might find smoked mackerel
salad with a dill vinaigrette dressing or asparagus soup with toasted
croutons to start, followed by grilled escalope of salmon with a chive
and anchovy butter with apple strudel with cinnamon ice cream to
finish.

BATH   Queensberry Hotel

Russel Street, Bath, Avon, BA1 2QT
Tel: (01225) 447928   *Fax:* (01225) 446065   **£45**
Open: lunch & dinner Mon-Sat (closed 1 wk Xmas)
Meals served: lunch 12-2, dinner 7-10

The Queensberry is a rather special oasis set in heart of Georgian Bath, a short walk from its architect John Wood's other, more celebrated achievements—the Royal Crescent, the Circus and the Assembly Rooms. Luxurious, stylish, decorative and intimate, Penny and Stephen Ross's privately-owned town house hotel, built in 1772, is located in a quiet residential street to the north of the town centre. Lovely, spacious bedrooms (bathrooms too) have deep comfortable seating and quality extras. The Olive Tree restaurant is a bright and airy room, full of cool sophistication, a good match for Stephen's con-

temporary English/French, bistro-inspired menus. Choose between the no-choice fixed-price lunch or dinner or the short à la carte. Tiger prawn, crab and couscous salad, followed by roast cod with a herb and pine nut crust, and a soft meringue roulade with fruits and raspberry sauce typify carte offerings. The elegant drawing room and cosy bar overlook a delightful secluded courtyard garden. Stephen is pictured with wife Penny.

Biography

Restaurants came into Stephen Ross's life at a fairly early age when his family bought the Cottage in the Wood Hotel at Malvern in 1965. Following an Economics degree at Bristol University, he moved on to
Stephen *stints at Thornbury Castle with Kenneth Bell; Popjoy's, Bath; and Homewood Park, Hinton Charterhouse, before*
Ross *acquiring the Queensberry Hotel and developing it into the successful establishment it is today. He first ran it without a restaurant but soon missed the stove, and is now delighted with the growing reputation of the Olive Tree restaurant within the hotel.*

BATH   Royal Crescent Hotel

16 Royal Crescent, Bath, Avon, BA1 2LS
Tel: (01225) 319090   *Fax:* (01225) 339401   739955   **£70**
Open: lunch & dinner daily
Meals served: lunch 12-2, dinner 7-9.30 (Fri & Sat to 10)

The luxurious Royal Crescent Hotel, at the centre of the crescent by the old magnolia tree, has no exterior signage as nothing is allowed to spoil the grand 500ft sweep of architect John Wood's masterpiece and rightly so: this is one of Europe's finest. Grand 18th-century elegance and luxury blend to perfection at this sophisticated hotel, which has 42

Biography

Steven Blake

Steven Blake started his apprenticeship with Trusthouse Forte, at the Hotel Russell then at Grosvenor House. He followed this with stints at The Piccadilly Hotel, and Le Talbooth, before taking up his role at the Royal Crescent. Steven believes that food should not be put into categories, and that any dish, done well, is good.

rooms and suites, all superbly fitted out in suitably elegant style, with half-testers or four-posters. This is where the Grand Old Duke of York of nursery rhyme fame (son of George III) lived during the late 18th century, along with other notables like the playwright Richard Brinsley Sheridan. The main hotel consists of the two central houses of the crescent, and within the grounds are the Pavilion and the magnificent Dower House, whose elaborate restaurant, with its gilded wall lights, marble busts and immaculate service, plays host to perhaps the greatest attribute of all, Steven Blake's exceptional culinary talent. Mixing tradition with modern, Steven delivers a theatrical repertoire of dishes which are as spectacular on the eye as they are on the palate. Minestrone of mussels with noodles scented with basil and tomato to start, followed perhaps by roast Lunesdale duckling with garlic croûtons, tomato and lardons of bacon and finish with baked chocolate cheesecake with a duo of sauces or a selection of British and Irish cheeses, complimented by delicious home-made walnut bread and biscuits. Interesting wine list with some reasonable prices.

BATH   Woods

9-13 Alfred Street, Bath, BA1 2QX
Tel: (01225) 314812   *Fax:* (01225) 443146   **£30**
Open: lunch daily, dinner Mon-Sat (closed 25 & 26 Dec)
Meals served: lunch 12-2.30, dinner 6.30-11

Woods is housed in a Georgian building next to the Assembly Rooms. Chef Kirk Vincent and his young team offer daily-changing menus in relaxed brasserie-style surroundings. The fixed-price dinner menu is exceptionally good value at only £10.95 for three courses, with the likes of turkey with a Tuscan bean sauce, pork casserole or poached fillet of cod served on a ratatouille sauce with mozzarella topping. Daily specials offer a wide choice, with around half a dozen options at each stage: grilled Derbyshire black pudding with shallot marmalade; Thai squid and Japanese-style pickled vegetables; roast quail with home-made boursin; and sirloin steak with a sun-dried tomato, basil and garlic butter. The lunch-time carte is simpler, with choices including bangers and mash or salmon and coriander fish cakes. Desserts, under the title of Cholesterol Corner, feature banoffi pie, sunken chocolate and prune soufflé and pear and butterscotch tart.

BATTLE — Netherfield Place

Battle, East Sussex, TN33 9PP
Tel: (01424) 774455   *Fax:* (01424) 774024   **£55**
Open: lunch & dinner daily (closed 21 Dec—10 Jan)
Meals served: lunch 12-2, dinner 7-9.30

A luxurious, 14-bedroomed, Georgian-style country retreat surrounded by 30 acres of garden and parkland. The kitchen is supplied with fresh fruit, vegetables and herbs picked daily from the walled garden. Well-balanced menus offer a modern British style of cooking: whole roasted quail filled with a light chicken mousse, served with a redcurrant and grape sauce; a trio of vegetable ravioli on a delicate cream sauce infused with basil; griddled medallions of venison on a rich port sauce with apple tart; and steamed supreme of halibut with a prawn and watercress sauce typify the range across à la carte and fixed-price menus. Good puds. Buffet Sunday lunches feature local seasonal fish, roast beef, pork or chicken with a bread sauce, plus the likes of individual steak puddings. Separate vegetarian menus offer ample choice. A haven of peace and tranquillity in a grand setting.

BEANACRE — Beechfield House

Beanacre, Nr Melksham, Wiltshire, SN12 7PU
Tel: (01225) 703700   *Fax:* (01225) 790118   **£65**
Open: lunch & dinner daily
Meals served: lunch 12-2, dinner 7-9.30

An elegant example of the ornate architectural style of the Victorian era. The Bathstone house is set in eight acres of mature garden with specimen trees and the 24 bedrooms are named after them. Sixteen of the bedrooms are in the main house, the remainder are in the adjacent coach house (linked to the main house by the orangery), and overlook the swimming pool. The restaurant, serving modern British cuisine, looks out on to a pretty walled garden which features a fountain. Fishing can be arranged on the River Avon which is only a few minutes walk from the hotel.

BEAULIEU — Montagu Arms

Beaulieu, New Forest, Hampshire, SO42 7ZL
Tel: (01590) 612324   *Fax:* (01590) 612188   **£55**
Open: lunch & dinner daily
Meals served: lunch 12.30-2, dinner 7.30-9.30,
   (Fri & Sat 7.30-10)

Situated in the centre of this picturesque village at the head of Beaulieu River, this 24-bedroomed hotel with terraced gardens dates back to the 13th century. Oil paintings, antiques and burning log fires in winter create a homely feel. In the summer, you can relax in the garden in the shade of the old magnolia tree and enjoy a cream tea or quiet read. Enjoy the mix of traditional and modern cooking in the comfort of the conservatory dining room. The hotel also has a health club in the nearby village of Brockenhurst, a six-mile drive away through the forest.

BECKINGHAM — Black Swan

Hillside, Beckingham, Lincolnshire, LN5 0RF
Tel: (01636) 626474   **£50**
Open: lunch & dinner Tue-Sun (closed 25 & 26 Dec)
Meals served: lunch 12-2 for bookings only,
    dinner 7-10 (booking preferred)

The Black Swan is at its most popular on fine Sundays afternoons, when the riverside garden and old village pub atmosphere of this 17th-century coaching inn really come into their own. Situated on the banks of the River Witham, the restaurant enjoys a delightful setting for light summer lunches alfresco. The regular five-course, fixed-price menus offer a varied and interesting choice of English and continental dishes: seafood soup served with fish and tarragon quenelles; warm pigeon breast salad; raspberry sorbet as a trou normand; lemon sole gratin on a basil and tomato sauce; guinea fowl casserole in brown beer sauce with parsley dumplings; vegetable and cashew nut cutlet on a tomato vinaigrette. Lovely puds, with hot rum and raisin soufflé a speciality.

BERWICK — Funnwayt'mekalivin'

41 Bridge Street, Berwick-upon-Tweed, Northumberland,
    TD15 1ES
Tel: (01289) 308827   **£40**
Open: lunch daily, dinner Wed-Sat (closed 25 & 26 Dec, 1 Jan)
Meals served: lunch 11.30-2.30, dinner at 8

Says chef-patron Mrs Middlemiss: "Quality is our passion. Test us and see!". We did and there's really nothing funny about the way Elizabeth Middlemiss makes her living. This is a serious restaurant, with the best of intentions. Menus are short and straightforward: a carte at lunchtime, fixed-price in the evening. Dine on Stilton and leek soup, followed by Arbroath smokie mousse then beef bourguignon with parsnip and potato cake. Finish with dark chocolate pot and Lanark blue cheese. Other offerings might include pigeon and steak pie or wild venison braised with beetroot. The lunch-time carte is lighter, with options such as pizza, three-cheese flan and lasagne. Three letting bedrooms have now been added, providing comfortable overnight accommodation to fall in to after a hearty, satisfying dinner.

BIBURY   The Swan

Bibury, Gloucestershire, GL7 5NW
Tel: (01285) 740695   *Fax:* (01285) 740473   **£80**
Open: lunch Sun, dinner daily (closed 24 Dec-8 Jan)
Meals served: lunch 12.30-2, dinner 7.30-9.45

This is a gem of a place in a sleepy Cotswold village. The creeper-clad
exterior by the bridge is a picture postcard setting which belies the not-
so-traditional goings-on within. Here you'll find a stylish all-day
brasserie (Jankowski's, open 10am-10pm), alongside a grand, chande-
liered, damask-draped dining room. The reception area has an auto-
matic grand piano which plays in the evenings, while the lounge
features pale oak panelling, flagstone floor and a mural depicting the
hotel's transformation. The kitchen provides modern English and
French dishes to the dining room under the direction of new chef Guy
Bossom; while Jankowski's brasserie offers an extensive, cosmopolitan
à la carte of Mediterranean dishes and grills. The brasserie and bar
open on to the old stable courtyard with fountain. The 18 bedrooms are
furnished and serviced to high standard, the best having four-poster
beds, spa baths or a luxurious, old-fashioned tub. Alex Furtek and Liz
Hayles have totally made over this delightful hostelry on the north side
of the River Coln, where there has been an inn or hostelry almost since
records began.

BIGBURY-ON-SEA   Burgh Island Hotel

Burgh Island, Bigbury-on-Sea, Devon, TQ7 4AU
Tel: (01548) 810514   *Fax:* (01548) 810243   **£60**
Open: lunch & dinner daily (closed Mon-Fri Jan & Feb)
Meals served: lunch 12.30-2.30, dinner 7.30-9

Built in 1929 at the behest of a wealthy industrialist, this great, white,
Art Deco palace is a memorial to that era, and to the Jet Set of the '30s.
Agatha Christie stayed and based two of her books here; the Prince of
Wales brought Wallis Simpson here to escape the press; Mountbatten
and Noël Coward followed. It's steeped in history and stories: it was
once a notorious haunt for smugglers. The most famous, Tom Crocker,
is now said to haunt the ancient, 1336 Pilchard Inn, which is also
owned, like the hotel and island, by Tony and Bea Porter. At high tide,

the island is completely cut off from the
mainland and visitors have to be brought
over on the world's only giant sea tractor.
The hotel has 14 suites, all of which are
designed to fully exploit the island setting,
with magnificent sea views in every direction. Splendid lounges feature terrazzo
steps, an ornamental goldfish pond, and a
staircase flanked by jet black glass and pink
mirrors which leads to the magnificent ballroom where dinner is served. Fixed-price
menus offer lobster, crab and locally caught
fish during the summer; other options
might include Highland venison loin with
glazed turnips and parsnips in a red wine
shallot sauce. Exotic desserts and local
cheeses to finish.

BILBROUGH	Bilbrough Manor

Bilbrough, York, North Yorkshire, YO2 3PH
Tel: (01937) 834002   *Fax:* (01937) 834724   **£55**
Open: lunch & dinner daily (closed 24-30 Dec)
Meals served: lunch 12-2, dinner 7-9.30 (Sun to 9)

Located just outside York, this lovely old manor house is ideally suited for visitors to the city, the race course or to the beautiful dales and moors of Yorkshire. Colin and Sue Bell's 15-bedroomed historic house is comfortable and elegant with extensive gardens set amidst 100 acres of farm and woodland. A new chef joined in 1994 but the intention was that the tradition be continued of using fresh local ingredients to good effect.

BILLESLEY	Billesley Manor

Billesley, Alcester, Nr Stratford-upon-Avon, Warwickshire,
    B49 6NF
Tel: (01789) 400888   *Fax:* (01789) 764145   **£60**
Open: lunch & dinner daily
Meals served: lunch 12.30-2, dinner 7.30-9.30 (Fri & Sat to 10)

Follow in Shakespeare's footsteps—from all accounts he was a regular visitor to Billesley Manor and possibly wrote *As You Like It* here—it's just three miles from Stratford-upon-Avon. At this recently refurbished 16th-century manor house set in 11 acres of grounds which include a stunning topiary garden, old blends with new to good effect. Oak panelling throughout the hotel is the unifying theme. Bedrooms, like the lounges, are spacious and comfortable. From the 41 rooms, choose between traditional four-poster or sumptuously decorated modern ones. Mark Naylor's modern British/French cooking is sound. Simple traditional dishes such as grilled Dover sole or the day's roast share the seasonal à la carte menu with more inventive ones: pressed terrine of red mullet, monkfish and salmon; breast of Gressingham duck with a confit of the leg and sweet spice sauce; hot pineapple soufflé or chocolate and banana marquise to finish. Vegetarians have a separate menu. Good leisure facilities, which include a heated swimming pool, tennis, croquet and nearby fishing.

BILLINGSHURST	The Gables

Pulborough Road, Parkbrook, Billingshurst, Kent, RH14 9EU
Tel: (01403) 782571   **£40**
Open: lunch Tue-Fri & Sun, dinner Tue-Sat
    (closed 2 wks Jan/Feb)
Meals served: lunch 12.30-2, dinner 7.15-9 (Fri & Sat to 10)

Nicholas Illes follows in family footsteps at this timbered 15th-century restaurant south of town. Father Othmar is chef-patron of Cisswood House, Lower Beeding, and brother Carl has the same role at The Willows in Ashington. And they all help each other out, taking it in turns to make early morning runs around the London markets. Nicholas and partner Rebecca Gilroy, who runs front-of-house, offer a seasonal menu with plenty of choice and something to tempt everyone. Simple, straightforward dishes (plain grilled fillet steak, grilled or poached salmon, Dover sole Colbert) are featured alongside more adventurous and sophisticated dishes such as grilled baby poussin with creamed red pepper sauce or sautéed halibut fillets with salmon caviar and chive sauce.

BIRDLIP   Kingshead House

Birdlip, Nr Gloucester, Gloucestershire, GL4 8JH
Tel: (01452) 862299   **£50**
Open: lunch Tue-Fri & Sun, dinner Tue-Sat
    (closed 24-27 Dec, 1 Jan)
Meals served: lunch 12.30-1.45, dinner 7.30-9.45

The menu changes at least twice a week at this relaxed, informal country restaurant, a former coaching inn run by chef-patronne Judy Knock and husband Warren. Judy's fixed-price dinners and à la carte lunches, the latter served in the bar if you prefer, offer an imaginative repertoire of modern English and French dishes which always include a vegetarian option. Popular Sunday lunches and culinary evenings; plus taxi vouchers given to diners who wish to take full advantage of the splendid and affordable wine list! Alternatively, stay overnight (but there's only one delightful en-suite bedroom).

BIRMINGHAM   Sloans

27 Chad Square, Hawthorne Road, Edgbaston, Birmingham,
    B15 3TQ
Tel: 021-455 6697   *Fax:* 021-454 4335   **£60**
Open: lunch Mon-Fri, dinner Mon-Sat
    (closed Bank Holidays, 1 wk from 25 Dec)
Meals served: lunch 12-2.15, dinner 7-10

At this smart, split-level, suburban restaurant in a shopping precinct, John Narbett has put time and trouble into offering affordable eating and a broader range of dishes. Chef Simon Booth offers a fixed-price lunchtime menu of two or three courses, such as soft poached eggs with spinach or cream of rabbit and mushroom soup followed by braised oxtail faggots or John Dory with fresh pasta and pesto sauce. The dinner carte offers wider choice along similar lines. Savoury French sausage with truffle and Madeira sauce, half a lobster with garlic butter and herbs, rib of beef bordelaise, breast of wood pigeon with glazed onion, parsnips and smoked bacon. Desserts might feature pear tart with Devon cream, apple crumble or a trio of sorbets on meringue base with sauce anglaise. John obviously has an eye for a winner judging on past form—not only his son, Roger, who after a stint here went on to the Dorchester and is now at The Lygon Arms, but also Idris Caldora, formerly at The Swallow in Birmingham and now at the Portman Churchill, London. Now Simon Booth is firmly in the frame.

BIRMINGHAM   Swallow Hotel

12 Hagley Road, Five Ways, Birmingham, West Midlands, B16 8SJ
Tel: 021-452 1144   *Fax:* 021-456 3442
Sir Edward Elgar: **£65**
Open: lunch Sun-Fri, dinner daily
Meals served: lunch 12.30-2.30, dinner 7.30-10.30 (Sun to 10)
Langtry's: **£50**
Open: lunch & dinner Mon-Sat (closed Bank Holidays)
Meals served: lunch 11.30-2.30, dinner 6.30-10.30

Birmingham's first five-star hotel set in the heart of the city's commercial centre, is an oasis of luxury and elegance combined with the comforts you might expect of a modern hotel, though the original building is of imposing Edwardian proportions. Italian marble, polished mahogany and crystal chandeliers create a magnificent first impression in the foyer. The drawing room and library are no less impressive, both providing a quiet retreat in which to enjoy a newspaper or browse through a book, while 98 bedrooms offer spacious, light accommodation. The main restaurant, the intimate, classic Sir Edward Elgar room, echoes the city's importance for the Midlands-born composer, whose greatest choral pieces had their first performance in Birmingham at the turn of the century. The room is luxurious, with striking hand-painted trompe l'oeil murals and a pianist playing six nights a week. In addition to the à la carte and table d'hôte menus, there is a special £25 post-theatre supper menu available by prior arrangement. Jonathan Harrison's menu has modern flavours with well-chosen combinations: tomato risotto with chanterelles, lobster and monkfish salad with spring onion and ginger dressing, pot-roast lamb with ratatouille, roast duck with baby onions, lardons of bacon and green lentils. The wine list is strongest in the French section with token selections from other countries. In a setting reminiscent of an Edwardian conservatory, Langtry's serves regional English cuisine, innovatively prepared. Cool greens and creams, Lloyd Loom chairs, Art Nouveau statuary and trellis work provide a cool, chic setting in which to sit down to spring chicken and leek soup, or roasted red pepper filled with ricotta and spinach. The menu offers a wide choice: plaice with a tomato and shell-fish sauce, Langtry's mixed grill, Malvern rabbit pot and traditional grilled fillet of beef. Traditional puds: baked rice pudding with jam, English trifle, rhubarb fool scented with honey.

BISHOP'S TAWTON   Halmpstone Manor

Bishop's Tawton, Barnstaple, Devon, EX32 0EA
Tel: (01271) 830321   *Fax:* (01271) 830826   **£45**
Open: lunch by arrangement, dinner daily (closed Jan)
Meals served: dinner 7-9

Unwind beside a crackling log fire in peaceful surroundings at this small 16th-century manor house, part of a working farm, with lovely views of the valley and rolling hills beyond. You are quickly made to feel at home by Jane and Charles Stanbury—he was born at the manor. Squashy sofas and romantic four-posters are offset by family memorabilia dotted about the place. Excellent breakfasts and inventive fixed-price four and five-course dinner menus are cooked by Jane. Relax in the panelled dining room to enjoy starters like smoked salmon roll or crab soufflé, followed by a champagne sorbet, then fillet of Devonshire beef with caramelised shallots or roasted fillet of monkfish with a grain mustard sauce. The cooking is English and French in style, with soufflés and game as specialities.

BLACKPOOL   September Brasserie

15-17 Queen Street, Blackpool, Lancashire, FY1 1PU
Tel: (01253) 23282   **£45**
Open: lunch & dinner Tue-Sat (closed 2 wks summer,
    2 wks winter)
Meals served: lunch 12-2, dinner 7-9.30

It was, indeed, a bold step for chef-patron Michael Golowicz to take. A stone's throw from the promenade, in a city not noted for its culinary appreciation, this first-floor brasserie above a hairdresser's shop was opened in 1989 right at the start of the recession. But it paid off. Michael is a dedicated chef with an impressive and varied background, from top London restaurants and clubs to the Sydney Opera House. His return to England brought him to Blackpool and within a year of opening, this talented and adaptable chef had put Blackpool on to the culinary map. The eclectic menu changes every month and is supplemented by daily blackboard specials. Organic produce is used whenever possible and a strictly organic wine list offers a wide choice of some 45 bins. A typical starter might be tripe cooked with calvados, cider, red lentils and fresh herbs, followed by beef fillet with shallot, thyme and a Shiraz jus. Finish with iced Grand Marnier soufflé on a nougatine and chocolate sauce or the likes of grapefruit and orange ramekin in a Côteaux de Layon jelly and passion fruit sorbet. The lunch-time carte is simpler, featuring dishes like seafood pancake with Gruyère or veal sausages with olive oil mash.

BLANDFORD FORUM   La Belle Alliance

Whitecliff Mill Street, Blandford Forum, Dorset, DT11 7BP
Tel: (01258) 452842   *Fax:* (01258) 480053   **£45**
Open: lunch by arrangement, dinner Tue-Sat
  (& Bank Holiday) (closed 2 wks Jan)
Meals served: dinner 7-10

Philip and Lauren Davison offer the interesting concept of either a
bistro or gourmet menu at their six-bedroomed house in this handsome
Georgian town. The style of cooking however is similar in both menus
with an additional course for the gourmets. Mussels in provençale
sauce are glazed with chervil hollandaise, or you could try a hot smoked
cheese soufflé or a terrine of mushrooms and garlic, then there's marinaded fillet of salmon with a basil sauce, fillets of brill with bacon,
spinach and white wine sauce or roast breasts of pigeon on lentils with
red wine sauce. Tempting puddings such as a hot raspberry sponge
with vanilla sauce, profiteroles of butterscotch cream with hot chocolate
sauce or pear tart with caramelised peach slices and chilled cider sauce.
The 60 or so wines provide good variety from around the World.

BOLLINGTON   Mauro's

88 Palmerston Street, Bollington, Nr Macclesfield,
  Cheshire, SK10 5PW
Tel: (01625) 573898   **£45**
Open: lunch & dinner Tue-Sat (closed 25 & 26 Dec,
  3 wks Aug/Sep)
Meals served: lunch 12-2, dinner 7-10

A friendly, neighbourhood Italian restaurant, recently extended with a
new bar. Fresh fish, shellfish, home-made pasta (in many different
guises) and home-made sweets are the specialities. The menu covers a
wide choice of traditional Italian favourites, with some bias towards
dishes from the North. Traditional antipasti and soups are followed by
the likes of gnocchi alla sorrentina or ravioli alla caprese (filled with
cheese and ham and topped with a tomato sauce). Market-fresh fish
accompanied by a sauce of your choice is available daily though fresh
lobster requires 48 hours' notice. Meat and veal are well represented
and the wine list is exclusively Italian.

BOLTON ABBEY   Devonshire Arms

Bolton Abbey, Nr Skipton, North Yorkshire, BD23 6AJ
Tel: (01756) 710441   *Fax:* (01756) 710564   **£65**
Open: lunch & dinner daily
Meals served: lunch 12-2, dinner 7-10, Sun 7-9.30

A traditional hotel on the Duke and Duchess of Devonshire's Bolton
Abbey estate. Handsome throughout, the hotel (a former coaching inn)
has been carefully restored under the personal supervision of the
Duchess and is furnished with paintings and antiques from Chatsworth,
their Derbyshire estate. Chef Gavin Beedham's blend of classical and
modern cooking results in an imaginative menu—marinated herrings in
lettuce parcel, layers of foie gras, mango and duck, followed by millefeuille of veal with air-dried ham and Gruyère, grilled Dover sole or
breast of Gressingham duckling served with plum sauce and hazelnut
dumplings. Most of the 40 bedrooms are in the main house.

BONCHURCH — Winterbourne Hotel

Bonchurch, Isle of Wight, PO38 1RQ
Tel: (01983) 852535   *Fax:* (01983) 853056   **£40**
Open: dinner daily (closed Nov-Feb)
Meals served: dinner 6.45-9 (later by arrangement)

Charles Dickens wrote most of David Copperfield here, from July to October, 1849. Images of Dickens are conjured up throughout the house and according to hearsay some of the book's characters were based on Bonchurch locals whom he met during the course of his stay. From all accounts he fell in love with house and grounds instantly—"I think it is the prettiest place I ever saw in my life, at home or abroad," he wrote to his wife, Kate. The most outstanding feature of this 17-bedroomed house is the garden, with extensive lawns, waterfalls, stream and sea views.

BOTLEY — Cobbett's

15 The Square, Botley, Southampton, Hampshire, SO3 2EA
Tel: (01489) 782068   **£55**
Open: lunch Tue-Fri, dinner Mon-Sat
   (closed Bank Holidays, 2 wks summer, 2 wks winter)
Meals served: lunch 12-2, dinner 7.30-10

Lucie Skipwith's cooking, based on the traditions of her native Bordeaux, finds a delightful English setting in this centuries-old, timber-framed building in the main street. Together with chef Giles Hester, Lucie offers a monthly-changing menu of French regional dishes, always with a choice of around three vegetarian options. The same menu is offered at lunch and dinner, with a choice of two or three courses. Typical dishes range from starters such as seafood risotto to main courses such as pan-fried sirloin flamed with brandy, served with a port wine sauce and Stilton butter. Read the slate in the bar for the daily fish dish. Desserts might include orange charlotte on a Cointreau-steeped orange syrup, but I would opt for the flaky pastry filled with apple and browned under the grill with a topping of nuts and cinnamon.

Good local restaurant with a loyal following.

BOUGHTON MONCHELSEA — Tanyard Hotel

Wierton Hill, Boughton Monchelsea, Nr Maidstone,
   Kent, ME17 4JJ
Tel: (01622) 744705   *Fax:* (01622) 741998   **£50**
Open: lunch Tue-Fri, dinner Tue-Sat (closed 2 wks Jan)
Meals served: lunch 12-2, dinner 7-9

An attractive medieval house with plenty of beams. Jan Davies is a friendly hostess who creates a house party atmosphere. Small menus are now available to non-residents as well as to guests at the hotel.

BOURNEMOUTH — Royal Bath Hotel

Bath Road, Bournemouth, Dorset, BH1 2EW
Tel: (01202) 555555   *Fax:* (01202) 554158   **£55**
Open: lunch & dinner daily
Meals served: lunch 12.30-2.15 (Garden: Sun only 12.30-2.15),
    dinner 7-10.15 (Garden: 7-9.15)

Victorian seaside hotel which relies heavily on the business and tourist market, but maintains the personal touch with friendly, courteous staff. The clifftop position is a big attraction, as is the magnificent Leisure Pavilion. The hotel has 131 rooms, many of which take advantage of the views, and there are two restaurants. Breakfast and a traditional menu in the evenings is available in the lovely Garden Restaurant, while Oscar's offers a more intimate setting amidst uncharacteristically discreet memorabilia of Oscar Wilde. Here, the food is of international style, with a bias towards France. With Wayne Asson at the stove, the results on the plate are well above average.

BOWNESS-ON-WINDERMERE — Gilpin Lodge

Crook Road, Bowness-on-Windermere, Cumbria, LA23 3NE
Tel: (0153 94) 88818   *Fax:* (0153 94) 88058   **£60**
Open: lunch & dinner daily
Meals served: lunch 12-2.30, dinner 7-8.45

Christine and David Cunliffe have turned their ancestral lakeland home into a comfortable nine-bedroomed hotel. Christine joins chef Christopher Davies in the kitchen while John looks after a lively front-of-house. Dinner is a five-course affair, relaxed and informal. Typical dishes include oyster and sage soup en croûte, chilled Roquefort mousse wrapped in air-dried Cumbrian ham, beef with cognac sauce, calf's liver with an onion confit and Guinness sauce, and medallions of monkfish and salmon with three pastas and three sweet pimento and Madeira sauces. Lunch-time offers a carte, except on Sundays.

BOWNESS-ON-WINDERMERE — Linthwaite House

Bowness-on-Windermere, Cumbria, LA23 3JA
Tel: (0153 94) 88600   *Fax:* (0153 94) 88601   **£70**
Open: lunch Sun, dinner daily
Meals served: lunch 12-1.30, dinner 7.15-8.45

It would be hard to find a more commanding view of the Lakes than the one enjoyed by Linthwaite, overlooking Lake Windermere. The hotel has 18 rooms, carefully designed by interior designer Amanda Rosa. There is a relaxed, casual atmosphere, which carries through to candlelit dinner in the dining room where Ian Bravey delights with dishes of modern British cooking. Quenelles of lemon sole and trout with a champagne and dill sauce, followed by Swiss cheese and potato soup is a fair example of how things might start. Main courses might feature creamy vegetable stroganoff with home-made buttered pasta, baked halibut topped with herb crumbs and presented on a tomato and tarragon coulis, or simply garnished tender fillet of Scottish beef cooked to your requirements. Good desserts and a spectacular range of British farmhouse cheeses: from hand-made Cooleney Camembert made in Moyne, Southern Ireland, to Somerset Brie and St Andrews from Howgate farm in Scotland. Less choice at lunchtime when the choice is lighter and served in the conservatory.

BRADFIELD COMBUST — Bradfield House

Bradfield Combust, Bury St Edmunds, Suffolk, IP30 0LR
Tel & Fax: (01284) 386301   **£40**
Open: dinner Tue-Sat
Meals served: dinner 7-9

Small, 17th-century hotel—four rooms only—and restaurant set in two
acres of English gardens, complete with old, protected trees, yew
hedgerows and kitchen gardens. The cooking is based on traditional
English fare, with rural French influences: fish soup bouillabaisse-style;
venison pie or fallow deer casserole topped with a shortcrust lid;
sautéed chicken breast on spinach and pea sauce; and beef Dijonnaise.
Antiques, parlour palms and old French wood-burning stoves create
character and charm throughout.

BRADFORD — Restaurant 19

19 North Park Road, Heaton, Bradford, West Yorkshire,
  BD9 4NT
Tel: (01274) 492559   *Fax:* (01274) 483827   **£60**
Open: dinner Mon-Sat
Meals served: dinner 7-9.30 (Sat to 10)   🏵

Messrs Smith and Barbour have now completed a decade at their
delightful restaurant in this city born of the industrial revolution. They,
too, were a revolution in pioneering fine cuisine in a gastronomic
wilderness some ten years ago. Stephen prepares four-course menus
with plenty of choice except for the fixed soup of the day. You might be
lucky to start with roast teal with onions, bacon, apple and croûtons, or
a pudding of chicken livers and mushrooms with a sun-dried tomato
sauce. An unusual carrot soup with coriander and saffron risotto to follow, and then choose roast partridge with chestnuts, red cabbage and
cider, steamed turbot with mussels and leeks, or fillet of pork stuffed
with wild mushrooms and stir-fried vegetables. For pudding a warm
treacle tart with vanilla custard or perhaps rhubarb jelly with pastry
cream and madeleines. Robert Barbour looks after the restaurant and
can advise on the excellent wines.

BRADFORD-ON-AVON — Leigh Park Hotel

Leigh Road West, Bradford-on-Avon, Wiltshire, BA15 2RA
Tel: (01225) 864855   *864885*   **£40**
Open: lunch & dinner daily
Meals served: lunch 12-2, dinner 7-9.30

The original house dating back to 1574 was a gift from Elizabeth I to
the Earl of Leicester. It has 22 bedrooms and five acres of grounds
which include a vineyard and walled garden. Fruit and vegetables are
thus home grown, and the cooking is predominantly English, with one
or two digressions towards France—main courses range from fruity
fowl (chicken with Cointreau and orange glaze) to prime beef steak
and French Barbary duck. The last 12 months have seen major refurbishment throughout, with bedrooms upgraded and redecoration in
the restaurant.

BRADFORD-ON-AVON   Woolley Grange

Woolley Green, Bradford-on-Avon, Wiltshire, BA15 1TX
Tel: (01225) 864705   *Fax:* (01225) 864059   865630.   **£65**
Open: lunch & dinner daily   *It all makes for a*
Meals served: lunch 12.15-2, dinner 7.15-10   *very good weekend.*

Woolley Grange is a Jacobean stone manor house built from mellow
Bath stone in the early 17th century by the Randolphs. A family home
for nearly 400 years, the house was in the hands of the Baskervilles for
almost two centuries, and it is doubtful that it has seen better days than
today. Current owners, the Chapmans are the most engaging of hosts,
with just the right amount of relaxed informality. Their principle concern is that the house be unstuffy in all aspects, and this they achieve.
The house is full of character: nooks and crannies, beams, antiques
and paintings, many of which were commissioned. It you're looking
for some sort of exercise, there's the Chapmans' collection of antique
bicycles, which include a '20s tandem, an Indian trishaw, a Moulton
and curiously a modern, pink-penny farthing! Chef Colin White is
establishing a sound reputation for himself here, with sophisticated
country-style cooking. Dishes such as wild mushroom risotto, saddle of
lamb stuffed with walnuts and rosemary, salt-baked black bream with
Thai spices, and chocolate tart with espresso sauce show the kind of
fare you might be offered. From noon to 10pm there's a more informal
menu served either in the conservatory or on the terrace. Good wine
list with some reasonable prices. It is also ideal for families, with the
old coach house converted into a large games room, complete with
nanny. The family livestock—house spaniel, cat and two pigs—go
down a treat with children. Lots of facilities, and a splendid view
towards the Salisbury Plain and White Horse at Westbury.

BRAITHWAITE   Ivy House

Braithwaite, Nr Keswick, Cumbria, CA12 5SY
Tel: (0176 87) 78338   **£40**
Open: dinner daily (closed Jan)
Meals served: dinner at 7.30

This small, elegant 17th-century house stands at the foot of the fells,
and is run with warm hospitality by Nick and Wendy Shill. Relax with a
book in front of the log fire after a long day's walk—the area is a
walker's paradise—before indulging in a candlelit supper in the handsome dining room where Wendy's five-course dinner might begin with
Thai pork saté or goujons of sole with tartare sauce, followed by local
trout with prawns and almonds or venison with a three berry sauce.
Neat and tidy bedrooms are furnished in traditional style with fine old
pieces and objets d'art. There is one suite with a four-poster.

BRAMLEY — Garden Restaurant

4a High Street, Bramley, Nr Guildford, Surrey, GU5 0HB
Tel: (01483) 894037 **£40**
Open: lunch Sat & Sun, dinner Fri & Sat (closed 2 wks Jan)
Meals served: lunch 12-3, dinner 7-9.30

This place recently changed its name from *Le Berger* but the owners remain the same. The fixed-price menu, available lunch and dinner, offers a choice of five starters and five main courses. Typical starters include mushroom gratin and duck and pistachio terrine. Main course selections might include monkfish kebab on a tomato concassé, pork with Calvados or steamed salmon with a wild mushroom sauce.

BRAMPTON — Farlam Hall

Hallbankgate, Brampton, Cumbria, CA8 2NG
Tel: (0169 77) 46234   Fax: (0169 77) 46683 **£65**
Open: dinner daily (lunch certain festive occasions)
     (closed 25-31 Dec)
Meals served: dinner 8-8.30

A former 17th-century farmhouse converted to a manor house in Victorian times, this charming country house hotel set in lovely grounds, complete with stream and ornamental lake, now offers 12 tastefully decorated, Victorian-style rooms, with modern, well-equipped bathrooms. Half-board terms include dinner served promptly at 8pm. Barry Quinion's four-course menu changes daily and offers three choices at each course. Typical starters might include courgette and rosemary soup, hot Arbroath smokies and hot seafood terrine. Typical main courses could be grilled fillet of lemon sole with banana and coconut and a sherry and cream sauce, or pan-fried medallions of beef on a potato and herb cake with a pink peppercorn, brandy and cream sauce. Desserts range from blackberry crème brûlée to rum and ginger mousse or grape and brandy trifle.

BRAY-ON-THAMES   The Waterside Inn

Ferry Road, Bray-on-Thames, Berkshire, SL6 2AT
Tel: (01628) 20691   Fax: (01628) 784710   **£130**
Open: lunch Wed-Sun, dinner Tue-Sun (Tue-Sat in winter)
    (closed Bank Holidays (open lunch 25 Dec), Xmas-Jan)
Meals served: lunch 12-1.30 (Sun 12-2.30), dinner 7-10

It's hard to think of a more delightful setting than her on the river at Bray where Michel Roux and his team, headed by chef Mark Dodson and restaurant manager Diego Masciaga, embody everything the name Roux stands for: consistency, professionalism and inspiration. Everyone who's anyone knows of the Waterside, of the beautiful peach-coloured dining room with its Thames-side terrace and riverside views. Not everyone knows that aperitifs and coffee can be taken in one of the summer houses or on the electric hotel launch, The Waterside Inn II, in fine weather. Or that the six bedrooms, each stunning, beautifully designed and only a staircase away, offer the same sense of blissful luxury and exclusivity which has become the hallmark of the restaurant itself. Alternatively, the River Cottage offers total sanctuary from the outside world, with its own drawing room, courtyard garden and kitchen, and unparalleled beauty of design. But it's for the food, first and foremost, that the culinary pilgrims flock to Bray. Discover the delights of exceptional dishes in a feast of small portions on the five-course menu exceptionnel, or on the à la carte which is always available, along with

fixed-price menu gastronomique at lunchtime and a seasonal dinner menu (October to Spring). Classic ingredients and time-honoured skills. Michel is of course a fabulous pâtissier: this is not somewhere not to have room for dessert! Outstanding wine list. Michel Roux was one of the first to reach the top of the gastronomes' tree in Great Britain and he's still there.

I can think of nothing better than arriving by boat on a summer's day, sipping a glass of Charles Heidsieck champagne.

Biography

Michel Roux

An articulate, many-sided character with opinions and exceptional talent, Michel Roux was born in Charolles, Saone et Loire. After his apprenticeship in pâtisserie, he then worked as commis pâtissier/cuisinier at the British Embassy, Paris, followed by work for such wealthy aristocrats as Mlle Cécile de Rothschild, the Bismarcks and the Schneiders. After this he came to England to join his brother Albert in starting Le Gavroche; followed by The Waterside Inn. Michel has won many international prizes and distinctions in pâtisserie and cuisine, and with his brother, is also well known for their best-selling cookery books and TV programmes. One of the most influential figures of the profession today.

BRIDPORT   Riverside Restaurant

West Bay, Bridport, Dorset, DT6 4EZ
Tel: (01308) 422011   **£35**
Open: lunch Tue-Sun, dinner Tue-Sat (& Bank Holiday Mon)
    (closed late Nov-early Mar)
Meals served: lunch 11.30-3 (Sat & Sun to 4), dinner 6.30-8.45
    (varies with season)

The key to success here lies in the simple preparation of fresher-than-fresh seafood and fish dishes and the setting on stilts. The regular menu features an extensive range: grilled red mullet, John Dory, Dover sole, plaice, lemon sole and sardines, along with scallops, local lobster, Abbotsbury oysters, squid, crab and mussels. There's a handful of grills and hot dishes—steak and chips, chili con carne—plus salads, omelettes, and more sophisticated daily specials such as hake provençale or black bream fillets with roquette herb crust. They also serve late breakfasts, snacks (egg and chips, hamburgers) and teas; and there is a patio for alfresco eating. A very good affordable selection of white wines. The restaurant overlooks the sea and river at West Bay. An unpretentious and friendly restaurant.

Well done the Watsons—long may they continue here!

BRIGHTLING   Jack Fuller's

Oxley's Green, Brightling, Nr Robertsbridge,
    East Sussex, TN32 5HD
Tel: (0142 482) 212   **£25**
Open: lunch Tue-Sun, dinner Tue-Sat
    (closed 25 Dec, dinner Bank Holidays, Tue & Wed Oct-Mar)
Meals served: lunch 12-3 (Sun to 4), dinner 7-11

A pub-turned-country restaurant offering traditional and regional British dishes, with the emphasis on main courses, vegetables and puds. Roger and Shirl Berman have created a cheerful restaurant which focuses on good, home, country cooking—an exciting repertoire of pies, puddings, casseroles and stews: gammon and onion pudding; beef stew and dumplings; chicken casserole; steak and kidney/mushroom pie or pudding; prawn and halibut pie; cauliflower crumble. Excellent, carefully prepared vegetable side dishes, followed by nursery puds which include vegetarian spotted dick. Beautiful gardens, with panoramic views.

BRIGHTON   Grand Hotel
King's Road, Brighton, East Sussex, BN1 2FW
Tel: (01273) 321188   *Fax:* (01273) 202694   **£65**
Open: lunch & dinner daily
Meals served: lunch 12-2, dinner 7-10
Right on the seafront, with 200 rooms; a grand luxury hotel with excellent leisure and conference facilities. Own health club and night club.

BRIGHTON   Le Grandgousier

15 Western Street, Brighton, BN1 2PG
Tel: (01273) 772005   **£35**
Open: lunch Sun-Fri, dinner Mon-Sat (closed 5 days Xmas)
Meals served: lunch 12.30-2, dinner 7.30-9.30

French country cooking in French country style. Not a place for romantic candlelit suppers: tables are for four and you may have to share, but
the excellent value food is the main event here. They have a well-
deserved reputation for straightforward, down-to-earth French dishes.
You can lunch on crudités, plat du jour and excellent, ripe brie for a
fiver.

BRIGHTON   Langan's Bistro

1 Paston Place, Brighton, East Sussex, BN2 1HA   *Good local bistro, the*
Tel: (01273) 606933   *best in Brighton* **£55**
Open: lunch Tue-Fri & Sun, dinner Tue-Sat
   (closed 26 Dec, 2 wks Jan, 2 wks Aug)
Meals served: lunch 12.30-2.15, dinner 7.30-10.15

The familiar Langan's style menu and chic, colourful decor of this
bistro near the marina make this one of the best restaurants in
Brighton, all thanks to Mark and Nicole Emmerson who have run the
place along Langan's house style lines since it opened six years ago.
The short menu of simply prepared, enjoyable dishes is full of tempta-
tion: a trio of salmon, crab bisque, scallop salad and country terrines to
start; followed perhaps by monkfish with a red onion confit, entrecôte
with red wine sauce or roast quail with a vegetable compote. Leave
room for dessert -charlotte with three chocolates, steamed syrup pudding. The menu changes regularly and is supplemented by a simpler,
set menu at lunchtime.

BRIGHTON   La Marinade

77 St George's Road, Kemp Town, Brighton, East Sussex, BN2 1EF
Tel: (01273) 600992   **£45**
Open: lunch Tue-Fri & Sun, dinner Tue-Sat
Meals served: lunch 12-2, dinner 7-10

French cooking in a popular, unpretentious little restaurant serving traditional bistro-style classics such as avocado and crispy bacon salad,
mussels in a creamy curry sauce or home-made soup to start, followed
by chicken in a cream, calvados and mushroom sauce, fillet steak in a
Madeira sauce, lobster thermidor or the day's fish dish of the day. Less
choice at lunch-time but similar fare.

BRIGHTON   Topps Hotel

17 Regency Square, Brighton, East Sussex, BN1 2FG
Tel: (01273) 729334   Fax: (01273) 203679   **£50**
Open: dinner Thu-Sat & Mon & Tue (closed 25 & 26 Dec, Jan)
Meals served: dinner 7-9

Situated at the heart of Brighton, in a beautifully restored Regency
building, this 15-bedroomed hotel is only 100 yards from the seafront.
Rooms are spacious and full of character (two have four-posters and
balconies); service is friendly and warm. The basement restaurant
serves unpretentious, mainly English cooking, with the emphasis on
freshness and simplicity. Specialities include steak and kidney pie and
fish soup. Everything, including the excellent bread is home-made.
Other typical dishes include prawn, sole and scallop pie; new season
lamb with onion sauce; casserole of pigeon breast; fresh salmon fish
cakes with a tomato sauce. Excellent breakfasts.

BRIMFIELD   Poppies Restaurant

The Roebuck, Brimfield, Hereford & Worcester, SY8 4NE
Tel: (01584) 711230   *Fax:* (01584) 711654   **£60**
Open: lunch & dinner Tue-Sat
    (closed 25 & 26 Dec, 2 weeks Feb, 1 week Oct)   🏵
Meals served: lunch 12-2, dinner 7-10

Carole Evans believes that food should be fun but going by the results
on the plate, the input from the kitchen is still highly professional. Set
in a former coach house attached to the village pub, this is a classy
restaurant both in terms of decor and cooking. Try perhaps roast turbot in a light Vermouth sauce followed by marmalade steamed pudding
with vanilla custard or home-made ice creams and sorbets. An extensive selection of cheeses, warranting their very own menu, is served
with home-made oatcakes and walnut and sultana bread. The bar menu
features a wide range of lighter versions of the more formal dishes,
from crab pot with Melba toast to Helford oysters, baked cod with a
tomato and onion sauce or chicken in cider pie. Organic produce is
used as much as possible. Good-value set lunch (£15). Three charming,
immaculate bedrooms, all en-suite, offer every modern comfort. Wake
up to a fabulous breakfast choice which features home-made preserves
and honey (from their own bees), local cow's or ewe's milk yoghurt,
smoked bacon, home-made pork sausage, black pudding, local free-
range eggs, Loch Fyne kippers—a true feast on which to start the day.
See you for breakfast!

BRISTOL	Bistro Twenty One

---

21 Cotham Road South, Kingsdown, Bristol, Avon, BS6 5TZ
Tel: (0117) 9421744   **£35**
Open: lunch Mon-Fri, dinner Mon-Sat (closed Bank Holidays)
Meals served: lunch 12-2.30, dinner 7-11.30

A straightforward menu of traditional bistro-style dishes, cosy atmosphere and friendly service are the hallmarks here. A la carte or set menus offer the likes of fish soup, smoked salmon platter and spinach and cream cheese pancakes, turbot supreme with a saffron sauce, roast lamb with a ginger and honey sauce or steaks. Good selection of desserts too: sorbets, lemon tart, strawberry sabayon and flambéed pancakes with Grand Marnier and chocolate ice cream.

Still a Bristol favourite after many years

BRISTOL	Harveys Restaurant

---

12 Denmark Street, Bristol, Avon, BS1 5DQ
Tel: (0117) 9275034   *Fax:* (0117) 9253003   **£65**
Open: lunch Mon-Fri, dinner Mon-Sat (closed Bank Holidays)
Meals served: lunch 12-1.45, dinner 7-10.45

Wine is centre stage at this comfortable restaurant in 13th-century cellars below Harveys of Bristol's head office, which first opened for business in 1796. The wine list is, not surprisingly, fantastic, with some exceptional clarets and expert notes to guide you through the thoroughly comprehensive range. The cooking is British, and is the domain of chef-manager Ramon Farthing. Light lunches of two and three courses offer the likes of traditional Guinness and steak pie.

Specialities include home-cured bresaola, and hot orange soufflé. Dinner menus (à la carte and fixed-price) feature carefully thought-out dishes such as fillet of beef filled with braised onion, parma ham and thyme, finished with a sherry vinegar sauce. Separate vegetarian menu available on request. Great puds—warm chocolate tart served with roasted clementines and a Cointreau cream or Harveys speciality apple dessert. British and Irish farmhouse cheeses to finish, plus coffee with petits fours.

Biography

As a boy Ray Farthing enjoyed cooking, so when his father encouraged him to join a trade, it seemed the obvious choice. He began as an apprentice at the Pier at Harwich, and came under the expert supervision of Chris Oakley. From here he moved to Le **Ramon** *Talbooth, then spent time as personal chef to the Earl* **Farthing** *and Countess Spencer. His next post was at the Castle Hotel, Taunton, then Calcot Manor and finally Harveys. Two things give him particular satisfaction: to see his brigade progressing and learning well; and to receive the appreciation of his customers at the end of the day.*

BRISTOL   Howard's

1A-2A Avon Crescent, Bristol, Avon, BS1 6XQ
Tel: (0117) 9262921   **£35**
Open: lunch & dinner Mon-Sat (closed 25 & 26 Dec)
Meals served: lunch 12-2.30, dinner 7-11.30

An informal, very friendly restaurant in a Georgian, listed building on
the city's historic, Victorian dockside, with views of the Clifton
Suspension Bridge. Everything from bread to petits fours is home-
made on the premises. Chef David Roast has been at the helm in the
kitchen for the past eight years serving an international range of
dishes, with fresh local game, and hot and cold smoked fish as specialities. There's always a vegetarian choice on the well-thought-out seasonal à la carte menu, as well as extra daily blackboard specials
featuring fish of the day and seasonal treats. Good-value weekday table
d'hôte menus and affordable wines.

A bustling, busy local restaurant, well worth a visit.

BRISTOL   Hunt's

26 Broad Street, Bristol, Avon, BS1 2HG
Tel & Fax: (0117) 9265580   *Good local restaurant*   **£55**
Open: lunch Tue-Fri, dinner Tue-Sat
   (closed Bank Holidays, 2 wks Xmas, 1 wk Easter, 1 wk Aug)
Meals served: lunch 12-2, dinner 7-10

Good cooking in small, intimate surroundings has gained a loyal following here. Daily menus feature starters such as fish soup provençale,
smoked haddock soufflé and roast sweet pepper salad. Fish is listed on
a separate menu each day according to market availability—fresh-
dressed Cornish crab salad or baked sea bass with lemon and dill
would be typical presentations. Carnivores might choose between veal
cutlet with a wild green lavender and lemon butter or Hereford duck
with honey, ginger and Madeira. Among desserts you might find blueberry tart or a trio of chocolate hearts (each with its own sauce).
British cheeses are served with delicious walnut bread. Good-value
fixed-price lunch menus offer two courses (£10.50) or three (£12.50).

BRISTOL   Restaurant Lettonie

9 Druid Hill, Stoke Bishop, Bristol, Avon, BS9 1EW
Tel: (0117) 9686456   *Fax:* (0117) 9686943   **£70**
Open: lunch & dinner Tue-Sat (closed 2 wks Xmas, 2 wks Aug)
Meals served: lunch 12.30-2, dinner 7-9

Martin and Siân Blunos's tiny French restaurant on the outskirts of
town in a suburban shopping parade is well worth a visit, and is not
likely to disappoint. Talent, imagination, attention to detail and dedication all go hand in hand here. Lunchtime offers a short fixed-price
menu with two or three choices for each course. Dinner likewise is a
fixed-price affair but with considerably more choice. Start with clear
rabbit soup served with a pressed rabbit terrine or tortellini of langoustine; then main course dishes such as honey-roast duck leg stuffed with
boudin blanc, stuffed pig's trotter with pork and chicken served with a
mace and Madeira sauce or pan-fried salmon with capers and a warm
olive oil dressing. A cheaper supper menu, similar to the lunchtime
menu, is available Tuesday to Thursday. This very talented couple win
the day with their dedication and determination.

BRISTOL   Markwicks

43 Corn Street, Bristol, Avon, BS1 1HT
Tel & Fax: (0117) 9262658   **£50**
Open: lunch Mon-Fri, dinner Mon-Sat
    (closed Bank Holidays, 1 wk Xmas, 1 wk Easter, 2 wks Aug)
Meals served: lunch 12-2, dinner 7-10.30

Stephen Markwick's elegant and interesting restaurant located in a former bank vault offers a well-thought-out range of interesting, uncomplicated dishes on both fixed-price and à la carte menus. Seafood
pancake, fillet of brill baked in cider, steamed fillet of grey mullet with
ginger and soy sauce are what he likes to cook and what his customers
like to eat. Dedicated meat eaters might prefer the likes of veal with a
morel sauce, venison soubise with juniper and port sauce or breast of
duck with sautéed apples, honey and cider vinegar. Finish with hot
orange and Grand Marnier soufflé pancakes, fig and frangipane tart, or
French and British cheeses with walnut bread. Around 15 interesting
house wines on a well-chosen list.

BRISTOL   Michael's Restaurant

129 Hotwells Road, Bristol, Avon, BS8 4RU
Tel: (0117) 9276190   **£55**
Open: lunch Sun, dinner Tue-Sat
    (closed 25 & 26 Dec, 1 Jan 4 days Aug)
Meals served: lunch 12.30-2.30, dinner 7-11

Just west of the city centre, this well-established restaurant keeps up
with trends, offering a menu which is both modern and eclectic. Game
terrine with an apple-spiced chutney, smoked haddock risotto with
saffron and fresh parmesan, turbot with a herb crust and lemon butter,
or sauté of fillet of beef with caramelised baby onions, glazed chestnuts
and red wine jus are followed by a good selection of desserts including
iced Armagnac mousse with caramel sauce and mango coulis, and ginger pudding with stem ginger anglaise. The decor is Victorian in style,
the atmosphere relaxed and informal. A cosy, elegant bar-lounge provides a relaxing setting for pre- or post-dinner drinks.

BRISTOL   Muset

16 Clifton Road, Bristol, Avon, BS8 1AF
Tel: (0117) 9732920   — switch board for group **£35**
Open: dinner Mon-Sat
Meals served: dinner 7-10.30

Tucked away behind the sedate façade of a Bristol crescent, this popular little city-centre restaurant, is made up of a maze of interconnecting rooms. The two or three-course fixed-price menu plenty of choice, with starters ranging from crepes to chef's salad or soup of the day. Main courses might include pan-fried fillet of pork with linguine and Stilton sauce, a salmi of game with onions, smoked bacon and lentils or grilled salmon with a crab and prawn-flavoured butter. Vegetarians might find the likes of carrot and parsnip rösti with a tomato, chili and coriander sauce or asparagus and spinach tartlet. Daily fish and meat specials complement the carte, and there are a number of home-made speciality breads on offer.

BRISTOL   Neil's

112 Princess Victoria Street, Bristol, Avon, BS8 4DB
Tel: (0117) 9733669   **£45**
Open: dinner daily (closed 1 wk Xmas)
Meals served: dinner 7.30-11.30

Neil's began life in the heart of Clifton as a bistro and remained so for 25 years. Neil Ramsay has decided to exchange the bistro image for that of a more formal restaurant. The menu remains refreshingly simple, retaining one or two favourites from the old bistro-style menu such as the classic seafood soup. The atmosphere in this quaint little restaurant is one of warmth and charm thanks to Neil himself who runs front of house, while son Pete keeps up the standards in the kitchen. The sensibly short à la carte features a handful of choices for each course. Typical starters include French onion soup and pan-fried Cornish scallops with smoked bacon. Main courses could be roast duck with honey and orange or roast rack of lamb with a cream potato and tarragon cream sauce. Finish perhaps with hot prune and Armagnac tart, orange and lemon syllabub or banana crème brûlée.

BRISTOL — Swallow Royal Hotel

College Green, Bristol, Avon, BS1 5TE
Tel: (0117) 9255100   *Fax:* (0117) 9251515   **£55**
Open: dinner Mon-Sat (closed Bank Holidays)
Meals served: dinner 7.30-10.30

The Palm Court with its spectacular stained glass roof three storeys up makes a grand setting for dinner at this Victorian hotel which enjoys an enviable position next to the Cathedral and overlooking the College Green. The recent refurbishment has enhanced the original grandeur of the build-ing and added a basement leisure club of Roman Baths design. Chandeliers, polished marble and brass, and rich mahogany give a magnificent first impression as you enter. Classic traditional style and contemporary comforts go hand in hand. In its earlier hey-day, the hotel was host to Queen Victoria, and then to Churchill who was known to favour the place, I even spent some time there myself – as an apprentice chef! The 242 bedrooms are luxuriously furnished and many offer superb views over the city and

■ **Michael Kitts, chef**

harbour. A second restaurant, the Terrace, looks out on to the cathe-dral square, offering an equally grand setting and a menu which includes simple grills.

BROADHEMBURY — Drewe Arms

Broadhembury, Devon, EX14 0NF
Tel: (01404) 841267   **£45**
Open: lunch daily, dinner Mon-Sat (closed 25 Dec)
Meals served: lunch 12-2, dinner 7-10

A thatched pub in Devon may seem an unlikely setting for a Swedish chef (no Muppet chicken jokes, please!) but Kerstin Burge's tiny restaurant offers some excellent dishes. The blackboard lets you know what fish is good that day: crab, lobster, scallops, turbot, John Dory, salmon, bass and red mullet are popular items. A small wine list ranges for £6.95 for house selections to just £28.50 for champagne.

BROADWAY — Collin House

Collin Lane, Broadway, Hereford & Worcester, WR12 7PB
Tel: (01386) 858354   **£40**
Open: lunch & dinner daily (closed 24-29 Dec)
Meals served: lunch 12-1.30, dinner 7-9

A mile north of Broadway is this lovely, 16th-century Cotswold stone house with its oak-beamed bar and restaurant, ancient mullioned win-dows and heartwarming inglenook fireplace. Local farm produce and game are specialities, as is Sunday lunch. In the evenings there's a light supper menu as well as the more formal dinner menu; and lunchtime options include light meals in the bar or garden. Choose from double mousse of Finnan haddock and Arbroath smokies for starters; and for main courses: oxtail casserole with herb dumplings, fresh fish gratin, or venison with a gin and mulberry sauce. The hotel is situated in its own grounds with pleasant gardens and an open-air swimming pool. The seven bedrooms are spacious, with a cottagey, rustic feel.

BROADWAY   Dormy House

Willersey Hill, Broadway, Hereford & Worcester, WR12 7LF
Tel: (01386) 852711   *Fax:* (01386) 858636   **£60**
Open: lunch Sun-Fri, dinner daily (closed 25 & 26 Dec)
Meals served: lunch 12.30-2 (Sun to 2.30),   ✤
    dinner 7.30-9.30 (Sat to 9)

Exposed stonework, beams, and tiled floors give period character to this luxuriously converted 17th-century farmhouse with 50 bedrooms overlooking the local golf course and Cotswold countryside. Bedrooms, housed in converted outbuildings are cottagey and comfortable with timbered ceilings. Food is served in a number of different settings: choose between the less formal, rustic-style bar, the bright conservatory or more formal, subtly-lit dining room. The menu range is extensive—there are à la carte, fixed-price, gourmet, vegetarian and children's supper menus. The cooking is modern English and French style, and typical dishes could be open ravioli with pan-fried chicken livers, shallots and lentils served with a light curry butter sauce and coriander to start; followed by sea bass with a tarragon mousse and pan-fried scallops in red wine sauce, or supreme of duck with a honey soy and sherry sauce. Good French cheeses served with walnut and raisin bread. Former sous chef Alan Cutler stepped into John Sanderson's shoes as head chef mid-1994.

BROADWAY   Hunters Lodge

High Street, Broadway, Hereford & Worcester, WP 7DT
Tel: (01386) 853247   **£40**
Open: lunch Sat & Sun, dinner Tue-Sat
    (closed 3 days Xmas, 3 wks Feb, 3 wks Aug)
Meals served: lunch 12.30-1.45, dinner 7.30-9.45

Kurt and Dottie Friedli are the warmest of hosts at this creeper-clad, Cotswold-stone house with its candlelit restaurant. Kurt's à la carte and fixed-price menus offer refreshingly straightforward dishes. Crispy crabmeat croquettes, or quails with sage stuffing and cider to start perhaps, followed by sirloin with shallots, grilled Dover sole with lemon butter or pan-fried pork steak with Roquefort and rosemary. Traditional puds to finish.

*A friendly and unfussy restaurant where you can relax
and enjoy yourself*

BROADWAY — Lygon Arms

High Street, Broadway, Hereford & Worcester, WR12 7DU
Tel: (01386) 852255   *Fax:* (01386) 858611
Open: lunch & dinner daily
Meals served: lunch 12.30-2, dinner 7.30-9.15

£70

The Lygon Arms has always ranked as one of the finest hostelries in the country. Its setting in picturesque Broadway helps, and there are few more lovely sights than the elegant High Street with its honey coloured stone buildings set amongst lawns and trees. The hotel is impeccably run by Kirk Ritchie and offers all that you could wish for. Dine in the vaulted Great Hall where new chef Roger Narbett has just joined. We know Roger of old from his Birmingham and London days and look forward to seeing the effects of his influence here. Needless to say, the wine list is all that it should be: a selection of the best from around the world, plenty of halves and moderate prices. Good leisure facilities in the country club. One of the best hotels in the country at which to spoil yourself.

BROCKENHURST — Le Poussin

The Courtyard, Brookley Road, Brockenhurst,
   Hampshire, SO42 7RB
Tel: (01590) 23063   *Fax:* (01590) 22912
Open: lunch Wed-Sun, dinner Wed-Sat (closed 2 wks Jan)
Meals served: lunch 12-1.30, dinner 7-9

£55

An elegant country restaurant in a courtyard setting, with four tables for alfresco dining. Chef-patron Alex Aitken (right) and his wife, Caroline, who runs front of house, have created a stylish yet intimate setting between them, with the help of son Justin who manages the wine list. The menu changes daily, offering two choices at each stage, so it's the kind of the place you'll want to return to again and again to try out more of Alex's cooking, which is refreshingly unfussy yet refined and well executed. Local game and seafood, from Lymington and Keyhaven, and wild mushrooms  picked by the family's fair hands when they've a moment, form the backbone of menus. Excellent range of wines by the glass.

BROCKENHURST — Rhinefield House

Rhinefield Road, Brockenhurst, Hampshire, SO42 7QB
Tel: (01590) 22922   *Fax:* (01590) 22800
Open: lunch Sun-Fri, dinner daily
Meals served: lunch 12.30-2, dinner 7.30-10

£50

Neo-Elizabethan 34-bedroomed house in the New Forest, with ornamental canals and Hampton Court-style maze in the grounds. Beautiful Alhambra room and striking leisure club based around the theme of the lost city of Atlantis.

BROMSGROVE — Grafton Manor

Grafton Lane, Bromsgrove, Hereford & Worcester, B61 7HA
Tel: (01527) 579007   *Fax:* (01527) 575221   **£55**
Open: lunch Sun-Fri, dinner daily
Meals served: lunch 12.30-1.30, dinner 7.30-9.30
   (Sat to 9.30, Sun at 7.30 only)

Home to the Morris family since 1947, this Elizabeth manor house has
a relaxed and welcoming atmosphere. It's set in six acres of grounds,
complete with water gardens, lake and formal herb garden, laid out in
decorative chessboard pattern and containing over 100 herbs which are
regularly put to use in the hotel kitchen by Simon Morris. The Great
Parlour has an ornate ceiling and open fireplace and houses the hotel
bar, but the 18th-century dining room is the real focal point of Grafton.
Simon's cooking is imaginative and beside the classics expect to find
dishes like breast of chicken with a mushroom and truffle sauce.
Desserts feature a good selection of regional puds—Worcestershire
pear pudding with an elderflower sorbet or the speciality whisky
steamed pud. A separate vegetarian menu is available on request.

BROUGHTON — Broughton Park

418 Garstang Road, Broughton, Nr Preston, Lancashire, PR3 5JB
Tel: (01772) 864087   *Fax:* (01772) 861728   **£45**
Open: lunch Sun-Fri, dinner daily
Meals served: lunch 12-2, dinner 7-9.45

Extensive leisure and conference facilities make this 98-bedroomed
Victorian manor house close to the M55 and M6 a popular choice for
business users. Bedrooms are well equipped and comfortable, the best
being in the newer south wing; three enjoy the added luxury of four-
poster beds. The Courtyard Restaurant, in the original part of the
house, is an attractive setting in which to enjoy classic, traditional and
seasonal dishes such as poached delice of sole and lobster, potted
Manx crab and Lancashire cheese with walnut and pine kernel salad,
steamed suet pudding of lamb and mushrooms, salmon and shrimp
pithiviers and roast duckling with orange and mulled wine sauce. To
finish, try gâteau Opéra on a raspberry coulis or apple and ginger tart
tatin with caramel ice cream.

BROXTED	Whitehall

Church End, Broxted, Essex, CM6 2BZ
Tel: (01279) 850603 *Fax:* (01279) 850385 **£75**
Open: lunch & dinner daily (closed 25-30 Dec)
Meals served: lunch 12.30-2, dinner 7.30-9.30

Next door to the village church, this 15th-century Elizabethan manor
house has been run with care and commitment by the Keane family for
almost ten years. Lovingly restored, the hotel features a spectacular
timbered, vaulted dining room, whose 600-year-old crooked timbers
provide an atmospheric setting for young Liverpudlian Paul Flavell's
delicate, artistic cooking, which takes full account of modern tastes
without being fussy. Hot soufflé of haddock, champ and whole-grain
mustard, steamed fillet of sea bass with potato and crab pancakes and
pan-fried fillet of Scottish beef with a foie gras sauce and purée of
parsnip are his sort of cooking. To finish, perhaps light ginger mousse
or hot raspberries in puff pastry. Twenty five bright and cheery bedrooms all have views of either the tranquil walled Elizabethan garden
or rolling countryside around. Spectacular conference and function
facilities in the ancient, beamed and galleried Barn House.

BRUTON	Claire de Lune

2-4 High Street, Bruton, Somerset, BA10 0EQ
Tel: (01749) 813395 **£45**
Open: lunch Sun, dinner Tue-Sat
   (closed Bank Holidays, 2 wks Jan)
Meals served: lunch 12-2, dinner 7-10

Claire de Lune combines bistro, grill, brasserie and pizzeria all in one
homely setting. Enjoy French onion soup, deep-pan pizza, steaks and
scampi, or go for the more formal, traditional approach in the
brasserie: ricotta and spinach tortellini, butterfly king prawns, grilled
venison with a wild mushroom and Madeira sauce, fillet of beef bordelaise with a red wine sauce and braised shallots. To finish, perhaps, a
Belgian chocolate mousse with piroulines, or cappuccino ice cream
with lychees. A friendly, helpful wine list in support.

BRUTON	Truffles Restaurant

95 High Street, Bruton, Somerset, BA10 0AR
Tel: (01749) 812255 **£45**
Open: lunch & dinner Tue-Sun
Meals served: lunch 12-2, dinner 7-10

Martin and Denise Bottrill's cottage in the small town of Bruton provides a delightful, intimate setting in which to enjoy Martin's adventurous cooking. Monthly menus offer a three course menu with five
choices for each course.

BUCKLAND Buckland Manor

Buckland, Nr Broadway, Hereford & Worcester, WR12 7LY
Tel: (01386) 852626   *Fax:* (01386) 853557   **£80**
Open: lunch & dinner daily
Meals served: lunch 12.30-1.45, dinner 7.30-8.45

Few country house hotels can date their origins as early as Buckland—first records of a house on the site are around 700 AD; while the present house dates back to the 13th century. Famous visitors through history include Queen Mary (grandmother to the present Queen), who is said to have visited Buckland during the Second World War when the house was occupied by the Red Cross. It's now a 13-bedroomed, Cotswold-stone manor house set in ten acres of immaculately maintained grounds in a peaceful, secluded Cotswold setting. Antique furnishings throughout the hotel provide character and a discreet sense of elegance and luxury. Bedrooms are no less impressive. The light, airy restaurant takes advantage of views over the rolling Cotswold hills and makes a magnificent setting for Martyn Pearn's skilful traditional cooking. Typical dishes from the seasonal à la carte include a pavé of oak-smoked salmon with oysters and chives, pan-fried loin of Brecon venison on a bed of celeriac and glazed fillets of brill with leeks and mussels. Puds include the likes of warm lemon tart with raspberry coulis, and hot mango tarte tatin served with a coconut sorbet. International wine list with some reasonable prices.

BURFORD Bay Tree

Sheep Street, Burford, Oxfordshire, OX8 4LW
Tel: (01993) 822791   *Fax:* (01993) 823008   **£50**
Open: lunch & dinner daily
Meals served: lunch 12-2, dinner 6.30-9.30, Sun 6.30-8.30

Built in 1584 as the home of Elizabeth I's Lord Chief Baron of the Exchequer, this delightful hotel in picturesque Burford retains much of its heritage: oak-panelled rooms, huge stone fireplaces, flagstone floors and the high raftered hall with galleried stairs.

Whether Elizabeth I actually slept here is a matter of conjecture, for she is known to have visited Burford. There are 23 rooms, four with four-posters (rumoured never to have left the building), some located in an adjoining cottage. A beautiful walled garden, complete with ancient apple trees, roses and an ornamental pond, is the perfect place to relax. The cooking is imaginative, concentrating on mainly traditional British ingredients with modern presentation. From the table d'hote lunch menu, start perhaps with coarse liver pâté served with an apple chutney, followed by char-grilled lamb cutlets served with a port sauce or fillet of cod steamed and placed on a bed of spinach and served with a red wine butter sauce, and finish with summer pudding or a selection of British cheeses.

BURFORD   Lamb Inn

Sheep Street, Burford, Oxfordshire, OX18 4LR
Tel: (01993) 823155   *Fax:* (01993) 822228   **£45**
Open: lunch Sun, dinner daily (closed 25 & 26 Dec)
Meals served: lunch Sun 12-2, dinner 7-9.30

Tucked down a quiet side street in one of the most attractive towns in
the Cotswolds, the 15th-century Lamb with its flagged floors, gleaming
copper and brass, log fires and antiques, and mellow Cotswold stone, is
everyone's dream of what an ancient English inn should be. Cottagey
bedrooms are furnished with antiques and pretty floral fabrics, some
have four-poster or half-tester beds, and standards of housekeeping are
high. The pretty, pillared restaurant serves predominantly British fare,
with influence from France. The price of a three-course meal depends
on the choice of main course, typified by dishes such as tuna and
thyme ravioli with crispy leeks and a tomato cream sauce, tournedos
Rossini with a Madeira sauce, or West Country duck with glazed red
cabbage and a pear and brandy sauce.

BURGH LE MARSH   Windmill

46 High Street, Burgh-le-Marsh, Nr Skegness,
    Lincolnshire, PE24 5JT
Tel: (01754) 810281   **£40**
Open: lunch Sun, dinner Tue-Sat (closed 25 Dec)
Meals served: lunch 12-2, dinner 7-9.15

After a visit to the Windmill Museum, a meal at the Windmill
Restaurant is a logical progression. Tim Boskett is the chef-patron and
wife Janette runs the restaurant. A varied menu offers around seven
dishes for each course with price determined by the selection of the
main dish. 'Tonight's Pot Luck Dish' is sure to inspire curiosity!

BURY   Normandie Hotel & Restaurant

Elbut Lane, Birtle, Nr Bury, Greater Manchester, BL9 6UT
Tel: 061-764 3869   *Fax:* 061-764 4866   **£50**
Open: lunch Tue-Fri, dinner Mon-Sat
    (closed Bank Holidays, 1 wk Easter, 2 wks Xmas)   ❀
Meals served: lunch 12-2, dinner 7-9.30 (Sat to 10)

It was in the late 1950s that Yves Champeau bought this old inn having
decided that it was high time that French cuisine was introduced to the
north west of England. Forty years on this now well-established hotel
still benefits from the skills of a Frenchman: Burgundian Pascal
Pommier whose modern style maintains the fine reputation of his pre-
decessor. Rillettes of duck with French bean salad, salmon marinaded
in citrus juices or a delicate mousse of cauliflower with mixed vegetable vinaigrette are typical first courses. Sea bass stuffed with a
mousse of sole is served with provençale vegetables, scallops flavoured
with coriander come with black noodles, noisettes of venison with
poivrade sauce or perhaps braised ham with herb and bacon
dumplings and Madeira sauce to follow. Try puddings such as fresh
fruit sorbets on a passion fruit coulis, caramel mousse with bananas
and hazelnuts or a classic tarte aux pommes with honey ice cream.
Carefully chosen wines are reasonably priced. Max and Gill Moussa
(mother and son) are the friendly hosts at this delightful hotel.

Biography

Pascal Pommier

Having combined work experience with his catering qualifications in France, Pascal Pommier came to England. First he worked at the Mill House, Kingham, during which time he did 'stages' with Raymond Blanc and Michel Roux, then he moved on to the Normandie Hotel where he has remained, to great acclaim both locally and nationally.

BURY ST EDMUNDS   **Angel Hotel**

Angel Hill, Bury St Edmunds, Suffolk, IP33 1LT
Tel: (01284) 753926   *Fax*: (01284) 750092   **£45**
Open: lunch & dinner daily
Meals served: lunch 12.30-2, dinner 7.30-10
42-bedroomed, Virginia creeper-clad hotel serving customers since 1452 when it first became an inn. Room fifteen was immortalised by Dickens, whose Mr Pickwick stayed in it overnight.

BURY ST EDMUNDS   Mortimer's

31 Churchgate Street, Bury St Edmunds, Suffolk, IP33 1RG
Tel: (01284) 760623   Fax: (01284) 752561   **£40**
Open: lunch Mon-Fri, dinner Mon-Sat
    (closed Bank Holidays & 1 day following, 2 wks
    Xmas/New Year, 2 wks Aug)
Meals served: lunch 12-2, dinner 7-9

The elder of two Mortimers, the other being in Ipswich: here, amid straightforward decor, seafood is the order of the day. Anything from Loch Fyne oysters, seafood gratin or grilled tiger prawns could be available to start, with steamed, grilled, baked or breadcrumbed offerings as main-course fish dishes. Char-grilled Scottish salmon béarnaise, sea bass with tarragon, steamed halibut Florentine or grilled fillet of brill are all good choices. The choice is extensive and the fish is fresh. Reasonably priced wine list.

CALSTOCK   Danescombe Valley Hotel

Lower Kelly, Calstock, Cornwall, PL18 9RY
Tel & Fax: (01822) 832414   **£60**
Open: dinner Fri-Tue (closed Nov-Easter, open Xmas)
Meals served: dinner at 7.30

Situated in a lane running parallel to the river Tamar in the hidden valley of Danescombe, this five-bedroomed hotel enjoys an enviably romantic setting half a mile west of Calstock village. All of the rooms overlook the river, with the best leading on to a shared verandah running around three sides of the house. There is also a self-catering cottage along the lane. The kitchen under chef-patron Anna Smith takes full advantage of local ingredients to produce four-course, no-choice dinners, and any dietary limitations are discussed when booking. Fine West Country farmhouse cheeses and a good wine list which is strong on Italians. Booking is essential (note limited opening times) as the dining room only seats 12. In fact, ideal for your own house party without the worry, so you could book all five rooms and treat yourself and friends.

CAMBRIDGE   22 Chesterton Road

22 Chesterton Road, Cambridge, Cambridgeshire, CB4 3AX
Tel: (01223) 351880   **£50**
Open: dinner Tue-Sat (closed 1 wk Xmas)
Meals served: dinner 7-9.45

Popular with locals this small candle-lit, Victorian-style restaurant offers a short fixed-price, monthly-changing dinner menu of classically inspired dishes with a modern approach. Start with cream of leek and onion soup, mushroom tart or rillettes of fresh trout with cucumber dill. Follow perhaps with delicious chicken sausages on a bed of creamed potatoes with a shallot sauce or rich venison casserole with wild rice. Carefully chosen European and New World wines in evidence, and every six weeks there are gourmet wine evenings and tastings.

This is a very special place

CAMPSEA ASHE   Old Rectory

Campsea Ashe, Nr Woodbridge, Suffolk, IP13 0PU
Tel: (01728) 746524   **£40**
Open: dinner Mon-Sat (closed 25 & 26 Dec)
Meals served: dinner 7.30-8.30

Dine by log fires in the winter or in the airy conservatory during the summer at Stewart Basset's retreat. A homely nine-bedroomed house is a perfect base for exploring the fascinating East Anglian coastline. The menu is simple and gives no choice, but lemon sole with a crab mousse, fillet of lamb with chestnut purée in puff pastry followed by a rich chocolate brandy cake sounds delicious anyway!

CANTERBURY   County Hotel

High Street, Canterbury, Kent, CT1 2RX
Tel: (01227) 766266   *Fax:* (01227) 451512   **£45**
Open: lunch & dinner daily
Meals served: lunch 12.30-2.30, dinner 7-10

This 73-bedroomed city-centre hotel on the pedestrianised high street
is steeped in history and dates back to 1588. A timbered foyer, Tudor
bar and ornate carving set the scene, but chef Eric Gavignet adds the
contemporary touch with menus in the modern mould: venison and
hazelnut terrine with cranberry and orange sauce; ravioli filled with
ricotta and spinach served with dolcelatte sauce as starters; followed by
pan-fried noisettes of pork with mustard sauce and pleurottes, roast
poussin with creamed ginger sauce and coriander, or pan-fried sea
bass with red wine sauce and bone marrow. The car park is at the rear
of the hotel, adjacent to the Stour Street entrance.

CARTMEL   Uplands

Haggs Lane, Cartmel, Cumbria, LA11 6HD
Tel & Fax: (0153 95) 36248   **£55**
Open: lunch & dinner Tue-Sun (closed Jan & Feb)
Meals served: lunch 12.30 for 1, dinner 7.30 for 8

John Tovey of Miller Howe has a hand in this charming, five-
bedroomed Edwardian country hotel co-owned and run in the Miller
Howe manner by former employees Tom and Diana Peter. The house
stands on a hillside in its own grounds with distant views of
Morecambe Bay. Dinner is based on a modern British approach, with
dishes such as hot salmon soufflé wrapped in smoked salmon with
watercress sauce to start; followed by baked fillet of brill with a leek
and prawn sauce, or local guinea fowl with brandied apricots and a rich
game sauce. Desserts might feature home-made prune and Armagnac
ice cream or fresh figs with Pernod and crème fraîche.

CASTLE CARY   Bond's

Ansford Hill, Castle Cary, Somerset, BA7 7JP
Tel & Fax: (01963) 350464   **£35**
Open: dinner daily (closed 1 wk Xmas)
Meals served: dinner 7-9.30 (Sun & Mon to 7.30)

Situated just 300 yards from the station, this seven-bedroomed listed
Georgian house with its creeper clad façade offers a genuinely warm
welcome. Light lunches are served outside or in the lounge; dinner is a
fixed-price affair, with many options. Choose from the short weekly or
daily menus. Red Leicester and Gorgonzola soufflé, aubergine and
mussel casserole, venison bourguignon, herb-encrusted rack of lamb
with redcurrant glaze, and a medley of fish—salmon, monkfish and
haddock served with a carrot and coriander sauce. Kevin and Yvonne
Bond, he fronting, she behind the scenes working wonders in the
kitchen, offer truly personal service. As it's only a small hotel, you can
book in as a party for the weekend, and take over the whole place, but
book well in advance; it's becoming popular. Breakfasts (healthy, old-
fashioned, continental, traditional) are also available to non-residents.

CASTLE COMBE — Manor House

Castle Combe, Nr Chippenham, Wiltshire, SN14 7HR
Tel: (01249) 782206   *Fax:* (01249) 782159
Open: lunch & dinner daily
Meals served: lunch 12.30-2, dinner 7.30-10

£75

Once voted the prettiest village in England, Castle Combe is very popular with tourists. The hotel, parts of which date back to the 14th century, has a cosy, relaxing but luxurious feel, and the surrounding grounds, complete with lily pond and bordered on one side by the trout-filled River Bybrook, are delightful. There are 36 beautifully decorated rooms, either in the main house or in picturesque cottages nearby, but it is the profusion of little extras that count. The cooking is modern English. Soufflés are a speciality, appearing in many guises, both in their own right and as accompaniments. Mark Taylor's cooking is skilful and at times quite outstanding. Typical meals could consist of a warm salad of oak-smoked scallops and sole with langoustine oil, followed by Scottish salmon with a creamy lobster sauce; or goat's cheese soufflé followed by smoked fillet of beef draped in a rosemary and tomato sauce. There is an outstanding British cheese menu with detailed, descriptive notes. Excellent desserts and an interesting, varied wine list with helpful notes.

CHADDESLEY CORBETT — Brockencote Hall

Chaddesley Corbett, Nr Kidderminster,
    Hereford & Worcester, DY10 4PY
Tel: (01562) 777876   *Fax:* (01562) 777872
Open: lunch Sun-Fri, dinner daily
Meals served: lunch 12.30-1.30, dinner 7-9.30

£50 .

Nothing is too much trouble for Alison and Joseph Petitjean at this classically-styled 17-bedroomed house set in 70 acres of landscaped grounds, complete with dovecote, lake, gatehouse and sheep—much of the land is let as grazing. A warm, friendly and professional atmosphere pervades throughout, and the feel is very much French, as befits the Petitjean family. Bedrooms, either in the main house or in the new adjoining extension, are spacious and stylish, and bathrooms are luxurious. The elegant restaurant with its views across the grounds is a worthy setting for head chef Eric Bouchet's traditional French menus, complemented by seasonal and regional specialities: poached Scottish Gigas oysters wrapped in courgette and served with a saffron cream; boned and roast saddle of lamb with wood mushrooms; braised sturgeon in vermouth served with Beluga caviar; roast Angus beef fillet cooked in a beef consommé. Locally cured sausages, bacon, ham, farmhouse eggs and wild Wyre Forest mushrooms (when in season) provide a splendid breakfast to start to the day.

CHADLINGTON · The Manor

Chadlington, Oxfordshire, OX7 3LX
Tel: (01608) 676711 **£60**
Open: dinner daily
Meals served: dinner 7-8.30

Head for the church and you'll find this old Cotswold manor just beside it, set in extensive grounds and offering a wonderfully relaxing stay thanks to Chris and David Grant and their team of staff. Accommodation is provided in seven splendidly furnished rooms and the cooking by Chris is both sound and reliable. The five-course fixed-price dinner menu starts with a soup (celery and lovage perhaps), followed by a choice of three second and main courses. Try venison patties with redcurrant and wine sauce or spinach mousseline with tomato sauce followed by red mullet with chive cream, saddle of lamb with kidney sauce or noisettes of the same cooked with orange, ginger and garlic. Home-made sweets feature a number of favourites like bread-and-butter pudding, as well as more exotic choices like rich chocolate pavé with praline cream sauce.

CHAGFORD · Gidleigh Park

Chagford, Devon, TQ13 8HH
Tel: (01647) 432367   *Fax:* (01647) 432574 **£100**
Open: lunch & dinner daily
Meals served: lunch 12.30-2, dinner 7-9 ☘

The wonderfully remote setting on the edge of Dartmoor of this mock-Tudor country house is among the finest in the land. Gidleigh Park is set in 40 acres of magnificent grounds on the North Teign River within the confines of Dartmoor National Park. Paul and Kay Henderson have brought the house and its gardens to the peak of perfection and new chef, 25-year-old Devonian Michael Caines, has taken on the difficult task of stepping into Shaun Hill's shoes in the kitchen. But Michael's pedigree—ex-Le Manoir under Raymond Blanc, and more recently a spell in Paris with Joël Robuchon of Jamin—bodes well. The menu format will remain the same: fixed-price menu, lunch and dinner, plus a no-choice, seven-course speciality menu in the evening; but the repertoire is Michael's own. The kitchen was busy perfecting the new techniques as we went to press, but expect the likes of crab ravioli with ginger and lemon grass, or foie gras and lentil soup, followed by main-course dishes such as stuffed rabbit leg served with a fricassée of wild mushrooms and lettuce, or beef fillet with roast shallots and red wine sauce. First reports speak of dishes which "linger in the mind" so we are looking forward to a bright new star on the culinary scene in this young man. Meanwhile, Paul Henderson's award-winning wine list continues to go from strength to strength. There are 15 rooms, including two suites and a woodland cottage across the river. Rooms are charged according to size and view. The hotel is two miles from Chagford Square, and enjoy the winding drive that brings you to the door.

CHAPELTOWN — Greenhead House

84 Burncross Road, Chapeltown, South Yorkshire, S30 4SF
Tel: (01742) 469004 **£65**
Open: dinner Tue-Sat (closed Bank Holidays,
  2 wks Xmas, 2 wk Easter, 2 wks Aug)
Meals served: dinner 7-9

Neil Allen cooks in robust and careful manner at this pretty little restaurant north of Sheffield—he and wife Anne have been running it now for over a decade. Monthly-changing menus offer an absorbing choice which draws in the regulars. Start perhaps with smoky salmon quenelles or galantine of quail—part-boned and filled with its own mousse and more, before choosing between the likes of casseroled guinea fowl with smoked bacon and red wine or cotriade—fish stew made to a traditional Northern French recipe. Round off with lemon tart, traditional Breton prune pudding or choose from a selection of English farmhouse cheeses.

CHARINGWORTH — Charingworth Manor

Charingworth, Nr Chipping Camden, Gloucestershire, GL55 6NS
Tel: (01386) 78555   Fax: (01386) 78353 **£70**
Open: lunch & dinner daily
Meals served: lunch 12.30-2, dinner 7.30-9.30 (Sat to 10)

Here you can experience a taste of gracious country house living, in an idyllic setting amidst the soft, rolling, Cotswold countryside. The ancient manor dates back to the early 14th century and the medieval origins can clearly be seen. For functions there is an impressive Long Room with breathtaking views, a billiards room with full-size table and a splendid leisure spa for relaxation. The 24 bedrooms and suites are charming, with antique furnishing and oak beams in some, while others in the Courtyard and Cottage annexes (created from the original stables and farm buildings) are contemporary and elegant. The John Greville restaurant is a series of low-ceilinged, beamed rooms where you can enjoy chef Bill Marmion's sound and imaginative cooking. Terrine of game and orange chutney; ragout of sea bass with mussels and asparagus; venison with wild mushroom ravioli; dark chocolate mousse with banana and coffee bean sauce might well be on his menu. Gentlemen are requested to wear jacket and tie for dinner.

CHARLBURY — The Bull at Charlbury

Sheep Street, Charlbury, Oxfordshire, OX7 3RR
Tel: (01608) 810689 **£40**
Open: dinner Tue-Sun (closed 4 days Xmas)
Meals served: dinner 7-9

The ground floor of this Cotswold stone pub is almost totally taken over by the bistro-cum-restaurant. There are bar snacks at lunchtime and an à la carte menu plus blackboard specials in the evening. Cooking is simple in concept, featuring many traditional favourites: lamb casseroles, lemon chicken, beef stroganoff, steak and venison pie and salmon with creamy asparagus sauce. Vegetarians are surprisingly well-looked-after, with choices such as cashew nut slice with korma sauce, vegetable stroganoff or Portuguese nut roast.

CHARTHAM   **Thruxted Oast**

Mystole, Chartham, Nr Canterbury, Kent, CT4 7BX
Tel: (01227) 730080
Open: bed & breakfast only (closed Xmas)
A converted late-18th-century oast house with three bedrooms, close to
Canterbury, surrounded by hop gardens and orchards. Breakfast with eggs from
their own hens is served in the large farmhouse kitchen.

CHEDINGTON   Chedington Court

Chedington, Nr Beaminster, Dorset, DT8 3HY
Tel: (01935) 891265   *Fax:* (01935) 891442   **£60**
Open: dinner daily (closed 2 Jan-2 Feb)
Meals served: dinner 7-9

The Chapmans promise peace and tranquillity at their ten-bedroomed
Jacobean-style country house. The house is set in ten acres of beautiful
gardens, with ponds, a grotto, water garden, sculptured hedge, giant
1,000-year-old gnarled yew tree, and lichen-encrusted tombstones (a
reference to the Saxon village church which once stood within the
hotel grounds) included among the attractions. The theme within is
true country house, in deference to the historic heritage of the manor
house which dates back to 1316, though the present building was
rebuilt on the site of previous manors in 1845. It's doubtful that previous occupants of the manor were quite as particular in their culinary
outlook as Hilary Chapman and her team who use hormone-free,
humanely reared and killed produce wherever possible. Dinner is the
main event here, with daily-changing menus which are short but well-
conceived, with the emphasis in planning being on flavour and popularity. Examples include lobster terrine with fresh tomato coulis and
grilled breast of turkey with herb sauce.

CHELTENHAM   Bonnets Bistro at Staithes

12 Suffolk Road, Cheltenham, Gloucestershire, GL50 2AQ
Tel: (01242) 260666   **£45**
Open: dinner Mon-Sat (closed Bank Holidays,
    1 wk Xmas, 2 wks summer)
Meals served: dinner 7-10

This former restaurant-turned-bistro, run by Paul and Heather Lucas
(she front-of-house, he in the kitchen) offers a seasonal carte of essentially British dishes with around half-a-dozen choices for each course.
Onion soup enriched with cream and flavoured with a hint of cider or
caramelised bacon salad to start, followed by escalope of fresh tuna
with a brown butter sauce, breast of Cotswold chicken with a garlic
cream sauce or fillet of beef with a red wine and thyme sauce to follow.
Good choice of desserts.

Now called Staithes Restaurant – same team

CHELTENHAM   Le Champignon Sauvage

24-26 Suffolk Road, Cheltenham, Gloucestershire, GL50 2AQ
Tel: (01242) 573449   **£70**
Open: lunch Mon-Fri, dinner Mon-Sat
    (closed Bank Holidays, 1 wk Xmas)
Meals served: lunch 12.30-1.30, dinner 7.30-9.15

David Everitt-Matthias sets his culinary imagination to work with great
success from what is essentially a classical French background, in this
cool grey and pink restaurant hung with contemporary prints. Choose
from the weekday menu du jour or daily table d'hôte after a compli-

mentary appetiser. A typical
meal might consist of
pressed foie gras with
mushy peas and ham hock
served with a warm green
bean and black pudding
salad, followed by chump of
Cinderford lamb in a herb
crust, or roast Wye Valley
salmon and squid with red
peppers and onion and a
light tomato dressing. For
dessert, you might try
tiramisu with coffee syrup
or iced honey and apricot
terrine. A recently introduced, well structured wine
list offers something for
everyone, including around
29 half bottles.

Biography

*From the age of seven, David Everitt-Matthias wanted to be a chef.
Starting off at The Inn on the Park in Mayfair, (during which time he
attended Ealing College to gain his City & Guilds qualifications) he
then helped set up a restaurant in Putney*

David

Everitt-Matthias

*specialising in Seychellois fish. After a spell at
Fingals, Fulham, he then achieved his main
ambition by opening his own restaurant in
Cheltenham. Here, he puts into practice a style that he says is
constantly evolving in accordance with his experience.*

CHELTENHAM   Epicurean

81 The Promenade, Cheltenham, Gloucestershire, GL51 1PJ
Tel: (01242) 222466   *Fax:* (01242) 222474   **£80**
Open: lunch Tue-Sun, dinner Tue-Sat
Meals served: lunch 12.30-2.30, dinner 7.30-9.30
   (Fri & Sat from 7; later by arrangement)

The Epicurean has now moved to a new address on the Promenade
where, in keeping with its name, even more sensual pleasures are on
offer. The first-floor restaurant continues in familiar style—Patrick
Macdonald's cooking continues to thrill gourmets and epicures alike.

The small menu offers starters like terrine
of pork knuckle and foie gras, sea scallops
with squid ink and ginger, or a risotto of
wild mushrooms and white truffle. To follow, there might be a confit of duck with
haricot beans and foie gras, roast salmon
with basil and tomato or a shellfish bouillon. Finally, enjoy a glazed lemon tart;
prune and vanilla parfait; or chocolate tart.
Moving down, the ground floor bistro has a
good choice of soup or salads to start, then
pasta, casserole dishes, grills and roasts. 20
wines by the glass, 50cl or bottle measures.
Down further to the basement where the
café/bar has a few tapas (now a generic
term for small dishes) a few tarts, wines
and beers throughout the day. We wish the
Macdonalds every deserved success with
their exciting venture.

■ **Patrick Macdonald**

CHELTENHAM   The Greenway

Shurdington, Cheltenham, Gloucestershire, GL51 5UG
Tel: (01242) 862352   *Fax:* (01242) 862780   **£70**
Open: lunch & dinner daily (closed Bank Holidays, 5 days Jan)
Meals served: lunch 12.30-2, dinner 7-9.30

Not far from the main road and set amid parkland with the gently
rolling Cotswolds beyond, this creeper-clad Elizabethan manor, a mile
or two south west of Cheltenham, is professionally run by Tony Elliott,
as it has been for the last 15 years. Excellent, warm, friendly service
and spacious, comfortable bedrooms are two of its greatest strengths.
The 19 bedrooms are located either in the main house or in the splendidly restored coach house annexe; all enjoy views of the gardens and
parkland. The restaurant, with its conservatory, looks out on to a
delightful sunken garden and lily pond. Chris Colmer produces interesting but not over-complicated dishes which might include fillet of
beef with a Stilton and walnut mousse, seared salmon with a
mignonette pepper crust and morel sauce, or braised pig's trotter filled
with a black pudding mousseline. Three vegetarian dishes are always
available—creamed risotto with wild mushroom perhaps. The shorter
fixed-price luncheon menu tends towards simpler dishes like boiled
ham hock with mashed potato or steak and chips. You could finish with
a warm rhubarb and custard tart with crumble topping. Good-value
New World wines on a predominantly French list.

CHELTENHAM   On The Park

Evesham Road, Cheltenham, Gloucestershire, GL52 2AH
Tel: (01242) 518898   *Fax:* (01242) 511526   **£45**
Open: lunch & dinner daily (closed 1 wk mid-Jan)
Meals served: lunch 12-2 (Sun to 2.30), dinner 7.30-9.30 (Sat to 10)

With the relocation of Patrick Macdonald's Epicurean from its location
within On the Park to a new town centre site (see previous entry), the
way has been cleared for a new style of operation at this town house
hotel and restaurant. The new restaurant concessionaires are Eamonn
and Nicola Webster, who were just settling in as we went to press.
Early menus (carte and set) offered the likes of mussel, celery, cream
and vermouth stew followed by chump of lamb, mint-roasted with lime,
orange, ginger and lemongrass, with a crunchy praline parfait
flavoured with pernod and served with a compote of blackberries to finish. The hotel side of the operation remains in the capable hands of
Darryl and Lesley-Ann Gregory. Twelve bedrooms are individually
designed with every modern comfort, and the suites are especially luxurious. Standards of maintenance are excellent throughout, as indeed
is the level of service.

CHELWOOD   Chelwood House

Chelwood, Bristol, Avon, BS18 4NH
Tel: (01761) 490730   *Fax:* (01761) 490730   **£50**
Open: lunch Sun, dinner Mon-Sat (closed 2 wks Jan)
Meals served: lunch Sun 12.30-1.15, dinner 7.30-9

A warm, welcoming atmosphere and outstanding views across the
rolling hills and meadows towards Bath (just ten miles away) are what
greet you on arrival at Chelwood. The former dower house, built in
1681, retains much of its original panelling. Bavarian-born chef-patron
Rudolf Birk and his wife are excellent hosts who clearly love the place.
Rooms are individually designed and there are three themed rooms
(French, Chinese and Victorian) which have the added luxury of four-
posters. High standards of food and service combine with Rudi's capable cooking in the bright, conservatory-style restaurant, complete with
fountain, gazebo and lush greenery. Typical dishes from Rudi's
European repertoire include home-made liver pâté with spicy pumpkin
preserve, Bavarian pasta with mushroom ragoût, prime haunch of
venison braised in red wine and served with baked apple and redcurrant jelly, or traditional roast rack of lamb with a rich rosemary
gravy. Angling enthusiasts may be attracted by nearby Chew Valley
Lake.

CHESTER   Chester Grosvenor

Eastgate Street, Chester, Cheshire, CH1 1LT
Tel: (01244) 324024   *Fax:* (01244) 313246
Arkle Restaurant   **£70**
Open: lunch Tue-Sun, dinner Mon-Sat (closed
    Bank Holidays, 2 wks from 25 Dec)
Meals served: 12-2.30, dinner 7-9.30
La Brasserie: **£40**
Open: all day daily (closed 25 & 26 Dec)
Meals served: lunch 12-2.30, dinner 7-9.30

Located within the ancient city walls, this 86-bedroomed hotel has been at the centre of Cheshire life for centuries. The restaurant offers modern cuisine in stylish, sophisticated surroundings with service to match. Executive chef Paul Reed (right) offers a wide choice of menu options, and for a lighter, more informal meal you can eat in the elegant, French-style brasserie which is open throughout the day. Head for the flagship Arkle restaurant, though, to sample the likes of woodland mushroom risotto, Loch Fyne oysters, shellfish stew or the dish of the day, carved from the silver trolley. The Brasserie menu is excellent too, with char-grills a feature alongside dishes such as pan-fried breast of duck with honeyed parsnips, and beef and horseradish sausages'n'mash. All in all, a grand and luxurious hotel, well deserving of its first-class reputation for quality, consistency and professionalism.

CHESTER   Crabwall Manor

Parkgate Road, Mollington, Chester, Cheshire, CH1 6NE
Tel: (01244) 851666   *Fax:* (01244) 851400   **£65**
Open: lunch & dinner daily
Meals served: lunch 12.30-2, dinner 7-9.45 (Sat to 10, Sun to 9)

Just north of Chester, set in 11 acres of formal gardens and parkland, this 48-bedroomed hotel offers a high level of luxury and comforts. The house dates back to mid-Victorian times: the exterior boasts distinctive turrets and there's a beautiful arched doorway over the clocktower entrance. Spacious rooms with excellent bathrooms are reached via a splendid stone staircase. A pianist plays in the evening, audible to the ears of the diners in the smart conservatory restaurant, where chef Michael Truelove's modern European-style dishes are served. Thinly-sliced scallops dressed with fruity olive oil and sweet basil, garnished with a clear tomato jelly or poached eggs set on spinach and glazed with cheese sauce to start, followed by roast best end of lamb served with a thyme jus and onion and shallot confit or fillets or red mullet served with basil flavoured olive oil and tomato confit. To finish, chilled caramelized rice pudding with a caramel syrup or hot lemon soufflé served with a lime sauce.

CHESTER — Francs

14 Cuppin Street, Chester, Cheshire, CH1 2BN
Tel: (01244) 317952   *Fax:* (01244) 340690   **£35**
Open: all day daily
Meals served: 11-11

Pop in for a quick snack or relax over a meal at this busy French brasserie, enlivened by the sound of background French rock music. A popular place throughout the day, with an extensive menu which includes many traditional favourites: bangers'n'mash, Francs fish'n'chips (dipped in a beer and crumb batter, then fried), moules Bretagne, mushrooms Bovary, crepes and salads, salmon hollandaise and boudin de Gaulle—a Caerphilly cheese pudding rolled and grilled. Good for family Sunday lunch.

CHICHESTER — Comme Ça

67 Broyle Road, Chichester, West Sussex, PO19 4BD
Tel: (01243) 788724   **£45**
Open: lunch Tue-Sun, dinner Tue-Sat (closed Bank Holidays)
Meals served: lunch 12-2, dinner 5.30-10.30

A pub-turned-French restaurant which is just a short walk from the Festival Theatre, so handy for pre- and post-theatre suppers. Jane and Michel Navet offer a sound, classically-based, extensive repertoire of dishes: from home-made soups to grilled peppered halibut béarnaise, entrecôte bordelaise, pan-fried calf's liver with sage, or medallions of pork with a ginger and lime sauce. Good choice of salads and similarly extensive choice on the two- and three-course lunch menus. An impressive list of wines is principally French with good representation of the main regions, a few New World wines creep in at the back pages. Take les enfants down on Sundays for a traditional French family lunch.

CHICHESTER — The Droveway

30a Southgate, Chichester, West Sussex, PO19 1DR
Tel: (01243) 528832   **£50**
Open: lunch & dinner Tue-Sat (closed 25 Dec, 2 wks Jan)
Meals served: lunch 12.30-2, dinner 7-10

Jonas Tester and his wife Elly have been running this smart, first-floor restaurant for over three years (though it has recently had a change of name), and in that time have built up a loyal following, as evidenced by the tone of the restaurant's quarterly newsletter. Menus combine classical and modern styles, with the new, simpler table d'hôte evening menu offering a simpler, plainer set of choices—supreme of chicken Mexicaine, escalope of salmon with thyme are typical. A separate vegetarian menu might offer a gratin of artichokes and courgettes or braised leeks in puff pastry. Good-value table d'hôte lunch, and delicious-sounding carte options such as wood pigeon, bacon and rocket salad. Those with a sweet tooth should leave room for desserts like saffron brûlée, bread and butter pudding or quenelles of bitter chocolate with an amaretto sauce.

CHILGROVE   White Horse Inn

Chilgrove, Nr Chichester, West Sussex, PO18 9HX
Tel: (01243) 535219   *Fax:* (01243) 535301   **£55**
Open: lunch Tue-Sun, dinner Tue-Sat (closed Feb, last wk Oct)
Meals served: lunch 12-2, dinner 7-9.30 (Sat to 10)

Lovers of wine will have plenty to delight in here. Barry Phillips has
spent 25 years building up his cellar and chef Neil Rusbridger provides
a happy complement for it with his culinary skills. Built as a hostelry in
1765, the White Horse has continued in that tradition to this day. The
cooking is honest and robust, using local fish and game with excellent
result in dishes such as sauté of local pheasant with artichoke and
horseradish sauce or civet of duck in Sauternes; fish dishes are prepared according to market availability and recited to you at your table,
but lobster and crab are frequent specialities. Menus take their influence from England and France, from both traditional and more modern
stables.

CHIPPING CAMPDEN   Cotswold House

The Square, Chipping Campden, Gloucestershire, GL55 6AN
Tel: (01386) 840330   *Fax:* (01386) 840310   **£55**
Open: lunch Sun only, dinner daily (closed 24-28 Dec)
Meals served: lunch 12-2, dinner 7.15-9.30,
    (light meals in Greenstocks 9.30am-10pm)

The Greenstocks run this 15-bedroomed late Georgian/early Regency
hotel in the centre of town with relaxed, easy-going charm, and staff
are cheerful and friendly. Themed bedrooms provide plenty of comfort
and are furnished in part with lovely period pieces and antiques. Enjoy
the comfort of the lounges in winter with roaring open fires, and in the
summer you can sit in the willow-shaded courtyard over a drink or
light meal from the adjoining continental-style café-bar. Alternatively,
the Garden Room restaurant provides a delightful setting overlooking
the walled garden for Scott Chance's English and continental-based
cuisine -a duo of warm fish terrines with champagne butter sauce followed by saddle of hare with port wine gravy, or grilled sea bass with
tarragon cream are a few of the dishes on offer. A very reasonably
priced house menu is also available.

CHIPPING CAMPDEN   Seymour House

High Street, Chipping Campden, Gloucestershire, GL55 6AH
Tel: (01386) 840429   *Fax:* (01386) 840369   **£55**
Open: lunch & dinner daily
Meals served: lunch 12-2, dinner 7-10

This 18th-century Cotswold-stone hotel boasts a 90-year-old vine in the
restaurant and a 500-year-old yew tree in the small rear garden overlooked by a patio. The bedrooms have quality Italian furnishings to
offset the original stonework and exposed beams. There is also a
garden cottage which houses some of the 16 bedrooms on offer.

CHOBHAM — Quails Restaurant

1 Bagshot Road, Chobham, Surrey, GU24 8BP
Tel: (01276) 858491 £45
Open: lunch Tue-Fri & Sun, dinner Tue-Sat (closed 26 Dec)
Meals served: lunch 12.30-2, dinner 7-10

This efficiently run family restaurant offers imaginative, well-executed cooking combining classic dishes such as soupe de poissons au rouille with more adventurous ones like filo parcel of monkfish with smoked bacon, grain mustard and Japanese seaweed. Boudin blanc is served on garlic crostini with honey and soy, while lamb's liver comes with smoked bacon and rich onion gravy. Desserts are high calorie and irresistible: nutty toffee tart, steamed treacle pudding with clotted cream or fruit sorbets in a brandy snap basket with red berry coulis. During the week and at Sunday lunch there are fixed price menus which offer good value. More than 100 wines from France and the New World have been well selected and have good tasting notes.

CHRISTCHURCH — Splinters Restaurant

11/12 Church Street, Christchurch, Dorset, BH23 1BW
Tel & Fax: (01202) 483454 £55
Open: lunch & dinner daily (closed 26-30 Dec, 2 wks Jan)
Meals served: lunch 12-2.30, dinner 7-10.30
   (light meals Number 11 Brasserie 10.30-2.30)

A small, friendly, informal French restaurant near the Priory. Chef Eamonn Redden joins the team here and makes the most of local produce; you might find dishes such as potted rabbit with home-made ale bread and Mrs W's apple chutney to start, followed by pan-fried fillet of salmon niçoise (a butter of black olives, french beans, tomatoes and herbs). Finish perhaps with British and Irish cheeses, Splinters' summer pudding made with brioche and berries served with clotted cream, or toasted strawberries with an elderflower sabayon, then coffee or tea served with home-made truffles. The lunch-time carte is simpler: mushroom and Gruyère omelette; lamb and pepper brochette on a bed on minted couscous. A sensibly priced wine list has four house wines under £10 and good value from all around the world.

CLANFIELD . The Plough at Clanfield

Bourton Road, Clanfield, Oxfordshire, OX18 2RB
Tel: (0136 781) 222   *Fax:* (0136 781) 596   **£70**
Open: lunch & dinner daily
Meals served: lunch 12-2, dinner 7-10 (Sun to 9.30)

This 16th-century Cotswold-stone manor house is covered in roses and wisteria and has six cosy bedrooms (some with whirlpool baths). Fixed-price menus come in many shapes and guises (l'épicure/gastronome/house) but you can always mix'n'match if you like. Lunch brings a single set-price menu or you can choose from the bar menu. The pleasant dining room earns its nomenclature (the Tapestry Room) from three framed tapestries on the walls, and it's a fine setting for Stephen Fischer's competent English and French cooking. Millefeuille of salmon and sole with a chive butter sauce, hot tartlet of Cornish crab and baby leeks with an apple and hazelnut salad, roast beef fillet with an onion soubise and tomato, basil and pine kernel sauce, or steamed fillet of turbot with a ratatouille and home-made noodles are typical of his range. An extensive Sunday brunch menu offers many traditional favourites like chicken chasseur, beef and Yorkshire pudding or the wrong-way-around-sounding Yorkshire pudding filled with steak and kidney.

CLAYGATE Les Alouettes

7 High Street, Claygate, Surrey, KT10 0JW
Tel: (01372) 464882   *Fax:* (01372) 65337   **£45**
Open: lunch Sun-Fri, dinner Mon-Sat
    (closed 1 wk Xmas)
Meals served: lunch 12-2.15, dinner 7-9.30 (Sat to 10)

The new fixed-price brasserie-style menu (Mon-Fri) offers some excellent value, both at lunchtime and in the evening. Start perhaps with French onion soup or deep-fried Whitby scampi with sauce tartare; follow with grilled skate wings, steak and kidney pie or Cumberland sausage with creamed potatoes and onion sauce. The carte is a little more modern and European in outlook, and includes a number of chargrilled dishes, from Dover sole to steaks or calf's liver and bacon. Elsewhere on the menu you might find deep-fried tempura of tiger prawns, hot smoked salmon on a tomato, mussel and basil sauce, or roast Gressingham duck with cassis and apple. Pretty decor.

CLITHEROE Browns Bistro

10 York Street, Clitheroe, Lancashire, BB7 2DL
Tel: (01200) 26928   **£50**
Open: lunch Mon-Fri, dinner Mon-Sat
    (closed 25 & 26 Dec, 1 Jan)
Meals served: lunch 12-2, dinner 7-10

Good, reliable cooking in this homely bistro where David Brown's Anglo-French menu pleases allcomers. Plenty of good fish and moderately priced wines but save yourself for the amazing range of ports. You can pick from 24 vintages spanning the years from '63 to '83!

COATHAM MUNDEVILLE   Hall Garth

Coatham Mundeville, Nr Darlington, Co Durham, DL1 3LU
Tel: (01325) 300400   *Fax:* (01325) 310083   **£45**
Open: lunch daily, dinner Mon-Sat
  (closed 24-26 Dec)
Meals served: lunch 12-2, dinner 7-10

Beautiful grounds surround this solid stone golf and country club which in parts dates back to 1540. Accommodation varies from the more traditional in the main house, furnished in period style and probably the best, to more modern yet comfortable rooms in a separate block. You can either eat in the dining room or a conservatory extension overlooking the grounds, which include a pretty walled garden full of fresh herbs. Choose from reliably cooked dishes such as peppered watercress soup, and pan-seared fillet of catfish on chili-flavoured noodles. Excellent leisure facilities include a heated outdoor pool and new nine-hole golf course.

COCKERMOUTH   Quince & Medlar

13 Castlegate, Cockermouth, Cumbria, CA13 9EU
Tel: (01900) 823579   **£35**
Open: dinner Tue-Sun (closed Bank Holidays, 2/3 wks
  Jan, Sun Xmas-Easter)
Meals served: dinner 7-9.30

Not far from Cockermouth Castle, in a Georgian building, you'll find this small, family-run vegetarian restaurant, run on informal, friendly lines by Colin and Louisa Le Voi. The wood-panelled, candle-lit dining room is comfortable and intimate. Colin's cooking is careful and creatively presented. The à la carte features about five or six options for each course. Typical starters include Stilton cheese soufflé, warm French onion tart and cream of watercress soup and main courses could include spinach and mushroom pasta, mushroom and smoked Westmorland cheese roulade or nut terrine. A short wine list includes a number of organic, non-alcoholic and English country wine.

COGGESHALL   Baumann's Brasserie

4-6 Stoneham Street, Coggeshall, Essex, CO6 1TT
Tel: (01376) 561453   *Fax:* (01376) 563762   **£55**
Open: lunch Tue-Fri & Sun, dinner Tue-Sat
  (closed Bank Holidays, 2 wks Jan)   *Good local restaurant*
Meals served: lunch 12.30-2, dinner 7.30-10

The monthly-changing à la carte menu at this friendly brasserie offers a well-thought-out selection of dishes. Start with chicken liver parfait and toasted brioche with a Cumberland onion marmalade or creamy Jerusalem artichoke soup. Move on to a mid-course offering such as blackcurrant and Gewurztraminer granita or smoked salmon parcels, before getting to grips with main-course dishes such as char-grilled guinea fowl in an Indonesian satay sauce or game stew of venison and pheasant with juniper and rösti potatoes. The decor is a legacy from its earlier incarnation under Peter Langan; young and enthusiastic staff. Look out for another branch in Colchester.

COGGESHALL — White Hart Hotel

Market End, Coggeshall, Essex, CO6 1NH
Tel: (01376) 561654   *Fax:* (01376) 561789   **£55**
Open: lunch daily, dinner Mon-Sat
Meals served: lunch 12-2, dinner 7-10

Flagstone floors, low beams, an inglenook fireplace and, reputedly, res-ident ghosts make this centuries-old, family-run inn an atmospheric choice. There are 18 en-suite bedrooms in all, six in the original house, the rest in a new extension. The Italian menu ranges from a variety of pastas to risottos, char-grilled steaks and fish, and game, with dishes such as grilled breast of duck served with Amaretto showing the range. Desserts include Fausto's speciality—tiramisu. Sunday lunch sees an anglicised menu come to the fore, with beef and Yorkshire pudding or Scottish salmon en croûte holding the fort. Bar snacks available for lighter lunchtime appetites.

COLERNE — Lucknam Park

Colerne, Wiltshire, SN14 8AZ
Tel: (01225) 742777   *Fax:* (01225) 743536   **£90**
Open: lunch & dinner daily
Meals served: lunch 12.30-2, dinner 7.30-9.30
(Sat to 9.45)

An elegant 42-bedroomed Georgian house, quintessentially English, is approached via a straight, mile-long, beech-lined drive on the southern edge of the Cotswolds, just six miles from Bath. Chef Michael Womersley (right) has a modern English repertoire that does justice to the elegance and beauty of the house. Regional produce is the mainstay of his menus. Try half a home-smoked lobster with garden herbs to start, or tortellini of lamb in mutton broth scented with lime leaves, or glazed scallops and langoustine with a spinach mousse. Main-course offerings might include supreme of Trelough duck served with sautéed foie gras and sherry sauce, roast monkfish with a crisp sesame seed coating and soy ginger butter sauce or, for vegetari-ans, a lasagne of wild mushrooms with coriander sauce, spiked with the finest-cut vegetables and lentils. The lunch-time menu is a little more down-to-earth, with the likes of lamb broth or oriental-spiced hot pot of Cornish fish leading the way for pan-fried salmon with saffron sauce or a roast brace of quail served on cabbage and bacon with truf-

fle sauce. For dessert, keep an eye out for the hot chocolate pudding served simply, with dollops of Devonshire clotted cream, or for some-thing a little lighter opt for the day's soufflé. Good leisure facilities include a pool, beauty room and tennis court.

COLTISHALL   Norfolk Place Restaurant

Point House, High Street, Coltishall, Norfolk, NR12 7AA
Tel: (01603) 738991   **£60**
Open: dinner Wed-Sat (closed 3 days Xmas)
Meals served: dinner 7.30-9

Some of you will remember Nick Gill as the chef who put Hambleton Hall on the culinary map some years ago. He has moved east to Norfolk and opened a small restaurant with Phillipa Atkinson in this small village. Dinner is chosen from a fixed-price menu and whilst you do so a house aperitif is offered, along with an appetiser such as tartlets of crab. There are five first courses, perhaps a terrine of foie gras with Burgundy poached pears, a feuillete of asparagus with chive butter or lamb's sweetbreads and smoked bacon with a salad of basil. Fish features strongly on the main dishes: a whole roast lobster served with saffron tagliatelle, poached salmon with fennel cream sauce or perhaps tuna fish with white wine, tomatoes and thyme. Pot-roast guinea fowl is flavoured with white truffles and barbary duck with blackberries and cassis. Farmhouse cheeses follow, and then imaginative puddings, a vanilla omelette flavoured with sauce Suzette, a hot soufflé of passion fruit, oranges and brandy or a light sorbet of fresh mangoes and elderflower. House wines start at under £8 and there are some excellent bottles at reasonable prices.

CORFE CASTLE   Mortons House Hotel

45 East Street, Corfe Castle, Dorset, BH20 5EE
Tel: (01929) 480988   *Fax:* (01929) 480820   **£50**
Open: lunch & dinner daily
Meals served: lunch 12-2, dinner 7-9

Mortons is a privately-owned, 16th-century Elizabethan manor house, linked by underground passages to the Norman castle of Corfe, where Edward, first king of England, was martyred in 978 AD. The present house was built in 1590. A walled garden overlooks the thatched roofs of the village, and there is a terrace and courtyard for alfresco relaxation. The 17 en-suite bedrooms are decorated in mostly traditional style, some with four-posters and spa baths. Traditional English cuisine with a nod here and there towards the Continent.

CORSE LAWN   Corse Lawn House

Corse Lawn, Nr Gloucester, Gloucestershire, GL19 4LZ
Tel: (01452) 780771   *Fax:* (01452) 780840   **£60**
Open: lunch & dinner daily
Meals served: lunch 12-2, dinner 7-10

An elegant Queen Anne House run by the Hine family since 1978, Corse Lawn is set back from the village green, in 12 acres of grounds. The house is fronted by an unusual ornamental pond, originally built as a coach wash into which you could drive and turn a coach-and-four. The 19 spacious bedrooms are prettily furnished with floral fabrics and antiques, and good bathrooms have generous towelling and robes. Baba Hine and her young team produce everything from the bread to the chocolates served with coffee. Menus offer modern interpretations of mostly classic French and English dishes: hot crab sausage with tomato sauce and chick peas; fresh water crayfish with chives and noodles; poached halibut with watercress sauce; pigeon breasts in red wine; hot butterscotch pudding. For lighter meals there's the popular bistro in the bar area—it has attracted a loyal local following. A separate vegetarian menu offers an excellent choice with French onion tart to start perhaps, followed by wild mushroom pancake with white wine and cream, and rhubarb bavaroise.

Total family commitment makes Corse Lawn an enjoyable and relaxing place to stay.

CORSHAM   Rudloe Park

Leafy Lane, Corsham, Wiltshire, SN13 0PA
Tel: (01225) 810555   *Fax:* (01225) 811412   **£35**
Open: lunch & dinner daily
Meals served: lunch 12-2, dinner 7-10
Steve and Ros Slater have now taken over the reins at this small country house hotel. Geoff Bell remains as head chef.

COWAN BRIDGE   Cobwebs

Leck, Cowan Bridge, Nr Kirkby Lonsdale, Lancashire, LA6 2HZ
Tel: (0152 42) 72141   **£55**
Open: dinner Tue-Sat (closed Jan & Feb)
Meals served: dinner 7.30 for 8

Booking is essential at this intimate little 24-seater restaurant with rooms on the edge of the Yorkshire Dales. On arrival you will be ushered into the Victorian parlour for a pre-dinner drink where partner Paul Kelly will announce the evening menu, a daily-changing feast prepared by partner and chef Yvonne Thompson, with some excellent wines (Paul's domain) in support. Courtesy and old-fashioned traditional charm are the keynotes at this country restaurant. Stay overnight in one of the five rooms with a view over the Pennines and Lune Valley to make a real occasion of it all, and catch a classic country breakfast before heading off.

CRANLEIGH   La Barbe Encore

High Street, Cranleigh, Surrey, GU6 8AE
Tel: (01483) 273889   **£45**
Open: lunch Tue-Fri, dinner Tue-Sat (closed Bank Holidays)
Meals served: lunch 12-2, dinner 7-10

The ambience here is that of a quirky French bistro, with a warm and
cosy atmosphere. The cooking is in the capable hands of chef-patron
Jean-Pierre Bonnet, whose approach is essentially mainstream classic
French. Snails in garlic butter, magret de canard with pear, red wine
and cinnamon sauce, pan-fried steak and shallots, breast of chicken
filled with veal sweetbreads and mushrooms, and always a fish dish of
the day. A popular local following means it's best to book.

CROSBY-ON-EDEN   Crosby Lodge

High Crosby, Crosby-on-Eden, Nr Carlisle, Cumbria, CA6 4QZ
Tel: (01228) 573618   *Fax:* (01228) 573428   **£60**
Open: lunch daily, dinner Mon-Sat
    (closed 24 Dec-mid Jan)   ❖
Meals served: lunch 12-1.30, dinner 7.15-8.45 (Sun 7.15-8.45)

A Georgian country house with Victorian additions overlooking mature
parkland and the river. Eleven bedrooms, some in the main house and
others in the converted stable block, provide comfortable, mostly spacious accommodation, and the Sedgwicks (who have run this hotel for
almost 25 years) are dedicated hosts. The bar menu offers a wide
range of snacks and light meals, including grills; the restaurant a repertoire of traditional British and Continental fare: roast farm duckling
with orange sauce; roulade of beef braised in rich Burgundy sauce; croquettes of lentils and couscous served with pasta in tomato sauce; and
grilled Solway salmon hollandaise. Good wine list with some reasonable bargains.

CUCKFIELD   Murray's

Broad Street, Cuckfield, West Sussex, RH17 5LJ
Tel: (01444) 455826   **£45**
Open: lunch Mon-Fri, dinner Mon-Sat
    (closed Bank Holidays, 2 wks Feb, 2 wks Aug)
Meals served: lunch 12-1.30, dinner 7.15-9.30

There is a marked European influence to Sue Murray's interesting
repertoire at this cosy restaurant. The short, mixed menu features
starters such as leek and apple tart, taramasalata parcels and chicken
liver parfait, while a main course might be shoulder of lamb with flageolet beans. Prides itself on being more family orientated than most.
There's usually a choice of three or four dishes for vegetarians.

CUCKFIELD — Ockenden Manor

Ockenden Lane, Cuckfield, West Sussex, RH17 5LD
Tel: (01444) 416111   *Fax:* (01444) 415549   **£55**
Open: lunch & dinner daily
Meals served: lunch 12.30-2, dinner 7.30-9.30

A delightful Tudor manor, dating from 1520, with beautiful rear gardens overlooking the South Downs. The house is furnished with taste throughout, from the lovely panelled restaurant with stained glass windows to the 22 bedrooms, each named after members of the two families who have owned the house since 1520. The original part of the house has been sympathetically extended over the last two centuries, with recent additions including extra bedrooms and a conservatory. There are four-posters in some of the rooms.

DARLINGTON — Sardis

196, Northgate, Darlington, Durham, DU1 1QU
Tel: (01325) 461222   **£40**
Open: lunch & dinner Mon-Sat
Meals served: lunch 12-2.30, dinner 7-9.45

A cheerful town centre Sardinian restaurant run by enthusiastic partners. The three-course lunch is £11, three-course dinner £16, but both include half a bottle of wine. Traditional Italian and British dishes, mostly Italian wines.

DARLINGTON — Victor's Restaurant

84 Victoria Road, Darlington, Durham, DL1 5JW
Tel: (01325) 480818   **£45**
Open: lunch & dinner Tue-Sat (closed 1 wk Xmas)
Meals served: lunch 12-2, dinner 7-10.30

Local produce takes precedence at this popular local restaurant, run by Jayne and Peter Robinson, and once a year there's kid on the menu, specially bred for the restaurant by a local supplier! Everything, from bread to ice creams, is home-made. Dinner menus change monthly, lunch menus fortnightly, and the food is in modern British style. Start with onion and sage tart or coarse pork and liver pâté, followed by roast bacon with tarragon cream, steamed fillet of plaice with basil and orange butter sauce, or tenderloin of pork with apricots and celery. Lunch-time offerings are simpler—chicken and leek pie, smoked haddock fish cakes. Steamed ginger fudge pudding is a popular choice among desserts. Look out for the interesting local farm cheese.

Interesting cooking at this 30-seater restaurant.

DARTMOUTH   **Carved Angel**

2 South Embankment, Dartmouth, Devon, TQ6 9BH *An all-time favourite*
Tel: (01803) 832465   **£100**
Open: lunch Tue-Sun, dinner Tue-Sat (closed Bank Holidays
    except Good Friday, 6 wks Jan/Feb, 1st wk Oct)
Meals served: lunch 12.30-2, dinner 7.30-9

Joyce Molyneux uses only the best of local produce. Fresh shellfish,
sea bass, turbot, mullet, salmon and trout are joined by local beef, poultry and game, and local fruit and vegetables supplied by the same reliable source for over 20 years. A delightful restaurant overlooking the

harbour set in an impressive quayside timbered building, this is a gem, worthy of the
highest accolades. Stylish but unpretentious inside, one of the main events is seeing Joyce and chef Nick Coiley moving
around the open kitchen. The other main
event is eating the results. The cooking is
European with a Mediterranean bias.
Dishes such as provençal fish soup, turbot
with prawn sauce and tomato couscous,
calf's liver with gin and lime sauce, lamb
with rosemary and pheasant in red wine
with pig's trotters are all typical of the
range. What's more, the staff are charming
and the wine list is excellent.

Biography

**Joyce
Molyneux**

*Joyce Molyneux went into cooking for the sheer love of it, but with a
determination and efficiency that has been a hallmark of her career ever
since. After two years at Birmingham College of Domestic Science, a
year with an industrial caterer and a stint at the
Mulberry Tree, Stratford-upon-Avon, she then joined
George Perry-Smith at the Hole in the Wall in Bath,
before taking on the fresh challenge of opening The
Carved Angel. A major figurehead for the English cookery world, she has
been at the forefront of a revival of the reputation of English food in the
eyes of the world, and is one of the handful of woman chefs to have
reached the upper echelons of her chosen profession.*

DEDHAM   Fountain House & Dedham Hall

Brook Street, Dedham, Nr Colchester, Essex, CO7 6AD
Tel: (01206) 323027   **£45**
Open: lunch Sun, dinner Tue-Sat (closed Bank Holidays)
Meals served: lunch 12.30-3, dinner 7-9.30   ✤

Simple, well executed cooking by Wendy Sarton is the norm at this
attractive house that overlooks a walled garden, just outside Dedham.
Menus are fixed price but with bags of choice: there's lentil and ham
soup and scrambled eggs with smoked salmon amongst the starters
then devilled lamb's kidneys, trout with orange and walnut stuffing or
sirloin steak with garlic butter. The dessert menu also has good variety
and some interesting half bottles to drink with them. Budding
Constables may enjoy residential painting courses in the summer.

DEDHAM   Maison Talbooth

Stratford Road, Dedham, Nr Colchester, Essex, CO7 6HN
Tel: (01206) 322367   *Fax:* (01206) 322752

This tranquil, country hotel, in an area immortalised by John
Constable, offers an air of quiet luxury. The ten bedroom suites are
individually furnished and named after English poets: Wordsworth,
Shelley, Milton, Shakespeare, Keats, Browning, Tennyson, Brooke,
Kipling, Masefield. Several of the rooms boast sunken or spa baths,
superb country views or terraces with steps that lead out to the garden,
and also benefits from immaculate housekeeping and attention to
detail. This is part of the Gerald Milsom's Stour Valley enterprise
which includes the riverside Talbooth restaurant, a short drive away in
a courtesy car (see entry below). Room service with breakfast and light
meals (omelettes, sandwiches, steaks) is available up to 11pm.

DEDHAM   Le Talbooth

Gunhill, Dedham, Nr Colchester, Essex, CO7 6HP
Tel: (01206) 323150   *Fax:* (01206) 322752   **£50**
Open: lunch & dinner daily
Meals served: lunch 12-2, dinner 7-9.30   ✤

This beautifully located restaurant in a splendidly preserved, half-
timbered Tudor building on the banks of the River Stour is a delightful
place to eat, indoors and out. The dining room overlooks the riverside
terrace on which you can sit under large canvas parasols in summer.
Inside, soft pastel shades of pink and blue and ancient beams create a
charming setting for Henrik Iversen's fixed-price, two or three-course
menus which change weekly, alongside the seasonal carte. The cooking is modern with traditional undertones. Set menus offer the likes of
daily roasts and Irish stew alongside medallions of pork with a mushroom risotto and stroganoff sauce. The carte is similar in style but
offers greater choice: starters such as soufflé Talbooth (Finnan haddock and mushrooms topped with cheese soufflé), pan-fried queen
scallops or marinated king prawns; and main dishes which might feature steak and kidney pie or délice of sole Talbooth (filled with a light
prawn mousse and served with a Sauternes butter sauce).
Comprehensive, informative, good value wine list.

DENMEAD — Barnard's

Hambledon Road, Denmead, Nr Portsmouth,
  Hampshire, PO7 6NU
Tel: (01705) 257788   **£35**
Open: dinner Tue-Sat (closed Bank Holidays,
  1 wk Xmas, 2 wks Aug)
Meals served: dinner 7.30-10

David and Sandie Barnard continue to do things the French country
way in new premises in Denmead (previously they were on the high
street in Cosham). David's speciality, twice-baked Swiss cheese ouffles,
continue to be most popular, along with other starters such as fresh
crab spiked with a fennel fumet and served with glazed pink grapefruit.
Main courses might include roast guinea fowl breast with creamy
mushroom sauce, and the fish dishes are determined daily. The vegetarian choice might be stir-fried vegetables on a Stilton sauce wrapped
in crisp pastry. Excellent-value set menu in support of the carte, at only
£13.50.

DISS — Weavers

Market Hill, Diss, Norfolk, IP22 3JZ
Tel: (01379) 642411   **£40**
Open: lunch Mon-Fri, dinner Mon-Sat (closed Bank Holidays,
  1 wk Xmas, 2 wks Aug)
Meals served: lunch 12-2, dinner 7-9.30

This old, beamed town-house restaurant has plenty of character—the
house dates back to the 15th century when it was built as a chapel for
the local Weavers' Guild. It was converted for use as a restaurant in
1974 but it wasn't until a decade later that William and Wilma Bavin
moved in, completely refurbishing the place, exposing and treating all
the beams and generally making the most of the building's heritage.
All this provides a colourful backcloth in which to enjoy William's cooking. Starters might range from wild rabbit and pork terrine to poached
quenelles of crab mousseline on a Thermidor sauce; main courses offer
the likes of steamed salmon with a lemon and ginger glaze or fillet of
beef en croûte, topped with warmed chicken liver pâté. The menus mix
innovation and tradition, but the main emphasis is on modern interpretations of classic dishes. Lighter lunches in the wine bar mould—stir-
fried chicken tikka masala; home-made venison sausages;
Mexican-style turkey enchilladas.

DORCHESTER   Mock Turtle

34 High West Street, Dorchester, Dorset, DT1 1UP
Tel: (01305) 264011   **£45**
Open: lunch Tue-Fri, dinner Mon-Sat (closed dinner
    Bank Holidays, 26 Dec)
Meals served: lunch 12-2, dinner 7-9.30

Local seafood is among the specialities at this attractive, 17th-century
town house restaurant, made up of a number of interconnecting rooms.
Daily specials, including plenty of fish dishes, supplement the fixed-
price lunch and dinner menus which offer plenty of choice with an
international slant. Whole grilled Dover sole, or Chinese-style pork in
lemon sauce, English Lunesdale duck with a sesame seed crust or
lamb in Greek pastry with a Madeira sauce are examples of the dishes
on offer. Lunch-time brings a shorter, less expensive menu, and
desserts range from the classic lemon brûlée to the more exotic, such
as raspberry sablé or chocolate délice.

DORKING   Partners West Street

2-4 West Street, Dorking, Surrey, RH4 1BL
Tel: (01306) 882826   **£50**
Open: lunch Sun-Fri, dinner Mon-Sat (closed 25 & 26 Dec)
Meals served: lunch 12.30-2, dinner 7.30-9.30

Modern decor enhances this charming, intimate restaurant located on
two floors of a 16th-century building just off the main street. Just as we
went to press, a new chef joined—Anthony Robinson from the Dining
Room in Reigate, where he had built up a good following. However,
partner Tim McEntire still keeps a watchful eye on matters, and early
summer menus looked good: a tartlet of smoked haddock brandade
with lime and chive sauce to start, followed by fillet of scotch beef
topped with mozzarella and served with spinach and garlic potatoes
and truffle oil dressing, finishing with roast peach with a peach and
thyme sorbet. The entire restaurant is now non smoking.

DORRINGTON   Country Friends

Dorrington, Nr Shrewsbury, Shropshire, SY5 7JD
Tel: (01743) 718707   **£55**
Open: lunch & dinner Tue-Sat (closed Bank Holidays,
    2 wks Jul, 1 wk Oct)   ✻
Meals served: lunch 12-2, dinner 7-9 (Sat to 9.30)

A comfortable restaurant in a half-timbered building, with three rooms
for overnight guests in a coach house annexe. Chef-patron Charles
Whittaker produces dishes such as spinach fettucine with smoked
salmon, calf's liver with citrus fruit, local duck with a spiced plum and
ginger sauce and fillet steak with celeriac and an oriental sauce, and
there's always a fish dish of the day. Desserts might include traditional
bread and butter pudding or delicious apple galette with mint custard.
Good value set menus also available.

DREWSTEIGNTON	Hunts Tor House

Drewsteignton, Devon, EX6 6QW
Tel: (01647) 21228 **£40**
Open: dinner daily (closed Dec-Feb)
Meals served: dinner at 7.30

A restaurant with four rooms at the centre of Dartmoor village. After a restful overnight stay, ask for smoked salmon and scrambled egg as an alternative to the continental breakfast, to set you up for a day exploring. The in the evening come back to a no-choice, fixed-price dinner menu which might include the likes of smoked salmon blinis with sour cream and a timbale of broccoli with tomato sauce, then skate with black butter or guinea fowl with a prune and Armagnac sauce as maincourses. Finish perhaps with bread and butter pudding or crème brûlée.

DULVERTON	Ashwick House

Dulverton, Somerset, TA22 9QD   *A unique experience, well*
Tel: (01398) 23868   *Fax:* (01398) 23056   *worth trying.* **£50**
Open: lunch Sun, dinner daily
Meals served: lunch 12.30-1.45, dinner 7.15-8.30

In Dulverton, turn left at the end of the village and take the road alongside the river Bark, then drive up onto Exmoor, turning left after the first cattle grid to find Richard Sherwood's splendidly isolated Edwardian country house. There are six bedrooms, all spacious, with lovely views across the National Park. Sweeping lawns lead to large water gardens with lily ponds, providing an oasis for relaxation. This is old-world hospitality—bright and sunny with flowers in summer; cosy and candlelit, with log fires in the galleried hall in winter. Richard's dinners are a four-course affair with restricted choice, British cordon bleu in style, with a nod towards local traditions. Apple and coriander soup, noisettes of spring lamb with a port wine sauce, and bread and butter pudding, are the sort of thing he offers. A one-man show but with great attention to small detail and creature comforts.

DUNBRIDGE	Mill Arms Inn

Dunbridge, Nr Romsey, Hampshire, SO51 0LF
Tel: (01794) 340401 **£45**
Open: lunch & dinner daily
Meals served: lunch 12-2.30, dinner 7-10 (Fri & Sat to 10.30)

Real ales, good bar food and a restaurant which sets high standards are some of the attractions of Niall Morrow's village pub opposite the railway station. Daily blackboard specials in the bar range from home-made soup and sandwiches to steak and kidney pie and many traditional favourites. A skittle alley at the rear (for pre-booked parties only) offers further opportunities for indulgence—and exercise.

DUXFORD   Duxford Lodge

Ickleton Road, Duxford, Nr Cambridge, Cambridgeshire, CB2 4RU
Tel: (01223) 836444   *Fax:* (01223) 832271   **£40**
Open: lunch Sun-Fri, dinner daily
Meals served: lunch 12-2, dinner 7-9.30

This 15-bedroomed hotel in the pretty village of Duxford was host to
Douglas Bader during the Second World War. A quiet, well-run place
in an acre of tended gardens, it is comfortable, secluded and friendly.
The restaurant offers a classic, traditional menu with speciality coffees
from around the world to finish. Lobster thermidor, Dover sole meunière, chef's pie of the day, venison royale and rack of lamb, steaks and
grills, and a vegetarian dish of the day are all featured.

EAST BOLDON   Forsters

2 St Bedes, Station Road, East Boldon, Tyne & Wear, NE36 0LE
Tel: 091-519 0929   **£55**
Open: dinner Tue-Sat
Meals served: dinner 7-10

Look for the bottle-green exterior among a small row of shops, herald-
ing Barry Forster's pretty little seven-table restaurant which is an
appealing and comfortable place in which to enjoy his predominately
French and English style of cooking, Barry lists Cheddar cheese and
chive soufflé and Thai-style king prawns among his specialities—the
menu is both imaginative and eclectic. You could start with snails in
sizzling garlic butter or pork and liver pâté with home made apricot
chutney. For main courses, there's roast beef with mustard, herbs and
red wine or roast loin of venison with braised cabbage, bacon and caraway. Desserts range from white chocolate truffle cake laced with
Grand Marnier to sticky toffee pudding.

EAST BUCKLAND   Lower Pitt

East Buckland, Barnstaple, Devon, EX32 0TD
Tel & Fax: (01598) 760243   **£45**
Open: dinner Tue-Sat (closed 25 Dec)
Meals served: dinner 7-8.30

This is a pretty, 16th-century, white-washed farmhouse with warm, cottagey appeal, located on the edge of Exmoor. Fresh produce from the
kitchen garden and local suppliers is the mainstay of the cooking.
Relax in the elegant conservatory dining room to enjoy Suzanne Lyons'
tempting dinner menus which offer plenty of choice. Mediterranean
king prawns with mayonnaise dip to start; followed by lamb Kashmir-
style, escalope of salmon with lemon butter sauce, veal escalopes or
beef stroganoff. Lunches by arrangement. There are three double
rooms for overnight guests, all en-suite and centrally heated.

EAST GRINSTEAD   Gravetye Manor

Vowels Lane, East Grinstead, West Sussex, RH19 4LJ
Tel: (01342) 810567   *Fax:* (01342) 810080   **£60**
Open: lunch & dinner daily (closed dinner 25 Dec)
Meals served: lunch 12.30-2, dinner 7.30-9.30 (Sun to 9)

Peter Herbert sets high standards for the running of country house
hotels. This beautifully restored Elizabethan stone mansion, built in
1598, with its 1000 acres of grounds complete with lake is among the
finest hotels in the land. The gardens are the legacy of former owner
and landscape gardener William Robinson who bought the house in
1884, restoring much of it to its original beauty, and realising many of
his ideas for the English natural garden style which was later to be
copied worldwide. As much painstaking care and attention goes into
preserving and maintaining the gardens here as into the house itself.
Beautifully designed bedrooms, of which there are 18, are models of
good taste and are named after trees on the estate; bathrooms are
sumptuous. Equally high standards are upheld in the kitchens, with a
delightful balance between modern and traditional in French and
English cuisine. Fish is a prominent feature and the hotel has its own
smokehouse: home-smoked venison, delicate fish sausage, tortellini of
crab and confit of duck are specialities. Fabulous wine list with some
reasonably priced good bottles under £20, plus their own water from a
spring which has served the Manor since 1598. Service throughout is
faultless.

EASTBOURNE   Grand Hotel

King Edward's Parade, Eastbourne, East Sussex, BN21 4EQ
Tel: (01323) 412345   *Fax:* (01323) 412233   **£55**
Open: lunch & dinner Tue-Sat (closed Bank Holidays, 2 wks Jan)
Meals served: lunch 12.30-2.30, dinner 7-10.30

This, as the name suggests, is one of the spacious and gracious grand
luxury hotels. The whitewashed hotel on the seafront has sea-facing
balconies in some of the larger of its 164 rooms, as well as good family,
leisure, and conference facilities. The Mirabelle restaurant is fittingly
elegant, and offers English- and French-inspired dishes served by
smart staff—menus show flair and imagination. A well-conceived à la
carte is supplemented by daily set menus at both lunch and dinner.
Dishes such as warm salad of lobster with orange and tarragon, Dover
Sole normande and the more simpler lunchtime offering of pan-fried
lamb's liver and bacon served with bubble'n'squeak and devil's sauce
are typical of the range.

EDBURTON — Tottington Manor

Edburton, Nr Henfield, West Sussex, BN5 9LJ
Tel: (01903) 815757   *Fax:* (01903) 879331   **£80**
Open: lunch & dinner daily (closed 25 & 26 Dec,
   dinner Sun Jan-Easter)
Meals served: lunch 12-2.15, dinner 7-9.15

This small, six-bedroomed hotel in its own grounds, has views over the South Downs and Sussex Weald. The main part of the house dates back to the 16th century but the origins of the site go back to medieval times. Ex-Ritz chef-patron David Miller offers a variety of seasonal game, coastal, river and shellfish specialities, and makes good use of local produce. Dishes on the à la carte and fixed-price menus, which are essentially English in style, include dishes such as char-grilled chicken and tarragon sausage with a grain mustard sauce to start; followed by poached fillet of salmon in a pink champagne and pink peppercorn sauce. Smashing breakfasts offer locally oak-smoked kippers and own new-laid eggs.

EDENBRIDGE — Honours Mill Restaurant

87 High Street, Edenbridge, Kent, TN8 5AU
Tel: (01732) 866757   **£70**
Open: lunch Tue-Fri & Sun, dinner Tue-Sat (closed 1-2 wks Xmas)
Meals served: lunch 12.15-2, dinner 7.15-10

Martin Radmall's well-thought-out fixed-price menus offer some careful French and English cooking of reliably good standard in this charming, converted mill owned by the Goodhew brothers. Starters might include onion soup topped with a cheese soufflé, crab-filled ravioli with a caviar and chive sauce or casserole of snails and wild mushrooms. Main courses could be along the lines of pot-roast foie-gras-stuffed pheasant. Fish and shellfish depend on the day's market. Among desserts you might find Martin's speciality: Sussex pond pudding, or fresh lime tart. Good-value fixed-price lunch at £14.50.

ELCOT — Jarvis Elcot Park

Elcot, Nr Newbury, Berkshire, RG16 8NJ
Tel: (01488) 58100   *Fax:* (01488) 58288   **£40**
Open: lunch & dinner daily
Meals served: lunch 12.30-2, dinner 7.30-9.30

Royal gardener Sir William Paxton left his mark here at Elcot Park in 1848, the gardens surrounding this 75-bedroomed Georgian house are his work. The house was built in 1768 and among its earlier inhabitants was the poet Shelley's mother who came here shortly after her son's death. Bedrooms are in the main house, in a new wing connected to the house by a lovely conservatory, or in the courtyard mews annexe. The new health and leisure club includes the services of a resident masseur and beauty therapist, on duty four days a week, making this an ideal retreat for business or leisure purposes. Cooking is in the modern British mode: starters such as woodland mushroom and tarragon casserole or warm chicken salad with a light soy vinaigrette could be followed by roast pheasant with lentils, monkfish wrapped in bacon or the more traditional grilled Dover sole or char-grilled sirloin steak.

ELTON   Loch Fyne Oyster Bar

The Old Dairy Building, Elton, Cambridgeshire, PE8 6SG
Tel: (01832) 280298   **£35**
Open: all day daily (closed 25 & 26 Dec)
Meals served: 9-9 (Fri & Sat to 10, Sun to 5)

One of several offshoots of the Highland restaurant of the same name
(see Cairngow, Scotland). Stop for a plate of fresh rock oysters, a
seafood platter or fish from the Loch Fyne smokehouse in relaxed surroundings. Almost everything on the menu is of West Highlands origin: shellfish soup or spicy seafood chowder, scallops in white wine,
smoked eel and trout, plus daily fish and vegetarian specials. Scottish
smoked venison and steak for meat eaters.

ELY   Fen House Restaurant

2 Lynn Road, Littleport, Ely, Cambridgeshire, CB6 1QG
Tel: (01353) 860645   **£50**
Open: dinner Tue-Sat (closed 25 & 26 Dec)
Meals served: dinner 7.30-9   *Great little place*

A friendly welcome and comfortable surroundings are the perfect
accompaniment to ex-Savoy and Buckingham Palace chef David Warne
and wife Gaynor's intimate restaurant. Fresh seasonal ingredients dic-
tate the bi-monthly-changing dinner menus which feature classically
inspired dishes. To start: parsnip and apple soup, confit of duck, or soft-
boiled quail's eggs in a nest of French beans with a creamy dressing;
for main course: breast of guinea fowl with lentils and bacon, fillets of
monkfish with mustard and a vegetable brunoise, or cabbage parcel
filled with a carrot and orange purée served on a bed of Star Anise
sauce. Lunches by arrangement.

ELY   Old Fire Engine House

25 St Mary's Street, Ely, Cambridgeshire, CB7 4ER
Tel: (01353) 662582   **£45**
Open: lunch daily, dinner Mon-Sat (closed Bank Holidays,
     2 wks Xmas/New Year)
Meals served: lunch 12.30-2, dinner 7.30-9

Built for the fire service in the 18th century, the house was converted
into an art gallery/restaurant in the late '60s. You'll find there's plenty
of atmosphere in the main room, with tiled flooring, kitchen tables and
pew seating; other dining areas are more formal and elegant. This is
good old traditional English cooking, the sort that warms the cockles
of your heart! Home-made soups (white onion/ham and lentil/Scotch
broth/watercress...), steak and kidney or turkey pie, pigeon casserole,
jugged hare, pike in white wine, roast beef and Yorkshire pudding,
pork chops in Suffolk cider, lemon sole with prawns and fennel, apple
pie and cream, rhubarb crumble. A hundred or so wines are lengthily
described and moderately priced.

EMSWORTH   36 On The Quay

The Quay, South Street, Emsworth, Hampshire, PO10 7EG
Tel: (01243) 375592   **£65**
Open: lunch Wed-Fri, Sun & Mon, dinner Mon-Sat
    (closed Bank Holidays, 2 wks Oct)
Meals served: lunch 12-2, dinner 7.15-9.45

Pretty, yellow-painted restaurant down by the quay.
Frank Eckermann chef has brought a lighter,
more informal touch to this stylish little French
restaurant since he took over mid-1992, and his
more recent introduction of the menu gastronomique has become a popular feature. Set
menus, both lunch and dinner, provide ample alternatives to choose from, including specials for two
such as poached lobster or beef bordelaise, and are
seasonally-inspired.

ERPINGHAM   Ark

The Street, Erpingham, Norfolk, NR11 7QB
Tel: (01263) 761535   **£40**
Open: lunch Sun (midweek by arrangement),
    dinner Tue-Sat (closed Tue in winter, 2 wks Oct)
Meals served: lunch 12.30-2, dinner 7-9.30

Restaurant with rooms where Sheila Kidd and family cook some imaginative dishes. Try mussels with apple, celery and cider, a trio of vegetable
pâtés (carrot, black olive and spiced mushroom). Salmon with herb butter
and sun-dried tomatoes, a rich daube of beef with red wine, tomato and
olives, or a vegetarian aubergine parmigiana with porcini. A very carefully
composed wine list has eight house wines at £8 and some serious claret and
burgundy.

ETON   Antico

42 High Street, Eton, Berkshire, SL4 6BD
Tel: (01753) 863977   *Fax:* (01628 30045)   **£60**
Open: lunch Mon-Fri, dinner Mon-Sat (closed Bank Holidays)
Meals served: lunch 12.30-2.30, dinner 7-10.30

Traditional Italian cooking and old world atmosphere are the hallmarks
at Ernesto Cassini and Ennio Morassi's popular restaurant. Much loved
after nearly 20 years on the site, Antico has a more than loyal following
among the locals. Comprehensive selection of Italian wines, including
the lovely Brunello de Montalcino from Tuscany.

EVERSHOT   Summer Lodge

Evershot, Dorchester, Dorset, DT2 0JR
Tel: (01935) 83424   *Fax:* (01935) 83005   **£60**
Open: lunch & dinner daily (closed 2 wks Jan)
Meals served: lunch 12.30-1.45, dinner 7.30-9

A graceful Georgian building is home to Nigel and Margaret Corbett's 17-bedroomed hotel and restaurant, in the pretty village of Evershot. The comfortable, well-maintained lounges are cosy and welcoming, while the bedrooms (some in a converted stable block) are well set up to guarantee a good night's sleep. Modern British menus are perfectly in tune with Summer Lodge and with a mixture of two-, three- and four-course set menus as well as the carte, you can be sure of something to suit everyone. Innovative use of the best produce available results in starters like brandade of smoked haddock with soured cream and keta caviar, or seafood sausage with a white butter sauce and lobster oil, or celery and apple soup. Main courses range from a simply grilled and fresh Dover sole with hazelnut butter, or braised belly of pork served with its own juices and a confit of shallots and garlic, to rack of Dorset lamb with a small tartlet of its kidney. Delicious and irresistible deserts might include a classic lemon tart served with a passion fruit sauce, chocolate marquise with a pistachio cream or gratin of fruits with a champagne sabayon. If you prefer to end the meal on a savoury note the plate of local farmhouse cheese served with celery, apples and home-made raisin bread is just the thing. An extensive wine list credits suppliers and compilers, and is a perfect foil to the cooking. New chef John Bishop (former sous at Clivedon) joined the team here as we went to press and, according to Nigel Corbett, will uphold the standards and style of menu, bringing a slightly lighter touch.

All in all a lovely place

EVERSLEY   New Mill Restaurant

New Mill Road, Eversley, Hampshire, RG27 0RA
Tel: (01734) 732277   *Fax:* (01734) 328780   **£45**
Open: lunch Sun-Fri, dinner daily (closed 26 & 27 Dec, 1 Jan)
Meals served: lunch 12-2, dinner 7-10 (Sun 12.30-8)

A charming restaurant within a 16th-century watermill, with picture windows overlooking the River Blackwater. New chef Steven Read prepares a British menu to match the setting. Typical dishes range from individual steak and kidney puddings and braised knuckle of lamb to pan-fried breast of Gressingham duck with citrus fruits and a confit of leg, local river trout coated in oats on a light lemon mousse, and salmon fillet with sorrel sauce. The more informal Grill Room situated in the oldest part of the mill offers straightforward traditional fare: casseroles and stews in winter, salads and grills in summer, and a selection of favourites like moules marinières and salmon fishcakes. Try the three-course Meal for a Tenner menu (lunch and dinner, weekdays only).

Have drinks on the terrace or in the gardens in summer or enjoy the warmth of log fires in winter.

EVESHAM   Evesham Hotel

Cooper's Lane, off Waterside, Evesham,
  Hereford & Worcs, WR11 6DA
Tel: (01386) 765566   *Fax:* (01386) 765443   **£45**
Open: lunch & dinner daily (closed 25 & 26 Dec)
Meals served: lunch 12.30-2, dinner 7-9.30

Not at all the traditional British hotel—it has even been described as
"slightly potty". Although professionalism and attention to guests is
very much at the forefront of policy here, the Jenkinsons firmly believe
in having fun as opposed to playing a more formal hand. A family hotel,
this is a largely Georgian building with Tudor origins, set in secluded
grounds on the edge of town. Touches of humour abound throughout.
Keys to the mostly characterful, traditionally furnished bedrooms come
attached to miniature teddy bears, and rubber ducks lie in wait in the
well-equipped bathrooms. The elegant, Regency-style restaurant provides weekly-changing, well-thought-out menus, with separate menus
for vegetarians and children. Cooking is competent, offering a balance
of traditional and more inventive dishes. The wine list is strong on New
World wines, with no French or German; the A-Z list of liqueurs is a
work of art. Families really come into their own here: extensive facilities include baby listening, baby-sitting, baby baths, indoor and outdoor play areas and a host of games.

EVESHAM   Riverside Hotel

The Parks, Offenham Road, Evesham,
  Hereford & Worcester, WR11 5JP
Tel: (01386) 446200   Fax: (01386) 40021   £55
Open: lunch Tue-Sun, dinner Tue-Sat
Meals served: lunch 12.30-2 (Sun to 1.30), dinner 7.30-9

The Willmotts' comfortable seven-bedroomed hotel on the banks of the
River Avon is difficult to reach by road—checking directions when
booking is essential. Alternatively, take advantage of the hotel's mooring and arrive by boat (the hotel offers mooring and fishing rights, and
has its own boats for hire). All of the rooms have wonderful views over
the gardens to the river beyond; likewise the dining room, where
Rosemary Willmott offers fixed-price, daily-changing menus with a
good choice of dishes. The cooking is English and French, and makes
the most of local ingredients. A typical dinner menu might include
lamb's sweetbreads with mushroom and a Madeira jus, followed by
crisp tiger prawns in filo pastry, or baked Scotch salmon with crème
fraîche, tarragon and lime. Traditional puds to finish.

EXETER   St Olaves Court

Mary Arches Street, Exeter, Devon, EX4 3AZ
Tel: (01392) 217736   *Fax:* (01392) 413054   **£50**
Open: lunch Mon-Fri, dinner daily (closed Xmas/New Year)
Meals served: lunch 12-2, dinner 6.30-9.30

Close to the Cathedral, hidden amid narrow side streets, this 1827
house stands in a secluded walled garden which boasts an ancient mulberry tree that still produces fruit for the kitchen. The 20 bedrooms are
furnished in Georgian style, each with an adjoining bathroom and all
modern facilities. The candlelit restaurant is building up a loyal local
following, thanks to the talented new kitchen brigade under 23-year-old
head chef Jason Horn whose light, modern touch is expressed with
competence and imagination. Starters might include a tian of crab meat
and smoked trout with a chive cream sauce or terrine of pheasant and
lentils with a whole-grain mustard dressing. Main courses range from
roasted hare wrapped in smoked bacon with red wine and a juniper
berry sauce to a tartlet of crisp vegetables and parsnip soufflé with an
orange and chive-scented cream. Desserts include baked fig in thin
leaves of pastry with frangipane.

EXETER   White Hart
South Street, Exeter, Devon, EX1 1EE
Tel: (01392) 79897   *Fax:* (01392) 50159   **£45**
Open: lunch Sun-Fri, dinner daily (closed 24-26 Dec)
Meals served: lunch 12-2, dinner 7-9.30
Ancient 15th-century inn, a former resting place for monks. Cobbled courtyard
and wine bar/garden, grill room and bar food. Traditional fare, old ales, lots of
character: 59 rooms in a modern extension. Change of ownership likely as we
went to press.

EYTON   Marsh Country Hotel

Eyton, Leominster, Hereford & Worcester, HR6 0AG
Tel: (01568) 613952   **£45**
Open: lunch Sun, dinner daily
Meals served: lunch 12.30-2, dinner 7.30-9

A delightful, 14th-century timbered hideaway with five rooms, in the
sleepy rural hamlet of Eyton, personally run by owners the Gillelands.
Lovely gardens surround the house, supplying home-grown herbs and
vegetables to the kitchen where Jacqueline's English style of cooking
places much of the emphasis on flavour. Imaginative cooking produces
dishes such as a goat's cheese, leek and hazelnut soufflé, roast local
duckling with kumquats, apricot stuffed saddle of lamb and for puds,
poached pear in puff pastry with butterscotch sauce or Alsace rhubarb
tart with ginger meringue ice cream. Fifty moderately priced wines and
more than twenty of them in halves. Sunny yellow walls, high-backed
chairs and old beams provide the setting for meals. Bedrooms are
named after birds; and the Gillelands also share a passion for garden-
ing—the gardens include a stream and lily pond complete with newts
and frogs.

FALMOUTH — Seafood Bar

Quay Street, Falmouth, Cornwall, TR11 3HH
Tel: (01326) 315129   **£40**
Open: dinner daily (Mon-Sat in winter) (closed 24-26 Dec, 2 wks Nov)
Meals served: dinner 7-10.30

A daily-changing menu of fresh fish and seafood is the attraction at this basement restaurant reached down a passageway and some steps. The array is quite astonishing—Helford oysters, Catalan prawns, fresh langoustine from Scotland, sea bass, skate, lemon sole, local scallops Veronique, lobster and a lot more. Carpetbagger steak stuffed with oysters and plain sirloin with mushrooms or au poivre also make an appearance on the menu for those who just can't resist meat.

FARNHAM — Krug's

84 West Street, Farnham, Surrey, GU9 7EN
Tel: (01252) 723277   **£45**
Open: dinner Mon-Sat
Meals served: dinner 7-11

Karin and Gerhard Krug's Austrian restaurant offers authentic national cuisine, competently cooked and consistently reliable. Expect to find a selection of fondues for sharing, including mixed meat, beef fillet, cheese and smoked cheese varieties. There are plenty of veal and steak options and a fine selection of home-cooked desserts. The sign over the door here reads: "Wine for truth, beer for strength and water for germs". What more can I say!

FAVERSHAM — Read's

Painter's Forstal, Faversham, Kent, ME13 0EE
Tel: (01795) 535344   *Fax:* (01795) 591200   **£75**
Open: lunch & dinner Tue-Sat
    (closed Bank Holidays)
Meals served: lunch 12-2, dinner 7-10

Don't let the exterior of David and Rona Pitchford's restaurant deter you, for once inside you will soon realise that the food, wines and service are far from uninteresting. Menus change with the seasons to make most use of fine produce. Well-judged combinations such as fillet of pink trout in a courgette envelope on lobster sauce, a hot cheese soufflé made with Montgomery cheddar on ratatouille, or a simple tart of plum tomatoes baked in the oven with olive oil, shallot and basil—and that's just to start! A breast of farmyard chicken comes with roasted peppers and artichokes, rösti potatoes and dry-baked tomatoes, roast chump of lamb with millefeuilles of aubergines and a rosemary jus, and undyed smoked haddock topped with a poached egg on tomato and chive sauce. Excellent British cheese, or how about a hot Grand Marnier soufflé, or honey and ginger ice cream with caramelised fruits and mango sauce, or for reckless chocoholics, a plate which combines chocolate mousse, chocolate marquise and chocolate ice cream! The choice of pudding wines is a match for the puds with some superb half bottles and some by the glass. Kids are welcomed and not humiliated by being offered fish fingers and burgers!

FELSTED	Rumbles Cottage

Braintree Road, Felsted, Essex, CM6 3DJ
Tel: (01371) 820996   **£50**
Open: lunch Sun, dinner Tue-Sat (closed Bank Holidays)
Meals served: lunch 12-2, dinner 7-9

Fields of home-grown produce go into the making of this charming little restaurant in a 16th-century cottage. Joy Hadley grows her own curly kale, fennel, aubergines, marrows, beans, salsify... it's a case of you name it, it's there, almost. Local farms and specialist suppliers make up the rest, with seasonal produce featuring strongly on the menus. Give a helping hand (Tues-Thurs nights) by opting for the Guinea Pig menu—a snip at £12.50 if you fancy trying out new dishes for customer feedback. Alternatively, you can play safe with the regularly-changing à la carte. The style of cooking is "very definitely British", they say, but the response from the kitchen to the great British culinary tradition is clearly a contemporary one, and there are influences from much further afield. Typical menu items include twice-baked soufflés, salmon bavarois, chicken and asparagus Wellington, and Arabian lamb casserole. Puds might include rhubarb and elder-flower soup, tropical syllabub or white chocolate brandy Alexander (a 1991 creation which passed the Guinea Pig test). Late-night pasta menu on Fridays.

FLETCHING	Griffin Inn

Fletching, East Sussex, TN22 3NS
Tel: (01825) 722890   **£35**
Open: lunch daily, dinner Mon-Sat (closed 25 Dec)
Meals served: lunch 12-2.15, dinner 7.30-10

Lots of character and a predominantly '30s feel to this old country inn with its beamed front bar, corner fireplace and squared oak panelling. Good wholesome fare in the bar and theme nights in the restaurant make it very popular with locals. The bar features a wide range of traditional favourites and local specialities such as beef and Guinness pie, local plaice and chips or Fletching sausages with bubble'n'squeak, as well as soups, salads, poultry and grills. Thursdays see the arrival of fresh fish from Newhaven so the theme in the restaurant that night is obviously fish. Start with coquilles St Jacques or stuffed mussels, followed by grilled cod marinated in lime and coriander, red mullet with pimento or delicious prawn curry. On the regular à la carte expect to find chicken satay, char-grilled steaks with caramelised onions, Sussex smokies, cottage pie or roast guinea fowl with an orange and Madeira sauce. In warm weather, eat in the garden or on the terrace, with lovely views over Sussex. Local ales on hand-pump and a good selection of wines. The inn has four comfortable bedrooms.

FLITWICK	Flitwick Manor

Church Road, Flitwick, Bedfordshire, MK45 1AE
Tel: (01525) 712242   *Fax:* (01525) 712242   **£80**
Open: lunch & dinner daily
Meals served: lunch 12.15-1.45, dinner 7.15-9.30

Beautiful, rolling gardens, complete with folly and ornamental pond provide a tranquil setting for this late 17th/early 18th-century house—

all 15 bedrooms enjoy garden views. The restaurant offers modern, international cooking under the watchful eye of Duncan Poyser. The fixed-price dinner menus offer plenty of choice and include a vegetarian section which in itself is no mean feat, with dishes like wild mushroom risotto with parmesan and lemon; or broccoli, tomato and hazelnut tartlet. Non-vegetarians could start with hot scallop soufflé or a mosaic of sweetbreads and crab, before tucking in to pot-roast local chicken basted with cèpes.. Choose between traditional British and French farmhouse cheeses or one of Duncan's imaginative desserts like melting chocolate tart with crème fraîche and cappuccino anglaise.

FOLKESTONE   Paul's

2a Bouverie Road West, Folkestone, Kent, CT20 2RX
Tel: (01303) 259697   **£40**
Open: lunch & dinner daily (closed 25 & 26 Dec)
Meals served: lunch 12-2.30, dinner 7.30-9.30 (Sat from 7)

The menu changes frequently at Paul and Penny Hagger's pretty, pastel-coloured restaurant, and Paul's imaginative cooking is well worth the visit. Home-made soups are a regular feature among starters, along with the likes of dressed, baked crab topped with brie or haggis samosa in filo pastry with whisky cream. Main courses might feature Barnsley lamb chops with a tangy honey and rosemary sauce or delicious pheasant crumble. Seafood and fresh fish are mainstays, something like Dover sole might come poached in cream with prawns and a tipple of Chablis. All in all a refreshing menu of a homely, yet inventive, nature. Vegetarians are catered for with a choice of two starter-size dishes as main course.

FOWEY   Food for Thought

Town Quay, Fowey, Cornwall, PL23 1AT
Tel: (01726) 832221   *Fax:* (01726) 832060   £40
Open: dinner Mon-Sat (closed Jan & Feb)
Meals served: 7-9

The Billingsley family's neat restaurant offers a quayside setting in which to enjoy some good, well-presented food. Choose from the fixed-price menu, or there's a three-course set dinner menu offering two choices per course – not surprisingly, fish is predominant on both. You might sample local sea scallops cooked with olive oil, garlic and herbs or moules marinière to start, followed by fillet of Fowey river bass simply cooked with saffron cream and butter sauce or, for non-fish eaters, roasted rack of Cornish lamb with a rosemary herb sauce. Delicious puds to finish – sticky toffee pudding with toffee sauce and clotted cream, tangy lemon tart or summer pudding set on a fruit sauce.

FRAMPTON-ON-SEVERN   Saverys Restaurant

The Green, Frampton-on-Severn, Gloucestershire, GL2 7EA
Tel: (01452) 740077   **£50**
Open: dinner Tue-Sat
Meals served: dinner 7-11.30

Small country restaurant off junction 13 of the M5. Carefully prepared, elaborately cooked dinners in English country style. You might start with onion cream and anchovy tart, followed perhaps by roats loin of lamb on port and redcurrant sauce with deep-fried leeks, finishing with meringue next filled with home-made vanilla ice cream, topped with dark bitter chocolate and pistachio sauce.

FRESHFORD   Homewood Park

Hinton Charterhouse, Freshford, Bath, Avon, BA3 6BB
Tel: (01225) 723731   *Fax:* (01225) 723820   **£70**
Open: lunch & dinner daily
Meals served: lunch 12-1.30, dinner 7-9.30

Homewood Park stands in 10 acres of well-cared-for grounds on the edge of the Limpley Stoke Valley, an area of outstanding beauty. Frank and Sara Gueuning maintain the highest of standards in this small, stylish, privately-owned, 15-bedroomed hotel. The same can be said of chef Tim Ford's domain. His cooking is noted for its light touch and lack of fussiness. Table d'hôte menus offer plenty of choice, with always a vegetarian option such as ratatouille crumble with a light tomato sauce. Non-vegetarians may expect a choice between the likes of grilled Cornish sea bass with mussels and a lightly spiced saffron sauce, or pink-roasted Gressingham duck served with a brandy and pink peppercorn sauce. A typical dessert would be the delicious-sounding butterscotch cream tart served with banana fritters and banana ice cream.

FRESSINGFIELD   Fox and Goose

Fressingfield, Nr Diss, Suffolk, IP21 5PB
Tel: (0137 986) 247   *Fax:* (0137 986) 8107   **£50**
Open: lunch & dinner Wed-Sun (closed Sun dinner in winter,
   25 & 26 Dec, 2 wks Nov)
Meals served: lunch 12-2.15, dinner 7-9.15

Great time and care is taken over the purchases for the kitchen at this handsome black-and-white inn which was built in 1500 as a guildhall. The menu is truly eclectic, a world tour no less, and only the best raw ingredients are used, with specialist suppliers from local farms to London's Chinatown providing the goods. Chef-patronne Ruth Watson runs a tight ship, with much attention to every detail, and together with chef Brendan Ansbro turns out a spectacular array of dishes. Snails with garlic butter, salmon and haddock fish cakes and deep-fried prawn and scallop tempura feature alongside cold starters such as Morecambe Bay potted brown shrimps on toast or Italian salamis. Main courses run from breast of free-range chicken à la king or braised beef casserole with Norfolk dumplings to local cod fillet with sun-dried tomato and herb crust. Sunday lunch is popular but you must pre-order 24 hours in advance for roast Scotch sirloin with Yorkshire pudding. Excellent home cooking with a mouthwatering choice. Good-value two- and three-course menu options at lunch-time and a selection of dishes is always available in the bar. Children are given a warm welcome indoors and out, where there's a sandpit and see-saw for their entertainment. This is a lovely place with a rustic feel created by beams and the tiled floor, and it's great on atmosphere.

GARSTANG   ·   El Nido

Whinney Brow Lane, Forton, Garstang, Lancashire, PR3 0AE
Tel: (01524) 791254   **£40**
Open: lunch & dinner Tue-Sun (closed Bank Holidays)
Meals served: lunch 12-2, dinner 7-10

Spanish restaurant offering all the traditional favourites: gazpacho, paella, garlic prawns, tortilla and lots of grills and meat; but with a difference—in the preparation of sauces, which display some English and French influences; and in the existence of a vegetarian paella on the à la carte.

GILLINGHAM   Stock Hill House

Stock Hill, Gillingham, Dorset, SP8 5NR
Tel: (01747) 823626   *Fax:* (01747) 825628   **£65**
Open: lunch & dinner daily
     (closed lunch check when booking)
Meals served: lunch 12.30-1.45, dinner 7.30-8.45

Nita and Peter Hauser have spent years restoring this late-Victorian house and grounds to their present lovely state, but it is the personal hospitality of the owners which is the crowning glory at this unusual and interesting eight-bedroomed hotel in Hardy country. Austrian-born Peter rules the kitchen, displaying French, Austrian, English and Balkan influences. Main courses range from grilled local calf's liver naped with cassis and blackcurrants, or Welsh Show fillet of beef Wellington served on Madeira glaze, to Balkan cevapcici (char-grilled fingers of minced meat) on Bosnian rice and Cornish venison with Austrian-style dumplings. Make sure you leave room for desserts—true to his native traditions, Peter takes them far more seriously than most—house meringue suchard or rhubarb and ginger soufflé will not disappoint.

Some interesting wines on the reasonably priced list.

Biography

Peter

Hauser

Peter began with three years' training in Linz, Austria, then cooked his way round Europe to gain experience. After ten years in the Channel Islands at Sark's Aval du Creux where he met his wife Nita, Peter bought Stock Hill House in Dorset and set about proving that a chef can own and run a country house without any help from anybody else. Peter has only one ambition left: to cook as well as his mother. Considering what Peter has achieved, she must be a very hard act to follow!

GITTISHAM   Combe House

Gittisham, Nr Honiton, Devon, EX14 0AD
Tel: (01404) 42756   *Fax:* (01404) 46004   **£45**
Open: dinner daily (closed 26 Jan-9 Feb)
Meals served: dinner 7.30-9.30

A stylish hotel has been created by the Boswell family, based on the philosophy that it should be the type of hotel in which they themselves would like to stay. It has a picturesque setting amidst lawns, rhododendrons and cedar trees. Thérèse Boswell wears many hats—hostess, artist and sculptress—yet still finds time to don a toque in the kitchen to produce her distinctive cooking. The Boswells certainly are a resourceful family: son Mark's wine company supplies the hotel, resulting in a list of jolly good value.

GLASTONBURY   No. 3 Restaurant & Hotel

3 Magdelene Street, Glastonbury, Somerset, BA6 9EW
Tel: (01458) 832129   **£65**
Open: dinner Wed-Sat (closed Dec & Jan)
Meals served: dinner only 7.30-9

In this 18th-century house next to the abbey ruins, seasonal Cornish lobster, fish and seafood come into their own on chef Ann Tynan's four-course dinner menus for residents and their guests. Enjoy salmis of game, aga-grilled fillet of brill with lemon butter or, if meat is out, walnut and cashew en croûte. Non-residents are welcome, space permitting. Oil paintings and antiques lend a gracious feel throughout the house, and some of the rooms are in a modern annexe at the foot of the garden. Most unusually in such a small hotel, guests can now also benefit from beauty, massage and aromatherapy facilities.

GLOUCESTER   Hatton Court

Upton Hill, Upton St Leonards, Gloucester, GL4 8DE
Tel: (01452) 617412   *Fax:* (01452) 612945   **£45**
Open: lunch & dinner daily
Meals served: lunch 12-2, dinner 7.30-10 (Sun to 9)

This is an ivy-clad, 17th-century Cotswold manor house set in its own grounds three miles from Gloucester. The hotel has 45 rooms, some lavishly furnished and with whirlpool baths, others (in the adjoining wing) more uniformly. The Carringtons Restaurant also boasts panoramic views over the surrounding hills, while the cooking finds its roots in both French and English cuisine. There's a terrace for summer lunching.

GOLANT   Cormorant Hotel

Golant, Nr Fowey, Cornwall, PL23 1LL
Tel & Fax: (01726) 833426   **£55**
Open: lunch & dinner daily
Meals served: lunch 12-2, dinner 7-9

A riverside setting in a small fishing village, with lovely views over the
Fowey estuary, is the big attraction of the Cormorant; and those looking for a peaceful break away from it all will not be disappointed here.
Most lounges, the indoor pool and all of the hotel's 11 bedrooms have
magnificent views over the river Fowey. The restaurant offers imaginative cooking with fresh locally caught fish and seafood being the speciality. Everything, from breakfast rolls and marmalade to soups,
terrines, pasta, pastries and sorbets, is made on the premises, and
there are home-grown organic vegetables available at most times of the
year. Special menus for vegetarians or diabetics are prepared on
request with the same imaginative flair as everything else. Many
improvements and refurbishments have taken place during '94.

GORING-ON-THAMES   The Leatherne Bottel

Riverside Inn & Restaurant, Goring-on-Thames,
    Berkshire, RG8 0HS
Tel: (01491) 872667   **£60**
Open: lunch & dinner daily (closed 25 Dec)
Meals served: lunch 12.15-2 (Sat & Sun to 2.30),
    dinner 7.15-9 (Sat to 9.30)   *Well worth a visit, summer or winter*

Keith Read and Annie Bonnet's delightful restaurant on the banks of
the Thames is unique, and has just about everything going for it. The
garden and riverside terrace are overflowing with hanging baskets,
wild herbs and flowers—Annie's domain. There's also a beautifully
restored Edwardian saloon launch which you can charter for pre-prandial drinks or relaxation: they will supply anything from champagne
and canapés to picnics and barbecues for special occasions, and serve you on board while you cruise. There
is no set-price luncheon menu. You can pop in for a
salad, a light snack or simply meet for a glass of
champagne down by the river among the flowers.
This is a relaxed, informal, yet highly civilised establishment, run with care and commitment. Everything,
from bread and chutneys to chocolates, is made on
the premises and the kitchen garden provides a
constant supply of herbs, salads, vegetables and
summer berries. The overriding emphasis in
Keith's and Clive O'Connor's cooking is simplicity and true flavours. Typical dishes on
the à la carte menu include the likes of
home-grown leaf and herb salad; fish
soup with lemon leaves and lemon
grass; crab cakes with coriander; char-grilled local venison
liver with lemon thyme jelly;
and shoulder of lamb with roast
black pudding. Marquees can
be set up beside the river.

GRASMERE   Michael's Nook

Grasmere, Nr Ambleside, Cumbria, LA22 9RP
Tel: (0153 94) 35496   *Fax:* (0153 94) 35765   **£85**
Open: lunch & dinner daily
Meals served: lunch 12.30 for 1, dinner 7.30 for 8,
   (booking essential)

The interior of this 14-bedroomed hotel, which takes its name from the humble dwelling of the shepherd in Wordsworth's poem, reflects owner Reg Gifford's other passion, namely antiques. The public rooms are truly impressive, with classically elegant decor, beautifully restored antique features, and a predominantly English collection of prints, rugs, furniture and porcelain, all of which combine to create an immediate sense of well-being and intimacy from the moment you enter this grand Victorian house. However, the feeling, enhanced by the presence of the owner's two Great Danes, exotic cats and a parrot, is that of an eccentric home rather than of a showpiece. Kevin Mangeolles provides an international repertoire of dishes, but with the emphasis on English style. Fixed-price menus feature additional daily specials, offering plenty of choice. Start perhaps with creamed swede and bacon soup or sweetbread ravioli, followed by guinea fowl pot au feu in a light Sauternes sauce, cassoulet of seafood garnished with herb sausage and a saffron sauce, or salmis of rabbit with noodles and sweet wine sauce. There's a separate vegetarian menu with some very decent offerings— white onion and cider soup served with a sage quiche, vegetable and pasta stew served in a truffle sauce—and desserts are mouthwatering. The wine list is also appropriate to the setting.

GRASMERE   White Moss House

Rydal Water, Grasmere, Cumbria, LA22 9SE
Tel: (0153 94) 35295   **£60**
Open: dinner Mon-Sat (closed Dec-Feb)
Meals served: dinner 7.30 for 8

Not lakeland's largest hotel but certainly one of its best, this comfortable house was once owned by Wordsworth, and is now run by friendly hosts, Peter and Sue Dixon. The main house has just five antique-laden rooms, and nearby Brookside cottage can be taken as a suite or used as family accommodation. Peter's cooking is meticulous: he prepares a five course dinner which will depend on fresh daily produce. A fennel and celery soup, then a soufflé of Argyll salmon poached with champagne on leeks and asparagus is married with Wastwater sea trout smoked with oak and bracken and Westmoreland cheese. Next comes a roast saddle of Cumbrian venison marinaded with juniper and Pomerol served with woodland mushroom sauce accompanied by a superb variety of vegetables. For pudding, an impossible choice between steamed pudding with raisins and currants with Malmsey sauce, raspberry Pavlova or apple and blackcurrants baked with a mild ginger topping. Still more to come! Up to a dozen British farmhouse cheese are offered with home-made oat biscuits. 200 bins on the wine list merit careful consideration. Apparently Wordsworth used to stop at White Moss House and rest in the porch during his walks between Rydal and Grasmere—I'm sure that if Peter had been cooking then he would have stopped over for dinner!

GRASMERE   Wordsworth Hotel

Grasmere, Nr Ambleside, Cumbria, LA22 9SW
Tel: (0153 94) 35592   *Fax:* (0153 94) 35765   **£65**
Open: lunch & dinner daily
Meals served: lunch 12.30-2, dinner 7-9 (Fri & Sat to 9.30)

Tradition and modernity go hand in hand at this tranquil, 37-bed-roomed hotel in landscaped grounds bordering the neighbouring churchyard where Wordsworth is buried. Bold, colourful fabrics grace many of the rooms; bedrooms are more traditional, with antiques and pretty floral fabrics. Menus, the domain of Bernard Warne, have a modern leaning: chilled leek and asparagus soup served with grilled scallop; fresh tagliatelle with calf's sweetbreads and broccoli; pork chop flavoured with French mustard; and to finish, the speciality: Wordsworth daffodil with a duet of iced creams.

GRAYSHOTT   Woods Place

Headley Road, Grayshott, Nr Hindhead, Surrey, GU26 6LB
Tel & Fax: (01428) 605555   **£45**
Open: lunch & dinner Tue-Sat
Meals served: lunch 12-2.30, dinner 7-11

Here you will find authentic Swedish cooking with a rustic slant, in the unlikely bistro-style setting of a former butcher's shop. Chef-patron Eric Nörrgren is the brother of Anna at Anna's Place (London) and the menu here bears a strong resemblance to that of his sibling. Homely, uncomplicated continental dishes encompass a wide range, from fresh and smoked salmon burger on a bed of lentils through to breast of turkey stuffed with chestnuts, or saddle of hare in a juniper-scented cream. Simple sweets like lemon tart or little pancakes with blueberry ice-cream are well made and the short wine list is chosen with care.

Handy if you need to nip out from Grayshott Hall Health Club!

GREAT DUNMOW   The Starr

Market Place, Great Dunmow, Essex, CM6 1AX
Tel: (01371) 874321   *Fax:* (01371) 876337   **£70**
Open: lunch Sun-Fri, dinner Mon-Sat (closed 1 wk Jan)
Meals served: lunch 12-1.30, dinner 7-9.30

There has been a hostelry on the site of the Starr for over 600 years. Today the handsome 400-year-old timber-framed building with Georgian façade houses a contemporary style but beamed restaurant overlooking Great Dunmow's market place, and there are eight nicely converted rooms in a converted stable block at the rear. Mark Fisher gets most of his raw materials from London markets, or from local suppliers. The blackboard menu might offer Mediterranean fish soup, or quenelles of pike, as possible starters; main course options might include peppered loin of venison with cognac and cream or escalope of salmon in champagne with elderflowers. Lunch-time features a light menu which includes simpler preparations like home-made curry, pies, pasta, chicken and vegetarian dishes of the day. Home-made puds tend towards the sticky varieties served with custard.

GREAT GONERBY — Harry's Place

17 High Street, Great Gonerby, Lincolnshire, NG31 8JS
Tel: (01476) 61780 **£85**
Open: lunch & dinner Tue-Sat (Sun & Mon by arrangement;
   closed Bank Holidays)
Meals served: lunch 12.30-2, dinner 7-9.30

You have the undivided attention of Harry and Caroline Hallam at this elegant, ten-seater, three-tabled restaurant in the centre of the village. The informal and intimate dining room is a fitting scene in which to enjoy Harry's culinary skills. The market-led menus (lunch and dinner) are exceptionally well balanced given the restricted choice of two options for each course, with main course options including one fish, one meat. Start perhaps with a soup of pheasant and lentils followed by fillet of Scottish turbot sautéed with olive oil, lemon juice, white wine, Pernod, rosemary and fennel. Bread-and-butter pudding or hot Bramley apple and Calvados soufflé to finish. An interesting wine list. Worth booking all three tables and having your own dinner party here.

GREAT MILTON Le Manoir aux Quat'Saisons

Church Road, Great Milton, Oxfordshire, OX44 7PD
Tel: (01844) 278881   *Fax:* (01844) 278847 **£130**
Open: lunch & dinner daily
Meals served: lunch 12.15-2.15, dinner 7.15-10.30

"The idea that food is simply fuel to get us through the duties and functions of daily existence is a hideous and unacceptable thought," says Raymond Blanc. Essentially light, his style through the years has not changed as such, but rather evolved, based on the purity and nobility of ingredients, fired by a creative spirit which, he says, is driven by honesty. Raymond's style is not limited by traditions; he uses influences selectively to enrich the palette of flavours, and is not one to simply follow fashion. In short, he is an artist, constantly looking for perfection, a genius whose technical execution of dishes is quite superb. Witness the man's accolades displayed in the hotel foyer. Head chef Clive Fretwell, here since 1984, ensures that standards in the kitchen never drop. Expect dishes such as marinated red mullet fillets layered in a purée of salted cod or an emincé of fresh truffles, onions and smoked bacon, baked in puff pastry leaves to start (both specialities); followed by the likes of roasted fillet of scorpion fish on pan-fried squid with herbs, served with a bouillabaisse jus. Elsewhere you may find roasted new season Highgrove lamb with pan-fried sweet-

**Raymond Blanc:
biography next page**

breads, kidney and liver; or corn-fed Bresse squab in its own juices and boudin blanc served on an emincé of leeks and truffles. Look out for the orange parfait wrapped in a fine nougatine box among desserts, it's pure heaven. Le Manoir is set in secluded private grounds seven miles

Biography

Raymond Blanc has earned a reputation of being one of the finest chefs in Europe. He came to England from France to work in restaurants, and set up his first in Oxford, before settling in at Le Manoir, where he makes superlative use of available **Raymond Blanc** produce, shaped by his own experience. He is driven by a burning desire to understand every aspect of the whole operation, and produces dishes of brilliance and artistic integrity. It is his combination of colours, flavours, and textures that sets him apart.

south of Oxford in the rural Cotswold countryside. Sweeping lawns and beautifully landscaped garden surround the 15th-century mellow stone house originally built for a French nobleman—fitting, then, that it is now home to the cuisine of one of the greatest French chefs of our time. There are 19 luxurious rooms, including a medieval dovecote in the gardens which has been transformed into a romantic honeymoon suite, and many of the rooms have their own private terrace with wrought-iron patio furniture. Bathrooms are magnificent, as are the breakfasts. The wine list reflects the aspirations and standards of the rest of the establishment, but still includes some affordable wines.

GREAT MISSENDEN   La Petite Auberge

107 High Street, Great Missenden, Buckinghamshire, HP16 0BB
Tel: (01494) 865370   **£55**
Open: dinner Mon-Sat (closed Bank Holidays, Xmas/New Year)
Meals served: dinner 7.30-10.30

A smart, local French restaurant—from the wine and wording on the menu through to the totally French cheeseboard. This is wholehearted French cooking: fresh foie gras de canard, hot scallop mousse with a coral sauce, or oysters and mussels in puff pastry to start; followed by sea bass in white wine with a tarragon butter sauce, medallions of veal with a ginger sauce or fillet of beef with marrow. To finish, hot apple with cinnamon ice cream. Try the ten-year-old Pineau des Charentes; or go for the grand finale with an equally aged Castarede armagnac.

GREAT YARMOUTH — Seafood Restaurant

85 North Quay, Great Yarmouth, Norfolk, NR30 1JF
Tel: (01493) 856009   **£45**
Open: lunch Mon-Fri, dinner Mon-Sat (closed Bank Holidays
ex Good Friday, 3 wks Xmas)
Meals served: lunch 12-1.45, dinner 7-10.45

This is a small, friendly, family restaurant which works on the principle that nothing is too much trouble. Super-fresh seafood and shellfish arrive daily from Lowestoft, including live lobsters for the tank. Fish can be served grilled, poached, in batter or with a sauce—hot, spicy cod Creole; skate with black butter; brill with port wine. Meat eaters can choose from a range of fillet and pepper steaks—or opt to mix'n'match with the surf'n'turf options—steak with prawns, crawfish tails or half a lobster. A fabulous choice of seafood here, and appropriately 20 champagnes head the comprehensive list of wines.

GRIMSTON — Congham Hall

Lynn Road, Grimston, King's Lynn, Norfolk, PE32 1AH
Tel: (01485) 600250   *Fax:* (01485) 601191   **£50**
Open: lunch Sun-Fri, dinner daily
Meals served: lunch 12.30-2, dinner 7.30-9.30

Relax in this haven of peace and quiet situated in 40 acres of parkland to the east of King's Lynn. This is a homely, Georgian country house with good leisure facilities and 14 rooms, each individually decorated by owners Christine and Trevor Forecast, pictured. Flowers grace the place from top to bottom, and the herb garden boasts over 400 varieties. The grounds also include a cricket pitch, used by the village team, orchards, tennis court and clay-pigeon range. New chef, local man Jonathan Nicholson (ex-Harveys, The Canteen and Le Talbooth) cooks a wide selection of imaginative British-based dishes which reflect modern trends. Creamy local fish soup perfumed with anise liqueur, ravioli of veal sweetbreads with spinach and forest mushrooms, poached oyster with caviar in champagne and chive sauce; followed by grilled lobster with tarragon and tomato glaze, poached fillets of skate with mussel and saffron risotto and confit of rabbit with grilled aubergine and pesto. Lovely views over the lawns and parklands as you eat.

GUERNSEY   Absolute End

St George's Esplanade, St Peter Port, Guernsey
Tel: (01481) 723822   *Fax:* (01481) 729129   **£40**
Open: lunch & dinner Mon-Sat (closed Jan)
Meals served: lunch 12-2, dinner 7-10

Cottagey seafood restaurant specialising in French and Italian dishes.
Typical dishes include lobster bisque, home-smoked seafood platter,
oysters florentine, sole St Malo, grilled ray, brill basquaise and crab
italienne. The menu goes on for pages, and includes choices for vegetarians and carnivores—fried Brie in pepper sauce, saltimbocca,
chicken estragon, tournedos with Madeira sauce. The menu is simple
and unpretentious, with no surprises. Good-value set lunch and a garden terrace for the summer months.

GUERNSEY   La Frégate

Les Cotils, St Peter Port, Guernsey
Tel: (01481) 724624   *Fax:* (01481) 720443   **£40**
Open: lunch & dinner daily
Meals served: lunch 12.30-1.30, dinner 7-9.30

Virtually all of the bedrooms at this 18th-century manor house set on a
hillside above the town enjoy splendid views of the harbour and neighbouring islands, and some have their own private balconies. The best
place to enjoy the view, though, is with a nice cool glass of champagne
on the terrace next to the bar and restaurant. Dinner is a jacket-and-tie
affair, with locally caught seafood a main feature but few surprises on
the mostly traditional menu of classic French dishes. Start with brandy-
flavoured lobster bisque, goujons of sole or seafood pancake, followed
by roast rack of lamb with herbs, veal chasseur, roast monkfish tail
provençale, scallops in a light curry sauce or the plateau de fruits de
mer.

GUERNSEY   La Grande Mare Hotel

Vazon Bay, Castel, Guernsey
Tel: (01481) 56577   *Fax:* (01481) 56532   **£45**
Open: lunch & dinner daily
Meals served: lunch 12-2, dinner 7-9.30

Run in friendly, relaxed style, this 34-bedroomed hotel on the west
coast of the island offers a choice of rooms, suites and self-contained
apartments. Lovers of golf and fishing will find plenty to amuse them,
with an 18-hole golf course and a network of tiny streams running into
freshwater lakes within the grounds, stocked with carp and perch—
relax fishing by the bank, or take a picnic perhaps. Enjoy freshly
caught fish from the island waters or a speciality dish flambéed at your
table. Adrian Jones, who has trained at Gidleigh Park in Devon and
with the Roux brothers, cooks a modern British and European repertoire, showing flair and imagination with dishes such as herb and truffle risotto with young spinach, grilled scallops with salsa verde and
pancetta, and sea bass with saffron-creamed potatoes and roast peppers
being typical. The set lunch menus offer less sophisticated but equally
delightful combinations like salmon with bubble'n'squeak and brill with
stir-fry greens. Good breakfast menu.

GUERNSEY   Louisiana

South Esplanade, St Peter Port, Guernsey
Tel: (01481) 713157   *Fax:* (01481) 712191   **£35**
Open: lunch & dinner Tue-Sun
    (closed Bank Holidays)
Meals served: lunch 12-2.30, dinner 6.30-10.30

Marinated Guernsey scallops, baked jumbo prawns, linguine Creole,
spiced almond risotto milanese, grilled Guernsey brill, lobster à la nage
or Cajun prime rib steak Mardi Gras are just some of the many dishes
you can enjoy while soaking in the panoramic view of the bay and
nearby islands (Herm and Sark) at this restaurant. Upstairs the new
Bâton Rouge Brasserie extends the choice even further, with the likes
of spare ribs and chicken wings, chargrills, baby chicken à la rouge or
teriyaki appearing on the menu. Vegetarian dishes on both menus.
Desserts follow suit, with Cajun, French and Italian elements:
Mississippi mudcake, tiramisu, flambéed crepes and pears Louis XV.
Traditional Sunday roasts, carved at the table, light lunches are served
in the brasserie.

GUERNSEY   Le Nautique

The Quay Steps, St Peter Port, Guernsey
Tel: (01481) 721714   *Fax:* (01481) 721786   **£50**
Open: lunch & dinner Mon-Sat (closed 1st 2 wks Jan)
Meals served: lunch 12-2, dinner 7-10

Vito Garau has ruled the kitchen roost for 10 years at this French fish
restaurant on the harbour. Local seafood is the speciality, with everything from scallops to skate served in a number of ways. Local
Guernsey lobster can be enjoyed cold with mayonnaise and salad,
grilled and flambéed with Scotch whisky or Thermidor. Starters offer
soups, island oysters, seafood cocktails, pancakes and eggs florentine.
Meaty options include various steaks, lamb noisettes with tarragon,
duck and veal, each in three different ways. And if your old favourite
isn't there, just ask! The chef is willing to prepare a dish of your choice,
whenever time permits.

GUERNSEY   Old Government House

Ann's Place, St Peter Port, Guernsey, GY1 4AZ
Tel: (01481) 724921   *Fax:* (01481) 724429   **£40**
Open: lunch & dinner daily
Meals served: lunch 12.30-2, dinner 7-9.30

The former Governor's residence, the OGH, as it is affectionately
known, is situated in the heart of St Peter Port. The hotel has 72 bedrooms and three bars, one of which hosts regular dances and is something of a local haunt. You can eat in the elegant Regency Restaurant,
with its blend of local specialities and traditional classical favourites—
flambées are a speciality; or take a light luncheon in the Centenary Bar
or poolside terrace. Good vegetarian choices and a separate children's
menu. The Gardner's Coffee Shop extends the choice even further,
with its all-day brasserie-style menu which is popular with families. A
charming hotel where traditional standards of service are maintained.

GUERNSEY   St Pierre Park

Rohais, St Peter Port, Guernsey, GY1 1FD
Tel: (01481) 728282   *Fax:* (01481) 712041   **£40**
Open: lunch Sun-Fri, dinner Mon-Sat
Meals served: lunch 12.15-2.15, dinner 7-10

Forty-five acres of purpose-built luxury is how they sum it up here.
Surrounded by parkland, with excellent leisure and conference facilities, this is one of the island's best resort hotels. All of the 135 bedrooms are well furnished and have a terrace or balcony with views over
the grounds, lake and Tony Jacklin-designed 9-hole golf course. Three
outdoor tennis courts, a 25m indoor pool and health and leisure complex complete the picture. Enjoy a buffet breakfast in the La Fontaine
room overlooking the lake, fine wines and French cuisine in the Victor
Hugo restaurant, a more informal setting and lighter meals in the Café
Renoir, or alfresco eating on the terrace. Something for everyone, from
Japanese tempura butterfly prawns, pizzas, prime Scottish steaks and
carvery dishes in the Renoir to Herm Island oysters, local sea scallops,
Guernsey lobster, chargrills and game in the Victor Hugo restaurant.

GULWORTHY   The Horn of Plenty

Gulworthy, Tavistock, Devon, PL19 8JD
Tel & Fax: (01822) 832528   **£60**
Open: lunch Tue-Sun, dinner daily (closed 24-26 Dec)
Meals served: lunch 12.15-2, dinner 7.15-9.30

Ian and Elaine Gatehouse's 200-year-old house overlooking the Tamar
Valley is surrounded by beautifully cared-for gardens. There are seven
well-appointed, pine-furnished bedrooms in a converted stable block
and each has its own balcony which affords views of the valley. The
kitchen is the domain of Peter Gorton, pictured, whose modern international repertoire owes something to time spent during 1993 at Joel
Robuchon's Jamin restaurant in Paris. Table d'hôte lunch and dinner

menus (the carte now discontinued)
offer starters such as tempura-fried
sole with Thai sauce, terrine of foie
gras with home-made brioche and a
ginger-scented nage of shellfish. Main
courses might include medallions of
venison with apple compôte and black
pepper cider sauce, pan-fried sea bass
and leeks with a sweet and sour
sauce, or roast pigeon with tagliatelle
and asparagus served with foie gras.
Tempting desserts, or English and
continental cheeses to finish. Monday
nights have been transformed with
much success by the introduction of
the three-course £16.50 Pot Luck
menu. Reasonably priced wine list.

HADLEY WOOD   West Lodge Park Hotel

Cockfosters Road, Hadley Wood, Hertfordshire, EN4 0PY
Tel: 0181-440 8311   *Fax:* 0181-449 3698   **£45**
Open: lunch & dinner daily
Meals served: lunch 12.30-2, dinner 7.15-9.45

Set in its own parkland, complete with arboretum and lake, this 19th-century country house has 45 individually furnished bedrooms which, together with the reception rooms, create a civilised atmosphere in which to relax. The split-level dining room is host to chef Peter Leggatt's daily-changing menus—a well-thought-out selection of between eight and ten dishes for each course. Start with Anglesey mussel soup or venison terrine with wild mushrooms and a port and apple dressing. Then move on to whole baked rainbow trout with garlic and prawn butter or medallions of pork fillet served with a wild mushroom cream sauce. To finish: a good selection of British cheeses and interesting desserts.

HALFORD   Sykes House

Queen Street, Halford, Shipston-on-Stour,
    Warwickshire, CV36 5BT
Tel: (01789) 740976   **£75**
Open: lunch by arrangement, dinner Wed-Sat (closed 24-31 Dec)
Meals served: dinner 7.30-8.15 (booking essential)

This is the home of David and Peggy Cunliffe, a lovely 16th-century Cotswold-stone house in the old part of Halford. Guests may dine in one of two rooms: at a large oak table in the inglenook dining room, or in the smaller, stone-mullioned bailiff's study after relaxed, pre-prandial anticipation and welcoming appetisers in the lovely garden room. David prepares a balanced, no-choice six-course dinner which changes daily according to the freshest ingredients available. Recent menus have featured interesting soups (cep/nettle/cream of salsify), followed by the likes of wild salmon escalope with a buttery court bouillon. Main courses have starred John Dory, Cornish lamb and Lunesdale duckling, and are followed by interesting salads (caramelised apple and blue cheese/Somerset Brie in a herb crust), usually a sorbet course and then dessert -rich, bitter chocolate quenelle with a coffee sauce was a recent offering, and jolly good it was, too.

HAMPTON WICK   Le Petit Max

97A High Street, Hampton Wick, Middx, KT2 5NB
Tel: 0181-977 0236   **£50**
Open: lunch Sun only, dinner daily
    (closed 4 days beginning of each month)
Meals served: lunch 12.30 & 3.45, dinner 7-10.30 (Fri & Sat to 11)

A bizarre mix perhaps but this café-by-day becomes a serious restaurant by night! Egg and chips give way to terrine of foie gras, baked beans disappear in favour of a cocktail of fresh brown shrimps and bangers step aside to let in ribs of Aberdeen Angus beef, char-grilled with sea salt and herbs with a bearnaise sauce. It's small, so no wonder booking is essential with such goodies on offer—no licence, so take your own wine (£2 corkage). The Renzland brothers have now opened another restaurant in Fulham (see entry—London, Chez Max) where I believe by contrast construction workers are not welcome for breakfast!

HANCHURCH   **Hanchurch Manor**

Hanchurch, Nr Stoke-on-Trent, Staffordshire, ST4 8JD
Tel: (01782) 643030   *Fax:* (01782) 643035   **£55**
Open: lunch & dinner daily (residents only)
Meals served: lunch 12.30-2, dinner 7.30-9.30
Elegant Tudor-style house, reputedly designed by Sir Charles Berry of Palace of
Westminster fame. Own grounds with fishing lake, and five delightful bedrooms.

HANDFORTH   Belfry Hotel

Stanley Road, Handforth, Nr Wilmslow, Cheshire, SK9 3LD
Tel: 0161-437 0511   *Fax:* 0161-499 0597   **£40**
Open: lunch & dinner daily (closed Bank Holidays, dinner 25 Dec)
Meals served: lunch 12.30-2, dinner 7-10

Attention to detail and dedication are the hallmarks of this hotel, run
for over 30 years by the Beech family. Mainly a hotel catering for business people, it has a functional looking exterior, all modern facilities
are provided as well as a warm welcome, comfortable reception areas
and well fitted bedrooms. The restaurant, in the capable hands of Mark
Fletcher, offers an extensive range across à la carte and fixed-price
menus, which include something for everyone. From the simple—like
carrot and coriander soup or liver and bacon, to classics, or the more
exotic—steamed chicken and Roquefort mousse on a basil and lentil
cream; and crispy duckling with a cherry and Kirsch sauce. Good-
value wines on an international list, with an excellent French section.

Useful for Manchester Airport—courtesy coach available

HARROGATE   Bettys Café & Tea Rooms

1 Parliament Street, Harrogate, North Yorkshire, HG1 2QU
Tel: (01423) 502746   *Fax:* (01423) 565191   **£30**
Open: all day daily (closed 25 & 26 Dec, 1 Jan)
Meals served: 9-9

The original of the four (others in York, Northallerton and Ilkley) and
first opened in 1919, Bettys is an institution. Its success is based on the
principle that to get things right you have to do them yourself.
Everything is made by hand at Bettys Bakery—cakes, chocolates,
breads, pastries, the lot!—over 400 different lines in all. Everything is
available, from a light snack or brunch to dinner (when a resident
pianist plays), with one of the best selections of coffee in the country.
Betty herself is a mystery: her identity remains a family secret.

HARROGATE   Café Fleur

3 Royal Parade, Harrogate, North Yorkshire, HG1 2SZ
Tel: (01423) 503034   **£20**
Open: dinner daily (closed 25 & 26 Dec, 1 Jan)
Meals served: dinner 6-9.30

You will come away more than satisfied at the value for money obtained at this lively, informal, brasserie-style restaurant which offers both fixed-price and à la carte menus. Have just two courses, such as soup of the day followed by grilled ribsteak or lasagne, for as little as £4.95 before 7.30pm (£6.95 thereafter). Specialities include steak sandwich in a baguette, Toulouse sausages, oxtail casserole, leek and onion tart or fisherman's pie with prawns. More sophisticated options include the likes of lamb with a redcurrant and rosemary sauce or poached salmon with an orange and basil sauce. This is good, simple bistro fare at very reasonable prices and only champagne breaks the £20 barrier, with the majority of wines below £10.

HARROGATE   Drum & Monkey

5 Montpellier Gardens, Harrogate, North Yorkshire, HG1 2TF
Tel: (01423) 502650   **£35**
Open: lunch & dinner Mon-Sat
Meals served: lunch 12-2.30, dinner 7-10.15

This is the sort of place you can return to time and time again. It's a bustling, fish-dedicated restaurant on two floors, with a menu which ranges from oysters and mussels to cream of whiting soup, sea trout salad, seafood pie, lobster in several guises (hot and cold), and sole likewise—try it grilled whole or in fillets with sauce Florentine, Bonne Femme or with prawns, mushrooms and a white wine sauce. The lunch menu is similar, but prices are lower.

*The Drum still packs them in and you can see why:
quality food, reasonable prices*

HARROGATE   The Dusty Miller Restaurant

Low-Laithe, Summerbridge, Harrogate,
    West Yorkshire, HG3 4BU
Tel: (01423) 780837   **£55**
Open: dinner Tue-Sat (closed 25 Dec, 1 Jan, 2 wks Aug)
Meals served: lunch , dinner 6.30-11

Brian and Elizabeth Dennison's restaurant offers something out of the ordinary: as well as the fixed-price proprietors' menu and the à la carte there's a late menu (after 9.30pm except Saturdays) consisting of just one main course which offers a choice of three dishes such as escalope of salmon and chives, beefsteak and kidney pie with oysters or suprême of chicken chasseur. The cooking is predominantly English, with a dash of French and a tickle of Irish; classically inspired dishes and robust traditional favourites are prepared with imagination and flair. Start perhaps with lobster, tomato and basil filo parcels (I would opt for a plate of Irish oysters); follow with crisp roast duckling cooked with apple and Calvados or saddle of venison with port. Tempting selection of desserts, plus a choice of English, French and Irish cheeses.

HARROGATE   Miller's, The Bistro

1 Montpelier Mews, Harrogate, North Yorkshire, HG1 2TG
Tel: (01423) 530708   **£45**
Open: lunch & dinner Tue-Sat (closed Bank Holidays,
     10 days Xmas)
Meals served: lunch 12-2, dinner 7-10

Eat outdoors in the cobbled courtyard in fine weather at this smart, modern bistro in a pretty mews development at the centre of town. With seats for only 38, it's best to book to enjoy Simon Gueller's short, concise carte of light, contemporary dishes: salad of goat's cheese with hazelnut vinaigrette, grilled sea scallops with sauce vierge, risotto of ink with roast squid, and lobster macaroni among starters; followed by turbot Viennoise with a grain mustard sabayon, Scottish sirloin with wild mushrooms and caramelised shallots, or pan-fried calf's liver, served with crispy bacon, puréed potatoes and devilled sauce. Carefully chosen wines complement the excellent food. Simon's wife, Rona, supervises the friendly service.

HARVINGTON   The Mill at Harvington

Anchor Lane, Harvington, Hereford & Worcester, WR11 5NR
Tel: (01386) 870688   *Fax:* (01386) 870688   **£50**
Open: lunch & dinner daily (closed 23-29 Dec)
Meals served: lunch 11.45-1.45, dinner 7-8.45

A converted Georgian malting mill in eight acres of wooded parkland in the Vale of Evesham, transformed and run with professionalism and charm by Simon and Jane Greenhalgh. Fifteen immaculately-kept bedrooms enjoy lovely garden views and the dining room opens on to the lawn and gardens, which stretch down to the River Avon where fishing from the hotel grounds is available. Good use is made of local Evesham produce in Jane's kitchen and the menus are changed frequently according to what's available. Typical starters include the likes of warm fish terrine, seafood sausage and grilled goat's cheese salad, while main courses might include walnut-coated rack of lamb, chicken with Comté cheese and steak, kidney and oyster pudding. Good desserts and coffee that comes with home-made fudge.

HASLEMERE   Morels

23 Lower Street, Haslemere, Surrey, GU27 2NY
Tel: (01428) 651462   **£45**
Open: lunch Tue-Fri, dinner Tue-Sat (closed Bank Holidays
     ex Good Friday, 3 wks Sep/Oct)   ✿
Meals served: lunch 12.30-2, dinner 7-10

A delightful restaurant of the type more common in small French towns than in English ones like Haslemere. Haslemere, however, has long been established as a centre for artisans and Jean-Yves Morel (see next page)is a master craftsman in his kitchen. There is tremendous value on his fixed price menus available from Tuesday to Friday, from which you could select a Mediterranean fish soup, follow it with pigeon served with pasta and red wine sauce and finish with a delicious apricot and Amaretto liqueur soufflé. Some of the best cooking in Britain at under £10! The carte provides a greater variety of equally well-composed dishes. Excellent service and a comprehensive wine list.

Biography

Jean-Yves Morel began his cooking career at the age of twelve, by helping out in a local restaurant, then undertook an apprenticeship in charcuterie in Lyon, France. He was taken

Jean-Yves *on by the Roux brothers, first at their own charcuterie and*
Morel *then at Le Gavroche, before moving down to Haslemere,*

where he transformed a previously run-down restaurant into the successful place it is today. Without doubt, it is here that he has really blossomed.

HASTINGS   Röser's

64 Eversfield Place, St Leonards on Sea, Nr Hastings,
    E Sussex, TN37 6DB
Tel: (01424) 712218   **£45**
Open: lunch Tue-Fri, dinner Tue-Sat (closed Bank Holidays,
    1 wk Jan, 1 wk Aug)   🍀
Meals served: lunch 12-2, dinner 7-10

This snug little seafood restaurant opposite the pier, with booth seating and dark-panelled walls, is in a class of its own when it comes to food. Gerald Röser takes his lead from French and German cooking and adds his own innovative touch. A well balanced meal might comprise smoked salmon blinis with crème fraîche, then line-caught local sea bass coooked and served Mediterranean-style, with one of Gerald's delicious desserts to finish—they're so popular that his local clientele clamour for their favourites to stay on the menu. His is reckoned to be the ultimate chocolate mousse, and I for one won't argue with that!

Every seaside resort should have one like this.

HATFIELD HEATH   Down Hall
Hatfield Heath, Nr Bishop's Stortford, Hertfordshire, CM22 7AS
Tel: (01279) 731441   *Fax:* (01279) 730416   **£45**
Open: lunch & dinner daily
Meals served: lunch 12.30-2, dinner 7-9.45
An ideal conference venue with over 100 bedrooms, swimming pool and tennis courts.

HAVANT   Cockle Warren Cottage

36 Seafront, Hayling Island, Havant, Hampshire, PO11 9HL
Tel: (01705) 464838   **£55**
Open: dinner daily
Meals served: dinner 7.30 for 8, residents only

Food is of primary importance at this delightful, five-bedroomed, cottagey hotel, minutes from the beach, but with its own garden and swimming pool. Breakfast features a host of specialities, such as devilled kidneys, duck eggs, finnan haddock, Arbroath smokies, kippers, home-made marmalade and brioches. Candlelit dinner is based on traditional English and French country cooking. The menu is planned around the best local ingredients available each day: South Downs lamb, local game and trout, Hayling Island crab, lobster and Dover sole. Other produce comes direct from France, namely cornfed guinea fowl and barbary duck, and French flour for the breads and viennoiserie, all made on the premises. A short wine list, but carefully chosen, features French or English wine from nearby Hambledon. Bedrooms are individually designed and all rooms have pleasant views, either across the Solent or overlooking the garden and pool. There is a four-poster room and a pretty, cottage room in Victorian style with half-tester bed just a few feet from the house. Chef-proprietors Diane and David Skelton have much to be proud of here.

HAWORTH   Weavers

15 West Lane, Haworth, Nr Bradford,
   West Yorkshire, BD22 8DU
Tel: (01535) 643822   **£30**
Open: lunch Sun in winter, dinner Tue-Sat
   (closed Bank Holidays,
   2 wks Xmas, 2 wks summer)
Meals served: lunch 12-1.30, dinner 7-9

An informal, friendly restaurant and bar with four rooms for overnight guests, converted from a group of cottages in the very heart of historic Haworth. Everything is made on the premises and most of the vegetables are home-grown. Straightforward, no-nonsense British dishes are Colin and Jane Rushworth's forte: pan-fried calf's liver with a gin and lime sauce; crisp roast duck with rhubarb sauce; fillet of pork with cracklin' and scrumpy gravy; Pennine beef steak pie; fisherman's bake; parsnip and cashew nut loaf. Old-school puds or Nanny's meringue for afters.

HAYFIELD	**Bridge End Restaurant**

7 Church Street, Hayfield, Derbyshire, SK12 5JE
Tel: (01663) 747321   *Fax:* (01663) 742121   **£45**
Open: lunch Sun, dinner Tue-Sat (closed 1 wk Jan)
Meals served: lunch 12.30-2.30, dinner 7.30-10   *Very good local restaurant*

This attractive little country restaurant with rooms occupies a 19th-century stone building opposite the village church. Unassuming though that may sound, Bridge End is in fact streets ahead of many and the national acclaim it has received for its cooking is thoroughly justified. Chef Jonathan Holmes brings his globe-trotting to bear on weekly menus, though the main focus is on English and French cuisine. Goat's cheese tart to start perhaps, followed by grilled salmon with chive sauce or guinea fowl marinated in lime, then fried in batter and served with fresh tomato sauce. The atmosphere in the dining room is laid-back and chatty. Four cottagey bedrooms for overnight accommodation.

HAYTOR	**Bel Alp House**

Haytor, Nr Bovey Tracey, Devon, TQ13 9XX
Tel: (01364) 661217   *Fax:* (01364) 661292   **£75**
Open: dinner daily (closed Dec-Feb)
Meals served: dinner 7.30-8.30

The Curnocks have done much to improve this delightful Edwardian house since their arrival here in 1983. An air of peace and quiet pervades throughout, with homely touches making you feel more like a house guest than hotel client. Light, airy, spacious bedrooms include two with Edwardian tubs, and housekeeping throughout is immaculate. The house enjoys a wonderful location (south-facing and sheltered), nestling into the hillside on the south-eastern edge of Dartmoor, with magnificent views across South Devon. In charge of the kitchen, Sarah Curnock offers a daily, five-course dinner menu based on English and French country cooking.

HELFORD	**Riverside**

Helford, Nr Helston, Cornwall, TR12 6JU
Tel: (01326) 231443   *Fax:* (01326) 231103   **£70**
Open: dinner daily (closed Nov-Feb)
Meals served: dinner 7.30-9

A pretty, cottagey retreat with an idyllic setting alongside a wooded creek in Daphne du Maurier country. Here, Sue Darrell cooks in French provincial style with confidence and simplicity, relying on local produce whenever possible. Locally-caught fish and seafood feature strongly, in dishes such as warm mussel and fresh crab salad, and steamed turbot with local clams and a chive butter sauce. Meat-lovers might opt for the likes of roasted stuffed quail followed by best end of West Country lamb in puff pastry with a rosemary and red wine sauce. Desserts might include crème brûlée or bread-and-butter pudding. This is a fixed-price, four-course dinner menu with around four or five choices at each course. Husband Edward's passion for wine is reflected in the excellent and reasonably priced list, which is strong on New World options and offers plenty of half bottles and old vintages. The six bedrooms are luxurious, with many fine features such as Oriental rugs and antiques. Breakfast on the terrace in fine weather.

HELMSLEY	Monet's

19 Bridge Street, Helmsley, North Yorkshire, YO6 5BG
Tel: (01439) 70618 £40
Open: dinner Tue-Sun (Tue-Sat in winter) (closed 24-27 Dec)
Meals served: dinner 7-9.30

English restaurant-with-rooms in a large private house just outside the town. Excellent daytime meals—steak and oyster pie, poached salmon with herb butter—and more elaborate fixed-price evening menus.

HEREFORD Steppes Country House Hotel

Ullingswick, Nr Hereford, Hereford & Worcester, HR1 3JG
Tel: (01432) 820424 £50
Open: dinner daily (closed Dec & Jan, open Xmas)
Meals served: dinner 7.30-9

A small 17th-century hotel with six traditional-style bedrooms converted from timber-framed barns. Rich in heavy oak beams, inglenook fireplaces, cobbled floors and antique furnishing, it is a place which suggests old-fashioned quiet and hospitality, the values of yesteryear. Nestling in a rural hamlet, the house has provided shelter and refreshment for generations of yeoman farmers over the last 400 years. Excellent breakfasts offer Loch Fyne kippers, Arbroath smokies, Norfolk bloaters, devilled kidneys and more traditional favourites.

HERM White House

Herm, GY1 3HR
Tel: (01481) 722159 *Fax:* (01481) 710066 £35
Open: lunch & dinner daily (closed Oct-Mar)
Meals served: lunch 12.30-2, dinner 7-9.30

The only hotel on the car-free island, the White House has 38 bedrooms, the best of which enjoy sea views and balconies, as well as a number of self-catering cottages and flats for those who really want to get away from it all. The hotel has its own pub, the Ship Inn, where you can eat in the carvery dining room, but a more formal alternative is provided by the restaurant. No surprises on an essentially British repertoire: beef Wellington, hake with a cheese and chive crust on lemon sauce, and oysters from the hotel's own farm. Friendly and relaxed.

HERNE BAY L'Escargot

22 High Street, Herne Bay, Kent, CT6 5LH
Tel: (01227) 372876 £35
Open: lunch Sun-Fri, dinner daily (closed 1 wk Jan, 1 wk Sep,
   Thu in winter)
Meals served: lunch 12-2, dinner 7-9.30

A friendly, informal restaurant run with charm by Alain and Joyce Bessemoulin. Largely classic French in outlook, Alain cooks with competence and a sense of simplicity. Good-value fixed-price menus complement the à la carte. Typical starters range from lobster bisque with a dash of brandy to deep-fried Camembert with a gooseberry sauce, or king prawns served either hot with garlic butter or cold with a spicy cocktail sauce. Main courses are typified by sirloin steak with red wine sauce and shallots, or best end of roast lamb with rosemary sauce. Desserts are simple, and in keeping with the general lack of fuss which pervades in Alain's methods.

HERSHAM	The Dining Room

10 Queens Road, The Village Green, Hersham, Surrey, KT12 5LS
Tel: (01932) 231686 **£40**
Open: lunch Sun-Fri, dinner Mon-Sat (closed Bank Holidays,
1 wk Xmas)
Meals served: lunch 12-2 (Sun to 2.30), dinner 7-10.30 (Sat from 6.30)

An unpretentious, neighbourhood restaurant specialising in good, honest food, served up in good-sized portions at affordable prices. A maze of tiny, interconnecting rooms (from what was once two old cottages) provide the setting for Richard Moore's competent cooking. Typical starters on the essentially English menu include hot Gloucester cheese and ale pot with toast, and duck liver pâté on Cumberland sauce. Main-course choices range from Welsh lamb and mint pie to traditional steak and kidney pudding or duck and raspberry casserole under a savoury crumble top. Inventive sweets include Sussex Pond pudding and Hersham Mess—a concoction of pineapple, meringue, whisky and cream. A fixed-price, two-course menu is also available in the evening from Monday to Friday.

HERSTMONCEUX	Sundial Restaurant

Gardner Street, Herstmonceux, East Sussex, BN27 4LA
Tel: (01323) 832217 **£60**
Open: lunch Tue-Sun, dinner Tue-Sat
(closed 2/3 wks Aug/Sep, Xmas-mid Jan) 🎗
Meals served: lunch 12.30-2.30, dinner 7.30-9.30 (Sat to 10)

A homely, long-established village restaurant located in a pretty 17th-century cottage, with garden and terraces for alfresco summer eating. Giuseppe and Laurette Bertoli have run this restaurant for over 25 years—she front of house, he in the kitchen. Expect to be treated more like guests at a dinner party than in formal fashion. His menu is largely classical, mainly French in outlook but with some Italian influences. The choice across menus is quite astonishing, with daily specials supplementing the fortnightly à la carte and twice-weekly-changing fixed-price menus. Specialities include bouillabaisse, grouse Vigneronne and turbot Belle Sophie.

Biography

Giuseppe Bertoli

Giuseppe Bertoli trained for nearly 13 years in various European countries before coming to England and finally finding what he was looking for—a small, 17th-century cottage in the pretty Sussex village of Herstmonceux, which he turned into the Sundial Restaurant. In those early days, Giuseppe's style was really classic French cooking, but over the years it has become more inventive, and he is constantly improving and studying new dishes.

HETTON   Angel Inn

Hetton, Nr Skipton, North Yorkshire, BD23 6LT
Tel: (01756) 730263   **£50**
Open: lunch Sun, dinner Mon-Sat (closed 3rd wk Jan)
Meals served: lunch 12-2, dinner 6.30-9.30, (light meals
   in the bar: 12-2, 6-10, earlier in winter)

The Angel has undergone a major refurbishment behind the scenes, with over £70,000 spent on modernising the kitchens. Pride of place goes to the new Bonnet of Lyons cooking range (only the 7th Bonnet to be installed in the UK) designed by partners Denis Watkins (pic-

tured) and chef John Topham it will allow more chefs to work on service at any one time, speeding up delivery to both the brasserie and restaurant proper. Long famous anyway for its food, there is now even more opportunity to enjoy what's on offer. The brasserie keeps up with modern trends: chilled gazpacho Andaluz, bruschetta, hot salad of provençal vegetables, sirloin with Caesar salad, chicken baked in filo with Thai spices. The set din- ner in the restaurant offers ample choice of greater sophistication in dishes such as Tuscan vegetable terrine with a tape- nade crostini, followed by roast leg of farmed rabbit stuffed with tar- ragon butter and wrapped in pancetta, then served on a pool of creamed potato and mustard sauce. Fish is brought and prepared on a daily basis. The investment in the kitchen is a good sign of confidence and greater things to come.

Go there! You won't be disappointed.

HIGH ONGAR   Shoes Restaurant

The Street, High Ongar, Essex, CM5 9ND
Tel: (01277) 363350   *Fax:* (01279) 871117   **£60**
Open: lunch Sun-Fri, dinner Mon-Sat
   (closed 1 wk Xmas/New Year)
Meals served: lunch 12-2.30, dinner 7-9.30

Since her arrival mid 1993, from the Grand Hotel in Brighton, chef Sue Kesseck has strengthened the growing local reputation of this English restaurant in a 17th-century former coaching inn in the tranquil village of High Ongar. Home-made bread, pasta, ice cream, sorbets and petits fours are standard. The menu shows a creative mind at work on tradi- tional dishes, as in white onion soup topped with a Stilton croûton, home-made venison sausage with a wild berry jus or wild mushroom consommé with herb dumplings to start. Main courses offer dishes such as whole roast poussin in a red wine sauce, pan-fried lemon sole coated in toasted sesame seeds with a soy butter sauce, or roast rack of lamb filled with a light chili and tarragon mousse, the whole wrapped in puff pastry and served with a tarragon and cream sauce. Afterwards try caramelised rice pudding or a selection of British and Continental cheeses served with home-made walnut and sultana bread. There's a resident harpist on Friday evenings and classical guitarist on Sundays at lunchtime.

HIGHAM   The Knowle

School Lane, Higham, Nr Rochester, Kent, ME3 7HP
Tel: (01474) 822262   **£50**
Open: lunch Tue-Sun, dinner Tue-Sat
Meals served: lunch 12-2, dinner 6.30-9.30

Built in 1840 by the rector of Higham, Lyn and Michael Baragwanath's large Victorian mansion home is set in three acres of private gardens. The menu changes regularly, offering generous portions of mostly traditional English fare. Start with salmon and cucumber mousse or cheese soufflé royale before tucking into one of a varied selection of fish and steak dishes. Specialities include chicken Portuguese, pot-roast pheasant and beef stroganoff. A cheaper, bistro menu operates in addition to the à la carte on Tuesday to Thursday evenings.

HINTLESHAM   Hintlesham Hall

Hintlesham, Nr Ipswich, Suffolk, IP8 3NS
Tel: (01473) 652334   *Fax:* (01473) 652463   **£55**
Open: lunch & dinner daily   ♣
Meals served: lunch 12-2, dinner 7-9.30

The Georgian facade of this 33-bedroomed Grade I listed house belies its Elizabethan origins: the house in fact dates back to the 1570s. The Hall is a haven of gracious living and has been much enhanced by lavish refurbishment over the last couple of years. It is set 175 acres of splendid grounds which include an 18-hole golf course and country club. Chef Alan Ford has an outstanding talent, and his menu offers a host of culinary delights. Start with a duo of lightly curried crab barquettes and seared scallops set on a cucumber cream, roasted quail with pistachio nut galette and Sauternes wine sauce, or a smooth foie gras parfait with port jelly on warm baby brioche. Follow with Dover sole filled with saffron mousse and served with a Vermouth sauce or a tournedos of Scottish beef with a stunning dark watercress sauce. Menus are seasonal and offer plenty of choice. Elegant accommodation is divided between the main house and courtyard block. I first fell in love with Hintlesham during Robert Carrier's distinguished reign and my affection didn't diminish when it was run by Ruth and David Watson; it's still as strong as ever now that the Hall is overseen by Tim Sunderland.

This place still casts its spell.

HOCKLEY HEATH   Nuthurst Grange

Nuthurst Grange Lane, Hockley Heath, Warwickshire, B94 5NL
Tel: (01564) 783972   *Fax:* (01564) 783919   **£55**
Open: lunch Sun-Fri, dinner daily (closed 1 wk Xmas)
Meals served: lunch 12-2, dinner 7-9.30

The approach to Nuthurst, a long avenue bringing you through seven
and a half acres of landscaped grounds towards an elegant Victorian
building, gives you time to contemplate the delights in store once you
arrive at the Randolphs' 15-bedroomed country hotel. Chief amongst
these has to be the ground-floor restaurant, a fitting showpiece for
David's cooking which embraces the best of both classic and modern,
British and French. A typical menu might offer broccoli and almond
soup or chicken liver parfait, followed by either chicken with ginger
sauce or whole roasted pigeon with a Burgundy and thyme sauce, with
raspberry brûlée or steamed date pudding with toffee sauce to finish.
Two choices for each course on the fixed lunch and dinner menus, but
considerably more on the carte. A separate vegetarian menu offers the
likes of ragout-stuffed peppers or spicy layered ratatouille. A variety of
meeting and conference rooms are available.

HOLBETON   Alston Hall
Alston Cross, Holbeton, Nr Plymouth, Devon, PL8 1HN
Tel: (01752) 830555   *Fax:* (01752) 830494   **£50**
Open: lunch & dinner daily
Meals served: lunch 12-2, dinner 7-9.30
Ivy-clad, 20-bedroomed Edwardian mansion in four acres of lightly wooded park-
land, with splendid views across soft, rolling hills to the sea beyond. French and
English cuisine. Own leisure club.

HOLDENBY   Lynton House

Holdenby Road, Holdenby, Northamptonshire, NN6 8DJ
Tel: (01604) 770777   **£50**
Open: lunch Tue-Fri, dinner Mon-Sat (closed Bank Holidays)
Meals served: lunch 12.30-1.45, dinner 7.30-9.45

Carol and Carlo Bertozzi bring a taste of Italy to this country restaurant
with five bedrooms. The English/Italian carte offers a wide choice and
is supplemented by fixed-price lunch and dinner menus. Escalopes of
veal with rosemary, roast duck or venison and hen pheasant feature
alongside traditional Italian favourites such as gnocchi alla romana,
seafood brodetti or home-made lasagne.

HOLT   Yetman's

37 Norwich Road, Holt, Norfolk, NR25 6SA
Tel: (01263) 713320   **£55**
Open: lunch Sat & Sun, dinner Wed-Mon
    (Wed-Sun in winter) (closed Bank Holidays)
Meals served: lunch 12.30-2, dinner 7.30-9

A short, hand-written menu which changes daily is Alison and Peter
Yetman's technique for success. Choose from starters such as pea and
ham soup, sautéed squid, mussels and prawns on toasted bruschetta or
terrine of duck livers with spiced figs; followed by braised rabbit in
white Burgundy with fresh sage, mustard and Puy lentils or local beef
with a tarragon and orange hollandaise. Crème brûlées, lemon tart and
toasted apricot pancakes are typical desserts.

HORLEY   Langshott Manor

Langshott, Horley, Surrey, RH6 9LN
Tel: (01293) 786680   *Fax:* (01293) 783905   **£60**
Open: lunch by arrangement, dinner daily (closed 24-30 Dec)
Meals served: dinner 7.30-9.30

New Zealanders Patricia and Geoffrey Noble run this small Elizabethan
manor house with great charm, in a relaxed, informal manner. With
just five bedrooms, it is small enough to make a homely impression.
Antiques grace the pretty bedrooms which offer a host of home comforts, and there's a courtesy Jaguar car for the short trip to Gatwick airport. The hotel is tucked away down a quiet country lane amidst
tranquil gardens and ponds, and in spite of its proximity to the airport,
it provides a peaceful ambience—all in all a gem of a find for these
parts. The tiny, dining room serves portions of hearty English home
cooking from a fixed-price menu which changes according to local seasonal produce. Sorrel soup or lettuce and lovage soup could be followed by "Rosemaried" lamb, pheasant with Calvados or steak, kidney
and oyster pie. Menus usually offer a choice between fish, beef, game
and lamb dishes.

HORNCASTLE   Magpies Restaurant

73-75 East Street, Horncastle, Lincolnshire, LN9 6AA
Tel: (01507) 527004   **£35**
Open: lunch Tue-Fri & Sun, dinner Tue-Sat
    (closed Bank Holidays, 2 wks Sep)
Meals served: lunch 12.30-2, dinner 7.15-10

A family restaurant offering excellent value for money. Fixed-price,
weekly-changing lunch and dinner menus (from £8.95 and £13.95
respectively) are supplemented by a monthly-changing à la carte. Start
perhaps with a warm confit of duck on a bed of onion and orange or
home-made French onion soup, followed by Scottish salmon on a basil
cream sauce, pan-fried medallions of pork with a prune and sloe sauce,
or supreme of chicken with spring onion, wrapped in filo pastry on a
honey and ginger sauce. Typical lunchtime menus might include traditional main courses such as roast chicken with sage and onion stuffing
or roast rib of local beef.

HORNDON-ON-THE-HILL Bell Inn

High Road, Horndon-on-the-Hill, Essex, SS17 8LD
Tel: (01375) 673154 *Fax:* (01375) 361611 **£40**
Open: lunch & dinner daily (closed 25 & 26 Dec)
Meals served: lunch 12.15-2, dinner 7-10

A former 15th-century coaching inn now run by the Vereker family, this is the focal point of village life and is steeped in history and tradition. One such is the hanging, on Good Friday each year, of a hot-cross bun from a beam over the bar—a tradition which has run for 90 years! The Bell offers imaginative English and international cuisine on a daily-changing menu which is available in either the restaurant or the bar. Dishes range from the simple to the more unusual: fish'n'chips, steaks, beef and pigeon broth, steamed venison pudding, pan-fried calf's liver and bacon, or lamb cutlets baked in pastry with a haggis mousse. Fish is also well represented by dishes such as Dover sole with dill butter or monkfish baked with lemon, garlic and chives.

HORNDON-ON-THE-HILL Hill House

High Road, Horndon-on-the-Hill, Essex, SS17 8LD
Tel: (01375) 642463 *Fax:* (01375) 361611 **£40**
Open: lunch Tue-Fri, dinner Tue-Sat (closed 25-31 Dec)
Meals served: lunch 12.15-2, dinner 7.30-9.45

Continuing the family tradition the Verekers have expanded their horizons with the opening of Hill House. Built about 1685, Hill House was formerly a prestigious residence in the village. Extensive renovation has resulted in a restaurant with 11 bedrooms, the pretty dining room offering more formal eating than at the The Bell (see above) a couple of doors away. Here, there's imaginative, skilful cooking with very enjoyable results on the plate, and there's plenty of choice. Starters could include asparagus with lemon hollandaise, chicken and guineau fowl sausage or blue cheese and avocado samosa. Main-course choice might offer lamb fillet with a tarragon mousse baked in filo, plain-grilled sirloin steak or salmon supreme baked with ginger, coriander and tomato sauce. Lovely puds such as lime and ginger mousse, orange and Grand Marnier trifle and apple and rhubarb crumble.

HORTON   French Partridge

Horton, Nr Northampton, Northamptonshire, NN7 2AP
Tel: (01604) 870033   *Fax:* (01604) 870032   **£50**
Open: dinner Tue-Sat (closed 2 wks Xmas & Easter, 3 wks Aug)
Meals served: dinner only 7.30-9

Over their 23 years at the helm, the Partridge family have built up strong local following here. The clubby dining room, with oil paintings, polished mahogany tables creates a traditional yet unpretentious setting for this dinner-only restaurant. The well-thought-out, four-course, fixed-price menu changes every couple of months or so, but you could start with cream of watercress soup, duck liver parfait and plum sauce or marinated salmon and sardine fillets, followed by a second course of cheese fondue pancake. Braised oxtail with herb dumplings or poached chicken with a mild curry sauce are typical of main-course selections. Leave room for dessert though—brown sugar meringues with cream or ice cream should not go amiss. Good wine list. Pictured, David Partridge.

Always a warm welcome from the Partridge family.

HORTON-CUM-STUDLEY   Studley Priory

Horton-cum-Studley, Nr Oxford, Oxfordshire, OX33 1AZ
Tel: (01865) 351203   *Fax:* (01865) 351613   **£50**
Open: lunch & dinner daily (closed Bank Holidays)
Meals served: lunch 12.30-1.45, dinner 7.30-9.30

Close to Oxford, set in 13 acres of wooded grounds, this striking Elizabethan manor enjoys views over the Chilterns (to the east), The Cotswolds (to the west) and the Vale of Aylesbury. Formerly a Benedictine convent, it was dissolved by Henry VIII passing next into the hands of the Croke family whose coat-of-arms can be seen in the stained glass windows and cornicework in the hall. There are six traditional-style bedrooms in the main house, one of which boasts a four-poster dating from 1700; but the majority of rooms (more modern and smaller) are in the Jacobean wing.

HULL   Le Bistro

400 Beverley Road, Hull, Humberside, HU5 1LW
Tel: (01482) 43088   **£35**
Open: dinner Mon-Sat (closed 26-28 Dec, 2 wks Aug)
Meals served: dinner 7-10

Something of a fun place: a cosy, intimate bistro, with games, and quizzes available for those who like to play while they eat. The daily-changing blackboard menu has plenty of scope for both carnivores and vegetarians. Starters range from soups and snails in garlic butter to deep-fried camembert or nut roasts. Main-course favourites include beef bourguinonne, roast duck with apple and cider, bean curry with rice or cidered hot pot. Excellent value for money.

HULL   Ceruttis

10 Nelson Street, Hull, Humberside, HU1 1XE
Tel: (01482) 28501   *Fax:* (01482) 587597   **£50**
Open: lunch Mon-Fri, dinner Mon-Sat (closed Bank Holidays
    1 wk Xmas)
Meals served: lunch 12-2, dinner 7-9.30

The Cerutti family's friendly, harbourside restaurant has built up a
sound reputation over the last 20 years. The emphasis is firmly on fish
and local seafood, with the favourite, Dover sole, prepared in a number
of different ways by long-serving chef Tim Bell. Irish oysters, scampi
Oscar Wilde, scallops wrapped in bacon, monkfish with black peppercorns, seafood rendezvous in a creamy chive sauce—the choice is
excellent. The dedicated meat-eater has a choice of steaks, poultry or
lamb; and there's the likes of mushroom stroganoff for vegetarians.

HUNSTRETE   Hunstrete House

Hunstrete, Chelwood, Nr Bath, Avon, BS18 4NS
Tel: (01761) 490490   *Fax:* (01761) 490732   **£55**
Open: lunch & dinner daily
Meals served: lunch 12-2, dinner 7.30-9.30

A 17th-century Georgian 24-bedroomed manor house, complete with
deer park, situated in 90 acres of parkland and beautiful gardens on the
edge of the Mendip Hills, ten miles from Bristol and Bath. New owners
have now completed refurbishment, bringing Hunstrete back into line
with the best of English country house hotels. The walled vegetable
garden supplies much of the kitchen's needs, and new chef Robert
Clayton is on hand to do the rest. His menus offer a good balance, with
dishes such as chicken and Madeira boudin with cep sauce, followed
by steamed guinea fowl with Calvados and lime served with a
Burgundy sauce, and salmon in a buttery court bouillon with garden
vegetables. Menus are refreshingly straightforward, with the emphasis
firmly placed on modern English country cooking. Arrive in the Spring
and you will be greeted by swathes of daffodils along the drive and an
abundance of bluebells, cherry blossom and tulips within the walled
garden. Come the summer and it's all roses, crimson wallflowers and
white tulips. Genuinely warm and welcoming service.

HUNTINGDON   Old Bridge Hotel

1 High Street, Huntingdon, Cambridgeshire, PE18 6TQ
Tel: (01480) 52681   *Fax:* (01480) 411017   **£60**
Open: lunch & dinner daily (closed dinner 25 Dec)
Meals served: lunch 12-2, dinner 7-10,
    (light meals on the Terrace 12-2.30, 6-10.30)

This handsome, creeper-clad Georgian hotel has gardens which run
down to the River Ouse yet it is only 500 yards from the centre of the
market town which was Oliver Cromwell's birthplace. The walls in the
Terrace Brasserie comprise a single mural by artist Julia Rushbury, a
work of art which took over four months to complete, and the effect is
summery and bright. The formal oak-panelled dining room is home to
chef-patron Nick Steiger's intelligent and imaginative cooking, and

offers a comprehensive à la carte menu of traditional English dishes such as trolley-carved prime roast beef, local game and Fenland vegetables. Lamb and lemon soup, iced lobster soufflé as starters; main courses might include baked suet pudding of hare in a rich fennel and sultana sauce, or chargrilled calf's liver with spinach, bacon, red onion and light red wine sauce. An excellent selection of British cheeses with classic puds including sticky toffee pudding. One of the best wine lists in the country. The hotel has 26 beautifully furnished rooms with carpeted bathrooms. Courteous staff throughout.

HUNTSHAM	Huntsham Court

Huntsham, nr Bampton, Devon EX16 7NA
Tel: (01398) 6365   *Fax*: (01398) 6456   *Ideal for groups of friends or family*   **£60**
Open: dinner daily
Meals served: dinner 8-10   ✤

Laid-back, casual and friendly—a little eccentric to some, perfect for others—this is a fun place in which you're more likely to relax, particularly if music is your love. Here, you're more likely to find a grand piano and pre-war radio sets in your room than a TV or telephone. Bathrooms boast Victorian tubs not jacuzzis. The hotel is a music lover's paradise: rooms are named after composers; there are brass instruments lying around to play if you wish and a4,000-strong record collection to choose from. There are only 14 bedrooms at Huntsham and the long, single dining-table seats 28. The Bolwigs (she Greek-Australian, he Danish) have spent years fine-tuning the very special atmosphere of this unique Victorian Gothic hotel hidden away in the middle of the countryside a few miles from Tiverton. Eating is communal—to the sound of classical music played *forte* in the evenings—and if you need something you simply wander into the kitchen yourself. Dinner—not nouvelle by any means—is a choice between vegetarian or carnivore; there are five courses, and post-prandial conversation has been known to run till 2am. Breakfast includes free-range eggs, local bacon, traditional local sausages and home-baked bread which is baked in log-fired ovens. A very special place indeed.

HURLEY	Ye Olde Bell

High Street, Hurley, Nr Maidenhead, Berkshire, SL6 5LX
Tel: (01628) 825881   *Fax*: (01628) 825939   **£45**
Open: lunch & dinner daily
Meals served: lunch 12.30-2.30, dinner 7.30-9.30, Sun 7.30-10

Dating back to around 1135, this is allegedly the oldest inn in England. A Norman entrance arch leads to a heavily beamed, characterful bar with lots of old brass. The 36 bedrooms range from traditional in the main house and neighbouring malt house, to modern-style annexe rooms. Relax in the oak-panelled restaurant to enjoy David Perrin's mix of English and continental dishes. Home-made tagliatelle with Meaux mustard dressing, loin of lamb en croûte, Scotch fillet steak with rich Burgundy sauce and grilled Dover sole show the range.

HURSTBOURNE TARRANT   Esseborne Manor

Hurstbourne Tarrant, Nr Andover, Hampshire, SP11 0ER
Tel: (01264) 736444   *Fax:* (01264) 736473   **£40**
Open: lunch & dinner
Meals served: lunch 12.30-2, dinner 7.30-9.309

A stylish country house about a mile north of Hurstbourne Tarrant
where attention to detail is very much apparent. Well-appointed bedrooms, with views over the gardens and beyond, are furnished to a
high standard, and some—the most spacious—are housed in a converted courtyard stable block a short distance from the main house.
Andy Norman's skilful, modern handling of English and French cuisine
produces a well-balanced menu. Start with piping hot spinach and
potato soup or mousseline of puréed vegetables, before breast of duck
with apple and honeyed Armagnac gravy or provençal beef stew with
slices of warm crusty olive bread. Good warm bread rolls, friendly service and a cosy atmosphere complete the event with much success.

ILKLEY   Bettys

32-34 The Grove, Ilkley, West Yorkshire, LS29 9EE   ·
Tel: (01943) 608029   *Fax:* (01943) 816723   **£30**
Open: all day daily (closed 25 & 26 Dec)
Meals served: 9-6

One of four Bettys dotted around Yorkshire—the others being in
Harrogate (the original), York and Northallerton—all displaying the
Bettys' formula of "fresh and dainty". Over 400 lines of home-made
cakes, pastries, breads, chocolates, breakfast/brunch dishes, light
snacks and hot meals, and the best selection of coffees in the country.
Not to be missed if you're in the area.

ILKLEY   Box Tree

37 Church Street, Ilkley, West Yorkshire, LS29 9DR
Tel: (01943) 608484   *Fax:* (01943) 816793   **£75**
Open: lunch Tue-Fri & Sun, dinner Tue-Sat
    (closed Bank Holidays, 2 wks Jan)
Meals served: lunch 12.30-2, dinner 7-10.30

Back up to full speed again, the Box Tree is as much of an institution as
ever, thanks to the care of Madame Avis and of new chef Thierry
Leprêtre-Granet (some of you may remember Thierry's cooking at
Whitechapel Manor, South Molton, so will know the standard you can
expect here). Fixed price menus offer good variety: sautéed Cornish
scallops with globe artichoke or sautéed duck foie gras with morel
cream and veal jus might be on offer as starters. For main course,
steamed bass with braised fennel comes with anchovy butter sauce,
roast pigeon with spring cabbage and spice sauce and tournedos of
beef with cep fumet. A superb wine list stops off at all the finest points
around the world.

ILKLEY   Rombalds Hotel

West View, Wells Road, Ilkley, West Yorkshire, LS29 9JG
Tel: (01943) 603201   *Fax:* (01943) 816586   **£40**
Open: lunch & dinner daily (closed 27-30 Dec)
Meals served: lunch 12-2 (Sun brunch 9am-1.30pm), dinner 7-9.30

Situated on the edge of Ilkley Moor in a sandstone terrace, this 15-bedroomed hotel is run with friendliness and charm. It's modestly furnished but accommodation is generous: all rooms have sitting rooms and there is round-the-clock room service. The kitchen offers a repertoire of dishes of global influence, though the style is essentially English and Continental. Roast beef and Yorkshire pudding and the locally famous Sunday brunch known as the "Edwardian Breakfast" are favourites. Good-value table d'hôte menus, plus self-serve buffet at lunchtime. Despite its wonderfully remote location on the edge of the moor, Rombalds, run by Ian Guthrie and his wife Jill, provides a level of personal and business services which rivals many.

IPSWICH   Mortimer's on the Quay

Wherry Quay, Ipswich, Suffolk, IP4 1AS
Tel: (01473) 230225   *Fax:* (01473) 752561   **£40**
Open: lunch Mon-Fri, dinner Mon-Sat (closed Bank Holidays
    & 1 day following, 2 wks Xmas/New Year, 2 wks Aug)
Meals served: lunch 12-2, dinner 7-9 (Mon 6.30-8.15)

Named after the 19th-century watercolour artist whose canvases adorn the walls, this is a quayside seafood restaurant offering good fresh fish and crustaceans in a number of straightforward, simple preparations. Lots of choice among starters, including a selection of smoked fish, plus daily specials like fresh salmon terrine or char-grilled Brittany sardines. Main courses include around a dozen choices, from lemon sole Bonne Femme to monkfish in fennel, steamed wing of skate with a black butter sauce or North Sea plaice in breadcrumbs. Finish with chocolate pot—Swiss chocolate and fresh cream with Pusser's Navy rum—or Mortimer's lemon chiffon—a lemon and cream filling on a biscuit base.

Bustling bistro style with pleasant and helpful staff.

IPSWICH   Singing Chef

---

200 St Helen's Street, Ipswich, Suffolk, IP4 2LH
Tel: (01473) 255236   **£40**
Open: lunch by arrangement, dinner Tue-Sat
    (closed Bank Holidays)
Meals served: dinner 7-11

A family restaurant with a history which dates back to the first Singing Chef at Marble Arch in London, in 1960. Ken and Cynthia Toye take their inspiration from the French countryside. This is a fun place—the songs start once the eating is over, if Ken hasn't already started singing from the kitchen. Expect classic regional French dishes: onion tart, soup au pistou, poulet basque with chorizo sausage, steak fines herbes and wild boar stew. Or bring along a pot and take it all home with you. The takeaway service needs 24 hours' notice and offers a 20% reduction on restaurant prices. Or perhaps you'd like to book Ken to cook at home for you (Sunday and Monday evenings only).

IXWORTH   Theobald's

68 High Street, Ixworth, Bury St Edmunds, Suffolk, IP31 2HJ
Tel: (01359) 231707   **£55**
Open: lunch Tue-Fri & Sun, dinner Tue-Sat
(closed Bank Holidays)
Meals served: lunch 12-1.30, dinner 7-9.30

It's over ten years since Simon and Geraldine Theobald moved into this
1650s-built property and converted it into the reliable restaurant it is
today. An abundance of beams and log fires set the scene for the work
of this talented chef. Simon changes his menus frequently to incorporate the best a season can offer, and there is plenty of choice. Twice-
baked cheese soufflé with a crisp cheese top is a favourite among
starters, while main courses run from winter offerings such as hare
wrapped in bacon on croutons, served with a blackcurrant-laced game
sauce to more summery items like roast halibut stuffed with ginger-
flavoured crab in white wine sauce or Spring lamb with rosemary,
tomato and celeriac, with sherry sauce. On Fridays, there's a special
Fish Supper menu which changes monthly. Good wine list with some
reasonable prices.

JERSEY   Chateau la Chaire

Rozel Valley, Rozel, Jersey, JE3 6AJ
Tel: (01534) 863354   *Fax:* (01534) 865137   **£50**
Open: lunch & dinner daily
Meals served: lunch 12.30-2, dinner 7-10

Nestling on the slopes of Rozel Valley, surrounded by terraced gardens, this 14-bedroomed hotel enjoys one of island's most beautiful and
peaceful locations. Built in 1843, it is an elegantly proportioned house
with lovely period details. The oak-panelled restaurant reflects the
island's influences with a menu of French and English cuisine on
which seafood naturally dominates: home-cured gravadlax with Jersey
crab, steamed supreme of turbot with a champagne and mussel beurre
blanc, brill with chervil and orange butter. Dishes are well executed,
with some fine saucing.

JERSEY — De Vere Grand

Esplanade, St Helier, Jersey, JE4 8WD
Tel: (01534) 22301   *Fax:* (01534) 37815   **£45**
Victoria's:
Open: lunch daily, dinner Mon-Sat
Meals served: lunch 12.30-2, dinner 7.30-10.30
Regency Room:
Open: dinner daily
Meals served: dinner 7.30-9.30

This impressive, seafront hotel, with gabled façade and ornate pillared entrance, is popular with both tourist and business trade for its traditional values and historic heritage. It was once the most fashionable place on the island and many distinguished guests, from royalty to Debussy (who composed *La Mer* during a stay here) have been through its doors. There are 115 rooms, including five suites, and a choice of two restaurants. Victoria's offers nightly dancing to a resident trio and a classic French repertoire which includes grills, flambés, seafood and pasta dishes. Alternatively there's the more sedate setting and table d'hôte menu in the Regency Room: well-prepared dishes, such as hollandaise-glazed brill tartlets, monkfish printanière and magret de canard with olive sauce. Good leisure facilities.

JERSEY — Hotel Chateau Valeuse

Rue de la Valeuse, St Brelade, Jersey, JE3 8EE
Tel: (01534) 46281   *Fax:* (01534) 47110   **£35**
Open: lunch & dinner daily (closed mid Oct-Apr)
Meals served: lunch 12.45-1.45, dinner 8-9
Quiet, 33-bedroomed hotel overlooking the bay; well-kept gardens and heated outdoor pool. Simple, well-prepared food—a classic repertoire from scallops to sole Walewska, chateaubriand to veal à la crème.

JERSEY — Hotel L'Horizon

St Brelade's Bay, Jersey, JE3 8EF
Tel: (01534) 43101   *Fax:* (01534) 46269   **£55**
Open: lunch & dinner daily
Meals served: lunch 12.30-2, dinner 7.30-10

Minutes away from the sandy beaches of St Brelade's Bay, this 106-bedroomed hotel has good leisure facilities in the Club L'Horizon and a choice of three restaurants. Make a real trip of it by chartering the  hotel's 40ft motor yacht for the day before returning to the hotel to choose between the all-day brasserie, intimate Star Grill or elegant Crystal Room for dinner. The range is international on chef Peter Marek's (ex-Savoy) Crystal Room repertoire: blackened red snapper on pepper and apricot dressing; pan-fried beef topped with crabmeat with sauce béarnaise; rainbow trout with roasted almonds and lemon butter. Traditional puds and a good range of British and Continental farmhouse cheeses to finish.

JERSEY   Jersey Pottery Garden Restaurant

Gorey, Jersey, JE3 9EP
Tel: (01534) 851119   *Fax:* (01534) 856403   **£45**
Open: all day Mon-Sat (Mon-Fri in winter)
    (closed Bank Holidays, 10 days Xmas)
Meals served: 11.30-4.30

With the Jersey Pottery rated as the number one tourist attraction on
the island, it's no surprise that this attractive conservatory restaurant
with climbing vines gets packed out. Beautifully fresh seafood salads
and plateaux de fruits de mer are joined on the extensive menu by
dishes such as peppered lady crab (recommended for experienced
crab pickers only), mussels in Jersey cider, grilled Dover sole with
herb butter and salmon Cameron. One or two meat options are
included but you really ought to make the most of feasting on the
locally-caught seafood. The self-service café operation next door offers
a range of light snacks and seafood salads.

JERSEY   The Lobster Pot

L'Etacq, St Ouen, Jersey, JE3 2FB
Tel: (01534) 482888   *Fax:* (01534) 481574   **£35**
Open: lunch & dinner daily
Meals served: lunch 12.30-2, dinner 7.30-10

Popular seafood restaurant overlooking the bay, with a menu to please
everyone. Lobster is star of the show, appearing in at least seven different outfits, with a large cast in support: from scampi, scallops, snails
and sole to steaks and pheasant. It's a familiar list on the whole and a
long one, which includes traditional soups, pasta dishes and popular
favourites like beef stroganoff, chicken Maryland and duck with orange
sauce.

JERSEY — Longueville Manor

St Saviour, Jersey, JE2 7SA
Tel: (01534) 25501   *Fax:* (01534) 31613   **£70**
Open: lunch & dinner daily
Meals served: lunch 12.30-2, dinner 7.30-9.30

The best place on the island for being cossetted and pampered, this 32-bedroomed hotel, now in the third generation of same-family ownership, is set in a wooded valley and offers high standards of service, accommodation and food. There are two dining rooms, the more formal being the ancient oak-panelled room—the manor dates back to the 13th century and boasts many features of architectural interest. Chef Andrew Baird (pictured) caters for many tastes. Specialities include steamed Jersey sea bass with crab soufflé and shellfish cream, and poached turbot with langoustine tortellini. Much emphasis is placed on local produce, with the kitchen garden and well-established hothouses serving the kitchen's needs. Beautifully decorated bedrooms, named after roses, offer traditional comforts and elegance and the hotel grounds, complete with trickling stream and lake, home to black swans and mandarins, are enchanting. An oasis of peace and tranquillity. Good leisure facilites include pool, tennis and croquet, and beautiful walks.

JERSEY — Old Court House Inn

St Aubin, Jersey
Tel: (01534) 46433   Fax: (01534) 45103   **£35**
Open: lunch & dinner daily (closed 25 & 26 Dec)
Meals served: lunch 12.30-2.30, dinner 7.30-10.30

Ten-bedroomed inn, with plenty of character. Bergerac fans will recognise the barge-shaped Mizzen Mast bar. Good pub food and pleasant restaurant with courtyard terrace. Superb views, a pretty place.

JERSEY — Sea Crest

Petit Port, St Brelade, Jersey, JE3 8HH
Tel: (01534) 46353   *Fax:* (01534) 47316   **£45**
Open: lunch & dinner Tue-Sun (closed Sun in winter, Feb)
Meals served: lunch 12.30-2 (Sun to 3), dinner 7.30-10

Hand-made English furniture and soft French furnishings grace the seven bedrooms of this small, intimate hotel above the picturesque bay. All of the rooms boast superb views and most have balconies, with sun lounger provided. In the restaurant, the international menu, strong on local fish and shellfish, appeals to most tastes; or there's a delightful sun lounge and terrace overlooking the pool where a light meal or drinks can be enjoyed throughout the day. Owners Julian and Martha Bernstein provide a warm welcome.

JEVINGTON — Hungry Monk Restaurant

The Street, Jevington, Nr Polegate, East Sussex, BN26 5QF
Tel: (01323) 482178   *Fax:* (01323) 483989   **£50**
Open: lunch Sun, dinner daily (closed Bank Holidays, 3 days Xmas)
Meals served: lunch 12-2.15 (Mon-Sat by arrangement), dinner 7-10

The Mackenzies now have more than 25 years behind them at this much-loved, charming, beamed restaurant. Pay no attention to the hungry monk reference: no sparsity here. Claire Burgess and Thai La Roche cook with inspiration and a touch of the exotic: crab fishcakes with mild curry sauce; medallions of beef with venison sausage, celeriac purée and an intensely flavoured sauce; or calf's liver with pink peppercorns served on fresh paglia e fieno. End with banoffi pie or perhaps a warm orange, ginger and almond tart served with crème fraîche.

KENDAL — The Moon

129 Highgate, Kendal, Cumbria, LA9 4EN
Tel: (01539) 729254   **£35**
Open: dinner daily (closed 24-25 Dec, 1 Jan)
Meals served: dinner 6.30-10 (Sat from 6)

This quaint bistro opposite the Brewery Arts Centre dedicates half its menu to vegetarians. The menu changes monthly and everything is based on the use of fresh local produce. Interesting dishes such as prawn kebabs marinated in garlic, lime and coriander or spinach and feta cheese pancake with tomato coulis to start, followed by the likes of mushroom and broad bean korma or two-layer vegetarian lasagne. Meat eaters have plenty of choice with options like Mexican-spiced pork-filled tortillas, beef and venison in red wine with parsley and horseradish dumplings, or spiced lamb and apricot bobotie. The restaurant runs a Pudding Club, so sweets are high on the list of priorities here—sticky toffee pudding, spiced steamed fruit suet pudding, and Italian chocolate nut truffle cake.

KENILWORTH — Restaurant Bosquet

97a Warwick Road, Kenilworth, Warwickshire, CV8 1HP
Tel: (01926) 52463   **£50**
Open: lunch by arrangement, dinner Tue-Sat
   (closed 1 wk Xmas, 3 wks Aug)
Meals served: dinner 7-9.30

In an unpretentious, converted house on this busy road, Bernard Lignier cooks with flair and imagination in the classical mould. Daily fixed-price and seasonal menus offer traditional and classical dishes presented in Bernard's own way. Breast of woodcock in pastry with game sauce or cassoulet soup to start, followed by supreme de canard (cooked with pear and ginger and served with a lime sauce), parmesan- and sage-coated saddle of lamb with a tomato and white wine sauce, or the fish dish of the day. Home-made petits fours with cafetière coffee to finish. David's wife, Jane, runs front of house.

KENILWORTH — Simpson's Restaurant

101-103 Warwick Road, Kenilworth, Warwickshire, CV8 1HL
Tel: (01926) 864567 £40
Open: lunch Mon-Fri, dinner Mon-Sat (closed Bank Holidays)
Meals served: lunch 12.30-2, dinner 7-10

Andreas and Alison Antona offer a seasonally changing menu of classic European and English dishes—fresh, contemporary interpretations of bourgeois and regional cuisine. French café feel with walls decorated with menus from famous restaurants where Andreas and head chef Andy Walters have worked. On the fixed-price menu (shorter at lunchtime) you might find dishes such as cappuccino of carrot and orange soup, two-fish terrine with avocado sauce, or Lyons sausage salad, to start; bavette of beef with red wine shallot sauce, sea bass with bouillabaisse, seafood sausages with noodles and lobster sauce. Puds on offer include iced yoghurt and honey parfait.

KESWICK — Brundholme Country House

Brundholme Road, Keswick, Cumbria, CA12 4NL
Tel: (0176 87) 74495 £50
Open: dinner daily (closed Dec-Jan)
Meals served: dinner 7.30-8.45

Set on the slopes of Latrigg, looking down on Keswick and the cascading River Greta, this is an oasis of rural tranquillity. Wordsworth thought so—he brought Dorothy here—and Coleridge was no stranger either. The Georgian mansion house we see today dates from a conversion in the style of Nash which took place in the early 19th century. Eleven bedrooms, all with romantic views over the valley and mountain grandeur of the lakes. Chef-patron Ian Charlton produces a classic, English menu, with a bias towards robust meat and game.

KEYSTON — Pheasant Inn

Village Loop Road, Keyston, Nr Bythorn,
   Cambridgeshire, PE18 0RE
Tel: (01832) 710241   *Fax:* (0180 14) 340 £40
Open: lunch & dinner daily (closed dinner 25 & 26 Dec)
Meals served: lunch 12-2, dinner 6-10

Located in the peaceful village of Keyston, this 150-year-old inn is divided into a number of interconnecting rooms. You can eat either in the bar with its open log fire, or in the Red Room—the menu is the same. Eat as much or as little as you please, too. In the 12 months or so that he's been here, ex-Walnut Tree (Abergavenny) chef Roger Jones has introduced modern Italian, Mediterranean and Oriental influences. Dishes such as warm, baked Piedmontese peppers, salmon and courgette tempura with a dashi dip, seared chicken with daikon and a teriyaki sauce share the well-balanced carte with traditional favourites, classics and more innovative creations, such as beef with Yorkshire pudding, wild boar sausages with Dijon and onion sauce or roast monkfish with black noodles and a light butter sauce. A wide range of puds might include hot pancakes with a coconut ice cream and maple syrup, or raspberry and redcurrant brûlée. A very good value wine list.

KINGS LYNN   ROCOCO

11 Saturday Market Place, Kings Lynn, Norfolk, PE30 5DQ
Tel: (01553) 771483   **£55**
Open: lunch Tue-Sat, dinner Mon-Sat
Meals served: lunch 12-2.30, dinner 7.30-10.30

The Andersons make the most of local produce on a varied menu,
which offers a choice of two or three courses. Despite influences from
further afield, the overall concept remains English at this 40-seater.
Smoky kipper and orange pâté or rich creamy mousse of wild mushrooms among starters; followed by the likes of steamed Finnan haddie
with saffron sauce or pan-fried fillet of beef topped with glazed shallots
and wild mushrooms. I'm looking forward to the hazelnut and butterscotch steamed sponge pud! Interesting wine notes and some reasonable prices on list.

KINGHAM   Mill House Hotel & Restaurant

Station Road, Kingham, Nr Chipping Norton,
    Oxfordshire, OX7 6UH
Tel: (01608) 658188   *Fax:* (01608) 658492   **£50**
Open: lunch & dinner daily
Meals served: lunch 12.15-1.45, dinner 7-9.45

An idyllic pastoral scene, complete with stream, is the setting for this
23-bedroomed Cotswold-stone hotel. Bedrooms are pretty, with fine
views over the surrounding countryside, and exposed beams and local
stone provide overall character and warmth to the place. Fixed-price
menus offer plenty of choice and the style of cooking is traditional
English with a modern approach. Start with warm quenelles of salmon
or asparagus hollandaise; move on to pan-fried calf's liver with bacon or
grilled Dover sole (a speciality). A relaxed, friendly atmosphere
created by attentive, thoughtful staff.

KINGSTON-UPON-THAMES   Restaurant Gravier

9 Station Road, Norbiton, Kingston-upon-Thames,
    Surrey, KT2 7AA
Tel: 081-547 1121   **£55**
Open: lunch Mon-Fri, dinner Mon-Sat
    (closed Bank Holidays, 1 wk Xmas, 1 wk Aug)
Meals served: lunch 12.15-2, dinner 7-10

Well-established, 40-seater, seafood restaurant on the outskirts of town.
The Graviers, Jean-Philippe and Joanne, he at front-of-house, she in the
kitchen, offer a concise menu which is almost doubled by dishes of the
day, recited at the table by Jean-Philippe, whose Billingsgate trips provide wife Joanne with a constantly-changing repertoire. She is a very
competent cook and the carte features many classics, from snails,
palourde clams provençale and moules marinières to lobster thermidor
and sole normande. Daily specials might include salmon in champagne
sauce, sea bass nantais or turbot hollandaise. For meat eaters, there's
Welsh lamb with a port wine sauce or steak béarnaise. Smart table settings and exposed brick walls are offset by displays of hops. Small terrace for the lucky few in summer.

KINGTON   Penrhos Court

Penrhos, Kington, Hereford & Worcester, HR5 3LH
Tel: (01544) 230720   *Fax:* (01544) 230754   **£55**
Open: dinner daily (Mon-Sat in winter) (closed Feb)
Meals served: dinner 7.30-9

The oldest part of Penrhos Court is the cruck hall built around 1280,
when Edward I took Kington away from the Welsh. Later additions
resulted in the establishment of a farm on the site during the 19th century, but after fire damage and neglect, the house fell on hard times.
Then came Martin Griffiths and Daphne Lambert who have lovingly
restored the property complete with beams and flagstones. Set in six
acres of grounds looking west over the Welsh hills, Penrhos is now a
delightful hotel with 19 rooms, but it is the restaurant which takes centre stage. Daily-changing menus offer plenty of choice, with three or
four options for each course. A typical menu might feature warm
chicken liver salad, followed by sea bream grilled with aromatic oils or
charcoal-grilled chicken with wild mushrooms, rounded off with carrot
cake and Greek yoghurt. Daphne's research into medieval cooking has
resulted in a number of theme nights on former medieval holidays
throughout the year. These are fun events at which the spirit of jollity
associated with the Middle Ages is brought to life, both in terms of the
ambience and cooking.

KINTBURY   Dundas Arms

53 Station Road, Kintbury, Nr Newbury, Berkshire, RG15 0UT
Tel: (01488) 58263   *Fax:* (01488) 58568   **£55**
Open: lunch Tue-Sun, dinner Tue-Sat (closed Xmas/New Year)
Meals served: lunch 12-2, dinner 7.30-9.15

This 18th-century canalside (the Kennet & Avon) inn has been a pub
for over 200 years. The old stable block has been converted to house
five bedrooms, which are spacious and traditional in style, with sliding
picture windows which lead out on to a terrace garden on the ground
floor. Food is served in the small cocktail bar in the pub, but with
David Dalzell-Piper in the kitchen it would be a mistake not to book
yourself in for a meal in the French auberge-style restaurant which
looks out directly on to the canal. David's menus are refreshingly
straightforward and unpretentious. Choose between starters such as
fresh pear and gorgonzola salad or red and white cabbage with warm
chorizo sausage, followed by breast of duck with mint and lemon
sauce, or rack of new English lamb with rosemary sauce. This is modern English cooking executed with flair and skill in honest, unfussy
fashion. Great wine list in support.

KNUTSFORD   Brasserie Belle Epoque

60 King Street, Knutsford, Cheshire, WA16 2DT
Tel: (01565) 633060   *Fax:* (01565) 634150   **£50**
Open: lunch Mon-Fri, dinner Mon-Sat
   (closed Bank Holidays, 1 wk Jan)
Meals served: lunch 12-2, dinner 7-10

The Parisian Belle Epoque comes to life inside the Art Nouveau dining room of this eccentric-looking Edwardian showpiece building in the high street. A new direction towards lighter, brasserie-style fare brings a new lease of life after 21 years to the Mooneys' restaurant with rooms. Try fresh and home-smoked fishcakes with coriander and tomato or the finest Lancashire tripe cooked in cider to start, followed by char-grilled tuna steak with tapenade, breast of guinea fowl braised in mushrooms and Madeira consommé or fish and chips—made from Fleetwood haddock and served with mushy peas. There are seven delightful bedrooms.

KNUTSFORD   Cottons Hotel
Manchester Road, Knutsford, Cheshire, WA16 0SU
Tel: (01565) 650333   *Fax:* (01565) 755351   **£45**
Open: lunch Sun-Fri, dinner daily
Meals served: lunch 12-2, dinner 7-10
82-bedroomed hotel handy for Manchester Airport. French New Orleans is the dominant design theme, with speciality Creole and Cajun dishes featuring on the menu. Good leisure and conference facilities.

LACOCK   At The Sign of The Angel

6 Church Street, Lacock, Nr Chippenham, Wiltshire, SN15 2LB
Tel: (01249) 730230   *Fax:* (01249) 730527   **£55**
Open: lunch Tue-Sun, dinner daily (closed 22-30 Dec)
Meals served: lunch 12.30-2, dinner 7.30-8.30

If you want to show some overseas visitors what Britain is all about,

this is it. Lacock is owned by The National Trust and this converted 15th-century wool merchant's house features strongly in the life and image of this beautiful village. The abbey still retains its 13th-century cloisters and sacristy and was once the home of pioneer photographer Fox Talbot, whose work can be seen in a museum near the gate houses. Antiques abound and there is a wonderful feeling of tranquillity and security within the hotel's solid walls. The food is unpretentious and sound from Stilton and walnut paté or smoked haddock fishcakes with wild boar sausages with Cumberland sauce or beef and tomato rissoles with horseradish. Save room for Mrs Levis's treacle and walnut tart with clotted cream, home-made meringues or the English cheeseboard. Wines have been meticulously chosen and there are one or two irresistible bottles for the connoisseur. Everyone should visit Lacock, and there are ten antique-filled rooms here in which to stay.

LAND'S END   The Land's End Hotel

Land's End, Sennen, Cornwall, TR19 7AA
Tel: (01736) 871844   *Fax:* (01736) 871599   **£50**
Open: lunch & dinner daily
Meals served: lunch 12.30-2, dinner 7-9.30 (Sun to 9)

This is a 34-bedroomed hotel embracing a dramatic clifftop setting. Ann Long, formerly of Long's in Blackwater, has resurfaced at the Land's End Hotel just as we went to press. We were unable to get here in time for this year's Guide, but there's plenty of excitement in store. Early four-course menus promised the likes of vegetable soup, followed by sliced smoked duck placed round a purée of cherry and orange with a main course of grilled bass set on a bed of mange tout and courgette with a light cream sauce. We await with interest what developments will occur. Watch this space—or better still, send me your comments. The ones I think are closest to my observations on my next visit, will receive a bottle of Charles Heidsieck Champagne!

LANGAR   Langar Hall

Langar, Nottinghamshire, NG13 9HG
Tel: (01949) 60559   *Fax:* (01949) 61045   **£65**
Open: lunch & dinner Mon-Sat (closed 25 Dec)
Meals served: lunch 12.30-2, dinner 7-9.30

Art lovers will enjoy Imogen Skirving's collection of 19th- and 20th-century art at this delightful, 1830s, 12-bedroomed sandstone house next to the village church. The house is set in its own grounds, in the heart of the beautiful Vale of Belvoir. An air of informality creates a relaxed and homely feel throughout the house, and simplicity reigns in the kitchen, where Imogen, with Toby Garratt, produces wholesome, hearty dishes in the modern mould, with a bias towards French and British traditions: potato pancake with smoked eel, ribs of beef with chips and sauce béarnaise, wing of skate with anchovy dressing.

LANGHO   Northcote Manor

Northcote Road, Langho, Nr Blackburn, Lancashire, BB6 8BE
Tel: (01254) 240555   *Fax:* (01254) 246568   **£65**
Open: lunch & dinner daily (closed 1 & 2 Jan)
Meals served: lunch 12-1.30 (Sun to 2),   ⚘
     dinner 7-9.30 (Sat to 10)

Small private hotel with 14 rooms, now in its tenth year under the enthusiastic management of Craig Bancroft and Nigel Haworth. Prettily decorated bedrooms include nice touches such as board games and there's an old-world charm which predominates—beams, panelling and roaring log fires. Fabulous breakfast start the day, with home-made jams, local farm eggs, local sausages and black pudding on the menu. Nigel is a talented chef whose cooking has a distinctly northern character. He has trained in Switzerland and at Gleneagles and is a founder member of the Northern Circle of Chefs. Try the house speciality—prime fillet of beef with garden herbs and a truffle dressing, the plate of tiny Lancashire delicacies or Bury black pudding interestingly served with pink trout and watercress sauce.

LAVENHAM   Great House

Market Place, Lavenham, Suffolk, CO10 9QZ
Tel: (01787) 247431   **£40**
Open: lunch Tue-Sun, dinner Tue-Sat (closed 5-25 Jan)
Meals served: lunch 12-2.30, dinner 7-9.30 (Sat to 10.30)

There's plenty of village-England appeal at this cosy 15th-century restaurant with rooms overlooking the market place in the medieval town of Lavenham. The four rooms for overnight guests feature old beams and antiques. Frenchman Régis Crépy offers an extensive carte, supplemented by fixed-price menus (brasserie-style at lunchtime). Essentially, it's French and English country cooking. Start with tender parcels of cheese fondue with garlic mayonnaise, warm leek gateau, mussels or French onion soup. Follow with roast rack of lamb provençale, coq au vin, beef bourguignon or osso buco; cod dieppoise, skate with black butter or salmon in a puff pastry cage. Be prepared for some hard decisions along the way! There's a new conservatory with bistro menu and pretty courtyard with tables for alfresco summer eating. Interesting wine list with some exceptional wines at affordable prices.

LAVENHAM   The Swan

High Street, Lavenham, Nr Sudbury, Suffolk, CO10 9QA
Tel: (01787) 247477   *Fax:* (01787) 248286   **£45**
Open: lunch & dinner daily
Meals served: lunch 12.30-2, dinner 7-9.30

The 47-bedroomed Swan at Lavenham is an American's dream. The place is oozing with history, dating back to the prosperity of the wool era, and the building is a splendid example of Elizabethan architecture. The medieval-looking dining room is a later addition, Elizabethan too, but Elizabeth II, not the I. It was built in 1965 and 400 tons of oak were used in its construction. No wonder that it is one of Forte's provincial flagships. Chef Andrew Barrass, here since 1988, offers a good choice of carefully-executed dishes of traditional British design. What else in such venerable surroundings? You might find on the menu the likes of cream of cauliflower and thyme soup, grilled Scottish salmon and garden herbs, roast rack of lamb with rosemary wine sauce and redcurrant compote, and breast of chicken with a red wine and bacon sauce.

LEAMINGTON SPA   Mallory Court

Harbury Lane, Bishop's Tachbrook, Leamington Spa,
   Warwicks, CV33 9QB
Tel: (01926) 330214   *Fax:* (01926) 451714   **£70**
Open: lunch & dinner daily (closed 10 days Jan)
Meals served: lunch 12-2, dinner 7.30-9.45 (Sat to 10, Sun to 9)

It is almost 20 years since Allan Holland and Jeremy Mort bought this
country house and set about making it into one of the most elegant and
distinctive of small hotels, with a fine reputation for cuisine and service.
They have maintained high standards, and, indeed, improved on them
during these two decades and their beautiful hotel in leafy
Warwickshire has won international acclaim. Allan taught himself to
cook and has developed an individual style based on classic French
principals. His gourmet menu offers a stunning opportunity to put this
talented chef though his paces and surprise you with his originality; or
if you prefer to exercise more control go for one of the set menus
which include about three choices per course. Try perhaps dressed
Cornish crab with avocado and pink grapefruit followed by grilled
sirloin steak with a wild mushroom friccassée and finish with Charlotte
of milk chocolate on an orange sauce. Fine wines complement the
cooking with good value amongst bottles from outside the classic areas
of France. The hotel is ideally suited near the National Exhibition
Centre and is close to historic Stratford-upon-Avon and Warwick.

LEDBURY   Hope End

Hope End, Ledbury, Hereford & Worcester, HR8 1SQ
Tel: (01531) 633613   *Fax:* (01531) 636366   **£70**
Open: dinner daily (closed mid Dec-early Feb)
Meals served: dinner 7.30-8.30

John and Patricia Hegarty's nine-bedroomed hotel is a haven of tranquillity. By no means a traditional country house—fewer frills than
most—but it is stylishly and tastefully furnished throughout, with
homely touches like piles of books by sofas and log-burning stoves.
Bedrooms are discreetly decorated, and cork-and-tile bathrooms are
supplied with a selection of bath oils. Patricia (author of *An English
Flavour*) cooks in the English country tradition, and puts as much love
and care into her chutneys and breads as she does into her fixed-price
dinner menu which is prepared from fresh local produce wherever
possible, much coming from the kitchen garden. A typical meal might
begin with a home-made soup (carrot and coriander seed/artichoke
and tomato/smoked haddock and potato), followed by rump steak with
a mustard and tarragon sauce, baked halibut with sweet pepper ragoût
or chestnut soufflé with mushroom sauce. Lovely desserts include the
likes of lime tart with honey ice cream. A selection of rare English
farmhouse cheeses should not be overlooked. Once the childhood
home of Elizabeth Barrett-Browning, the house is mostly of 18th-
century origin and nestles in 40 acres of wooded parkland amid a
Georgian, landscaped garden which contains a temple, a grotto and
ruins. This is an area of outstanding natural beauty, close to the
Malvern Hills.

LEEDS	Brasserie Forty Four

44 The Calls, Leeds, West Yorkshire, LS2 7EW
Tel: (0113) 2343232   *Fax:* (0113) 2343332   **£40**
Open: lunch Mon-Fri, dinner Mon-Sat (closed Bank Holidays)
Meals served: lunch 12-2.30, dinner 6.30-10.30

A stylish, modern, riverside brasserie where chef Jeff Baker cooks some exciting, innovative dishes. Smoked haddock and saffron risotto, deep-fried shredded duck pancake with plum sauce and sautéed foie gras with shallots and balsamic vinegar feature amongst starters. Main dishes range from a substantial Toulouse sausage with lentils to a subtle escalope of salmon with linguini and lemon butter sauce. Good vegetables, salads and pasta accompany main dishes and there are weekly specials dependent on the market. It's essential to book and if you dine between 6.30 and 7.15 or after 10.00 you'll get a 25% discount on the food. Real value!

LEEDS	Bryan's of Headingley

9 Weetwood Lane, Headingley, Leeds, West Yorkshire, LS16 5LT
Tel: (0113) 2785679   **£25**
Open: all day daily (closed 25 Dec)
Meals served: 11.30-11.30 (Sun 12.30-8)

Opened in 1934 by John Bryan and handed down through his family, from father to son and later grandson, Bryan's finally changed families in 1984 when it was bought by its present owner, Jan Fletcher. But the principle goes on, ensuring that this 120-seat restaurant on the outskirts of Leeds maintains its worldwide reputation for some of the best fish'n'chips in the land.

LEEDS	42 The Calls

42 The Calls, Leeds, West Yorkshire, LS2 7EW
Tel: (0113) 2440099   *Fax:* (0113) 3244100
Open: lunch Sun-Fri, dinner Mon-Sat (closed 5 days Xmas)
Meals served: lunch 12.00-2.30 (Sun dinner 6.30-10.30 (Sat to 11)

Housed in the riverside shell of an old grain mill, 42 The Calls breaks the pattern of city centre hotels. Located at the heart of the city, minutes from the business, arts and commercial districts, each of the 41 bedrooms and suites is furnished to a high level of comfort and sophistication, yet still making the most of the building's original features, like painted stone walls, arches and warehouse beams. All rooms have excellent facilities for work, including a large work desk, three phones, a CD stereo system and coffee percolator. Peace, quality and genuine, first-class service complete the package. Excellent business and conference facilities. Top marks for style and contemporary thinking. Jonathan Wix, the brains behind this and Brasserie 44 next door, widened his horizons just as we went to press, joining forces with his business associate here, Michael Gill, and welcoming the Gills' out-of-town enterprise at Pool Court to a new city-centre home. So in the down time between this Guide going to press and you reading this, preparations should be completed for the autumn opening of Pool Court at the Calls. We look forward to developments here with great excitement—watch this space!

LEEDS	Haley's Hotel

Shire Oak Road, Headingley, Leeds, West Yorkshire, LS6 2DE
Tel: (0113) 2784446   Fax: (0113) 2753342   **£45**
Open: lunch Sun, dinner daily (closed 26-30 Dec)
Meals served: lunch 12.30-2, dinner 7.15-9.45

Lovely Victorian house transformed into a stylish hotel with 22 rooms. Bedrooms are well equipped, with nice touches here and there—each has a lifesize toy cat named Haley, which you put out at night if you don't want to be disturbed! The recent arrival of chef Chris Baxter bodes well too, with some imaginative dishes appearing on the carte alongside more traditional fixed-price menu offerings. Start with pan-fried salmon supreme with balsamic butter or thick parsnip soup, followed by baked chicken breast with grape and herb stuffing perhaps or fillets of brill grilled under a crumb crust with vermouth and chive sauce. Traditional puds, such as warm treacle sponge or charlotte royale, followed by coffee and mignardises.

LEEDS	Leodis Brasserie

Victoria Mill, Sovereign Street, Leeds, West Yorkshire, LS1 4BJ
Tel: (0113) 2421010   *Fax:* (0113) 2430432   **£45**
Open: lunch Mon-Fri, dinner Mon-Sat
    (closed lunch Bank Holidays, 25 & 26 Dec)
Meals served: lunch 12-2, dinner 6-10 (Fri & Sat to 11)

Stylish modern decor contrasts with exposed brick walls, arched ceilings and old timbers in this ground-floor brasserie, housed in a Victorian mill just south of the city centre. Popular with the smart local set, the brasserie offers a varied and modern menu with plenty of choice, around 20 starters and main courses, and about a dozen puds. Start with gazpacho, wild mushroom and asparagus tart, chicken liver parfait with chutney or tuna fish niçoise, before tucking into Leodis' bangers and mash, Burgundy- braised oxtails or the house speciality—roast beef carved at the table, with Yorkshire pudding et al. Fishy offerings range from char-grilled swordfish with blackened herbs or red snapper fillet in a coriander, pine nut and lime crumble to simply grilled Dover sole.

LEEDS — Olive Tree

Oaklands, Rodley Lane, Leeds, West Yorkshire, LS13 1NG
Tel: (0113) 2569283 **£40**
Open: lunch Sun-Fri, dinner Mon-Sat (closed 25 Dec, 1 Jan)
Meals served: lunch 12-2, dinner 6-11

Excellent Greek Cypriot restaurant in a large Victorian house, of all things! Located to the west of town, overlooking the roundabout where the A657 meets the ring road, this is an unusual setting for some of the best baklava in town. You may have seen chef-patron George Psarias on BBC2's Food and Drink programme in the Spring of 1994, or come across the entry in the Guinness Book of Records for the world's longest-ever kebab. This is not a restaurant which rests on its laurels, rather the owners are constantly striving to improve whenever possible. Typical dishes include a range of seafood starters, such as deep-fried squid with garlic sauce, stuffed vegetable dishes (dolmades, Imam Bayeldi), kleftiko and a good choice of fish—swordfish, red mullet and salmon. More conventional palates and minds may prefer familiar options like moussaka or the Olive Tree steak—sirloin which has been sautéed in butter and finished in wine, fresh tomato and cream sauce. Bouzouki night on Tuesdays.

Go there, this man is an enthusiast!

LEEDS — Sous le Nez en Ville

Basement, Quebec House, Quebec Street, Leeds,
   West Yorkshire, LS1 2HA
Tel: (0113) 2440108   Fax: (0113) 2450240 **£35**
Open: lunch Mon-Fri, dinner Mon-Sat (closed Bank Holidays)
Meals served: lunch 12-2.30, dinner 6-10.30

This is one restaurant where I would start with the wine list and then decide from the menu what food would best accompany it! Literally a world-wide selection with 13 house wines and something for everyone in halves, bottles or magnums. There's no shortage of choice on the menu, either—you can have bits and pieces at the bar, fixed price menus until 7.30pm or choose from the imaginative carte. A good range of fish and lots of vegetarian dishes so collect a few thirsty friends, go along and enjoy yourself.

LEICESTER — Welford Place

9 Welford Place, Leicester Leicestershire, LE1 6ZH
Tel: (0116) 2470758   *Fax:* (0116) 2471843   **£30**
Open: all day daily
Meals served: 8am-11pm

An all-day eating house, reading room, meeting place and watering hole, Welford Place is housed in a delightful Victorian building in the heart of Leicester. The food is English with Mediterranean and international influences. Menus may be mixed'n'matched at will and represent good value for money. Straightforward set-price lunch and dinner menus feature dishes such as brown onion soup with cheese croûtons followed by beef casserole, or fillet of cod with mushrooms and a vermouth butter sauce. The à la carte is a little more formal, there is an excellent breakfast menu and a daily supplementary menu featuring sandwiches and light snacks. Under the same ownership as Lincoln's Wig & Mitre.

LEW — Farmhouse Hotel & Restaurant

University Farm, Lew, Oxfordshire, OX18 2AU
Tel: (01993) 850297   *Fax:* (01993) 850965   **£40**
Open: dinner Mon-Sat (closed Xmas/New Year)
Meals served: dinner 7-7.30 (Fri & Sat to 9)
Small country restaurant in a 17th-century Cotswold stone farmhouse which is part of a working farm. 6 rooms for overnight guests. Homely and hospitable.

LEWDOWN — Lewtrenchard Manor

Lewtrenchard, Lewdown, Nr Okehampton, Devon, EX20 4PN
Tel: (0156 683) 256   *Fax:* (0156 683) 332   **£60**
Open: lunch Sun, dinner daily
Meals served: lunch 12.15-1.45, dinner 7.15-9.30

Surrounded by soft, green, Devon countryside (close to Dartmoor), this lovely, old stone manor house built around 1600 is proving to be the ideal country retreat under proprietors James and Sue Murray, who run it with quiet charm. Inside, all is mellow, with many original features adding warmth and character. The house has eight bedrooms, two with four posters, and all benefit from extensive views over the garden and surrounding countryside. The oak-panelled dining room, hung with oil paintings, is an appropriate setting for Patrick Salvadori's cooking, which is best described as traditional at heart with modern influences. Dishes such as steamed fillets of red mullet with a saffron butter sauce, new season's lamb with honey and pepper sauce and brill poached in a fennel and Pernod stew sit happily on the menus alongside cod with parsley butter sauce or roast beef with Yorkshire pudding. Fine French and English cheeses served with oatmeal biscuits  and walnut bread. Desserts follow a similar pattern to that of the menu, with imaginative creations like hot pistachio soufflé perhaps sharing the limelight with local strawberries and clotted cream.

LIFTON   Arundell Arms

Lifton, Devon, PL16 0AA
Tel: (01566) 784666   *Fax:* (01566) 784494   **£60**
Open: lunch & dinner daily (closed 2 days Xmas)
Meals served: lunch 12.30-2, dinner 7.30-9

People come to the Arundell Arms to fish, shoot, go riding, walk, play golf, or do a spot of birdwatching. This former coaching inn dating back to Saxon times is situated in a valley of five rivers close to Dartmoor. The hotel has its own rod and fishing tackle room housed in the 250-year-old circular stone cockpit (one of the few surviving in England) in the garden, and owner Anne Voss-Bark owns 20 miles of rights on the Tamar and its tributaries. This has been one of country's premier fishing hotels for over half a century; they teach fishing here, sell the tackle, give advice, provide maps. The atmosphere changes with the seasons, with the guests. Autumn brings the shooting parties, shifting the focus of conversation from spate rivers to snipe. The kitchen is supplied with excellent local meat—the butcher breeds his own hormone-free herd—and a superb supply of fresh fish, including Tamar salmon and sea trout. Chef Phillip Burgess keeps up-to-date with modern fads; witness red mullet soup with anchovy toasts, grilled fillet of Tamar salmon with a green herb butter and leaf salad or roasted fillet of hake with a red pepper dressing.

LINCOLN   The Jew's House

15 The Strait, Lincoln, Lincolnshire, LN2 1JD
Tel: (01522) 524851   **£45**
Open: lunch Tue-Sat, dinner Mon-Sat
   (closed Bank Holidays except Good Friday)
Meals served: lunch 12-1.30, dinner 7-9.30

Choose between à la carte, light lunch or fixed-price menus at Richard Gibbs' little restaurant at the bottom of the steep hill leading up to the cathedral. There are six tables in the stone-walled dining room, and the small first-floor lounge is set aside for aperitifs. Largely French-influenced, Richard lists mussels marinières, venison and duck with an Armagnac and shallot sauce among his specialities. Home-made soups feature regularly among starters—mussel and leek with saffron is a favourite; while main courses might include roast guinea fowl with rosemary and bacon and beef bordelaise. Creativity and flair are evident from the moment you read the menus. Finish with perhaps lemon tart with cream. The house dates back to 1180 and its fascinating history is related on the back of the menu.

LINCOLN   Wig & Mitre

29 Steep Hill, Lincoln, Lincolnshire, LN2 1LU
Tel: (01522) 535190   *Fax:* (01522) 532402   **£30**
Open: all day daily (closed 25 Dec)
Meals served: 8am-midnight

Maximum results with the minimum of fuss is the principle behind
Michael and Valerie Hope's all-day, mix'n'match menus at this sister
establishment to Welford Place in Leicester. But the principle goes
beyond mere food, for here you can pop in for a drink, a chat, a meal or
a meeting. Feel free, eat what you like when you like and enjoy yourself—anything from a steak sandwich or a light meal to full-blown
three-course dinners. The wine list roams the world with some interesting selections.

LINTON   Wood Hall

Tripp Lane, Linton, Nr Wetherby, West Yorkshire, LS22 4JA
Tel: (01937) 587271   *Fax:* (01937) 584353   **£50**
Open: lunch Sun-Fri, dinner daily
Meals served: lunch 12.30-2, dinner 7-9.30
A large and historic house that now has 43 bedrooms and extensive leisure facili-
ties. Competent cooking by Andrew Mitchell who produces modern French
dishes using good local ingredients.

LISKEARD   Well House

St Keyne, Liskeard, Cornwall, PL14 4RN
Tel: (01579) 342001   **£55**
Open: lunch & dinner daily
Meals served: lunch 12.30-2, dinner 7.30-10

A small, intimate hotel, down a country lane in the Looe Valley. The
house was built at the turn of the century by a Victorian tea planter
who clearly had an eye for the light. It is beautifully situated in small,
landscaped gardens, and offers a menu which makes the most of local
fish and meat in British and traditional local dishes. The set menu (two,
three or four courses) comes complete with canapés, coffee and petits
fours, offering around half a dozen choices at each stage. Typical are
Cornish fish soup with garlic croutons, roast wood pigeon with braised
Puy lentils and smoked bacon, and steamed escalope of salmon with an
asparagus and dill beurre blanc. Friendly, relaxing place.

LITTLE WALSINGHAM — Old Bakehouse

33 High Street, Little Walsingham, Norfolk, NR22 6BZ
Tel: (01328) 820454 **£50**
Open: dinner Tue-Sat (Wed-Sat in winter) (closed 2 wks Jan/Feb)
Meals served: lunch one Sun a month: 12.30,
dinner 7-9.30 (earlier in winter)

At its peak, Walsingham was second only to Canterbury as a centre for pilgrimage; the village has been a Christian shrine since the Middle Ages and the village museum has all the evidence you need. The Old Bakehouse, which dates back to Tudor times, was indeed the village bakery until just some 25 years ago. Today the Georgian-inspired dining room plays host to an interesting menu of traditional and more inventive English-inspired dishes: from steak, kidney and oyster pie, steak and guinea fowl pie and roast beef and Yorkshire pudding to dishes such as fillet of sole with a scallop mousseline. Home-made puds include the likes of spotted dick, or Alaskan meringue cream with Grand Marnier. A separate vegetarian menu is available. Three bedrooms (one en-suite; two double-bedded, one twin) offer clean, comfortable accommodation.

LIVERPOOL — Armadillo

20 Mathew Street, Liverpool, Merseyside, L2 6RE
Tel: 051-236 4123 **£50**
Open: lunch & dinner Mon-Sat (closed 25 & 26 Dec, 1 Jan)
Meals served: lunch 12-3, dinner 7-10.30,
(early supper 5-6.30 Mon-Fri)

Situated in the re-christened Cavern Quarter of town (Beatles' country), this is a relaxed, bistro-style eaterie owned by two brothers, John and Frank Kenny. Try a single course if you wish -a bowl of home-made soup of the day, or home-made venison sausage with creamed potatoes and a rich onion sauce; or a full-blown meal of such dishes as lamb sweetbreads in a Madeira sauce, Roquefort and walnut pie, followed by apple crumble, lemon tart or a range of homemade ices.

LIVERPOOL — Jenny's Seafood Restaurant

The Old Ropery, off Fenwick Street, Liverpool,
Merseyside, L2 7NT
Tel: 051-236 0332 **£35**
Open: lunch Tue-Fri, dinner Tue-Sat (closed 2 wks Aug,
1 wk Xmas/New Year, Bank Holidays)
Meals served: lunch 12-2.15, dinner 7-10

Choose from the good fixed-price menu or the carte at this well-established city-centre restaurant. Seafood stew based on a wine and saffron sauce, grilled halibut with orange sauce, monkfish à la bourguignonne, whole fresh lobster, crab and Mediterranean prawns are just a few of the many different guises of fish and seafood offerings. Both menus offer a number of poultry, beef and lamb dishes (devilled chicken, blanquette of lamb) but it is seafood which commands the show.

LONG CRENDON   The Angel

Bicester Road, Long Crendon, Nr Aylesbury,
   Buckinghamshire, HP18 9EE
Tel: (01844) 208268   **£30**
Open: lunch daily, dinner Mon-Sat (closed Xmas)
Meals served: lunch 12-2.30, dinner 6.30-10

You can spend as little or as much as you like in Mark (ex-Sweeney Todd, Oxford) and Ruth Jones' brasserie-style pub-restaurant which dates back to the early 1500s. British and continental in style, the menu has a strong Mediterranean bias but Lancastrian roots. Anything from big steaks and bangers'n'mash to provençale-style fish soup with rouille, or salads, sandwiches and soup. Mark gets his fish direct from Billingsgate twice weekly so there's always a choice of fresh fish dishes on the hand-written menu: whitebait with crunchy spinach, perhaps, or Italian seafood platter. Continental breads and freshly baked baguettes add to the pleasure, and the wine list, though limited, has some good New World selections. Four en-suite bedrooms with TV complete this delightful pub set-up.

LONG MELFORD   Chimneys

Hall Street, Long Melford, Sudbury, Suffolk, CO10 9JR
Tel: (01787) 379806   **£65**
Open: lunch daily, dinner Mon-Sat
Meals served: lunch 12-2, dinner 7-9.30

A beautiful 16th-century timbered building in the centre of the village where lunch and dinner offer fixed-price menus with ample choice. Start perhaps with a terrine of smoked fish with a pepper purée or pan-fried marinated pigeon breast served with walnuts and grapes. Main courses might offer roast leg of lamb with thyme and garlic, grilled turbot on a bed of fennel and onion with tomato vinaigrette sauce or fillet of pork with broccoli mousse. Chef Steven Wright has taken over from owner Sam Chalmers in the kitchen, but little else has changed. This is a good local restaurant, with some reasonably priced wines and pleasant, informal service.

LONGHORSLEY   Linden Hall

Longhorsley, Nr Morpeth, Northumberland, NE65 8XF
Tel: (01670) 516611   *Fax:* (01670) 788544   **£50**
Open: lunch & dinner daily
Meals served: lunch 12-2, dinner 7-9.45
Elegant country house hotel with health spa, just outside Newcastle-upon-Tyne.

LONGRIDGE   Paul Heathcote's Restaurant

104-106 Higher Road, Longridge, Nr Preston,
  Lancashire, PR3 3SY
Tel: (01772) 784969   *Fax:* (01772) 785713   **£75**
Open: lunch Fri & Sun, dinner Tue-Sun
Meals served: lunch 12-2 (Sun to 2.30) (open lunch 6 days in Dec),
  dinner 7-9.30

Young chef-patron Paul Heathcote's return to his native Lancashire
after years of experience with some of the best, including time at Le
Manoir (Great Milton), Sharrow Bay (Ullswater) and The Connaught
(London), is a happy event for those in the North. Paul, pictured, with
the support of his head chef Andrew Barnes and a dedicated team, is

fast establishing this split-level restaurant
(set in a pretty whitewashed cottage, with
exposed stone walls and beams and immaculate table settings) as the new Northern star.
Paul cooks a modern repertoire, essentially
British, with great flair and imagination.
Menus change frequently according to the
seasonal availability of the best local produce.
The set lunch offers around five choices at
each stage, with dishes such as a confit of
duck with pea purée and wild mushrooms,
followed by pot-roasted rump of beef served
with oxtail, tongue and parsnip purée in ale
sauce. The carte offers even greater choice. Start with Heathcote's
black pudding served on a bed of crushed potatoes with baked beans
and bay leaf sauce or a mosaic of lamb fillet and provençal vegetables
with sun-dried tomato salad. Follow perhaps with ravioli of lobster
served with basil, truffle and lobster juices, then breast of local
Goosnargh corn-fed chicken, the skin lightly filled with truffle and
thyme, served with a truffle oil-scented casserole of artichoke and
asparagus; or roast fillet of mullet served with fondant potatoes,
savoury vegetables and mussel juices. Wonderful puds to finish, such
as hot banana soufflé, or bread-and-butter pudding with sauce anglaise
and clotted cream; or as a savoury, baked goat's cheese crusted in
parmesan, served with a nut salad. For a real treat, try the seven-course
gourmet menu. Paul Wiltshire's wine list is impressive; he's an excellent sommelier who is happy to advise.

*Egon Ronay's Guides' Chef of the Year status has undoubtedly
helped put him firmly on the map.*

LOUTH	Ferns

---

40 Northgate, Louth, Lincolnshire, LN11 0LY
Tel: (01507) 603209   *Fax:* (01507) 600828   **£40**
Open: lunch Mon-Fri, dinner Tue-Sat
Meals served: lunch 10-2, dinner 7-9.30

Nick and Kim Thompson offer good value for money with their fixed-price, weekday menu at just £9.90, supplemented by an à la carte. The cooking is essentially British, with much local influence and a continental vein too. Typical starters might include traditional black pudding grilled with apple and a splash of Calvados, or lobster bisque. Main courses could be breast of Barbary duck in Cointreau, chateaubriand steak béarnaise, or Lincolnshire Hog—dry-cured, smoked bacon chops, cooked on a moist bed of apples and onions, and there's always a fish dish of the day. To finish, there's brown bread ice cream, hot steamed puddings and chocolate truffle torte.

LOWER BEEDING	Cisswood House

Sandygate Lane, Lower Beeding, Nr Horsham,
   West Sussex, RH13 6NF
Tel: (01403) 891216   *Fax:* (01403) 891621   **£50**
Open: lunch & dinner Mon-Sat (closed 10 days Xmas/New Year)
Meals served: lunch 12.15-2, dinner 7-9.30 (Sat to 10)

Built in the late 1920s, this mock Tudor house with later extensions takes its name from those of the then chairman of Harrods, Sir Woodman Burbridge, and his wife Cissily. Now a 34-bedroomed hotel, it has been run by Othmar and Elizabeth Illes since 1979. Known locally in its younger days as "Harrods in the Country", much of the mock-period details of the house were done by Harrods' craftsmen, including panelling and plasterwork and the quality of their workmanship has stood the test of time. Bedrooms are traditionally furnished, with the largest in the most recent extension boasting separate walk-in showers. The traditional-style restaurant looks on to the lawns and dovecotes and is a fittingly elegant setting for Othmar's skilful and confident cooking, which is based mainly on classic French traditions. The two-or three-course table d'hôte menu offers plenty of choice, with best dishes being straightforwardly simple—pan-fried sea bass with a light orange butter sauce; chateaubriand béarnaise or breast of magret duck with a raspberry vinegar sauce. Great choice of desserts includes pecan pie served with a nutty ice cream and vanilla sauce.

LOWER BEEDING   South Lodge

Brighton Road, Lower Beeding, West Sussex, RH13 6PS
Tel: (01403) 891711   *Fax:* (01403) 891766   **£60**
Open: lunch & dinner daily
Meals served: lunch 12.30-2 (Sun to 2.30),
    dinner 7.30-10 (Sat to 10.30)

Formerly the home of explorer and botanist Frederick Ducane
Godman, flora plays more than a mere supporting role at this grand,
wisteria-clad Victorian country house set in 90 acres of well-tended gardens and parkland looking over the South Downs. Fresh flowers adorn
the rooms, and the gardens boast many rare trees and shrubs, including the largest rhododendron in England. Indoors, heavily carved wood
panelling, chandeliers and ornate ribbed ceilingwork create a warm
and graceful atmosphere. Thirty-nine individually designed bedrooms
are furnished with reproduction and original antiques, and boast luxurious Italian marble bathrooms; some are housed in the converted stable
block built around an indoor garden. The south-facing, dado-panelled
dining room enjoys fabulous views over the Downs and is traditional in
style, unlike the more modern outlook of the cooking. Ravioli of red
mullet, spicy chicken sausage baked in a rich brioche with wild mushrooms and a truffle sauce to start; mains of crispy aromatic duck with
an olive jus, steamed chicken filled with Cornish lobster and spinach
with a simple cream sauce, hot smoked tuna steak with a butter of
lemon and dill, or steamed turbot with a champagne and caviar butter
sauce demonstrate the range of dishes. Interesting and unusual
desserts might include a lavender honey and walnut mousse with
poached kumquats, or winter berries in a champagne and lemon jelly.
Good-value set lunch. Reasonably priced wine list.

LOWER BRAILES   Feldon House

Lower Brailes, Nr Banbury, Oxfordshire, OX15 5HW
Tel: (01608) 685580   **£50**
Open: lunch & dinner daily (closed 2 wks autumn)
Meals served: lunch 12.30-2, dinner 7-8.30

Allan and Maggie Witherick's comfortably furnished home on the edge
of the Cotswolds provides the setting for what is essentially a restaurant with rooms. The four rooms, two in the main house and two in the
coach house, are tastefully decorated and enjoy many thoughtful extras
to make you feel at home. The food, however, is really the main event
here. Both lunch and dinner are by arrangement only and the fixed-
price, no-choice menus are specifically designed to meet customer
tastes. It's a charming place, though, sadly, Maggie tells me they may
soon be moving on, but all was still quiet as we went to press.

LOWER SLAUGHTER Lower Slaughter Manor

Lower Slaughter, Nr Bourton-on-the-Water,
Gloucestershire, GL54 2HP
Tel: (01451) 20456   *Fax:* (01451) 22150   **£75**
Open: lunch & dinner daily (closed 2 wks Jan)
Meals served: lunch 12-2 (Sun 12.30-2.30), dinner 7-9
(Fri & Sat to 9.45)

A wonderfully relaxing place to stay, this peaceful Georgian manor
house in beautiful Cotswold country is just outside the village. Within
the walled garden is an ancient six-gabled 15th-century dovecote which
boasts over a thousand nesting boxes. Inside the manor, rooms are
beautifully proportioned and fine features abound throughout. The
house is owned and run by Audrey and Peter Marks, ex-Rookery Hall
(Nantwich). In the kitchen is Julian Ehlers whose classy, refined modern French cooking offers dishes such as parsley and shallot ravioli,
pig's trotter "our way" served with glazed onions and crispy potato,
seared scallops with Thai pancake on a Cabernet Sauvignon butter
sauce or Dover sole, served grilled or meunière. For dessert, try pear
galette with warm caramel sauce or a hot soufflé of Cotswold honey
and lime served with citrus fruit salad and orange sorbet. Expertly chosen and interesting wine list. A very special place to stay.

LUDLOW   Feathers Hotel

Bull Ring, Ludlow, Shropshire, SY8 1AA
Tel: (01584) 875261   *Fax:* (01584) 876030   **£45**
Open: lunch & dinner
Meals served: lunch 12-2, dinner 7-9

Old-world charm, comfort and traditional hospitality lie behind the
impressive, timbered, gabled façade of this 40-bedroomed hotel dating
back to the 17th century. Ornate plasterwork, wood panelling, log fires
and bright floral fabrics make up the decor. Once described as the
most handsome inn in the world, the Feathers has been owned and run
by the Edwards family for the last 50 years. In the restaurant, trolley-
carved roasts are a speciality and the style of cooking is predominantly
British.

LUPTON   Lupton Tower Vegetarian Country House
Lupton, Carnforth, Nr Kirkby Lonsdale, Cumbria, LA6 2PR
Tel: (0153 95) 67400   **£40**
Open: dinner Tue-Sun
Meals served: dinner 7.30 for 8
Six-bedroomed 18th-century house which has received much acclaim for its
innovative vegetarian cooking and non-smoking environment.

LYMINGTON — Gordleton Mill

Silver Street, Hordle, Nr Lymington, Hampshire, SO41 6DJ
Tel: (01590) 682219 *Fax:* (01590) 683073 **£80**
Open: lunch & dinner daily (closed 2 wks Jan)
Meals served: lunch 12-2.30, dinner 7-10

The atmosphere at this small seven-bedroomed hotel and restaurant is quite delightful. The 17th-century watermill enjoys a pretty riverside location, with views from the terrace and dining room. Mill pond, sluice gates, weir, rustic bridges, lily pond and gardens provide masses of charm, but the main event really is the restaurant, Provence, with its modern French and Mediterranean repertoire. Home-smoked salmon, foie gras maison and paper-thin slices of assorted fish served with fish butter sauce and a paysanne of vegetables are typical of starters on the à la carte. Main courses might offer poached sole with quenelles of pearl barley and a cockle and lemon sauce; grilled guinea fowl served with couscous and a spicy sauce; or fillet of beef served with foie gras ravioli and red wine sauce. Special Provence nights are a big attraction, with dishes such as stuffed squid with lobster-flavoured sauce and carré d'agneau topped with ratatouille and lamb mousse, served with thyme sauce. There's plenty of choice across all menus, both à la carte and fixed-price. Owner William Stone has a talent for finding good chefs and Toby Hill follows some distinguished names including that of Jean-Christophe Novelli, who is now at London's Four Seasons Hotel.

LYMINGTON — Stanwell House

High Street, Lymington, Hampshire, SO41 9AA
Tel: (01590) 677123 *Fax:* (01590) 677756 **£40**
Open: lunch & dinner daily
Meals served: lunch 12-2, dinner 7-9.30

An attractive, 18th-century town house hotel with 35 well-appointed bedrooms. Reception rooms include a smart cocktail bar and a pretty lounge. The restaurant offers a wide choice of menus, refreshingly simple in approach: crab and prawn salad with a sweet pepper dressing; poached supreme of smoked cod with a cheese and chive sauce; pan-fried Barbary duck breast with a light mustard sauce might be on offer. Lovely desserts include the likes of apple and lemon tart with clotted cream.

LYMPSTONE — River House

The Strand, Lympstone, Devon, EX8 5EY
Tel: (01395) 265147   **£60**
Open: lunch Tue-Sun, dinner Tue-Sat (closed Bank Holidays)
Meals served: lunch 12-1.30, dinner 7-9.30 (Sat to 10.30)

A delightful location on the estuary of the River Exe at the heart of picturesque Lympstone is a major attraction at Michael and Shirley Wilkes' restaurant with rooms. The views from the upstairs restaurant and ground-floor bar are quite spectacular. The restaurant has its own garden supplying fruit, vegetables and herbs to the kitchen where Shirley Wilkes executes her skill to great acclaim. Menus offer plenty of choice from two courses to five, with dishes such as crab pancakes, beef casserole in Guinness and port, and home-made fudge typical. This is classically-based English cooking of well-conceived dishes on a well-planned repertoire. Sunday lunch is popular. The restaurant has 14 pretty, en-suite bedrooms available for overnight accommodation: Michael and Shirley are excellent hosts.

LYNDHURST — Parkhill Hotel

Beaulieu Road, Lyndhurst, Hampshire, SO43 7FZ
Tel: (01703) 282944   *Fax:* (01703) 283268   **£55**
Open: lunch & dinner daily
Meals served: lunch 12-2, dinner 7-9

Formerly the elegant country home of the Duke of Clarence, the house was built in 1740 and restored in 1850. Situated in secluded grounds, complete with well-stocked lake, right on the edge of the New Forest, you could hardly find a more peaceful setting than this. The 20 bedrooms are comfortable and well furnished in mostly traditional style. Four rooms are in a separate coach house and a self-contained cottage suite boasts its own private walled garden. Wake to the sound of birdsong or animals scampering across the lawns. The light and airy restaurant has benefitted from a new conservatory extension and the cooking, nouvelle-ish in style but not in size, is essentially a blend of modern and classical English. Typical dishes from the seasonal carte might in autumn include the likes of light chicken soup with fresh sweetcorn and asparagus, pot-roasted partridge with orange and ginger and a rich claret sauce, or baked Dover sole with lemon grass and thyme.

MAIDEN NEWTON | Le Petit Canard

Dorchester Road, Maiden Newton, Dorset, DT2 0BE
Tel: (01300) 320536   **£45**
Open: dinner Tue-Sat
Meals served: dinner 7-9

This intimate 30-seat restaurant has monthly changing menus with
international influences. Light cream of asparagus, prawn and mushroom soup; smoked salmon soufflé; roast chicken breast with sweet
onion on a mild satay sauce; char-grilled venison with mustard and
shallot sauce; slow-roasted black bean and cracked pepper duck on
sautéed Chinese leaf; baked fillet of hake with a tarragon cream sauce
are the sort of dishes you might find. Finish with passion fruit tartlet
with an unusual black pepper ice cream or coconut rum sorbet with a
mango coulis. A sensibly- sized, moderately-priced wine list has been
extremely well chosen and has selections from around Europe and the
New World.

MAIDENHEAD | Fredrick's

Shoppenhangers Road, Maidenhead, Berkshire, SL6 2PZ
Tel: (01628) 35934   *Fax:* (01628) 771054   **£65**
Open: lunch Sun-Fri, dinner daily (closed 24-30 Dec
   except lunch 25 Dec)
Meals served: lunch 12-2, dinner 7-9.45

A luxury hotel and restaurant designed with the senior executive in
mind: complimentary champagne on arrival sets the tone. A modern
reception area with marble waterfall leads to a winter garden overlooking the patio—Fredrick Losel has lavished much time and money on
creating a European style decor in this traditional English building.
Bedrooms, whether in the original house or bright, new wing are classically-styled and well-serviced. The luxurious dining room, with
cream-painted panelling and chandeliers, makes a fitting venue for
Brian Cutler's traditional French and English cuisine. A typical menu
might feature grilled squid on roasted peppers, smoked quail salad or
watercress soup among starters; before veal Pojarski on wild mushroom sauce, braised oxtail bourguignonne or sea bass baked in a salt
crust. British and Continental cheeses precede coffee and petits fours.
Conference facilities available.

MALVERN	The Cottage in the Wood

Holywell Road, Malvern Wells, Hereford & Worcester, WR14 4LG
Tel: (01684) 573487   *Fax:* (01684) 560662 **£60**
Open: lunch & dinner daily
Meals served: lunch 12.30-2, dinner 7-9 (Sun-Thu to 8.30 in winter)

It was around 20 years ago on a lovely summer's day that I first visited the Cottage in the Wood. The food was excellent, the staff were charming: a real delight. And I'm pleased to say that there's still a warm welcome and fine food to be enjoyed at this family run hotel located amongst the beautiful Malvern hills. Kathryn Young offers dishes like a goat cheese and fig tart, salmon and trout terrine, spinach patties or Greek salad. Main courses might include saddle of goat with blackcurrant sauce, lamb's kidneys with juniper and mint or quail en croute with pistachio and raisin stuffing. Fine English cheeses and good home-made puddings round off the menu. A good wine list begins with a selection from four local English vineyards and a promise: that if you order one of these wines and find that you don't like it, the patron will drink it and refund your money.

MALVERN	Croque-en-Bouche

---

221 Wells Road, Malvern Wells, Hereford & Worcester, WR14 4HF
Tel: (01684) 565612 **£75**
Open: dinner Wed-Sat (closed Xmas/New Year, 2 wks Sep)
Meals served: dinner 7.30-9 (Sat to 9.30)

Husband and wife Robin and Marion Jones have been running this restaurant two miles south of Malvern since 1978, attracting diners from near and far. Robin takes charge of the wine list (and how!) while Marion looks after the culinary side of things. Robin's wine list is exceptional, and Marion cooks with flair and imagination. The six-course dinner menu is changed weekly, but typical offerings might include a puréed soup of split green peas, leek and sorrel, followed by Cornish skate with mango, ginger and coriander salsa and new season lamb marinated with a parsley pesto, then roasted with bulgar stuffing and served with a rosemary gravy and paloise sauce. A salad follows the main course, prior to the arrival of some excellent British farmhouse cheeses. Desserts such as a glazed lemon tart with wild strawberry purée, toffee rice pudding or a frozen meringue with preserved ginger and Kahlua served with coffee sauce are all memorable.

Biography

Marion Jones

Marion Jones is a remarkable lady, and all the more so in that she is one of a select band of extremely highly-rated but entirely self-taught chefs currently working in Britain. She has been making her mark in a quiet but determined way since she and her husband, Robin (a restaurateur in Battersea prior to this) first opened the 'Croque' as it is affectionately known. The essence of this modest lady's success is her determination to maintain standards, and husband and wife team-work.

MANCHESTER   Lime Tree

8 Lapwing Lane, West Didsbury, Greater Manchester, M20 8WS
Tel: 0161-445 1217   **£40**
Open: lunch Sun, dinner daily (closed Bank Holidays)
Meals served: lunch Sun 12-2.30, dinner 6.30-10.30

Hearty cooking served in busy bistro-style surroundings served by
cheerful, friendly staff: this is a well-established, attractive place in tranquil suburbs, four miles south of the city. A well-balanced meal might
be oriental-style king scallops followed by roast duckling with a raspberry sauce, and walnut tart with vanilla crème anglaise or a selection
of French cheeses to finish. There's always a vegetarian option. All in
all, a popular place, particularly for Sunday lunch, when roast beef with
Yorkshire pudding comes into its own.

MANCHESTER   Market Restaurant

104 High Street, Smithfield City Centre,
   Greater Manchester, M4 1HQ
Tel: 0161-834 3743   **£45**
Open: dinner Wed-Sat (closed 1 wk Xmas, 1 wk Easter, Aug)
Meals served: dinner 6-9.30 (Sat from 7)

Not a stone's throw from Manchester's up-and-coming gourmet district
near Smithfield Market, this friendly, homely restaurant run by the
O'Gradys has enormous appeal, with its slightly faded decor and 1940s'
feel. The monthly-changing menu ranges far and wide for influence
with African-inspired bobotie, Sussex-braised beef in a mushroom, port
and stout gravy and Thai sweetcorn fritters being typical of a menu,
which roams from the exotic to the more traditional without missing a
beat. Reasonably priced wine list. The Pudding Club may be of interest,
to those who read menus back to front; or there's the Starters' Society
for those who like to on a feast of small savoury bites. Both meet a
handful of times a year on Tuesdays.

MANCHESTER   Victoria & Albert Hotel

Water Street, Greater Manchester, M60 9EA
Tel: 0161-832 1188   *Fax:* 0161-834 2484   **£60**
Open: lunch Sun-Fri, dinner daily
Meals served: lunch 12-2, dinner 7-10,
     (light meals Café Maigret 10am-10.30pm daily)

The new flagship Granada hotel opposite the television studios by the
River Irwell was voted Best New Hotel of the Year by travel executives
in a recent magazine survey. The hotel was built as a warehouse in the
19th century: more recently it became the prop store for the TV studio
and when the Granada Studios Tour began to take off, someone had the
bright idea of creating the hotel. Bedrooms are themed on popular
Granada dramas, so TV addicts will be delighted to stay in the
Brideshead Revisited room, for instance. Amenities include the
Sherlock Holmes restaurant where chef John Benson-Smith cooks with
style and panache. Gourmet themed suppers offer plenty to talk about,
and the lunchtime carte is a teaser when it comes to choice. Hot spicy
Thai salad (prawns, mango, apricot and cashew nuts) is a bestseller,
along with many traditional old English favourites, such as Yorkshire
pudding with onion gravy (among starters), grilled sausage and mash
with more of the same, crispy battered haddock and chips with mushy
peas or the wittily presented "formerly known as beef stroganoff"—
strips of fillet with green peppercorns and brandy. Culinary alternatives
are also available in the Café Maigret; malt whisky and cask-conditioned
ales in Watson's Bar. Good team work from staff across the board.

MANCHESTER   Woodlands

33 Shepley Road, Audenshaw, Greater Manchester, M34 5DJ
Tel: 0161-336 4241   **£40**
Open: lunch & dinner daily (closed 1 wk Jan,
     1 wk Easter, 2 wks Aug)
Meals served: lunch 12-2, dinner 7-9.30 (Sat to 10)

A popular family restaurant run by the Crank family, with son-in-law
Mark Jackson offering sound, classic French cuisine without fuss:
smoked salmon and prawn salad, lobster bisque with Armagnac, grilled
fresh scallops with spring onions and garlic, whole lobster with a
cheese and mustard sauce and fillet of lamb with two tarragon sauces.
Three guest rooms next to the main building are now in operation.

MANCHESTER AIRPORT   Moss Nook

Ringway Road, Moss Nook, Greater Manchester, M22 5WD
Tel: 0161-437 4778   **£70**
Open: lunch & dinner Tue-Sat (closed Bank Holidays,
     2 wks Xmas)
Meals served: lunch 12-1.30, dinner 7-9.30

The well-established Moss Nook is home to Kevin Lofthouse's quality
cooking. Surrounded by warm red walls and sparkling crystal, you
could start perhaps with thinly sliced marinated beef garnished with
Anglesey oysters, fresh lobster with a raspberry dressing, or spiced
chicken livers sautéed with bacon and apples. For your main course you

might find a choice between chicken marinated in limes on a tomato and tarragon sauce, or grilled fillet of salmon with spinach noodles and a watercress sauce. If you like the element of the unexpected, put yourself in Kevin's hands for the seven-course surprise menu. There's a good-value five-course tasting menu at lunchtime for just £16.50.

MANNINGTREEM   Stour Bay Café

39-41 High Street, Manningtree, Nr Colchester,
  Essex, CO11 1AX
Tel: (01206) 396687   **£40**
Open: lunch Sat & Sun, dinner Tue-Sat (closed Bank Holidays,
  2 wks Jan, 2 wks Sep)
Meals served: lunch 12-2.30, dinner 7-10

Short handwritten à la carte menus (lunch and dinner) announce the eclectic range of dishes available at this brasserie-style restaurant. Start, perhaps, with the day's soup (cream of tomato and lentil), Stour Bay crab cakes with lemon pepper aiöli or spinach, mushroom and Stilton tart with macadamia nuts. Follow with pan-seared grouper fillet in a light Thai red curry sauce, grilled whole Dover sole in ginger brown butter, roast rack of lamb in a hazelnut crust with a Cabernet cassis sauce or the more straightforward honey-glazed loin of pork.

MARY TAVY   The Stannary

Mary Tavy, Nr Tavistock, Devon, PL19 9QB
Tel: (01822) 810897   *Fax:* (01822) 810898   **£65**
Open: dinner Tue-Sat
Meals served: dinner 7-9.30

The cooking at this vegetarian restaurant is resourceful enough to tempt the appetite of committed carnivores, and the ambience is warm and welcoming. A restaurant with three rooms, housed in a 16th-century house with Victorian additions, it is unique in its policy of catering for every possible dietary restriction—from gluten-free to dairy-free to yeast-free alternatives. The cost of the three-course dinner of generous portions is inclusive of canapés on arrival, specialist breads with starters, and coffee and home-made chocolates to finish. Choose from starters such as truffle pâté or wild mushroom and pink peppercorn vol-au-vents, followed by hazelnut nests on a leafy herb sauce or hokypoky (nettle) pancakes. And for dessert: bilberry crepes with bilberry cream; citrus and walnut wedge; or ginger pillow—a slab of chewy ginger puff pastry served hot, with cinnamon custard, Greek yoghurt and clotted cream. Home-grown vegetables. The extensive range of wines might even tempt teetotallers no fewer than 13 champagnes on offer and representative bottles from around the world.

MATLOCK   Riber Hall

Matlock, Derbyshire, DE4 5JU
Tel: (01629) 582795   *Fax:* (01629) 580475   **£60**
Open: lunch & dinner daily
Meals served: lunch 12-1.30, dinner 7-9.30

Set in the foothills of the Pennines, on the edge of the Peak District, this 11-bedroomed Elizabethan manor house in its own grounds has a delightful walled garden, orchard and conservatory. The Hall dates from the early 1400s and was restored from near derelict condition in the early 1970s. Bedrooms are half-timbered and prettily furnished, with antique four-posters or half-testers, and are located in converted stables across a courtyard. Two elegant dining rooms, reflecting different periods in the history of the Hall, are the setting for the kitchen's extensive repertoire of modern French and English cuisine. Game pie in a rich wine jus and short pastry crust, stir-fried Oriental salmon with a hint of soy sauce, or poached chicken stuffed with lemon and parsley mousse with basil and tomato coulis might be on offer. An usually wide choice of puds, plus imaginative vegetarian options.

MAWNAN   Meudon Hotel

Mawnan, Nr Falmouth, Cornwall, TR11 5HT
Tel: (01326) 250541   *Fax:* (01326) 250543   **£55**
Open: lunch & dinner daily (closed Jan & Feb)
Meals served: lunch 12.30-2, dinner 7.30-9

The accent is on peace and quiet at the Pilgrim family's 32-bedroomed hotel. One of the main attractions here are the sub-tropical gardens, designed by Capability Brown, which lead down to a private beach and are at their most colourful between March and June. Bedrooms overlook the gardens and there are two balcony suites each with its own sitting room. The restaurant provides an international repertoire of dishes, with a bias towards traditional English fare. Specialities include Falmouth Bay diver-picked scallops cooked with lemon, spring onion, butter and garlic, local dressed crab, or lobster Thermidor. Light lunches are served in the bar, lounges or in the garden. The house was built at the turn of the century and a new wing has been sympathetically added in matching stone. Free golf is available to residents at the nearby golf club, plus sea and river fishing.

MAWNAN   Nansidwell

Mawnan, Nr Falmouth, Cornwall, TR11 5HU
Tel: (01326) 250340   *Fax:* (01326) 250440   **£55**
Open: lunch & dinner daily (closed Jan)
Meals served: lunch 12.30-1.30, dinner 7-9.30

Jamie and Felicity Robertson offer real hospitality in their 12-bed-roomed country house hotel set right between the sea and the Helford river. You'll enjoy Anthony Allcott's cooking in the homely dining room. His well-conceived, fixed-price menus offer such treats as quail and asparagus tartlet with lemon and vermouth sabayon, flaky pastry case of prawns with garlic and tarragon butter or a simple leek and potato soup. Fillet of brill with chervil and grape butter, medallions of monkfish with a lobster ragout and chanterelles, or a saddle of rabbit with chestnuts and bacon on port wine sauce. Good cheeses and superb puds to follow. A small wine list but some excellent Spanish wines from Laymont and Shaw in nearby Truro.

MEDMENHAM   Danesfield House

Medmenham, Marlow, Buckinghamshire, SL7 3ES
Tel: (01628) 891010   *Fax:* (01628) 890408   **£75**
Open: lunch & dinner daily
Meals served: lunch 12-2, dinner 7-10 (Sun to 9.30)

High above a bend in the Thames and with superb views, Danesfield is a sumptuous mix of architectural styles. The house was built at the end of the last century for Robert Hudson of soap family fame. Features include a baronial, tapestry-hung hall with hammerbeam roof and min-strel's gallery (the snooker room), sunlit atrium and loggia, glittering chandelier-lit Versailles room. This is haute period elegance, which extends to the formal parterre gardens which include an Italian water garden overlooking the Thames. The restaurant, supplied with wild mushrooms from the hotel grounds, takes over the panelled Oak Room with a weekly-changing table d'hôte menu of English- and French-inspired dishes.

MELBOURN — Pink Geranium

Station Road, Melbourn, Nr Royston, Hertfordshire, SG8 6DX
Tel: (01763) 260215   *Fax:* (01763) 262110   **£70**
Open: lunch Tue-Sun, dinner Tue-Sat (closed 26-29 Dec)
Meals served: lunch 12-2.30, dinner 7-10.30

Housed in a pretty thatched cottage dating back to around 1500, Steven Saunders' Pink Geranium is surrounded by a neat garden—pink both inside and out, including, of course, the geraniums featured in the decor and upholstery. Steven has a new chef this year, Philip Guest, who with an enthusiastic kitchen team produce dishes such as warm salad of roasted quail and aspara-gus with a Gewurztraminer jus, and millefeuille of halibut and fresh crab with a light fish cream. Home-made puds range from classic crème brûlée to warm hazelnut tart with home-made butterscotch ice cream.

Well worth a visit

■ **Steven and Sally Saunders**

MELKSHAM — Toxique

187 Woodrow Road, Melksham, Wiltshire, SN12 7AY
Tel: (01225) 702129   **£55**
Open: lunch Sun, dinner Wed-Sat (closed 2 wks winter,
   2 wks summer)
Meals served: lunch Sun 12.30-2, dinner 7-10

This is a slightly eccentric place, not only for its name but also for its farmhouse setting and decor—an abstract mural and ordinary chairs disguised with loose coverings sum it up. But around these parts, it's a real find. Peter Jewkes and chef-partner Helen Bartlett offer a fixed-price menu of three courses with plenty of choice. Unusual flavour and texture combinations are a feature as demonstrated by dishes such as chestnut and almond soup with lemon grass, buffalo mozzarella with sun-dried tomatoes and basil tortino, spring lamb with charred sweet peppers and tomatoes, and garlic-seared monkfish with coriander. Interesting desserts—honey-dipped nut pastry with vanilla ice cream, and fig and orange tart with whipped cream. Wines have been very well chosen with some interesting lesser known items and a comprehensive range of sweet wines in half bottles to sip with those puddings. There are also four en-suite rooms.

MELMERBY — Village Bakery

Melmerby, Penrith, Cumbria, CA10 1HE
Tel: (01768) 881515   *Fax:* (01768) 881848   **£25**
Open: all day daily (closed 25-27 Dec, 1 Jan)
Meals served: light meals 8.30-5 (lunch 12-2)

The restaurant attached to what is indeed the village bakery offers a wide choice, starting with breakfast, and continuing throughout the day with light meals and snacks (quiches, sandwiches, aduki bean pie and the like). Housed in a converted stone barn with a bright, airy conservatory, the restaurant overlooks the village green. Longstanding owners Andrew and Lis Whitley are committed to using ingredients produced by organic methods. Lunch-time menus offer more substantial meals, starting perhaps with a leek and potato cream soup, followed by main dishes such as grilled Cumberland sausage, pheasant casserole, hot prawn salad or brown lentil and red wine moussaka. Traditional puds to finish. All the baking is done in a wood-fired, brick oven. It's good to see so many of their bakery products more widely available, even in southern supermarkets, Several brownie points to the Whitleys for this achievement!

MELTON MOWBRAY — Olde Stocks

Grimston, Nr Melton Mowbray, Leicestershire, LE14 3BZ
Tel: (01664) 812255   **£45**
Open: dinner Tue-Sat
Meals served: dinner 7-10

Organically-reared local lamb and beef, local farm-grown asparagus, Stilton cheese from nearby Colston Basset and vegetarian dishes to order are just some of the attractions at this small restaurant in the shadow of an old chestnut tree by the original Grimston stocks. A frequently-changing blackboard menu presents a small but novel à la carte with dishes like duck turnovers with Madeira and duck broth, individual beef Wellingtons with a brandy and green peppercorn sauce or poached salmon, monkfish and king prawns on a bed of seaweed with a spring onion sauce. Desserts range from the traditional: sticky toffee, bread-and-butter—to the more elaborate: iced strawberry terrine with crushed meringue and nougatine served with pistachios and a butterscotch sauce. Exciting, unusual vegetarian dishes are also available.

MIDDLE WALLOP — Fifehead Manor

Middle Wallop, Nr Stockbridge, Hampshire, SO20 8EG
Tel: (01264) 781565   *Fax:* (01264) 781400   **£55**
Open: lunch & dinner daily (closed 2 wks Xmas/New Year)
Meals served: lunch 12-2.30, dinner 7.30-9.30
Friendly and informal, 16-bedroomed manor house whose foundations are said to date back to the Middle Ages, standing in several acres of gardens.

MIDHURST   Angel Hotel

North Street, Midhurst, West Sussex, GU29 9DN
Tel: (01730) 812421   *Fax:* (01730) 815928   **£50**
Open: lunch & dinner daily
Meals served: lunch 12-2.30, dinner 7-10 (brasserie from 6)

This 16th-century former coaching inn with white-painted Georgian
façade is a warm and friendly place run by Nicholas Davies and Peter
Crawford-Rolt. Sympathetic restoration to retain as many original features as possible has gone hand-in-hand with contemporary comforts.
Bedrooms, of which there are 21 (including four new ones due to come
on line at the end of 1994), are spacious and comfortable, whether in
the main house or in the modern block to the rear. All are en-suite and
some have four-posters. Peter rules the kitchen, producing traditional
and modern English and French cuisine. There are two restaurants:
one an informal brasserie-style operation, with the emphasis on
seafood, and a daily-changing menu of hearty roasts, casseroles, pies
and the like; the other a more formal dining room, with its extensive
menu featuring char-grilled meats and fish along with more sophisticated dishes such as fillet of steamed turbot with asparagus and saffron
cream sauce, or canon of local roe deer with apple chutney and port
sauce. Lovely desserts include warm plum and almond tart with praline
and Armagnac ice cream. A marquee can be erected on the lawns for
parties.

*Those of you who ate at Beechfield House in
the early '80s will appreciate Peter Crawford-Rolt's
capable cooking here at the Angel.*

MIDHURST   Maxine's

Elizabeth House, Red Lion Street, Midhurst,
    West Sussex, GU29 9PB
Tel: (01730) 816271   **£30**
Open: lunch Sun, dinner Wed-Sat (closed 2 wks Jan)
Meals served: lunch 12-2, dinner 7-11

Expect a warm welcome at Robert and Marti Jäger's dining room,
where a fixed-price weekday menu (£12.95) is supplemented by a
sensibly-thought-out à la carte which includes a good choice of fish,
meat and game. Good home-cooked dishes might include crispy duck
with black cherry sauce, lamb casserole, pork stroganoff, sweetbreads
with mushrooms and thyme in a white wine sauce are typical. You
might start with home-made soup of the day, Robert's special fish soup,
crab cakes with ginger, tomato and coriander or salmon mousse with
avocado.

MILFORD-ON-SEA   Rocher's

69-71 High Street, Milford-on-Sea, Hampshire, SO41 0QG
Tel: (01590) 642340   **£55**
Open: lunch Sun only, dinner Wed-Sat (closed 2 wks Jun)
Meals served: lunch 12.30-1.45, dinner 7.15-9.45

Choose from a variety of menus at this charming little French restaurant where Alain Rocher and his wife Rebecca offer some excellent cooking in elegant surroundings. With only seven tables and a strong local following, booking is essential. Alain's style of cooking is classically-based with modern touches. Expect dishes such as fish terrine served with a light curry dressing, delicate home-made carrot mousse with coriander, Scotch beef with grain mustard sauce or fillet of lamb with a port and Roquefort cheese sauce. Monkfish may be complemented with a red pepper sauce, salmon with a creamy garlic one. Alain works singlehandedly in the kitchen, picks his own wild mushrooms, grows his own herbs and flowers; Rebecca provides a warm and friendly welcome front of house. The wine list is totally French and there are sound choices amongst the classics and a very comprehensive selection from the patron's native Loire valley.

MINSTER LOVELL   Old Swan
Minster Lovell, Nr Witney, Oxfordshire, OX8 5RN
Tel: (01993) 774441   *Fax:* (01993) 702002   **£45**
Open: lunch & dinner daily
Meals served: lunch 12-2, dinner 7-10
Charming Cotswold inn dating back to the time of Richard III, with own grounds, 57 rooms and a beamed restaurant leading out on to the garden. Fly fishing or punting on the Windrush.

MONKTON COMBE   Combe Grove Manor
Brassknocker Hill, Monkton Combe, Nr Bath, Avon, BA2 7HS
Tel: (01225) 834644   *Fax:* (01225) 834961   **£60**
Open: lunch & dinner daily
Meals served: lunch 12-2.30, dinner 7-9.30
Glorious views over the Limpley Stoke valley to the White Horse of Westbury from this 41-bedroomed Georgian manor. Breathtaking views from the rooms, and state-of-the-art leisure facilities.

MONTACUTE   Milk House

The Borough, Montacute, Nr Yeovil, Somerset, TA15 6XB
Tel: (01935) 823823   **£45**
Open: lunch Tue-Fri, dinner Wed-Sat (closed 25 & 26 Dec)
Meals served: lunch 12.30-2, dinner 7.30-9

Set in a pretty Somerset village, the 15th-century Milk House indeed sold milk from its stable block for many hundreds of years until just 20 years ago, when it became the small, two-bedroomed hotel with restaurant that it is today. With the accent placed on meat and fish, there is nevertheless always a serious vegetarian option on the menu, and much emphasis is placed on additive-free ingredients, even down to the wine list which includes a number of organic wines. Good, simple, classic dishes are the order of the day. Main dishes might include fillet of wild salmon with a sorrel sauce or pork with a Somerset brandy sauce. This is a rambling old house, with lots of character—roaring log fires in winter, ancient beamed ceilings, antiques, a creeper-clad terrace and pretty walled garden.

MORETON-IN-MARSH   Annie's

3 Oxford Street, Moreton-in-Marsh, Gloucestershire, GL56 0LA
Tel: (01608) 651981   **£50**
Open: lunch Sun, dinner Mon-Sat (closed 3 wks Jan/Feb)
Meals served: lunch 12-2, dinner 7-10

Supervising front of house, Annie Ellis proffers a warm welcome to guests at this romantic, candlelit restaurant with cottagey appeal. Husband David is meanwhile busy at the stove, producing unpretentious French and English country cooking. Start perhaps with fresh salmon fishcakes served with a white wine and salmon cream sauce or light spinach roulade with oak-smoked salmon. Move on to poussin with a lemon mustard sauce, pan-fried calf's liver with caramelised onions or a fish dish of the day. Home-made bread and puddings, such as pecan pie with toffee ice cream.

MORETON-IN-MARSH   Marsh Goose

High Street, Moreton-in-Marsh, Gloucestershire, GL56 0AX
Tel: (01608) 52111   **£55**
Open: lunch Tue-Sun, dinner Tue-Sat (closed 26 Dec, 1 Jan)
Meals served: lunch 12.15-2.30, dinner 7.30-9.45

A happy balance is struck by chef Sonya Kidney at this pleasant Cotswold restaurant where modern interpretation vies with classic traditions. A light lunchtime carte offers half-a-dozen or so dishes to be enjoyed as starters or light meals, such as hot mushroom fritters with grain mustard sauce or warm chicken salad. Dinner shifts to a table d'hôte arrangement, with plenty of choice. Expect to find the likes of marinated salmon with sweet mustard dressing or braised Puy lentils and shallots served with an escalope of foie gras, followed by grilled red mullet with red peppers and garlic butter sauce or breast of guinea fowl with braised flageolet beans and chorizo sausage.

MORSTON   Morston Hall

Morston, Holt, Norfolk, NR25 7AA
Tel & Fax: (01263) 741041   **£50**
Open: lunch Sun, dinner daily (closed Jan & Feb)
Meals served: lunch Sun 12.30 for 1, dinner 7.30 for 8

Many buildings in this typical North Norfolk coastal village are of local flint, and you could hardly find a more traditional setting, with village pub, 13th-centry church and fisherman's quay. Morston Hall completes the picture: a 17th-century house in its own secluded grounds. Running the show are three ex-Miller Howe (Windermere) professionals, who hope to make Morston one of the best small country house hotels in the country. Galton Blackiston shows a light and refined touch in the kitchen, with dishes such as smoked salmon risotto or warm Stilton cheesecake to start, followed by the likes of roast Aberdeen Angus sirloin with an onion marmalade or breast of duck Teriyaki-style on Chinese leaves and sesame seeds. The fixed-price four-course menu offers no choice except for desserts which might include rich white chocolate torte or warm apple soufflé with poached rhubarb. Bedrooms, all large, have lovely views over grounds and surrounding farmland. They are sunny, and well equipped.

MOTTRAM ST ANDREW　　　　　**De Vere Mottram Hall**

Mottram St Andrew, Prestbury, Cheshire, SK10 4QT
Tel: (01625) 828135　*Fax:* (01625) 829284　　　　　**£50**
Open: lunch Sun-Fri, dinner daily
Meals served: lunch 12.30-2, dinner 7-9.45,(Sat 7-10)
133-bedroomed hotel, an impressive Georgian mansion in 270 acres of parkland. Extensive leisure facilities, including golf course, club house and terrace restaurant.

MOULSFORD-ON-THAMES　　Beetle & Wedge

Moulsford-on-Thames, Oxfordshire, OX10 9JF　*Wonderful setting, good food and charming staff*
Tel: (01491) 651381　*Fax:* (01491) 651376
Restaurant:　　　　　**£80**
Open: lunch Tue-Sun, dinner Tue-Sat (closed 25 Dec)
Meals served: lunch 12.30-2, dinner 7.30-10
Boathouse Brasserie:　　　　　**£45**
Open: lunch & dinner daily (closed 25 Dec)
Meals served: lunch 12-2, dinner 7.30-10

Kate and Richard Smith (ex-Royal Oak, Yattendon) attend to every detail at this riverside hotel and restaurant, once the home of Jerome K Jerome of *Three Men in a Boat* fame. Lunch in the dining room or in the lovely, old beamed Boathouse on the water's edge, complete with terrace for riverside eating. The atmosphere here is buzzy and informal, the menu long—huge choice of imaginative dishes, including soups, casseroles and a wide selection of fresh fish and game from the charcoal grill. Alternatively, you can relax in the elegant dining room

where Richard offers a daily-changing à la carte menu, with dishes such as sautéed foie gras with lyonnaise onions followed by whole grilled Cornish lobster with tarragon butter sauce, roast loin of venison with morels and Armagnac sauce or escalope of halibut with langoustine and lobster sauce. Wonderful desserts follow, then a selection of farmhouse cheeses, coffee and petits fours. It's almost too good to be true. There are ten bedrooms, almost all with riverside views, and breakfasts are truly excellent too.

Biography

Richard Smith

Richard Smith grew up in South London and freely admits that his mother's cooking had a profound and lasting influence upon him. His first post was by default, when wife Kate applied for job at Langan's Brasserie in London but ended up by talking Richard Shepherd into hiring her husband instead! After this, there was a brief spell at the Greenhouse, Mayfair, followed by time at The Royal Oak, Yattendon, before he and Kate settled at the Beetle & Wedge. Richard's food is for a hearty appetite.

MOULTON — Black Bull

Moulton, Nr Richmond, North Yorkshire, DL10 6QJ
Tel: (01325) 377289   *Fax:* (01325) 377422   **£50**
Open: lunch daily, dinner Mon-Sat (closed 24-27 Dec)
Meals served: lunch 12-2.30 (Sun to 3), dinner 6.45-10.15

The gregarious George Pagendam's somewhat eccentric pub and railway carriage restaurant has pulled diners from far afield for almost 30 years to enjoy the delicious seafood on offer. Hot crab mousse with chive butter sauce, seafood pancake thermidor, queenie scallops with garlic butter or grilled Dublin Bay prawns are just a few of the first courses. Follow them with sole, lobster, salmon, turbot, sea bass or the wonderful seafood platter. George is equally proud of his Aberdeen Angus beef, so chateaubriand, sirloin or fillet steak will delight meat eaters. His selective wine list has some good bottles at reasonable prices.

NANTWICH — CHURCHE'S MANSION

Hospital Street, Nantwich, Cheshire, CW5 0RY
Tel: (01270) 625933   *Fax:* (01270) 74256   **£55**
Open: lunch Tue-Sun, dinner Tue-Sat (closed 1 wk Jan)
Meals served: lunch 12-2.30, dinner 7-9.30

Original oak beams, exposed brickwork and open fireplaces are the setting for Graham Tucker's cooking, which he describes as modern British with French and Italian undertones. Everything is either produced on the premises—bread, biscuits, pastry, ice-creams, sorbets, pasta, home-smoked meats and fish—or bought in from the best of local suppliers. Winter and spring favourites include home-made black pudding with mashed potato, egg poached in red wine with a truffled Madeira sauce, shank of lamb on a parsnip purée with flageolet beans and rosemary, oxtail crepinette with roast vegetables, and par-smoked, pan-fried salmon. Summer menus include the likes of crayfish tortellinis with a citrus vinaigrette or seared red mullet with a Caesar salad and polenta croutons. For dessert you could be tempted by a nougatine parfait with caramel ice cream and cappuccino sauce.

NANTWICH   **Rookery Hall**

Worleston, Nr Nantwich, Cheshire, CW5 6DQ
Tel: (01270) 610016   *Fax:* (01270) 626027   **£60**
Open: lunch & dinner daily (closed 25-31 Dec)
Meals served: lunch 12-2, dinner 7-9.45

Fifty years after it was originally built (in the latter half of the 19th century), a Bavarian merchant banker bought the house and added the distinctive schloss-like tower we see today, to remind him of his homeland. There is a definitive sense of space here -no less apparent in the bedrooms than in the baronial-style reception rooms which boast many fine features and antiques. The elegant dining rooms are a fitting backdrop to David Alton's well-thought-out menus. The à la carte is supplemented by fixed-price menus, with dishes such as warm shellfish sausage on a prawn and dill butter, casseroled loin of spring lamb with tarragon dumplings or baked breast of chicken with rich, wild mushroom, brandy and peppercorn sauce showing the range. There are extensive grounds, with lovely walks by the river, plus a stylish, self-contained conference centre in the converted Coach House.

NAYLAND   **Martha's Vineyard**

18 High Street, Nayland, Suffolk, CO6 4JF
Tel: (01206) 262888   **£45**
Open: dinner Tue-Sat (closed 2 wks summer, 2 wks winter)
Meals served: dinner 7.30-9.30

Gutsy home cooking coupled with warmth and friendliness are the hallmarks of this pleasant country restaurant. Chef and co-owner Larkin Rogers offers an à la carte menu that is short but sensible; while the cooking is competent and individual. A typical menu might include mussel and bacon fritters with a tartare sauce or spicy black bean chili to start, followed by West Indian braised rib of beef with peppers, Californian mixed fish stew or pan-roasted pheasant with a cranberry and orange relish. Finish with something like chocolate bread-and-butter pudding, ice creams and sorbets, or a selection of farmhouse cheeses.

NETHER LANGWITH — Goff's Restaurant

Langwith Mill House, Nether Langwith, Mansfield,
   Nottis, NG20 9JF
Tel: (01623) 744538   **£40**
Open: lunch Tue-Fri & Sun, dinner Tue-Sat
   (closed Tue after Bank Holidays, 1 wk Sep, 1 wk Mar)
Meals served: lunch 12-2.30, dinner 7-9.30

Look out for the ramshackle old cotton mill about a mile east of the village to find this delightful restaurant with rooms in the adjacent mill house. The restaurant has two dining rooms, both pretty and candlelit, one intimate, the other less so but more spacious. Fish from Abergavenny (on Tuesdays) plays a major role on Darren Shears' menus, which are supplemented on a daily basis by a short selection of specials. Typical dishes might be gravadlax of tuna with fresh coriander and vegetable dressing; fillet of salmon with cucumber spaghetti and tomato tarragon sauce; and pan-fried beef with herb and vegetable casserole. Imaginative use of familiar ingredients is the keynote to many of the dishes. Save room for dessert—glazed figs with mascarpone, bread-and-butter pudding, lemon soufflé with fresh pink grapefruit.

NEW ALRESFORD — Hunters

32 Broad Street, New Alresford, Hampshire, SO24 9AQ
Tel: (01962) 732468   **£35**
Open: lunch & dinner Mon-Sat (plus lunch Sun in winter)
   (closed 25-30 Dec)
Meals served: lunch 12-2, dinner 7-10

This is a wine bar-cum-brasserie run by the Birmingham family in friendly, laid-back style. Dinner offers seasonal à la carte or nightly table d'hôte menus while lunch-time provides a choice of light snacks or main meals from a short carte which represents excellent value. The cooking is essentially English and French, with dishes such as pan-fried scallops and a shellfish sauce followed by roast wood pigeon with a red wine sauce. The lunch menu includes the likes of home-made Stilton and broccoli quiche and pork and herb sausages with mashed potatoes and gravy. The restaurant offers overnight guests three delightful, en-suite bedrooms overlooking Broad Street.

NEW BARNET — Mims Restaurant

63 East Barnet Road, New Barnet, Hertfordshire, EN4 8RN
Tel: 0181-449 2974   **£55**
Open: lunch Tue-Fri & Sun, dinner Tue-Sun (closed 25-30 Dec, 1 wk Sep)
Meals served: lunch 12-2.30, dinner 6.30-11, (light meals Sun 12-10.30)

Don't be put off by the rather unfashionable location of this very good restaurant—in a parade of shops next to a petrol station—for once inside you'll find cooking refined and skillful with a Mediterranean bias. A long-standing local favourite—some folk come for miles—this is a gem of a place. Simple, yet striking, green decor is the setting for Ismail Al-Sersy's daily-changing menus (fixed-price for lunch; à la carte for dinner). Dishes are imaginative and artistic: start perhaps with langoustine salad, roast quail and herbed noodles or cream of smoked leek soup; followed by dishes such as roast red mullet with vegetables provençale or beef with a turnip confit, mushrooms and a mustard sauce. Finish with lemon tart, bread and butter pudding or a light mixed sorbet.

NEW MILTON	Chewton Glen

Christchurch Road, New Milton, Hampshire, BH25 6QS
Tel: (01425) 275341   *Fax:* (01425) 272310
Open: lunch & dinner daily
Meals served: lunch 12.30-2 (Sun to 2.30),
    dinner 7.30-9.30

£60

Nothing is overlooked at Martin and Brigitte Skan's exclusive 58-bed-roomed hotel half way between Bournemouth and Lymington. The quality of staff and service is faultless, the setting (in 70 acres of grounds) magnificent. The stunning leisure and health club is classical in style, with trompe-l'oeil frescoes, and balcony lounge overlooking the pool. Garden rooms have balconies and terraces, and breakfast is a regal affair, with everything from kippers to kedgeree on offer. Chef Pierre Chevillard completes the picture with his modern classical British cuisine. Flavours are subtle, textures divine, and menus are straightforward and unpretentious. Look forward to dishes such as a terrine of duck foie gras flavoured with green walnut wine, wafer-thin pastry tarts filled with leeks and truffles, fillet of turbot served on a tapenade crouton, crispy roasted salmon with grilled celeriac and onion jam or black Angus beef with a rich marrowbone sauce. Menus, both fixed-price and à la carte, offer an

imaginative and exciting choice. A wonderful place to indulge yourself in every way. Martin and Brigitte are pictured.

NEWARK	Gannets Café-Bistrot

35 Castlegate, Newark, Nottinghamshire, NG24 1AZ
Tel: (01636) 702066
Open: lunch & dinner Wed-Sat (closed 25 & 26 Dec)
Meals served: lunch 12-2, dinner 6.30-9.30,
    (light meals ground floor café daily 10-4.30)

£35

Casual, informal bistro run by Hilary and David Bower, with a ground-floor café serving an all-day menu and an upstairs bistro where background music, candlelit tables and mirrored walls provide an attractive, relaxing setting for dishes such as Roquefort and onion soufflé, lamb's liver and bacon with gin and lime sauce and sticky toffee pudding. In the café, you can look forward to an astonishing range: from hot buttered muffins and home-made soups to spicy lamb casserole, country fish pie, Castilean hash and chicken and mint crumble. The influences are both Mediterranean and Oriental, though the cooking is essentially British. The new garden room extension is a major attraction, allowing outdoor eating in summer.

NEWBURY   Regency Park Hotel

Bowling Green Road, Thatcham, Newbury, Berkshire, RG13 3RP
Tel: (01635) 871555   *Fax:* (01635) 871571   **£45**
Open: lunch & dinner daily
Meals served: lunch 12.30-2.30, dinner 6.30-10.30, Sun 7-9.30
Triple glazing, private balconies and a purpose-built business centre at this
Edwardian house, set in five acres of established grounds. Good facilities make
this a popular business and conference hotel.

NEWCASTLE-UPON-TYNE   Blackgate

Milburn House, The Side, Newcastle-upon-Tyne,
    Tyne & Wear, NE1 3JE
Tel: 0191-261 7356   **£55**
Open: lunch Mon-Fri, dinner Tue-Sat (closed Bank Holidays)
Meals served: lunch 12-2, dinner 6.30-10

This restaurant, housed in a former staff dining room in an old office
blockhas a Victorian feel to it. The cooking is modern British in style
with a choice between set menus and à la carte. Beef and oxtail broth
or home-soused herring with an onion compote are typical of starters.
Main-course dishes might include casserole of chicken with chives and
forest mushrooms, or Northumbrian venison with walnuts and an apricot timbale. To finish, apple flan or brown bread trifle, or a choice of
British cheeses.

NEWCASTLE-UPON-TYNE   Café Procope

35 The Side, Newcastle-upon-Tyne, Tyne & Wear, NE1 3JE
Tel: 0191-232 3848   **£40**
Open: all day Tue-Sun (closed 25 Dec, 1 Jan)
Meals served: 11-10.30

Informal bistro-style restaurant with an eclectic à la carte menu showing many different influences: Mediterranean, West African, Mexican,
Malaysian and Indian, to name but a few. Typical starters: baby
shrimps in a Spanish-style tomato sauce; Lithuanian potatoes—sautéed
onions, bacon and potatoes in a sour cream sauce; and carrot kofta with
a red lentil sauce. Main courses range from pan-fried trout with a hot,
garlicky tomato sauce to Ho Sonia! – a generous T-bone steak with
roast onion gravy and home-made herby pease pudding. There's lots of
choice within courses. Local art is exhibited on the premises, the exhibitions changing every six weeks.

The menu has travelled almost as much as that of
Pomegranates in London!

NEWCASTLE-UPON-TYNE — Courtney's

5-7 The Side, Quayside, Newcastle-upon-Tyne,
Tyne & Wear, NE1 3JE
Tel: 0191-232 5537 **£55**
Open: lunch Mon-Fri, dinner Mon-Sat (closed Bank Holidays,
2 wks May)
Meals served: lunch 12-2, dinner 7-10.30

Simple, yet elegant, this restaurant in the city's trendy gastronomic quarter offers good, sound cooking with an English bias. To start, there could be scallop mousse with a lemon and basil vinaigrette, goat's cheese and leek filo with a walnut salad or terrine of guinea fowl with a thyme dressing. Main courses from the à la carte include dishes such as beef fillet with a sherry and truffle sauce or grilled calf's liver with bacon, while vegetarian choices, of which there are always several, might include tomato and aubergine gratin, vegetable stroganoff or spinach and Swiss cheese tart. To finish, floating islands with praline, raspberry crème brûlée or hot apple strudel with honey ice cream. Lunch-time sees the addition of a fixed price two- or three-course menu.

NEWCASTLE-UPON-TYNE — Fisherman's Lodge

7 Jesmond Dene, Jesmond, Newcastle-upon-Tyne,
Tyne & Wear, NE7 7BQ
Tel: 0191-281 3281 *Fax:* 0191-281 6410 **£55**
Open: lunch Mon-Fri, dinner Mon-Sat (closed Bank Holidays)
Meals served: lunch 12-2, dinner 7-11

Seafood is the speciality at this long-established restaurant in the North East, situated in the middle of Jesmond Dene Park, just two miles from Newcastle city centre. Fresh lobster, salmon with scallops and asparagus or a medley of pan-fried fish and shellfish in a langoustine sauce are examples. There are plenty of meat options too: prime local beef and Northumbrian lamb are also specialities. Expect to find traditional dishes like steak Diane alongside more exotic, unusual creations like Chinese-style beef satay with a prawn pilaff. The extensive à la carte and fixed-price dinner menus are complemented by a vegetarian one, and lunchtime offers a good choice of lighter meals.

NEWCASTLE-UPON-TYNE   21 Queen Street

21 Queen Street, Princes Wharf, Newcastle,
  Tyne & Wear, NE1 3UG
Tel: 0191-222 0755   *Fax:* 0191-230 5875   **£70**
Open: lunch Mon-Fri, dinner Mon-Sat (closed Bank Holidays,
  2 wks Aug)
Meals served: lunch 12-2, dinner 7-10.45

Chef-patron Terence Laybourne's sophisticated, pastel coloured,
French restaurant is a real find in this part of the world. Careful planning and execution of dishes resulting in delightful
rewards on the plate. Start perhaps with seared
scallops with black bean chili and salsa or warm
potato pancake with smoked salmon, caviar and
crème fraîche, followed by turbot with lobster
mousse, classic tournedos Rossini or medallions of Kielder venison with a spicy lentil compote. Lovely desserts might feature lemon
brûlée, orange tart or a wicked chocolate
extravaganza! The lunchtime menu offers a
heartier, simpler choice, such as asparagus
risotto, monkfish fricassée and spicy lamb
sausage with couscous salad. Pictured,
Terence Laybourne.

NORTH HARROW   Percy's Restaurant

66-68 Station Road, North Harrow, Middlesex, HA2 7SJ
Tel: 0181-427 2021   *Fax:* 0181-427 8134   **£50**
Open: lunch & dinner Tue-Sat (closed 27-30 Dec)
Meals served: lunch 12-3, dinner 6.30-10

This bright, wine bar-turned-restaurant is run by former turf accountant Tony (front of house) and wife Tina (in the kitchen) Bricknell-
Webb. Tina is completely self-taught: her style of cooking is a happy
blend of modern English and French, with some unusual yet interesting departures. Fresh vegetables and herbs are supplied by their own
40-acre farm in Devon. Starters might include grilled chèvre with a
mild rouille, crab, asparagus and lobster chowder and fricassée of frogs
legs; main courses—wild venison haunch (a speciality), skate fillet
encasing buffalo mozzarella and spinach, or sautéed calf's livers with
mushroom, marsala and peppercorn jus. Desserts range from lime and
cardamon crème brûlée to home-made ices and sorbets, plus British
and French farmhouses cheeses.

NORTHALLERTON   **Bettys**

188 High Street, Northallerton, North Yorkshire, DL7 8LF
Tel: (01609) 775154   *Fax:* (01609) 777552   **£30**
Open: all day daily (closed 25 & 26 Dec, 1 Jan)
Meals served: 9-5.30 (Sun from 10)

When in Yorkshire, go to Bettys. This is one of four, the others (qv) being in Harrogate, Ilkley and York. First established in Harrogate in 1919 by a Swiss confectioner, Frederick Belmont, today the operation is still in the hands of his descendants. The repertoire covers more than 400 lines of home cooking and baking: anything from warm Yorkshire oatcakes and delicious home-made soup and breads, to smoked salmon pasta and Amadeus torte -layers of sweet (or short-crust) pastry with a wild black cherry and cream filling, dusted with cocoa and cinnamon.

Essentially a wonderful tea shop with memories of yesterday in food and service.

NORTHLEACH   **Old Woolhouse**

Market Place, Northleach, Gloucestershire, GL54 3EE
Tel: (01451) 860366   **£75**
Open: dinner Tue-Sat (closed 1 wk Xmas)
Meals served: dinner 8-9.30   ✿

Sound, honest French cooking is the beauty of this small, low-beamed, Cotswold-stone restaurant run for 20 years with dedication and commitment by Jacques and Jenny Astic. At around 8pm, Jenny will read out to you the daily-changing, fixed-price menu of about six main

courses, while Jacques is busy creating it in the kitchen from the freshest ingredients available. Fish depends on the catch delivered. All-time favourite dishes include poulet au porto, and calf's sweetbreads and kidneys in cassis. First-class bread and coffee and some super wines. This is a tiny, much-loved restaurant where booking is essential.

Biography

Jacques Astic is a quiet, self-effacing man, who went into the restaurant business because of family connections in his birthplace, Lyon. After three years at hotel school, and some early experience in France, he

Jacques

Astic

came to England and worked in various good restaurants, before settling at The Old Woolhouse in Northleach, to the delight of those in the `know'. Customers flock to his door, and as far as he is concerned, knowing that his customers are happy is all Jacques needs—no fuss, no false compliments. But it is no false compliment to say that he is a very good chef indeed.

NORTHLEACH   Wickens

Market Place, Northleach, Gloucestershire, GL54 3EJ
Tel: (01451) 860421   **£45**
Open: lunch & dinner Tue-Sat (closed lunch in winter,
     Bank Holidays)
Meals served: lunch 12.15-1.30, dinner 7.20-9

"Everything is a pretext for a good dinner," (Jean Anouilh) recalls a
recent menu from Christopher and Joanna Wickens charming little
English restaurant at the heart of this typically English village. Here
you'll get modern English cooking minus much of the fuss: typical
dishes from Christopher might include Cotswold lamb casseroled in
nut brown ale and topped with horseradish dumplings or a steak of
hake baked in a garlicky breadcrumb crust with shellfish gravy. Joanna
is in charge of seasonal home-made puds which change daily. Light
lunches offer home-made soup, speciality open sandwiches, char-
grilled steaks or perhaps a trio of locally-made pork and leek sausages,
mashed potato and parsnip. Good local farmhouse cheeses. A really
innovative wine list gives you the rare opportunity to try over 20
English wines and as many again from the New World.

NORTON   Hundred House Hotel

Norton, Nr Shifnal, Shropshire, TF11 9EE
Tel: (0195 271) 353   *Fax:* (0195 271) 355   **£50**
Open: lunch & dinner daily
Meals served: lunch 12-2.30, dinner 6.15-10 (Sun 7-9)

Family-run, part creeper-clad Georgian inn with ten rooms, on the
Telford/Bridgnorth road, where chef Stuart Phillips brings things right
up-to-date with a menu which shows a distinctly modern outlook.
Starters include broccoli and almond soup; warm country pigeon salad
with mushrooms, croutons and bacon; pithiviers of salmon with pernod
sauce; main-course offerings might be blanquette of rabbit with cider
and artichoke sauce, home-made salmon fish cakes with tomato and
cumin sauce and free-range duck with blackcurrant sauce. Delicious
puds like hot treacle tart, poached pears with vanilla ice cream and butterscotch sauce—or a selection of all nine, plus fresh fruit and home-
made ice cream for an amazing £7.50! Traditional bar food (steak pies,
lasagne and moussaka) is available throughout the day in the bar. The
house takes its name from medieval times (from the hundred court
divisions—JPs met at the "hundred house"). Parts of the house (timbered and thatched) date back to the 14th century; a local court is said
to have been held in the old barn for centuries.

NORWICH   Adlard's

79 Upper St Giles Street, Norwich, Norfolk, NR2 1AB
Tel: (01603) 633522   **£75**
Open: lunch & dinner Tue-Sat (closed 1 wk Xmas)
Meals served: lunch 12.30-1.45, dinner 7.30-10.30

David Adlard's fine cooking seems to improve year on year, with perfectly judged combinations of ingredients. Hot foie gras comes with Puy lentils, sherry vinegar sauce and grapes; char-gilled smoked salmon with a tartlet of quail egg on beurre blanc. Main courses might be rack of lamb with tapenade crust served with grilled Mediterranean vegetables, roast garlic and gratin dauphinoise; whilst loin of venison with juniper sauce has red cabbage, spätzle and bacon to accompany it. Puddings are equally imaginative: caramelised pears with mascarpone cheesecake or a tulip of prune and armagnac ice cream with hot spiced compôte of prunes. Lunch is perhaps one of the best value meals in Britain, and as if choosing the food were not difficult enough the wine list has just about everything worth drinking at prices that make them drinkable!

A pleasant, relaxed restaurant with helpful, attentive service

NORWICH   Brasted's

8-10 St Andrew's Hill, Norwich, Norfolk, NR2 1DS
Tel: (01603) 625949   **£50**
Open: lunch Mon-Fri, dinner Mon-Sat (closed Bank Holidays)
Meals served: lunch 12-2, dinner 7-10

A cosy, intimate, little restaurant tucked away in the old part of the city, close to the Cathedral and Castle. English with a French influence is how chef Adrian Clarke describes his inspired cooking; and among his specialities he lists fish, and beef stroganoff. Start with Brasted's own cheese parcels served with a home-made apple and thyme jelly, or smoked haddock savoury custard, before going on to sample the roast quail with Madeira sauce or fillets of lemon sole Dieppoise. Daily specials, with the chef's own comment and explanation, are a nice personal touch.

NORWICH   **Greens Seafood Restaurant**

82 Upper St Giles Street, Norwich, Norfolk, NR2 1LT
Tel: (01603) 623733   *Fax:* (01603) 615268   **£50**
Open: lunch Tue-Fri, dinner Mon-Sat (closed Bank Holidays, 1 wk Xmas)
Meals served: lunch 12.15-2.15, dinner 7-10.45
Atmospheric seafood bar and restaurant, with sepia fishing prints on the walls.
Lighter options on a lunchtime blackboard menu, more sophisticated by night.

NORWICH   Marco's

17 Pottergate, Norwich, Norfolk, NR2 1DS
Tel: (01603) 624044   **£55**
Open: lunch & dinner Tue-Sat (closed Bank Holidays)
Meals served: lunch 12.30-2, dinner 7-10

Vibrant Marco Vessalio is likely to greet you from the door of his
kitchen where for the last 24 years, in steadfastly untrendy yet skilful
fashion, he has been producing quintessential provincial Italian dishes.
Warm beef carpaccio, gnocchi with wild mushroom sauce, tagliolini
with smoked salmon sauce, scallops of monkfish with pink pepper
sauce, beef fillet with Barbera wine sauce are the sort of thing he likes
to cook. Finish perhaps with Italian-style bread-and-butter pudding
served with a glass of prosecco, or classic zabaglione. The extensive
carte is supplemented at lunch-time by a fixed-price menu of somewhat
simpler design.

NORWICH   St Benedicts Grill

9 St Benedicts Street, Norwich, Norfolk, NR2 4PE
Tel: (01603) 765377   **£35**
Open: lunch & dinner Tue-Sat (closed 25 Dec, 1 Jan)
Meals served: lunch 12-2, dinner 7-10 (Fri & Sat to 10.30)

This is a brasserie-cum-restaurant run by husband-and-wife team Nigel
and Jayne Raffles. The menu is short, the prices reasonable, and the
service friendly. Chunky fish and tarragon sausages with creamed
spinach or tempura of giant prawns with an oriental dip might open the
meal; a cassoulet of crispy duck or roast chump of lamb with saffron
mash and a rosemary sauce for main courses. Nigel's cooking is both
competent and inventive.

NOTTINGHAM   Loch Fyne Oyster Bar

17 Kings Street, Nottingham, Nottinghamshire, NG1 2AY
Tel: (0115) 9508481   **£35**
Open: all day Mon-Sat (closed Bank Holidays)
Meals served: 9-8.30 (Thu-Sat to 10.30)

An offshoot of the mother establishment at the head of Loch Fyne in
Cairndow, Scotland, the oyster bar is supplied direct from Loch Fyne
overnight. Pop in for a seafood or smoked fish feast – Cairngow has its
own smokehouse—or simply indulge yourself in oysters! Other more
humble attractions include the likes of mussel stew and Arbroath
smokies.

NOTTINGHAM — Sonny's

3 Carlton Street, Hockley, Nottingham,
  Nottinghamshire, NG1 1NL
Tel: (0115) 9473041 **£35**
Open: lunch & dinner daily (closed 25 & 26 Dec, 1 Jan)
Meals served: lunch 12-2.30, dinner 7-10.30 (Fri & Sat to 11),
  (light meals in cafe Mon-Sat 11-3.30)

Sister to the branch in London (qv), this smart but informal restaurant is popular with a youngish clientele for its modern, appropriately informal decor as well as the excellent-value menus, styled to Rebecca Mascarenhas' fashion. The chef here is Graeme Watson, and he offers a fixed price or à la carte choice with the likes of goats cheese soufflé with roast beetroot and roquette, Yucatan grilled chicken breast with tomato salsa, or asparagus and sun dried tomato risotto. Like its London counterpart, Sonny's also offers a café menu from mid-morning to mid-afternoon.

OAKHAM — Hambleton Hall

Hambleton, Nr Oakham, Leicestershire, LE15 8TH
Tel: (01572) 756991   *Fax:* (01572) 724721 **£70**
Open: lunch & dinner daily
Meals served: lunch 12-2, dinner 7-9.30

In a spectacular lakeside setting in unspoilt Rutland country, Tim and Stefa Hart's elegant and imposing 15-bedroomed Victorian house is one of the finest in the country. Rooms combine luxury with homely comforts and are filled with Anne Taylor's magnificent flower arrangements. Young chef Aaron Patterson (pictured) heads a talented team which keeps up the standards set throughout the rest of the house. The cooking is essentially English and French and is of outstanding quality. Seasonal à la carte and fixed-price menus use first-rate raw materials—local game, and produce from the hotel's own garden. Typical starters could include ballotine of duck with slivers of duck ham, or Mediterranean vegetable gâteau with mussels and a saffron vinaigrette.  Roast loin of beef encased in a crispy Yorkshire pudding or honey-roasted Gressingham duck with beetroot, turnips and a jasmine tea sauce could follow, while fish creations might include brill in its own juices flavoured with chives, millefeuille of halibut and langoustines with an orange and parsley crust and fennel sauce, or tagliatelle with roasted scallops served with a light champagne sauce. Desserts are just divine: hot passion fruit soufflé, lemon tart with pears and a red wine sauce, and praline parfait in caramelised pastry with a compôte of rhubarb. British and Continental cheeses are served with delicious walnut bread. Interesting wine list with a range of prices and some good Californians. You will not be disappointed here.

OAKHAM — Whipper-In Hotel

Market Place, Oakham, Leicestershire, LE15 6DT
Tel: (01572) 756971   *Fax:* (01572) 757759   **£30**
Open: lunch & dinner daily
Meals served: lunch 12.30-2, dinner 7.30-9.30

Traditional charm and hospitality are the strong points at this 17th-century inn. Bedrooms, of which there are 24, are traditionally furnished with a mixture of antique and reproduction furniture. The cooking, under Carl Bontoft, is both sound and imaginative. Good-value set lunch (£9.95) and dinner (£12.95) and a short à la carte menu feature the likes of dishes such as smoked salmon tagliatelle in a creamy mushroom sauce, or Scotch beef with haggis and a whisky sauce. Oakham is just two miles from the largest man-made lake in Europe, Rutland Water, where there is fishing, sailing and surfing.

OLD BURGHCLERE — Dew Pond

Old Burghclere, Newbury, Berkshire, RG15 9LH
Tel: (01635) 278408   **£55**
Open: dinner Tue-Sat (closed 2 wks Jan, 2 wks Aug)
Meals served: dinner 7-10

Keith Marshall's cooking has established a fine reputation at this attractive family restaurant. The menu has predominantly French influences with the odd flourish of Eastern flavours. Six first courses might include a sausage of guinea fowl with caramelised apples and Calvados sauce, a mussel broth flavoured with saffron, coriander and chili garnished with tomato and spring onion, and rillettes of pheasant with garlic vinaigrette. Next you could try the fillet of sea bass with fennel and ginger- scented sauce, or roast brace of quail layered with potato rösti, apricots and almonds, or saddle of venison with pastry boats of creamed wild mushrooms on Madeira sauce. Lovely puddings too: hot chocolate soufflé comes with vanilla pod ice cream and bitter chocolate sauce, or a baked banana in puff pastry with almond cream and butterscotch sauce. Carefully selected wines begin at £8.00. A real find, and the perfect place to celebrate after a win at the local races.

OLD MINSTER LOVELL — Lovells at Windrush Farm

Old Minster Lovell, Oxfordshire, OX8 5RN
Tel: (01993) 779802   *Fax:* (01993) 779802   **£65**
Open: lunch & dinner Tue-Sun (closed 3 wks Jan)
Meals served: lunch 12-2, dinner 8-9.30

New chef Marcus Ashenford (previously at the Waterside Inn, Bray, and Calcot Manor, Tetbury with Ramon Farthing) brings a blend of classical and and international cuisine to this small, elegant dining room, set in 80 acres of grounds. Daily-changing fixed-price menus (no choice) are well thought-out, with lunch a three-course affair, and dinner a seven-course menu of beautifully balanced courses. A typical meal from an early autumn menu might commence with fish cakes with continental leaves and lemon oil, followed by onion and garlic soup, then fillet of turbot provençale, topped with brioche crumbs with a rosemary sauce. A pre-dessert course, perhaps a chaud-froid of peach tea and lime water ice, prepares the way for dessert itself—peach sabayon, caramel and almond ice cream in a brandy snap basket, followed by coffee and petits fours. Two rooms upstairs, in the main house, provide good overnight accommodation. The River Windrush flows through the grounds and Lovells has over a mile of fishing rights.

ORFORD   Butley-Orford Oysterage

Market Hill, Orford, Woodbridge, Suffolk, IP12 2LH
Tel: (01394) 450277   *Fax:* (01394) 450949   *Simple, down* **£30**
Open: lunch & dinner daily (closed 25 & 26 Dec)   *to earth and interesting.*
Meals served: lunch 12-2.15, dinner 6.30-8.30

Oyster lovers will find their fancies favoured here—oysters from their own beds are the speciality of the house. There's oyster soup, oyster cocktails, fresh Butley oysters with brown bread, grilled bacon and oysters on toast, hot salmon cutlet with oyster sauce—but it's not all oysters. Smoked mackerel, trout, sprats, cod roe, eel and wild Irish salmon, cured daily in their own smokehouses, are also here to tempt you. Daily blackboard specials depend on the local catch. Wash it all down with a glass of wine: the list, European only, includes the local English whites.

OSWESTRY   Restaurant Sebastian

45 Willow Street, Oswestry, Shropshire, SY11 1AQ
Tel: (01691) 655444   **£35**
Open: lunch Wed-Fri, dinner Tue-Sat (closed Bank Holidays)
Meals served: lunch 12-2, dinner 6.30-10.30

The cooking here is predominantly French provincial; the setting an old, beamed, low-ceilinged room with an open fire in the winter, and French music playing in the background. Fresh fish and shellfish is the speciality, collected personally by Mark (Sebastian) or Michelle Fisher from the North Wales coast: seafood bisque, prawn beignets, red mullet with citrus fruit on a coriander and cream sauce or pan-fried Dover sole meunière. For meat eaters, there's a choice of grilled steaks, beef en croûte, magret de canard au cassis or lamb topped with a mint mousse. Home-made foie gras de canard served on a Sauternes jelly with toasted brioche is a favourite among starters. Wide choice of light lunches from the Bouffe du Midi repertoire which includes a host of traditional brasserie-style favourites—soups, salads, steaks and crêpes.

OXFORD   Bath Place Hotel & Restaurant

4 & 5 Bath Place, Holywell Street, Oxford, Oxfordshire, OX1 3SU
Tel: (01865) 791812   *Fax:* (01865) 791834   **£70**
Open: lunch Wed-Sun, dinner Tue-Sat
Meals served: lunch 12-2, dinner 7-10 (Fri & Sat to 10.30)

There are ten rooms for overnight accommodation, some with four-posters, in this pretty, little, family-run establishment (a cluster of 17th-century cottages) down a cobbled lane in the oldest part of town. Head chef Jeremy Blake O'Connor brings a wealth of experience and his very own personal style to bear on the kitchen team. There are high hopes of things to come here. The no-choice residents' menu (£16.50, with £5 supplement for guests) is well-thought-out, simple and concise. Mediterranean influences abound: cassoulet, Italian-style lamb, fillet of hake Basque-style. The regular carte (non-residents and residents alike) offers more sophisticated combinations, a point made by the wordy descriptions on the menu. New season lamb fillet sliced and laid on a bed of ratatouille with potato pancake is served with a vegetable tartelette, timbale of spinach and potato fondant, for example. Elsewhere you'll find the likes of twice-baked Gruyère soufflé, terrine of venison and hare saddle and pigeon breast, or pan-fried Cornish red mullet with bouillabaisse butter sauce and sautéed scallop. A good selection of wines with lots of variety and plenty of good half bottles.

OXFORD   Browns

5-11 Woodstock Road, Oxford, Oxfordshire, OX2 6HA
Tel: (01865) 511995   *Fax:* (01865) 52347   **£35**
Open: all day daily (closed 25 & 26 Dec)
Meals served: 11am-11.30pm (Sun from 12)

Browns is almost as much a part of Oxford as the colleges, an integral part of life for students and locals alike. Eat what you fancy when you wish, be it breakfast, a sandwich or a substantial lunch or dinner. Kids love it, too, as they have their own menu and special tea parties that would make the Mad Hatter envious! Other branches of Browns can be found in Brighton, Bristol and Cambridge.

OXFORD   Cherwell Boathouse

Bardwell Road, Oxford, Oxfordshire, OX2 6SR
Tel: (01865) 52746   *Fax:* (01865) 391459   **£40**
Open: lunch Wed-Sun, dinner Tue-Sat
    (closed Bank Holidays, 1 wk Xmas)
Meals served: lunch 12-2, dinner 7-10.30

Not easy to find but well worth the effort on a sunny day! Anthony Verdin's converted boathouse on the river Cherwell offers short, three-course fixed price menus that change weekly, offering the likes of sea bream with basil and saffron, or grilled leg of lamb with redcurrant and port sauce. Vegetarians could have stuffed artichoke hearts with ratatouille and parmesan or peppers stuffed with creamy fennel and goat's cheese. Afterwards there's British cheese, sticky toffee pudding or perhaps marmalade ice cream. Wines are good and reasonably priced, so don't overdo it if you have to punt home! Now in its 27th year, the Cherwell Boathouse has served generations of students who make the pilgrimage back to enjoy its special ambience.

OXFORD — Restaurant Elizabeth

82 St Aldate's, Oxford, Oxfordshire, OX1 1RA
Tel: (01865) 242230   **£65**
Open: lunch & dinner Tue-Sun (closed Good Friday, 24-30 Dec)
Meals served: lunch 12.30-2.30, dinner 6.30-11 (Sun 7-10.30)

People come and go, but not Antonio Lopez, pictured, who has been in charge here for more than 35 years, with chef Salvador Rodriguez clocking up over 15 years at the stove. A relaxed atmosphere and a warm welcome await, along with a menu which centres on classical continental dishes, with a bias towards French, such as chicken liver pâté, quenelles of salmon, Basque-inspired piperade, beef stroganoff and sliced breast of duck with orange sauce. Simpler lunchtime set menu which offers good value at £15, with three choices at each stage. The wine list is a classic, too, with exceptional depth in burgundies and clarets.

OXFORD — 15 North Parade

15 North Parade Avenue, Oxford, Oxfordshire, OX2 6LX
Tel: (01865) 513773   **£50**
Open: lunch Tue-Sun, dinner Tue-Sat
   (closed some Bank Holidays)
Meals served: lunch 12-2, dinner 7-11

In a narrow street just north of the city centre, you'll find Georgina Wood's attractive little restaurant where son Sean and colleague Ben Gorman have brought about a new and more modern lease of life. Sean and Ben took over the cooking in April 1994, introducing an eclectic menu of contemporarily-inspired dishes. Set lunches and daily specials supplement the carte. Expect the likes of parsleyed ham and ox tongue terrine, Boston crab cakes with piquant mayonnaise, stewed squid Andalucian-style or a lightly curried corn chowder to start. For a main course, try the hamburger with spicy yellow catsup, red onion relish and chunky chips; calzone with roasted peppers or a tureen of seafood in a clear Thai-scented fish consommé. The cool, minimalist decor is a suitable match for the menu. Those who thought they knew 15 will find a whole new concept in operation. Lovely patio at the rear for alfresco dining.

OXFORD — GEE'S BRASSERIE

61a Banbury Road, Oxford, Oxfordshire, OX2 6PE
Tel: (01865) 53540   **£40**
Open: lunch & dinner daily (closed 25 & 26 Dec)
Meals served: lunch 12-2.30, dinner 6-11.30

This pretty, tiled conservatory offers a wide selection of brasserie-style dishes, prepared by chef Graham Corbett, who is particularly skilful in his use of herbs and spices. Good pasta and imaginative salads and starters are featured along with rack of lamb with a herb crust and onion confit, rare-grilled tuna fillet with a spicy Thai dip and traditional Sunday roast. A brunch/light lunch section of the carte features ham and cheese croûte with eggs, traditional English breakfast and a variety of omelettes. Staff are young, informal and friendly: flair and imagination in an unusual setting.

OXFORD — Old Parsonage Hotel

1 Banbury Road, Oxford, OX2 6NN
Tel: (01865) 310210   *Fax:* (01865) 311262   **£45**
Open: lunch & dinner daily (closed 23-27 Dec)
Meals served: lunch 12-3, dinner 6-11
(light meals in bar 7am-11pm)

With a history that includes being a sanctuary for persecuted clergy, a stronghold for Royalists during the Civil War and home for the likes of Oscar Wilde, the honey-coloured Old Parsonage has 30 individually-decorated bedrooms, each with its own marble-fitted bathroom. The Parsonage Bar serves good food at reasonable prices with dishes ranging from salmon cakes served with lemon mayonnaise, grilled bacon and goat's cheese salad to grilled sirloin steak with french fries and salad. Well-chosen wine list (over ten wines by the glass) and friendly service help to make this a special place.

PADSTOW   **Seafood Restaurant**

Riverside, Padstow, Cornwall, PL28 8BY
Tel: (01841) 532485   *Fax:* (01841) 533344   **£65**
Open: lunch & dinner Mon-Sat
  (closed late Dec-end Jan, May Day)
Meals served: lunch 12.30-2.15, dinner 7-9.30

Rick Stein (pictured below) is to fish what Armani is to fashion—a modern classicist! During the last two decades he has established a unique restaurant alongside the harbour of this picturesque, Cornish fishing village. It has the buzz of a busy London restaurant drawing 'afishionados' from far and wide to enjoy his superb cooking. Try a mixture of hot shellfish served with olive oil, garlic and lemon juice, scallops and squid with black noodles and parsley, quenelles of gurnard with lobster sauce, John Dory with olives, capers and rosemary or just a few Helford oysters. To follow you might have char-grilled fillets of monkfish and Dover sole with a sauce of sun-dried tomatoes, garlic and tarragon, red mullet

with spiced fish sausages, grilled Padstow lobster with herbs, turbot with mussels or a groaning platter of seafoods served in the shells. There is sirloin steak if you must! The Steins have now bought St. Petroc's hotel just a few yards down the road, providing an additional eight bedrooms and giving Rick the chance to demonstrate further his culinary skills in the bistro. Here you will find equally tempting food such as salmon fishcakes with aiöli, warm salad of smoked duck breasts with new potatoes and dandelions (yes, dandelions, delicious!), baked hake with lemon, bayleaf, onion and garlic or grilled Tywardreath sausages with spring onion, mashed potato and onion gravy. Who needs London?

Biography

A chef's curriculum vitae tends usually to be a lengthy list of work experience. Not so for Rick Stein—his is short and sweet—six months as a management trainee at the Great Western Hotel, Paddington; a degree
Rick   *in English at Oxford University—and that's that! Opening*
          his charming seafood restaurant was prompted by childhood
Stein   *memories of his parents' holiday home in Cornwall and his*
          father's fishing boat. From here Rick has evolved his individual style and enjoys what he considers to be his greatest pleasure, developing new recipes and seeing them work.

PAINSWICK   Painswick Hotel

Kemps Lane, Painswick, Gloucestershire, GL6 6YB
Tel: (01452) 812160   *Fax:* (01452) 812059   **£55**
Open: lunch Sun, dinner daily
Meals served: lunch Sun only 12.30-2, dinner 7-9.30 (Sun to 8.30)

Painswick is often referred to as "the Queen of the Cotswolds" because
architecturally it is so interesting. The hotel is tucked away in the centre behind the church, down narrow streets, and is the former rectory.
The house is Palladian in style, much of it dating back to the end of the
18th century. In the spacious, relaxing dining room, choose from the à
la carte or seafood menu: perhaps a filo skillet of home-smoked
chicken with aubergine, sun-dried tomatoes and a mozzarella glaze, or
a warm salad of pigeon with beetroot and orange to start, followed by
either medallions of venison with a timbale of barley and bacon served
with a red wine sauce or grilled cutlet of monkfish with mussels and
fennel. To finish, perhaps hot Cumbrian apple pudding served with
sauce anglaise or a selection of mainly Gloucestershire cheeses with
homemade oatcakes. The Moore family run their 20-bedroomed establishment in relaxed style, in contrast to the apparent grandeur and elegance within. Accommodation varies from spacious rooms in the
original building to smaller, more modest ones in the new wing.
Breakfast, with freshly-squeezed orange juice and some lovely smoky
bacon, is the one meal not to be missed!

PAULERSPURY   Vine House

100 High Street, Paulerspury, Northamptonshire, NN12 7NA
Tel: (01327) 811267   *Fax:* (01327) 811309   **£50**
Open: lunch Tue-Fri, dinner Mon-Sat (closed 26-30 Dec)
Meals served: lunch 12-2.30, dinner 7-10.30

Marcus and Julie Springett's aim is to offer a relaxing home-from-home
atmosphere at their six-bedroomed house, a 300-year-old limestone cottage in rural Northamptonshire. Everything, from bread to petits fours,
is home-made. There is a cosy bar with log fire for pre-dinner drinks
before you go into the bright yet characterful dining room for whatever
daily treats Marcus has in store. This is English country cooking—
breast of duckling with mushy peas and a fresh mint sauce, and home-
made chicken and bacon sausage with bread sauce and sage gravy are
examples of the main courses. Coffee with sweetmeats to finish. There
are six en-suite rooms, one with four-poster. The house stands in its
own grounds and has a delightful cottage garden.

PENKRIDGE — William Harding's House

Mill Street, Penkridge, Stafford, Staffordshire, ST19 5AY
Tel: (0178 571) 2955   **£45**
Open: lunch first & last Sun in month only, dinner Tue-Sat
(closed Bank Holidays)
Meals served: lunch at 1, dinner 7.30-9.30

This small, cottagey restaurant run by Eric and Fiona Bickley is a welcome find in the gastronomic wilderness of Staffordshire. The cooking (Eric's domain) is both classic and innovative; his fixed-price menus offer plenty of choice and change every eight-ten weeks: ragoût of shellfish in cream and vermouth; sliced roulade of smoked salmon; escalopes of veal on a herb green sauce; rich chocolate flan; orange and rice brûlée. The dining room operates on a one-sitting-only basis, so feel free to linger over your meal. A newly launched supper club meets once a month and offers great value.

PENZANCE — Abbey Hotel

Abbey Street, Penzance, Cornwall, TR18 4AR
Tel: (01736) 66906   *Fax:* (01736) 51163   **£50**
Open: dinner daily (closed 24-26 Dec)
Meals served: dinner 7.30-8.30

The abbey dates back to 1660, and has been lovingly restored by owners (since 1976) Michael and Jean Cox. The building is perched above the quay, overlooking the town and St Michael's Mount beyond and is decorated with antiques and comfortable sofas. The atmosphere is relaxed and friendly and the tiny, informal restaurant, with only six tables, offers sound French cooking. A table d'hôte offers three choices for each course. Courgette and blue cheese soup or quenelles of salmon with cream to start; followed by roast quail with a lemon and orange sauce or roast breast of duck on a bed of aubergine provençale; and to finish—chilled soufflé of lemon and lime or purée of chestnut and chocolate slice.

PLUMTREE — Perkins Bar & Bistro

Old Railway Station, Station Road, Plumtree,
Nottinghamshire, NG12 5NA
Tel: (01602) 373695   *Fax:* (01602) 376405   **£35**
Open: lunch & dinner Tue-Sat (closed Bank Holidays, 1 wk Xmas)
Meals served: lunch 12-2.30, dinner 6.30-9.45

The demise of British Rail has actually created more activity in Plumtree station than was ever probably seen during its heyday! Tim and Wendy Perkins have created an attractive bar and bistro within its walls and serve a good-value mix of modern and classic French cooking. Old favourites such as onion soup gratinée and poached egg Florentine vie with warm salad of seared scallops, samphire with mint vinaigrette and tomato, olive, mozzarella and pesto tart. Traditional dishes like entrecote bearnaise and osso bucco are offered along with a magret of duck with apricot and prune stuffing or brochette of monkfish and bacon with chive butter sauce and basmati rice. The well-composed menus change frequently and daily specials are available. In the summer there's additional seating on the old platform—luckily, no trains!

PLYMOUTH	Chez Nous

13 Frankfort Gate, Plymouth, Devon, PL1 1QA
Tel: (01752) 266793   *Fax:* (01752) 660428   **£65**
Open: lunch & dinner Tue-Sat (closed Bank Holidays,
   3 wks Feb, 3 wks Sep)
Meals served: lunch 12.30-2, dinner 7-10.30

Friendly, informal bistro-style restaurant in a parade of shops where Jacques Marchal cooks with skill, confidence and spontaneity: Cuisine Spontanée is what he calls it. He is content to remain faithful to his origins yet still seeks and finds new inspiration. French blue-painted tables and chairs, dado darkwood-panelling and attractive wall posters create a pretty and authentic French setting for what follows. Choose from the blackboard, set menus or à la carte: French onion soup, chicken liver mousse with walnut brioche, chicken breast with ginger, pork with tamarind sauce and fillet of beef with pleurottes or béarnaise sauce are typical. Eat as you please, there's no pressure to stick to a traditional format here.

Jacques continues to go from strength to strength here.

PLYMOUTH	Piermasters Restaurant

33 Southside Street, The Barbican, Plymouth, Devon, PL1 2LE
Tel: (01752) 229345   **£50**
Open: lunch & dinner Mon-Sat (closed Xmas,
   Bank Holidays except Easter)
Meals served: lunch 12-2, dinner 7-10 (later for post-theatre suppers)

It is mainly for the fish and seafood that many come to this bustling, quayside restaurant. You could start perhaps with gratin of crab and spinach, provençal fish soup or duck galantine. Main course fish dishes might include Dover sole with a Noilly Prat sauce, whole grilled lemon sole, monkfish with fresh herbs or grilled sea bass with Tuscan olive oil. Carnivores might choose between steak with wild mushrooms or medallions of venison with mushrooms and a truffle essence. Simple traditional desserts and unlimited coffee to finish. Good-value set lunch and weekend menus. Reasonably priced house wine selection plus full list.

POLPERRO	Kitchen at Polperro

The Coombes, Polperro, Cornwall, PL13 2RQ
Tel: (01503) 72780   **£30**
Open: dinner daily (Tue-Sat in winter) (closed Bank Holidays)
Meals served: dinner 7-9.30

The short walk from the village car park will whet your appetite for some fish at Ian and Vanessa Bateson's charming restaurant. The à la carte menu offers a wide range of choice, listing half a dozen or so fish, shellfish, poultry, meat and vegetarian main options. Start with chargrilled Cornish sausages and onion marmalade, deep-fried prawns or crab cocktail, before sampling dishes such as swordfish steak with cream, coriander and lemon. Other main-course options include the likes of crab Dijonnaise, chicken piri-piri, Thai beef, char-grilled Angus beef, mixed bean goulash or mushroom ravioli. An unpretentious wine list starts at £8.60. Excellent value for money.

POOLE   Haven Hotel

Banks Road, Sandbanks, Poole, Dorset, BH13 7QL
Tel: (01202) 707333   *Fax:* (01202) 708796
La Roche Restaurant   **£65**
Open: dinner Tue-Sat (closed 25 & 26 Dec)
Meals served: dinner 7-10.30
Sea View Restaurant   **£45**
Open: lunch & dinner daily
Meals served: lunch 12.30-2, dinner 7-9.30   ❖

At the entrance to the country's second-largest, natural harbour, right on the water's edge, you'll find this 94-bedroomed hotel overlooking Poole Bay, Brownsea Island and the Purbeck Hills. This is primarily a holiday venue with two restaurants, conservatory and terrace, plus excellent facilities in the leisure club staffed by fully qualified instructors, including everything from American hot tub and massage to the latest fitness techniques. The club offers a range of events such as pool parties, barbecues and sporting competitions. Eat in either the Sea View or La Roche restaurants, and choose from table d'hote or à la carte menus respectively. Eclectic dishes from chef Karl Heinz Nagler might include curried chicken soup, ragout of angler fish and tiger prawns, baked stuffed quail in filo pastry with port wine sauce, paupiette of beef with potato rösti, or a simple herb omelette topped with vegetable panaché and cheese. Traditional roast beef with Yorkshire puddings on Sundays.

POOLE   Mansion House

11 Thames Street, Poole, Dorset, BH15 1JN
Tel: (01202) 685666   *Fax:* (01202) 665709   **£45**
Open: lunch Sun-Fri, dinner Mon-Sat
Meals served: lunch 12.30-2, dinner 7.30-9.30 (Sat from 7)

Despite its central location—a stone's throw from the bustling quay and adjacent to St James Church—this 28-bedroomed hotel is an oasis of Georgian-inspired calm at the heart of this unique old town which counts Anthony Caro's sculpture, Sea Music, and the Arts Centre (home of the Bournemouth Symphony Orchestra) among its attractions. The marble-pillared portico and tall, arched windows are the epitome of Georgian elegance. The clubby dining room is smart and relaxed, offering a balanced table d'hôte of modern English cuisine, with local seafood and game well represented. A new bistro, JJs, offers cheaper, more informal eating at both lunch and dinner—anything from poached eggs on spinach with a cheese sauce to grilled rump steak and chips or a salmis of pheasant in its own jus. Blackboard specials feature homemade starters, soups and fish dishes of the day and there are a number of quick fixed-price options. The hors d'oeuvres table at lunch-time has become something of a feature since its recent introduction.

POOL-IN-WHARFEDALE Pool Court

Pool Bank, Pool-in-Wharfedale, Otley, West Yorkshire LS21 1EH
■ See under 42 The Calls, Leeds

PORLOCK Oaks Hotel

Porlock, Somerset, TA24 8ES
Tel & Fax: (01643) 862265 **£45**
Open: dinner daily (closed Jan-Feb)
Meals served: dinner 7-8.30

Looking down on the pretty village and bay of Porlock, Exmoor, this is
a friendly, ten-bedroomed, homely hotel in an Edwardian house surrounding by lawns and majestic old oaks. It's run by Tim and Anne
Riley and Anne's four-course dinners are something of an event. The
daily-changing menu, with ample choice, makes the most of seasonal
produce: the cooking is essentially English, with venison a speciality.
Start with soup (cream of watercress, vegetable, or celery, apple and
tomato) or Stilton beignet soufflé; follow with a fish course—grilled
salmon with cream sauce, scallops in filo pastry or hot smoked
haddock mousse. Main courses could be grilled Devonshire fillet steak
béarnaise, duck with orange or black cherry sauce, or grilled Exmoor
venison with a redcurrant and port wine sauce. For pudding warm
treacle tart with clotted cream is very popular.

POWBURN Breamish Country House Hotel

Powburn, Alnwick, Northumberland, NE66 4LL
Tel: (01665) 578266 *Fax:* (01665) 578500 **£50**
Open: lunch Sun, dinner daily (closed 1 Jan-14 Feb)
Meals served: lunch 12.30-1, dinner 7.30-8

Doreen and Alan Johnson promise peace and quiet at this 11-bed-
roomed house which began life in the 17th century as a farmhouse and
was later converted to a hunting lodge in the 1800s. The gardens are
ablaze with colour in spring, and rooms are named after trees indige-
nous to the surrounding woodland. The kitchen serves traditional
English fare, with game the speciality: mallard, partridge, pheasant,
woodcock, venison and locally-farmed wild boar, plus fish supplied
direct from the quayside at Amble.

PRESTBURY   White House Manor

New Road, The Village, Prestbury, Cheshire, SK10 4HP
Tel: (01625) 829376   *Fax:* (01625) 828627   **£50**
Open: lunch Tue-Sun, dinner Mon-Sat
Meals served: lunch 12-2, dinner 7-10

Nine suites offer a variety of styles of
decor and facilities in the Wakehams' opulent converted manor house. The restaurant is located in a separate building: here,
Ryland Wakeham oversees the cooking of
contemporary British dishes. A well-
planned menu offers Welsh mussels with
mushroom and saffron sauce, croustade
of shellfish in filo pastry with lobster
sauce, a warm pear and Wensleydale
cheese tart or perhaps a warm duck liver
mousse with sprouting lentils and smoked
bacon. Main courses of roast cod with a
vegetable ragoût and aiöli, half a crispy
duck with apple rösti and Calvados sauce,
or perhaps medallions of lamb with black
pudding on bubble and squeak with
tomato and tarragon jus. Also not lacking
imagination are the puddings which range
from caramel orange tart with honey
sabayon to profiteroles filled with blue-

berry cream on toffee sauce. Many of the wines are listed by style—
fruity white, medium bodied, full bodied and so on, which is a helpful
idea.

PUCKRUP   Puckrup Hall

Puckrup, Tewkesbury, Gloucestershire, GL20 6EL
Tel: (01684) 296200 *Fax:* (10684) 850788   **£55/£45**
Open: dinner Wed-Sat
Meals served: dinner 7-9.30, (light meals Brasserie:
    12.30-2.30, 6.30-10 (Fri & Sat to 10.30))

All change here over the last year. The original hotel, with 16 bedrooms, is now an annexe linked by a glass walkway to the main building, a brand new, beautifully designed hotel complex, bringing the total
number of rooms up to 84. The hotel stands in 140 acres of parkland
and is surrounded by its own 18-hole golf course. The choice of places
to eat now stands at four. There's the Regency Room in the original
house, offering a modern British repertoire with dishes such as warm
quail salad with orange followed by roast sea bass with carrots and net-
tles or collops of beef with foie gras and sherry (dinner only). The
more upbeat Balharries Brasserie (named after the chef) offers an
eclectic range of international and traditional dishes, everything from
hoisin chicken and billy can soup to Irish beef and Guinness pie, pizzas, pastas and Bal's burgers – menu sections include the Best of
British, Thrills and Grills, The Italian Job, Sand Which? and Chicken
Lickin' favourites. Something for everyone. Good leisure and conference facilities and golf course complete the picture.

PULBOROUGH — Stane Street Hollow

Codmore Hill, Pulborough, West Sussex, RH20 1BG
Tel: (01798) 872819 — **£50**
Open: lunch Wed-Fri & Sun, dinner Wed-Sat
 (closed 24-27 Dec, 2 wks Jun, 2 wks Nov)
Meals served: lunch 12.30-1.15, dinner 7.15-9.15

Originally two farm cottages built some 450 years ago, Stane Street Hollow still retains a homely, cottagey feel under the influence of owners René and Ann Kaiser, who have run the place for almost 20 years. Swiss-born René offers a short but interesting menu which changes monthly to allow for the best of seasonal produce. He describes his cooking in the broad-reaching terms of European country-style. They grow many of their vegetables, herbs and soft fruit; keep their own ducks and chickens; and smoke their own meat and fish. This is good, sound, capable cooking at its best. Excellent value at lunch-time is the two-course, no-choice menu, which offers main course and dessert – cassoulette of duckling, pheasant and bacon with lentils, perhaps, followed by apple and blackberry pancake for just £8.25. An excellent, comprehensive wine list with a good choice of halves complements the menu and is reasonably priced.

PURTON — Pear Tree

Church End, Purton, Nr Swindon, Wiltshire, SN5 9ED
Tel: (01793) 772100 *Fax:* (01793) 772369 — **£60**
Open: lunch Sun-Fri, dinner daily
Meals served: lunch 12-2, dinner 7-9.30

The Pear Tree, though 400 years old, has only been in its present location since the turn of the century, when it was moved stone by stone from beside the church to its present site on the outskirts of the village. Immaculately kept and well run, the Pear Tree has 18 rooms and suites, each named after local village figures across the ages – anyone from Anne Hyde, mother of Queen Mary and Queen Anne, to the cricketer E H Budd! Good English cooking, makes the most of fresh local produce in dishes such as wild mushroom and chicken consommé or three-cheese mousses to start. Pan-fried lamb's liver, bacon and glazed onions with a tawny port sauce, or grilled fillet of Scotch beef topped with walnut butter on a bed of diced bacon and peppers are possible for main-course selections. Exotic desserts to finish or a good selection of British farmhouse cheeses.

QUORN — Quorn Grange

88 Wood Lane, Quorn, Leicestershire, LE12 8DB
Tel: (01509) 412167 *Fax*: (01509) 415621 — **£55**
Open: lunch Sun-Fri, dinner daily
Meals served: lunch 12-2.30, dinner 7-9.30 (Sat to 10, Sun to 9)
Stylish 17-bedroomed, ivy-clad Victorian house in landscaped gardens. Conservatory bar-lounge and modern English cooking skilfully prepared by chef Gordon Lang.

RAMSBOTTOM — Village Restaurant

18 Market Place, Ramsbottom, Nr Bury,
   Greater Manchester, BL0 9HT
Tel: (01706) 825070   **£25**
Open: lunch Wed-Sun, dinner Wed-Sat
Meals served: lunch 12-2.30 (Sun at 1.30), dinner 7.45

A good local establishment, offering simple, unpretentious, everyday food, but prepared from the highest quality raw ingredients—organic or conservation-grade produce wherever possible. Ros Hunter continues to do the cooking though the old restaurant has now gone, being replaced by this refurbished bistro-style room, furnished with pew seating—the long-legged may find things a little cramped. While salt is provided on all tables, Ros and partner, Chris Johnson, have an aversion to using it in the actual cooking. Weekday lunches from the blackboard menu and four-course Sunday lunch, with prime roast and organic vegetables. Dinner offers three courses, with a choice of around six main courses which determine the overall price. Typical dishes are traditional—everything from smoked salmon and soup starters to cottage pie, smoked meats and char-grilled steaks and fish. An interesting and unusual wine list is available. Ros and Chris have changed with the times and gone the simpler and less expensive route, but it didn't stop them opening their dinner party shop, The Ramsbottom Victuallers, in 1994.

Call for details of their wine tastings.

RAMSEY — Harbour Bistro
5 East Street, Ramsey, Isle of Man
Tel: (01624) 814182   **£40**
Open: lunch daily, dinner Mon-Sat (closed 2 wks Jan, 1 wk Oct)
Meals served: lunch 12-2, dinner 6.30-10.30
Friendly, relaxed bistro near the quay, with fresh seafood and steaks the specialities.

REETH — Burgoyne Hotel
The Green, Reeth, Richmond, North Yorkshire, DLll 6SN
Tel & Fax: (01748) 884292   **£50**
Open: dinner daily (closed Jan & Feb)
Meals served: dinner at 7.45
Small, intimate, eight-bedroomed hotel overlooking the village green, run by friendly, enthusiastic owners. Traditional English cooking.

REIGATE — La Barbe

71 Bell Street, Reigate, Surrey, RH2 7AN
Tel: (01737) 241966   **£50**
Open: lunch Mon-Fri, dinner Mon-Sat (closed Bank Holidays)
Meals served: lunch 12-2, dinner 7-10

A bright and cheerful bistro is the venue for long-serving chef Laurent Pacaud's classic and regional French cuisine. Fixed-price menus, lunch and dinner, which change every two months, are supplemented by a daily two-course blackboard menu. Begin with the likes of guinea fowl and asparagus mousse; followed by beef and morel casserole, fillet of turbot in a champagne velouté or pork fillet cooked in a Roquefort cheese sauce. For dessert, you may find fresh pancake filled with banana cooked in butter and rum, or chestnut mousse topped with fresh Chantilly cream. Menus include wine suggestions which are helpful and instructive.

REIGATE   The Dining Room

59a High Street, Reigate, Surrey, RH2 9AE
Tel: (01737) 226650   **£35**
Open: lunch Mon-Fri, dinner Mon-Sat (closed 2 wks Xmas,
    1 wk Easter, 1 wk Aug)
Meals served: lunch 12-2, dinner 7-10

Paul Montalto keeps a close eye on things front of house at his smart
new restaurant in the high street (above a furniture shop). Chef
Anthony Tobin takes charge in the kitchen, offering both à la carte and
fixed-price menus, all refreshingly short and concise but with ample
choice. His modern style of cooking retains a certain robustness, with
dishes such as sautéed scallops on crispy potato cake with chive cream
followed by baked brill with provençale vegetables or roast lamb with
spicy bean cassoulet. Delicious home-made puds might feature upside
down caramelised pear tart with vanilla ice cream or a chocolate marquise marbled with biscuit and raisins. Round it all off in hedonistic
fashion with a glass of spicy, brambly Fonseca port – or a glass of
Charles Heidsieck champagne.

REMENHAM   The Little Angel

Remenham, Henley-on-Thames, Oxfordshire, RG1 5NN
Tel: (01491) 574165   *Fax:* (01491) 411879   **£35**
Open: lunch & dinner daily (closed 26 Dec)
Meals served: lunch 12-2.15, dinner 7-10.30

Just south of Henley by the bridge, this is a popular pub-restaurant
wich offers an extensive range of dishes in generous portions, from
light snacks to full-blown meals. Eat in the bar, bistro area or restaurant—booking is recommended if you need guaranteed space, otherwise it can get pretty hectic, especially in summer!

RICHMOND   Burnt Chair

---

5 Duke Street, Richmond, Surrey, TW9 1HP
Tel: 0181-940 9488   **£45**
Open: lunch Mon-Fri, dinner Mon-Sat
    (closed 1 wk Xmas, 1 wk Aug)
Meals served: lunch 12-2.30, dinner 6-11

Former accountant Weenson Andrew Oo has put his heart into this
little restaurant around the corner from the Richmond Theatre. In col-
laboration with the theatre, chef-patron Weenson offers a combined
theatre-supper ticket which gives discount for post-theatre diners at the
restaurant. His enthusiasm for his trade is clearly evident in an à la
carte which is both interesting and adventurous: pumpkin risotto with
deep-fried sage leaves; spicy mussel stew with okra; poached fillet of
beef with chervil and oregano; steamed fillet of cod with a sesame oil,
ginger and sherry vinegar sauce. The early evening set dinner at £15
(till 8pm, 7pm Fri and Sat) provides excellent value.

RICHMOND — Café Flo

149 Kew Road, Richmond, Surrey, TW9 2PN
Tel: 0181-940 8298   *Fax:* 0181-332 2598   **£40**
Open: lunch & dinner daily (closed 25 & 26 Dec)
Meals served: lunch 12-4 (Sat to 4.30, Sun to 5),
      dinner 6-11.30 (Sat from 6.30, Sun from 7)

Good-quality, French-style food, reasonably priced and with no preten-
tions is the recipe for success here. However unlike its sister establishments, where you can pop in for just a coffee or for breakfast, the
Richmond Flo, up the road from Kew Gardens, is run more as a restaurant. A traditional bistro-style à la carte menu is complemented at lunch
by two- and three-course fixed-price menus, and by specialities of the
day. There's also an early evening happy-hour menu of soup, steak and
frites. Typical carte offerings include pan-fried king prawns with garlic
and parsley butter, Toulouse-style sausages with mashed potatoes and
roast lamb with a Madeira sauce. A young capable team, ably lead by
Dawn Painter.

*Outside tables much sought after in sunny spells,
so be sure to book.*

RICHMOND — King's Head

Market Place, Richmond, North Yorkshire, DL10 4HS
Tel: (01748) 850220   *Fax:* (01748) 850635   **£40**
Open: lunch Sun, dinner daily
Meals served: lunch 12-2, dinner 7-9.15

Formerly a coaching inn in the early 1700s, today the hotel's Georgian
façade dominates the town's cobbled market square. Antiques grace
the reception rooms and the Clock Room, used as a lounge, boasts a
large collection of working clocks which chime throughout the day.
The 28 bedrooms, with excellent bathrooms, include premier rooms
with four-poster or half-tester beds. Enjoy a pint of local Theakstons in
the bar or sample the traditional English fare on offer in the restaurant
which looks out on to the square and castle. Traditional Dales sausage,
Yorkshire Dales game terrine, a choice of steaks—au poivre, Diane or
béarnaise, game and poultry are all featured. There's Dales ice cream
and home-made puds with fresh cream to finish.

RICHMOND   Petersham Hotel

Nightingale Lane, Richmond, Surrey, TW10 6UZ
Tel: 0181-940 7471   *Fax:* 0181-940 9998   **£55**
Open: lunch & dinner daily (closed 25 & 26 Dec)
Meals served: lunch 12.15-2.15, dinner 7-9.45 (Sun to 8.45)

The Victorian Petersham Hotel, just a stone's throw from the Royal Park, commands splendid views over the Thames and boasts an impressive, grand cantilever staircase of Portland stone (the longest flight in the country) which extends from the black-and-white tiled lobby floor to the painted ceiling five floors above. The hotel has 54 traditional-style bedrooms, many of which enjoy the fine views from its elevated position on Richmond Hill. The restaurant with its own fabulous views offers reliable cooking from Tim Richardson, whose menus offer something for everyone, with traditional English and French dishes treated with a modern touch.

RIDGEWAY   Old Vicarage

Ridgeway Moor, Ridgeway, Nr Sheffield, Derbyshire, S12 3XW
Tel: (01742) 475814   *Fax:* (01742) 477079   **£70**
Open: lunch (reservations only) & dinner Tue-Sun
   (closed Bank Holidays, 1 wk Xmas)
Meals served: lunch 12.30-2.30, dinner 7-10.45, (light meals in
   Bistro 12.30-2.30, 7-10.45 (closed dinner Sat)

Tessa Bramley has two basic policies: that food is meant to be enjoyed not worshipped; and that whatever is being cooked be of the highest and freshest quality. Local and home-grown produce are the mainstay of the kitchen, which supplies exciting dishes for both the restaurant and conservatory bistro. The main dining room, decorated in soft pastel shades and hung with oil paintings, makes an elegant and romantic setting, particularly at night when the candles are lit; while the conservatory overlooking the gardens, weather permitting, is beautifully bright and sunny. Bistro offerings include dishes such as pork fillet with lentils or cod fillet with a rarebit glaze; while the restaurant might offer a dinner of caramelised and roasted tomato tart with spinach sauce, followed by delicious fillet of cod baked in provençale herb crust with artichokes in a warm tomato dressing, and to finish passion fruit and lime tart with banana and lime sorbet perfumed with muscat. This is a very special establishment and deserves its continued success.

Tessa is undoubtedly one of our best women chefs.

RIPLEY   Michels'

13 High Street, Ripley, Surrey, GU23 6AQ
Tel: (01483) 224777   **£55**
Open: lunch Tue-Fri & Sun, dinner Tue-Sat
    (closed 25 & 26 Dec, 1st wk Jan)
Meals served: lunch 12.30-1.30, dinner 7.30-9 (Sat 7-9.30)

When the season is right, Erik and Karen Michel are out picking wild mushrooms to supplement their supply of home-grown herbs and locally-grown produce for Erik's kitchen. The setting is stylish and elegant, with a small sunken bar area at the heart of the ground-floor dining room behind the restaurant's classical Georgian facade at the centre of the village. A meal here is a culinary delight, an adventure. The dishes conceived by this talented chef show a high degree of complexity and sophistication which seems to work every time. Imagination and the challenging juxtaposition of ingredients in certain dishes are the keynotes here. Don't expect not to be surprised by the menu! Cream of nettle soup, pan-fried frogs' legs with potato cage and fennel salad, green asparagus with a mousseline of oysters or a light mixed herb salad tossed in truffle oil dressing are typical of starters. Main courses feature dishes such as poached corn-fed chicken in a cream of watercress sauce, roast sea bass with wild mushrooms cooked in veal jus, roast loin of wild boar with horseradish and caper sauce or Madeira-sauced pig's trotter boned and filled with a mousse of sweetbreads, mushrooms and Parma ham before being gently rolled in puff pastry. Splendid desserts are no less imaginative or complex, but if simplicity is what you need at this stage, opt for a plate of British farm cheeses.

RIPPONDEN   Over the Bridge Restaurant

Millfold, Ripponden, Sowerby Bridge, West Yorkshire, HX6 4DL
Tel: (01422) 823722   **£50**
Open: dinner Mon-Sat (closed Bank Holidays)
Meals served: dinner 7-9.30

Close to the church and the old packhorse bridge, this small, well-established restaurant is host to the talent of Sue Tyer, whose fixed-price, four-course dinners have a local loyal following. Start perhaps with apple and brie tartlet with caramelised onions or a brochette of black pudding and smoked bacon with an onion sauce; choose one of two soups to follow—a recent menu featured parsnip and orange and a prawn bisque. Main courses could be roast young partridge, rich game pie with port wine gravy, or escalope of Dutch veal Dijonnaise, though there is always a fish choice too, such as baked sea bass with tomato, spring onion and ginger. Friendly and relaxed.

Good local restaurant, worth booking.

ROADE	Roadhouse Restaurant

16 High Street, Roade, Northamptonshire, NN7 2NW
Tel: (01604) 863372   **£50**
Open: lunch Tue-Fri & Sun, dinner Tue-Sat
   (closed Bank Holidays, 2 wks Jul/Aug, 1 wk Dec)
Meals served: lunch 12.30-1.45, dinner 7-9.30

A village restaurant (formerly the ale house) with suitably informal service makes for a leisurely, relaxed place run by chef-patron Christopher Kewley and wife Susan. The shortish à la carte menu is supplemented at lunch-time by a set menu. This is good, sound cooking without gimmicks. A typical menu offers home-made soup of the day among a choice of six starters such as salad of soused herrings, quails eggs, olives and bacon, potato pancake with smoked salmon and sour cream, followed by a similar range of choice for main courses: fillet of beef served with a beetroot and horseradish relish and a port sauce, steamed fillet of salmon with a butter and red pepper sauce or sautéed calf's liver with sage and a compote of onions. Desserts range from classic favourites, a crumble or steamed pudding, to the more unusual.

ROCHFORD   **Hotel Renouf & Renoufs Restaurant**

Bradley Way, Rochford, Essex, SS4 1BU
Tel: (01702) 544393   *Fax:* (01702) 549563   **£45**
Open: lunch Sun-Fri, dinner Mon-Sat (closed 26-30 Dec)
Meals served: lunch 12-1.45, dinner 7-9.45
A 24-bedroomed hotel, whose restaurant specialises in pressed duck—since its 1978 opening. To date it boasts having served over 16,000!

ROMALDKIRK	Rose and Crown

Romaldkirk, Durham, DL12 9EB
Tel: (01833) 650213   *Fax:* (01833) 650828   **£50**
Open: lunch Sun, dinner Mon-Sat (Sun residents only)
   (closed 25 & 26 Dec)
Meals served: lunch 12-1.30, dinner 7.30-9

Situated in one of the prettiest villages in England, the Rose and Crown overlooks the village green, with its original stocks and water pump, as it has done since the early 18th century when it began life as a coaching inn. Today the heart of the 12-bedroomed inn is still in the kitchen where puddings and bread are baked daily, and where chef-patron Christopher Davy prepares his daily-changing menus with care, enthusiasm and a bias towards local produce: game from the moors, fish from the East Coast and from over the Border, beef and lamb from the local butcher. The cooking is essentially English: start perhaps with a hot tartlet of Scotch salmon, oyster mushrooms and chives before poached halibut hollandaise. Alternatively try the excellent bar and supper snacks and real ales served in the cosy, traditional bar with its old black-and-white pictures of the village. This is a unspoilt corner of England, a land of high contrasts, dramatic waterfalls (including High Force, the highest waterfall in England), tiny becks, white-washed farms and stone-built cottages, grouse moors and village greens.

ROMSEY   Old Manor House

21 Palmerston Street, Romsey, Hampshire, SO51 8GF
Tel: (01794) 517353   **£45**
Open: lunch Tue-Sun, dinner Tue-Sat (closed 1 wk Xmas)
Meals served: lunch 12-2, dinner 7-9.30

France meets Italy in a quintessential English setting at Mauro
Bregoli's delightful restaurant in a cottagey Tudor town house. Start
with home-made spicy Italian salami served hot with lentils or a
delicious clam soup, before Lymington lobster served cold with mayonnaise, braised ox cheek with polenta, escalope of salmon with a light
sorrel sauce or stuffed leg of duck with blackberry sauce. If the balance
isn't quite clear already, the dessert menu is a symphony of the

national influences which come to bear in
this traditional English setting. Choose
from warm pear and hazelnut tart, home-
made Amaretto ice cream, Grand Marnier
mousse, tiramisu or crème brûlée with
raspberries. Excellent cooking on a menu
which is both interesting and refreshingly
down-to-earth. The fixed-price lunch and
dinner menu offers excellent value.

Biography

*Mauro Bregoli went straight into an apprenticeship after leaving school
at fifteen, working his way through the various aspects of the industry,*
Mauro   *before coming to England (originally to learn the lan-*
guage), but then buying the beautiful 15th-century build-
Bregoli   *ing which he turned into his well-known restaurant. It's a*
*quintessentially English setting for some genuine Italian
food, for he tries to avoid the compromises that he feels have ruined the
name of traditional Italian cooking in England.*

ROSS-ON-WYE   Pheasants

52 Edde Cross Street, Ross-on-Wye,
   Hereford & Worcester, HR9 7BZ
Tel: (01989) 565751   **£50**
Open: lunch & dinner Tue-Sat (closed Bank Holidays, 1 wk Xmas)
Meals served: lunch 12.30-2 (bookings only Nov-Mar), dinner 7-10

Eileen Brunnarius has created a real home-from-home atmosphere at
this homely, little, ten-table restaurant in a former pub. Simplicity is the
golden rule. Start with fresh vegetable soup; follow with breast of
Trelough duck with sauce gastrique, fresh Cornish fish or venison pan-
fried with sweet spices, red wine gravy and fried breadcrumbs. Sweet
delights might include a pear tatin, trio of sorbets or raw-sugar
meringue with apple cheese. Speciality coffees and bitter chocolate to
finish. Good-value fixed-price dinner (£18.50) and a more informal,
blackboard menu at lunchtime. New Zealander Adrian Wells heads
front of house and is happy to advise you on the best choice of wine for
your meal. Two modestly furnished bedrooms share a bathroom.
Hearty breakfasts.

ROTHERWICK   Tylney Hall

Rotherwick, Nr Hook, Hampshire, RG27 9AZ
Tel: (01256) 764881   *Fax:* (01256) 768141   **£65**
Open: lunch & dinner daily
Meals served: lunch 12.30-1.45, dinner 7.30-9.30 (Fri & Sat to 10)

The present Tylney Hall was built at the turn of the century as the home
of Sir Lionel Phillips, since when it has been a hospital, a shipping base
and later a boarding school. The house is as impressive in its palatial
proportions as in its setting—66 acres of stunning parkland, featuring
cascading waterfalls, fountains, water tower, sunken garden, pavilion,
rose and azalea gardens, woodland and lakes; not to mention the extensive leisure facilities also available today—archery, clay shooting, hot-air
ballooning—the list seems endless. Inside, the hall features the original
carved oak panelling and high, moulded ceilings, as well as ornate
Italian walnut panelling and an Italian ceiling from the Grimation Palace
in Florence—evidence that no expense was spared when the house was
built in 1898. The 91 bedrooms are spacious though all share the same
basic pink/green colour scheme, and there are three cottage suites
overlooking a small lake in the grounds. Stephen Hines' modern style of
cooking is precise and service is friendly and correct. Specialities from
the kitchen include such dishes as salad of gambas, sea scallops and
mussels with a warm lime and coriander dressing; spring lamb with a
basil mousse and port wine jus; and iced praline nougat served with an
orange, pink grapefruit and passion fruit sauce. The à la carte is extensive but adventurous and is supplemented by a fixed-price menu of traditional English fare. The cellar befits the style of the house with some
very fine wines at proportional prices.

ROWDE   George & Dragon

High Street, Rowde, Wiltshire, SN10 2PN
Tel: (01380) 723053   **£40**
Open: lunch & dinner Tue-Sat (closed 25 & 26 Dec, 1 Jan)
Meals served: lunch 12-2, dinner 7-10

A village pub with a difference: good food and good wine! Tim Withers
cooks and Helen Withers looks after the customers in the small dining
room. Tim's cooking offers sound innovative dishes such as mussels
steamed with lemongrass and coriander; or how about trying fishcakes
with hollandaise, lamb's kidneys and sweetbread served in a piquant
tomato salsa or a simple salad of cold roast sirloin with potato and pickles? Puddings range from rhubarb fool to crème brûlée to bread-and-
butter pudding, and coffee comes with fudge. An imaginative variety of
wines is very reasonably priced and you can ring the changes as at
least a dozen of them can be ordered by the glass. Why can't all pubs
be like this?

ROWSLEY   Peacock Hotel
Rowsley, Matlock, Derbyshire, DE4 2EB
Tel: (01629) 733518   *Fax:* (01629) 732671   **£45**
Open: lunch & dinner daily
Meals served: lunch 12-2, dinner 7-9
Popular fisherman's haunt—trout and grayling on the Derwent at the bottom of
the garden, plus rights on the Wye. 17th-century manor house, with 14 bed-
rooms. A hotel since 1820, famous guests have included the poet Longfellow and
Maximilian, Emperor of Mexico (1867).

RUSHLAKE GREEN   Stone House

Rushlake Green, Heathfield, East Sussex, TN21 9QJ
Tel: (01435) 830553   *Fax:* (01825) 764673   **£60**
Open: dinner daily residents only (closed 24 Dec-5 Jan)
Meals served: dinner 7.30-9

The house dates back to 1495 and has been in the hands of the Roberts
Dunns family ever since. Set in acres of unspoilt countryside on the
Kent and Sussex border, the house offers eight bedrooms, all comfortably and carefully furnished. Excellent fishing and pheasant shoot facilities for those who like the outdoor life, and Glyndebourne is just up
the road. Jane Dunn's good, wholesome cooking is the other big attraction here. A typical meal might include fresh tomato soup with basil,
home-grown asparagus with a lemon butter sauce or layered smoked
salmon pancakes with crème fraîche to start. Main courses might be
tranche of salmon with a sorrel sauce, saddle of lamb with spinach
leaves and a lemon stuffing with a Madeira and rosemary sauce, or
salmon and turbot mousse stuffed with prawns and squid, served with
a chive and prawn sauce; and to finish, perhaps rich lemon tart or
chocolate Amaretto torte with raspberry sauce. A full wine list with
some good half bottles.

RYE   Landgate Bistro

5/6 Landgate, Rye, East Sussex, TN31 7LH
Tel: (01797) 222829   **£50**
Open: dinner Tue-Sat
Meals served: dinner 7-9.30

The straightforward handwritten menu at this quaint and friendly
bistro is indicative of the whole style of the place, which is relaxed and
unfussy. Chef Toni Ferguson-Lees cooks in the modern way, with seasonal ingredients being used to their full advantage whenever possible,
but doesn't lose sight of classical tradition. Typical items on the menu
might be a leek and Roquefort tart, salad of confit of duck with green
lentils, a "very fishy stew", sea bass hollandaise, wild rabbit with garlic
and thyme, or fillet of beef in pastry with sauce béarnaise. Eight wines
served by the glass on a concise, well-chosen list.

RYE — Mermaid Inn

Mermaid Street, Rye, East Sussex, TN31 7EU
Tel: (01797) 223065   *Fax:* (01797) 225069   **£55**
Open: lunch & dinner daily
Meals served: lunch 12.30-2.15, dinner 7.30-9.15

The cobbled streets of ancient Rye provide the setting for this once infamous inn, with a history of smuggling and black deeds. It's got to be one of England's oldest and most characterful places, with a wealth of old timbers and roaring log fires in winter. In the 1300s, The Mermaid brewed its own ale and charged a penny a night for lodging. Built of wattle and daub, lath and plaster, it was destroyed by the French towards the end of that century and rebuilt in 1420. In the early 20th century, it was home to a literary club, welcoming the likes of Rupert Brooke, Dame Ellen Terry and Oscar Wilde's Bosey (Lord Alfred Douglas). It is now in the hands of a small local consortium whose love of the place has resulted in a new lease of life. There are 28 rooms (most overlooking the town) up creaky staircases and a number boasting four-posters. With foundations which date back to 1156 and Norman cellars, it's one of the most historically romantic places in the country.

ST AUSTELL — Boscundle Manor

Tregrehan, St Austell, Cornwall, PL25 3RL
Tel: (01726) 813557   *Fax:* (01726) 814997   **£50**
Open: dinner daily (closed Nov-Mar)
Meals served: dinner 7.30-8.30

Andrew and Mary Flint fell in love with this secluded, 18th-century manor house at first sight in 1978 and have been continuously improving and developing it ever since. The house is furnished with many fine antiques and paintings and is run along the lines of a private house; Andrew cooks breakfast and runs front-of-house while Mary cooks dinner, a three-course set menu with two or three choices for each course, making the most of local Cornish produce. Breakfast is served in the delightful conservatory overlooking the garden. There are seven bedrooms in the manor itself, one in the garden room and two in the garden cottage.

ST IVES — Pig'n'Fish

Norway Lane, St Ives, Cornwall, TR26 1LZ
Tel: (01736) 794204   **£55**
Open: lunch & dinner Tue-Sat (closed Nov-mid Mar)
Meals served: lunch 12.30-1.30, dinner 7-9.30

When you consider that we are an island country, there is a dire shortage of decent fish restaurants around our coastline and a positive wilderness inland. Paul Sellars is doing his best to redress the balance in this attractive artist's retreat of St Ives. A range of shellfish dishes, fish soup or salads precedes the selection of cod, lemon sole, salmon, brill, monkfish or skate cooked in a medley of ways. There may be a bourride or bouillabaisse to enhance the variety. A few good puddings and a short list of mainly white wines complete the picture at this unpretentious restaurant. Why aren't there more like it?

ST MARGARET'S   Wallett's Court

West Cliffe, St Margaret's, Dover, Kent, CT15 6EW
Tel: (01304) 852424   *Fax:* (01304) 853430   **£50**
Open: dinner Mon-Sat (closed Xmas, 1 wk Jan, 1 wk Nov)
Meals served: dinner 7-9

This lovely old Manor House is an ideal overnight stop for travellers
crossing over to France. Set in its own well-tended grounds, it has
some rooms in the main house and others across the garden in a converted granary. The history of the house goes back to Domesday and
is documented on scrolls on one of the dining room walls; but the
enchanting atmosphere is mostly created by oak beams to walls and
ceilings—and the careful attention of the Oakley family. The kitchen is
in the capable hands of father Chris, who might offer the likes of
Kentish huntsman's platter of game terrine and smoked duck breast
with Cumberland sauce, or linguine with local seafood in saffron sauce,
then English lamb braised in white wine with barley and seasonal vegetables, or jugged Kent hare. Luscious puds are displayed on a tray for
you to select. Well-priced wine list.

ST MAWES   Idle Rocks Hotel

Tredenham Road, St Mawes, Cornwall, TR2 5AN
Tel: (01326) 270771   *Fax:* (01326) 270062   **£45**
Open: lunch Sun, dinner daily
Meals served: lunch 12-2.30, dinner 7-9.15

Get away from it all on the 55ft ketch of this 24-bedroomed harbourside
hotel: the hotel boat has the wind in its sails twice a week weather permitting. This is a delightful, picture-postcard setting, with a water's
edge terrace which runs the length of the hotel and a restaurant looking out across the bay. Menus are classically based, with the emphasis
on British traditions: potted crab and smoked trout mousse; plain-
grilled lamb cutlets or roast rack of west-country lamb with a sultana
and brioche crumb crust, served with mint and redcurrant sauce; and
grilled turbot on a bed of wild mushrooms served in a Madeira cream.
A fixed-price menu, in support, offers three choices at each stage. A
good selection of wines are classified by their styles.

SALCOMBE	Spinnakers

Fore Street, Salcombe, Devon, TQ8 8JG
Tel: (01548) 843408   **£35**
Open: lunch daily, dinner Mon-Sat (closed Mon & Tue in winter, Dec & Jan)
Meals served: lunch 12-2, dinner 7-9.30
Waterside restaurant and bar with views of the estuary. Straightforward, informal lunches served in the bar or patio, plus formal evening fare. Eclectic menu, from the traditional (steak pie) to the more exotic (Mexican chicken), strong on fish, which is displayed on the blackboard.

SANDIWAY   Nunsmere Hall

Tarporley Road, Sandiway, Cheshire, CW8 2ES
Tel: (01606) 889100   *Fax:* (01606) 889055   **£55**
Open: lunch & dinner daily
Meals served: lunch 12-2, dinner 7-10

Originally the home of the Brocklebanks of Cunard fame, Nunsmere's past is entwined with England's maritime history and with those aristocratic liners of the 20th century, the Queen Mary and the QE2. Enjoying a secluded woodland setting surrounded by a 60-acre lake the hall, despite its proximity to Manchester airport, is the epitome of an English country house, a haven of calm, an oasis of beauty. Elegant reception rooms, reminiscent of a bygone age, and 32 spacious, stylishly-furnished bedrooms, together with good conference facilities make it ideal for the business market. Chef Paul Kitching offers fixed-price lunch and dinner menus, plus an à la carte and vegetarian menus that are classic French in style, but modern in method. Typical dishes might include: a lightly curried cream of mussel, scallop and lobster tail herb bisque followed by grilled baby Cornish sea bass or roast end of Cumbrian lamb with a thyme and game sauce.

SARK   Aval Du Creux

Sark, GY9 0SB
Tel: (01481) 832036   *Fax:* (01481) 832368   **£35**
Open: lunch & dinner daily (closed Oct-Apr)
Meals served: lunch 12-2, dinner 7-9

Traffic-free Sark eight miles east of Guernsey makes for a peaceful retreat from the hurly burly of 20th-century life. This former farmhouse is now a friendly, 12-bedroomed hotel run by Peter and Cheryl Tonks, and is an ideal place for family holidays. See the island in style from a Victorian horse-drawn carriage, before relaxing over a four-course candlelit dinner in the Lobster Restaurant (including oyster bar), popular with the islanders and international yachtsmen who come for the seafood. Lunchtime offers alfresco eating on the terrace, and there's a pool and miniature splash pool for children. They say everyone is friendly on Sark: no wonder! The absence of traffic works like balm on the mind, body and soul.

SARK   Dixcart Hotel

Sark, GY9 0SD
Tel: (01481) 832015   *Fax:* (01481) 832164   **£30**
Open: lunch & dinner daily
Meals served: lunch 12-1.30, dinner 7-9

The oldest hotel on the island, set in peaceful sloping gardens, has private access to the beach and has played an important part in the island's history. Prince Henry, Victor Hugo and Edward VII all stayed here. The hotel occupies the original 16th-century feudal longhouse, surrounded by medieval hand-terraced gardens, woodland and fields. As one of Sark's original feudal tenements, the property carries its own seat in the local parliament and is represented by the head of the family when the Court sits three times a year. The Brannam family, with Michael Egan in the kitchen, offer one of the best value table d'hôte dinner on the island, using freshly caught fish, local lamb and beef as the mainstay for Michael's three-course menus. Start perhaps with a a sauté of king prawns in garlic butter followed by your own choice of Sark-caught brill, Dover sole or sea bass, cooked plain or with a sauce, as you wish. Finish with home-made Sark ice cream and retire to the cosy lounge for coffee.

SARK   La Sablonnerie Hotel

La Sablonnerie, Sark, GY9 0SD
Tel: (01481) 832061   *Fax:* (01481) 832408   **£45**
Open: lunch & dinner daily (closed mid Oct-Easter)
Meals served: lunch 12-2.30, dinner 7-9.30

A horse-drawn carriage will pick you up at the tiny harbour and take you to the Perrées' beautiful 22-bedroomed inn located on the remote, southernmost part of the island known as Little Sark. This is a delightful unpretentious hotel which is virtually self-suffcient: it has its own farm which produces organic dairy products, meat and vegetables for the table, and only the locally-caught fish and seafood are needed to complete matters. Dinner starts with canapés in the bar and is a five-course affair: oysters, salmon and lobster, Spring lamb with garlic and fresh garden herbs, home-reared pork with apples and Calvados, and fillet steak with wild mushroom hollandaise. The cooking is international, with a French bias. Lighter meals and afternoon teas are served in the pretty tea garden a few yards from the main building which is surrounded by flower-filled gardens. Bright, comfortable accommodation in and around the hotel—some of the rooms are housed in Duvallerie Farm and at La Pipeterie, both about 50 yards from La Sablonnerie.

SARK   Stocks Island Hotel

Sark, GY9 0SD
Tel: (01481) 832001   *Fax:* (01481) 832130   **£40**
Open: lunch & dinner daily (closed Oct-Apr)
Meals served: lunch 12-2.30, dinner 7-9

Sark rabbit sausage, Sark lobster grilled with lemon beurre blanc and
Sark lamb are some of the local delights you can enjoy at this 24-bed-
roomed family-run hotel which lies in a wooded valley about 20 minutes' walk from the harbour. Stocks has long been a favourite haunt of
writers and artists, including the likes of Victor Hugo and Mervyn
Peake among its honoured guests. The Cider Press restaurant offers a
daily table d'hôte and monthly-changing carte, with the emphasis on
British and continental dishes. Alternatively, you can eat in the
Courtyard Bistro or alfresco by the pool in summer. A peaceful place,
relaxing and homely.

SEAFORD   Quincy's

42 High Street, Seaford, East Sussex BN25 1PL
Tel: (01323) 895490   **£50**
Open: lunch Sun, dinner Tue-Sat
Meals served: lunch 12-2, dinner 7-10

An eclectic menu, with a leaning towards English traditions and modern influences. Starters range from home-made potato and leek soup
with chorizo to crab and sweetcorn cakes with red pepper sauce. Main
courses feature locally caught fish, along with dishes like pan-fried
calf's liver with lime and peppercorns, duck with a prune and honey
sauce, or salmon with crayfish ravioli and ginger sauce. Interesting
vegetarian options might include leeks and gruyère baked in a pancake
with asparagus and a herby lemon sauce. Dawn Dowding looks after
front of house with charm, while husband Ian takes charge in the
kitchen.

SEAHOUSES   Olde Ship Hotel

9 Main Street, Seahouses, Northumberland, NE68 7RD
Tel: (01665) 720200   *Fax:* (01665) 721383   **£30**
Open: lunch & dinner daily (closed Dec & Jan)
Meals served: lunch 12-2, dinner 7-8.30

Formerly a farmhouse built in the mid-1700s, this characterful old inn
overlooks the harbour and Farne Islands, and has been run by Alan
and Jean Glen since 1969. The menu changes daily—ranging from bar
lunches to excellent-value, three-course dinners of good home cooking
served in the dining room which is adorned with nautical paintings by
local marine artists. In fact, the pub is a veritable treasure trove of
antique nautical pieces—brass lamps, navigating instruments, obsolete
fishing artefacts, lifeboat oars, 19th-century ship figureheads.
Bedrooms, of which there are 15, are homely and two have four-
posters.

SEATON BURN   Horton Grange

Seaton Burn, Nr Newcastle-upon-Tyne, Tyne & Wear, NE13 6BU
Tel: (01661) 860686   *Fax:* (01661) 860308   **£70**
Open: dinner Mon-Sat (closed 25 & 26 Dec)
Meals served: dinner 7-8.45

Andrew and Sue Shilton's nine-bedroomed house used to belong to a
farming family; you'll find the house on the edge of a large working
farm. When you arrive, your bags will be taken up to your room to
allow you a moment's respite after the journey over a complimentary
drink. The idea here is that the moment you enter you will feel it's
started: that holiday, the pampering and so on. Go to your room and
you'll find the menu (which changes daily) on hand to browse through
at your ease. The five-course dinner prepared by Steve Martin offers
plenty of choice and sophistication. Bedrooms are delightful; those in
the Peach House in the garden offer more privacy and seclusion.

SEAVIEW   Seaview Hotel

High Street, Seaview, Isle of Wight, PO34 5EX
Tel: (01983) 612711   *Fax:* (01983) 613729   **£45**
Open: lunch daily, dinner Mon-Sat (closed 25 Dec)
Meals served: lunch 12-2, dinner 7.30-9.30

A small, 16-bedroomed, family-run hotel set back from the sea front,
with snug lounges, a characterful, nautical bar and patio from which
you can sit and watch the world go by. Bedrooms, some with views
over the Solent, are designed to make you feel cossetted, with crisp
linen, firm mattresses and fluffy towels. The dining room makes the
most of the island's own garlic, wine, lobster, crab and flat fish. Dine
there by candlelight in a discreetly elegant yet homely setting, or go
down in time for a hearty breakfast of porridge and kippers in winter.
Good snacks are served in the bar or on the terrace. Delicious garlic
bread is made from oak-smoked Island garlic, or there's a crispy olive
oil and herb variety. Seaview is a small, unassuming, Victorian seaside
resort whose tidy streets dip down to a pretty bay.

SETTLE	**Blue Goose**

Market Square, Settle, North Yorkshire, BD24 9EJ
Tel: (01729) 822901   **£40**
Open: lunch & dinner Mon-Sat
Meals served: lunch 11-2, dinner 7-9.30
English cooking with a Continental slant at this wine bar and restaurant. Chef-patron Willi Rehbock also has a cookery school on the premises.

SEVENOAKS   Royal Oak

High Street, Sevenoaks, Kent, TN13 1H7
Tel: (01732) 451109   *Fax:* (01732) 740187   **£60**
Open: lunch Sun-Fri, dinner daily
Meals served: lunch 12.30-2, dinner 7.30-10.30

The stone Georgian façade belies the cosy interior of this 18th-century coaching inn. Comfortable rooms, good value varied menus with a very good selection of imaginatively-prepared dishes and a cosy bar. Wines by the glass and bottle.

SHAFTESBURY   La Fleur de Lys

---

25 Salisbury Street, Shaftesbury, Dorset, SP7 8EL
Tel: (01747) 853717   **£45**
Open: lunch Tue-Sun, dinner Mon-Sat   *A wine list to suit*
Meals served: lunch 12-2.30, dinner 7-10   *most people at very good prices.*

Good-value cooking with a definite French accent means a loyal local following at this restaurant, run with panache by the ex-Lewtrenchard Manor trio, David Shepherd, Mary Griffin and Marc Preston. Fixed-price dinner menus and lunch and dinner à la cartes offer excellent choice across a range of exciting, well-composed dishes. Starters include the likes of hot lobster and langoustine soufflé served with sautéed shellfish in a champagne sauce, or tomato and Cornish crab consommé. Main courses range from pan-fried fillets of Dutch veal with devilled kidneys in a creamy Dijon mustard sauce to sautéed collops of monkfish in a lemon and ginger coat served with spring onions, apples and shallots in a light lemon sauce. Exotic desserts and a fine selection of quality wines.

SHANKLIN OLD VILLAGE   The Cottage

---

8 Eastcliff Road, Shanklin Old Village, Isle of Wight, PO37 6AA
Tel: (01983) 862504   *Fax:* (01983) 867512   **£50**
Open: lunch & dinner Tue-Sat (closed 26 Dec,
     4 wks Feb/Mar, Oct)
Meals served: lunch 12-2, dinner 7.30-9.45

Neil Graham takes his inspiration from both sides of the Channel in this cosy cul-de-sac restaurant made up of three old cottages on the town side of the old village; and the locals and visitors love it. His partner of over 20 years, Alan Priddle, looks after front-of-house with relaxed dedication and charm. Lunch is a fairly simple fixed-price affair (plaice Bonne Femme, roast leg of lamb anglaise), while dinner presents an à la carte of considerable choice. Poached tiger prawns with ginger vinaigrette; quenelles of sole with tarragon sauce; chilled vichyssoise; vegetarian stroganoff; sole Véronique; supreme Durhamaise (boned breast of chicken wrapped in bacon with a Stilton butter, poached and served on a Madeira sauce); and fillet Shakespeare cooked "As you like it" are what Neil offers, with delicious home-made desserts to finish.

SHEFFIELD   **Charnwood Hotel**

10 Sharrow Lane, Sheffield, South Yorkshire, S11 8AA
Tel: (0114) 2589411   *Fax:* (0114) 2555107   **£55**
Open: dinner Tue-Sat (closed Bank Holidays)
Meals served: dinner 7-10
22-bedroomed Georgian hotel a mile from the centre of Sheffield. Good conference facilities.

SHEFFIELD   The Harley

334 Glossop Road, Sheffield, South Yorkshire, S10 2HW
Tel: (0114) 2752288   *Fax:* (0114) 2722383   **£35**
Open: lunch Mon-Fri, dinner Mon-Sat (closed 25 & 26 Dec, 1 Jan)
Meals served: lunch 12-2.30, dinner 7.30-10.30

Named for the numerous Harley Street practitioners who used to lodge here, today the Harley is a 22-bedroomed hotel offering a good standard of accommodation with a wide choice of culinary styles. Eat simply—a light lunch—or choose from Ian Morton's extensive carte. Typical starters include tomato and olive pasta salad or marinated smoked salmon. Main-course offerings range from roast duck with orange and cognac sauce to fillet steak or pan-fried Dover sole.

SHEPTON MALLET   Blostin's Restaurant

29 Waterloo Road, Shepton Mallet, Somerset, BA4 5HH
Tel: (01749) 343648   **£35**
Open: dinner Tue-Sat (closed 2 wks Jan, 2 wks Jun)
Meals served: dinner 7-9.30

Nick and Lynne Reed's intimate restaurant provides the kind of good value, reliable bistro-style cooking that ought to be found in every small town in Britain. Hand-written, fixed-price menus might offer a warm salad of chicken and smoky bacon, mussels steamed with white wine, shallots and parsley, or fish soup with rouille followed by escalope of salmon with sorrel, crispy duck with bacon, mushrooms and Burgundy sauce, or breast of chicken with asparagus and tarragon sauce. There is also an à la carte, and vegetarians are well cared for. Puddings are not for slimmers. Wines listed by grape variety are reasonably priced.

SHERBORNE   **Eastbury Hotel**

Long Street, Sherborne, Dorset, DT9 3BY
Tel: (01935) 813131   *Fax:* (01935) 817296   **£45**
Open: lunch & dinner daily
Meals served: lunch 12.30-2, dinner 7.30-9.30
Deep in Hardy country, this Georgian town house with 15 bedrooms is a comfortable and elegant place to stay.

SHERE	Kinghams Restaurant

Gomshall Lane, Shere, Surrey, GU5 9HB
Tel: (01483) 202168   **£40**
Open: lunch Tue-Sun, dinner Tue-Sat (closed 25 & 26 Dec)
Meals served: lunch 12-2.30, dinner 6.30-9.30

"One cannot work well, feel well, love well, unless one has eaten well."
This is the motto which heads brothers Paul and Jason Baker's concise
but well-thought-out à la carte. Begin perhaps with Mexican prawns or
half a lobster. Move on to venison with a gin and juniper sauce or vegetarian risotto. Finish with treacle tart and clotted cream, light lemon
mousse with a cassis coulis or a selection of fine English cheeses.
Good, uncomplicated cooking. A blackboard comes into play at lunch-
time, displaying a £10 two-course menu; in the evenings it displays the
fish dishes of the day or daily specials. The restaurant is cottagey in
style and dates back to 1620. Former owners include a family of sheep
thieves, one of whom is said to have been hanged at the gibbet, just
north of Shere!

SHIFNAL	Weston Park

Weston Park, Shifnal, Shropshire, TF11 8LE
Tel: (0195 276) 201   *Fax:* (0195 276) 430   **£70**
Open: lunch & dinner by arrangement (closed 25 & 26 Dec)

Weston Park is only open for residential parties and corporate entertaining but is occasionally open to the public for gourmet dinner
evenings and concerts. The magnificent house set in 1000 acres of
parkland is the Earl of Bradford's Estate and as a well- known restaurateur and gastronome, he maintains high standards in the kitchen.
There are 19 elegant bedrooms available during special events and for
corporate bookings. It's worth asking for details of their Gourmet
Evenings or treat 30 or so of your best friends to a weekend in a Stately
Home!

SHINFIELD	L'Ortolan

Old Vicarage, Church Lane, Shinfield,   ❀
    Nr Reading, Berkshire, RG2 9BY
Tel: (01734) 883783   *Fax:* (01734) 885391   **£100**
Open: lunch Tue-Sun, dinner Tue-Sat
    (closed last 2 wks Aug, last 2 wks Feb)   🍾
Meals served: lunch 12-2.15, dinner 7-10   ✤

In the same class as the Waterside Inn at Bray and Raymond Blanc's
Le Manoir (Great Milton), L'Ortolan is a culinary masterpiece. John
Burton-Race and wife Christine set the highest of standards here, both
in the kitchen and at front-of-house. His creative flair, enthusiasm and
dedication just seems to run on and on. This is without doubt one of
the finest restaurants in the country and the setting, in a former vicarage surrounded by beautiful gardens, is truly delightful. Dishes,
menus rather, are so exciting and rewarding that somehow, somewhere, you feel there's a touch of magic in the air. And so there is.

Look forward to signature dishes like langoustine lasagne—layers of tarragon-scented langoustine bound with its own mousse, between steamed leaves of fresh pasta masked with a delicate truffle oil. Other delights might include classic French onion tart scented with herbs, spiked with lardons and gratinated; slices of sea bass steamed in champagne and served with oyster jus; and wild pigeon breast béarnaise, laced with a Cahors fumet. Wonderful desserts are equally impressive, as is the wine list, service, coffee and petits fours—indeed everything about the place. There are two conservatories either side of the simple but elegant main dining room which overlooks the garden; one is used as a drawing room for aperitifs and digestifs, the other provides a more summery aspect for dining.

SILVERTON   Silverton Inn

Fore Street, Silverton, Devon, BX5 4HP
Tel: (01392) 860196   **£40**
Open: lunch Sun, dinner Tue-Sat (closed 1 wk Xmas/New Year)
Meals served: lunch 12-3, dinner 7-10.30
Simple setting offers unexpectedly fine cooking from a blackboard menu—robust no nonsense food is the order of the day. Short wine list with nothing over £15.

SISSINGHURST   Rankins

The Street, Sissinghurst, Kent, TN17 2JH
Tel: (01580) 713964   **£55**
Open: lunch Sun, dinner Wed-Sat (closed Bank Holidays)
Meals served: lunch 12.30-1.30, dinner 7.30-9

Hugh and Leonora Rankin's winning formula at this charming, white, cottage restaurant is to produce enjoyable and varied dishes on a short, imaginative table d'hôte. Hugh's menus are refreshingly even as you read them, short and unfussy. Start perhaps with crab and lentil soup, followed by pan-fried breast of pigeon with rich mushroom sauce, Lunesdale duck with Cumberland sauce, or salmon, corn and bacon chowder. Typically English puds to finish. Short, well selected and reasonably priced wine list.

SIX MILE BOTTOM   Swynford Paddocks

Six Mile Bottom, Nr Newmarket, Cambridgeshire, CB8 0UE
Tel: (01638) 570234   *Fax:* (01638) 570283   **£50**
Open: lunch Sun-Fri, dinner daily (closed Xmas/New Year)
Meals served: lunch 12.30-2, dinner 7-9.30 (Sun 7-8.30)

Swynford Paddocks is the former home of Lord Byron's half-sister, Augusta and it is here that their romance is said to have blossomed in the summer of 1813. Reception rooms set a period tone, while bedrooms are generally light and pretty, with lovely views over the grounds. Specialities from the kitchen include roast black pudding wrapped in bacon; chef Patrick Collins' cassoulet of snails; prime fillet steak filled with prawns; roast crispy duckling in an orange-flavoured brandy sauce; and baked smoked haddock in a whisky sauce.

SLOUGH   Tummies Bistro

5 Station Road, Cippenham, Slough, Berkshire, SL1 6JJ
Tel: (01628) 668486   *Fax:* (01628) 663106   **£35**
Open: lunch Sun-Fri, dinner daily (closed 25 & 26 Dec, 1 Jan)
Meals served: lunch 11.30-3 (Sun 12-4), dinner 5.30-12 (Sun 7-11)

This friendly bistro, with open kitchen, offers dishes from around the world, starting with mussels with pesto and garlic, taramasalata with cucumber salad or perhaps pasta with smoked chicken and wild mushrooms from around a dozen first courses. Blackened Cajun chicken, halibut steak with tomato and olive butter or oriental-style pork with saffron rice might tempt you afterwards. Children are well catered for and there are traditional roasts for Sunday lunch.

SOLIHULL   Jarvis George Hotel

The Square, Solihull, West Midlands, B91 3RF
Tel: 021-711 2121   *Fax:* 021-711 3374   **£40**
Open: lunch & dinner daily
Meals served: lunch 12-2.30, dinner 7-9.45

Close to the National Exhibition Centre, this 127-bedroomed hotel, a former coaching inn dating back in parts to the 16th century, forms a quadrangle around the old bowling green at the rear. The beamed Club Bar is very much a focal point for both locals and visitors and there is a second bar adjoining the restaurant. Bedrooms vary from standard to executive to luxury Townhouse suites—mock street doors lead off a themed corridor into spacious rooms with galleried bedrooms, complete with slippers, fax, work table, stress toys, additional bedside TV and many other extras.

SOUTH MOLTON   Whitechapel Manor

South Molton, Devon, EX36 3EG
Tel: (01769) 573377   *Fax:* (01769) 573797   **£70**
Open: lunch & dinner daily
Meals served: lunch 12-1.45, dinner 7-8.45   🏵

If it's peace, calm and solitude you're after, this Grade I listed Elizabethan manor house is the place to go to get away from it all. The house is set in 14 acres of terraced garden, surrounded by woodland in the foothills of Exmoor. Chef/patron Patricia Shapland (pictured with husband John) shares the cooking with Martin Lee. They use local game and seafood according to the seasons, fresh local vegetables and Devon cheeses. Try fillet of trout with lemon grass and sorrel butter sauce, roast tenderloin of pork with a cider and Calvados sauce or fillet of Devon beef with roast shallots and a Madeira sauce. Coffee and petits fours are served in the Great Hall drawing room which features 18th-century pan-  elling and warming log fires. The house has ten rooms with larger ones overlooking the garden, and breakfasts are excellent.

SOUTHAMPTON   **Browns Brasserie**

Frobisher House, Nelson Gate, Commercial Road,
    Southampton, Hampshire, SO1 0GX
Tel: (01703) 332615   **£45**
Open: lunch Sun-Fri, dinner daily (closed 25 & 26 Dec,
    1 Jan, 2 wks Aug)
Meals served: lunch 12-2.30, dinner 6.30-10.30
    (5.30-11.30 for theatre-goers)

Richard and Patricia Brown's small lively restaurant in downtown Southampton continues to provide quality cooking. Spinach soufflé with anchovy, pan-fried foie gras with lemon and lime dressing or a fricassée of scallops and prawns with oyster butter sauce or perhaps a roasted loin of rabbit with Dijon mustard and a boudin of rabbit to start. Aylesbury duck comes cooked in three styles, the breast roasted, the leg as a confit and then a duck sausage, all served in a thyme and orange sauce. Oxtail is braised, boned and served with parsnip purée, a vegetarian walnut roulade is poached with asparagus, quail eggs and hollandaise.

SOUTHEND-ON-SEA   **Slassor's**

145 Eastern Esplanade, Southend-on-Sea, Essex, SS1 2YD
Tel: (01702) 614880   **£35**
Open: lunch Tue-Fri, dinner Mon-Sat
    (closed Bank Holidays in summer)
Meals served: lunch 12-2, dinner 7-9.30

Leslie Slassor, a one-man band, has created an unusual, almost whimsical menu at this unlicensed restaurant (corkage 75p except on bottles of Charles Heidsieck champagne which is uncorked for free). A daily blackboard menu featuring hearty brasserie-style favourites from around the world supplements the carte which features some good fish selections, a range of steaks, and specialities such as chicken breast with spring onions with a lemon, gin and cream sauce. Good vegetarian menu with lots of choice—vegetable Wellington with herb sauce or saffron rice Spanish-style.

SOUTHSEA   **Bistro Montparnasse**

103 Palmerston Road, Southsea, Hampshire, PO5 3PS
Tel: (01705) 816754   **£35**
Open: dinner Tue-Sat (closed Bank Holidays, 2 wks Jan)
Meals served: dinner 7-10

Catching the ferry to Spain or France? If so, schedule in a stopover here, at Peter and Gillian Scott's friendly bistro, close to the main shopping centre. Gillian's frequently-changing menus are eclectic, well-thought-out and inventive. Starters might include chestnut tortelli with brown butter and parmesan, or Chinese-style steamed bun with chicken. Main courses could be game pie, pan-fried calf's liver with sage and onion stuffing; osso buco with gremolata; steak and wild mushroom pie; or aubergine and roasted garlic custard tart. Finish with lime and tangerine sorbets in tuile flowers or hot apple cake with raspberry sauce and custard. Weekday specials on the blackboard. A comprehensive wine list is well priced and includes three local Wickham wines.

SOUTHWOLD — The Crown

90 High Street, Southwold, Suffolk, IP18 6DP
Tel: (01502) 722275   *Fax:* (01502) 724805   **£45**
Open: lunch & dinner daily (closed 1 wk Jan)
Meals served: lunch 12.30-1.45, dinner 7.30-9.30

With Adnams brewery just up the road, a perfect pint is nigh on certain at this Adnams-owned Georgian pub-restaurant with 12 rooms. This is an inn, not a grand hotel, but help is always at hand: staff here are helpful and friendly. Bar meals are served in the front room facing the High Street, ranging from home-made soups with seeded cob rolls to tandoori lamb kebabs or wild rabbit and ale casserole. In the restaurant, menus change daily, with around five choices at each stage. Steamed turbot Andaluz, Dover sole Colbert and chicken supreme in almonds with amaretto sauce are some of the main courses. Besides the very good wine list, they have an excellent monthly selection of 20 wines by the glass, an ideal way to try them if you're not sure of your palate!

SOUTHWOLD — The Swan

Market Place, Southwold, Suffolk, IP18 6EG
Tel: (01502) 722186   *Fax:* (01502) 724800   **£45**
Open: lunch & dinner daily (closed lunch Mon-Fri Jan-Easter)
Meals served: lunch 12-1.45, dinner 7-9.30

At some hotels, the wine list is an afterthought; here it's the raison d'etre! Simon Loftus of Adnams in Southwold is amongst one of the most innovative and knowledgable wine merchants in Britain and it's therefore no surprise to find that the Swan has such a stunning choice of quality wines. There's not one suspect selection amongst the 120-odd bottles. Pricing is kept within most pockets, Adnam's champagne at just £20 and ten other house wines are available by the glass. Oh, I almost forgot, there's good food to accompany the wines! Unfussy, modern English cooking in fact, with dishes like honey-baked leg of lamb with port wine sauce, roast beef and Yorkshire pudding, game casserole, baked cod with mussels and to finish there's a wicked spotted dick with custard (don't forget a glass of pudding wine). Centrally located in Southwold, this charming hotel is ideal for visiting the Aldeburgh Festival Hall, or for just catching up on this delightful seaside town.

SPARK BRIDGE — Bridgefield House

Spark Bridge, Ulverston, Cumbria, LA12 8DA
Tel: (01229) 885239   *Fax:* (01229) 885379   **£45**
Open: dinner daily (closed 25 Dec)
Meals served: dinner 7.30 for 8

This is a place which prides itself on giving a genuinely warm welcome to guests. The Glister family's small five-bedroomed hotel overlooking the beautiful Crake valley is homely and refreshingly modest, with attitude and comfort, not gloss, being the primary concern. Moreover Rosemary Glister's daily-changing, six-course dinner menus are well conceived and beautifully presented. This is traditional country cooking in contemporary style. A typical menu, with limited choice, might feature a choice of three appetisers: lamb sweetbreads in a mustard and cream sauce; pineapple and seedless grapes in a tarragon cream dressing; or filo pastry tartlets filled with white crabmeat in mayonnaise with marinaded sweet peppers. Move on to cream of Jerusalem artichoke soup with almond toast, before fillet of wild Scottish salmon poached in white wine with a saffron and cream sauce. Take a breather over apple-mint water ice before tackling dessert, perhaps rhubarb and banana cream fool with shortbread. Good cheese, with coffee and brandy to finish.

SPEEN	The Old Plow Inn at Speen

Flowers Bottom Lane, Speen, Nr Princes Risborough,
  Bucks, HP27 0PZ
Tel: (01494) 488300   **£60**
Open: lunch Tue-Sun, dinner Tue-Sat (closed Bank Holidays)
Meals served: lunch 12-2, dinner 7-9

Eat from the bistro-inspired menu in the bar, with dishes such as avocado and brie salad, grilled haggis and black pudding, char-grilled home-made herby sausages or grilled Scotch salmon with a light yoghurt and East Indies spiced sauce. Alternatively, opt for the à la carte in the pretty candlelit dining room. English game terrine, giant Mediterrean prawns with a spicy cocktail sauce or seafood platter are starters here. Roast breast of duck with prunes and a cider sauce or lamb with an onion and red wine preserve might be the main courses. Desserts include caramelised old English lemon tart with clotted cream. Interesting wine list with some good buys. Well worth a drive to enjoy this unfussy but professionally run establishment.

Biography

Malcolm Cowan

Malcolm Cowan was born in Scotland, and an early love of cooking provoked a career decision when he was only fifteen. After an apprenticeship at the Queen's Hotel, Portsmouth, his first job was as a commis on RMS Queen Elizabeth. He then got down to some serious cooking in London, working his way round Simpson's-on-the-Strand, The Ritz, Verry's, Walton's and Odin's, and followed this by six years as executive head chef at The Westbury Hotel, and four years as executive head chef at Maxims de Paris in London. Finally, he found exactly what he was looking for at the quaintly named and located Old Plow at Speen.

STADDLEBRIDGE McCoy's

The Cleveland Tontine, Staddlebridge, Nr Northallerton,
  North Yorkshire, DL6 3JB
Tel: (01609) 882671   *Fax:* (01609) 882660   **£70**
Open: dinner Tue-Sat (closed 25 & 26 Dec, 1 Jan)
Meals served: dinner 7-9.30, (light meals Bistro 12-2, 7-10 daily)

The three McCoy brothers' unique restaurant with six rooms is renowned for its originality and eccentricities. An extraordinary place; don't expect anything standard here. There's a certain decadence about the decor, with its laid-back, personal style, 1940s tired furnishings, scattered cushions and flamboyant use of colour. Bedrooms boast Givenchy wallcoverings, double glazing to cut out the noise of traffic which swirls around the tontine, a little plot of land by the road intersection where the McCoys reign supreme. Wake up to a wonderful breakfast, using free-range eggs from their own black hens—the real event here is the food. The bistro in the basement is extremely popular, offering more informal dining from a blackboard menu, but for the full McCoy you've got to eat in the ground-floor dining room where the more sophisticated menu is available. Start with caviar scallops in red wine sauce, foie gras with brioche and Madeira-stewed grapes or langoustine pasta served with a shellfish sauce. The choice is extensive, including Irish oysters, polenta and always a home-made soup such as celery and red pepper. The hallmark here is that while imagination is given free rein in creating new and exciting robust dishes, there are always traditional favourites on offer for the less adventurous palate. Steak and chips is never off the menu, and can be enjoyed in many traditional ways -au poivre, Dijonnaise or béarnaise, as you please. Alternatives could include honey-roasted pigeon with pulses, sea bass with spicy lentils or fillet of lamb with rosemary and poivre sauce. Desserts are a wow too, with the range following a similar pattern, from the traditional to the exotic.

STAMFORD The George of Stamford

71 St Martins, Stamford, Lincolnshire, PE9 2LB
Tel: (01780) 55171   *Fax:* (01780) 57070   **£65**
Open: lunch & dinner daily
Meals served: lunch 12.30-2.30, dinner 7.15-10.30,
  (light meals Garden Lounge: 12-10.30)

There's been a hostelry on this spot for over 900 years. Look out for the gallows sign above the door to herald entrance to this charming old-world pub, once home to travellers waiting for the passing highway coach. Expectations are met by flagstone floors strewn with rugs, exposed stone walls and ancient beams, a cosy lounge with open fire and the lovely covered garden lounge with its wrought-iron furniture where families can eat informally. There are 47 bedrooms, some overlooking the cobbled courtyard, some with four-poster beds. The oak-panelled dining room is a formal jacket-and-tie affair. Chef Matthew Carroll offers traditional and modern English cooking, with Oriental and Mediterranean influences. The range runs from starters such as spicy Thai crab cake with lime and coconut sauce to grilled Dover sole, calf's liver with lemon and sage butter, pan-fried pigeon breast on chargrilled polenta with a lentil and port sauce and traditional roasts like beef which comes on the silver carving trolley. Light, quick lunch menu (two courses for £15.50). More informal eating in the garden lounge or ivy-clad courtyard area, including toasted club sandwiches, cold buffet, pasta dishes and grills.

STAPLEFORD   Stapleford Park

Stapleford, Nr Melton Mowbray, Leicestershire, LE14 2EF
Tel: (01572 787) 522   *Fax:* (01572 787) 651   **£65**
Open: lunch & dinner daily
Meals served: lunch 12-2.30, dinner 7-9.30 (Fri & Sat to 10.30)

At the sumptuous yet casual Stapleford Park, the young staff dispense
with traditional pomp to provide pure hospitality without any hint of
snobbery. A majestic 16th-century stately home in 500 acres of mature
parkland who spares no expenses in being transformed into one of the
most sophisticated country house hotels in Britain. The 42 bedrooms
are luxuriously appointed, and include 25 signature rooms individually
created by famous designers, a sort of museum of interior design, and
more recently, a cottage on the estate has been converted into four
rooms with private kitchen and function room. There are two dining
rooms, the stone-arched Old Kitchen and the ornate Grinling Gibbons
room. Diners get a whole home-baked loaf on a marble breadboard to
accompany evening meals.Unfussy and international, with
Mediterranean notes, the dinner menu offers dishes such as wild mushroom fricassée, juniper berry-scented gravadlax, charred sea bass with
herb fettuccine, pork loin with pecan rice or a simple risotto. Desserts
look across the Atlantic to deliver chocolate pecan pie with caramel
sauce and black-bottom pie along with traditional bread-and-butter pudding with maple syrup or the refreshingly unusual lemon soup with
fresh berries. Coffee and truffles to finish. An all-day lounge menu offers
sandwiches, salads, pasta and the all-time-American-favourite steak
sandwich. An impressive and comprehensive wine list is arranged by
grape variety, providing something for all palates.

STOKE-BY-NAYLAND   Angel Inn

Stoke-by-Nayland, Suffolk, CO6 4SA
Tel: (01206) 263245   *Fax:* (01206) 37324   **£35**
Open: lunch Wed-Sun, dinner Tue-Sat (closed 25 & 26 Dec, 1 Jan)
Meals served: lunch 12-2, dinner 6.30-9

Six comfortably furnished guest rooms, beamed bars with log fires in
the winter, good food, good wine and local ales: this is the 16th-century
Angel Inn, which stands at the crossroads in the centre of this ancient
village. Landscape artist John Constable was born nearby and found
much of his inspiration in the area. Eat in the bar or in the striking Well
Room, with its 52ft well. The menu changes twice daily, with choices
ranging from home-made soups and home-cooked gammon salad to
griddled wing of skate or steamed steak and kidney pudding with an
onion gravy. Good choice of puds.

STOKESLEY	CHAPTERS

27 High Street, Stokesley, North Yorkshire, TS9 5AD
Tel & Fax: (01642) 711888 £50
Open: lunch by arrangement, dinner Mon-Sat
Meals served: dinner 7-9.30 (Sat to 10)

Alan Thompson moved his restaurant here four years ago, taking over the former Golden Lion hotel and has transformed the place. On the ground floor is a bistro with blackboard menu—Indonesian chicken satay, paella Valenciana, Toulouse sausage cassoulet, lamb with Dijon sauce, and there's a similar bistro-style lunch menu available in the dining room if you prefer a more formal setting and fancy a choice of pasta dishes, too. Dinner is à la carte, short and concise, with a choice of eight dishes or so at each stage. Try the Scottish rope-grown mussels à la marinière, grilled goat's cheese on walnut-dressed salad or thin hot cheesey tart (made from Dolcelatte, olives, basil and tomato) to start, followed perhaps by a trio of sole, salmon and turbot baked in filo pastry, served on crayfish sauce. Thirteen rooms are available at special weekend rates for those eating in the restaurant. A new attraction is the beauty and relaxation centre on the first floor—reflexologist, hypnotherapist, massage and more!

STON EASTON	Ston Easton Park

Ston Easton, Nr Bath, Avon, BA3 4DF
Tel: (01761) 241631   *Fax:* (01761) 241377 £85
Open: lunch & dinner daily
Meals served: lunch 12.30-2, dinner 7.30-9.30 (Fri & Sat to 10)

Palladian luxury is what Ston Easton is all about; even the upstairs-downstairs tradition has been preserved in a lower ground level which features kitchen museum, servants' hall and 18th-century linen room in use today. Ask for a tour if you're interested. Beyond the walls outside is another world of romance, with landscaped gardens created by Humphrey Repton, complete with wells, bridges across the River Norr which runs through the gardens and an 18th-century ice house. It's total indulgence all round, not least in the main dining room where gentle, pastel decor provides an elegant setting for Mark Harrington's classically styled menu. Sit down to the delights of grilled Loch Fyne oysters and smoked tuna glazed with a champagne sabayon or baked noisette of cod with a vinaigrette of sun-dried tomatoes and herb ravioli. Ease on through a fillet of veal with mushrooms perhaps, baked in brioche and puff pastry; or poached roulade of turbot and langoustine à la Newburg. Simpler options are also available for those who prefer, and desserts are an art—teardrop of two chocolates set on a coulis of Grand Marnier and oranges, or baked banana and clotted cream clafoutis with rum and raisin ice cream. All the little extras imaginable are provided: excellent breakfasts, excellent staff, 21 rooms, including some with original Chippendale and Hepplewhite four-poster beds.

STONEHOUSE	Stonehouse Court

Bristol Road, Stonehouse, Gloucestershire, GL10 3RA
Tel: (01453) 825155   *Fax:* (01453) 824611 £55
Open: lunch & dinner daily
Meals served: lunch 12.30-2, dinner 7.30-10
17th-century Grade II-listed stone mansion in parkland, overlooking Stroud Water, on the edge of the Cotswolds. Friendly staff and beautiful gardens. 36 rooms.

STONHAM   Mr Underhill's

Stonham, Nr Stowmarket, Suffolk, IP14 5DW
Tel: (01449) 711206   **£65**
Open: lunch by arrangement, dinner Tue-Sat
  (closed Bank Holidays (open 25 & 26 Dec))
Meals served: dinner 7.30-9

Chris Bradley runs a one-man band in the kitchen of this delightful
Suffolk restaurant where he serves a daily-changing dinner menu with
dishes such as warm asparagus salad with mushrooms to start, followed by Barbary duck with provençal herbs perhaps, rack of lamb
with sorrel and mint or fillet of beef with tarragon and wild oyster
mushrooms. The handwritten menus are straightforward and perfectly
balanced—you can discuss fads and dislikes at the time of booking.
For dessert, there is usually a choice of three or four, and the whole
event comes to a truly satisfying end with coffee and delicious home-
made petits fours. Chris's wife Judy is your charming hostess at the
table. Some reasonably priced wines on the list. It's good to see a chef-
patron operation in the countryside still turning out interesting and
good food year after year—the real heroes of the restaurant trade.

STONOR   Stonor Arms

Stonor, Nr Henley-on-Thames, Oxfordshire, RG9 6HE
Tel: (01491) 638345   *Fax:* (01491) 638863   **£65**
Open: lunch Sun only, dinner Mon-Sat
Meals served: lunch 12-2, dinner 7-9.30,
  (light meals in Blades 12-2, 7-9.30)

Friendly staff, imaginative cooking and a beautiful Thames Valley location are some of the bonuses of this attractively converted 18th-century
village pub in the tranquil village of Stonor. Eat in the brasserie (lunch
or supper) or in the elegant restaurant with conservatory where
Stephen Frost's frequently changing set menus offer dishes such as
cream of mussel and saffron soup or ballotine of quail to start; followed
by char-grilled beef fillet, tournedos of salmon with leeks and a shellfish sauce, or loin of rabbit wrapped in bacon with a prune stuffing,
roasted and served with mashed potatoes and wild mushrooms.
Perhaps try a hazelnut mousse or poached fruit savarin to finish. A reasonably priced wine list and friendly smiling staff make it just the place
to crack open a bottle of Charles Heidsieck champagne.

STORRINGTON — Abingworth Hall

Thakeham Road, Storrington, West Sussex, RH20 3EF
Tel: (01798) 813636   *Fax:* (01798) 813914 **£45**
Open: lunch & dinner daily
Meals served: lunch 12.30-1.45, dinner 7.15-9

There's a pretty lake within the grounds of this 20-bedroomed, white-painted house, which was built in the 1930s. The house reflects the style and affluence of that time when the British Empire was at its height. Canopied beds and soft pastel colours give the best of the 20 bedrooms an air of quiet luxury; others are more standard, and smaller. Reception rooms include a cosy, oak-panelled drawing room and elegant, rattan-furnished conservatory lounge. Long-serving chef Peter Cannon offers an eclectic repertoire of competently prepared, straightforward dishes—field mushroom soup with Madeira; grilled lamb cutlets with a redcurrant sauce; fine English cheeses with home-made walnut bread and a good choice of refreshing desserts—lemon tart, chocolate and orange mousse.

STORRINGTON — Little Thakeham

Merrywood Lane, Storrington, West Sussex, RH20 3HE
Tel: (01903) 744416   *Fax:* (01903) 745022 **£75**
Open: lunch Tue-Sun, dinner Mon-Sat
   (closed 2 wks Xmas/New Year)
Meals served: lunch 1-2, dinner 7-9

The beauty of Tim and Pauline Ractliff's nine-bedroomed house extends well beyond its walls. Designed by Sir Edward Lutyens, the house is set in superb gardens created in the style of Gertrude Jekyll and is approached via a long drive lined with walnut trees. It has been beautifully restored and tastefully furnished by the Ractliffs over the last 15 years. Among its many fine features are a minstrel's gallery, massive oak doors, original stone fireplaces, flagstoned polished floors and mullioned windows. On the culinary side, new chef Joanna Docherty produces short fixed-price menus of Mediterranean and English design. Bruschetta with roasted peppers and balsamic dressing, Sussex potted cheese with carrot chutney, and courgette and fennel soup with croutons precede dishes such as roast rack of Southdown lamb with tarragon hollandaise, grilled red snapper with leek and white wine sauce or beef with a pink peppercorn and brandy sauce. Dinner is a four-course affair.

STORRINGTON   Manley's

Manleys Hill, Storrington, West Sussex, RH20 4BT
Tel: (01903) 742331   **£55**
Open: lunch Tue-Sun, dinner Tue-Sat (closed 1st 2 wks Jan)
Meals served: lunch 12-2, dinner 7-9.15

Chef Karl Löderer turns out sophisticated, accomplished dishes with a great deal of care and flair, at this attractive, low-beamed, Sussex-stone restaurant located in a Queen Anne building at the foot of the South Downs. His continental repertoire is essentially classic in style, with many dishes harking back to his Austrian roots. Start perhaps with pan-fried scallops with braised leeks, or crab gratin, before tucking into dishes such as local mallard duck with port or pan-fried turbot with a shellfish crust and langoustine sauce. The fixed-price lunch and dinner menus are fully inclusive of service, coffee, amuses-bouches and petits fours. Speciality Austrian sweets and vegetarian dishes on request. Overnight guests can stay in the large comfortable apartment which overlooks the garden and the Downs.

Biography

From an early age Karl Löderer has had a great love of cooking and took every opportunity to exercise his budding skills, first at school and then at college, in his native Vienna. He worked his way around Europe, before

Karl

Löderer

coming to Britain via La Frégate, Guernsey. The next twelve years Karl spent at Gravetye Manor, in Sussex, as chef de cuisine. This was where the public and the guides really began to take notice of him. But wanting to be his own boss, he moved on, bringing his `Midas touch' to Manleys in Storrington.

STORRINGTON   Old Forge

6a Church Street, Storrington, West Sussex, RH20 4LA
Tel: (01903) 743402   **£45**
Open: lunch Wed-Fri & Sun, dinner Tue-Sat
    (closed Bank Holidays, 1 wk spring, 3 wks autumn)
Meals served: lunch 12.30-1.30, dinner 7.15-9

Clive and Cathy Roberts offer an adventurous and eclectic choice of menus and dishes at this converted, beamed forge. Start perhaps with a smooth parfait of bacon and black pudding or Icelandic prawns bound in lime and ginger mayonnaise, before tucking into pan-fried cutlets of lamb with wild mushrooms and caraway or thinly-sliced goose supreme with a pink grapefruit and peppercorn sauce.

Vegetarians might find a baked lentil, onion and sage roulade served with a tomato coulis; fish lovers might opt for the likes of fresh Scottish salmon set on a lightly creamed mustard and chive sauce. Puds are no less mouthwatering, with rich butterscotch pudding or pineapple tarte tatin and cardamom ice cream among favourites. Coffee and petits fours are complimentary. Excellent value wines, strong on New World varieties, with Californian house wines.

STOURBRIDGE   Bon Appetit

38 Market Street, Stourbridge, West Midlands, DY8 1AG
Tel: (01384) 375372   **£45**
Open: lunch Tue-Sat, Sun in winter, dinner Tue-Sat
Meals served: lunch 12.30-2, dinner 7.30-10

This straightforward, friendly little restaurant is on two floors and chef-patron Simon Rudge has built up a loyal local following in the six years he has been here. Start with brochette of lambs kidneys with devilled potato salad or cream of cauliflower soup, before going on to Polynesian breast of chicken, or traditional Black Country faggots with onion gravy. Desserts include dishes such as warm walnut and treacle tart with cinnamon cream, or glazed lemon tart.

STOW BRIDGE   Swinton House

Stow Bridge, King's Lynn, Norfolk, PE34 3PP
Tel: (01366) 383151   *Fax:* (01366) 383151   **£40**
Open: lunch Sun, dinner Fri-Sat (closed 1 wk Xmas)
Meals served: lunch 12.15-2, dinner Fri & Sat only 7-9

A small, friendly, informal restaurant with the emphasis on quality and value for money. Chef-patron Graham Kitch offers short set menus with three or four choices for each course. A typical meal might consist of creamy soup of Jerusalem artichokes followed by poached fillet of turbot in a saffron sauce with mock caviar; and to finish, crunchy lemon tart with whipped cream.

STOW-ON-THE-WOLD   Fosse Manor Hotel

Fosse Way, Stow-on-the-Wold, Gloucestershire, GL54 1JX
Tel: (01451) 830354   *Fax:* (01451) 832486   **£40**
Open: lunch & dinner daily (closed 22-30 Dec)
Meals served: lunch 12.30-2, dinner 7.30-10

A traditional Cotswold stone house efficiently run by Bob and Yvonne Johnston. Twenty impeccable bedrooms and comfortable lounges make this a popular hotel with regular customers who seem to leave their hats hanging in the bar—I suppose it gives them another reason to return! The set menus offer plenty of choice with perhaps a leek soup, deep-fried mushrooms with Stilton or home-made pâté amongst the starters. Half a roast duck with orange sauce, lamb cutlets with piquant sauce or grilled steak to follow. Vegetarians and children are well catered for.

STOW-ON-THE-WOLD   Grapevine

Sheep Street, Stow-on-the-Wold, Gloucestershire, GL54 1AU
Tel: (01451) 830344   *Fax:* (01451) 832278   **£45**
Open: lunch & dinner daily (closed Bank Holidays, 24 Dec-11 Jan)
Meals served: lunch 12-2, dinner 7-9.30

In this lovely Cotswold-stone hotel set in the middle of one of the most
typical of Cotswold villages, beware of low beams as you explore the
lounges, bars and corridors to the bedrooms. Top of the range
amongst these is the aptly-named Rafters Room, and all are well maintained. The restaurant is in the vine-filled conservatory, and there you
can enjoy modern British cooking and charming service. Light lunches
are served in the bar.

STOW-ON-THE-WOLD   Wyck Hill House

Burford Road, Stow-on-the-Wold, Gloucestershire, GL54 1HY
Tel: (01451) 831936   *Fax:* (01451) 832243   **£70**
Open: lunch & dinner daily
Meals served: lunch 12.30-2.30, dinner 7.30-9.30 (Sat to 10)

This hilltop hotel with splendid views over the Windrush Valley and
100 acres of well-maintained gardens and woodland is considered by
many to be one of the finest hotels in the Cotswolds. The 31 rooms are
divided between the main house, the more secluded Coach House and
the Orangery; all are beautifully designed and luxuriously appointed.
The food, in the capable hands of Ian Smith, is essentially English,
though very much contemporary in design (in contrast to the rich traditional opulence of the dining room). Expect the likes of spicy chowder of Cornish shellfish, or tartlets of sautéed pheasant to start;
followed by pot-roasted rabbit cooked with burgundy wine or halibut
with a lemon and thyme crust. A lengthy wine list majors on France
with many bin ends at the top end of the market in price.

STRATFORD-UPON-AVON   Ettington Park

Alderminster, Stratford-upon-Avon, Warwickshire, CV37 8BS
Tel: (01789) 450123   *Fax:* (01789) 450472   **£65**
Open: lunch & dinner daily
Meals served: lunch 12-2, dinner 7-9.30 (Fri & Sat to 10)

Perhaps the most original, imaginative house of its type in
Warwickshire, this neo-Gothic stately home offers 48 luxury bedrooms
including nine suites, many of which look out on to the surrounding
countryside and Victorian gardens. The house is unique in that it has
remained within the tenure of the same family since the time of the
Domesday Book and possibly even further back, to the Norman
Conquest. Public rooms reflect the grandeur and historic importance
of the house. Notable features include the lovely conservatory leading
to the restaurant with its rococo ceiling; a very elegant, distinguished
lounge; and the splendid Long Gallery with book-lined walls and high,
wood-panelled ceiling—one of the most sought-after meeting rooms in
the country. Good leisure centre and their own fishing on the Stour;
French and English cuisine in the restaurant.

STRATFORD-UPON-AVON — Liaison

1 Shakespeare Street, Stratford-upon-Avon,
    Warwickshire, CV37 6RN
Tel: (01789) 293400   *Fax:* (01789) 297863   **£50**
Open: lunch Mon-Fri, dinner Mon-Sat (closed 2 wks Jan)
Meals served: lunch 12-2.30, dinner 6-10.30

Readers with a medium-length memory will remember a restaurant of this name in the 1980s in Solihull, and this incarnation is also in the capable hands of Patricia Plunkett and Ank Van Der Tuin. Now located in a converted Methodist church, they have a good setting in which to offer modern cooking with a Mediterranean slant. A fixed-price menu offers plenty of choice for each course, with typical dishes such as a marbled Mediterranean terrine, wild salmon gateau tartare and a rendezvous of seafruits on a light tomato and basil cream. Early evening and lunchtime sees the addition of an informal, single-dish menu called Liaison Lights—caviar and melon, red mullet on a ratatouille jus. Freshly made canapés and good petits fours begin and end full meals.

STREATLEY-ON-THAMES — Swan Diplomat

High Street, Streatley-on-Thames, Berkshire, RG8 9HR
Tel: (01491) 873737   *Fax:* (01491) 872554   **£60**
Open: lunch Sun-Fri, dinner daily
Meals served: lunch 12.30-2, dinner 7.30-9.30 (Sat from 7)

Over half of the 46 rooms here have wonderful river views, and some even have balconies at this water's edge hotel on the south bank of the Thames. It's a delightful location, and the hotel is run in friendly, professional style by manager Borge Karlsson and team. Relax in the riverside restaurant and enjoy Christopher Cleveland's cooking. A typical table d'hôte selection might include potted salmon with lemon vinaigrette and hot sauce followed by grilled lamb cutlet with sautéed mushrooms and deep-fried onions or pork fillet with Madeira sauce flavoured with Parma ham, tomato and sage. Alternatively, you can opt for a lighter lunch menu in the Duck Room, or for the full-blown carte in the evening to enjoy the likes of veal with pan-fried scampi and a lime and Pernod sauce and steak béarnaise. Conference and leisure facilities within the hotel and the Magdalen College Barge moored alongside.

STRETTON — Dovecliffe Hall

Dovecliffe Road, Stretton, Nr Burton-on-Trent,
    Staffordshire, DE13 0DJ
Tel: (01283) 531818   **£45**
Open: lunch Tue-Fri & Sun, dinner Tue-Sat
    (closed 1 wk Xmas, 2 wks Aug)
Meals served: lunch 12-1.45, dinner 7-9.30

This is a carefully restored, seven-bedroomed Georgian house dating from 1790, set in seven acres of garden and farmland overlooking the river Dove. Spacious, elegant lounges and large, comfortable bedrooms provide good accommodation, while the restaurant, with its outstanding views over the lawns and fountains, offers light and imaginative cooking, making the most of fresh, local produce. The restaurant has attracted a strong, local following, with owner Nicholas Hine very much in evidence front-of-house. Chef-patron Hilary Hine and her team offer monthly-changing fixed-price and à la carte menus. Typical of main courses are grilled breast of duck garnished with the leg meat and carved onto a Chinese spicy sauce, or fillet steak with peppercorn sauce. Fish and vegetarian dishes of the day are always in evidence, and the house speciality is a wicked bread- and-butter pudding, made with double cream and Cointreau-soaked raisins, served with crème anglaise and caramel.

STRETTON   Ram Jam Inn

Great North Road, Stretton, Nr Oakham, Rutland,
  Leicestershire, LE15 7QX
Tel: (01780) 410776   *Fax:* (01780) 410361
Open: lunch & dinner daily (closed 25 Dec)
Meals served: lunch 12-2.30, dinner 7-10, (light meals 7am-10pm)

You might be wrong in your expectations at this roadside inn with restaurant next to a service station on the A1. The Ram Jam, which takes its name from a 16th-century drink, is far more than a mere eating and drinking establishment. Inside, you'll find a number of smartly furnished eating places, including snack bar, bar proper, outdoor terrace and restaurant which overlooks the garden orchard, as do the seven tastefully decorated rooms. Here they really do care about the food. There are giant sandwiches, chopped steakburgers, huge Rutland sausages, half pints of prawns and farmhouse cheeses, all served as a snack with fresh crusty bread, or for a full-blown meal you can sit down in the restaurant for home-made soup and puddings, fresh fish and a variety of grills. This, indeed, is the place to stop if you're heading north from Stamford on the Al (southbound drivers take the B668 towards Oakham).

STROUD   Oakes

169 Slad Road, Stroud, Gloucestershire, GL5 1RG
Tel: (01453) 759950   **£65**
Open: lunch Tue-Sun, dinner Tue-Sat (closed Bank Holidays)
Meals served: lunch 12.30-1.45, dinner 7.30-9.30

An enjoyable meal at this restaurant in a former school house is guaranteed because chef-patron Chris Oakes is at the stove. Chris focusses religiously on local ingredients, creating interesting combinations, and his is one of the finest tables for miles around. This is gutsy country cooking, keen on flavours, inspired by English and French traditions. Start with pea soup served with croutons, breadcrumbed tiger prawn tails with tomato and chili salsa or home-made sausages—venison served with lentils, bacon and onion gravy perhaps, or lamb sausages with a red wine dressing. Follow with fillet of pike with ginger sauce, osso buco or breast of chicken with a hazelnut sauce. Excellent desserts to finish. Some reasonably priced wine on the list are the final component in creating a very good restaurant.

STUCKTON	**Three Lions**

Stuckton, Nr Fordingbridge, Hampshire, SP6 2HF
Tel: (01425) 652489   *Fax:* (01425) 656144
Open: lunch Tue-Sun, dinner Tue-Sat (closed Bank Holidays,
   1 wk Xmas, 2 wks Jul/Aug)
Meals served: lunch 12.15-1.30, dinner 7.15-9 (Sat to 9.30)

£55

Karl and June Wadsack pack them in at their informal restaurant. Blackboards advise the daily fare which changes at lunch and dinner. Old favourites are offered together with classic dishes—modern

Mediterranean to Thai or Indonesian. You might find—wiener schnitzel or skate with black butter alongside roasted black bream with olive oil and sun-dried tomatoes, nasi goreng and sambal, or Thai green curry. For pudding you could have bread-and-butter pudding, tiramisu, chocolate marquise or warm apple strudel. A superb wine list has equally varied selections to complement the food.

Biography

Karl Wadsack

Karl Wadsack was born in Hanover and trained there at the Hotel Regina, then spent his first two cooking years on luxury liners, cruising the Americas, the Atlantic and the Caribbean. On arriving in the Lake District, he worked at the Wild Boar Hotel, before joining Trusthouse Forte and opening the St George's Hotel in Liverpool for them. He then moved on to Quaglino's, then Chewton Glen before buying the Three Lions, which he runs with wife June

---

STURMINSTER NEWTON	**Plumber Manor**

Hazelbury Bryan Road, Sturminster Newton, Dorset, DT10 2AF
Tel: (01258) 472507   *Fax:* (01258) 473370
Open: lunch Sun, dinner daily (closed Feb)
Meals served: lunch 12.30-1.30, dinner 7.30-9.30

£45

The Prideaux-Brunes have been living at the manor house since it was built in 1665 by the forefathers of the present occupiers, Brian, Richard and Alison, who in 1973 took the decision to turn their home into this charming restaurant with rooms. Located at the heart of Hardy country, the house is an imposing Jacobean structure made of local stone, set in peaceful secluded grounds through which runs the Divelish stream, a tributary of the River Stour—making it an ideal place to escape the madding crowd! There are six bedrooms in the main house (approached by a gallery hung with family portraits); and six more in a converted stone barn within the grounds—the largest, with window seats overlooking the stream and garden; and finally a further four spacious rooms in the converted courtyard annexe. Brian's cooking remains the mainstay of the business. He provides a balance of imaginative and traditional cuisine of French and English style, using the finest of raw ingredients. Start perhaps with wild mushroom mille-feuilles, crab tartlets with a thermidor sauce or prawns with a light curry sauce, followed by beef Wellington or chateaubriand, Aylesbury duck with orange, chicken indienne or salmon hollandaise. Good wines support the cooking.

SUDBURY   Mabey's Brasserie

47 Gainsborough Street, Sudbury, Suffolk, CO10 7SS
Tel: (01787) 374298   **£45**
Open: lunch & dinner Tue-Sat (closed 5 days Xmas)
Meals served: lunch 12-2, dinner 7-10

Pine and pews create a bistro-style setting to match the blackboard menus at this bright, split-level restaurant-cum-brasserie, run by Robert and Johanna Mabey (he was at Hintlesham Hall). Daniel McClelland offers a varied range of dishes: crab and prawn filo parcels; Japanese-style tempura chicken; cod baked with a herb crust; char-grilled meats. This is good eclectic cooking with a light, homely touch.

SURBITON   Chez Max

85 Maple Road, Surbiton, Surrey, KT6 4AW   *Very good local*
Tel: 0181-399 2365   *restaurant.*   **£45**
Open: lunch Tue-Fri, dinner Tue-Sat
    (closed Bank Holidays, 24-30 Dec, open lunch Mothering Sunday)
Meals served: lunch 12.30-2, dinner 7.30-10

Well-executed French classics take centre stage at this pretty, peach-painted restaurant. Start with Mediterranean prawn salad, grilled goat's cheese with apple and walnut or classic moules marinières. Main course options will always feature fish of the day—grilled Dover sole, steamed monkfish with lobster sauce, or sea bass with fennel—along with the likes of guinea fowl with lime and raisin sauce, or fillet steak with mustard and pink pepper sauce. The fixed-price lunch menu reflects the style of the carte, with four choices for each course. Desserts include home-made sorbets and trolley sweets.

SUTTON   Partners Brasserie

23 Stonecot Hill, Sutton, Surrey, SM3 9HB
Tel: 0181-644 7743   **£40**
Open: lunch Tue-Fri, dinner Tue-Sat
    (closed Bank Holidays, 25 Dec-2 Jan)
Meals served: lunch 12-2, dinner 7-9.30   ❖

Sound cooking and friendly staff have earned a loyal local following at this brasserie in a shopping parade off the busy A24. Sister to the Dorking-based Partners West Street, it offers a well-balanced, varied carte with around six choices for each course, ranging from simple pasta dishes to calf's liver and bacon, or fish and shellfish hot pot. Traditional puds or British cheeses with celery and oat cakes to finish.

SUTTON COLDFIELD　　　　　New Hall

Walmley Road, Sutton Coldfield, West Midlands, B76 8QX
Tel: 0121-378 2442　　*Fax:* 0121-378 4637　　　　　　　**£60**
Open: lunch Sun-Fri, dinner daily
Meals served: lunch 12.30-2 (Sun to 2.15),
　　dinner 7-10 (Sun 7.30-9.30)

Reputedly the oldest inhabited moated house in Britain, New Hall is set in 26 acres of private gardens surrounded by a lily-filled Medieval moat which is fed by seven springs. The house dates back nearly 800 years and has a wealth of historic features and romantic, period charm. The cocktail bar and lounge overlook the terrace from which a wood-clad bridge leads over to the gardens, which include yew topiary, orchards, croquet lawns and delightful wooded arbours. Largest bedrooms are in the main house, the smaller ones in the modern courtyard wing. Excellent service throughout. New chef, Simon Radley, joined as we went to press – watch this space!

SWANAGE　　　　　　　　　Galley

9 High Street, Swanage, Dorset, BH19 2LN
Tel: (01929) 427299　　　　　　　　　　　　**£35**
Open: dinner daily (closed 2 wks Nov, Jan-Easter)
Meals served: dinner 7-9.30

Good home-made bread, fresh herbs and Nick Storer's competent cooking make this little restaurant close to the pier a popular choice with regulars. The fixed-price menu features local fish, seafood, game, poultry, meat and vegetarian dishes. Fresh oysters and lobster are usually available and there's plenty of choice across the courses. Expect the likes of venison and pheasant pudding or roast lamb with a Madeira gravy. The vegetarian menu might include a mushroom stroganoff or savoury strudel with hollandaise.

TADWORTH　　　　Gemini Restaurant

28 Station Approach, Tadworth, Surrey, KT20 5AH
Tel: (01737) 812179　　　　　　　　　　　　**£50**
Open: lunch Tue-Fri & Sun, dinner Tue-Sat
　　(closed 1 wk Xmas, 2 wks Jun)
Meals served: lunch 12-2, dinner 7-9.30

Robert and Debbie Foster's restaurant has a welcoming feel to it and the menu focuses on French cooking, with fish and game as specialities. Starters on the extensive, seasonal table d'hôte menu might range from warm crab tartlet to home-made tomato fettucine with mushrooms, asparagus and basil. Main courses might be breast of corn-fed guinea fowl on a bed of bubble'n'squeak with whisky and almonds, or stir-fry of monkfish, tiger prawns and scallops in a Pernod sauce. Home-made desserts (rum and sultana crème brûlée, mango bavarois mousse), English and French cheeses, and coffee with petits fours to finish. Good-value daily-changing lunch menus along with daily specials in the evening.

TAPLOW   Cliveden

Taplow, Nr Maidenhead, Berkshire, SL6 0JF
Tel: (01628) 668561   *Fax:* (01628) 661837   **£100**
Waldo's:
Open: dinner Tue-Sat
Meals served: dinner 7-10.30
Terrace Dining Room:
Open: lunch & dinner daily
Meals served: lunch 12.30-2.30, dinner 7-10.30

Cliveden is about elegance and sheer luxury. Formerly the home of Frederick, Prince of Wales, three dukes and the Astor family, and now in the very careful hands of John Tham, the 17th-century mansion sits majestically amidst 400 acres overlooking a picturesque stretch of the Thames. Words hardly do justice to the experience of staying here: sumptuous decor, impeccable service, two swimming pools, sauna, gym, horse riding, fishing, ten-nis, boating and so on. One

visit will convince you that this is a lifestyle to which you could readily become accustomed, and not least among the luxu-ries is the food. Head chef Ron Maxfield (pictured) has a string of accolades to his name and two showcases for his skills, the Terrace Dining Room and Waldo's. As much as possible is home made (breads, pastries, ice creams, preserves, pastas, chocolates) or locally bought (fruits, veg-etables, salads); though the produce is used in different ways. In the Terrace the emphasis is on traditional, clas-sic, simple English and European dishes—even his-toric ones such as 14th century chicken cooked with pine nuts, hyssop and summer savoury, and English summer pudding with elderflower ice cream. In Waldo's, Ron can give his imagination free rein and you eat dishes like lasagne of lobster and langoustine with a truffle-scented dressing, and hot mirabelle soufflé with liquorice ice cream. The wine list matches the setting and the cuisine and has great strength and depth, especially in the classics.

TAUNTON — Castle Hotel

Castle Green, Taunton, Somerset, TA1 1NF
Tel: (01823) 272671   *Fax:* (01823) 336066   **£45**
Open: lunch & dinner daily
Meals served: lunch 12.30-2, dinner 7.30-9

The Chapman family's hotel with 35 rooms has long been known for its serious approach to the revival of English culinary delights. The restaurant uses first-rate suppliers providing produce on a daily basis to ensure the very best possible standards at all times. Chef Phil Vickery does the rest, producing a well-balanced choice of menus which include a lighter menu option at each sitting. Try a stew of wild mushrooms, baked crab tart or Jerusalem artichoke soup with saffron and sorrel to start. Main courses could include saffron fettucine with poached egg and shallot butter sauce, pan-fried tournedos with celeriac and truffles or braised cornfed duck with star anise, lemon grass and green ginger. The choice is mouthwatering, the setting quite exceptional. Twelve centuries of history, from Saxon settlement to Norman fortress, razed to the ground and rebuilt three times, are the making of this eminent hotel, whose guest list reads like a pageant of history.

TAUNTON — Nightingales Restaurant

Bath House Farm, Lower West Hatch, Nr Taunton, Somerset, TA3 5RH
Tel: (01823) 480806   **£50**
Open: dinner Tue-Sat (closed 25 Dec)
Meals served: dinner 7-9.30
Under new ownership just as we went to press, so that we were unable to make a visit this time. However early menus read well, so write and tell me what you think. For the first ten reviews received that read the closest to our inspector's, I'll send a bottle of Charles Heidsieck champagne!

TAUNTON — Porters

49 East Reach, Taunton, Somerset, TA1 3EX
Tel: (01823) 256688   **£35**
Open: lunch Mon-Fri, dinner Mon-Sat (closed Bank Holidays)
Meals served: lunch 12-2, dinner 7-9.45

This is a good local place to eat with plenty of wines available by the glass and some tables in a courtyard. The blackboard menu, which changes several times a week, offers straightforward competent cooking. Deep-fried camembert with a redcurrant and raspberry sauce, or chicken liver and port pâté precede main-course dishes, which offer a good range from char-grilled steaks and lasagne to Brixham scallops, red mullet with ginger and spring onion or cashew and carrot roast with a tomato coulis for vegetarians. Sticky toffee pudding is the speciality among desserts.

TEDDINGTON   Spaghetti Junction

20 High Street, Teddington, Middlesex, TW11 8EW
Tel: 081-977 9199   *Fax:* 081-977 8890   **£40**
Open: lunch & dinner Tue-Sun (closed Bank Holiday Sundays)
Meals served: lunch 12-2, dinner 6-11.15 (6-10.30 Sun)

Despite the American-sounding name (or is it Birmingham?!), the over-riding influence here comes indeed from Italy, home of spaghetti. Typical dishes from the repertoire, which is simple and straightforward, include home-made minestrone, gnocchi with dolcelatte and cream, arrosto misto and cold escalope of veal topped with creamed tuna. Grills and roasts are also common, along with the likes of chicken Lucifero—topped with asparagus and sun-dried tomatoes, in a hot and spicy sauce. Tiramisu, zabaglione and cassata Siciliana feature among desserts. Set menus include one for children, and one for executives.

TEFFONT EVIAS   Howard's House

Teffont Evias, Dinton, Nr Salisbury, Wiltshire, SP3 5RJ
Tel: (01722) 716392   *Fax:* (01722) 716820   **£75**
Open: lunch Sun, dinner daily
Meals served: lunch 12.30-2, dinner 7.30-10

There's no bar but drinks are served at any time of the day at this small family-run hotel in the sleepy hamlet of Teffont Evias. Beautiful gardens surround this converted Tudor farmhouse, with evidence of their colour displayed in every room in the house. Chef-patron Paul Firmin cooks in modern country style, offering a fixed-price menu with plenty of choice. Start with curried parsnip soup with toasted cumin seed, followed by chicken supreme with a marjoram and sun-dried tomato mousseline or grilled sea bream with fresh basil and saffron sauce. Lovely puds might include a sorbet tulip with raspberry sauce or pear and almond tart with Amaretto crème anglaise. A very extensive wine list has some fine wines at reasonable prices. There are now nine luxurious bedrooms to tempt you to stay.

TEIGNMOUTH   Thomas Luny House

Teign Street, Teignmouth, Devon, TQ14 8EG
Tel: (01626) 772976   **£35**
Open: dinner daily (closed mid Dec-end Jan)
Meals served: dinner 7.30 for 8

This late 18th-century Georgian house in the old quarter of the seaside town is run by John and Alison Allan as a small, informal hotel with comfortable rooms. The dining-room is only open for residents and guests and the set menu is served around one large table. Simple, carefully prepared fare is produced from good local ingredients and a few wines are offered, all at the same price.

TETBURY   Calcot Manor

Tetbury, Gloucestershire, GL8 8YJ
Tel: (01666) 890391   *Fax:* (01666) 890394   **£50**
Open: lunch & dinner daily
Meals served: lunch 12.30-2, dinner 7.30-9.30

The rolling Cotswold hills provide a breathtaking setting for this 20-bedroomed hotel, originally part of a 14th-century farmhouse complex. Old beams and real log fires create a homely and welcoming feel. Some of the rooms are located in the converted stable annexe, including some of the best and most characterful. Splendid family suites offer plenty of thoughtful extras for the kids' entertainment, and an enclosed garden next door includes a play train. The restaurant, candlelit for dinner, is a lovely room with a beautiful old butcher's table at one end where home-made breads are displayed. New chef Alec Howard uses local organic beef and fresh Cornish fish to good effect on his short, imaginative carte. Typical starters include double-baked Cheddar soufflé with mustard sauce, bresaola with goat's cheese dressing and smoked haddock and whisky soup. Main courses might offer fillet of cod with thyme sauce, seared salmon with tomato butter sauce and beef Bordelaise served with onion rings. Look out for glazed rice pudding with exotic fruit sauce among desserts.

TETBURY   The Close

8 Long Street, Tetbury, Gloucestershire, GL8 8AQ
Tel: (01666) 502272   *Fax:* (01666) 504401   **£55**
Open: lunch & dinner daily
Meals served: lunch 12.30-2, dinner 7.30-9.45

This 15-bedroomed town house with its delightful walled garden is a peaceful, tranquil oasis at the heart of this little market town in the Cotswolds. Elegance and comfort go hand-in-hand, both in the lounges and in the bedrooms, which are individually designed and named (not numbered). Most rooms retain the character of a bygone era—the house was originally built in 1585 for a local wool merchant and was returned to its former glory in the early 1970s. The restaurant offers modern British cooking on a seasonal à la carte or daily fixed menu.

THAME — Spread Eagle

Cornmarket, Thame, Oxfordshire, OX9 2BW
Tel: (01844) 213661   *Fax:* (01844) 261380   **£45**
Open: lunch & dinner daily (closed 28-30 Dec)
Meals served: lunch 12.30-2 (Sun to 2.30), dinner 7-10
    (Sat from 7.30, Sun to 9)

Right in the town centre, this former coaching inn dates back to the 16th century. Charles II is said to have stayed here and French soldiers are rumoured to have been held in the hotel cellars during the Napoleonic Wars. The hotel found fame in the 1920s when John Fothergill bought it, turned his back on the regular locals and passing tradesmen, and attracted a new, distinguished clientele through his social and artistic connections. Politicians, Oxford dons, and most famous of all, Oscar Wilde, added their notoriety to the already renowned period charm of the place. There are 33 comfortable, en-suite bedrooms, including two suites; those in the main house are traditional, those in the newer wing have french windows which open on to a west-facing lawn and flower beds. The Fothergill restaurant provides classic English and French cuisine, with Anglo-Indian specialities.

THORNBURY — Thornbury Castle

Thornbury, Nr Bristol, Avon, BS12 1HH
Tel: (01454) 281182   *Fax:* (01454) 416188   **£70**
Open: lunch & dinner daily (closed 2 days Jan)
Meals served: lunch 12-2, dinner 7-9.30
    (Fri & Sat to 10, Sun to 9)

In 1510 Edward Stafford, 3rd Duke of Buckingham and Constable of England, received a licence from Henry VIII to build a castle at Thornbury. Ten years later, the king disposed of the Duke on the grounds of treason (beheaded) and appropriated the castle, which he retained for the next 33 years. In 1535 he and Anne Boleyn spent ten days here before she too suffered the same fate as the Duke. Then Mary Tudor lived here for some years and it was she who returned the Castle to Buckingham's descendants upon her ascension to the throne. Today, in some respects little has changed at this authentic Tudor castle for history and contemporary comforts blend to create an atmosphere of timelessness. Surrounded by vineyard, gardens and high walls, with views over the Severn into Gloucestershire and Wales, the Castle offers 18 bedrooms, several of which have large Tudor fireplaces, rough stone walls and oriel windows overlooking the walled garden. Furnishing and fabrics are stylish and elegant; many of the rooms have four-posters and are reached via the spiral stone staircase. Candlelit baronial public rooms include two dining rooms with panelled walls, heraldic shields and large open fires. Fixed-price menus offer a classic French and English repertoire with a choice of two or three courses at lunchtime. Excellent selection of British farmhouse cheeses, which include 75-year-old David Bone's Hurston Dunlop, made in a tiny Somerset dairy from the unpasteurised milk of his one and only Jersey cow.

Maurice Taylor continues to devote much money to improving and maintaining the structure of this extraordinary castle.

THORNTON CLEVELEYS   Victorian House

Trunnah Road, Thornton Cleveleys, Lancashire, FY5 4HF
Tel: (01253) 860619   *Fax:* (01253) 865350   **£45**
Open: lunch & dinner Mon-Sat (closed 2 wks Feb)
Meals served: lunch 12-1.30, dinner 7-9.30

Victorian is the overall theme, but the cooking at Didier and Louise Guérin's restaurant is decidedly French bourgeois. Choose from starters such as wild boar pâté with a Cumberland sauce, bacon and onion cream tart, or gratin Breton—creamed leeks and mushroom fondue with poached egg and cheese gratin; followed perhaps by braised salmon hollandaise, venison casserole in red wine with juniper berries and spices, or chicken supreme with tarragon. The house is set in two acres of lovely gardens surrounded by mature trees; and there are three en-suite traditional-style bedrooms available for those who wish to stay overnight. Light lunches (Tue-Sat) served in the conservatory.

THORNTON-LE-FYLDE   River House

Skippool Creek, Thornton-le-Fylde, Nr Blackpool,
    Lancashire, FY5 5LF
Tel: (01253) 883497   *Fax:* (01253) 892083   **£45**
Open: lunch & dinner by arrangement (closed dinner Sun,
    some Bank Holidays)
Meals served: lunch Sun only 12.30 for 1, dinner 7.30-9.30

Bill and Carole Scott share the cooking at their charming restaurant with rooms: he looks after meat and fish, while Carole takes charge of starters and sauces. The motto is to put the customer first; and when it comes to looking after you, they make sure that they succeed. Quality is important: fresh fish from Fleetwood and Scotland, locally shot game, wild venison and lamb from the Fylde all feature strongly. Though strong on game, the menu is varied: starters such as soufflé suissesse, sautéed chicken livers or scallops in a creamy wine and herb sauce; might be followed by beef teriyaki, young grouse served with a redcurrant sauce, rare roasted venison with game sauce, and fish dishes which depend on the day's catch. Puddings are the domain of Karen Jones, and are in keeping with standards throughout the meal. For overnight guests there are five rooms, two of which feature splendid Victorian hooded bathtubs. It's worth noting that the road outside the hotel floods during spring tides.

THUNDRIDGE   Hanbury Manor

Thundridge, Nr Ware, Hertfordshire, SG12 0SD
Tel: (01920) 487722   *Fax:* (01920) 487692   **£65**
Open: dinner Mon-Sat (closed Bank Holidays)
Meals served: dinner 7.30-9.30 (Fri & Sat 7-9.45)

A handsome Jacobean mansion with 200 acres of splendid parkland
which includes a 30-acre arboretum and 18-hole championship golf
course. Recently converted, this is a fine, modern, 96-bedroomed country house hotel complete with sporting complex, palatial swimming
pool and good conference and banqueting facilities. The style and character of the old building have been retained in many features—carved
wall panelling, tapestries, marble fireplaces and the like. Bedrooms,
including 25 suites, are generally sumptuous, and are housed in the
main house or in the sympathetically-designed Garden Court annexe.
The kitchen is advised by Albert Roux of London's Le Gavroche, and
offers a varied choice of menus across three venues: all-day snacks and
light meals in Vardon's Grill and Bar above the health club; lunch in
the Conservatory; and dinner in the more formal setting of the elegant
Zodiac restaurant. A typical menu du jour might feature smoked
salmon tartelette or a terrine of sole and sea scallops; followed by duo
of sea bass and zander with fennel cream and white butter sauce or, on
Sundays, roast rib of beef with Yorkshire pudding and creamed horseradish. The carte is extensive, with Gavroche signature dishes like
soufflé suissesse to start, followed by baked turbot with wild mushrooms and ginger, or magret of duck with ceps, grapes and a muscat
sauce. The wine list is in keeping with the establishment—extensive,
but with some good buys on offer.

TINTAGEL   Trebrea Lodge

Trenale, Nr Tintagel, Cornwall, PL34 0HR
Tel: (01840) 770410   **£35** .
Open: dinner daily
Meals served: dinner at 8

At first sight you may get the impression that this is a cross between an
antique shop and a hotel, but this old Cornish manor house will soon
convince you of its prime objective; for an intimate atmosphere has
been created within the comfortable house and the dining room provides a stage for chef patron Sean Devlin's cooking. A hand written
menu offers no choice, and might start with baked smoked haddock
creams followed by grilled lamb chops with redcurrant and mint sauce.
Banoffi pie and finally Cornish yarg and Stilton cheeses complete a
simple but delicious dinner.

TORQUAY — Mulberry House

1 Scarborough Road, Torquay, Devon, TQ2 5UJ
Tel: (01803) 213639 **£35**
Open: lunch Wed-Sun, dinner Fri & Sat
Meals served: lunch 10-5, dinner 7.30-9.30, (light meals all day)

This is a small, well-established restaurant with three rooms, close to the seafront, run single-handedly by Lesley Cooper for the last eight years. A daily blackboard menu features a number of choices for each course, including one or two fish and one vegetarian option daily. Lesley's cooking is basically English with French overtones, but above all it is good, sound cooking. Start perhaps with smoked salmon bisque or French onion tart before tucking into local sole with a light caper sauce, roast duck with a Seville orange and brandy sauce or spinach and cream cheese filo parcels with a satay sauce. Good-value Sunday lunches (£11). All rooms are en suite. Breakfast includes home-made marmalade and their own Devon honey.

TORQUAY — Remy's Restaurant Français

3 Croft Road, Torquay, Devon, TQ2 5UF
Tel: (01803) 292359 **£35**
Open: dinner Tue-Sat
Meals served: dinner 7.30-9.30

Remy and Dolene Bopp have run this charming little classic French restaurant for the past ten years, providing excellent value for money with their good home cooking and relaxed, friendly atmosphere, all combined in the pleasant surroundings of a Victorian house. Loyal customers flock in for Remy's fixed-price three-course menus. Typical of his starters are snails in puff pastry with a creamy garlic sauce, creamed shellfish soup or stuffed mussels. Main courses are typified by entrecôte au poivre vert or saddle of lamb in a tarragon and tomato sauce. There's always a fish and vegetarian dish of the day, and an array of French sweets to finish. Some reasonably priced items on the wine list.

TORQUAY — Table Restaurant

135 Babbacombe Road, Babbacombe, Torquay, Devon, TQ1 3SR
Tel: (01803) 324292 **£60**
Open: dinner Tue-Sun (closed Bank Holidays,
    2 wks Feb, 2 wks Sep)
Meals served: dinner 7.30-9.30

Trevor Brooks and Jane Corrigan hardly put a foot wrong at this tiny restaurant to the east of the town. Trevor's fixed-price dinner menus are imaginative and well-executed. Start with red mullet soup with saffron and tomato or carpaccio of venison with Thai dressing perhaps, followed by Chinese vinegar-glazed duck breast with tarragon jus or one of several fish dishes announced daily according to what's on offer in the market. Finish with a lemon meringue dessert or traditional farmhouse cheeses. Excellent and charming service by Jane.

TRURO Alverton Manor

Tregolls Road, Truro, Cornwall, TR1 1XQ
Tel: (01872) 76633   *Fax:* (01872) 222989   **£40**
Open: lunch & dinner daily
Meals served: lunch 12-1.45, dinner 7.30-9.30
A beautifully situated Grade II listed building with 34 bedrooms, on the edge of town.

TUCKENHAY Floyd's Inn (Sometimes)

Bow Creek, Tuckenhay, Totnes, Devon, TQ9 7EQ
Tel: (01803) 732350   *Fax:* (01803) 732651   **£85**
Open: lunch Wed-Fri, Sun & Mon, dinner Wed-Sat & Mon
Meals served: lunch 12-3, dinner 7-9
   (light meals The Canteen: lunch 12-2.30, dinner 12-2.30)

Located on the quayside of the lovely Bow Creek and surrounded by woodland, Keith Floyd's delightful pub (dating back to 1550) has a relaxed, unconventional feel to it. You can eat in George's Restaurant, George being the suitably attired (bow tie, yellow-checked waistcoat) wine-sipping teddy bear seated at one of the tables. Here you might try the likes of warm duck liver mousse with Sauternes sauce, followed by roast loin of venison with braised lentils, finishing with delicious hot apple and plum strudel with clotted cream. Or try some of the snacks in The Canteen—smoked salmon with horseradish and capers, grilled chicken with stir-fried spinach and chili butter, Thai rice soup. If you don't want to drive home after dinner, stay in one of the three themed bedrooms in `Floyd's Barn'. The Dart Cabin is nautical with anchor, ship's telegraph and blue and white blinds; the Khun Akorn Chamber has satin sheets, carved wooden screens and a draped four-poster bed; while the Dukes Suite boasts green walls and curtains and dark antique furniture.

TUNBRIDGE WELLS Cheevers

56 High Street, Tunbridge Wells, Kent, TN1 1XF
Tel: (01892) 545524   *Fax:* (01892) 535956   **£55**
Open: lunch & dinner Tue-Sat (closed Bank Holidays,
   2 wks Jan)
Meals served: lunch 12.30-2 (Sat to 1.45), dinner 7.30-10.30

Rack of Sussex lamb with a herb crust is the signature dish at Tim Cheevers' attractive restaurant where fixed-price menus offer ample choice and dishes are described in simple, straightforward English—no false fuss or fads but plenty of imagination and good honest cooking. Mussel and fennel broth, hot calf's liver mousse with peppercorn sauce, monkfish sautéed with Pernod or crisp roasted duckling with spring onion and ginger are typical of what's on offer. Starters and puds are all £4 and main courses £9.50 on the lunchtime and week-day evening menu; the weekend fixed-price dinner of three courses is preceded by crudités and closes with coffee and sweetmeats. Lots of half bottles offer variety on the wine list.

TUNBRIDGE WELLS   Downstairs at Thackeray's

85 London Road, Tunbridge Wells, Kent, TN11 1EA
Tel: (01892) 537559   **£35**
Open: lunch & dinner Tue-Sat (closed 5 days Xmas)
Meals served: lunch 12.30-2.30, dinner 7-9.30

With a separate courtyard entrance, Downstairs has a really cosy bistro feel to it. Menus (à la carte dinner and fixed-price lunch) are varied and imaginative, with dishes like potted pork with green peppercorns and lightly curried vegetable soup among starters; followed by grilled Rye cod with parsley crust, braised oxtails in red wine with basil dumplings and breast of chicken with apples and Calvados. Desserts could feature banana burnt cream or chilled yoghurt mousse with orange caramel sauce. The garden patio with its flowering vine is an ideal place for a summer lunch.

Thackeray's remains THE venue in Tunbridge Wells.

TUNBRIDGE WELLS   Thackeray's House

85 London Road, Tunbridge Wells, Kent, TN11 1EA
Tel: (01892) 511921   **£50**
Open: lunch Tue-Sun, dinner Tue-Sat
    (closed Bank Holidays, 1 wk Xmas)
Meals served: lunch 12.30-2.30, dinner 7-10

Bruce Wass cooks a classical array of dishes for this lovely dining room (pale yellow walls hung with oils and watercolours), in what was once the novelist Thackeray's home. Good home-made bread rolls (walnut, brown and white) set things off to an excellent start for dishes such as hot artichoke and chicken liver mousse with hollandaise sauce or crab bisque with mussels. Main courses might offer steak au poivre with Armagnac and cream, brill baked in vermouth with Dijon mustard and chives or saddle of rabbit with borlotti beans and tarragon. There's a wide choice of menus, including midweek specials and a two-course lunch option for only £10. A good wine list reasonably priced and the charming bistro downstairs (see above) makes Thackeray's House the restaurant for many miles.

TURNERS HILL   Alexander House

East Street, Turners Hill, West Sussex, RH10 4QD
Tel: (01342) 714914   *Fax:* (01342) 717328   **£55**
Open: lunch & dinner daily
Meals served: lunch 12.30-2, dinner 7.30-9.30 (Sun to 9)

This is a place to dress up for and enjoy: an imposing, 17th-century country mansion, home to the present Earl and Countess Alexander. The house is set in 135 acres of private parkland, including tennis court, croquet lawn and archery range. The interior is grand and decorative, with many ornate features, antiques and original oil paintings. Bedrooms, including suites, overlook the surrounding countryside, and include a premium, four-poster suite. Make the most of dinner in this discreetly elegant, pastel-coloured dining room where tailcoated waiters attend your every need. Menus are inspired by French and English cooking of the highest order, with dishes such as soufflé Alexander (a lobster soufflé with brandy sauce) or glazed scallops and crayfish with home-made noodles to start. Grilled Dover sole tartare, carré d'agneau, magret de canard or steak Diane typify main courses on the carte. Set menus (daily, and at Sunday lunch) offer less conservative choices. Puddings draw mostly on French traditions: Grand Marnier soufflé, crepes Suzette, tarte aux pommes normande. Separate vegetarian menu. Don't, forget to dress for dinner-jacket and tie is expected!

TWICKENHAM   Hamiltons

43 Crown Road, St Margarets, Twickenham, Middlesex, TW1 3EJ
Tel: 0181-892 3949   **£45**
Open: lunch Tue-Fri & Sun, dinner Tue-Sat
    (closed Bank Holidays, 1 wk New Year)
Meals served: lunch 12-2.30 (Sun to 3.30),
    dinner 7-10.30 (Fri & Sat to 11)

The distinctive red and gold facade and stained glass windows of Hamiltons set an appropriate tone for the sumptuous, artistic interior within—massive walnut-framed mirrors, wall-to-wall French Impressionist paintings, drop chandeliers and gold ceiling fans—it's not surprising that when Poirot was filmed here in 1988, the restaurant interior was left largely untouched. The cooking is essentially Anglo-French: pan-fried black pudding, smoked haddock and chive fish cakes, Hamilton's steak and vegetable pie, chicken and ham cassoulet, grilled venison sausages and deep-fried goujons of monkfish might be on offer. Good-value set lunches (Tuesday to Friday) and popular Sunday lunches with live jazz.

TWICKENHAM   McClement's Bistro

2 Whitton Road, Twickenham, Middlesex, TW1 1BJ
Tel: 0181-744 9610   *Fax:* 0181-890 1372   **£45**
Open: lunch & dinner daily
Meals served: lunch 12-2.30, dinner 7-10.30 (Fri & Sat to 11)

This is John McClement's new venture, a small, cosy bistro decorated in pastel shades. The menu changes every two weeks and offers an extensive range of dishes. Offal is a strong feature, a passion of John's. Expect dishes, prepared by head chef Philip Rickerby, such as black pudding en croute with Dijon mustard sauce or something a little lighter like fresh oysters served with a simple lemon dressing among starters. Main courses might include roast pigeon with liver dumplings and cabbage, rib of beef with two herbs, or the assiette du boucher, where the offal really comes into its own, with a medley of trotter, sweetbread, oxtail and tongue. If that's taking things a little too far, try Kromeskie—the meat of the pig's trotter chopped and wrapped in Parma ham and fried in batter. This an interesting and varied bistro menu selection.

TWICKENHAM — McClements Restaurant

12 The Green, Twickenham, Middlesex, TW2 5AA
Tel: 0181-755 0176   *Fax:* 0181-890 1372 £65
Open: lunch & dinner Tue-Sat
Meals served: lunch 12-2.30, dinner 7-10.30

No matter what you choose, the execution of dishes is quite superb at John McClements' pretty little French restaurant (the original of his two ventures) opposite the green. Start with fresh oysters in the shell served with lemon dressing, wild mushroom charlotte in a pancake or a seafood risotto with shavings of parmesan. Main courses, with around eight choices, might include crispy sea bass with soya butter sauce, pan-fried cheek of skate, or stuffed pig's trotter, a speciality. The menu is short and imaginative, with offal and seafood predominating. Finish with lemon tart or perhaps a hot soufflé with Calvados sauce. The new bistro up the road (see previous entry) is a welcome addition to the scene. Pictured, John McClements.

UCKFIELD — Hooke Hall

250 High Street, Uckfield, East Sussex, TN22 1EN
Tel: (01825) 761578   *Fax:* (01825) 768025 £50
Open: lunch Mon-Fri & Sun, dinner Mon-Sat
Meals served: lunch 12-2.30, dinner 7-10

Panelled rooms and oak fires create a comfortable, homely feel in this elegant Queen Anne hotel run in relaxed fashion by husband-and-wife team, Alister and Juliet Percy. Bedrooms, of which there are nine, are named after famous mistresses and lovers. The new Italian restaurant, La Scaletta, with its own separate entrance, offers a short, concise à la carte of traditional and regional dishes, with modern interpretations. Look forward to the likes of mixed antipasti, risotto with cuttlefish, ravioli served simply with butter and parmesan or tagliatelle with a beef fillet sauce. Fish and meat options may offer calf's liver with onions alla veneta, veal with Marsala sauce or turbot in a fine potato crust with courgettes. The plan to introduce a light lunch-time/pre-theatre menu for around £10 should prove popular.

UCKFIELD   Horsted Place

Little Horsted, Uckfield, East Sussex, TN22 5TS
Tel: (01825) 750581   *Fax:* (01835) 750459   **£70**
Open: lunch & dinner daily
Meals served: lunch 12-2, dinner 7.30-9.30

Formerly the home of Lord and Lady Nevill, Horsted has been visited
in the past by the Queen and Prince Philip. Built in 1850, much of the
detail of Horsted is the work of Augustus Pugin, making it one of the
finest examples of Gothic revivalist architecture in the country; while
the grounds and gardens were landscaped by Geoffrey Jellicoe at the
behest of the Nevills. The house sits at the heart of its own 1,100-acre
estate which includes the East Sussex National Golf Club. The grand
hallway gallery stretches the full length of the house and a splendidly
carved, exuberant staircase leads up to the 17 luxurious bedrooms and
suites which retain many original features. Other delights include a
Gothic library, the indoor pool and a relaxing outdoor terrace. The
Pugin dining room, luxuriously appointed in keeping with the rest of
the house, is an appropriate setting for head chef Allan Garth's short,
well-balanced menu. Typical starters might include a clear oxtail soup
or salad of Finnan haddock and poached egg. Dover sole with a mushroom and tarragon purée and champagne sauce or pan-fried fillet of
beef with horseradish and a shallot sauce might be on offer as main
courses like the rest of Allan's cooking are imaginative without being
over-fussy. A separate vegetarian menu offers the likes of double-baked
goat's cheese soufflé and risotto with brown lentils and a gazpacho
sauce. There's also a light luncheon menu and an excellent choice of
breakfasts ranging from Continental to healthy or full English.
Altogether, a very special place.

ULLSWATER   Leeming House

Watermillock, Ullswater, Cumbria, CA11 0JJ
Tel: (0176 84) 86622   *Fax:* (0176 84) 86443   **£65**
Open: lunch & dinner daily
Meals served: lunch 12.30-1.45, dinner 7.30-8.45

A 40-bedroomed country house in a wooded setting on the shores of
Lake Ullswater, this is early 19th-century elegance with late 20th-cen-
tury comforts. The bedrooms at the front of the house enjoy views of
the lake and fells beyond, and almost half the rooms have either a private balcony or terrace. All are elegantly furnished and pretty, with floral decor. The drawing room and conservatory enjoy lovely views over
the 20 or so acres of grounds which boast rare species of trees from
around the world, and the beautifully-proportioned, south-facing dining
room also looks out towards the lake. Head chef Adam Marks and his
team prepare dishes of French and English origin, competently
cooked.

ULLSWATER Old Church Hotel

Watermillock, Ullswater, Cumbria, CA11 0JN
Tel: (0176 84) 86204 *Fax:* (0176 84) 86368 **£55**
Open: dinner daily (closed Nov-Mar)
Meals served: dinner 6-8

A stunning location on the water's edge is enhanced by the fact that here at the Whitemores' ten-bedroomed hotel you are made to feel more like a house visitor than a paying guest. Relaxing lounges are packed with board games and reading material while bold, brightly coloured bedrooms with crown canopies and half-testers provide comfort. Excellent breakfast start the day with Manx kippers, Cumberland sausages and Lakeland yoghurts as regular morning fixtures. The short dinner menu from the capable hands of Kevin Whitemore offers a choice of at least two main courses which, on a recent menu, featured sautéed chicken supreme with a tomato and basil sauce and roast rack of Lakeland lamb baked under a herb crust served with redcurrant jelly.

ULLSWATER Rampsbeck Country House

Watermillock, Ullswater, Cumbria, CA11 0LP
Tel: (0176 84) 86442 *Fax:* (0176 84) 86688 **£45**
Open: lunch & dinner daily (closed 6 wks Jan/Feb)
Meals served: lunch 12-1.30, dinner 7-8.30

Enjoy a drink on the patio at this family-run, 21-bedroomed hotel overlooking Lake Ullswater. The setting is quite spectacular, with the fells in the background and 18 acres of garden and surrounding parkland leading down to the lake. On the inside, the house is furnished in period style (the house dates back to the 18th century), and most of the rooms, the drawing room and restaurant enjoy the views. Chef Andrew McGeorge can be relied upon with his modern classical style to produce plenty of variation, with some interesting combinations. Eat from the set menu or à la carte, from choices such as assiette of veal where the fillet, sweetbreads and ragout of kidneys are served in a tartlet together with pickled walnut sauce. Locally farmed lamb, venison, Lunesdale duck and corn-fed chicken from specialist suppliers. A good wine list has lots of choice at well under £20.

ULLSWATER   Sharrow Bay

Howtown, Ullswater, Cumbria, CA10 2LZ
Tel: (0176 84) 86301   Fax: (0176 84) 86349
Open: lunch & dinner daily (closed Dec-Feb)
Meals served: lunch 1-1.30, dinner 8-8.30

£90

Located on the shores of Lake Ullswater and surrounded by 12 acres of superb gardens, Sharrow Bay, reputed to be the first country house hotel in Great Britain, has perhaps the most outstanding location of them all. From small beginnings in 1948 as a private house, Sharrow Bay has grown into a hotel of astonishing worldwide renown, all of which is a tribute to the work of two men, Francis Coulson and Brian Sack, here respectively since 1949 and 1952. More than 40 years on, the hotel continues to gain the highest accolades for its standards of comfort, luxury and taste. This is evident everywhere, but nowhere more so than in the food. "Cooking is an art and all art is pleasure" read the menus. And so it is. From the wonderful selection of breads at the start of a meal to the petits fours at the end, this is an experience which might easily be confused with dream. The first choice is whether to eat in the splendid lakeside setting of the main dining room, or next door in the Victorian conservatory with its genteel, spacious feel. Head chefs Johnnie Martin, Colin Akrigg and Philip Wilson follow a menu format

Francis Coulson and Brian Sack. Biography on next page

established by Francis and Brian many years ago. The set-price lunch and dinner menus encompass a range of dishes from the simple to the more elaborate; the style is predominantly British and steadfastly traditional. Your next decision is what to choose from a range of eight-ten starters: cream of leek and potato soup; ravioli of lobster in lemon and saffron pasta with a lobster sauce; Kyle of Lochalsh scallops with tarragon and soya-scented sauce; terrine of duckling, venison and hare with pistachio nuts; smoked salmon stuffed with fresh salmon tartare. Relax over the next two courses (no choice to make)—a recent menu featured fillet of brill Adrienne, served with a white wine sauce and Swiss cheese soufflé, followed by an elderflower granité. Main courses (again a choice of eight-ten dishes) might include corn-fed chicken with a mushroom and herb truffle served on a bed of noodles with a wild mushroom cream sauce; roast noisettes of English lamb stuffed with shallots, mushrooms, oregano and spinach; or fillet of sea bass with tomatoes and fennel, served with a wine sauce. English roasts and game in season are specialities of the house. Puds, I'm afraid, demand yet more choosing: Old English Regency syllabub; fresh fruit terrine; vanilla mousse with a summer fruit compote; traditional bread, butter and marmalade pudding with apricot sauce. Prime British cheeses close the dinner. The wine list is impressive, as might be expected, with both the New World and the traditional European areas equally well represented, with a good many offered by the glass. Bedrooms are furnished to a high standard. There are 12 bedrooms in the main house, eight en suite; there is also a nearby garden cottage and a charming Quaker cottage in the village of Tirril, four miles from the house. In addition there are six suites/rooms in the Edwardian gate-house by the hotel entrance and seven in a converted Elizabethan farmhouse, the Bank House, just over a mile away, all benefitting from the inimitable Sharrow touch. Approached by a sweeping drive, the views from the Bank House are spectacular. All the rooms and the stunning Refectory breakfast room look down on to the lake.

A real sense of occasion here, very special hosts, very special location

---

Biography

Francis Coulson and Brian Sack

Francis Coulson was there at the beginning of Sharrow Bay, but it was on the arrival of Brian Sack and the start of their successful partnership that the story of Sharrow Bay and the whole country house hotel genre began in earnest. They remain together to this day, Brian running the front of house while Francis takes care of the kitchen.

Season after season, they have re-invested profits to improve standards and comfort, and work out every detail of the hotel's development with love and concern, and over the years their enterprise and insistence upon high standards has paid off. They were both awarded much-deserved MBEs in 1994 for their service to the hotel industry.

ULVERSTON — Bay Horse Inn & Bistro

Canal Foot, Ulverston, Cumbria, LA12 9EL
Tel: (01229) 583972   *Fax:* (01229) 580502   **£50**
Open: lunch Tue-Sun, dinner daily
Meals served: lunch 12-2, dinner 7.30 for 8

A joint venture between Robert Lyons, ex-Miller Howe, and his former employer John Tovey. Robert took over the inn after many years at Miller Howe and has transformed it. There are six bedrooms for

overnight accommodation, five of which open on to a small terrace overlooking the Leven Estuary—the views are quite superb. In addition, there's a bar and conservatory restaurant, which is really the main event, though the bar food menu also offers some really tasty dishes. In the restaurant expect to find some Tovey-style classics such as smoked chicken and fresh spinach salad with quail eggs and a hazelnut oil dressing to start, followed by marinaded guinea fowl roasted with honey, orange and fresh thyme and served with a calvados apple sauce and finishing with cape brandy pudding with crème fraîche.

UPPER SLAUGHTER　　　Lords of the Manor

Upper Slaughter, Nr Bourton-on-the-Water,
　　Gloucestershire, GL54 2JD
Tel: (01451) 820243　*Fax:* (01451) 820696　　　　　**£80**
Open: lunch & dinner daily (closed 1-15 Jan)
Meals served: lunch 12.30-2 (Sun to 2.30),
　　dinner 7.30-9.30 (Fri & Sat from 7)

Historically the home of the parish rectors for 200 years, the house is
set amidst 8 acres of lake and parkland. The village itself, with its
Norman church, has changed little over the last 300 years. The River
Eye flows through both village and manor grounds, and half a mile
upstream Milton is said to have written his famous trilogy, Paradise
Lost. The 29-bedroomed hotel has a pretty walled garden, a charming
courtyard and lovely views from the front of the house of the English
countryside. Bedrooms are very English in style, with chintzy decor
and a welcoming decanter of sherry. The whole house has a restful
country feel, with lots of fresh flowers, and blazing log fires in winter.
The pretty dining room looks out on to the garden and patio. The cooking is country style with modern influences—sea bass with a sole and
chervil mousse and langoustine ravioli; roast Hereford duckling with a
spicy, pearl barley risotto and home-made chutney; rack of lamb studded with rosemary and garlic, served with mushy peas, foie gras and a
shallot sauce. Eat as much or as little as you like from the lunch-time
carte; dinner is a two- or three-course fixed-price menu with a good
choice of sweets.

UPPINGHAM　　　The Lake Isle

16 High Street East, Uppingham, Leicestershire, LE15 9PZ
Tel: (01572) 822951　*Fax:* (01572) 822951　　　　　**£55**
Open: lunch Tue-Sun, dinner Mon-Sat
Meals served: lunch 12.30-2, dinner 7-10

A small, friendly town-house hotel with ten bedrooms named after different wine-producing regions of France, situated in the centre of this
pretty market town. The bedrooms, all en-suite, range from first-floor
rooms with large windows to cottagey-style second-floor rooms; and
there are two cottage suites. The wood-panelled dining room, a former
barber's shop, offers fixed-priced menus of French and English cuisine
under the direction of chef-patron David Whitfield. Home-made soups
or wild-boar sausages might precede breast of pheasant with pears and
Calvados or filo parcels of scallops, prawns and sea bream. Good
English and French cheeses are served with home-made walnut bread
and nuts. An immense wine list offers real value for money with lots of
half bottles. There is a small, informal walled garden and an abundance
of flowering baskets in the yard which leads to the hotel entrance.

WADHURST — Spindlewood

Wallcrouch, Wadhurst, East Sussex, TN5 7JG
Tel: (01580) 200430   *Fax:* (01580) 201132   **£55**
Open: lunch & dinner daily (closed 4 days
   Xmas, lunch Bank Holidays)
Meals served: lunch 12.15-1.30, dinner 7.15-9

This eight-bedroomed Victorian hotel in five acres of gardens is lovingly furnished in traditional manner Long-serving chef Harvey Lee Aram offers a regularly changing fixed-price menu in the airy and attractive dining room. Half a dozen or so dishes at each course are supplemented by dishes of the day to provide plenty of choice. Game terrine with spiced apple jelly perhaps, followed by roast chicken with wild mushroom sauce or marinated venison with port, pear and redcurrant. A bar menu of light snack lunches (Mon-Fri) offers a range of home-made pastas, minute steaks, club sandwiches and the like.

WALKINGTON — Manor House

Northlands, Walkington, Beverley, Humberside, HU17 8RT
Tel: (01482) 881645   *Fax:* (01482) 866501   **£40**
Open: dinner Mon-Sat (closed 25 & 26 Dec, 1 Jan)
Meals served: dinner 7.30-9.15

Derek and Lee Baugh's peaceful late-Victorian house in the lovely Yorkshire Wolds offers seven rooms, all comfortable furnished with king-size beds, and views over the surrounding farmland. Local fish, shellfish and game are among Derek's specialities. Start perhaps with New Bridlington queen scallops or freshly poached mussels in chablis, followed by Manor House mixed grill – a modern version of the classic; pork roulade with a wild mushroom mousse and a Madeira demi-glace; or a mélange of fish and seafood including sea bream, halibut, brill, scallops, prawns... the whole served with a buttered chardonnay and citron sauce. Baking and pâtisserie come from under the more-than-capable hands of wife Lee.

WALTERSTONE — Allt-Yr-Ynys Hotel

Walterstone, Hereford & Worcester, HK2 0DU
Tel: (01873) 890307   **£40**
Open: lunch & dinner daily
Meals served: lunch 12-2, dinner 7.30-9.30

The name (pronounced "Allt-er-Innis") literally means "Hill of the Island", a reference to the two rivers which run either side, producing an island effect. Formerly a farmhouse and once the home of Robert Cecil, Allt-Yr-Ynys reputedly once played host to Elizabeth I. Situated on the wooded banks of the river Monnow, dominated by the great Welsh Fwddog Ridge, the house has been elegantly converted and retains much of its original historic appeal. There are 12 rooms, located in either the main house or adjoining annexe, formerly ancient outbuildings. Plenty of character, modern comforts, and a warm, friendly atmosphere prevail. Luxury suites adjoin the main building and there is an indoor swimming pool.

WANSFORD-IN-ENGLAND · The Haycock

Wansford-in-England, Peterborough, Cambridgeshire, PE8 6JA
Tel: (01780) 782223   *Fax:* (01780) 783031   **£60**
Open: lunch & dinner daily
Meals served: lunch 12-2.30, dinner 7-10.30
     (light meals Orchard Room 7.30am-11pm)

A mellow, traditional atmosphere pervades throughout this 17th-century coaching inn set in a delightful, unspoilt village. The busy, traditional bar is the hub of the hotel, and the celebrated gardens which stretch along the banks of the River Nene incorporate the village cricket pitch. The hotel hosted Mary Queen of Scots on her way to imprisonment at Fotheringhay in 1586; and Queen Victoria is said to have stayed in the Gainsborough Room in 1835 prior to her ascension to the throne. The 51 bedrooms are luxuriously appointed and the restaurant serves traditional English cooking of high standards. Head chef Peter Grant offers a seasonal menu such as prime sirloin of English beef carved from the trolley, local game and fish. Lighter meals and snacks are available on the extensive bar menu, which might include smoked kipper pâté and curd cheese, seafood pancake, beef steak and kidney pie, and lots more.

WAREHAM   Priory Hotel

Church Green, Wareham, Dorset, BH20 4ND
Tel: (01929) 551666   *Fax:* (01929) 554519   **£55**
Open: lunch & dinner daily
Meals served: lunch 12.30-2.30, dinner 7.30-10

This 16th-century priory with 19 bedrooms is set in four acres of immaculately-kept gardens which slope gently down to the River Frome. Lounges overlook the gardens and there is a small, cosy, traditional bar. Bedrooms feature handsome antique furniture, one room has a four-poster and whirlpool bath; and there is luxurious suite accommodation in the converted boathouse. The candlelit Abbots Cellar restaurant in the vaulted stone cellars of the priory makes an atmospheric, romantic setting for dinner. Michael Rust recreates traditional English dishes with his lighter, modern approach: grilled fillet of beef wrapped in Dorset air-cured ham with roast shallots and Madeira sauce; glazed Gressingham duck with ginger and honey on an orange and lemon jus. Menus offer great variety, showing skill and imagination at work in the kitchen. Breakfast and lunch are served in the Greenwood dining room.

WARMINSTER — Bishopstrow House

Boreham Road, Warminster, Wiltshire, BA12 9HH
Tel: (01985) 212312   *Fax:* (01985) 216769   **£75**
Open: lunch & dinner daily
Meals served: lunch 12-2, dinner 7.30-9.30

Splendid flower displays, Persian carpets, antiques, oil paintings and roaring log fires in winter greet you as you enter this 32-bedroomed, ivy-clad Georgian hotel which dates back to 1817. Bedrooms, either in the main house, or in garden or courtyard annexes, are spacious and well equipped. The striking indoor pool looks out on to the hotel gardens, through which runs the River Wylye. Chef Chris Suter's imagina-

tive modern cooking offers some wonderful delights such as risotto marinara with saffron, warm salad of honey-roast duck leg confit with Puy lentils, wild boar sausages and mash with an onion gravy, or fricassée of chicken with morels. Desserts include the likes of grape-flavoured crème brûlée with a Granny Smith sorbet, and rhubarb and strawberry gratin with a delicious rhubarb sorbet. Consistency and maturity are the hallmarks of Chris' talent.

Biography

Chris Suter

A career in catering was the obvious choice for a publican's son whose hopes of playing professional football were not to be realised. An apprentice at the Beeton Restaurant, Cheshire, Chris Suter attended a local college on day release. Following a spell at The Cumberland he then moved to 90 Park Lane; and Ettington Park. Prior to his present position, he spent time as both sous and head chef at Ménage à Trois, where he worked with Antony Worrall Thompson. He brings all this experience to bear in his present country location.

WATERHOUSES — Old Beams

Leek Road, Waterhouses, Staffordshire, ST10 3HW
Tel: (01538) 308254   *Fax:* (01538) 308157   **£75**
Open: lunch Tue-Fri & Sun, dinner Tue-Sat
Meals served: lunch 12-2, dinner 7-9.30

Nigel and Ann Wallis have transformed this former 18th-century inn into a charming restaurant with rooms. The five bedrooms in a converted smithy across the road boast hand-made Heal's beds (the ultimate in comfort, they say). Fresh flowers, old oak beams, an open fire and quality place settings provide a fitting backdrop for talented chef Nigel's carefully planned menus. Choose between the original dining room or the light, mural-painted, lush-green conservatory with its palm court atmosphere and grand piano. Caramelised onion tart, ravioli of Dublin Bay prawns in a lobster sauce, pan-fried foie gras on a Calvados sauce, roast calf's sweetbreads with a truffle sauce and ragoût of lamb on a bed of couscous with chili sauce demonstrate his versatility. Splendid desserts might be hot soufflés, crumbles and home-made ice creams. Copious coffee and home-made chocolates and petits fours to finish. The fixed-price lunch menu is simpler and more robust, with dishes like osso bucco or steak, Guinness and mushroom pie making an appearance. Consistently high standards are maintained here, both in the kitchen and front of house, under the supervision of wife Ann. Excellent wines, with good, helpful tasting notes.

The Ackerman Guide was the first to recognise this talented team in 1987. Thank goodness the other guides have followed suit.

WATH-IN-NIDDERDALE   Sportsman's Arms

Wath-in-Nidderdale, Pateley Bridge, Nr Harrogate,
    N Yorkshire, HG3 5PP
Tel: (01423) 711306   **£50**
Open: lunch & dinner daily (closed 25 Dec)
Meals served: lunch 12-2.30, dinner 7-10 (Sun to 8.30)

Fresh local lamb, pork, beef, trout and game in season (from the surrounding moors), woodcock, grouse and pheasant from the hotel's own shoot, free-range eggs and fresh fish delivered daily are some of the secrets to Ray Carter's success in this five-bedroomed restaurant with rooms, a former 17th-century inn. Fish and lamb top the speciality stakes: noisettes of Dales lamb cooked in fine pastry with herbs and sauce béarnaise; and poached Whitby turbot wrapped in smoked salmon and served with a sorrel and grape sauce. Ray makes the most of seasonal and market produce, cooking in classic style, with a glance or two towards the Continent. His summer pudding lives on through popular demand, and cheeses are outstanding. Excellent value among the wines, too.

WATLINGTON   Well House

34-40 High Street, Watlington, Oxfordshire, OX9 5PY
Tel: (01491) 613333   **£45**
Open: lunch Tue-Fri & Sun, dinner Mon-Sat
    (closed Bank Holidays, 1 wk Xmas)
Meals served: lunch 12.30-2, dinner 7-9.15 (Sat to 9.30)

A delightful beamed restaurant with ten rooms, run with charm and friendliness by Alan and Patricia Crawford for nearly 20 years. Patricia's sound, straightforward European-style cooking offers dishes such as home-made oxtail soup, smoked fish platter, or twice-baked crab soufflé to start; followed by veal cutlet with lemon sauce, roast monkfish wrapped in bacon on a sweet pepper sauce, or fillet steak with herb and mushroom topping on a tomato coulis. To finish try lemon roulade or crème brûlée. Lighter lunch-time snacks are available in the bar, and there's always a vegetarian menu alongside the short table d'hôte and carte menus. Over 100 wines with lots of good value at under £10.

WELLS   Ritchers Restaurant

5 Sadler Street, Wells, Somerset, BA5 2RR
Tel: (01749) 679085   **£45**
Open: lunch & dinner Tue-Sat (closed 26 Dec, 1 Jan)
Meals served: lunch 12-2 (reservations only), dinner 7-9
   (Sat to 9.30), (light meals Bistro: 12-2, 7-9 7 days)

This bistro and restaurant is tucked between two shops down an alley
in the centre of town. Venture down and you will find plenty of choice.
The all-day ground-floor bistro menu runs from steaks and pies to
home-made beefburgers and salads, and there are alfresco options in
the small courtyard area with its sliding roof. Upstairs the more formal
restaurant is more sophisticated, with typical dishes such as oven-
baked loin of pork en croute or grilled salmon with white crab meat on
a Vermouth cream.

WELLS-NEXT-THE-SEA   The Moorings

6 Freeman Street, Wells-Next-The-Sea, Norfolk, NR23 1BA
Tel: (01328) 710949   **£35**
Open: lunch Fri-Sun, dinner daily (closed 24-26 Dec,
   2 wks Dec, 2 wks Jun)
Meals served: lunch 12.30-2, dinner 7.30-9

Eat as much as you like—from one course to four—at this quayside
restaurant, which offers an extensive, daily-changing menu. A three-
course dinner (£15.95) could consist of local cockles, oysters, Norfolk-
style pork brawn or spicy fish soup to start, followed by venison pie,
breast of duck in blackberry vinegar sauce or salmon filo pastry with a
mild ginger and orange sauce. The menu has more unusual offerings
than most in the area.

WEST MERSEA Le Champenois Restaurant

Blackwater Hotel, 20-22 Church Road,
   West Mersea, Essex, CO5 8QH
Tel: (01206) 383338   **£45**
Open: lunch Wed-Mon, dinner Mon-Sat (closed 3 wks Jan)
Meals served: lunch 12-2, dinner 7-10

An authentic French family restaurant, part of the ivy-clad, seven-
bedroomed Blackwater Hotel. The food is wholesome and unfussy,
blending favourite classic dishes with a more inventive approach.
French onion soup, mushroom champenois, snails or mussels precede
rack of lamb, calf's liver with a mango and shallot sauce, fillet of beef
stroganoff or individual steak and kidney pies. Bedrooms are comfortable, some en suite.

WEYMOUTH — Perry's

4 Trinity Road, Old Harbour, Weymouth, Dorset, DT4 8TJ
Tel: (01305) 785799 **£45**
Open: lunch Tue-Fri & Sun, dinner daily (closed dinner Sun winter)
Meals served: lunch 12-2, dinner 7-9.30

Good fresh local seafood is the main attraction at this busy harbour restaurant whose blackboard menu of seafood dishes varies according to local catch. Perry's offers a good choice of meat dishes too—medallions of venison and pigeon with port and cranberries, supreme of duckling in filo pastry. Start perhaps with a terrine of game, Perry's home-made soup of the day or crab thermidor.

WHIMPLE — Woodhayes Hotel

Whimple, Nr Exeter, Devon, EX5 2TD
Tel: (01404) 822237 **£55**
Open: dinner daily
Meals served: dinner 7.30-9

Eleven miles from the Devon coast, in large park-like gardens complete with apple orchard, Woodhayes enjoys a delightfully peaceful, rural setting. The real strength of this small, six-bedroomed Georgian hotel, however, lies in the Rendle family who run it with warmth and style, creating a home-from-home feel. Katherine Rendle discusses her six-course menus with guests and special arrangements can be made for any dietary requirements. She obtains as much of her raw material as possible from local suppliers. Katherine has been vegetarian herself for 26 years, so there's little chance of vegetarians feeling left out or shortchanged here. However, a typical omnivores' dinner might consist of frisée and walnut salad, followed by vegetable consommé, then fillet of Dover sole with prawns and coriander; then fillet of beef with polenta and salsa verde; and to finish a choice of desserts and cheese—first-class, unpasteurised mature local Cheddar or Stilton, accompanied by oatcakes, grapes and walnuts. Excellent value for wine lovers with a dozen house selections at under £10 per bottle. Spacious, comfortable bedrooms.

WHITBY — Magpie Café

14 Pier Road, Whitby, North Yorkshire, YO21 3PU
Tel: (01947) 602058 **£30**
Open: all day daily (closed mid Nov-mid Mar)
Meals served: 11.30-6.30

Overlooking the harbour in the historic port of Whitby, the Magpie is housed in a distinctive black-and-white building which has a long association with the fishing and shipping industry. The premises were converted into a café in the late 1930s and has been owned by the McKenzie family for many years. The dining room, with its wheel-back chairs, is where you might eat fresh Whitby fish: up to 10 varieties are on offer daily—deep-fried, with a slice of bread and butter, is the speciality. Choose between cod, haddock, plaice, lemon sole, skate, halibut, monk—have it grilled or poached if you prefer. The extensive fish menu is supplemented by daily specials (fresh salmon in orange herb butter), a wide range of salads and home-made desserts (including low-fat, vegetarian, gluten-free and low-cal options). There are also a number of good-value fixed-price menus, the Special Fish Lunch, Steak Lunch or Salad Lunch menus, and a comprehensive children's menu, too. Reliably good, with the fish about as fresh as you can get.

WHITBY   Trenchers

New Quay Road, Whitby, North Yorkshire, YO21 1DH
Tel: (01947) 603212   *Fax:* (01947) 821025   **£30**
Open: all day daily (closed mid Nov-mid Mar)
Meals served: 11am-9pm

After a busy day on the beach or rambling through the narrow streets
and harbour of Whitby, Trenchers provides the exact fare that you
would expect to find in a Yorkshire fishing village. Fresh fish and
chips, or salads of Whitby crab and lobster can be followed by traditional puddings such as sherry trifle, apple pie or fruit crumble. There
is good value on the children's menu and an above-average choice of
wines: £8.50 for house selections up to £59 for Dom Perignon, which
may not be the perfect accompaniment to fish and chips but must be
the best price in Britain!

WHITSTABLE   Oyster Fishery Co

Royal Native Oyster Stores, Horse Bridge Beach, Whitstable,
     Kent, CT5 1BU
Tel: (01227) 276856   *Fax:* (01227) 770666   **£45**
Open: lunch & dinner Tue-Sun
Meals served: lunch 12-2.30, dinner 7-9.30

The restaurant is actually housed within a former
oyster store though the original, tidal holding tanks
are still in use for live shellfish. Lobster and crab vie
for star status with native Whitstable or Scottish
rock oysters, as fresh as you are likely to find them.
The menu is short and written up on a blackboard,
the decor simple, with bare wooden boards and
pretty gingham tablecloths. Even so, through the
glow of candlelight over dinner, the effect is warm
and welcoming. New potatoes (no chips!), salads
and simple saucing accompany dishes such as
baked haddock with gruyère cheese, sour cream
and spring onions, dressed Cornish crab or char-
grilled salmon fillet served with a dill mayonnaise.

WICKHAM   Old House Hotel

The Square, Wickham, Hampshire, PO17 5JG
Tel: (01329) 833049   *Fax:* (01329) 833672   **£60**
Open: lunch Tue-Fri, dinner Mon-Sat
     (closed Bank Holidays, 2 wks
     Xmas, 2 wks Aug)
Meals served: lunch 12-1.30, dinner 7-9.30

Here you will find a menu with a strong French provincial bias in a
civilised, unpretentious house of early Georgian origin. The rooms are
warm, comfortable and pretty, all are ensuite; the lounges are traditional in style, with solid period pieces about the place and fine panelling. Chef Nick Harman's French cuisine takes its instruction from
various regions of France, with an emphasis on Provence where Annie
Skipwith spent some time.

WILLITON   White House

Williton, Nr Taunton, Somerset, TA4 4QW
Tel: (01984) 632306   **£55**
Open: dinner daily (closed Nov-May)
Meals served: dinner 7 for 7.30 & 8.30 for 9

Whitewashed walls and shuttered windows set the simple tone of things to come at Dick and Kay Smith's attractive little hotel and restaurant, where local supplies are the foundation for a repertoire which is refreshingly honest and unfussy. The cooking is British with modern European influences. The fixed-price dinner menu (three to five courses) might offer a warm salad of pigeon breast with hot beet-root; crab soufflé, Korean-style pork with sesame, soy and ginger; black-baked chicken with fresh mango salsa and sweet potato purée; roast local Gressingham duck with plums; or monkfish, brill and sole lightly poached in saffron-flavoured broth. Lovely puds might include Mosimann's bread-and- butter pudding made with double cream and brioche, or choose English cheeses and home-made oatmeal biscuits. There are 12 rooms, nine of which are ensuite, either in the main house or converted coach house. A successful formula which the Smiths have developed lovingly over 30 years.

WILMSLOW   Stanneylands

Stanneylands Road, Wilmslow, Cheshire, SK9 4EY
Tel: (01625) 525225   *Fax:* (01625) 537282   **£55**
Open: lunch daily, dinner Mon-Sat
Meals served: lunch 12.30-2, dinner 7-10

Cosy, traditional accommodation within easy reach of Manchester Airport makes this family-run, red-bricked Victorian hotel in two acres of picturesque grounds a popular business hotel. Handsome reception rooms are classically styled and quietly luxurious. The impressive gardens feature a rare collection of over 36 varieties of tree from all over the world, and several of the bedrooms and function rooms enjoy views of the garden and the Cheshire countryside. The hotel's tradition of contemporary English cuisine successfully upheld by Steven Kitchen in the past has now become the domain of new head chef Matthew Barrett.

WINCHESTER   Lainston House

Sparsholt, Winchester, Hampshire, SO21 2LT
Tel: (01962) 863588   *Fax:* (01962) 772672   **£75**
Open: lunch & dinner daily
Meals served: lunch 12-2.30, dinner 7-10.30

Sixty-three acres of Hampshire parkland is the setting for this elegant William and Mary period house a couple of miles north-west of Winchester. The grounds hold many surprises for the stroller: a reputedly haunted 12th-century chapel, an 18th-century herb garden, a dovecote, and much more besides. The parquet-floored foyer is dominated by a large Delft-tiled fireplace, and the cedar-panelled bar is also splendid. Beautifully proportioned main-house bedrooms are stylish and there are also a number of very fine, spacious rooms in the newly-converted stable block. Good breakfasts and friendly staff. The cooking is English with overtones of French: pan-fried scallops with a beetroot terrine, Cornish crabmeat, roast cannon of lamb, and poached salmon with a sole mousse.

WINCHESTER	Old Chesil Rectory

Chesil Street, Winchester, Hampshire, SO23 8HU
Tel: (01962) 851555   **£50**
Open: lunch & dinner Tue-Sat (closed 25 Dec-10 Jan)
Meals served: lunch 12-2, dinner 6.30-9.30

This lovely old building dates back to 1430, and it's history is apparent in the old timbers and exposed brickwork, warmed by big log fires. The restaurant is on two-floors—casual on the ground floor, more formal on the first, but the same menu is available both rooms and you could eat Artbroath smokies au gratin, Hampshire pork sausages with mash and onion gravy, casserole of game and beef with chestnuts or strips of beef fillet in a mushroom sauce with Gruyère. The blackboard features daily fish and other specials—sauté of salmon with a tomato and basil vinaigrette, fish and shellfish soup. Popular puds to finish and a number of wines by the glass. A popular local restaurant, well run by Nicholas and Christina Ruthven-Stuart.

WINDERMERE	Holbeck Ghyll

Holbeck Lane, Windermere, Cumbria, LA23 1LU
Tel: (0153 94) 32375   *Fax:* (0153 94) 34743   **£65**
Open: dinner daily
Meals served: dinner 7-8.45

Formerly the hunting lodge of Lord Lonsdale, the man who bequeathed the Lonsdale Belt to British boxing champions, Holbeck Ghyll commands majestic views over Lake Windermere and offers the comforts of a traditional country house hotel. Comfortable lounges are traditionally furnished and there's a wonderful smell of polish as you enter the oak-panelled hall which has a fine inglenook fireplace in which a log fire burns most of the year round. Bedrooms and bathrooms show extra attention to detail, from decanters of sherry in the bedrooms to large bathrobes and sophisticated toiletries. The oak-panelled restaurant serves traditional English-style dishes ranging from pot-roasted guinea fowl French-style to delicate wholemeal pancakes filled with mushrooms and leeks, served with a cheese and chive sauce. Typical starters could include cream of tomato and tarragon soup or home-oak-smoked Barbary duck breast with a plum and port sauce. Home-made sweets and a farmhouse cheeseboard to finish. The hotel is ideally situated between Windermere and Ambleside, good base from which to tour the Lakes.

WINDERMERE	Miller Howe

Rayrigg Road, Windermere, Cumbria, LA23 1EY
Tel: (0153 94) 42536   *Fax:* (0153 94) 45664   **£75**
Open: dinner daily (closed early Dec-early Mar)
Meals served: dinner only at 8.30   ❀

With probably the finest views of any hotel in the Lake District, Miller Howe looks down over Lake Windermere and its grounds sweep down almost to the water's edge. Much work on the downstairs lounges over the last year or so has brought the decor into line with the Edwardian origins of the house. The kitchen has also undergone changes, with lighter-textured dishes replacing the old heavy cream sauces. Portions are smaller and strong, basic flavours are acknowledged. The end result is more aesthetic, aiming to titillate the eye as much as tempt the palate. Dinner starts with canapés in the lounge and is accompanied by freshly-baked bread. The essentially British five-course no-choice (except for dessert) dinner menu changes daily. Bedrooms are homely and cosy, with lots of cosseting extras. The best rooms enjoy balconies, complete with seating, wrought-iron tables and even binoculars! Start the day with a complimentary Bucks Fizz, which awaits you at the foot of the stairs, then tuck into an excellent breakfast repertoire. Watching the sun set over the distant  Cumbrian mountains—should you be so lucky—is a glorious way to end any day.

John Tovey, pictured, still keeps a watchful eye over this much-loved hotel & restaurant.

WINDERMERE   Roger's Restaurant

4 High Street, Windermere, Cumbria, LA23 1AF
Tel: (0153 94) 44954   **£40**
Open: dinner Mon-Sat (Sun Bank Holidays) (closed 1
    wk summer, 1 wk winter)
Meals served: dinner 7-9.30

Roger Pergl-Wilson and wife Alena created a little corner of France here in the heart of the English Lakes. However, local demand has increasingly introduced an English bent to Roger's previously French-dedicated menus, which he continues to execute with skill and flair at this cosy restaurant opposite the Information Centre. His repertoire is strong on provincial cooking (there are regular theme nights). Look out for hot parsnip mousse with roasted peppers and pesto sauce; warm red onion tart; roast rack of lamb with a herb crust and Madeira gravy; calf's liver with bacon, sage and Marsala; pan-fried Windermere char with lemon and parsley. Wicked desserts include the likes of rich chocolate and maple pecan pie. Over a hundred wines from America to Moldavia with plenty of more conservative choices!

WINDSOR   Oakley Court

Windsor Road, Water Oakley, Nr Windsor, Berkshire, SL4 5UR
Tel: (01628) 74141   *Fax:* (01628) 37011   **£65**
Open: lunch & dinner daily
Meals served: lunch 12.30-2, dinner 7.30-10

The grounds of this grand Victorian manor three miles from Windsor slope down to the River Thames. During the '60s and '70s when it was uninhabited, over 200 films were shot here, including *The Rocky Horror Show*, *Hammer's Dracula* and the *St Trinian's* series. The hotel has 92 bedrooms, including a number of luxurious suites in the original house, but most rooms are in the separate Riverside and Garden Wing extensions. This is a comfortable hotel, with impressive rooms which boast many original features, including an antique table in the Billiard Room. We have not had the opportunity to visit since long-standing chef, Murdo MacSwean, left Oakley Court. You can eat in the Oakleaf restaurant or in the informal Boaters Brasserie, where you can eat as much or as little as you like. There are nine-hole and par-three golf courses within the grounds, and almost a mile of fishing rights on the Thames, with punts and cruisers available for hire.

WINKLEIGH   Pophams

Castle Street, Winkleigh, Devon, EX19 8HQ
Tel: (01837) 83767   **£35**
Open: all day Mon-Sat (closed 25 Dec, all Feb)
Meals served: 9am-3pm

This little treasure is part of a village shop-cum-delicatessen and only
has three tables. Melvyn Popham's lunch-time blackboard menu offers
simple yet creative dishes. A typical menu might include carrot, leek
and artichoke soup, duck breast with Madeira and plum sauce or fresh
salmon in pastry with a red pepper and dry vermouth sauce. Enjoy a
three-course meal or a single dish as you please. The atmosphere is
chatty and relaxed, much like eating out at a friend's home, and in similar fashion you have to bring along your own wine!

WINSFORD   Royal Oak Inn

Winsford, Somerset, TA24 7JE
Tel: (0164 385) 455   *Fax:* (0164 385) 388   **£50**
Open: lunch Sun, dinner daily
Meals served: lunch 12-1.15, dinner 7.30-9

Charles Steven has run this picturesque, thatched village inn, dating
back to the 12th century, for over 20 years. Enjoy a light meal in one of
the bars—home-made pies, home-cooked hams, pâtés, steak sandwich,
giant Yorkshire pudding filled with steak, mushroom and ale casserole,
and the like—or go for the more formal option from the daily-changing
menus of unfussy, traditionally English dishes on offer in the pretty
beamed restaurant. Bedrooms, of which there are 15, nestle under
thatched eaves in the main house—cosy and cottagey; those in the converted courtyard annexe are equally attractive and include a self-contained family cottage. Good vegetarian and breakfast menus. A
delightfully relaxing place in a sleepy Exmoor village, in the heart of
Exmoor National Park, but very much a popular haunt among hunting
and fishing folk.

WINTERINGHAM   Winteringham Fields

Winteringham, Humberside, DN15 9PF   *A very special place.*
Tel: (01724) 733096   *Fax:* (01724) 733898   **£60**
Open: lunch Tue-Fri, dinner Mon-Sat (closed Bank Holidays,
    2 wks Xmas, 1 wk Aug)
Meals served: lunch 12-1.30, dinner 7.30-9.30

Chef-patron Germain Schwab, pictured,
describes his cooking as provincial, with
French and Swiss influences. His attractive
restaurant with rooms in a 16th-century
house is situated about four miles south west
of the Humber Bridge in a small farming
community. Seasonal menus are based on
local produce, with fresh fish from Grimsby
coming in plentiful supply. Specialities
include charcoal-grilled scallops with wild
asparagus and lobster sauce, wings of skate
with braised shallots and light beer and roast

guinea fowl with sage served in its own juices. Choose from a variety of menus, including the four-course menu surprise for a whole table. There are seven luxuriously furnished bedrooms, four in the main house, three in a converted courtyard stable annexe. Exposed ships' timbers, oak panelling and period fireplaces reflect the original character of the house, which now attracts visitors not only from Great Britain but also further field. An oasis of comfort, some very good food and a wine list that offers something for everyone.

WITHERSLACK — Old Vicarage

Church Road, Witherslack, Cumbria, LA11 6RS
Tel: (0153 95) 52381   Fax: (0153 95) 52373   **£50**
Open: lunch Sun, dinner daily
Meals served: lunch 12.30 for 1, dinner 7.30 for 8

Follow signs for the church once you reach the village to find this 15-bedroomed Victorian hotel, a former vicarage as the name implies. Personal, friendly service goes hand-in-hand with period charm and character. Whether you're staying in one of the homely main house rooms or in the more secluded Orchard House, you'll not be disappointed, and don't miss breakfast either, with its free-range eggs, Finnan haddock, kippers and home-cured bacon. For dinner, you'll be treated to some genuine British country house cooking, with regional specialities under head chef Stanley Reeve and his new ex-Langan's Brasserie (London) assistant, Paul Axford. Smoked duck breasts with a cranberry sauce, venison and Cumbrian ale casserole, and Waberthwaite pork with crackling are the sort of dish you'll find. Excellent selection of British farmhouse cheeses; popular Sunday gourmet theme dinners and good selection of half-bottles on the wine list.

WIVELISCOMBE — Langley House

Langley Marsh, Wiveliscombe, Nr Taunton, Somerset, TA4 2UF
Tel: (01984) 23318   Fax: (01984) 24573   **£55**
Open: dinner daily
Meals served: dinner 7.30-8.30

Unspoilt, rural Somerset is the setting for Peter and Anne Wilson's pretty, peach-coloured Georgian house with its award-winning gardens and cobbled courtyard, just half a mile north of Wiveliscombe. Eight stylish bedrooms offer comfortable accommodation and the beamed, candlelit restaurant is an appropriate apt setting for Peter's skilful modern English cooking. The four-course, no-choice (except for desserts) dinner menu changes daily. You could start with a warm quail breast salad followed by steamed fillet of red mullet and veal with apricot, coriander and walnuts. Then there's a choice of around five desserts or an excellent selection of local West Country cheeses. Among his specialities Peter lists his fillet of sea bass on a bed of leeks and Somerset lamb with onion tartlet and a cassis purée. Some interesting choices from the wine list. Good breakfasts.

WOBURN   Paris House

Woburn Park, Woburn, Bedfordshire, MK17 9QP
Tel: (01525) 290692   *Fax:* (01525) 290471   **£80**
Open: lunch Tue-Sun, dinner Tue-Sat
  (closed Bank Holidays, Feb)
Meals served: lunch 12-2, dinner 7-9.30

There's a great sense of occasion as you approach Paris House up the sweeping driveway through a deer park towards the part-timbered house. Peter Chandler continues to delight after more than ten years at

the helm, with his robust modern interpretations of classical French cuisine. Start perhaps with confit of crispy duck in blackcurrant coulis, pig's trotters béarnaise, curried mussels, fish soup or a delicious light tartlet of leeks and smoked haddock served with red pepper sauce. Follow with salmon in champagne, lamb cutlets in tarragon vinegar or rabbit in mustard sauce. A strong loyal following. Quite right, too.

Biography

Peter Chandler

Peter Chandler was born in Edinburgh, although most of his early childhood was spent in Singapore. A passion for cooking prompted him to enrol on an evening course at Carshalton Technical College, and his first cooking job was as an apprentice with the Roux brothers, working through the company (Le Poulbot, Brasserie Benoits (now Le Gamin), pastry laboratory, Le Gavroche, and The Waterside Inn). After an 'interlude' in France at La Réserve in Beaulieu working for Jules Picard, he returned to The Waterside Inn. In 1983 the opportunity arose to set up the kitchens at Paris House, in the beautiful grounds of Woburn Park, where Peter has continued to developed his own style, which is still influenced by his very classical background.

WOODSTOCK   Bear Hotel

Park Street, Woodstock, Oxfordshire, OX7 1SZ
Tel: (01993) 811511   *Fax:* (01993) 813380   **£55**
Open: lunch & dinner daily
Meals served: lunch 12.30-2.30 (Sun from 12), dinner 7-10 (Sun to 9.30)

This creeper-clad coaching inn in a side street near Blenheim Palace dates back to the 12th century and is full of charm and curiosities. Original oak beams in the dining room provide an atmospheric setting; menus are short, concise and straightforward, with dishes such as roasted scallops and king prawns with lemon grass and ginger or lobster and lentil bisque, preceding main-course selections like veal casserole with herb and prune dumplings.

WOODSTOCK   Feathers Hotel

Market Street, Woodstock, Oxfordshire, OX7 1SX
Tel: (01993) 812291   *Fax:* (01993) 813158   **£55**
Open: lunch & dinner daily
Meals served: lunch 12.30-2.15, dinner 7.30-9.30, (light meals
    Whinchat Bar 12.30-2.15, 7.30-9.30, closed dinner Sat & Sun)

At the heart of historic Woodstock, this
17th-century Cotswold-stone house has a
great deal of character and charm. The 17
bedrooms and suites are sumptously decorated and have excellent marbled bathrooms. The upstairs drawing room and
cosy, flagstoned bar, together with the
antique-panelled dining room, enhances
the air of quiet sophistication. The menu
changes daily and game is a speciality of
the house. Modern British in style, chef
David Lewis (pictured) produces dishes
such as smoked duck breast crostini, followed by marinated queen scallops with
chili and shallots or venison with green
peppercorns and port. The carte is com-
plemented by a no-choice fixed-price dinner which might include a
casserole of monkfish and salmon with saffron and vermouth. Tasty
puds range from sorbets to hot puddings. Round it all off with coffee
and truffles.

Definitely the place to stay in the Woodstock area.

WOOLTON HILL   Hollington House Hotel

Woolton Hill, Nr Newbury, Berkshire, RG15 9XR
Tel: (01635) 255100   *Fax:* (01635) 255075   **£55**
Open: lunch & dinner daily
Meals served: lunch 12-2.30, dinner 7-9.30

The hunt is on at this 20-bedroomed
Edwardian house in 14 acres of woodland
gardens south of Newbury. Australian owners John and Penny Guy have recently dis-
covered that the gardens are an early
example of Gertrude Jekyll's work and a
return to the original planting scheme
planned. The new games area and swimming
pool, created from the old stables, are the latest addition to what is already a delightful
hotel, with galleried oak-panelled inner hall,
lovely touches about the place and spacious
comfortable bedrooms. The restaurant is
also a handsome room with stone mullioned
windows, Tudor-style ribbon ceiling and
more panelling, and the focus of the cooking is on traditional English
fare, with favourites like steak pie usually featured alongside modern
European dishes.

WORCESTER   Brown's

24 Quay Street, Worcester, Hereford & Worcester, WR1 2JJ
Tel: (01905) 26263   **£70**
Open: lunch & dinner daily
   (closed Bank Holidays, 1 wk Xmas)
Meals served: lunch 12.30-1.45, dinner 7.30-9.45

In an award winning converted cornmill-cum-warehouse, with large picture windows overlooking the river, Brown's enjoys a delightful setting—one that is both spacious and relaxing. Longstanding owners the
Tansleys offer fully-inclusive set menus with limited but sufficient
choice. Typical starters include salmon mousse with dill sauce or sauté
of monkfish with a Japanese dressing; main courses might include
char-grilled langoustine and bacon kebabs, casserole of rabbit with
juniper and thyme, and braised beef with herb dumplings. There's
always a fresh fish dish of the day along with a vegetarian option.
Lunch menus are similar in style, if a little simpler and with less choice.

*This is the type of restaurant that is very rarely seen outside of
London and major cities and deserves its success.*

WORFIELD   Old Vicarage

Worfield, Bridgnorth, Shropshire, WV15 5JZ
Tel: (01746) 716497   *Fax:* (01746) 716652   **£60**
Open: lunch Sun-Fri, dinner daily
Meals served: lunch 12-2, dinner 7-9

An Edwardian parsonage has been carefully transformed by Peter and
Christine Iles to create a gracious, informal, country house which
reflects the peace and tranquillity of this tiny hamlet setting.
Individually-designed bedrooms are named after local villages and in
the Coach House there are four superior rooms which open on to a private garden with unspoilt views across the rural valley to the River
Worfe. A ground-floor suite is specially equipped for disabled guests
and families with children, like all guests, are warmly welcomed. Twin
conservatories make up a relaxing lounge with wicker chairs. The
kitchen prides itself on British cuisine. Typical dishes include the likes
of light celery soup with pesto and golden croûtons, chicken breast
wrapped in smoked bacon served with a whole grain mustard sauce
and Old Vicarage chocolate, fruit and nut tart served with Poire
William sabayon. Award-winning selection of British cheeses.
Wonderful, well-balanced wine list with a good selection of half-bottles.

WYCH CROSS   Ashdown Park Hotel

Wych Cross, Nr East Grinstead, East Sussex, RH18 5JR
Tel: (01342) 824988   *Fax:* (01342) 826206   **£50**
Open: lunch & dinner daily
Meals served: lunch 12.30-2, dinner 7.30-10 (Sun to 9.30)

Formerly a convent, American university and bank training centre, this
extensive Victorian mansion has seen more than a few minor changes

over the years, not least its conversion in late 1993 into a luxury hotel with 95 bedrooms. Set in 187 acres of splendid Sussex parkland, complete with wild deer, both the house and the estate are steeped in history, and there's even rumour of a ghost! Careful restoration and extensive refurbishment has created elegant reception areas with many of the house's original features back in place, including marble pillars, arched windows, plaster mouldings and oak panelling. Bedrooms vary in size but they are all similarly furnished with reproduction antique-style furniture, and some have the added romance of four-poster beds. Food in The Anderida Restaurant (the Roman name for the surrounding forest) is in the talented hands of John McManus, whose repertoire includes warm oyster and watercress tartlet, wild mushroom risotto with orange and chicory salad, pan-fried fillet of beef with artichokes and a delicious sticky toffee pudding. Cheeses, all British, include Ashdown Park's very own. Extensive, international wine list.

WYLAM   Laburnum House

Main Street, Wylam, Northumberland, NE41 8AJ
Tel: (01661) 852185   **£55**
Open: dinner Mon-Sat (closed 26 Dec, 1 & 2 Jan)
Meals served: dinner 6.30-10

Attractive table settings and wicker chairs provide the setting for some excellent cooking in this 18th-century house opposite the Ship Inn, but don't be put off by the simple exterior—chef Kenn Elliott knows just what he is doing. The short carte might offer fried squid with a salsa dip or smoked turkey with curry mayonnaise to start, followed by turbot with a crab sauce, roast pheasant English-style or chicken supreme with mushrooms and cognac. Menus change frequently. Partner Rowan Mahon takes charge front of house, and there are four neat rooms for overnight guests.

WYMONDHAM   Number Twenty Four

24 Middleton Street, Wymondham, Norfolk, NR18 0BH
Tel: (01953) 607750   **£35**
Open: lunch & dinner Tue-Sat (closed 25-31 Dec)
Meals served: lunch 10-2.30, dinner 7.30-9

Very popular since its 1991 opening, Richard and Sue Hughes' enterprise follows in the tradition of small family-run restaurants offering sound, reliable and imaginative cooking in friendly, informal surroundings. The acquisition of the premises next door enabled them to increase dining potential without losing the charm and character of the original building whose dining rooms are tiny, almost cottagey, by comparison to the new, spacious dining area. Richard flies the flag for local produce, using local farmshops, smokehouses, Fenland fruit and vegetables, shellfish from the Wash and Lowestoft fish markets. His aim here is to provide the sort of restaurant he would like to eat at en famille himself—top-class food at middle-of-the-road prices. Fixed-price lunch and dinner menus (plus a lunch-time blackboard) offer modern English cooking at its best. You might start with warm, tea-smoked salmon, ratatouille soup or a terrine of local pheasant and chicken, before escalope of Lowestoft cod with a Welsh rarebit topping and parsley cream, grilled sirloin with a mushroom and shallot sauce or pot-roasted chicken with a red wine and rosemary sauce. To finish, why not go for the Grand Dessert -a taste of all the desserts available? Good vegetarian choices on a separate menu.

YATTENDON **Royal Oak**

The Square, Yattendon, Nr Newbury, Berkshire, RG16 0UF
Tel: (01635) 201325   *Fax:* (01635) 201926   **£65**
Open: lunch & dinner daily
Meals served: lunch 12-2.30, dinner 7-10 (Sun to 10.30)

Pretty, wisteria-clad village inn with five rooms. Cromwell dined here before fighting the battle in 1644. Bar meals and restaurant. Complete rewiring and redecoration of rooms is planned, on line for completion in early 1995.

YEOVIL   Little Barwick House

Barwick Village, Nr Yeovil, Somerset, BA22 9TD
Tel: (01935) 23902   *Fax:* (01935) 20908   **£55**
Open: dinner Mon-Sat (closed 3 wks Jan)
Meals served: dinner 7-9 (Sat to 9.30)

Christopher and Veronica Colley aim to make you feel at home here the minute you walk through the door. The listed Georgian dower house with its secluded garden on the edge of the village makes a delightful place at which to stay. Six en-suite rooms offer good levels of comfort and tranquillity. In the kitchen, the recipe for success is simply good cooking using the very best of local ingredients. Extensive use is made of local fish and game, and everything from rolls to chocolates are made on the premises. The à la carte offers a good choice—opt for two or three courses—and vegetarians have their own menu. Starters range from baked pancakes to avocado and chicken tikka salad. Main courses include the likes of Little Barwick pie (beef and game), West Bay sole and butter-roast poussin with herbs.

YORK   Bettys

---

6 St Helens Square, York, North Yorkshire, YO1 2QP
Tel: (01904) 659142   *Fax:* (01904) 627050   **£30**
Open: all day daily (closed 25 & 26 Dec, 1 Jan)
Meals served: 9-9

One of four in the Bettys stable, the others being in Harrogate (the original), Ilkley and Northallerton. When in Rome... When in Yorkshire... Bettys is not to be missed. Founded in 1919 by a Swiss confectioner, the business has expanded and flourished over the years. Everything from cakes, pastries, breads and muffins to hot and cold dishes, salads, breakfasts and brunch is available, all freshly made. Evening specialities feature the likes of Masham sausages with casseroled red cabbage and rösti potatoes or chicken provençale. The pâtisserie selection is nothing short of amazing, with choices like hazelnut meringue, Venetian festival cake, Normandy apple torte, chocolate brandy roulade and toffee and brandy snap fanfare. Yorkshire cheeses—white and smoked Wensleydale—are served with Bettys' own oatcakes. Excellent selection of teas and coffees.

YORK — Grange Hotel

Clifton, York, North Yorkshire, YO3 6AA
Tel: (01904) 644744   *Fax:* (01904) 612453   **£50**
Open: lunch Sun-Fri, dinner daily
Meals served: lunch 12-2.30, dinner 7-10, (light meals in Brasserie 12-3, 6-11)

Just outside the city walls, this carefully restored Regency town house
hotel with 30 bedrooms has a relaxed and homely atmosphere. Good
management and friendly staff make it a good alternative to more uniform commercial rivals. Elegant furnishings and beautifully proportioned rooms feature antiques and English chintz, while the Ivy
restaurant still offers French and traditional country house cooking,
although new chef Christopher Falcus has brought in some more
European and Italian influences.

YORK — Melton's

7 Scarcroft Road, York, North Yorkshire, YO2 1ND
Tel: (01904) 634341   **£50**
Open: lunch Tue-Sun, dinner Mon-Sat
    (closed 24 Dec-12 Jan, 30 Aug-7 Sept)
Meals served: lunch 12-2, dinner 7-10

Adventure and tradition go hand in hand on the short Anglo-French
menu here. Chef Michael Hjort—ex-Roux restaurants—produces
dishes such as caramelised onion tart with rosemary sauce or bacon
and cabbage broth among starters. Main course might be ox tongue
with a piquant sauce served with mashed potatoes and spinach, or
roast duck with honey. Among his specialities he lists salad of scallops
and smoked bacon, venison with oranges, and salmon and smoked eel
in a red wine sauce. Daily specials complement the carte: seafood on
Tuesdays, puddings on Wednesdays and vegetarian specials on
Thursdays. Lovely desserts include the likes of pancake soufflé with
raspberries, brioche and orange pudding and walnut tart. British and
Irish cheeses to finish.

YORK — Middlethorpe Hall

Bishopthorpe Road, York, North Yorkshire, YO2 1QB
Tel: (01904) 641241   *Fax:* (01904) 620176   **£55**
Open: lunch & dinner daily
Meals served: lunch 12.30-1.45, dinner 7.30-9.45

Racegoers can't do better than stay at this magnificent William-and-
Mary house overlooking York racecourse. The Hall has been skilfully
restored to its former glory by Historic House Hotels, yet retains an
atmosphere of comfort and well-being. The gardens and parkland alone
are a sight to behold, with an array of specimen trees, a small lake,
walled garden, white garden and ha-ha to explore. There are 30 bedrooms, some in the 18th-century courtyard annexe. All are beautifully
furnished and have Edwardian-style bathrooms. Overlooking the gardens are the panelled dining rooms where you can relax in the knowledge that chef Kevin Francksen really knows his stuff. His style of
cooking is British, with dishes such as warm game salad in a pastry
case followed by pan-fried red mullet with orange and basil butter
sauce or roast pigeon with blueberries and figs. The choice of menus

includes a classically-inspired gourmet option of three or four courses. The Grill Room offers less formal dining if required. Good wine list.

YORK   19 Grape Lane

19 Grape Lane, York, North Yorkshire, YO1 2HU
Tel: (01904) 636366   **£45**
Open: lunch & dinner Tue-Sat
   (closed Xmas, 2 wks Jan/Feb, 2 wks Sep)
Meals served: lunch 12-1.45, dinner 7-10 (Sat to 10.30)

Call in at this attractive restaurant in a characterful, timbered building down a narrow lane close to York Minster for some contemporary English cooking. At lunchtime a blackboard offers a choice of simple hot dishes and snacks, including salads, home-made soups and sandwiches. Evening brings the carte and a fixed-price menu, with dishes such as duck and lentil terrine served with tarragon jelly followed by a medley of North Sea fish with tomato and brandy sauce or roast saddle of lamb served with a timbale of kidney and mushroom. Traditional puds are popular—bread-and-butter, Yorkshire treacle tart or sticky toffee pudding.

YORK   Ristorante Bari

15 The Shambles, York, North Yorkshire, YO1 2LZ
Tel: (01904) 633807   **£35**
Open: lunch & dinner daily (closed 25 & 26 Dec, 1 Jan)
Meals served: lunch 10.30-2.30, dinner 6-11

Situated in one of York's oldest and most picturesque streets, this is also appropriately the city's longest-established Italian restaurant. The menu offers an extensive range of traditional dishes, from starters like home-made minestrone to filetto Casanova (steak with Marsala, cream and brandy) or scaloppine alla crema (veal with white wine, mushrooms and cream). Particularly famous locally for its pizzas, pasta, seafood and steaks.

YORK   Taylor's Tea Rooms & Coffee Shop

46 Stonegate, York, North Yorkshire, YO1 2AS
Tel: (01904) 622865   *Fax:* (01904) 640348   **£30**
Open: all day daily (closed 25 & 26 Dec, 1 Jan)
Meals served: 9-5.30

Situated at the heart of medieval York, Taylor's was founded in 1886 by two brothers who, during the heady days of the Empire, supplied rare and exotic blends of tea and coffee to Victorian society. In 1962 it joined forces with that Yorkshire-based tea-room institution, the award-winning Bettys. Still a family business, the success of Taylor's, like Bettys, is founded on the principle that if you want things just right you have make them yourself. The range on offer is extensive; come for afternoon tea, toasts and muffins, sandwiches, salads, desserts, pastries, or a hot lunch.

Scotland Establishment Reviews

ABERDEEN — Courtyard on the Lane

1 Alford Lane, Aberdeen, Grampian, AB1 1YD
Tel: (01224) 213795   **£55**
Open: lunch Tue-Fri, dinner Tue-Sat
    (closed 25 & 26 Dec, 1 Jan, 2 wks Jul)
Meals served: lunch 12-2, dinner 7-9.30

Make your way to the junction of Holburn and Union streets to find this back-alley restaurant where Tony Heath cooks with flair and imagination. The short lunchtime and dinner cartes offer ample choice, with dishes such as squid and mussel stew served on a bed of noodles or lightly curried parsnip soup, followed by by local lamb cooked with a courgette and vegetable tian with sweet potatoes boulangère or grilled fillet of turbot and monkfish with Chablis and saffron sauce. International puds—tiramisu, caramelised apple tart, strawberry shortcake with soft fruit coulis. Friendly service from partner Shona Drysdale.

ABERDEEN — The Marcliffe at Pitfodels

North Deeside Road, Pitfodels, Aberdeen, Grampian, AB1 9YA
Tel: (01224) 861000   *Fax:* (01224) 868860   **£75**
Open: dinner Mon-Sat
Meals served: dinner 7-10,
    (light meals Conservatory: 12-2.15 & 6.30-10)

Aberdeen's newest hotel to the west of the city has got off to a good start under the ownership of experienced local hoteliers Stewart and Sheila Spence. Forty-two bedrooms provide well-designed, spacious accommodation and there are two restaurants to choose from. The stylish, split-level Conservatory offers a short but interesting choice of traditional dishes, from beef, mushroom and Guinness pie with flaky pastry top to roast beef and Yorkshire pudding or a selection of char-grilled steaks served with French fries and salad. The Invery Room provides a more formal dinner setting for Norman Mundie's four-course menu. Fishy options might include char-grilled halibut with chive butter sauce or grilled salmon with sun-dried tomato and herbs.

ABERDEEN	Silver Darling

Pocra Quay, North Pier, Aberdeen, Grampian, AB2 1DQ
Tel: (01224) 576229   **£65**
Open: lunch Mon-Fri, dinner Mon-Sat (closed 2 wks Xmas)
*Meals served:*lunch 12-2, dinner 7-10

Barbecue seafood restaurant in the old customs house down by the quay, with views of the city and old port. The food is cooked in full view of diners through a large window and the choice is vast. Orkney oysters, large tiger prawns, mussels and princess scallops cooked in French cider with shallots and chives; followed by a trio of grilled fish (sea trout, rock turbot and monkfish), cooked on the barbecue and served with red pepper and basil coulis, or whisky-flambéed brill with redcurrant and gooseberry cream sauce. If it's meat you want, ask the waiter for the speciality of the day. Similar lunchtime carte.

ABERFELDY	Farleyer House

Weem, Aberfeldy, Tayside, PH15 2JE
Tel: (01887) 820332   *Fax:* (01887) 829430   **£60**
Open: dinner daily summer, Fri & Sat winter
Meals served: dinner 7.30 for 8 (Bistro 10-2 & 6-9.15)

Once the main residence of the Clan Menzies, this attractive house in the Tay valley is ideally situated for sightseeing or fishing. Richard Lyth's cooking will impress with dishes such as thin slices of Tay salmon flavoured with coriander, a soup of wild mushrooms or herb-baked turbot with saffron sauce. Pause for breath, then enjoy the fine selection of Scottish cheeses such as Ettrick, Caboc and Drumlock before the sheer luxury of a raspberry crème brûlée with honey ice cream. There are some attractive bottles of fine wine from good vintages on the serious wine list. In the bistro you could try wild boar sausages with Arran mustard sauce, Swiss potato cake with Ayrshire bacon and puddings like gooseberry crumble and cream.

ABERFOYLE	Braeval Old Mill

Braeval, By Aberfoyle, Central, FK8 3UY
Tel: (01877) 382711   **£65**
Open: lunch, dinner Tue-Sat
     (closed Bank Holidays, 1 wk Feb, 1 wk May/Jun, 1 wk Nov)
Meals served: lunch 12.30-1.30, dinner 7-9.30

Nick Nairn's fixed-price menus offer no choice, simply the very best that the market has to offer that day: a straightforward approach for an unpretentious setting of rough stone walls hung with fabrics, flag-stoned floor and black polished wooden tables. A typical meal might start with lettuce, pea and mint soup and move on to game terrine served with smoked bacon and Cumberland sauce, then roast salmon with mashed potatoes served with a champagne and chive velouté. Desserts do present a choice (the only one) from six, and it won't be easy. Typical are strawberry pavlova with raspberry sauce, Armagnac parfait with prunes and Earl Grey syrup and caramelised apple tart with Calvados cream. Nick's cooking places the emphasis firmly on modern British and Scottish cuisine; local game, fish and shellfish are the specialities.

ACHILTIBUIE   Summer Isles

Achiltibuie, by Ullapool, Highland, IV26 2YG
Tel: (01854) 622282   *Fax:* (01854) 622251   **£70**
Open: dinner daily (closed mid Oct-Easter)
Meals served: dinner at 8, (light meals Café: 10.30am-9pm)

Chris Firth-Bernard has been at this idyllically situated, family-run
hotel since 1986 and his sound cooking never fails to please. Fresh
local produce is used to good effect in his fixed dinner menus. You
might be offered smoked haddock and potato soup served with buck-
wheat and caraway loaf, followed by carpaccio of beef with tomato and
anchovy relish, then baked wild salmon with a herb crust. There's a
choice of four puddings- perhaps tarte tatin, lemon and lime soufflé,
praline and vanilla ice cream or a glazed fruit flan. Scottish cheeses and
coffee follow. The owner, Mark Irvine writes 'there's a marvellous
amount of nothing to do in Achiltibuie', I would recommend a vigorous
day's walking to work up an appetite and a considerable amount of time
to peruse the impressive wine list!

ALEXANDRIA   Cameron House

Loch Lomond, Alexandria, Strathclyde, G83 8QZ
Tel: (01389) 55565   *Fax:* (01389) 59522   **£75**
Open: lunch Sun-Fri, dinner daily
Meals served: lunch 12-2, dinner 7-10

Good leisure and crèche facilities make this 68-bedroomed Georgian
house ideal for families. The house stands on one mile of private land
on the shores of Loch Lomond, has its own private marina (sailing,
windsurfing, water skiing), children's playground, nine-hole golf
course, and indoor leisure club, good enough to rival many. Panelled
walls, marble fireplaces and fine Italianate ceilings set the tone indoors.
Food comes in plentiful supply in a number of venues: choose between
the chandelier-hung Georgian Room, the Grill Room, the Brasserie
overlooking the pool and loch, or the Marina Clubhouse by the water's
edge. Specialities include ravioli of salmon and asparagus, haggis, and
hot pear soufflé with dark chocolate sauce; and while the main focus is
on Scottish cooking, continental influences abound.

ALYTH   Drumnacree House
St Ninians Road, Alyth, Tayside, PH11 8AP
Tel: (0182 83) 2194   **£45**
Open: dinner Tue-Sat (closed 23 Dec-31 Mar)
Meals served: dinner 7-10
Small, modest hotel where patron Allan Cull's skilful cooking is earning just
recognition.

ANSTRUTHER   Cellar

24 East Green, Anstruther, Fife, KY10 3AA
Tel: (01333) 310378   **£65**
Open: lunch & dinner Tue-Sat (closed 10 days Xmas)
Meals served: lunch 12.30-1.30, dinner 7.30-9

A delightful cellar restaurant near the harbour, with stone walls and
real fires burning in the grate at either end of the room in winter. Chef-
patron Peter Jukes offers a short carte with ample choice and fish is the
speciality. Crayfish and mussel bisque, cold dressed crab served with
toast and mayonnaise, omelette filled with smoked haddock or a trio of
cold-cured salmons: oak-smoked, marinated and kiln-roasted, served
with a dill and sweet mustard sauce. And that's only starters! Main
courses might feature fresh tuna with a crushed black peppercorn
sauce, turbot and west coast scallops braised in Chardonnay with
cream or pan-fried beef with oyster mushrooms and a creamy Dijon
mustard sauce. It's popular and has only eight tables, so book in
advance.

APPIN   Invercreran Country House Hotel

Appin, by Oban, Highland, PA38 4BJ
Tel: (0163 173) 414   *Fax:* (0163 173) 532   **£60**
Open: lunch & dinner daily (closed Nov-Feb)
Meals served: lunch 12.15-1.45, dinner 7-8

The Kersleys (three generations of them) aim to please at this low,
white-washed, '70s-built hotel in spectacular surroundings, overlooking
Glen Creran with the mountains beyond. There are nine bedrooms,
designed for a variety of tastes; many enjoy panoramic views and all are
ensuite. The lounge and dining areas are housed at the centre of the
building, overlooking the terrace and surrounding landscape. Tony
Kersley prepares Scottish dishes, with game and seafood high on his
list of interests.

ARISAIG   Arisaig House

Beasdale, Arisaig, Highland, PH39 4NR
Tel: (0168 75) 622   *Fax:* (0168 75) 626   **£80**
Open: lunch & dinner daily (closed Nov-Apr)
Meals served: lunch 12.30-2, dinner 7.30-8.30

John and Ruth Smither's lovely house is set amid
beautiful gardens on the road to the isles. A warm
welcome and comfortable bedrooms await the
weary traveller, and David Wilkinson's cooking will
revive the spirits. Set menus offer two courses,
sometimes a terrine, a sauté of forest mushrooms or
a quail egg tartlet to start, then a soup or salad to follow. Local game, fish or meat will be the main
course, with a choice of four puddings or cheese at
the end. When weather permits, have a light lunch
on the terrace.

AUCHENCAIRN   Balcary Bay Hotel

The Shore, Auchencairn, Dumfries & Galloway, DG7 1QZ
Tel: (0155 664) 217   *Fax:* (0155 664) 272   **£40**
Open: lunch by arrangement, dinner daily (closed mid Nov-Feb)
Meals served: dinner 7-8.30 (summer to 9)

Comfortable family-run hotel in a spectacular, secluded setting on the
edge of Balcary Bay. A former smugglers' haunt, this 17-bedroomed
hotel is now managed in friendly, relaxed fashion by the Lamb family
who have been in situ for just two years. The cocktail bar with patio
offers splendid views of nearby Heston Isle and the cooking is sound, if
mostly traditional. Choose from the fairly lengthy carte which includes
cullen skink and feather fowlie among the list of home-made soups.
The choice extends to straightforward grills, poached or grilled
salmon, Dover sole, trout with orange herb butter, and lobster served
three ways—as a salad, Thermidor or Hebridean (flambéed in brandy).

AUCHENCAIRN   Collin House

Auchencairn, Castle Douglas, Dumfries & Galloway, DG7 1QN
Tel: (01556) 640292   *Fax:* (01556) 640276   **£60**
Open: dinner daily (closed 3-4 wks Jan/Feb)
Meals served: dinner 7.30 for 8

Situated on Scotland's Galloway coast in a conservation area, this is a
delightful, peaceful location in which to relax and enjoy chef-patron
John Wood's refreshingly straightforward, set dinner menus, which
depend on the very best of local produce. Fresh fish and local game are
a strong feature—start with smoked salmon parcel stuffed with a crayfish mousse or smoked duck salad with an orange and brandy dressing; followed by tomato and tarragon soup; then wild venison with
peppercorns and a red wine sauce or fillet of salmon trout in a buttery
court bouillon. Good desserts, plus Scottish and French cheeses to finish. The small wine list has been carefully compiled to give variety and
value. The pretty, pinkwashed house stands in 20 acres of grounds, on
a hillside setting, and dates from around 1750, which is probably about
the time the magnificent Lebanese cedar was planted in the garden.
Partner Pam Hall runs front of house with style and charm. The six,
well-proportioned bedrooms are furnished with many period pieces
and all have spacious, well-appointed bathrooms. There are beautiful
views across the Auchencairn Bay from both the dining room and
drawing room.

AUCHTERARDER   Auchterarder House

Aucterarder, Tayside, PH3 1DZ
Tel: (01764) 663646   *Fax:* (01764) 662939   **£80**
Open: lunch Sun, weekdays by arrangement, dinner daily
Meals served: lunch 12-3, dinner 7-9.30

A splendid baronial mansion retaining the feel of a family home. Fixed-price menus offer dishes such as a warm salad of goat's cheese with hazelnut crumbs, crisp bacon and avocado, west coast mussel stew flavoured with Pernod served with herb dumplings, or rillettes of rabbit flavoured with juniper and served with walnut bread and plum and port chutney. To follow, there could be medallions of red deer with a timbale of chicken, barley and tarragon with red wine sauce, or braised turbot with light pesto on warm dill and tomato dressing. A Taste of Scotland menu featuring local produce cooked in imaginative ways is available at lunch and dinner. An exceptional wine list merits attention.

AUCHTERARDER   Gleneagles Hotel

Auchterarder, Tayside, PH3 1NF
Tel: (01764) 662231   *Fax:* (01764) 662134   **£90**
Open: lunch & dinner daily
Meals served: lunch 12.30-2.30, dinner 7.30-10

You don't have to have an interest in golf to enjoy yourself at Gleneagles, but if you do, there is nowhere better to indulge your hobby. Here you can play, talk, and live the sport to your heart's content. The new 18-hole golf course, The Monarch's was designed by Jack Nicklaus and opened in 1993, adding a fourth course to the three already established (the King's, Queen's and Wee). Though the name is synonymous with golf, however, there's no shortage of other sporting facilities available—Jackie Stewart's shooting school, the Mark Phillips equestrian centre and the British School of Falconry among them. Fishing, riding and shooting are big sports in this part of the world and Gleneagles is at the centre of all of them. Outside, the views are breathtaking; inside, all is sumptuous. This is, indeed, the Palace of the Glens, as it calls itself. The hotel has 234 rooms, three restaurants, and various bars and grills from which to choose. Start the day with kippers; end perhaps with Angus beef, Tay salmon, venison or Highland grouse from one of the Taste of Scotland menus. The repertoire from the kitchen is quite staggering, and includes as many as 20 soups or more on the Gleneagles Soup Kettle menu (Brown Windsor, Hebridean fish stew, brown beer and onion, to name a few). Lunch and dinner offer buffet menus alongside set menus and carte.

AUCHTERHOUSE	Old Mansion House

Auchterhouse, By Dundee, Tayside, DD3 0QN
Tel: (0182 626) 366   *Fax:* (0182 626) 400   **£70**
Open: lunch & dinner daily (closed 25 & 26 Dec, 1st wk Jan)
Meals served: lunch 12-1.45, dinner 7-9.15 (Sun to 8.30)

Nigel and Eva Bell have created an elegant small hotel from this substantial 16th-century house. Campbell Bruce adds a Scottish influence to basic French cooking and offers a comprehensive vegetarian menu. Breakfast is substantial with tempting Arbroath smokies or hearty black pudding with potato scones.

AYR	Fouters Bistro

2a Academy Street, Ayr, Strathclyde, KA7 1HS
Tel: (01292) 261391   **£35**
Open: lunch Tue-Sat, dinner Tue-Sun (closed 25-27 Dec, 1-3 Jan)
Meals served: lunch 12-2, dinner 6.30-10.30 (Sun 7-10)

There's lots to see in this attractive resort, excellent beaches, the fishing harbour and in nearby Alloway the thatched cottage where Robert Burns was born, now preserved as a museum. Opposite the Town Hall there's also Fouter's Bistro, which certainly shouldn't be missed. Starters include smoked trout from Fence Bay fisheries, a brioche filled with shrimps and mushrooms or a "Taste of Scotland" platter which has smoked chicken, smoked salmon, shrimps, poached home cured salmon, pâtés and salad: a meal in itself! To follow there's a rendezvous of local seafood, char-grilled steaks of Scottish beef or perhaps local salmon with asparagus. The fixed price bistro menu is good value.

AYR	The Stables

Queen's Court, 41 Sandgate, Ayr, Strathclyde, KA7 1BD
Tel: (01292) 283704   **£40**
Open: all day daily (closed Sun Oct-Jun, 25 & 26 Dec, 1 & 2 Jan)
Meals served: 10-4.45 (Sun 12.30-4.45)

Part of a group of Georgian and Victorian buildings which constitute an attractive shopping area which was extensively restored in the early 1980s with old paving stones, original period lamps and timber lintels, the Stables restaurant is part of the Stables Coffee House which serves a wide selection of pastries, light snacks and meals, as well as traditional country wines (raspberry/elderflower/silver birth), English and European wines and a select choice of single malt whiskies and de-luxe blends. Light snacks include traditional stovies—a dish of potatoes, turnips, onions and carrots—and haggis served with rumbledethumps and mashed turnip. Main meals offer the likes of ham and haddie pie (bacon and smoked haddock in a white sauce), the 18th-century Tweed Kettle recipe (a spicy casserole of salmon), simple steaks and salads. The family smokehouse at Auchterarder supplies a wide range of smoked meats and fish. This is good home cooking firmly rooted in tradition; owner Edward Baines has an extensive knowledge of Scottish culinary history.

BALLATER   Balgonie House

Braemar Place, Ballater, Grampian, AB35 5RQ
Tel: (0133 97) 55482   *Fax:* (0133 97) 55482   **£65**
Open: lunch & dinner daily
Meals served: lunch 12-2, dinner 7-9

Edwardian-style country house on the outskirts of the village with four
acres of mature gardens overlooking the golf course and the hills of
Glen Muick beyond. Balgonie has nine rooms, each named after a fishing pool on the Dee. Dinner is a four-course, fixed-price affair; lunch
the same minus one course. Local produce goes into providing sound
Scottish cuisine, with dishes like local venison terrine with a chestnut
parfait or warm mousseline of Orkney scallops to start; followed by
fillet of turbot topped with a basil crust, roast local wood pigeon on a
red burgundy game jus, or roast local pheasant on a bed of honey
braised red cabbage to follow. Dessert may be a hot Grand Marnier
soufflé, or you might prefer the Scottish cheeses.

BALLATER   Craigendarroch Hotel

Braemar Road, Ballater, Grampian, AB35 5XA
Tel: (0133 97) 55858   *Fax:* (0133 97) 55447   **£45**
Open: lunch Sun, dinner daily
Meals served: lunch 12-2, dinner 7-10

On the banks of the River Dee Craigendarroch (the former home of
the illustrious Keiller family) nestles among the great oaks of
Craigendarroch Hill in a serene Highland landscape of outstanding natural beauty. The hotel offers a wealth of sporting and leisure facilities,
two bars (one with live entertainment) and three restaurants: the Oaks
for modern international cuisine; the Lochnagar for Scottish game and
seafood and local specialities; and the Clubhouse, an informal setting
for light snacks or full meals. The hotel has 50 bedrooms including two
suites: one with four-poster and sumptuous whirlpool bath; the other
with an elegant drawing room and two individual bedrooms.

BALLATER   Tullich Lodge

Ballater, Grampian, AB35 5SB
Tel: (0133 97) 55406   *Fax:* (0133 97) 55397   **£55**
Open: lunch & dinner (closed Dec-Mar)
Meals served: lunch only at 1, dinner 7.30-9

Beneath the majestic Lochnagar in the valley of the Dee, this turreted
mansion offers real hospitality. Hosts Hector Macdonald and Neil
Bannister have run Tullich Lodge for nigh on 20 years and maintain
high standards. Neil's cooking can be enjoyed in the elegant panelled
dining room where jacket and tie are de rigueur. The set menu offers
no choice but the four courses are well balanced. You might start with
mussels au gratin followed by consommé with tomato, basil and
Madeira. Skate wings with black butter follow and then a warm fruit
salad with glazed cream or fine Scottish cheeses to finish. Why not visit
in August to coincide with the Ballater Highland games?

BANCHORY   Raemoir House

Raemoir, Banchory, Grampian, AB31 4ED
Tel: (01330) 824884   *Fax:* (01330) 822171   **£55**
Open: lunch & dinner daily (closed 1st 2 wks Jan)
Meals served: lunch 12.30-2, dinner 7.30-9

For 50 years the Sabin family have cared for guests at their 25-bed-roomed hotel, an 18th-century mansion set in a 3500 acre estate. Chaises longues feature in bedrooms, tapestried walls and fine antiques throughout the house. Some of the bedrooms are housed in the 16th-century Ha'Hoose behind the mansion, thought to be one of the finest examples of its type. The restaurant offers an extensive menu, with some bias towards Scottish traditions. Chef Derek Smith lists roast local wild boar with sage and walnut stuffing, Raemoir pheasant braised in claret, and smoked salmon and lobster in a champagne and dill sauce in filo pastry basket among his specialities. A good selection of Scottish cheeses and an international wine list are additional treats.

BEARSDEN   Fifty Five BC

128 Drymen Road, Bearsden, Glasgow, Strathclyde, G61 3RB
Tel: 041-942 7272   *Fax:* 041-942 9650   **£50**
Open: lunch & dinner daily
Meals served: lunch 12-2, dinner 7-10

Hamish McLean's smart designer bar with the restaurant at the rear has not taken long to catch on. The cooking is in the modern European mode. Look forward to starters like salmon and truffle terrine, chicken liver parfait or steamed Loch Etive mussels à la marinière, followed by Scottish salmon wrapped in lattice puff pastry with cream and vegetable sauce perhaps, roast monkfish, char-grilled steak or rack of lamb with orange and rosemary jus. Delicious desserts like iced Grand Marnier soufflé precede Scottish cheeses served with oatcakes and biscuits. Good bar menu with plenty of choice, plus special children's menu.

BLAIRGOWRIE   Kinloch House

Kinloch, By Blairgowrie, Tayside, PH10 6SG
Tel: (01250) 884237   *Fax:* (01250) 884333   **£60**
Open: lunch & dinner daily (closed 2 wks Dec)
Meals served: lunch 12.30-2, dinner 7-9.15

Blairgowrie is an attractive little town, an angling resort and the centre of a prosperous strawberry- and raspberry-growing region. Just to the west of town is the fine Scottish house where the Shentalls' welcome guests to share their hospitality in 25 acres of parkland. Menus for the restaurant change daily, making good use of fresh local produce. The wine list is superbly composed with some fine wines from excellent vintages and a huge selection of half bottles.

CAIRNDOW   Loch Fyne Oyster Bar

Clachan Farm, Cairndow, Strathclyde, PA26 8BH
Tel: (0149 96) 264   *Fax:* (0149 96) 234   **£35**
Open: all day daily (closed 25 & 26 Dec, 1 & 2 Jan)
Meals served: 9-9 (Nov-Mar 9-6)

The original Loch Fyne oyster bar, situated at the head of the loch, with seats outside during the fine weather. It has spawned a number of siblings below the border, supplying them direct from Cairndow. A wonderful array, from oysters and langoustines to smoked trout, eel, salmon, mussels and mackerel from the restaurant's own smokehouse. Plus haggis with tatties and neeps—how could they leave it out! Pop in for a quick bite or a feast at this straightforward, no-nonsense bar.

CALLANDER   Roman Camp Hotel

off Main Street, Callander, Tayside, FK17 8BG
Tel: (01877) 330003   *Fax:* (01877) 331533   **£70**
Open: lunch & dinner daily
Meals served: lunch 12-2, dinner 7-9

The pink-turreted 17th-century Roman Camp looks something like a French château. A house of grand proportions with ornate features including painted ceilings, this was once the hunting lodge of the Dukes of Perth. The River Teith is a short cast from the hotel entrance so it's popular with fishermen, and the grounds offer ample scope for a quiet read or gentle walk. That's if you can tear yourself away from the library—this is a beautiful room with secret chapel concealed behind panelled walls. Cooking is in the modern Scottish mould, with dishes such as home-made sweetbread and wild mushroom sausage with truffle sauce followed by whole boned poussin stuffed with prunes, walnuts and apple, served on tarragon gravy.

CANONBIE   Riverside Inn

Canonbie, Dumfries & Galloway, DG14 0UX
Tel: (0138 73) 71512   **£50**
Open: dinner daily (closed 25 & 26 Dec, 1 Jan, 2 wks
   Feb, 2 wks Nov)
Meals served: dinner 7.30-8.30

Robert and Susan Phillips have owned the Riverside for 20 years and have fine tuned the art of innkeeping. Comfortable bedrooms and high standards in the kitchen are the keys to their success. They have a blackboard menu in the bar which opens for lunch and dinner, and in the dining room there's a fixed price dinner menu offering homely cooking of fine ingredients. Baked garlic oysters or air dried Cumbria ham could be followed by crispy roast duck, breast of corn-fed chicken or perhaps fillet of salmon. Good local cheeses, tempting puddings and a well composed wine list. A delightful stopover just north of the border.

COLBOST   Three Chimneys Restaurant

Colbost, By Dunvegan, Isle of Skye, Highland, IV55 8ZT
Tel: (01470) 511258   **£55**
Open: lunch & dinner Mon-Sat (Sun Bank Holidays)
    (closed Nov-Mar)
Meals served: lunch 12.30-2, dinner 7-9

Scottish beef, lamb and game, and local seafood and fish form the basis of Shirley Spear's excellent Scottish cooking at this charming restaurant, housed in a converted crofter's cottage. Most of the seafood is creel-caught, rope or raft-grown in the sea lochs surrounding Skye or nearby Minch and Mooner bays. Various 4-course dinner menus cater for everyone, including vegetarians who have their own, but the big attraction has got to be the Grand Seafood Platter menu for two: start with fresh squat lobster broth followed by hot crab tart with lemon butter sauce, then relax and await the arrival of the grand platter itself: fresh Skye langoustines, queenie scallops, mussels, oysters, velvet crab, claws, half a fresh lobster, and more. There's a wide choice of delicious, homely puds to follow, such as warm curdie cake with hot lemon curd sauce or hot marmalade pudding with Drambuie custard. Home-made breads and up to 12 varieties of Scottish cheese.

CONTIN   Coul House Hotel

Contin, by Strathpeffer, Highland, IV14 9EY
Tel: (01997) 421487   *Fax:* (01997) 421945   **£50**
Open: lunch by arrangement, dinner daily
Meals served: dinner 7-9 (light meals Bar: 12-2)

This former country mansion, belonging to the ancient Mackenzies of Coul, enjoys a secluded location looking out on to the Strathconon mountains. Today, it is in the hands of Martyn and Ann Hill, who together with lovable labradors, Skye and Ramsay, give a warm Highland welcome to guests at this 21-bedroomed hotel. The Taste of Scotland carte is supplemented by a fixed-price dinner menu which combines Scottish specialities with Continental-inspired dishes. Typical examples from the Scottish repertoire include mussels Mackenzie (flamed in whisky and finished with cream), poached fillet of Loch Inver haddock and sirloin steak Rob Roy (filled with haggis and served in its own jus).

CRINAN   Crinan Hotel

Crinan, By Lochgilphead, Strathclyde, PA31 8SR
Tel: (0154 683) 261   *Fax:* (0154 683) 292
Westward Restaurant: £60
Open: dinner daily
Meals served: dinner 7-9
Lock 16:   £80
Open: dinner Tue-Sat (closed 3 days Xmas, Oct-Apr)
Meals served: dinner at 8

The Ryans' hotel in the tiny fishing village of Crinan (population 58) at the northern end of the canal which connects Loch Fyne with the Atlantic has 22 rooms, all enjoying at least a peep of the surrounding

waters. The hotel has been at the centre of the community for over 200 years, no less so nowadays. Look down over the village and loch from the roof bar and seafood restaurant, known as Lock 16, served daily by the local fishing fleet which unloads just 50 yards from the hotel kitchen, giving chef Nick Ryan the pick of the catch for his evening table. Superb shellfish: jumbo prawns, clams, lobsters, mussels and oysters offer a feast which is as fresh as it can be! Alternatively you might prefer to dine in the main ground-floor restaurant on prime Scottish beef, Kintyre lamb and salmon from the loch which comes either fresh or smoked. Menus are fixed-price with limited choice and change nightly—awaiting the arrival of the boats before final decisions are made. Wonderful desserts—try the hot lime soufflé with chocolate sauce. For lunch, it's down to the bar at the east end of the hotel for something a little lighter. Boat trips on large fishing-type vessels can be arranged.

CUMBERNAULD   Westerwood Hotel

St Andrews Drive, Westerwood, Cumbernauld,
    Strathclyde G68 0EW
Tel: (01236) 457171   *Fax:* (01236) 738478   £50
Open: lunch Sun, dinner Wed-Sun
Meals served: lunch 12-2.45, dinner 6.45-9.45
    (Fri & Sat only in Jan & Feb)

Well located for either Edinburgh or Glasgow, this custom-built hotel, golf and country club is a golfer's dream! An 18-hole golf course with golf school, tennis courts, gym, swimming pool or more tranquil snooker or bowls will keep all sportsmen happy. After whichever exercise you choose, you can later relax in the circular dining room and enjoy Tom Robertson's excellent cooking. Smoked Tay salmon, breasts of quail on green lentils and smoked bacon with port wine sauce, canon of lamb on creamed aubergine with a whisky and pickled walnut sauce or a vegetarian potato rösti with oriental spiced mushrooms and goat's cheese are sure to please. Simpler dishes are offered in 'The Tipsy Laird'.

CUPAR   Ostlers Close

25 Bonnygate, Cupar, Fife, KY15 4BU
Tel: (01334) 655574   **£55**
Open: lunch & dinner Tue-Sat (closed 25 & 26 Dec,
    1 & 2 Jan, 2 wks Jun)
Meals served: lunch 12.15-2, dinner 7-9.30

Fresh produce is the essential element in Jimmy Graham's kitchen at
this small restaurant in the thriving market town of Cupar. He combines ingredients in interesting ways: saddle of roe venison with wood
pigeon breast are served in a red wine sauce, Pittenweem turbot with
West Coast scallops in herb butter sauce, a roast breast of duck with
duck leg confit on Puy lentils. Puddings command no less attention. He
might prepare a honey, Drambuie and oatmeal ice cream or baked
lemon tart served with lemon sorbet, creating a lovely contrast of textures. Try the excellent Scottish cheeses. Lunch-time sees lower prices
but no less imaginative cooking.

DRUMNADROCHIT   Polmaily House
Drumnadrochit, Highland, IV3 6XT
Tel: (01456) 450343   **£40**
Open: lunch & dinner daily
Meals served: lunch 12-2.30, dinner 7.30-9.30
Ten-bedroomed house in 18 acres of woodland and gardens, looking southward
to Glen Urquhart and Loch Ness. A beautiful house in a beautiful setting and one
which gives a warm welcome to families. Traditional Highland breakfasts, lunch
by the pool.

DRYBRIDGE   Old Monastery Restaurant

Drybridge, Buckie, Grampian, AB56 2JB
Tel: (01542) 832660   **£50**
Open: lunch & dinner Tue-Sat (closed Bank Holidays,
    3 wks Jan, 2 wks Nov)
Meals served: lunch 12-1.30, dinner 7-9.30

I remember my first visit to the Old
Monastery back in 1987 when Maureen and
Douglas Gray had just moved into their hilltop refuge. After almost giving up all hope of
finding them (trying to follow directions given
by a previous owner), I finally succeeded and
was warmly welcomed by Maureen who
explained their aspirations for the newly-
acquired restaurant. Seven years have sped
by. They seem to have achieved their goals
and established a regular following who
return to enjoy their hospitality and Douglas's
cooking. The menu has developed well; local
produce is much in evidence: Aberdeen
Angus beef, Highland venison, salmon and
Scottish artisan cheeses served with oatcakes.
The wine list has grown in volume and stature
with over a hundred listings drawn from
around the world, more than 20 of them in halves. Still offering sanctuary, The Old Monastery is a triumph of mind over matter!

DRYBURGH	Dryburgh Abbey Hotel

St Boswells, Dryburgh, Borders, TD6 0RQ
Tel: (01835) 22261 *Fax:* (01835) 23945   **£45**
Open: lunch & dinner daily
Meals served: lunch 12.30-2.15, dinner 7.30-9.30

This splendid Victorian sandstone house adjacent to the abbey ruins
stands on the banks of the Tweed and is an ideal venue for salmon or
trout fishing or shooting parties. Owned by the Grose family, the house
has undergone extensive restoration and now offers the traditional
peace and comfort of a country house hotel. Patrick Ruse prepares traditional Scottish and British dishes with a classic, modern outlook. The
Tweed restaurant, with views over the river, is an elegant setting in
which to enjoy his daily table d'hote menus which reflect the abundance of local ingredients. Terrine of Highland venison studded with
pistachios, halibut topped with a provençale crust on white wine cream,
Border lamb in its own juices, honey-roasted Lunesdale duckling with
plum sauce, traditional desserts and a Scottish cheeseboard. Light
lunches—sandwiches, salads and hearty hot dishes—are served in the
lounge, the bar or on the terrace in fine weather. A well-judged miscel-
lany of wines to please all palates.

DULNAIN BRIDGE	Auchendean Lodge

Dulnain Bridge, Grantown-on-Spey, Highland, PH26 3LU
Tel: (01479) 851347   **£55**
Open: dinner daily (closed 4 wks Nov or 4 wks Jan)
Meals served: dinner 7.30-9

This is a perfect place for a holiday at any time of the year with so
many local activities: salmon fishing on the Spey, skiing in the
Cairngorms, plenty of local golf courses or more gentle bird watching
in the Abernethy reserve—there's something for everyone. Eric Hart
presides over the cooking, preparing limited-choice fixed-price menus
with fish and game featuring prominently. Ian Kirk looks after the
guests and offers a fine selection of wines, particularly from his native
New Zealand.

DULNAIN BRIDGE	Muckrach Lodge

Dulnain Bridge, Grantown-on-Spey, Highland, PH26 3LY
Tel: (01479) 851257 *Fax;* (01479) 851325   **£50**
Open: lunch & dinner daily (closed 3 wks Nov)
Meals served: lunch 12-2, dinner 7.30-9
Highland hospitality in a converted Edwardian hunting lodge with 12 rooms.
Scottish cuisine. Nearby skiing in the Cairngorms and canoeing on the River
Spey.

DUNBLANE   Cromlix House

Kinbuck, Dunblane, Central, FK15 9JT
Tel: (01786) 822125   *Fax:* (01786) 825450   **£75**
Open: lunch & dinner daily (closed mid Jan-end Feb)
Meals served: lunch 12.30-1.15, dinner 7-8.30

New management, under David and Ailsa Assenti, has brought a new
lease of life to this distinguished 14-bedroomed country house, set in
3,000 acres of parkland and estate. The house, complete with private
chapel where Sunday service is held, was built in 1874 as a family residence and the estate has belonged to the same family for 500 years.
Dinner in the ornate, elegant, beautifully proportioned dining room is
to be savoured and enjoyed to the fullest. The finest local trout, salmon,
game, beef and lamb, soft fruits and vegetables are all available on the
estate or bought from local suppliers in season. Typical dishes on the
fixed-price dinner menu might include baked brie wrapped in Parma
ham and filo pastry with citrus coulis, and rosemary-flavoured cream of
smoked chicken and leek soup, followed by beef with woodland mushroom and Arran mustard sauce or grilled halibut on saffron butter with
prawns and capers. They have their own fishing and shooting—watch
out for the rods and wellies in the entrance hall.

DUNKELD   Kinnaird

Kinnaird Estate, Dalguise, By Dunkeld, Tayside, PH8 0LB
Tel: (01796) 482440   *Fax:* (01796) 482289   **£55**
Open: lunch & dinner daily (closed Feb)
Meals served: lunch 12.30-1.45, dinner 7.15-9.30

The view, looking down over the
River Tay, from this 9-bedroomed
hotel in 9000 acres of grounds is
quite spectacular. The house was
built in the 18th century, and has
been lovingly (no expense spared)
renovated and refurbished in country
house style by owner Constance
Ward. Bedrooms are lavish, as are
bathrooms, and a delightful, red
cedar-panelled drawing room is
made homely by the presence of
flowers and family memorabilia. The
dining room is elegance itself, with
views across the Tay and beautiful,
Arcadian-themed, painted panels
vying for attention, along with John

Webber's (pictured) modern British cooking. Menus show innovation
and respect for tradition. Typical dishes include crab and cod cakes,
risotto of smoked duck breast, braised boned oxtail, grilled sausage of
guinea fowl and honey-roast breast of quail with essence of wild mushrooms. Fishy options might include sautéed fillet of turbot with red
wine and thyme butter. Leave room for a dessert—light pear and sultana pie, apple and cider mousse, hot marzipan soufflé are typical.

DUNOON	**Chatters**

58 John Street, Dunoon, Strathclyde, PA23 8BJ
Tel: (01369) 6402   **£50**
Open: lunch & dinner Mon-Sat (closed Jan)
Meals served: lunch 12-2.30, dinner 6-9.30
Good home cooking based on French and Scottish influences, with local seafood, fish and game as specialities.

EDINBURGH   Alp-Horn

167 Rose Street, Edinburgh, Lothian, EH2 4LS
Tel: 0131-225 4787   **£45**
Open: lunch & dinner Mon-Sat (closed 25 & 26 Dec, 1 wk Jan)
Meals served: lunch 12-2, dinner 6.30-10

Informal Swiss restaurant off Charlotte Street, with Alpine mountain scenes and cowbells lending an authentic air to the two dining rooms. Air-dried Swiss beef and ham, veal sausage with Madeira sauce, cheese and beef fondues (for two or more) and Swiss wines are faithful to their origins. Lighter meals at lunch-time offer a two-course Square Deal Lunch for just £5.50. Vegetarian platters on request.

EDINBURGH   The Atrium

Saltire Court, 10 Cambridge Street, Edinburgh, Lothian
Tel: 0131-228 8882   **£55**
Open: lunch Mon-Fri, dinner Mon-Sat (closed 1 wk Xmas)
Meals served: lunch 12-3, dinner 6-10.30

There's an arty, post-modernist approach to the decor at Andrew Radford's restaurant which matches his style of cooking. Scottish and international dishes get contemporary treatment at this striking restaurant where you eat at railway sleeper tables lit by glass kerosene lamps. The towering glass-roofed atrium comes into its own at lunchtime when things are busy. Andrew's style is both sound and imaginative. Choices from the twice-daily-changing carte might include crab cake with spinach and lemon butter, Arctic char with leek and lovage, venison with roast roots and ginger or a gratin of leek and asparagus on brioche for vegetarians. Lovely desserts to finish—white chocolate truffle cake with cocoa sorbet, chocolate and amaretto ice cream. Pre-theatre suppers too, plus short snack menu at lunchtime as alternative to the carte.

EDINBURGH   L'Auberge

56 St Mary Street, Edinburgh, Lothian, EH1 1SX
Tel: 0131-556 5888   *Fax:* 0131-556 2588   **£45**
Open: lunch & dinner daily (closed 25 & 26 Dec, 1 & 2 Jan)
Meals served: lunch 12.15-2, dinner 6.30-9.30

Classic French menus emerge from the kitchen of Fabrice Bresulier and in true French style offers fixed price as well as à la carte menus (extremely good value at lunch). Dishes are well composed: try delicate fish mousseline bound in crème fraîche with a julienne of carrots and leeks, or a parfait of chicken livers with onion marmelade, grilled lamb cutlets with a light rosemary and honey sauce or duck breast with bitter-sweet sauce and caramelised carrots. The puddings are equally well-thought-out, a mousse of green apple with cinnamon-flavoured syrup, a Swiss chocolate mousse flavoured with Armagnac and served with a dark, bitter Belgian chocolate sauce. There's a rare opportunity for those of you who remember crêpes Suzette to have them once again prepared at your table; and for those who don't remember, now's the time to become acquainted with this classic dessert!

EDINBURGH   The Balmoral

Princes Street, Edinburgh, Lothian, EH2 2EQ
Tel: 0131-556 2414   *Fax:* 0131-557 3747   **£75**
Open: lunch Mon-Fri, dinner daily
Meals served: lunch 12-2.15, dinner 7-10.30

One of the grand hotels of the Victorian era provides an elegant and luxurious base to stay in Edinburgh. Nothing is omitted: there's a large pool, gymnasium, Turkish steam room, aerobics studio and of course a hairdresser. Almost 200 rooms and suites are opulently furnished, and there are private function suites and conference facilities. The Grill Room at No.1 Princes Street is elegant and formal in a modern style, while still retaining a grand feel. Scottish produce is cooked in interesting ways and served up by helpful staff at well spaced tables. There is also a brasserie for more informal meals.

EDINBURGH   Caledonian Hotel

Princes Street, Edinburgh, Lothian, EH1 2AB
Tel: 0131-225 2433   *Fax:* 0131-225 6632
Carriages Restaurant   **£55**
Open: lunch & dinner daily
Meals served: lunch 12-2.30, dinner 6.30-10
The Pompadour Room: **£80**
Open: lunch Mon-Fri, dinner Mon-Sat
Meals served: lunch 12.30-2, dinner 7.30-10.30

The "Caley", as it is known locally, stands on the site of the old Caledonian railway station. With 239 rooms, some of which overlook Edinburgh Castle, it is one of the capital's top hotels and is popular with tourists. Built at the turn of the century, it was designed to be one of the most opulent hotels in the country; thus space and splendour go hand in hand here. Visitors can call in for afternoon tea in the Caley lounge, a tradition which goes back nearly a century. Diners have a choice, between the elegant Pompadour restaurant or more informal Carriages, which offers a bistro-style menu of soups, salads, hot pots, grills, pastas, pies and haggis, with some emphasis on traditional Scottish fare. Meanwhile, in the Pompadour, chef Tony Binks produces a mostly modern French repertoire, with a nod here and there to Scotland itself: cream of hazelnut and  chanterelle soup; Loch Fyne oysters with creamed leeks and brie, glazed with a champagne sabayon; wild Tay salmon stuffed with oyster mushrooms bound in yoghurt; and maize-fed poussin stuffed with Roquefort, apple and prunes. The Caley vies for fame with the Castle itself: no small claim, but one which is justified.

EDINBURGH   Channings

South Learmonth Gardens, Edinburgh, Lothian, EH4 1EZ
Tel: 0131-315 2226   *Fax:* 0131-332 9631   **£40**
Open: lunch & dinner daily (closed 24-28 Dec)
Meals served: lunch 12.30-2, dinner 6.30-9.30

In a quiet, cobbled street close to the city centre, this privately-owned
hotel is made up of a series of Edwardian town houses. With a traditional country house feel, the hotel is rich in traditional ornate features—oak panelling, high moulded ceilings, antiques and
prints—while the 48 bedrooms, some of which overlook the old quarter of Edinburgh, are furnished in more contemporary style. There's a
relaxed, club-like atmosphere here, engendered by helpful, friendly
staff who pride themselves on good, old-fashioned service. The hotel
brasserie is a popular local haunt, and there is a cosy traditional bar,
where chess can be played. Comfortable fire-lit lounges, and a tranquil
library which can be used for conferences.

EDINBURGH   Denzlers 121

---

121 Constitution Street, Leith, Edinburgh, Lothian, EH6 7AE
Tel: 0131-554 3268   **£50**
Open: lunch Tue-Fri, dinner Tue-Sat
   (closed Bank Holidays, 1 wk Jan)
Meals served: lunch 12-2, dinner 6.30-10

Sister to the Alp-Horn though with an altogether different look -this
one is housed in a former bank so it has a somewhat imposing exterior
(amidst the bonded warehouses of Leith) rather than chalet-style
decor. Once inside, however, similarities are more obvious since like
its sibling, the restaurant offers solidly traditional Swiss favourites: veal
zurichoise, air-dried meats, fondues; along with traditional Scottish
dishes: rich venison stew, pigeon pie; and classic modern preparations:
fillets of sole in a mild curry sauce, poached salmon with an orange-
flavoured hollandaise. There is plenty of choice on both the lunch-time
and evening cartes, including simple steaks au poivre, salmon rissoles
and the likes of stuffed pancakes with a chicken and mushroom sauce.

EDINBURGH   Howard Hotel
36 Great King Street, Edinburgh, Lothian, EH3 6QH
Tel: 0131-557 3500   *Fax:* 0131-557 6515   **£45**
Open: dinner daily (closed 24-27 Dec, 1st wk Jan)
Meals served: dinner 7-9.30
Small, intimate, 16-bedroomed hotel created out of three Georgian town houses.
Quiet luxury and comfort.

EDINBURGH   Kelly's

---

46 West Richmond Street, Edinburgh, Lothian, EH8 9DZ
Tel: 0131-668 3847   **£45**
Open: dinner Tue-Sat (closed Oct-New Year)
Meals served: dinner 5.30-9.30

Jeff and Jacquie Kellys' small L-shaped restaurant in a former baker's
shop is situated in a Georgian block close to the city's theatreland.
Jacquie's cooking is modern British and the menu offers four or five
choices at each stage. Smoked haddock roulade with a basil and citrus

sauce and fish soup with rouille and croutons among starters; followed by tarragon pistou-encrusted Border lamb served with caramelised aubergine and onion confit or sautéed collops of monkfish with West Coast scallops coated in a rosemary and saffron cream sauce. Desserts might include traditionally-baked cheesecake or dark chocolate roulade with chocolate sauce. British and French cheeses; coffee and petits fours.

EDINBURGH — Malmaison Hotel et Brasserie

One Tower Place, Leith, Edinburgh EH6 7BD
Tel: (0131) 555 6868 (Hotel), (0131) 555 6969 (Brasserie)
Fax: (0131) 555 6999   **£45**
Open: lunch & dinner daily
Meals served: lunch 12-2.30, dinner 6-11 (light meals Bar 12-6)

The first of Ken McCulloch's new openings (the other in Glasgow, see separate entry), this contemporary hotel with its traditional French café wine bar and brasserie has already become one of the most fashionable addresses in Edinburgh. The 25 rooms, some with views over the Forth Estuary, are decorated in combinations of green/cream, blue/cream and beige/cream and offer all the latest mod cons. The bar, to the left of the lobby, features wicker chairs, elaborate iron work and etched glass and alternately blue and red blinds, a theme which continues into the brasserie where you can enjoy French regional and Mediterranean-style food. Chef Roy Brett comes from Le Caprice, and although we did not have a chance to eat here before we went to press, his pedigree, combined with Ken McCulloch's experience, indicate a sure winner.

EDINBURGH — Le Marché Noir

2/4 Eyre Place, Edinburgh, Lothian, EH3 5EP
Tel: 0131-558 1608   *Fax:* 0131-556 0798   **£45**
Open: lunch Mon-Fri, dinner daily
    (closed 25 & 26 Dec, 1 & 2 Jan)
Meals served: lunch 12-2.30, dinner 7-10
    (Fri & Sat to 10.30, Sun 6.30-9.30)

"I welcome anyone interested in good food, good wine and merriment," says owner-manager Malcolm Duck at this friendly, relaxed restaurant which is popular with locals. The menu (written in French) shows inspiration and a strong French bias, though cooking is based firmly on local produce wherever possible—smoked salmon with asparagus and quail's eggs; roast hare with a port and cassis sauce; beef with saffron rice and a brandy and green peppercorn sauce might be on offer. Desserts might feature peach bavarois, cinnamon and nut pudding or a good crème brûlée. `Le lunch' menus are good value as indeed is `Le list' which also leans strongly towards France.

EDINBURGH	Martin's

70 Rose Street, North Lane, Edinburgh, Lothian, EH2 3DX
Tel: 0131-225 3106   **£55**
Open: lunch Tue-Fri, dinner Tue-Sat (closed 4 wks
    Dec/Jan, 1 wk Jun, 1 wk Oct)
Meals served: lunch 12-2, dinner 7-10 (Fri & Sat to 10.30)

Not an easy place to find but worth the trouble. Situated between
Frederick Street and Castle Street in the cobbled North Lane off Rose
Street, this is among the city's best. Forbes Stott's short daily-changing
menus won't fail to please. Start with a warm salad of smoked salmon,
mussels and chorizo or a feuilleté of langoustines with spinach and nettle sauce, followed by halibut with a provençal crust and tomato coulis,
grilled fillet of lamb with Puy lentils, shallots and spring onions, or sea
bass with leek, chili and fennel sauce. The lunchtime menu is shorter
but similar, if a little simpler. Fresh herbs are supplied by owner
Martin Irons' father. A cosy, well-established place, now in its 11th
year. Decor is simple and highlighted by masses of fresh flowers
around the room.

EDINBURGH	Round Table Restaurant

31 Jeffrey Street, Edinburgh, Lothian, EH1 1DH
Tel: (0131) 557 3032   **£30**
Open: all day Tue-Sat
Meals served: 10-10

Full Scottish breakfast starts the day at this bistro-style restaurant,
served till noon when the blackboard and light Shoppers Lunch menus
come into operation. Dinner offers a fixed-price menu or à la carte of
Gaelic specialities. This is good, straightforward, unfussy cooking by
chef-patron Robert Winter. Typical dishes include haggis dumpling
with whisky sauce, Otter Ferry smoked salmon, Auld Reekies fowl (a
supreme of chicken in wild mushroom, malt whisky and cream sauce),
grilled fillet of trout with shrimps and Scottish cheddar. Fish is popular
and depends on the day's catch. Good vegetarian options, like courgettes provençale, and home-made soups.

EDINBURGH	The Shore

3/4 The Shore, Leith, Edinburgh, Lothian, EH6 6QW
Tel: 0131-553 5080   **£40**
Open: lunch & dinner daily (closed 25 & 26 Dec, 1 & 2 Jan)
Meals served: lunch 12-2.30 (Sun from 12.30), dinner 6.30-10,
    (light meals 11am-midnight)

Situated on the Leith waterfront about a mile from the city centre, this
is a no-nonsense seafood restaurant offering a twice-daily changing
menu which is guided by the day's catch, ensuring that the freshest
possible raw ingredients are used. Eat in the bar or in the no-smoking
dining room. Typical dishes—sautéed squid with cumin and lemon;
home-made soups (courgette and lemon/broccoli and apple); salmon
with a tarragon beurre blanc; poached turbot steak with coriander and
orange; chicken supreme with bacon and chestnuts; and to finish,
sticky toffee pudding or home-made ices.

EDINBURGH — Vintners Room

The Vaults, 87 Giles Street, Leith, Edinburgh, Lothian, EH6 6BZ
Tel: 0131-554 6767   *Fax:* 0131-554 8423   **£60**
Open: lunch & dinner Mon-Sat (closed 2 wks Xmas)
Meals served: lunch 12-2.30, dinner 7-10.30

The Vintners' Guild old sale room with its
ornate 17th-century Italian plasterwork and
candle lighting makes an atmospheric setting for excellent cooking from Tim
Cumming, pictured. A light informal lunch
(two or three courses) is served in the wine
bar, while dinner is more formal. The
refreshingly short and concise carte might
offer aubergine fritters with provençal
tomato sauce, west coast oysters or sautéed
scallops with capers and Pernod to start; followed by lemon sole with crevettes and vermouth sauce, guinea fowl with bacon, lentils
and red wine or fillet of Aberdeen Angus

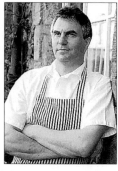

beef with sauce amoureuse. Good wine list with fair pricing in support.

ERISKA — Isle of Eriska

Eriska, Ledaig, by Oban, Strathclyde, PA37 1SD
Tel: (0163 172) 371   *Fax:* (0163 172) 531   **£80**
Open: dinner daily (closed Nov-Mar)
Meals served: dinner 8-9

The Buchanan-Smith family have enjoyed the peace and tranquility of
island life for over 20 years—Eriska is virtually a nature reserve. If you
want to get away from it all, this is the place to do it. A packed lunch
and collection of wellies by the front door provide the basics, Eriska
the rest. The house was designed by architect Hippolyte Blanc and was
built in 1824. Stern grey granite blends with warm red sandstone to
provide an imposing exterior in the Scottish baronial style. Inside, burr
oak panelling, log fires and a selection of malt whiskies in the library
provide an atmosphere of relaxed, easy-going informality. Bedrooms,
each individual, are named after neighbouring Hebridean islands, and
a good night's sleep is inevitable amidst all this pure, clean air. If walking's not your thing, there's an all-weather tennis court, watersports at
the pier, and a host of other less energetic activities to keep you busy.
Dinner is a candlelit, five-course affair, something of a house party—
with so few distractions on an island, you soon get to know the rest of
the guests. There's a choice of two courses at each stage of the meal.
You might find dishes such as chicken liver parfait with Oxford sauce,
followed by parsnip and pear soup or Loch Etive oysters served with
lemon. Main courses might include roast leg of Scottish lamb with a
mint gravy or pan-fried breast of chicken with a tarragon cream sauce.
Dessert is followed by a savoury, like rarebit, then comes Stilton and
Scottish cheeses. Mrs Buchanan-Smith remains at the helm in the
kitchen, with local Oban man Alan Clark at her side. A great many people return here year after year. Perhaps they just can't resist coming
back to watch the nightly ritual of badger feeding from the French windows of the bar. A private vehicle bridge keeps you easily in touch with
the mainland, if you don't want to feel too isolated.

FAIRLIE   Fins Restaurant

Fencefoot Farm, Fairlie, Nr Largs, Strathclyde
Tel: (01475) 568989   **£50**
Open: lunch Tue-Sun, dinner Tue-Sat (closed 25 & 26 Dec)
Meals served: lunch 12-2.30, dinner 7-10

The 350-year-old barn, with rough stone walls, green-painted concrete floor and pine furniture, part of a working fish farm and smokehouse, provides a suitably simple setting for Alastair McCullum's cooking. The menu is devoted of course to seafood, with just one daily-changing meat and vegetarian option offered. Beech-smoked Scottish salmon, local oysters au naturel or quickly grilled with savoury butter, pan-fried Atlantic salmon on a pool of port wine, grape and root ginger sauce, lightly poached Colonsay cod with orange and lemon butter sauce, Jura monk-fish casserole, creel-caught lobster and Cumrae langoustine are all typical. Finish with a Hook Line & Sinker!—home-made desserts (banoffi pie, sticky toffee pud) and Scottish cheese platter.

FORT WILLIAM   Crannog Seafood Rest.

Town Pier, Fort William, Highland, PS33 7NG
Tel: (01397) 705589   **£40**
Open: lunch & dinner daily (closed 25 Dec, 1 Jan)
Meals served: lunch 12-2.30, dinner 6-9.30

A converted quayside ticket office and bait house, Crannog specialises in fresh seafood, some of which is caught in the restaurant's own boats, then smoked in the adjoining smokehouse. Local langoustines are a speciality. The simple menu includes a vegetarian dish of the day, and a Scottish-only cheeseboard, all served up in a simple setting with scrubbed tables.

FORT WILLIAM   The Factor's House

Torlundy, Fort William, Highland, PH33 6SN
Tel: (01397) 705767   *Fax:* (01397) 702953   **£45**
Open: dinner Tue-Sat (closed mid Nov-mid Mar)
Meals served: dinner 7-9.30

This was once the Inverlochy estate manager's house—from here he controlled fishing rights on the Loch and activities on the Great Glen cattle ranch. Today, it is a charming seven-bedroomed guest house at the foot of Ben Nevis, with magnificent views of the surrounding countryside. Visit Loch Ness or take to the water in the hotel's sailing boat, but get back in time for dinner. Margaret McLellan's cooking is eclectic, but char-grilled steaks and fresh local fish are staple elements. Owner Peter Hobbs points out that his two black labradors are generally a big hit with the youngsters. This is very much a family-friendly place.

FORT WILLIAM   **Inverlochy Castle**

Torlundy, Fort William, Highland, PH33 6SN
Tel: (01397) 702177   *Fax:* (01397) 702953
Open: lunch & dinner daily (closed Dec-Feb)
Meals served: lunch 12.30-2, dinner 7-9.30

£90

The castle has now completed 25 years as one of the country's finest hotels, and throughout these years Grete Hobbs and her team have maintained impeccable standards. The kitchen of Simon Haigh, pictured, perpetuates the reputation for fine food, and his fixed-price menus of well-presented, well-judged dishes make choosing difficult. You might be offered dishes like chilled oysters with watercress cream; ballotine of foie gras with Sauternes jelly; confit of duck between layers of potato with a nut-oil-dressed salad; braised turbot with broad beans; tomato, basil and scallop mousse; fillet of Angus beef with braised root vegetables; or breast of Gressingham duck with a sliver of foie gras. The 50-page wine list can't fail to please, and the surroundings are a delight.

GAIRLOCH   Creag Mor

Charleston, Gairloch, Highland, IV21 2AH
Tel: (01445) 2068   *Fax:* (01445) 2044
Open: dinner daily
Meals served: dinner 6.30-9.30

£55

17-bedroomed, family-run hotel overlooking Old Gairloch harbour. Warm, relaxed hospitality, neat bright accommodation and traditional Scottish cuisine. Restaurant, plus all-day Buttery for informal light meals. A hundred malt and blended whiskies on offer in the bar, frequented by locals and fishermen.

GLAMIS   **Castleton House**

Glamis, By Forfar, Angus, Tayside, DD8 1SJ
Tel: (01307) 840340   *Fax:* (01307) 840506
Open: lunch & dinner daily
Meals served: lunch 12-2.30, dinner 7-9.30,
    (light meals Conservatory: 12-10)

£55

Located just outside Glamis, this comfortable, small hotel is capably run by William and Maureen Little. The kitchen is William's domain and he will provide five-course fixed menus in addition to the à la carte. Game and fish are much in evidence, and there are some excellent sweets.

GLASGOW Brasserie on West Regent Street

176 West Regent Street, Glasgow, Strathclyde, G2 8HF
Tel: 0141-248 3801   *Fax:* 0141-248 8197   **£40**
Open: all day Mon-Sat (closed Bank Holidays)
Meals served: 12-11

This Brasserie draws its identity from local and seasonal produce, with a bias towards French brasserie-style dishes on the short à la carte. Start with scampi provençale in puff pastry, seafood bisque or fresh oysters, before tucking in to poached salmon hollandaise, rack of lamb with a shallot jus or steak au poivre. There are good-value post-theatre suppers and a Something Lighter menu which features half a dozen or so single dishes such as Cumberland sausage with onion gravy; dolcelatte, walnut and apple salad; or goujons of sole with chips.

GLASGOW   Buttery

Delightful styling, exuberant decor!

652 Argyle Street, Glasgow, Strathclyde, G3 8UF
Tel: 0141-221 8188   **£55**
Open: lunch Mon-Fri, dinner Mon-Sat (closed Bank Holidays)
Meals served: lunch 12-2.30, dinner 7-10.30

At first sight this place seems rather more like a London club than a converted Victorian pub in Glasgow, but that's what it is and it's where Stephen Johnson cooks with flair and imagination. Try the pigeon and blackberry pie with an oatmeal glaze, steamed mussels in scampi and prawn sauce or ravioli of Italian sausage in black olive and basil sauce. Main courses might be a breast of guinea fowl on lentil and oatmeal stuffing with citrus sauce or grilled fillet of brill on a dark peppercorn butter. Fixed price menus at lunch and a vegetarian menu with a choice of no fewer than nine dishes! A hundred wines start at just under £14.

GLASGOW   D'Arcy's
Basement Courtyard, Princes Square, Glasgow, Strathclyde, G1 3JN
Tel: 0141-226 4309   **£25**
Open: all day daily (closed 25 & 26 Dec, 1 & 2 Jan)
Meals served: 9.30am-12 midnight (Sun 11-6)
International menu of popular dishes, from all-day snacks, salads, burgers and sandwiches to mussels marinière, steaks and fish, with good-value, fixed-price dinner menu served in the Back Room.

GLASGOW   Glasgow Hilton

1 William Street, Glasgow, Strathclyde, G3 8HT
Tel: 0141-204 5555   *Fax:* 0141-204 5504   **£80**
Open: lunch Mon-Fri, dinner Mon-Sat
Meals served: lunch 12-2, dinner 7-11

A skyscraper with heart! 20 storeys, more than 300 bedrooms, ballroom, business centre, pool and gymnasium—all in the centre of Glasgow. The Cameron Restaurant offers traditional Scottish produce cooked in innovative ways whilst Minsky's New York Deli has a variety of pizzas, pastas, sandwiches and salads.

GLASGOW — One Devonshire Gardens

1 Devonshire Gardens, Glasgow, Strathclyde, G12 0UX
Tel: 0141-339 2001   *Fax:* 0141-337 1663   **£85**
Open: lunch Sun-Fri, dinner daily
Meals served: lunch 12.30-2, dinner 7-10.30   ✿

This is Glasgow's most stylish hotel with its almost theatrical decor of bold colours and rich fabrics. It doesn't just look good, everything about this small hotel is quality, from the sumptuous bedrooms with marble bathrooms to superb service, fine food and an impressive wine list. Andrew Fairlie, pictured, cooks in modern style offering small menus of well-prepared dishes such as fish ravioli with pleurottes and a light basil sauce or fillet of beef with red onion marmalade. Delicious desserts feature the likes of apple Napoleon with a caramel lime sauce or rhubarb crème brûlée. Definitely the place to stay in Glasgow. Ken McCulloch is rightly proud of his achievements here—standards remain high year on year—no mean feat in anyone's book!

GLASGOW — Puppet Theatre

11 Ruthven Lane, Glasgow, Strathclyde, G12 9BQ
Tel: 0141-339 8444   *Fax:* 0141-339 7666   **£60**
Open: lunch & dinner daily
Meals served: lunch 12-2.30, dinner 7-11

A chic West End restaurant opposite Hillhead metro station, down a narrow lane. The building dates back to the early 19th century and you have a choice of two rooms: one featuring details from the Sistine Chapel paintings and a mirrored wall, the other an unusually-shaped conservatory room towards the rear. Excellent raw materials are combined to excellent effect by chef Douglas Painter. Skewered scallops with lentils and coriander, char-grilled squab on a bed of pulses and grape sauce, rich venison pie, calf's liver with lime and caramelised onions, roast leg of lamb and a ragout of monkfish, salmon and mussels in herb butter sauce are typical. Good-value two- and three-course set lunch menu.

GLASGOW — Ristorante Caprese

217 Buchanan Street, Glasgow, Strathclyde, G1 2JZ
Tel: 0141-332 3070   **£40**
Open: lunch Mon-Fri, dinner Mon-Sat (closed Bank Holidays)
Meals served: lunch 12-2.30, dinner 5.30-11
Old-style basement Italian restaurant with traditional menu, supplemented by daily specials on the blackboard. A favourite with locals, cheeful and atmospheric. Handy for the Royal Concert Hall.

GLASGOW   Malmaison Hotel et Brasserie

278 West George Street, Glasgow, G2 4LL
Tel: 0141 221 6400 (Hotel) 0141 221 6401 (Brasserie)
Fax: 0141 221 6411   **£45**
Open: lunch & dinner daily
Meals served: lunch 12-2.30, dinner 12-6 (light meals Bar 12-6)

Conveniently located just 15 minutes from Glasgow airport, five minutes from both stations and close to Glasgow's theatres and shopping, the second of Ken McCulloch's new ventures (see other entry in Edinburgh) offers stylish accommodation in its 21 rooms, which include four suites. Good food (French regional or Mediterranean-style) at reasonable prices can also be had in its café/wine bar and brasserie, decorated in art nouveau style.

GLASGOW   Rogano

11 Exchange Place, Glasgow, Strathclyde, G1 3AN
Tel: 041-248 4055   *Fax:* 041-248 2608   **£65**
Open: lunch Mon-Sat, dinner daily (closed Bank Holidays)
Meals served: lunch 12-2.30, dinner 6.30-10.30,
     (light meals in café 12-11, Fri & Sat 12-12, Sun 6-10)

Worth a visit just for the classic 1930s' decor but it would be a great shame to miss the food! There is a ground floor restaurant and Café Rogano in the basement—different menus, different prices. Chef Jim Kerr majors on seafood but there are plenty of meat dishes to satisfy all tastes. White wines make up the lion's share of the restaurant list to accompany the fish, and a separate list in the café has some interesting wines from around the world.

Rogano is a must when you're in Glasgow.

GLASGOW   Two Fat Ladies

88 Dumbarton Road, Glasgow, Strathclyde, G11 6NX
Tel: 041-339 1944   **£55**
Open: lunch Tue-Sat, dinner Mon-Sat (closed 12 days early Jan)
Meals served: lunch 12-2.30, dinner 5.30-10.30

Market-fresh fish is the speciality at chef-patron Calum Matheson's relaxed little restaurant. The straightforward handwritten carte offers plenty of choice and the cooking is modern. Char-grilled scallops with aubergines and basil pesto, halibut teriyaki, cod and prawn fishcake with parsley sauce or char-grilled sea bass with tomato salsa are the sort of thing you'll be offered. Vegetarians are catered for and there are one or two meat dishes available, plus daily specials marked up on the blackboard.

GLASGOW — Ubiquitous Chip

12 Ashton Lane, Glasgow, Strathclyde, G12 8SJ
Tel: 041-334 5007   *Fax:* 041-337 1302   **£55**
Open: lunch & dinner daily (closed 25 Dec, 31 Dec-2 Jan)
Meals served: lunch 12-2.30, dinner 5.30-11

Known locally as The Chip, this split-level restaurant in a cobbled lane near the university has been pulling in the crowds for over 20 years. Chef-patron Ronald Clydesdale cooks in the modern idiom with the emphasis on Scottish traditions. The setting was converted from a former coach house and stables so there's plenty of character about the place, not least at lunchtime when it's buzzing. The choice is vast, from a lengthy handwritten carte and fixed-price menu in the restaurant proper to an equally lengthy carte in the café-bistro operation, Upstairs at the Chip. Starters such as shellfish bisque with cream and ginger, warm salad of west coast shellfish with bacon and tarragon vinaigrette, venison or vegetarian haggis'n'neeps and wild mushroom and pearl barley risotto; followed perhaps by breast of Perthshire wood pigeon with game and chocolate sauce, Ayr-landed cod on a bed of clapshot with roasted peppers and chili oil, or Aberdeen Angus steak with onion and leek marmalade. Lovely menus, which show imagination and a gutsy approach.

GLENELG — Glenelg Inn

Glenelg, by Kyle of Lochalsh, Highland, IV40 8JR
Tel: (0159 982) 273   *Fax:* (0159 982) 373   **£40**
Open: dinner daily (closed Nov-Easter)
Meals served: dinner 7.30-9

Enthusiastic Christopher Main's small inn located in this sleepy hamlet is reached by a twisting road from Shiel Bridge, and the climb over Ratagan Pass affords spectacular views of the mountains known as the Five Sisters of Kintail. Six spacious bedrooms look out to the Isle of Skye. Simple fixed price menus have local seafood as their mainstay together with local venison and lamb from the surrounding hills. Have a hearty Scottish breakfast, go to see the Iron Age Broch Towers and then ask Christopher about a cruise around the sea lochs in the Swallow of Glenelg.

GULLANE — Greywalls Hotel

Muirfield, Gullane, Lothian, EH31 2EG
Tel: (01620) 842144   *Fax:* (01620) 842241   **£75**
Open: lunch & dinner daily (closed Nov-Mar)
Meals served: lunch 12.30-2, dinner 7.30-9

Built in 1901 by Sir Edward Lutyens, Greywalls opened as a hotel in 1948 and remains in the Weaver family's competent hands. It's a golfer's paradise situated next to the championship course of Muirfield, and it boasts an impressive guest list. Arnold Palmer, Lee Trevino, Greg Norman and Nick Faldo have all enjoyed the comforts of this elegant house. Paul Baron's cooking is another good reason to stay. Local fish, game and meats are well prepared and will satisfy even the most healthy appetite after 18 holes!

GULLANE   La Potinière

Main Street, Gullane, Lothian, EH31 2AA
Tel: (01620) 843214   **£65**
Open: lunch Sun-Tue & Thu, dinner Fri & Sat
    (closed 25 & 26 Dec, 1 & 2 Jan, 1 wk Jun, Oct)   🎋
Meals served: lunch at 1, dinner at 8

This small, pretty dining room with huge floral display and dried flowers hanging from old ceiling beams makes a delightful setting for the
joint talents of chef Hilary Brown and husband David. David is the
most charming of hosts and Hilary's cooking is faultless. Taking her
inspiration from France, she shows a light and sophisticated approach
in finely balanced dishes. There's no
choice, and dinner is at a fixed hour
with everyone eating together, so be
prepared to wait for other diners
between courses if need be. The
simple handwritten menu usually
begins with a soup (cream of red
pepper, tomato and mint), then
fish—perhaps pan-fried salmon with
Puy lentils, followed perhaps by
apricot-stuffed guinea fowl, then
cheese or dessert. Advance booking
strongly advised.

Biography

Hilary Brown

*Hilary trained at the Glasgow College of Domestic Science specialising
in food and nutrition. This is the formal training of someone who has been described as one of the best cooks in
Scotland, with an intuitive understanding of ingredients.
Accuracy, honesty and complete consistency are the key to
her cooking: quality guaranteed.*

INGLISTON   **Norton House**
Ingliston, Nr Edinburgh, Lothian, EH28 8LX
Tel: 031-333 1275   *Fax:* 031-333 5305   **£60**
Open: lunch Sun-Fri, dinner daily
Meals served: lunch 12-2, dinner 7-9.30
Virgin-owned, 47-bedroomed hotel within easy reach of the capital. Own pub tavern in converted stable block which is popular with locals and ideal for families.

INVERNESS   **Culloden House**

Inverness, Highland, IV1 2NZ
Tel: (01463) 790461   *Fax:* (01463) 792181   **£70**
Open: lunch & dinner daily
Meals served: lunch 12.30-2, dinner 7-9

Among famous visitors to Culloden was Bonnie Prince Charlie who fought his last battle by the park walls after seizing the house during the Jacobite Rising of 1745. Remodelled as a Palladian mansion in 1772, this handsome Georgian mansion stands in 40 acres of elegant grounds. Glistening chandeliers, marble fireplaces, massive pillars and classical Adam-style plasterwork reliefs feature in the decor of the house, which has been run by resident owners the McKenzies for more than a decade. The bedrooms, in keeping with the Georgian style of the rest of the house, are traditionally furnished, several boasting four-posters and spas. The cooking, a blend of classical and Scottish traditional, is in the capable hands of long-serving chef Michael Simpson who delivers an à la carte at lunch-time and a fixed-price affair for dinner. He might offer you grilled West Coast scallops dipped in breadcrumbs and glazed with a light onion and herb butter; calf's liver sautéed in butter, garnished with orange and grapefruit on a red wine vinegar sauce; guinea fowl breast with a wild mushroom mousse on a mustard sauce; and always a vegetarian option—Crowdie cheese and pine kernels in filo pastry on a pimento sauce, for example excellent Scottish cheeses. House claret is £9.25, Château d'Yquem 1976 is £549.35 but there's plenty in between, with several bottles under £15.

INVERNESS   **Dunain Park**

Inverness, Highland, IV3 6JN
Tel: (01463) 230512   *Fax:* (01463) 224532   **£50**
Open: lunch & dinner daily (closed 3 wks Jan/Feb)
Meals served: lunch 12.30-1.30, dinner 7-9

A mile from Inverness on the road to Loch Ness, this 14-bedroomed hotel is set in its own grounds surrounded by woodland. Two acres of walled garden and fresh local produce supply most of what Ann Nicoll needs in her kitchen. The cooking is Scottish with classic influences: mousseline of smoked haddock and whiting with sabayon sauce; cheese soufflé with a mild grain-mustard cream sauce; fillet of Highland beef Wellington with red wine sauce; or fillet of Shetland salmon baked in sea salt, served with a white port, lime and ginger sauce. Hearty breakfasts. Bedrooms, some with four-posters, are located in the main house or in the converted coach house within the grounds. Don't leave without sampling one of the 85 malt whiskies available from the bar!

INVERURIE   Thainstone House Hotel

Inverurie Road, Inverurie, Grampian, AB51 9NT
Tel: (01467) 621643   *Fax:* (01467) 625084   **£50**
Open: lunch & dinner daily
Meals served: lunch 12-2, dinner 7-9.30

The grand portal entrance to this 19th-century Palladian mansion house sets the tone for the stately elegance which lies within, matched by state-of-the-art leisure and conference facilities: the hotel boasts one  of the best-equipped country leisure clubs in the North. Outdoor activities are no less impressive, ranging from golf and fishing to clay pigeon shooting and falconry. Or perhaps you'd prefer the excitement of the only malt whisky trail in the world which starts from Thainstone and takes you through some of the Grampian Highlands' finest scenery. However you choose to pass the time until dinner, you can look forward to chef Bill Gibb's refined cooking across a range of fixed-price menus which include one for vegetarians. Start perhaps with roasted monkfish with stir-fry vegetables on a spicy capiscum sauce, followed by collops of venison in a pink peppercorn and cognac sauce served with a timbale of rice. Lovely home-made soups such as lobster bisque with malt whisky cream, oxtail consommé with tarragon quenelles and cream and woodland mushroom and chervil.

KENTALLEN OF APPIN   Ardsheal House

Kentallen of Appin, Highland, PA38 4BX
Tel: (0163 174) 227   *Fax:* (0163 174) 342   **£75**
Open: lunch & dinner daily (closed mid Jan-mid Feb)
Meals served: lunch 12-1.45, dinner 8-8.30

The approach, bordering Loch Linnhe, to this 13-bedroomed hotel is quite spectacular in itself. The house, which dates back to the early 1500s, is set in 900 acres of hills, woods, gardens and shore front. Destroyed by the uprisings of 1745, it was rebuilt shortly afterwards on the same foundations. New owners Neil and Philippa Sutherland offer a Scottish and international cuisine at the hands of chef George Kelso who has stayed on following the departure of the previous owners. Local seafood, fish, meat and game in season are the staple elements, along with home-grown fruit and vegetables, home-baked breads, preserves and their own brown eggs. Lunch is taken on the lawn in fine weather, dinner in the elegant, conservatory dining room.

KILCHRENAN   Ardanaiseig

Kilchrenan, By Taynuilt, Strathclyde, PA35 1HG
Tel: (0186 63) 333   *Fax:* (0186 63) 222   **£45**
Open: lunch & dinner daily (closed Oct-Apr)
Meals served: lunch 12-2.30, dinner 7.30-9
Baronial-style mansion with beautiful woodland gardens on the edge of Loch Awe. 14 bedrooms with views of the loch or gardens, plus fishing and hotel boat. Scottish cuisine.

KILCHRENAN   Taychreggan Hotel

Kilchrenan, By Taynuilt, Strathclyde, PA35 1HQ
Tel: (0186 63) 211   *Fax:* (0186 63) 244   **£60**
Open: lunch & dinner daily
Meals served: lunch 12.30-2.15, dinner 7.30-8.45

Nestled between the hills on the shores of the awe inspiring Loch Awe, Taychreggan enjoys spectacular views. Annie Paul continues her programme of refurbishment, gradually improving the whole of this delightful hotel. Happily unchanged, however, is Hugh Cocker's precise cooking of daily changing set menus. A typical dinner might start with avocado with hot smoky bacon and chive cream, then a choice of mushroom soup or mandarin sorbet; next comes pot-roast breast of chicken on a truffle galette with Madeira. Honey and malt whisky parfait is served with bitter chocolate sauce and followed by cheeses and then coffee. Plenty of choice on the wine list, with selections at under £10.

KILDRUMMY   KILDRUMMY CASTLE

Kildrummy, Alford, Grampian, AB33 8RA
Tel: (0197 55) 71288   *Fax:* (0197 55) 71345   **£60**
Open: lunch & dinner daily (closed Jan)
Meals served: lunch 12.30-1.45, dinner 7-9

This is castle country—Grampian has more than 70 castles, many just a short drive from this 15-bedroomed hotel overlooking the ruins of the original 13th-century castle. Kildrummy is a grandiose affair, a castellated country house built in 1900, in a lovely setting with beautiful gardens which boast rare shrubs, trees and Alpine plants. Inside there is a grand, baronial entrance hall, Adam-style drawing room and ornate staircase, (flanked at the foot by two carved lions), which leads up to the elegant, comfortable and spacious bedrooms. There are also some charming attic rooms higher up. Well-motivated, friendly staff, take their lead from longtime owner Thomas Hanna. The hotel has over three miles of fishing on the River Don and is ideally placed for many nearby outdoor pursuit centres: shooting, stalking, riding, skiing on the ski slopes; and over 30 golf courses within an hour's drive. There are set menus offering traditional cooking and the extensive wine list has some real bargains.

KILFINAN   Kilfinan Hotel

Kilfinan, By Tighnabruaich, Strathclyde, PA21 2AP
Tel: (01700) 82201   *Fax:* (01700) 82205   **£50**
Open: lunch Sun, dinner daily
Meals served: lunch 12-2, dinner 7.30-9.30

A remote setting along a single track road down the finger of land that sits between Loch Fyne and the Kyles of Bute, but the warm welcome from charming hosts Rolf and Lynne Mueller soon dispels any feeling of isolation and Rolf's cooking will soon put to flight any pangs of hunger, as you relax in the cosy candlelit dining rooms. Try fillet of rabbit on leaf spinach served with Madeira sauce, canon of lamb in sesame seeds to follow, or langoustine tails in garlic and herb sauce. Local cheese are worth trying, as well as puddings like honey and poppyseed parfait or lime and rum syllabub.

KILLIECRANKIE   Killiecrankie Hotel

Killiecrankie, By Pitlochry, Tayside, PH16 5LG
Tel: (01796) 473220   *Fax:* (01796) 472451   **£60**
Open: dinner daily (closed Jan & Feb)
Meals served: dinner 7-8.30

Home to its owners, Carole and Colin Anderson, Killiecrankie is set in
four acres of wooded grounds overlooking the River Garry. The house
has a cosy atmosphere; and the ten pine-furnished bedrooms are comfortable and bright, though some do not have sea views. Don't be surprised if you wake to the sound of red squirrels or roe deer
nearby—the area is rich in Scottish wildlife. Bar lunches and light suppers are available in the cosy, mahogany-panelled bar whilst the restaurant offers modern Scottish cuisine with a nod towards ethnic flavours
and styles -locally smoked leg of lamb, marinaded venison fillet, spicy
Malaysian fish curry soup. The hotel logo commemorates the story of
Donald MacBean (one of William of Orange's soldiers) who fled from
the loyalist Jacobite victors at the Battle of Killiecrankie in 1689 by
leaping 18ft across the high gorge of River Garry, losing his shoe and
his sword to the waters below, but living to tell the tale. The site of
Donald's leap is just a five-minute walk from the hotel.

KILMORE   Glenfeochan House
Kilmore, Oban, Strathclyde, PA34 4QR
Tel: (0163 177) 273   *Fax:* (0163 177) 624   **£70**
Open: dinner daily (closed Nov-Feb)
Meals served: dinner at 8
Chef-owner Patricia Baber produces stylish food here using mostly home-grown
raw materials. There are just three bedrooms in this charming house set amidst
its own estate to the South of Oban.

KILMUN   Fern Grove
Kilmun, Strathclyde, PA23 8SB
Tel: (0136 984) 334   *Fax:* (0136 984) 424   **£45**
Open: lunch & dinner Wed-Mon (closed Nov & Mar)
Meals served: lunch 12-2.30, dinner 7-9.30
Daily-changing menus based on fresh local produce; even the bread is home-
made at Ian and Estralita Murray's restaurant overlooking the Holy Loch, with
three bedrooms for overnight guests.

KINCLAVEN BY STANLEY   Ballathie House

Kinclaven by Stanley, Tayside, PH1 4QN
Tel: (01250) 883268   *Fax:* (01250) 883396   **£50**
Open: lunch & dinner daily   ❖
Meals served: lunch 12-2, dinner 7-9

Turreted, baronial-style house, with rooms overlooking the River Tay.
Sit by a roaring log fire in winter and sip your way through some of the
excellent malts on offer! The house is set in 1,500 acres of grounds,
with lawns which slope down to the river bank. Inside, all is space and
grace, with many fine original features. The restaurant also boasts river
views and is an elegant setting for dinner, a fixed-price affair which
offers plenty of choice at each stage. West Coast seafood, Perthshire
lamb and game feature strongly in Kevin MacGillivray's modern
Scottish repertoire. Plenty of good value on an extensive, well chosen
wine list.

KINGUSSIE   The Cross

Tweed Mill Brae, Ardbroilach Road, Kingussie,
    Highland, PH21 1TC
Tel: (01540) 661166   *Fax:* (01540) 661080   **£60**
Open: lunch & dinner Wed-Mon
    (closed Dec-Feb, open New Year)
Meals served: lunch 12.30-2, dinner 7-9)

The Hadleys' enthusiasm flourishes in their new setting of a converted tweed mill. Ruth's cooking is still some of the best in Scotland and Tony's fabulous wine list offers some of the best value available anywhere. The menu is fixed but with choices, and Saturday's gastronomic menu is worth trying. Choose between a boudin (scallops, prawns and turbot) with tomato vinaigrette or quail stuffed with chicken liver, spinach and mushrooms on a dressed salad. Next, an onion and cider soup to be followed by home-smoked Shetland salmon with avocado and pesto dressing. To cleanse the palate a garden mint sorbet, then back to deciding between fillet of red deer with a juniper, thyme and red wine sauce, Gressingham duck (half a half-wild duck as Tony describes it) with blackcurrants and beetroot, or a breast of guinea fowl flavoured with herb butter and a tarragon sauce. Next a fine selection of predominantly Scottish cheese to be followed by chocolate roulade

filled with orange cream with lemon curd ice cream. Not just worth tasting, but obligatory! Tony even takes time to select a few wines that he feels best complement Ruth's menu. Comfortable bedrooms and a waterside terrace where you can take breakfast—if you can eat any more that is!

Biography

Ruth

Hadley

Ruth Hadley had no formal training as a chef before she and her husband Tony bought The Cross. The decision to start a restaurant came about as a result of disillusionment with the general standards of eating out - a feeling of `I can cook better than that'. Armed with books, magazines and her own instincts, she launched herself upon the kitchen. Her subsequent acclaim is still looked upon by Ruth with a certain amount of bewilderment.

KIRKNEWTON	**Dalmahoy Hotel**

Kirknewton, Lothian, EH27 8EB
Tel: 031-333 1845   *Fax:* 031-335 3203   **£55**
Open: lunch Sun-Fri, dinner daily
Meals served: lunch 12-2, dinner 7-9.15

Just west of Edinburgh, this 116-bedroomed hotel is a golfer's dream, with two courses surrounding it and a restaurant and rooms which overlook one of the courses. Sleep, eat and breathe the game to your heart's content. Lakes, woodland and streams add to the beauty of the setting at the foot of the Pentland Hills, and a host of other sports and leisure facilities provide plenty of alternative ways to pass the time. There are two restaurants, the poolside Terrace and more formal setting of the main restaurant where Gary Bates offers a menu of both classical and seasonal dishes: terrine of Highland game, braised oxtail soup, char-grilled fillet of Aberdeen Angus beef, roast local wood pigeon with warm shallot and saffron vinaigrette, oven-baked loin of lamb with pesto mousse, Scotch salmon fillet baked in garden herbs and served with a vermouth cream sauce. Good vegetarian choices and a fabulous list of British farmhouse cheeses, including Scottish Howgate Brie. Good puds, too.

LINLITHGOW	**Champany Inn**

Champany, Linlithgow, Lothian, EH49 7LU
Tel: (0150 683) 4532   *Fax:* (0150 683) 4388   **£80**
Open: lunch Mon-Fri, dinner Mon-Sat
   (closed 25 Dec, 1 Jan)
Meals served: lunch 12.30-2, dinner 7-10

People have been flocking to Clive and Anne Davidson's Champany Inn for more than ten years, endorsing the theory that if you have the best raw materials simple cooking is the best way to enjoy them. Wonderful Aberdeen Angus beef, Scottish lamb, Shetland salmon and lobsters from their own sea-water tanks are best enjoyed either charcoal-grilled, cooked on a skillet or simply steamed in the case of fish. There are good salads and vegetables to accompany them and an excellent selection of wines.

LINLITHGOW	**Champany Inn Chop & Ale House**

Champany, Linlithgow, Lothian, EH49 7LU
Tel: (0150 683) 4532   *Fax:* (0150 683) 4388   **£40**
Open: lunch & dinner daily (closed 25 Dec, 1 Jan)
Meals served: lunch 12-2 (Sun 12.30-2.30),
   dinner 6.30-10 (Sat from 6)

For a taste of what the Champany (see entry above) is all about, try one of the less expensive, smaller steaks served in the younger, more informal, sibling room, along with the likes of Aberdeen Angus burgers, char-grilled chicken and a cold buffet bar. Ten courtyard tables for alfresco dining.

MARKINCH   Balbirnie House

Balbirnie Park, Markinch, by Glenrothes, Fife, KY7 6NE
Tel: (01592) 610066   *Fax:* (01592) 610529   **£50**
Open: lunch & dinner daily
Meals served: lunch 12-2, dinner 7-9.30

An elegant 30-bedroomed hotel in the golfers' paradise of Fife, set in
well-kept gardens, efficiently run by the Russell family. The menus
offer a wide variety of dishes and the wine list is almost as long as the
adjacent Balbirnie golf course, with over 200 listings!

MARYCULTER   Maryculter House

South Deeside Road, Maryculter, Grampian, AB1 0BB
Tel: (01224) 732124   *Fax:* (01224) 733510   **£60**
Open: lunch daily, dinner Mon-Sat (closed 26 & 27 Dec)
Meals served: lunch 12-2.30, dinner 7-9.30

Take a step back into the days of the Knights Templar at this riverside
hotel, on the site where Walter Bisset founded a college for the pilgrim
protectors in the early 13th century. The oldest room in the house, now
a cocktail bar and lounge, has high stone walls and a splendid vaulted
ceiling and is built above cellars dating back to 1225. Set in five acres of
woodlands on the banks of the River Dee, Maryculter House is just
eight miles from Aberdeen and offers 23 pretty, traditional-style bedrooms. The Victorian-style Poachers Bar enjoys splendid views over
the riverside patio and landscaped gardens. Light lunches and suppers
are available in the bar or candlelit dinners (traditional Scottish and
classic French dishes) in the Priory Room.

MAYBOLE   Ladyburn

Maybole, Strathclyde, KA19 7SG
Tel: (0165 54) 585   *Fax:* (0165 54) 580   **£55**
Open: lunch Tue-Sat, dinner Tue-Sun (closed Feb)
Meals served: lunch 12.30-1.30, dinner 7.30-8.30

The Hepburns opened their house to guests some four years ago and
run it in true country house style. The atmosphere is homely and comfortable with masses of fresh flowers and family memorabilia dotted
around. Jane Hepburn's cooking is equally homely, with dishes such as
Aunt Ella's chicken and mushroom pie, roast sirloin with Yorkshire
pudding, salmon with hollandaise sauce, all served with home-grown
vegetables. The Ladyburn Tart should not be missed!

MELROSE   Burts Hotel

Market Square, Melrose, Borders, TD6 9PN
Tel: (0189 682) 2285   *Fax:* (0189 682) 2870   **£45**
Open: lunch & dinner daily (closed 24-26 Dec)
Meals served: lunch 12-2, dinner 7-9.30 (Sun 7-9)

Centrally located in the market square of this historic border town,
Burts has been owned by the Hendersons for over 20 years.
Comfortable rooms and a cosy atmosphere provide an ideal stopping
point from which to explore the local places of interest. There's a wide
choice in the bar or in the restaurant, which has fixed-price lunch and
dinner menus.

MOFFAT   Well View Hotel

Ballplay Road, Moffat, Dumfries & Galloway, DG10 9JU
Tel: (01683) 20184   **£50**
Open: lunch Sun-Fri, dinner daily
Meals served: lunch 12.30-1.15, dinner 6.30-8.30

Former teachers, husband-and-wife team John and Janet Schuckardt
run this small, 6-bedroomed hotel in relaxed style. The house was built
for two shoemaker brothers in 1864 and is named after one of the sul-
phurous wells which led to Moffat's growth as a spa town in Victorian
times. Jane's four-course, fixed-price dinner menus offer some choice,
and John is only too pleased to advise on wines. One of the distinguished visitors to Moffat who came to take the waters was Robert
Burns and whilst there, composed the drinking song `O Willie brew'd a
peck o' maut'. I think I'll stick to the wine!

MUIR-OF-ORD   Dower House

Highfield, Muir-of-Ord, Highland, IV6 7XN
Tel & Fax: (01463) 870090   **£65**
Open: lunch & dinner daily (closed Xmas, 1 wk Oct)
Meals served: lunch 12.30-2, dinner 7.30-9

Situated in three acres of mature grounds
between the Beauly and Conan rivers, the
Dower House is the home of Robyn and Mena
Aitchison. Fine cottage-style bedrooms are
comfortably furnished and the elegant dining
room is a serious stage for Robyn's cooking.
Four-course menus may feature steamed
monkfish with lemon grass or black pudding
with sautéed apple and mustard vinaigrette. To
follow, a cream of Jerusalem artichoke soup;
then a further choice of breast of duck with
peppered pineapple and lime sauce, or mixed
seafoods in a pastry case. Finally, a gratin of
preserved summer fruits, or a chocolate crepe
with orange Armagnac mousse, or cheese if
you prefer. Home-made truffles come with the
coffee.

NAIRN   Clifton Hotel

Viewfield Street, Nairn, Highland, IV12 4HW
Tel: (01667) 453119   *Fax:* (01667) 452836   **£55**
Open: lunch & dinner daily (closed Nov-Mar)
Meals served: lunch 12.30-1, dinner 7-9.30

Whilst most restaurants and hotels reflect to some extent the character
of their owners, few do so with more unabashed nonconformity and
flourish than Gordon Macintyre's 12-bedroomed hotel. It could so easily have been the Clifton Theatre, with its dramatic decor and theatrical
touches—this is not the domain of Laura Ashley! Menus are written
with the same vigour, and dishes are predominantly of French origin.
The wine list is as veritable a tome as the works of Shakespeare but
makes lighter reading, with over 50 champagnes, magnums of several
clarets and burgundies and just a few half bottles for a drink in the
interval. Curtain up!

A very special place that provides all-round entertainment.

NEWTON STEWART   Kirroughtree Hotel

Newton Stewart, Dumfries & Galloway, DG8 6AN
Tel: (01671) 402141   *Fax:* (01671) 402425   **£60**
Open: lunch & dinner daily (closed 3 Jan-early Mar)
Meals served: lunch 12-1.30, dinner 7-9.30

Striking 18th-century mansion built in 1719 for the Heron family,
whose friendship with Robert Burns brought the young poet here on
many occasions. The hotel is situated on the crest of a hill in eight
acres of landscaped grounds and new owners are making all the right
moves to upgrade and enhance the place. Roux-trained chef Ian
Bennett produces short set dinner menus which are both well-conceived and well-executed. Typical dishes from Ian's stable include roast
guinea fowl with cranberries and lime, and steamed fillet of grey mullet
with celeriac and ginger sauce. This is Anglo/French cooking in the
modern mode. Wines range from the unpretentious to extravagant vintages of Claret and Burgundy.

NEWTONMORE   Ard-na-Coille Hotel

Kingussie Road, Newtonmore, Highland, PH20 1AY
Tel: (01540) 673214   *Fax:* (01540) 673453   **£65**
Open: dinner daily (closed mid Nov-end Dec)
Meals served: dinner at 7.45

Situated beneath the massive Carn Ban mountain, Newtonmore is a
good centre for climbing or pony trekking in the Monadhliath mountains. Ard-na-Coille, is a converted shooting lodge in which Barry
Cotham and Nancy Ferrier provide a relaxed haven. Dinner is a set-
price, no-choice affair: smoked trout mousse with avocado might be followed by watercress and pear soup. A breast of wild duck comes next,
lightly roasted on a bed of lentils, bacon and pimento with a Madeira
and tarragon sauce. Cheese precedes the pudding. Menus are imaginative with attention to balance and variety and the wine list is full of New
World wonders.

NORTH MIDDLETON   Borthwick Castle

North Middleton, Nr Gorebridge, Lothian, EH23 4QY
Tel: (01875) 820514   *Fax:* (01875) 821702   **£65**
Open: dinner daily (closed Jan & Feb)
Meals served: dinner 7-9

It was to this historic castle built in 1430 with its twin-towered baronial keep, that Mary, Queen of Scots and her husband, the Earl of Bothwell, fled in 1567, spending their last days of freedom together before she was finally executed on the scaffold. A hundred years later Oliver Cromwell's forces besieged the castle, leaving the mark of the cannon on the castle walls. The early warrior-like Borthwicks are said to have engaged in the sport of inviting prisoners in the keep to jump the 12ft gap between the twin towers, their hands tied behind their backs, in exchange for their liberty should they succeed! Atmosphere is the main attraction at this castle, and of the 10 bedrooms, reached by a spiral staircase, the best is the Mary, Queen of Scots four-poster chamber. Dine by candlelight in the magnificent Great Hall with 40ft Gothic arch, minstrel's gallery and hooded fireplace, and enjoy the three-course set menu of modern British cooking using only local produce wherever possible. Probably the most genuinely atmospheric medieval castle in the country.

OBAN   Knipoch Hotel

by Oban, Strathclyde, PA34 4QT
Tel: (0185 26) 251   *Fax:* (0185 26) 249   **£60**
Open: lunch by arrangement, dinner daily
    (closed mid Nov-mid Feb)
Meals served: dinner 7.30-9

Loch Feonan and its surrounding woodland provide the setting for the Craig family's 17-bedroomed Georgian house. The bar is stocked with a rare selection of malt whiskies and cognacs, and fireside armchairs invite a nip or two. In the kitchen are Jenny and Colin Craig whose daily-changing menus are both modest and refined. Start perhaps with Highland potato soup served with home-baked bread, followed by halibut and sole with champagne sauce and marinated pears in delicious creamy fudge sauce. Look out for the smoked salmon—it's home-smoked and available by mail order.

ONICH   Allt-nan-Ros Hotel

Onich, By Fort William, Highland, PH33 6RY
Tel: (0185 53) 210   *Fax:* (0185 53) 462   **£50**
Open: lunch & dinner daily (closed mid Nov-Xmas)
Meals served: lunch 12.30-2, dinner 7-8.30
With stunning views across Loch Linnhe towards Appin, Glencoe, Mavern and Mull, this old Victorian shooting lodge affords good hospitality food and wines in convivial surroundings.

PEAT INN   The Peat Inn

Peat Inn, By Cupar, Fife, KY15 5LH
Tel: (01334 840) 206   *Fax:* (01334 840) 530   **£65**
Open: lunch & dinner Tue-Sat (closed 25 Dec, 1 Jan)
Meals served: lunch 12.30 for 1, dinner 7-8.30

The Peat Inn has now been established for over 20 years and David
and Patricia Wilson can be justifiably proud of putting such a remote
setting on the gastronomic map. An Inn in the true sense of the word,
offering excellent hospitality, fine accommodation in wonderful suites,
superb food and wines in the restaurant, and above all bestowing on its
visitors a great feeling of well-being and contentment. David's cooking
relies on his well-established menu formula and standards are consistently high. Try the likes of sauté of scallops, monkfish and port with
spiced apple to start, followed by breasts of pigeon with wild mushrooms in a sauce with brandy and juniper and finish with caramelised
apple pastry with a caramel sauce. The wine list is as good as anywhere
in Britain with reasonable prices. The Peat Inn is a unique experience.

PEEBLES   Cringletie House

Peebles, Borders, EH45 8PL
Tel: (01721) 730233   *Fax:* (01721) 730244   **£55**
Open: lunch & dinner daily (closed Jan & Feb)
Meals served: lunch 1-1.45, dinner 7.30-8.30

Aileen Maguire and her team use fruit and vegetables from the hotel
garden and honey from their own hives in the kitchen of this 13-bed-
roomed baronial-style sandstone house, run for over 20 years with
immense warmth and charm by the Maguire family and with views
over the surrounding hills. Set lunch and dinner menus change daily
and always include a vegetarian dish. Main courses are typified by venison with whisky cream sauce, curried shoulder of lamb korma and pan-
fried monkfish with fennel and vermouth cream. Cringletie was built in
1861 and is set in 28 acres of grounds in rolling Scottish Border
country.

PERTH   Number Thirty Three

33 George Street, Perth, Tayside, PH1 5LA
Tel: (01738) 633771   **£40**
Open: lunch & dinner Tue-Sat (closed 10 days Xmas/New Year)
Meals served: lunch 12.30-2.30, dinner 6.30-9.30

Choose between the light menu in the oyster bar
or the more formal affair served in the dining room
at this art-deco seafood restaurant close to the
town centre. The former might feature chef-patron
Mary Billinghurst's seafood soup or assorted fresh
and smoked seafood platter; the latter might range
from pan-fried lemon sole with herb butter or fillet
of salmon in a parcel with thyme butter to seafood
casserole topped with langoustine or, for meat
eaters, breast of duckling with a chestnut and
apple stuffing. Coffee comes with home-made
fudge.

PORT APPIN   Airds Hotel

Port Appin, Appin, Strathclyde, PA38 4DF
Tel: (0163 173) 236   *Fax:* (0163 173) 535   **£80**
Open: lunch by arrangement, dinner daily (closed 10-31 Jan)
Meals served: dinner at 8

After nearly 20 years in this 250-year-old former ferry inn overlooking Loch Linnhe, the Allens have had ample time to get accustomed to their home and the impression you get when you enter is one of a comfortable, friendly and relaxed house. The 12 bedrooms vary in size and are furnished mostly with antiques. Mother and son, Betty and Graeme, share the kitchen stove, jointly producing their daily-changing four-course dinners. The philosophy is simple—use only the best and keep it simple but refined. Starters such as crab tart with salad and tomato coulis or sautéed scallops with shiitake and sweet and sour sauce; and cream of smoked haddock soup, followed perhaps by rack of lamb with sweetbreads, kidneys and onion marmalade or wild salmon with honeyed aubergines and sauce hollandaise. Lovely desserts to finish, such as mango mousse with walnut shortbread and coffee and pistachio iced soufflé glace served with coffee sauce. Scottish and French farmhouse cheeses, and finally coffee served in the drawing room.

PORTPATRICK   Knockinaam Lodge

Portpatrick, Nr Stranraer, Dumfries & Galloway, DG9 9AD
Tel: (01776) 810471   *Fax:* (01776) 810435   **£70**
Open: lunch & dinner daily (closed 2 Jan-25 Mar)
Meals served: lunch 12-2, dinner 7.30-9

This elegant, small hotel sits beside the Irish Sea, sheltered by the cliffs and warmed by the Gulf Stream. Portpatrick (just to the North) was the port from where steamers used to ferry passengers to and from Donaghadee, some 21 miles across the water in Ireland. That was some 150 years ago but I doubt that little has changed along this lovely coastline. However, Marcel and Corinna Frichot now run the Lodge and Stuart Muir cooks. Dinner sees classic French menus, dishes like goujonettes de sole aux grains de sesame et sa crème de lardon fumé. A well-composed wine list has bottles from most areas of repute, and plenty of halves.

QUOTHQUAN   **Shieldhill**

Quothquan, Biggar, Strathclyde, ML12 6NA
Tel: (01899) 20035   *Fax:* (01899) 21092   **£60**
Open: lunch & dinner daily
Meals served: lunch 12-2, dinner 7-9 (reservations essential)
Elegant yet homely 11-bedroomed baronial-style stone mansion surrounded by beautiful gardens and woodland, dating back to 1199 and home to the Chancellor family for seven centuries. Four nearby golf courses, plus fishing on the River Tweed.

ST ANDREWS   Grange Inn

Grange Road, St Andrews, Fife, KY16 8LJ
Tel: (01334) 472670   *Fax:* (01334) 478703   **£40**
Open: lunch & dinner daily
Meals served: lunch 12.30-2.15, dinner 6.30-9.15

Good local seafood and straightforward grills form the mainstay of the
menu in this cottagey inn and restaurant overlooking St Andrews and
the bay. Have a pint in the cosy pubby Ploughman's Bar before moving
next door to the panelled Caddies Room hung with prints of famous
golfers, the Bay Room or Patio Room for some good home cooking.
The same menu, lunch and dinner, offers half a dozen starters including locally smoked salmon and around ten main courses—from
seafood platter to grilled salmon or steaks. Homely puds to finish.

ST ANDREWS   Old Course Hotel

St Andrews, Fife, KY16 9SP
Tel: (01334) 474371   *Fax:* (01334) 477668   **£75**
Open: dinner daily
Meals served: dinner 7-10

Located at The Home of Golf, the Old Course Hotel is indeed home to
golfers from around the world who come to pay homage at the shrine.
There are high standards of comfort in this luxurious hotel and a well-
equipped health club. If your golf drives you to despair, the hotel will
organise some fishing or clay pigeon shooting instead. If that fails too,
you could try the Roadhole Bar and sip your way gently through the
100 odd single malt whiskies on offer!

ST FILLANS   Four Seasons
St Fillans, Nr Crieff, Tayside, PH26 2NF
Tel & Fax: (01764) 685333   **£50**
Open: lunch & dinner daily (closed mid Dec-Feb)
Meals served: lunch 12.15-2.15, dinner 7-9.30
A small, family-run hotel with striking views of Loch Earn. Six chalets are ideal
for families.

SCARISTA   Scarista House

Scarista, Isle of Harris, Highland, PA85 3HX
Tel: (01859) 550238   *Fax:* (01859) 550277   **£55**
Open: lunch by arrangement, dinner daily (closed mid Oct-Apr)
Meals served: dinner at 8.15

On the remote west coast of Harris with views straight out to the
Atlantic, Scarista commands a three-mile-long shell-sand beach. The
Georgian building was formerly the manse for Harris, and both decor
and architecture are in keeping with its history. Peat fires provide additional warmth in the lounges, and bedrooms take full advantage of sea
views. Dinner in the candle-lit no-smoking dining room, uses local
ingredients humanely farmed, to good advantage. Relax after dinner in
the first-floor drawing room and watch the sun go down—perfect!

SCONE	Murrayshall House

Scone, Tayside, PH2 7PH
Tel: (01738) 51171   *Fax:* (01738) 52595   **£55**
Open: lunch & dinner daily
Meals served: lunch 12-2, dinner 7-9.30

Murrayshall House is a stylish country house with 19 bedrooms, set in 300 acres of undulating parkland. Golf is a major attraction, with 18-hole course, new driving range, golf shop, buggies and clubs for hire, and separate Club House and bar serving a simple menu as part of the package. For the non-golf lover, there's fishing, shooting, tennis, croquet and bowls, as well as beautiful woodland walks. The basis of chef Andrew Campbell's menus is seasonal, using local produce to full effect in dishes such as Madeira-flavoured cream of wild mushroom soup or roast woodland deer served with a compote of sweet and sour red cabbage with blackcurrant port sauce. Elsewhere on the menu you'll find Murrayshall's own fish stew flavoured with Pernod and saffron or traditional beef casserole with Irish stout and a crisp pastry top. Check out the speciality coffees or opt for it straight and black with home-made sweetmeats. A varied and interesting menu.

SLEAT	Kinloch Lodge

Sleat, Isle of Skye, Highland, IV43 8QY
Tel: (01471) 833214   *Fax:* (01471) 833277   **£60**
Open: dinner daily (closed Dec-Feb)
Meals served: dinner 8-9.30

Built in 1680, this white stone building at the head of Loch Na Dal enjoys a spectacular setting in an isolated position in the south of the island. The home of Lord and Lady Macdonald, visitors are also made to feel at home, more like family friends than paying guests. The hotel has 10 rooms without phones or TV to disturb the peace. Lady Macdonald and Peter Macpherson prepare good home cooking in generous portions, while Lord Macdonald oversees the front-of-house. The five-course, fixed-price menu with limited choice might offer herb profiteroles filled with bacon and cheese or smoked trout pâté; followed by a soup (spinach, apple and turmeric); then roast leg of lamb with Reform sauce or baked fillet of cod in filo parcels. Traditional desserts are followed by coffee and fudge.

SPEAN BRIDGE	Old Station Restaurant

Station Road, Spean Bridge, Highland, PH34 4EP
Tel: (01397) 712535   **£40**
Open: lunch Sat & Sun, dinner daily (Thu-Sun in winter)
    (closed 25 & 26 Dec, 1 Jan)
Meals served: lunch 12-2.30, dinner 6-9

Richard and Helen Bunney's restaurant is located on the station platform in the converted ticket office and waiting room areas. The short well-thought-out carte offers an eclectic range despite its length, with dishes such as char-grilled Aberdeen Angus steak, scallopini of chicken with mushrooms and cream, grilled teriyaki salmon fillet and venison casseroled in port with herbed cobbler all appearing on the same menu. Excellent soups—there's always a soup of the day featured.

STEWARTON   **Chapeltoun House**

Stewarton-Irvine Road, Stewarton, Strathclyde, KA3 3ED
Tel: (01560) 482696   Fax: (01560) 485100   **£55**
Open: lunch & dinner daily (closed 1st 2 wks Jan)
Meals served: lunch 12-2, dinner 7-9
Eight-bedroomed hotel in private gardens, two miles out of Stewarton. Royal Troon and Old Prestwick golf courses are a 20-minute drive away.

STRACHUR   Creggans Inn

Strachur, Strathclyde, PA27 8BX
Tel: (0136 986) 279   *Fax:* (0136 986) 637   **£45**
Open: lunch & dinner daily
Meals served: lunch 12-2.30, dinner 7-9.30

Not unnaturally, seafood features strongly on Jean-Pierre Puech's menus at this lochside Inn, such as smoked salmon, oysters, Oban shrimps, baby scallops, mussels and a pâté of the legendary Loch Fyne kippers. Other local produce also appears: venison haggis with neeps 'n' tatties, Argyllshire pheasant, Aberdeen Angus steaks and local lamb. Perhaps the widest range of local produce appears at the end of the wine list where there are no fewer than 25 single malt whiskies, some famous, some not so 'well-kent' (well known) as Sir Fitzroy Maclean observes. After sampling these heady brews a brisk walk through the woods is just the job. If you prefer, Lady Maclean will arrange visits to nearby stately homes or gardens.

TIRORAN   Tiroran House

Tiroran, Isle of Mull, Strathclyde, PA69 6ES
Tel & Fax: (0168 15) 232   **£65**
Open: dinner daily (closed Oct-mid May)
Meals served: dinner at 7.45

In a remote location, the Blockleys offer a real welcome and true hospitality to their guests. Mull is a beautiful island of moorland, forest and peaks, and Tiroran overlooks the islands of Iona, Staffa, Colla and Tiree. The Blockleys' home becomes the visitor's home and Sue Blockley's cooking makes dinner a special treat. Local produce, of necessity, features strongly: wild Mull salmon, venison steak and kidney pie, local smoked oysters and Hebridean smoked trout all feature on the fixed price menu which offers a fixed main dish with choice of first course and pudding. The wines are well chosen and sensibly priced. A visit to Fingal's cave on Staffa inspired Mendelssohn's Hebrides overture: see what you can do with the peace and inspiration of Tiroran!

TROON	Highgrove House

Old Loans Road, Loans, Troon, Strathclyde, KA10 7HL
Tel: (01292) 312511   *Fax:* (01292) 318228   **£45**
Open: lunch & dinner daily
Meals served: lunch 12-2.30, dinner 6-9.30

Formerly the home of a retired sea captain, Highgrove enjoys panoramic views over the Ayrshire coastline to the Isle of Arran and Mull of Kintyre. It's a warm and friendly place which combines traditional charm with modern comforts. The house has nine pretty, ensuite bedrooms looking out on to the surrounding countryside. Chef-patron Bill Costley and his team produce a good choice of traditional and classic, gourmet dishes like beef with a Stilton mousseline, rich fish stew with dry vermouth and traditional bread-and-butter pudding.

TURNBERRY	Turnberry Hotel

Turnberry, Strathclyde, KA26 9LT
Tel: (01655) 31000   *Fax:* (01655) 31706   **£85**
Open: lunch Sun, dinner daily
Meals served: lunch 1-2.30, dinner 7.30-10

Custom-built in 1906 this elegant Edwardian hotel in a spectacular coastal setting overlooks two championship golf courses, the Ailsa having been host to three British Open Championships. The hotel, too, is world-class with 132 bedrooms, health spa, swimming pool, gymnasium, tennis courts, squash and just about anything else that you could wish for. Stewart Cameron is Turnberry's chef and his excellent cooking is just the job after 18 holes. Steamed west coast scallops and scampi with endive and spinach leaves and nantua dressing, turbot poached in champagne in sauce of crayfish, mushrooms and mussels, veal sweetbreads braised in amontillado with morels and tarragon flavoured spätzlis or fillet of Ayrshire lamb with potatoes and onions served with rosemary sauce are par for the course.

ULLAPOOL	Altnaharrie Inn

Ullapool, Highland, IV26 2SS
Tel: (01854) 633230   **£120**
Open: dinner daily (closed Nov-Easter)
Meals served: light lunches for residents only, dinner at 8

It's no small wonder that people talk of pilgrimages to this delightful restaurant with rooms on the edge of Loch Broom. The 10-minute trip across the loch from Ullapool quay by private launch (phone on arrival in Ullapool) makes this one of the most appetising approaches any restaurant could wish for. From the boat you can see the wisteria-clad house with cottage garden surrounded by woodland and heather. Log fires and fresh flowers grace the entrance where Fred Brown awaits with a warm welcome. Luxury and simplicity go hand in hand here—decor is stylish and charming, but when the generator goes off at night, it's candles and torches only! There are 8 lovely bedrooms which promise a peaceful night's sleep (no neighbours, just the lap of waves) before a splendid breakfast. The real event though is Gunn Eriksen's cooking. Make sure you're back in time to catch the hotel launch (six trips daily) for dinner if you venture back on to the other side of the

loch. With an artist's eye for detail, Gunn turns out a stunning repertoire for her nightly five-course dinners based on local produce. Fish
and shellfish are delivered straight to the private jetty, then stored live
in the sea in creels until required. There's no choice on the menu but
special requirements are discussed at the time of booking and the
menus are exceptionally well thought out. Beautiful views of the loch
from the restaurant.

ULLAPOOL   Ceilidh Place

14 West Argyle Street, Ullapool, Highland, IV26 2TY
Tel: (01854) 612103   *Fax:* (01854) 612886   **£50**
Open: dinner daily (closed 2 wks Jan)
Meals served: dinner 7-9, (light meals 9-6.30)

Ceilidh Place is fast becoming a local cultural centre in its own right.
The collection of buildings houses a bookshop, arts centre and venue,
restaurant (Scottish cooking), coffee shop (light snacks) and 13 prettily
decorated bedrooms. Cheaper, bunkbedded accommodation is also
available in the Clubhouse. Nightly entertainment in the summer, from
classical concerts to jazz and, of course, folk music. Relaxed and informal, this a good place for families.

WHITEBRIDGE   Knockie Lodge

Whitebridge, Highland, IV1 2UP
Tel: (01456) 486276   *Fax:* (01456) 486389   **£65**
Open: dinner daily (closed Nov-Apr)
Meals served: dinner at 8

Work up an appetite by walking the 22-mile military road which was
built in the 1730s to link Fort Augustus to the Spey valley, then go back
to the tranquility of Knockie Lodge for a relaxing dinner. Daily five-
course menus offer no choice until the pudding. Start with goujons of
haddock with tartare sauce, then a courgette and lemon soup, followed
by marinaded chicken with avocado and red peppers served on saffron
rice with vermouth sauce. Choose between clootie dumpling or a
grapefruit mousse with raspberry purée before tackling the Scottish
cheeseboard. A comfortable hotel with lots of character and charming
hosts.

Wales Establishment Reviews

ABERCYNON	**Llechwen Hall**

Abercynon, Nr LLanfabon, Mid Glamorgan, CF37 4HP
Tel: (01443) 742050   *Fax:* (01443) 742189   **£40**
Open: lunch & dinner daily
Meals served: lunch 12-2.30, dinner 7-10
17th-century farmhouse-turned-Victorian gentleman's residence, now a country hotel with 11 rooms. Beautiful valley location, lively local trade, traditional and French cuisine.

ABERGAVENNY	**Walnut Tree Inn**

Llandewi Skirrid, Abergavenny, Gwent, NP7 8AW
Tel: (01873) 852797   *Fax:* (01873) 859764   **£60**
Open: lunch & dinner Tue-Sat
  (closed Xmas, 2 wks Feb)
Meals served: lunch 12.15-3, dinner 7.15-10

This may look like a pub—whitewashed and decked with flowers—but it's not. Ann and Franco Taruschio's stylish Italian country restaurant has built up an enviable reputation over the years. Franco has been cooking in unpretentious style here since 1963 and the customers love it. He is a talented, skilful and, above all, enthusiastic chef who draws on his native Italy, the Mediterranean and the Orient for his inspiration. Start with carpaccio of salmon with lime, bruschetta of seafood or pasta with porcini mushrooms, truffles and Parma ham—an 18th-

century recipe. Follow with a mixed fish casserole, tagliolini with lobster sauce or calf's liver with sweet and sour onions. Plenty of choice—around 15-20 dishes at each stage, but leave room for one of Franco's desserts—Toulouse chestnut pudding, chocolate brandy loaf with coffee bean sauce or torte with three liqueurs. Lunch is served in the homely bistro-bar, dinner in the main dining room.

Biography

Franco Taruschio was born in Montefano, Italy, and went into the restaurant business because the catering industry was one of the few in Italy in 1958 that offered the opportunity of proper training with only a

Franco *grammar school education. Following hotel school in Bellagio, Lake Como, and work in various establish-*

Taruschio *ments in Italy, Switzerland and France he came to England and spent two years as restaurant manager at the Three Horseshoes Hotel in Rugby before buying the Walnut Tree Inn, now the most highly acclaimed restaurants in Wales.*

ABERSOCH   Porth Tocyn Hotel

Bwlchtocyn, Abersoch, Gwynedd, LL53 7BU
Tel: (01758) 713303   *Fax:* (01758) 713538   **£55**
Open: lunch & dinner daily (closed mid Nov-wk before Easter)
Meals served: lunch 12.30-2, dinner 7.30-9.30

Three generations of Fletcher-Brewers have safeguarded the family reputation for hospitality at this hotel high above Cardigan Bay, since 1948 when it was no more than a row of lead miners' cottages. The hotel has 17 rooms, many with sea views, and the house has a homely, cosy feel, with a playroom for children. Louise Fletcher-Brewer has been at the helm in the kitchen since 1981 producing short two- or five-course menus daily. The dining room, complete with huge picture window, enjoys a panoramic view over the bay to Snowdonia. Lunch tends to be a light, informal affair—a soup, salads, sandwiches and perhaps whisky cream pie to finish. Dinner sees the likes of hot hazelnut and goat's cheese soufflé, baked sea trout with plaice mousseline in filo pastry, casseroled guinea fowl with gin and juniper berries and, to finish, brandied fruit pudding with old English sauce or maybe tipsy trifle. A well-constructed wine list has good variety and plenty of half bottles.

ABERSOCH   Riverside Hotel

Abersoch, Gwynedd, LL53 7HW
Tel: (01758) 712419   *Fax:* (01758) 712671   **£50**
Open: lunch & dinner daily (closed mid Nov-Mar)
Meals served: lunch 12-2 (bar only), dinner 7.30-9

A 12-bedroomed, family-run hotel, situated on the harbour, with the River Soch running through the garden behind the house. Hospitality is the key word for dedicated hoteliers John and Wendy Bakewell, who have been here for 26 years. The hotel is bright and cheerful, with board games available in the lounge, and morning coffee served by the pool or on the patio. The Bakewells share the cooking, producing imaginative modern dishes such as a little toasted bread box of curried kidneys, tomato and goat's cheese tartlet with fresh thyme and tenderloin of pork with a creamy sloe gin sauce. Special diets catered for on request.

ABERYSTWYTH   Conrah Country Hotel

Chancery, Aberystwyth, Dyfed, SY23 4DF
Tel: (01970) 617941   *Fax:* (01970) 624546   **£50**
Open: lunch & dinner daily (closed 1 wk Xmas)
Meals served: lunch 12-2, dinner 7-9

Originally the estate mansion house, the hotel enjoys outstanding views to the north towards the Cader Idris mountains, and tranquility is the watchword here. Indoors, there are three comfortable drawing rooms—one where afternoon tea is served; another for writing; and a third which is simply named the Withdrawing Room. The hotel has 20 bedrooms, some of which are built around the courtyard. Don't be surprised if you wake to find the hotel donkey outside your door: it grazes on the Conrah fields along with the local farmer's sheep! The cooking is in the modern manner, with seafood, local lamb and beef put to good use. The Summer House has the pool and sauna, and local facilities for outdoor pursuits are plentiful.

BARRY	Bunbury's

14 High Street, Barry, South Glamorgan, CF6 8EA
Tel: (01446) 732075   **£45**
Open: lunch & dinner Tue-Sat (closed Bank Holidays)
Meals served: lunch 10.30-2.30, dinner 7.30-10 (Sat to 10.30)
Attractive '30s-style restaurant with eclectic menu. Blackboard specials at lunchtime include traditional favourites like cottage pie.

BEAUMARIS   Ye Olde Bulls Head

Castle Street, Beaumaris, Anglesey, Gwynedd, LL58 8AP
Tel: (01248) 810329   *Fax:* (01248) 811294   **£45**
Open: lunch Sun, dinner daily (closed 25 & 256 Dec, 1 Jan)
Meals served: lunch 12-1.30, dinner 7.30-9.30
    (light meals in Bar 12-2.30 Mon-Sat)

The Bull, originally a posting house for the borough, dates back to 1472, since when it has seen Cromwell's men, Dickens and Dr Samuel Johnson within its walls. There are 11 bedrooms, each named after characters Dickens created, and the whole place simply oozes old-world charm. This is a delightful inn, situated in the pretty town of Beaumaris on the south east corner of Anglesey. Bar lunches offer dishes such as pork and mushroom pie, sandwiches and dressed crab salad. Dinner goes à la carte, with the likes of roast local teal with Puy lentils and juniper berries or baked Padarn Lake Arctic char with watercress among main-course options. Alternatively, there's a no-choice, fixed-price menu which might feature tenderloin of pork in a smoked bacon, mushroom and sage sauce. There's a good selection of wines with lots of halves at affordable prices.

BUILTH WELLS   Caer Beris Manor

Builth Wells, Powys, LD2 3NP
Tel: (01982) 552601   *Fax:* (01982) 552586   **£45**
Open: lunch & dinner daily
Meals served: lunch 12.30-2.30, dinner 7.30-9.30

A 22-bedroomed Elizabethan manor set in 27 acres of parkland along-side the River Irfon. The restaurant offers a straightforward à la carte of traditional and continental-style dishes and there are good leisure facilities on site—multi-gym and sauna, clay-pigeon shooting, fishing, mountain biking. Nearby golf and swimming pool, too.

CAPEL COCH   Tre-Ysgawen Hall

Capel Coch, Nr Llangefni, Anglesey, Gwynedd, LL77 7UR
Tel: (01248) 750750   *Fax:* (01248) 750035   **£45**
Open: lunch & dinner daily
Meals served: lunch 12-2.30, dinner 7-9.30

The elaborate carving and plasterwork of recent years adds a certain grandeur to this Victorian mansion which boasts an impressive galleried central hall with skylight and handsome public rooms. The 19 bedrooms are stylish and generally spacious and the formal, conservatory-style restaurant extension is an elegant setting for Mark Colley's cooking. You might find the likes of seared scallops set on spicy stir-fried vegetables, flavoured with a soya and ginger sauce to start, followed by half roast guinea fowl served with creamy mashed potatoes and black pudding accompanied with a madeira sauce, then honey comb meringue filled with Welsh honey ice cream and served with a lemon sauce to finish. The hotel stands in three acres of grounds which include kennels for those with canine companions!

CARDIFF   Armless Dragon

97 Wyeverne Road, Cathays, Cardiff, South Glamorgan, CF2 4BG
Tel: (01222) 382357   **£45**
Open: lunch Tue-Fri, dinner Tue-Sat (closed 25 & 26 Dec, 1 Jan)
Meals served: lunch 12.15-2.15, dinner 7.15-10.30

David Richards' busy bistro serves up excellent value lunches when you can choose the number of courses to suit your appetite. In the evening there's even more choice with an extensive menu of imaginative, well-cooked dishes that have round worldwide influences.

CARDIFF   La Brasserie
60 St Mary Street, Cardiff, South Glamorgan
Tel: (01222) 372164   **£40**
Open: lunch & dinner Mon-Sat (closed 25 & 26 Dec)
Meals served: lunch 12-2.30, dinner 7-12
Atmospheric brasserie, specialising in grilled meats and seasonal game. Good-value 2-course lunch for a fiver.

CARDIFF   Le Cassoulet

5 Romilly Crescent, Canton, Cardiff, South Glamorgan, CF1 9NP
Tel: (01222) 22195   **£55**
Open: lunch Tue-Fri, dinner Tue-Sat
   (closed 2 wks Xmas, Aug)
Meals served: lunch 12-2, dinner 7-10

Toulouse rugby fan Gilbert Viader and his wife have decorated their traditional French restaurant in the centre of Cardiff in his home team colours of black and red. New chef Michael Wignall prepares a menu of traditional regional and classic French dishes which range from cassoulet toulousain and stuffed pig's trotter with Puy lentils to roast pigeon with pan-fried foie gras and a Madeira sauce or wild mushroom tart with a truffle butter sauce. Desserts might include a hot mango tart or cold soufflé of wild strawberries with an apricot sauce. French cheeses and petits fours to finish.

CARDIFF	Champers

61 St Mary Street, Cardiff, South Glamorgan, CF1 1FE
Tel: (01222) 373363 £40
Open: lunch Mon-Sat, dinner daily (closed 25 & 26 Dec)
Meals served: lunch 12-2.30, dinner 7-12
Popular restaurant-cum-wine bar with a Spanish slant to food and wine—over 100 Riojas.

CARDIFF	Le Monde

60 St Mary Street, Cardiff, South Glamorgan, CF1 1FE
Tel: (01222) 387376 £40
Open: lunch & dinner Mon-Sat (closed 25 Dec)
Meals served: lunch 12-2.30, dinner 7-12
Seafood and fish restaurant-cum-wine bar. A huge array, from oysters to Dover sole and more exotic fish like parrot, grouper and black bream. Plenty of atmosphere.

CARDIFF New House

Thornhill Road, Cardiff, South Glamorgan, CF4 5UA
Tel: (01222) 520280   *Fax:* (01222) 520324 £45
Open: lunch & dinner daily (closed 25 & 26 Dec, 1 Jan)
Meals served: lunch 12-2, dinner 7-10.30

On the edge of Cardiff, this Georgian mansion house boasts views over the city and the Vale of Glamorgan. The 20 bedrooms emulate the luxury of times past, with reproduction Chippendale, Sheraton and Hepplewhite furniture. The menu draws on traditional, classic dishes— beef with Yorkshire pudding, stuffed saddle of wild rabbit, venison in red wine, pot-roast baby guinea fowl—but shows a modern spirit at work in the kitchen too, in dishes such as sorbet of white peaches in sparkling wine and rosette of pork with a rhubarb and quince sauce in mulled wine.

CHIRK Starlings Castle

Bronygarth, Nr Chirk, Clwyd, SY10 7NU
Tel: (01691) 718464 £45
Open: lunch Sun, dinner daily
Meals served: lunch 12.30-2.30, dinner 7.30-9.30 (Sat & Sun to 10)

Ask for directions when booking at this 18th-century farmhouse, complete with pottery, just over the Clwyd border. Hidden from view by rhododendrons and conifer trees, this is more of a rustic hideaway than a castle. And it's delightful, with the added bonus of Anthony Pitt's cooking. The flagstoned dining room in a converted barn, with rough-stone walls and wood-burning stove is the perfect setting for Anthony's short but interesting à la carte. Glamorgan sausage with spiced tomato sauce; salmis of pigeon; baked hake in a crab crust; and tarte tatin. This is hearty, down-to-earth cooking executed with imagination, style and skill. The restaurant has ten antique-furnished rooms, eight of which share two bathrooms—but you needn't worry about the journey to the bathroom—silk dressing gowns are provided. The other two rooms are new, and are ensuite. Children are welcome -the Pitts have two of their own, and although there's no special children's menu they will always cater happily for them.

COLWYN BAY   Café Nicoise

124 Abergele Road, Colwyn Bay, Clwyd, LL29 7PS
Tel: (01492) 531555   **£45**
Open: lunch Thu-Sun, dinner Mon-Sat (closed 1 wk Jan, 1 wk Jun)
Meals served: lunch 12-2, dinner 7-10

A friendly, local restaurant, offering traditional and modern French cooking in a romantic setting with French background music. Typical dishes from Carl Swift's constantly changing repertoire might include warm salad of red mullet provençale, tournedos steak with glazed shallots and thyme and pear tart with an apricot sauce. The Menu Touristique offers good-value fixed-price two- and three-course menus available at lunchtimes and on weekday evenings.

CONWY   Sychnant Pass Hotel

Sychnant Pass Road, Conwy, Gwynedd, LL32 8BJ
Tel: (01492) 596868   *Fax:* (01492) 870009   **£40**
Open: lunch by arrangement, dinner daily
Meals served: dinner 7-9

Situated just a couple of miles to the East of Conwy, this friendly hotel is an ideal base from which to explore the magnificent castle, Telford's suspension bridge and the beautiful Bodnant Gardens. Bedrooms vary from traditional to modern, depending on which part of the house you're in; and many have fine views. Brian and Jean Jones are your hosts as well as your cooks, providing a mixed repertoire of French and British cooking. Pink rack of Welsh lamb with port wine and mint sauce, Conwy salmon poached in white wine with tarragon and deep-crust apple and summer fruit pie are fine examples of what's on offer.

COYCHURCH   Coed-y-Mwstwr Hotel

Coychurch, Nr Bridgend, Mid Glamorgan, CF35 6AF
Tel: (01656) 860621   *Fax:* (01656) 863122   **£55**
Open: lunch & dinner daily
Meals served: lunch 12-2.15, dinner 7.15-10.15

The appropriately named Coed-y-Mwstwr, which means "whispering trees", stands in 17 acres of ancient woodland high above the Vale of Glamorgan and village of Coychurch. On a fine day you can see the Bristol Channel and distant hills of Exmoor. The house exudes a homely charm, and elegant period decor is very much in evidence in this 23-bedroomed Victorian house which was once home to the politi-cally active Crawshay-Williams family, one member of whom was parlia-mentary secretary to Lloyd George. Go for a walk around the grounds, catch sight of a fox or badger, or even one of the buzzards and kestrels said to nest in the estate, before heading for the high-beamed, wood-panelled setting of the Elliot Room restaurant. Set-price menus and the à la carte, both feature local produce wherever possible. Warm roast pigeon with a grape and juniper sauce on a bed of puréed parsnip; roulade of salmon and cod on a saffron and chive cream; double-baked Cheddar and onion soufflé with a sage and capiscum sauce; grilled breast of pheasant with black pudding in a rich game sauce; crème caramel flavoured with hazelnuts and orange typify Gareth Passey's cooking. A well-stocked cellar and good Welsh, continental and British cheeses.

CRICKHOWELL — Bear Hotel

High Street, Crickhowell, Powys, NP8 1BW
Tel: (01873) 810408   *Fax:* (01873) 811696   **£45**
Open: lunch & dinner daily
Meals served: lunch 12-2, dinner 7-9.30

The long tradition of hospitality at the Bear dates back to the 16th century when it was a stop-off point on the London to West Wales coaching route. It's a quaint, friendly hotel (28 bedrooms) which is very much a focal point in this market town. The low, black beams and open fires of the bar make it a good place for a drink and chat or for light lunches, and there's a quiet residents' lounge upstairs. Bedrooms vary from cosy, traditional style to luxurious. A la carte menus offer a wide choice of traditional English and French dishes.

CRICKHOWELL — Gliffaes Country House

Crickhowell, Powys, NP8 1RH
Tel: (01874) 730371   *Fax:* (01874) 730463   **£45**
Open: lunch & dinner (closed Jan & Feb)
Meals served: lunch 12.30-2, dinner 7.30-9.15

Spectacular views from the drive down to the River Usk 150 feet below is the first thing to notice about this delightful, late-Victorian house, set in 29 acres of grounds, run by the Brabner family for almost half a century. Deep in fishing country, the hotel has its own fishing—from slow-flowing flat to runs of rapids on the Usk, and there is also coarse fishing nearby. Here you are greeted by friendly, informal hospitality and warmth from the moment you enter. The hotel has 22 rooms, all of which are spacious and comfortable in traditional country house style, some with views over the surrounding hills and river below. Cold buffet lunches, bar snacks and home-made afternoon teas, plus a wide choice of options from the fixed-price and à la carte menus in the evening, complete the experience.

DOLGELLAU — Dolmelynllyn Hall

Ganllwyd, Dolgellau, Gwynedd, LL40 2HP
Tel: (01341) 40273   *Fax:* (01341) 40273   **£55**
Open: dinner daily (closed Dec & Jan)
Meals served: lunch light lunches only, dinner 7.30-8.30

An informal, relaxed, family-run hotel with 11 bedrooms. Start the day with coddled eggs, Loch Fyne or Manx kippers, kedgeree, haddock, kidneys or sweet-cured ham—breakfast here is taken seriously. Later, head chef Joanna Reddicliffe and Nicola Parkes produce daily-changing dinner menus in the modern, classical style. Start with butter-fried wings of skate with a hot cherry tomato compote or warm, devilled crab and fennel tart on a watercress sauce; before local lamb baked in a sea salt crust with a carrot and cumin mousse or pigeon breasts in ale with prunes and pickled walnuts. The five-course fixed-price menus offer desserts and cheese in whichever order you prefer, and the cheese course always includes a savoury tart, fritter or toasty option. Superb wines from the cellars of Adnams in Southwold are keenly priced. Now an entirely non-smoking hotel.

DOLGELLAU   Dylanwad Da

2 Smithfield Street, Dolgellau, Gwynedd, LL40 1BS
Tel: (01341) 422870   **£35**
Open: dinner daily (closed Feb)
Meals served: dinner 7-9

Chef-patron Dylan Rowlands has built up a loyal, local following at his small, cosy restaurant in the centre of the old market town. International dishes share the short à la carte menu with more traditional homely fare. Polish salad, mushroom and bacon bake, smoked salmon mousse to start; followed by the likes of leek and Pernod chicken, Hungarian pork casserole or vegetable curry. To finish, Welsh cheeses or traditional puds. A short wine list with concise helpful notes.

EGLWYSFACH   Ynyshir Hall

Eglwysfach, Machynlleth, Powys, SY20 8TA
Tel: (01654) 781209   *Fax:* (01654) 781366   **£55**
Open: lunch Sun only, dinner daily
Meals served: lunch 12.30-1.30, dinner 7-8.45

Art lovers may get special pleasure from this 8-bedroomed Georgian house, once owned by Queen Victoria, as owner-artist Rob Reen uses his own paintings to decorate the house and has named each of the bedrooms after a famous painter. His most recent works feature in the dining room where you can mull over art and aesthetics as you tuck into a dinner in modern British style cooked by chef Tony Pierce. The fixed-price menu changes monthly and there are a couple of daily specials in support. Try a casserole of local mussels with home-made pasta or sausage of smoked salmon and trout mousse to start, followed by Welsh lamb with Puy lentils, shallot confit and light rosemary jus or sea bass with scallop mousse, black noodles and coriander butter sauce. Finish with hot pistachio soufflé perhaps or the citrus tartlet dessert. Good local suppliers, plus excellent Welsh cheeses.

EWLOE   St David's Park Hotel

St David's Park, Ewloe, Clwyd, CH5 3YB
Tel: (01244) 520800   *Fax:* (01244) 520930   **£45**
Open: lunch & dinner daily
Meals served: lunch 12.30-2, dinner 7-10

This is a smart, modern, purpose-built hotel with 121 spacious, well-designed rooms and good leisure, business and conference facilities. Set in landscaped gardens, its Georgian-style façade is designed around an inner courtyard with fountain. Good housekeeping and nice little touches in the rooms include the provision of robes and slippers. Rooms range from executive standard (gents' and ladies') to suites, studios, family and adjoining rooms, no-smoking rooms and rooms especially designed for the disabled. The restaurant offers a buffet-style table, plus an international menu of dishes. The hotel's new Northop Country Park golf club, created with championships in mind, opened in June 1994.

FISHGUARD — Three Main Street

3 Main Street, Fishguard, Dyfed, SA65 9HG
Tel: (01348) 874275 **£40**
Open: lunch & dinner Mon-Sat (Tue-Sat in winter) (closed Feb)
Meals served: lunch 12-2.30, dinner 7-9.30

A stone's throw from the sea, this informal, Georgian town house restaurant is decorated in vibrant colours with natural wood furnishing and a profusion of fresh flowers to create an atmosphere of warmth and hospitality. A well-balanced menu of modern, classical cooking, with the emphasis on natural flavours and light saucing, offers the best of local produce. Dinner menus might offer fresh, local, Cardigan bay scallops, tart basquaise (tomato, red onions and herbs), walnut pesto ravioli and home-made soups to start; followed by breast of chicken stuffed with Gruyère and rosemary, medallions of monkfish with glazed shallot and red wine butter sauce or peppered loin of venison with red cabbage and a poivrade sauce. Good choice of puds plus excellent local farmhouse cheeses and organic breads. There is also a coffee house which serves home-made pastries and a selection of light savoury dishes, plus a light lunchtime menu which includes pastas, salads, pizzas, soups, tarts and crepes. Three ensuite bedrooms provide comfortable and stylish accommodation for those who wish to stay overnight.

GOWERTON — Cefn Goleu Park

Cefn Stylle Road, Gowerton, West Glamorgan, SA4 3QS
Tel: (01792) 873099 **£50**
Open: lunch Sun, dinner Tue-Sat (closed 2 wks Jan)
Meals served: lunch 12.30-2, dinner 7.30-9.30

Built in 1880 for the bride of Sir Charles Berington, who tragically died before the couple ever had the chance to occupy the house, this distinctive Welsh manor house changed hands many times before Emma and Claude Rossi fell in love with it in 1987 and began the painstaking job of restoring it. Happily, in their case, love's labour has not been lost! A magnificent, vaulted central hall with a minstrel's gallery leads to the four master bedrooms which Emma has lovingly restored to their former Victorian elegance. Claude and son Bernard are in charge of the kitchen, which delivers hearty, full-flavoured, no-nonsense dishes. A wide choice of chicken, fish, steak and veal feature on the regular carte, along with fishy starters such as langoustines provençale and scampi meunière, while weekly-changing fixed-price menus offer seasonal specials such as fish of the day in a rich white wine, brandy, cream and crushed peppercorn sauce, and seafood cocktail parisienne. Good-value Sunday lunch (£12.50).

LAKE VYRNWY — Lake Vyrnwy Hotel

Lake Vyrnwy, (via Oswestry), Llanwyddyn, Powys, SY10 0LY
Tel: (0169 173) 692   *Fax:* (0169 173) 259   **£50**
Open: lunch & dinner daily
Meals served: lunch 12.15-1.45, dinner 7.30-9.15

If it's space you're looking for, this is the place. There are miles of splendid walks and lots of outdoor pursuits available, from canoeing or fishing on the lake to bird watching and cycling. The hotel has 37 rooms with views of the lake or surrounding countryside, including romantic four-poster rooms and family suites. The kitchen is well stocked with fresh herbs, fruits, edible flowers and vegetables from its own garden which is lovingly tended and watched over by the hotel gardener. Everything is home-made, from marmalade to petits fours at dinner; they even make their own mustards, preserves, chutneys and vinegars. The menu changes every day, making good use of fresh trout from the lake and game from the estate. The hotel has its own country pub in the grounds, serving light lunches and dinner on the terrace on warm evenings.

LLANBEDR — Llew Glas Brasserie

Llanbedr, Gwynedd, LL45 2LD
Tel: (01341) 23555   **£30**
Open: lunch & dinner Wed-Mon (Thu-Sat in winter)
Meals served: lunch 10.30-5, dinner 6.30-10 (7-10 Thu-Sat Winter)

Home cooking graded for dietary needs is the order of the day at Trevor and Marj Pharoah's small brasserie. From snails in garlic butter to `gobble and grunt pie' (turkey and ham!) or simple steaks to sizzling duck with black bean sauce. Kids' menu until 7.30pm.

LLANDRILLO — Tyddyn Llan

Llandrillo, Nr Corwen, Clwyd, LL21 0ST
Tel: (01490) 440264   *Fax:* (01490) 440414   **£55**
Open: lunch & dinner daily (closed Feb)
Meals served: lunch 12.30-2, dinner 7.30-9.30

Situated at the foot of the Berwyn Mountains amidst the serenity of the Vale of Edeyrnion, Tyddyn Llan is a haven of peace and tranquility in an area of great natural beauty, rich in wildlife. Llandrillo was for centuries a strategic point on the Drovers' Route used to drive livestock from as far away as Anglesey to the markets of England. From here you can explore ancient Roman routes across the Berwyns accompanied by a guide, or take advantage of the hotel's four miles of grayling, trout and salmon fishing on the River Dee with the help of an experienced local ghillie. The house is Georgian, made of stone, and has been run by the Kindreds for over a decade. Inside, it is all light and elegance, and all of the 10 bedrooms look out on to the surrounding gardens and country-side. The restaurant makes the most of local produce, making a point of serving Welsh cheeses, beef, lamb and local seafood. The three- or four-course daily-changing menu from chef Dominic Gilbert offers a good range—tagliatelle of oyster mushrooms with olives, pesto and pecorino cheese; darne of salmon with caper beurre noisette; free-range Hereford duckling with an apple and pear compote and cider sauce; baked lemon cream with warm white chocolate sauce.

LLANDUDNO   Bodysgallen Hall

Llandudno, Gwynedd, LL30 1RS
Tel: (0492) 584466   *Fax:* (0492) 582519   **£60**
Open: lunch & dinner daily   ✿
Meals served: lunch 12.30-2, dinner 7.30-9.30

Two hundred acres of parkland surround this 17th-century house
which has been sympathetically restored by Historic Hotels Ltd to provide some of the best country house hospitality in the country. There
are superb views of Snowdonia and delightful gardens including a rare
17th-century knot garden of box hedges filled with herbs, a walled rose
garden and a rockery. Bedrooms, either in the main house or courtyard cottages, provide elegant, well-appointed accommodation. A former stable block has been converted into a conference hall on two
floors and a new leisure complex is currently under construction 200
metres from the hotel, for completion in early 1995. The kitchen provides imaginative food prepared from fresh local produce, as well as
many traditional country-house-style dishes. Steamed herb pancake
filled with a seafood mousse; Welsh lamb with glazed shallots and a tarragon jus; dark chocolate and hazelnut mousse on coffee bean sauce;
Welsh and English cheeses and coffee and sweetmeats to finish.

LLANDUDNO   Richard's Bistro Restaurant

Church Walks, Llandudno, Gwynedd, LL30 2HD
Tel: (0492) 877924   **£40**
Open: dinner daily
Meals served: dinner 6.30-10
Richard Hendey's dinner-only bistro-cum-restaurant is open 365 nights a year.,
Good home cooking at reasonable prices. Friendly, welcoming atmosphere.

LLANDUDNO   St Tudno Hotel

The Promenade, Llandudno, Gwynedd, LL30 2LP
Tel: (0492) 874411   *Fax:* (0492) 860407   **£60**
Open: lunch & dinner daily
Meals served: lunch 12.30-1.45, dinner 7-9.30 (Sun to 9)

In 1861, Alice Liddell (later immortalised in Lewis Carroll's Alice's
Adventures In Wonderland) spent a holiday here. A hundred or so
years later, Martin and Janette Bland moved in and have been running
this 21-bedroomed promenade hotel, which looks out on to the bay,
ever since. The Blands provide a warm and friendly welcome, with
plenty of thoughtful, homely touches. Chef David Harding looks after
the culinary side of affairs, with a modern British style of cooking influenced by both Welsh and French traditions. Grilled goat's cheese with
hot crispy bacon or hotpot of Conwy mussels in cider and cream are
typical of the range of starters; main courses could include cutlets of
Welsh lamb with a minted butter sauce, collops of venison with pickled
walnuts and juniper sauce, sirloin with wild mushrooms and red wine
sauce, or turbot grilled with lemon and limes. Vegetarian options are
always included, as is chateaubriand for two, served with tarragon butter sauce. Interesting desserts, Welsh organic cheeses and home-made
sweetmeats.

LLANGAMMARCH WELLS   Lake Country House

Llangammarch Wells, Powys, LD4 4BS
Tel: (0159 12) 202   *Fax:* (0159 12) 457 **£55**
Open: lunch by arrangement, dinner daily
Meals served: lunch 12.45-1.45, dinner 7-8.45

An elegant Welsh country house with 19 bedrooms, set in 50 acres of grounds. It's popular with fishermen since the Irfon runs through the grounds which include a trout-stocked lake, and guests can also fish on the Wye and the Chewfru. Jean-Pierre and Jan Mifsud are enthusiastic owners who want your stay to be a peaceful and relaxing one. There are beautiful riverside walks and a host of activities which can be arranged, from hacking and trekking to clay pigeon shoots and golf. Bedrooms are richly and sumptuously furnished and enjoy lovely views over the grounds. Dinner is a daily-changing five-course, fixed-price affair with ample choice. Typical dishes include a light cheese and apple soufflé with whole grain mustard sauce or warm potato and dill pancakes topped with oak-smoked salmon followed by Welsh venison with chestnuts and juniper berries in a port wine and shallot sauce or codling baked with a lemon and herb crust on a mussel and prawn butter sauce.

| **LLANGYBI** | **Cwrt Bleddyn Hotel** |

Tredunnock, Nr Usk, Gwent, NP5 1PG
Tel: (06133) 450521   *Fax:* (01633) 450220 **£50**
Open: lunch & dinner daily ❖
Meals served: lunch 12-2.30, dinner 7-10.30
36-bedroomed country house hotel in an area known locally as the "Best Kept Secret" in Wales. Beautiful scenery, French cuisine and extensive leisure and business facilities.

LLANRUG   Seiont Manor

Llanrug, Caernarfon, Gwynedd, LL55 2AQ
Tel: (01286) 673366   *Fax:* (01286) 672840 **£45**
Open: lunch & dinner daily
Meals served: lunch 12-2.30, dinner 7-10

Welsh country mansion surrounded by 150 acres of parkland, with country club, conference (up to 100) and leisure facilities. The hotel's 28 rooms are housed in two separate, purpose-built blocks around a courtyard, and are furnished with antiques and period pieces. The house is built from the original farmstead of a Georgian manor house; inside, it's pretty, elegant and clean. Fishing rights on the Seiont, complimentary access to a nearby golf course, and proximity to Snowdonia provide a wealth of outdoor pursuits. The menu has a Welsh flavour but the overriding influence is French.

LLANSANFFRAID GLAN CONWY   Old Rectory

Llanrwst Road, Llansanffraid Glan Conwy, Gwynedd, LL28 5LF
Tel: (01492) 580611   *Fax:* (01492) 584555   **£60**
Open: dinner daily (closed 20 Dec-1 Feb)
Meals served: dinner 7.30 for 8

The Welsh motto of the Old Rectory means "a beautiful haven of peace", and so it is at this 6-bedroomed, Georgian house, furnished with antiques and a fine collection of Victorian watercolours. The house stands on a hillside with fabulous views over the Conwy estuary and Snowdonia. It is run in friendly, chatty style by the Vaughans, and is thoroughly homely—even down to irons and ironing boards in the rooms. Wendy Vaughan produces excellent, five-course set dinners in the kitchen while husband Michael attends to front of house. Everything from the bread rolls to pre-dinner nibbles are freshly prepared. You have the choice of dining separately or at the large communal table where dinner is served at 8pm. Good Welsh farmhouse cheeses and delicious puds.

LLYSWEN   Llangoed Hall

Llyswen, Brecon, Powys, LD3 0YP
Tel: (01874) 754525   *Fax:* (01874) 754545   **£80**
Open: lunch & dinner daily
Meals served: lunch 12.15-2.15, dinner 7.15-9.30

Set on the banks of the River Wye, this 23-bedroomed Edwardian hotel, owned by Sir Bernard Ashley of fabric fame, is one with a difference. No reception desk or hostage credit card control on arrival here; just friendly staff to take your coat and carry your bags up to your room. Beautifully restored, the house is handsome and elegantly furnished: rooms are well-proportioned, spacious and have plenty of natural light—all the luxuries of modern times as well as a historic and artistic heritage which rivals many. The oldest part of the surviving house, the South Wing, dates back to Jacobean times, but the present hall is the work of Portmeirion-famed architect Sir Clough Williams-Ellis. The restaurant makes the most of local specialist suppliers: Welsh farmed venison, Herefordshire Trelough duck bred in apple orchards; salmon from the Wye (the hotel has fishing rights on the Wye and the Irfon). The style of cooking follows the modern British mode, with Nigel Morris at the stove. Immaculately set tables are matched by immaculately presented dishes from well-balanced menus. Great breakfasts—the menu includes salmon kedgeree, grilled Welsh kippers, smoked haddock fish cake, Glamorgan sausages and English muffins, served with smoked salmon, poached egg and hollandaise sauce!

MISKIN   Miskin Manor
Penddylan Road, Pontyclun, Miskin, Mid Glamorgan, CF7 8ND
Tel: (01443) 224204   *Fax:* (01443) 237606   **£55**
Open: lunch & dinner daily
Meals served: lunch 12-2, dinner 7-9.45
Handsome 32-bedroomed mellow greystone manor overlooking the River Ely. Spacious luxuriously appointed rooms, health and leisure club with playroom and crèche, and conference facilities. Beautiful setting. Traditional/Welsh cuisine.

MUMBLES — Norton House

17 Norton Road, Mumbles, Swansea, West Glamorgan, SA3 5TQ
Tel: (01792) 404891   *Fax:* (01792) 403210   **£55**
Open: lunch & dinner daily (closed 25 & 26 Dec)
Meals served: dinner 7.30-9.30

A friendly little hotel (15 bedrooms) run by the Power family for the last five years. This is a pretty Georgian house with a wisteria-framed door and an unusual umbrella-vaulted ceiling in the bar. Homely touches in the bedrooms, some of which have four-posters, make all the difference, and the majority of the rooms are housed away from the main house in a new, modern wing. Traditional British cooking for the most part from the kitchen, with specialities like Welsh lamb coated in finely chopped mushrooms cooked in puff pastry and served with a mint gravy.

NEWPORT — Celtic Manor

The Coldra, Newport, Gwent, NP6 2YA
Tel: (01633) 413000   *Fax:* (01633) 412910   **£50**
Open: lunch Mon-Fri, dinner Mon-Sat
Meals served: lunch 12-2.30, dinner 7-10.30

This 73-bedroomed 19th-century manor house set in 300 acres of hillside and woodland is only a minute from junction 24 of the M4. High standards of decor and service, and impressive leisure and conference facilities make it popular across the board. There are two restaurants to choose between. You can eat in the Patio Grill conservatory, which is particularly popular at lunchtime, or in the elegant oak-panelled dining room, Hedley's Restaurant, which offers a more intimate romantic setting, with its candlelit tables and stained glass windows. There are plans to bring on line an 18-hole golf course and tennis club by the spring of 1995.

NEWPORT — Cnapan Country House

East Street, Newport, Nr Fishguard, Dyfed, SA42 0WF
Tel: (01239) 820575   *Fax:* (01239) 820878   **£40**
Open: lunch & dinner Wed-Mon (closed Feb, Xmas)
Meals served: lunch 12-2, dinner 7-9

Good value for money is the guiding principle of Cnapan. The Lloyds and the Coopers run this five-bedroomed listed house close to National Parkland with a relaxed informality, offering light lunches (flans, traditional Welsh fagggots in a rich onion gravy, local fresh crab salad) and a well-thought-out, imaginative à la carte in the evening. Food in fact is the main focus of the operation and local produce is used as much as possible. Start perhaps with two-taste pancake—spinach and wild mushroom layers—or spicy fish chowder with crispy anchovy bread; before duck breast marinated in soy sauce, honey and ginger, with a piquant bitter orange sauce or monkfish kebab with home-made tartare sauce. Local Dyfed cheeses to finish, plus interesting desserts which might include boozy ginger biscuit roll or old-fashioned baked mincemeat pudding served with a cinnamon and brandy custard. Wines from the New World, Chile and Italy feature on the wine list.

NORTHOP — Soughton Hall

Northop, Nr Mold, Clwyd, CH7 6AB
Tel: (01352) 840811   *Fax:* (01352) 840382   **£50**
Open: lunch by arrangement, dinner daily (closed 2 wks Jan)
Meals served: dinner 7.30-9.30 (Sat to 10, Sun to 8)

This former bishop's palace dating from 1714, in extensive parkland
and gardens, has been lovingly restored by the Rodenhurst family for
whom it is home. It's an ornate house with many fine architectural
features, yet there's a real family feel about the place despite the overall
grandeur of first impressions. Carved stone fireplaces, tapestries and
Persian rugs abound, but family memorabilia are equally in evidence.
The splendid State Dining Room on the first floor overlooks the garden
and is a stunning setting in which to enjoy Christopher Plummer's
modern English cuisine. The à la carte offers dishes such as warm ravioli of salmon, lobster and prawns served with pan-fried scallops, crispy
leeks and a light soy and ginger butter sauce, followed by poached
breast of local chicken filled with a leek and tomato mousseline and
served with a creamy sweetcorn and wild mushroom sauce.
Alternatively there's the special house menu which changes daily, with
the focus firmly on wholesome traditional fare. The hotel has 14
rooms—possibly the best accommodation in this part of the world—
and there is much excitement at present over the new 18-hole golf
course within the grounds.

PORTHKERRY — Egerton Grey

Porthkerry, Nr Cardiff, South Glamorgan, CF6 9BZ
Tel: (01446) 711666   *Fax:* (01446) 711690   **£45**
Open: lunch & dinner daily
Meals served: lunch 12-2, dinner 7-9.30

Down a lane between thatched farm cottages, this 10-bedroomed country house, a former rectory, enjoys an enviably secluded setting in a
wooded valley making it an ideal retreat from the pressures of 20th-
century life. Go for a walk around the grounds, where if the whim takes
you, you can knock about on the all-weather tennis court or play a
game of croquet, but alternatively find a spot with views down to
Porthkerry Park and the sea and simply take in the beauty before heading back for dinner. Some of the bedrooms include superbly restored
Edwardian bathrooms, as well as half-tester and four-poster beds, for
those who want to soak up the romance of it all.

PORTMEIRION   Hotel Portmeirion

Portmeirion, Gwynedd, LL48 6ER
Tel: (01766) 770228   Fax: (01766) 771331   **£55**
Open: lunch Tue-Sun, dinner daily (closed 8 Jan-2 Feb)
Meals served: lunch 12.30-2, dinner 7-9.30

I have always found Portmeirion one of the most mystical and attractive destinations in the British Isles, indeed the world. A cluster of Italianate buildings is set on a wooded peninsula between the rivers

Glaslyn and Dwyryd, designed by the eccentric genius Sir Clough Williams-Ellis who spent 46 years of his life on the project. The resultant 'village' is definitely more reminiscent of the Mediterranean coast than of Wales, and guests can choose to stay in the main hotel building or in the cottages dotted around the village. The hotel restaurant's kitchen is in the capable hands of Craig Hindley, whose modern menus bring Mediterranean touches to locally produced ingredients: Welsh lamb with a tagliatelle of creamed leek and garlic, poussin with caramelised onions and crisp Parma ham or a flan of Pencarrig cheese, broccoli and almonds with chive sauce. An excellent wine list with a tremendous choice of wines at under £15.00 makes for difficult selection. Many years ago I was wandering around the village and met the architect, resplendent in his customary plus fours and bow-tie. He joined me and proudly pointed out interesting features of his masterpiece. As we returned to the hotel he stopped and asked "Well, do you like it?". "I cannot imagine that anyone visiting such a unique and lovely place could fail to be totally captivated by it", I replied, and having been back many times since, I still experience the same feelings of almost disbelief. Try it!

PWLLHELI   Plas Bodegroes

Nefyn Road, Pwllheli, Gwynedd, LL53 5TH
Tel: (01758) 612363   *Fax:* (01758) 701247   **£70**
Open: dinner Tue-Sun & Bank Holiday Mon (closed Nov-Feb)
Meals served: dinner 7-9.30

The rugged sea cliffs and sandy coves of the Llyn Peninsula is the setting for this delightful Georgian manor house fronted by an avenue of 200-year-old beeches in wild, secluded woodland a mile west of Pwllheli. It's simply idyllic. More of a restaurant with rooms than an hotel, the emphasis is definitely on the food. Walls hung with modern Welsh art create a stylish scenario in which to enjoy Chris Chown's five-course, fixed-price menus. Based largely on local ingredients—the area is renowned for seafood, Welsh lamb and beef, free-range chickens and ducks (and their eggs)—the menus offer plenty of choice, and the cooking is skilful, with the emphasis being on natural flavours rather than over sophistication. The eight immaculately kept rooms have been designed by Chris' wife Gunna, whose Scandinavian flair for design is altogether evident. Taking on an additional restaurant (Hole in the Wall in Bath) does not seem to have diluted Chris' diligence at all—rather, it has doubled! We wish him well in his ventures.

REYNOLDSTON   **Fairyhill**
Reynoldston, Gower, Swansea, West Glamorgan, SA3 1BS
Tel: (01792) 390139   *Fax:* (01792) 391358   **£50**
Open: lunch Sun only, dinner daily
Meals served: lunch 12.30-1.15, dinner 7.30-9
A haven of peace and tranquillity in an area of outstanding beauty. Intimate 11-bedroomed hotel in 24 acres of grounds, complete with trout stream and lake. Splendid country breakfasts include Welsh kippers. Traditional cooking with a modern touch.

ROSSETT   **Llyndir Hall**
Llyndir Lane, Rossett, Nr Wrexham, Clwyd, LL12 0AY
Tel: (01244) 571648   *Fax:* (01244) 571258   **£45**
Open: lunch & dinner daily
Meals served: lunch 12-2, dinner 7-10
Elegant 38-bedroomed hotel, surrounded by lush lawns and beautiful gardens. A family-friendly place, with indoor pool and leisure facilities, all-day coffee shop and children's menu.

SWANSEA   Annie's Restaurant

56 St Helen's Road, Swansea, West Glamorgan, SA1 4BE
Tel: (01792) 655603   **£40**
Open: dinner Mon-Sat (Tue-Sat in winter) (closed Bank Holidays)
Meals served: dinner 7-10

Chef-patron Ann Gwilym continues to offer an imaginative menu in an informal, relaxed setting. Asparagus and Gruyère tart, terrine of wood pigeon with blueberry chutney, skate and crab fish cake and oeuf en cocotte with chicken livers and oyster mushrooms are typical of the range of starters on offer. Main courses might include shank of Welsh lamb braised in red wine; whole grilled baby guinea fowl with lime, rosemary and garlic; poached lemon sole on a bed of sorrel with white wine sauce; baked polenta pie or chestnut, walnut and lentil roast with a warm beetroot salad. A short list of French and Australian wines in support.

SWANSEA   Number One

1 Wind Street, Swansea, West Glamorgan, SA1 1DE
Tel: (01792) 456996   **£55**
Open: lunch Mon-Sat, dinner Wed-Sat
Meals served: lunch 12-2.30, dinner 7-9.30

An unpretentious bistro in every sense and a popular local venue, which means it's best to book, since seating is limited. Fixed-price lunches are good value, offering the likes of asparagus soup followed by chicken and chestnut mushroom pie or fillet of hake with sauce vierge. Plenty of choice on the à la carte—Welsh smoked salmon with hot potato scones; fillet steak en croute; venison with poached pear and port. Welsh cheeses and traditional puds. There's really good value on a well chosen wine list with house wines starting at under £7 a bottle.

TALSARNAU   Maes-y-Nevadd

Talsarnau, Nr Harlech, Gwynedd, LL47 6YA
Tel: (01766) 780200   *Fax:* (01766) 780211   **£65**
Open: lunch & dinner daily
Meals served: lunch 12.15-1.45, dinner 7-9.15

The Welsh equivalent of the Orient Express offers a rather shorter but
no less enjoyable experience as you travel the 27-mile round trip pulled
by the narrow gauge steam trains on the Ffestiniog railway between
Portmadog and Blaenau Ffestiniog. You may be wondering what this
has to do with a hotel in Talsarnau: it's simple. The food for this unique
experience is cooked by Peter Jackson from the Maes-y-Neaudd hotel!
However, to enjoy this treat you will need at least 30 like minded
friends and have to book through the hotel. You could just stay at the
hotel instead—it's a gem and Peter's cooking will ensure a memorable
stay. His menu offers choices at some of the courses. Start with either
a warm quail and scallop salad or a terrine of leeks and laverbread,
then comes a carrot, potato and oatmeal cawl followed by fillets of brill
in brown butter with cucumber. A main dish of venison with a herb
crust on pepper sauce, escalope of pork with apple gateau and tarragon
sauce or an aubergine gateau with tomato fondue for vegetarians.
Leave some room for delicious puddings and/or tempting Welsh
cheeses. Don't forget to catch the train!

TINTERN ABBEY   Royal George

Tintern Abbey, Nr Chepstow, Gwent, NP6 6SF
Tel: (01291) 689205   *Fax:* (01291) 689448   **£40**
Open: lunch & dinner daily   ✤
Meals served: lunch 12-2, dinner 7-9.30

The Royal George was built in 1598 as a cottage for the iron master
from the nearby mine: it was converted into a coaching inn in the 17th
century. The hotel stands at the foot of a wooded hillside in its own gardens, bordered by a stream in which the Cistercian monks from nearby
Tintern Abbey used to fish. Several of the 19 bedrooms have balconies
with views across the valley to the vineyard on the hills opposite, and
many are suitable for families. Owners Tony and Maureen Pearce are
friendly and welcoming—the hotel has colour and character, and a
relaxed, informal country feel. Local produce, including wine from the
village, is used in the kitchen, which produces French- and English-
inspired dishes.

TRELLECH   Village Green

Trellech, Nr Monmouth, Gwent, NP5 4PA
Tel: (01600) 860119   **£45**
Open: lunch Tue-Sun, dinner Tue-Sat
    (closed lunch Bank Holidays, 10 days Jan)
Meals served: lunch 12-1.45, dinner 7-9.45 (Sat to 10)

Restaurant and bistro with two cottagey rooms for overnight guests.
Blackboard menu in the bistro—seafood lasagne, Welsh lamb pie—and
classically-based à la carte in the restaurant. Warm, friendly owners
and good atmosphere.

WELSH HOOK　　　　　　　Stone Hall

Welsh Hook, Wolfscastle, Nr Haverfordwest, Dyfed, SA62 5NS
Tel: (01348) 840212　*Fax:* (01348) 840815　　　　　**£40**
Open: dinner Tue-Sun (closed some of Jan/Feb)
Meals served: dinner 7.30-9.30

Slate-flagged floors and rough-hewn oak beams bear witness to the
14th-century origins of this 5-bedroomed manor house in a secluded
setting down country lanes. It's more a restaurant with rooms than a
hotel, and French-born owner Martine Watson brings her native cuisine to the fore through the capable talents of chef Christophe Caron.
Warm goat's cheese salad, home-smoked salmon with chives and
cream, confit de canard with garlic cream and local scallops marinated
in lime and served with home-made pasta, plus local fish, home-baked
breads, and home-cured or smoked meats and fish. Ask directions
when booking.

WHITEBROOK　　　　Crown at Whitebrook

Whitebrook, Nr Monmouth, Gwent, NP5 4TX
Tel: (01600) 860254　*Fax:* (01600) 860607　　　　　**£55**
Open: lunch Tue-Sun, dinner Mon-Sat (closed 25 & 26 Dec,
　　2 wks Jan, 2 wks Aug)
Meals served: lunch 12-2, dinner 7-9 (Sat to 9.30)

The food is French-inspired at Sandra and Roger Bates' auberge-style
restaurant-with-rooms in the Wye Valley. Specialities include guinea
fowl poached in wine, Welsh loin of lamb with home-made faggots en
croute and fresh Wye salmon with a cream and brandy sauce. Good
starters range from warm salad of smoked duck breast to salmon
tartare on a tomato coulis. Sandra makes everything herself, from
bread to gravad lax. Lunchtime brings a simpler menu or a more informal lounge menu. The 12 rooms offer good overnight accommodation
and you can breakfast on the terrace in fine weather. Around 150 wines
to choose from, so allow plenty of time!

Northern Ireland Establishment Reviews

AGHADOWEY   Greenhill House

24 Greenhill Road, Aghadowey, Coleraine,
   Co Londonderry, BT51 4EU
Tel: (01265) 868241   **£25**
Open: dinner Mon-Sat (closed Nov-Feb)
Meals served: dinner only at 6.30

Greenhill is actually part of a working farm, where Elizabeth Hegarty offers comfortable accommodation and a warm welcome to her guests, along with some excellent home baking, all part of the hospitality. Dinner provides some sound, but simple, home cooking, but no wine in this house of temperance. Still, if it's a good feed you need, not an occasion, Elizabeth will certainly come up with the goods. Sit down perhaps to home-made vegetable soup followed by Agivey pork fillet and banoffi pie. The six rooms are attractive, with many thoughtful touches.

BALLYMENA   Galgorm Manor

136 Fenaghy Road, Ballymena, Co Antrim, BT42 1EA
Tel: (01266) 881001   *Fax:* (01266) 880080   **£55**
Open: lunch & dinner daily
Meals served: lunch 12-2.30, dinner 7-9.45 (Sun 6-9)

Under new ownership, Galgorm Manor is being transformed into one of the most attractivly located hotels in Northern Ireland. With the River Maine running through its grounds, a weir and waterfalls along its course, you can go for a delightful riverside stroll. Alternatively, you may prefer to try your hand against the brown trout along the hotel's stretch of the river, or put yourself in the hands of experts at the hotel's equestrian centre behind the hotel—it has 12 stables, a show jumping course and eventing cross-country practice area—and that's just for starters! Inside the house, a sense of luxury pervades now that refurbishment of the public areas has been completed and the restaurant, with glittering chandeliers and Arcadian murals, provides an elegant setting for competent cooking based on good local produce. For a less formal affair, you can eat from a full bar menu in the clubhouse or rustic Ghillies bar. The hotel has 23 rooms, some of which have spectacular views over the river.

BELFAST — Antica Roma

67-69 Botanic Avenue, Belfast, Co Antrim, BT7 1JL
Tel: (01232) 311121   *Fax:* (01232) 310787   **£50**
Open: lunch Mon-Fri, dinner Mon-Sat
   (closed 3 days Xmas, 31 Dec)
Meals served: lunch 12-3, dinner 6-11

Salvo Liberante draws on ancient Rome for the decor at this fashionable restaurant at the heart of the city's university district. Classical murals, columns, stucco and mosaic floor provide an enormously atmospheric setting for chef Vincenzo's first-class Italian dishes. Start with likes of rigatoni toscani (one of Tuscan cuisine's all-time greats— smoked bacon, tomato and brandy being the determining factors), or the delicious pappardelle with a rich game sauce. Smaller appetites can opt for granchi—gratinated oak-smoked crab claws cooked in a light bisque sauce, taleggio in crispy pastry or perhaps a warm winter salad of chicken livers. Main courses offer dishes such as roast duck with a sweet brandy and citrus sauce, saltimbocca cooked in rich white wine and butter sauce, or a darne of hake, with red mullet and monkfish, baked and served with mustard and dill sauce. Authentic Italian desserts complete this culinary odyssey.Good set menus at lunchtime.

BELFAST — La Belle Epoque

61-63 Dublin Road, Belfast, Co Antrim, BT2 7AG
Tel: (01232) 323244   *Fax:* (01232) 240666   **£45**
Open: all day Mon-Fri, dinner only Sat
   (closed 25 & 26 Dec, 12 & 13 July)
Meals served: 12-11.30 (Sat 6-11.30)

Now settled into its new location, La Belle Epoque continues to produce sound French cooking. Excellent-value lunchtime menus include a Lunch For A Tenner and Lunch For A Fiver options alongside the à la carte. The more sophisticated evening menu offers starters such as langoustines with garlic mayonnaise, duck terrine with an onion confit and grenadine syrup and pan-fried piegeon breast with a raspberry vinegar. Typical main courses range from the likes of pan-fried escalope of veal with a creamy artichoke sauce to sea bass with a Pernod butter sauce or lobster Thermidor. Vegetables (featured separately) include ratatouille, pommes dauphines and risotto milanese; while desserts might include delicious crispy filo parcels with strawberries or cream cheese bavarois with forest fruits.

BELFAST   Crown Liquor Salon

46 Great Victoria Street, Belfast, Co Antrim, BT2 7BA
Tel: (01232) 249476
Open: lunch & dinner daily (closed 25 Dec)
Meals served: lunch 12-3, dinner 7-11.15
The best-preserved and most famous bar in Belfast. High Victorian style, opu-
lent. The Edwardian Britannic Lounge includes original timbers from the SS
Britannic. Good bar snacks—Irish stew, steak and kidney pie, fish and shellfish.

BELFAST   Dukes Hotel

65 University Street, Belfast, Co Antrim, BT7 1HL
Tel: (01232) 236666   *Fax:* (01232) 237177   **£65**
Open: lunch Mon-Fri & Sun, dinner Mon-Sat
Meals served: lunch 12.30-2.30, Sun 1-2.30,
   dinner 6.30-10.15, Sat 6.30-10.45

A modern hotel created within a collection of Victorian buildings,
centrally located and popular with business clients. The spacious, cool
reception sets the scene, borne out by well-equipped bedrooms and the
minimalist decor of the dining room. There's a health club as well as
extensive conference facilities.

BELFAST   Roscoff

Lesley House, Shaftesbury Square, Belfast, Co Antrim, BT2 7DB
Tel: (01232) 331532   **£55**
Open: lunch Mon-Fri, dinner Mon-Sat
   (closed 11 & 12 Jul, 24-26 Dec, 1 Jan)
Meals served: lunch 12.15-2.15, dinner 6.30-10.30

The chicest restaurant in town, and the best. Paul Rankin, pictured
with wife Jeanne, has brought to his native Northern Ireland a wealth
of experience gained in
England and California.
Sophisticated, modern dishes
compliment the minimalist
designer decor to great success. Starters such as herb and
ricotta ravioli with walnut
pesto or marinated leeks and
beetroot with goat's cheese
toast precede main course
dishes such as spiced sesame-
fried hake and peppered duck
breast with wild mushrooms
and cream. Lunch-time brings
a set menu of similar design—
seafood risotto, char-grilled
rump of beef. Finish with an
unusual touch, with panettone
bread and butter pudding or
polenta cake. Interesting, rea-

sonably-priced wine list matches the standards set by the cooking and
service.

BELFAST — Speranza

16 Shaftesbury Square, Belfast, Co Antrim, BT2 7DB
Tel: (01232) 230213 — **£35**
Open: dinner Mon-Sat (closed 3 days Xmas, 12 Jul)
Meals served: dinner only 5-11.30

There's plenty of room at this large pizzeria-restaurant set on two floors. Pretty checked tablecloths and rustic decor provide an appropriately informal setting for the wide range of pasta and pizza, steaks and other hot dishes such as grilled fillet of sole served in a delicious spinach, prawn and smoked fish sauce. Children are well looked after, with high chairs available and their own menu on colouring mats with crayons supplied. Friendly, cheerful staff complete the picture.

BELFAST — Strand Restaurant

12 Stranmillis Road, Belfast, Co Antrim, BT9 5AA
Tel: (01232) 682266 — **£35**
Open: lunch & dinner daily (closed 25 & 26 Dec, 12 & 13 Jul)
Meals served: lunch Sun 12-3, dinner Sun 5-10,
  (light meals Mon-Sat 12-12)

The Complete Meal for only £3.95 (noon-11pm, till 7pm Fri/Sat) is surely a winner at Anne Turkington's popular wine bar and restaurant, with Charles Rennie Mackintosh-inspired furnishings. Situated within the university area, the Strand serves up one-plate dishes such as liver and bacon hot pot, steak and kidney pie with Guinness, cod and chips or French onion flan which come with appropriate accompaniments to form a substantial meal. Alternatively, you can opt for a more traditional arrangement from the à la carte, with choices such as oyster fritters, cabbage and hazelnut croquettes, peppered homemade burger, bacon-stuffed courgettes and pork gorgonzola. There's also an attractive upstairs conservatory bar.

BELFAST — Villa Italia

39 University Road, Belfast, Co Antrim, BT7 1ND
Tel: (02132) 328356   *Fax:* (01232) 234978 — **£45**
Open: dinner daily (closed 25, 26, 31 Dec, 12 Jul, Easter Sunday)
Meals served: dinner only 5-11.30 (Sat from 4, Sun 4-10)

Similar in style to its sister restaurant Speranza (see above), but slightly more upmarket, with a move towards more sophisticated Italian dishes, though plenty of pizza choices remain. Main course dishes include poached salmon steak with yellow pepper and chive sauces, numerous char-grilled steak dishes and chicken—the breast glazed in a light lemon sauce, then sautéed with smoked bacon and mushrooms. Friendly, efficient service and an air of informality make for a relaxing and satisfying meal.

BELFAST — The Warehouse

35-39 Hill Street, Belfast, Co Antrim, BT1 2LB
Tel: (01232) 439690   *Fax:* (01232) 230514   **£40**
Open: lunch Mon-Fri, dinner Tue-Sat (closed Bank Holidays)
Meals served: lunch 12-3, dinner 6-9

A colourful and lively place on two floors, housed in a converted warehouse. At lunch-time, the ground floor operates as a wine bar with a separate menu from the upstairs restaurant—sausage casserole, turkey satay, mushroom loaf. At night the two come together under one menu concept. Typical dishes range from starters such as Mr Price's seafood soup or spiced beef with onion compote, to main courses options like lentil and spinach casserole with fennel, breast of duck with a five-spice sauce and salmon fillet with herb butter sauce. A night-time snack menu is also available in the wine bar.

CRAWFORDSBURN — Old Inn
15 Main Street, Crawfordsburn, Co Down, BT19 1JH
Tel: (01247) 853255   *Fax:* (01247) 852775   **£60**
Open: lunch & dinner daily (closed 24-26 Dec)
Meals served: lunch 12.30-2.30, dinner 7-9.30, Sun 5-7.30
In one of the prettiest villages in the province, the Old Inn dates back to the 1600s—its history is apparent in the rooms. Popular with lovers of the outdoor life.

DUNADRY — Dunadry Inn

2 Islandreagh Drive, Dunadry, Co Antrim, BT41 2HA
Tel: (01849) 432474   *Fax:* (01849) 433389   **£40**
Open: lunch Sun-Fri, dinner daily (closed 24-27 Dec)
Meals served: lunch 12.30-1.45, dinner 7.30-9.45, Sun 5.30-9.45

First there was paper, then came linen: Dunadry today covers the site of the village which grew up around the converted riverside mill which is now at the heart of the hotel complex. There are 67 rooms, many with French windows leading out on to the garden or inner courtyard around which the rooms are arranged. The restaurant also overlooks the river and the popular Copper Bar, with its lunchtime buffet, has plenty of character. Free fishing on Six Mile Water which enjoys a late season run of dollaghan. Good leisure club, and handy for the airport—only a 10-minute drive.

GARVAGH — MacDuff's Restaurant

Blackheath House, 112 Killeague Road, Garvagh,
   Co Londonderry, BT51 4HH
Tel & Fax: (01265) 868433   **£45**
Open: dinner Tue-Sat (closed 4/5 days Xmas, 12 Jul)
Meals served: dinner 7-9.30

A really delightful place, whether you've come solely for dinner or are staying overnight in one of the Erwins' 5 comfortable rooms, which has lovely views over the gardens. But it would be a mistake not to eat in this excellent basement restaurant, where Margaret Erwin turns out some seriously good dishes. Starters might include individual cheese soufflés or halibut and prawns au gratin; main courses show variety, with dishes such as rack of lamb with mulled wine sauce, Premila Lal's chicken curry and a symphony of seafood. Lovely desserts—filo fruit and cream basket or rhubarb and passion fruit glory.

HELEN'S BAY   Deanes on the Square

7 Station Square, Helen's Bay, Co Down, BT19 1TN
Tel: (01247) 852841   **£45**
Open: lunch Tue-Sun, dinner Tue-Sat (closed 2 wks Jan, 1 wk Jul)
Meals served: lunch 12.30-2.30, dinner 7-10

Thanks to the 1st Marquis of Dufferin and his attempts to boost trade
in the little town of Helen's Bay, a railway station was built here in
1863, in the style of a Scottish baronial castle. It is this unusual station
building which is now the Deane brothers' restaurant. It's well worth a
visit, especially for Michael and Haydn's cooking which produces
dishes such as warm duck salad with soya and balsamic dressing, followed by grilled sirloin of beef with potato pancake, and chocolate
steamed pudding. The restaurant looks out on to the platform (still in
use). Small bar in the basement.

HOLYWOOD   Culloden Hotel

142 Bangor Road, Craigavad, Holywood, Co Down, BT18 0EX
Tel: (01232) 425223   *Fax:* (01232) 426777   **£50**
Open: lunch Sun-Fri, dinner daily (closed 24 & 25 Dec)
Meals served: lunch 12.30-2.30, dinner 7-9.45 (Sun to 8.30)

This 19th-century Scottish baronial house, with 91 rooms including
suites, overlooks Belfast Lough and County Antrim coastline. The interior is rich with fine antiques, Louis XV chandeliers, an Adam fireplace
and ornate plasterwork, though most of the bedrooms are housed in an
extension, not in the main house. The Mitre restaurant, with its baby
grand piano and small marble dance floor, overlooks the garden and
offers an international menu. Choices range from the likes of chicken
and spinach roulade with walnut and orange dressing or snails bourguignonne to Manhattan clam chowder, crispy duck with plum and
hazelnut sauce and a wide range of grills. Alternatively, try the menu at
the Cultra Inn within the hotel grounds for bar snacks and light meals.
Good leisure facilities in the Elysium Club. A short stroll through the
grounds of the Culloden and down a country lane will take you to the
shores of the lough.

HOLYWOOD   Sullivans

Sullivan Place, Holywood, Co Down, BT18 9JF
Tel: (01232) 421000   **£35**
Open: lunch Mon-Sat, dinner Tue-Sat (closed Bank Holidays)
Meals served: lunch 10-4, dinner 6.30-10

Bright and cheerful, Sullivans is more of a café by day, serious restaurant at night. Lunch-time sees a range of hot savouries appear from
Simon Shaw's kitchen—home-made soups (minestrone, cauliflower),
quiches, while the evening brings a short carte and a fixed-price menu,
with dishes such as baked goat's cheese topped with almonds, pheasant with braised onions and monkfish with a light saffron vinaigrette.
Bring your own wine—or buy some champagne Charles Heidsieck
from one of the nearby wine merchants on your way.

LONDONDERRY   Beech Hill House Hotel

32 Ardmore Road, Londonderry, Co Londonderry, BT47 3QP
Tel: (01504) 49279   *Fax:* (01504) 45366   **£40**
Open: lunch & dinner daily (closed 25 & 26 Dec)
Meals served: lunch 12-2.30, dinner 6-10

The hotel takes its name from the abundance of trees, including beech, which grace the grounds of this 1729-built house opposite Ardmore Chapel. Local private functions form an important part of the hotel's trade, though this is a family-run establishment where family values count. The pretty Ardmore restaurant, housed in what was once the billiard room, overlooks the gardens and makes an intimate setting for Noel McMeel's cooking. A typical menu might feature Dublin Bay prawns baked in a croissant pastry and served with a mustard and grain sauce, followed by casserole of Irish lamb or cannon of pork (wrapped in bacon, and served with home-made nodles and a rich tomato sauce). If the look of the dessert menu is anything to go by, this is Noel at his most flamboyant, with the likes of baked apple dumpling with a mango purée and butterscotch sauce or tea bavarois with red-currant sauce typical. Finish with Irish country cheeses.

PORTAFERRY   Portaferry Hotel

10 The Strand, Portaferry, Co Down, BT22 1PE
Tel: (0124 77) 28231   *Fax:* (0124 77) 28999   **£40**
Open: lunch & dinner daily (closed 25 & 26 Dec)
Meals served: lunch 12.30-2.30, dinner 7-9

John and Marie Herlihy's 14-bedroomed inn overlooks Strangford Lough at the foot of a peninsula, in an area designated as a bird sanc-tuary, wildlife and marine nature reserve. Portaferry itself is a centre for water sports (yachting, sea angling, deep-sea fishing, sub-acqua). The drawing room and many of the bedrooms have superb views of the lough, and the feeling throughout the house is one of homely elegance. The restaurant is renowned for its seafood, which lands daily in the neighbouring fishing villages of Portavogie and Ardglass, offering the hotel kitchen an abundance of freshly-caught prawns, turbot, brill, sole, scallops, lobster and mussels. The hotel is reached via a five-minute ferry crossing from mainland Strangford or a 30-mile drive down the peninsula from Belfast.

PORTRUSH   Ramore

The Harbour, Portrush, Co Antrim, BT56 8VM
Tel: (01265) 824313   **£45**
Open: dinner Tue-Sat (closed 25 & 26 Dec)
Meals served: dinner only 6.30-10.30

One of the best restaurants in the province, Ramore is quite an experience. George McAlpin's cooking is quite enough in itself, but there's much more to the picture—startlingly modern decor, buzzy ambience and a delightful waterside setting. The partly-open kitchen, well-trained floor staff and huge displays of home-made breads invite high expectation, which George then skilfully rewards with Californian- and Mediterranean-influenced dishes of character. Starters range from the hot and spicy, as in tempura prawns, to light and breezy salads. Main courses are their adult counterparts, as in supreme of duck and chargrilled Irish Spring lamb. The Complete Dishes option on the menu provides a choice of around four single main courses—paella or pasta of the day for example, for just £6.95. What time, I wonder, as I write, does the next plane to Belfast leave?

TEMPLEPATRICK   Templeton Hotel
882 Antrim Road, Templepatrick, Ballyclare, Co Antrim
Tel: (0184 94) 32984   *Fax:* (0184 94) 33406   **£40**
Open: lunch Grill only Mon-Sat, dinner daily (closed 25 Dec)
Meals served: lunch 12-2.30, dinner 7-9.45 (Grill 5-9 Mon-Thu, 5-10 Fri & Sat)
Interesting hotel 10 minutes from Belfast airport—historical themes form the basis for strikingly modern decor. Multi-level terrace overlooking beer garden and lake, plus grill room, atmospheric flagstoned bar and restaurant.

Republic of Ireland Establishment Reviews

ADARE	Adare Manor

Adare, Co Limerick
Tel: (061) 396566   *Fax:* (061) 396124   **£70**
Open: lunch & dinner daily
Meals served: lunch 12.30-2.30 (Sun to 3), dinner 7.30-10

An imposing setting on a gentle curve of the River Maigue and 19th century architecture (the house and gardens were created over about 30 years from 1832) combine to make Adare Manor an impressive place to visit. The 20 acres of well laid out and maintained gardens (within the 1,000 acre estate) draw the eye in to the equally well designed and maintained interior—vaulted plaster work ceilings, elegant chandeliers and fine oak panelling. In some of the 64 bedrooms, the fireplaces are individually carved. Since the manor was modelled to some degree on Versailles it's perhaps no surprise to find a classical French-based menu cooked by chef Gerard Costelloe, but with strong Irish overtones, taking the best of local produce and using it to good advantage on set dinner menus served in the gracious dining room. Predominantly French wine list but with some exploratory excursions to the New World.

ADARE	Dunraven Arms

Adare, Co Limerick
Tel: (061) 396633   *Fax:* (061) 396541   **£50**
Open: lunch & dinner daily (closed restaurant Good Friday)
Meals served: lunch 12.30-2.30, dinner 7.30-9.30, (bar food 12-6)

The Dunraven is at the heart of one of Ireland's prettiest villages, dating back to the Norman Conquest. This is the fox-hunting centre of Ireland; manager Bryan Murphy is a keen huntsman who can arrange for you to attend meets and ride with famous packs. Equestrian

holidays, in general, are a speciality at the Dunraven; salmon and trout fishing on the Maigue and golf, are also big attractions. The hotel offers 43 rooms, including the Princess Grace and Prince Rainier suite (in memory of their 1961 visit). This is a lively, buzzy place, serving excellent bar snacks and lunches in traditional surroundings—steaks, roasts and today's fisherman's catch are regular features. The Maigue restaurant makes much use of local produce, including some from the hotel garden. You might be offered a terrine of wild pheasant with light Cumberland sauce, followed by lightly roasted fillet of monkfish with a red wine sauce or pan-fried breast of guinea fowl served on a bed of straw potatoes with its own jus.

ADARE — Mustard Seed

Main Street, Adare, Co Limerick
Tel: (061) 396451   **£55**
Open: dinner Tue-Sat (closed Bank Holidays, Feb)
Meals served: dinner only 7-10

A pretty thatched cottage is the setting for some excellent cooking from Michael Weir. Michael uses local produce to good effect in modern dishes which look to France for their inspiration. A typical four-course dinner menu features dishes such as parcel of smoked salmon with a crab, mussel and ginger filling set in a fennel dressing; followed by smoked haddock and fish chowder with spicy rouille; and pan-fried breast and leg of pheasant on a bed of port-scented figs with a game jus. Desserts show imaginative variations on traditional favourites, such as the pyramid of baby profiteroles with sticky butterscotch sauce or baked pear in a jacket of filo pastry with cinnamon and a white chocolate ice cream. Delicious walnut bread and good farmhouse cheeses; excellent coffee and petits fours.

AHAKISTA — Shiro

Ahakista, Nr Bantry, Co Cork
Tel: (027) 67030   **£75**
Open: dinner daily
Meals served: dinner 7-9

One of a kind in the west of Ireland—indeed it would probably be so in many locations: Japanese cooking served with German housekeeping and standards of service by wife-and-husband team Kei and Werner Pilz. Styled as a Japanese dinner house, it also has cottage accommodation which bears the mark of Kei's other talent—painting. The menus are traditional Japanese—zensai, tempura, sashimi, yakitori, teriyaki— but with the occasional surprise: masu-yaki is gently roasted wild sea trout served with ginger, lemon and vegetables, a speciality of Sapporo. A charming experience.

ARDEE — The Gables

Dundalk Road, Ardee, Co Louth
Tel: (041) 53789   **£45**
Open: dinner Tue-Sat (closed 2 wks Jun, 2 wks Nov)
Meals served: dinner only 7-10

Snails bourguignonne, Irish oak-smoked salmon, stuffed brace of quail, roast guinea fowl with rich cognac- and tarragon-flavoured butter sauce and seafood according to the day's catch: chef-patron Michael Caine cooks in classic French bourgeois style, with rich saucing and familiar preparations which go down very well with local diners. Wife Glynis takes charge at front-of-house.

ATHY   Tonlegee House

Athy, Co Kildare
Tel: (0507) 31473   *Fax:* (0507) 31473   **£45**
Open: lunch by arrangement, dinner Mon-Sat (Sun residents only)
     (closed 24-26 Dec, Good Friday)
Meals served: dinner 7-9.30 (Fri & Sat to 10.30)

This 18th-century country house on the outskirts of town has been lovingly restored and refurbished, in homely period style, by its warm and friendly owners, the Molloys. The five bedrooms are spacious, offering plenty of light. Dinner, with husband Mark at the stove and Margaret front of house, is a five-course set menu with around half a dozen choices at each stage. This is good home cooking based on classical traditions. Starters such as a warm salad of pigeon with sherry vinegar sauce, or raviolis of crab; followed by fillet of beef with Roquefort cheese sauce, roast rack of lamb with a herb crust, served with a roast garlic and thyme sauce, or guinea fowl with wild mushroom sauce. Fish dishes according to the day's market. Classic puds to finish, plus Irish farmhouse cheeses served with a glass of port.

AUGHRIM   Schoolhouse Restaurant

Aughrim, Nr Ballinasloe, Co Galway
Tel: (0905) 73936   **£40**
Open: lunch Sun, dinner Tue-Sun (Tue-Sat in winter)
     (closed 24-26 Dec)
Meals served: lunch Sun 12.30-3, dinner 6.30-11

Michael Harrison and Geraldine Dolan's restaurant was indeed once a school, and in the couple of years that it has been open, visitors have learned that they are on to a good thing here. Avoiding the obvious ruse of a blackboard menu, there is seriously good food here—hot crab claws with lemon pasta, warm duck confit salad, fresh salmon poached with basil and white wine, breast of pheasant with a bacon and onion tartlet, moist chocolate torte with rumtopf, Irish cheeses with homemade onion confit. Concise wine list with helpful notes—top marks!

BALLINA   Mount Falcon Castle

Ballina, Co Mayo   *All round, a cosy and*
Tel: (096) 21172   *Fax:* (096) 21172   *comfortable place.*   **£65**
Open: dinner daily (closed Xmas, Feb & Mar)
Meals served: dinner only at 8

Constance Aldridge is the life and soul of her 10-bedroomed Victorian castle whose grounds extend down to the banks of the River Moy. The house is run in friendly, relaxed fashion, with Constance joining diners at a long, candlelit table in the evening (not obligatory, though—you can opt to dine separately if you wish), before retiring to the drawing room to discuss the next day's plans over a nightcap or two. This is good, honest Irish country house cooking—the menu (in written note format) offers two main courses, usually a roast and fish dish. Ideal for fishing, with the river and Lough Conn at close hand; also for walking—the house is situated on a 100-acre estate of mature woodland and park.

BALLYDEHOB   Annie's Restaurant

Main Street, Ballydehob, Co Cork
Tel: (028) 37292   **£45**
Open: lunch & dinner Tue-Sat (closed 25 & 26 Dec, 3 wks Oct)
Meals served: lunch 12.30-2.30, dinner 6.30-10

David and Anne Barry offer a short handwritten menu based on local produce at their small, intimate restaurant. Arrive and you will be directed to the pub across the road to wait while your meal presentations get underway. The menu, though short, is varied, with starters like home-made pâté with redcurrant jelly, and main courses typified by fillets of sole and brill stuffed with crabmeat, pork steak with apricot and Cointreau sauce and chicken Kiev. Desserts might include home-made mincemeat in filo pastry or chocolate fudge cake with cream.

BALLYFERRITER   Tigh an Tobair (The Well House)

Ballyferriter, Co Kerry
Tel: (066) 56404   **£20**
Open: lunch & dinner daily (closed Jan & Feb)
Meals served: lunch 12.30-2.30, dinner 6.30-9, (light meals 12-9)

At the opposite end of the village to owner Louis Mulcahy's pottery is his restaurant behind the grocery shop. Renovations revealed a beautiful old well around which Louis has created this informal restaurant, decorated with Louis' own ceramic and his weaver wife Lisbeth's colourful wares. The menu offers simple traditional home-cooking. Favourites such as Irish stew and Dublin coddle are offered alongside sandwiches, soups and salads, served with home-made breads. Louis' daughter Sally runs front of house.

BALLYHACK   Neptune Restaurant

Ballyhack, New Ross, Co Wexford
Tel & Fax: (051) 89284   **£40**
Open: lunch Sun, dinner Tue-Sun (also lunch & dinner
     Mon Jul & Aug) (closed Xmas-17 Mar)
Meals served: lunch 12.30-3, dinner 6.30-10 (Sat to 10.30)

Pierce and Valerie McAuliffe's attractive little bistro restaurant, standing in the shadow of the medieval Ballyhack castle, is delightful with its conservatory dining room overlooking the harbour. Seafood, not surprisingly, is a speciality, with dishes such as creamy fish soup, shrimp and ginger pot, local grilled salmon, and fillet of turbot with lobster sauce sharing the limelight with meat and game dishes (breast of chicken Thermidor, steak au poivre). No-nonsense cooking at very reasonable prices.

BALLYLICKEY   Ballylickey Manor House

Ballylickey, Bantry Bay, Co Cork
Tel: (027) 50071   *Fax:* (027) 50124   **£50**
Open: lunch & dinner Thu-Tue (Wed to residents) (closed Nov-Mar)
Meals served: lunch 12.30-2, dinner 7.30-9.30

Built as a shooting lodge by Lord Kenmare over 300 years ago, Ballylickey has been lovingly restored and extended by its present owners, the Graves. There are five suites in the main house and another seven rustic-style rooms in sheltered garden cottages in the grounds, through which the River Ouvane flows. The house is set in ten acres of award-winning gardens, which include the garden restaurant and swimming pool (with wonderful views over Bantry Bay), and their own fishing (salmon and trout).

BALLYLICKEY   Larchwood House

Pearsons Bridge, Ballylickey, Co Cork
Tel: (027) 66181   **£45**
Open: dinner Mon-Sat (closed 1 wk Xmas)
Meals served: dinner only 6.30-10

Sheila and Aidan Vaughan offer accommodation in five comfortable rooms, with those at the back of the house enjoying the best views. It is the restaurant, though, which is the main attraction here. Sheila's five-course set menus (priced according to main-course choice) offer plenty of variety (around a dozen options at each stage), with dishes being simultaneously imaginative yet uncomplicated. Grilled stuffed mussels with herbs and garlic, snails à la bourguignonne, peach and nettle soup and baked haddock with cream are typical openers. Main courses run from lamb with lemon and mint or chicken Calvados, to John Dory with sesame seeds, or lobster Thermidor. If you're staying overnight, don't miss breakfast.

BALLYLICKEY   Seaview Hotel

Ballylickey, Nr Bantry, Co Cork
Tel: (027) 50462   *Fax:* (027) 51555   **£45**
Open: lunch Sun, dinner daily (closed mid Nov-mid Mar)
Meals served: lunch 11.45-2, dinner 7-9.30

Kathleen O'Sullivan converted her family home to a hotel in the mid '70s and has gone from strength to strength at this 17-bedroomed hotel overlooking Bantry Bay. She has established quite a reputation over the years for her warm and friendly welcome and personal supervision of the place. Ask for a room with sea view if possible. Dinner is a daily-changing, five-course affair, with plenty of choice and variety. Local produce is the mainstay of the menu, with a natural emphasis therefore on seafood. Start perhaps with bacon, kidney and mushroom kebabs followed by rack of lamb with rosemary, grilled sirloin, or monkfish in a light wine sauce.

BALLYVAUGHAN — Gregans Castle Hotel

Ballyvaughan, Co Clare
Tel: (065) 77005   *Fax:* (065) 77111   **£60**
Open: lunch & dinner daily (closed Nov-Mar)
Meals served: lunch 12-3 in bar, dinner 7-8.30

The rocky limestone terrain of the Burren is the setting for this 22-bedroomed hotel run by the Haden family. The library features Raymond Piper's famous collection of mural paintings of Burren flora which you can refer back to after an adventurous walk over the ancient landscape, which is dotted with rare Alpine and Arctic flora. The hotel looks down over Galway Bay, a view which can be best enjoyed from the luxury of the elegant dining room where local Burren lamb and fresh local fish are specialities. Take a stroll around the gardens after dinner or enjoy a quiet drink in the drawing room. As an alternative to the main dining room, you can eat in the Corkscrew Bar which serves food throughout the day.

BALTIMORE — Chez Youen

The Pier, Baltimore, Co Cork
Tel: (028) 20136   **£50**
Open: lunch (summer only) & dinner daily (closed Nov, Xmas)
Meals served: lunch 12.30-2.30, dinner 6-11,
   (light meals 12.30-midnight in summer)

Chef/patron Youen Jacob (pictured) is a larger-than-life figure who has been wowing them in Baltimore since 1978. A mixture of set menus  and a carte, but from whatever format you choose fish and seafood is what you come for. Locally caught (not farmed) and accompanied whenever possible by organically-grown vegetables, the shellfish platter is a meal in itself—indeed the menu lists it as such, served simply but including in the price bread and butter, home-made mayonnaise, a dessert and coffee. The range will doubtless include the best quality prawns, shrimps, brown crab, velvet crab, lobster, crawfish and oysters. These and more besides tempt diners back time after time. Try poached cod with fennel one time, grilled haddock with garlic butter the next, scallops with brandy and cream after that—truly, I would never tire of eating here!

BIRR — Tullanisk

Birr, Co Offaly
Tel: (0509) 20572   *Fax:* (0509) 20572   **£45**
Open: dinner daily (closed 4 days Xmas)
Meals served: dinner at 8.30

Early birds are handsomely rewarded here—breakfasts are excellent, as are George Gossip's no-choice dinners which bring the customers back for more. Guests gather around the fire in the drawing room for pre-dinner drinks and eat at one large table overlooking the grounds. The house is beautifully furnished, with a fine mix of antiques, and a skilful eye has been at work on design. George and his wife, Susan, opened their 18th-century dower house five years ago and have gone from strength to strength. The house is surrounded by open parkland and mature woods, which are bursting with wildlife—glimpses of pheasant, fallow deer and fox have been reported.

BLACKLION — MacNean Bistro

Blacklion, Co Cavan
Tel: (072) 53022   **£40**
Open: lunch Sun only, dinner Tue-Sun (Thu-Sun in winter)
Meals served: lunch 12.30-3.30, dinner 5-10 (light meals 3-6)

Mother and son do one another proud at this front room restaurant on Blacklion's main street. The cooking is stylish, imaginative and skilful. Smoked eel with garlic mayonnaise and small salad or seafood chowder with herb cream are typical of starters, while main courses might include chicken sauté Bagatelle, honey-baked Thornhill duckling with ginger and pineapple sauce, or the surf-and-turf combination of salmon and beef with onions, lemon and garlic. Vera and Nevan Maguire should go from strength to strength. Traditional roast beef with Yorkshire pudding on Sunday along with popular favourites like pork stroganoff. A la carte at lunchtime, carte and set menus (including an Early Bird for £12) in the evening.

BOYLE — Cromleach Lodge

Ballindoon, Castlebaldwin, Nr Boyle, Co Sligo
Tel: (071) 65155   *Fax:* (071) 65455   **£60**
Open: lunch by arrangment, dinner daily (closed 18 Dec-30 Jan)
Meals served: dinner 7-9 (Sun 6.30-8)

Moira and Christy Tighe's hotel is quite unique: it's a modern country house in the hills above Lough Arrow. There are spectacular views of the lough from every room, including the lounges and dining room. Chef Moira puts her imagination to excellent use in dishes based on regional produce. Dinner is a five-course, fixed-price affair, with dishes such as grilled goat's cheese with pineapple and date chutney; leek and herb cream soup; Irish Mist and rosemary-scented loin of lamb; and venison with a vintage port sauce. Wonderful desserts—meringue tartlet of raspberry mousse and vanilla-poached nectarines with a tuile of ice cream are typical.

BUNRATTY   MacCloskey's

Bunratty House Mews, Bunratty, Co Clare
Tel: (061) 364082   **£55**
Open: dinner Tue-Sat (closed 20 Dec-25 Jan)
Meals served: dinner only 7-10

On the opposite side of the road to the historic Castle and the new Folk
Park, this white-washed cellar restaurant run by Gerry and Marie
MacCloskey has built up a considerable local and international reputation for its traditional five-course dinners. Start perhaps with half-a-
dozen native oysters or mussels, followed by a traditional roast, darne
of cod with parsley and lemon butter or salmon with lemon and chive
sauce. Finish with local farmyard cheeses, icky sticky pudding or
home-made ice cream.

CAHERDANIEL   Derrynane Hotel

Caherdaniel, Co Kerry
Tel: (066) 75136   *Fax:* (066) 75160   **£40**
Open: lunch & dinner daily (closed Oct-Apr)
Meals served: lunch 12.30-2, dinner 7-9

Well-run 75-bedroomed family hotel built in the 1960s, with beautiful
location on the south side of the famously spectacular Ring of Kerry.
Family rooms come complete with bunk beds and many of the rooms
enjoy magnificent sea views, as do the bar and restaurant overlooking
the pool. The small kitchen garden beside the hotel supplies some of
the basics to a kitchen which turns out some good honest dishes, complemented by excellent home-made breads. Changes were taking in
place in the kitchen as we went to press. This is a thoroughly modern
hotel with good facilities; the major attraction is the hotel's dramatic
setting overlooking the sea and mountains.

CAHERDANIEL   Loaves & Fishes

Caherdaniel, Nr Derrynane, Co Kerry
Tel: (066) 75273   **£40**
Open: dinner daily (Tue-Sun Jun-Aug, Wed-Sun Sep)
    (closed Oct-Easter)
Meals served: dinner only 6-9.30

Charming cottage restaurant decorated with a collection of old plates.
Modern European cooking is available on a short, inventive menu that
makes good use of local lamb and seafood. Good desserts.

CAHIRCIVEEN   Brennan's Restaurant

13 Main Street, Cahirciveen, Co Kerry
Tel: (066) 72021   **£50**
Open: lunch & dinner daily (closed 24-26 Dec, Nov, Feb)
Meals served: lunch 12-2.30, dinner 7-10

Conor Brennan's new venture in Cahirciveen is simple but stylish, like his menus, which at a glance
have a refreshingly straightforward appeal but on
closer inspection reveal a level of sophistication and
innovation which should bring new life to the culinary landscape of the Ring of Kerry. A galette of
crab to start is served with red pepper and potato in
a lime yoghurt sauce; tomato soup is actually
tomato and oregano consommé. Main courses can
feature pan-fried black sole, roast Kerry lamb with
rosemary and garlic sauce or a sauté of monkfish
with ginger and apples. These and the like are complemented by more traditional lines, such as breast
of Barbary duck with woodland mushrooms or fillet
of beef with tarragon and green peppercorn sauce.

CARLINGFORD   Jordan's Bar & Restaurant

Carlingford, Co Louth
Tel: (042) 73223   **£40**
Open: lunch Sun in summer, dinner daily
    (closed 25 & 26 Dec, 2 wks Jan)
Meals served: lunch 12.30-3.30, dinner 7-10

Expect a warm welcome from Harry and Marian Jordan at this friendly,
local restaurant. They bake their own soda bread and rolls and offer a
balance of modern and traditional dishes on their menu. Together with
a reasonably-priced wine list, it makes for a very enjoyable meal.

CARRIGALINE   Pew's Bistro

Main Street, Carrigaline, Co Cork
Tel: (021) 371512   *Fax:* (021) 371237   **£45**
Open: lunch Tue-Sun, dinner Tue-Sat
    (Sun in Jun-Aug) (closed 25 Dec)
Meals served: lunch 12.30-2.30
    (Sun to 5), dinner 7-11 (Sun to 10.30)

The decor at this cosy town-centre restaurant is perfectly in keeping
with the name. Bare floorboards and pew seating are finished off with
crisp white tablecloths for a menu of wide-ranging influences, supplemented by daily blackboard specials. Barry O'Connor, with time spent
in London restaurants behind him, has returned home to spread the
word. Typical of starters are brandy-flavoured fish soup, char-grilled
tiger prawns and wild game terrine served with caramelised onions and
balsamic vinegar dressing. Main courses include char-grilled steaks,
game and lamb, along with fresh fish and seafood dishes such as
grilled whole Dover sole with lemon balm and lime butter. Irish
cheeses served with a glass of port or a rich selection of desserts to
finish.

CARRIGTWOHILL   Niblicks Restaurant

Fota Island Golf Club, Carrigtwohill, Co Cork
Tel: (021) 883667   **£35**
Open: lunch daily, dinner Fri & Sat (closed 25 & 26 Dec)
Meals served: lunch 12.30-6, dinner 6.30-9.30 (Fri & Sat only)

Michael Ryan, brother of Declan of Arbutus Lodge fame, offers an
informal, bistro-like menu at this club-house restaurant in a converted
farm building. The choice is varied; starters and main courses are featured together, with two prices depending on whether you opt for a
dish as main or starter. Mediterranean stuffed pancakes, warm sesame
chicken salad and lamb curry are typical of dishes on the lunchtime
menu. Dinner is similar. Both menus always include a pasta dish, such
as ricotta-filled tortelloni with Gorgonzola, and fresh fish dishes are displayed daily on the blackboard. The afternoon menu offers a selection
of light snacks and more hot dishes, including steaks. Interesting
desserts such as chestnut and almond tart with vanilla ice cream and
twice-baked pressed chocolate cake and cream.

CASHEL   Cashel House

Cashel, Co Galway
Tel: (095) 31001   *Fax:* (095) 31077   **£65**
Open: lunch & dinner daily (closed 10-31 Jan)
Meals served: lunch 1-2 (in bar), dinner 7.30-8.30 (Sun 7.30-9)

One of the best things about Cashel House is its location—a hideaway
oasis on the Connemara coastline. There's a private beach as well as
award-winning gardens within the 50 acres of grounds. The 19th-
century house takes full advantage of the views, both from the well-
maintained bedrooms (32 in all) and the lounges (warmed by turf fires
in winter). The other best thing here is the food, cooked by Dermot
McEvilly and his team, served by his wife Kay. Local produce, especially seafood, is used to good effect—vegetables come from their own
garden. A five-course set dinner menu has choices at most courses so
that you might enjoy a home-made veal and quail terrine, fresh vegetable soup, then a lemon sorbet to refresh your palate before moving
on to grilled wild Atlantic salmon. Finish with wine jelly trifle or crème
caramel or Irish cheeses, and good coffee. Reasonably priced wine list.
All in all, a delightful place to stay and indulge in west coast pursuits
like pony trekking, golf and fishing.

CASHEL   Chez Hans

Rockside, Cashel, Co Tipperary
Tel: (062) 61177   **£45**
Open: dinner Tue-Sat (closed Bank Holidays, 3 wks Jan)
Meals served: dinner only 6.30-10

An unusual setting here—a converted Wesleyan chapel—for good
cooking by Hans-Peter Matthia. Seafood is the speciality, cooked in a
modern style from a classical base: half a dozen Rossmore oysters,
cream of mussel soup with a hint of saffron, steamed Irish scallops on a
bed of spinach, to name but a few. There are plenty of meat dishes, and
a separate dessert menu. Concise, reasonably priced wine list.

CASTLEDERMOT   Kilkea Castle

Kilkea, Castledermot, Co Kildare
Tel: (0503) 45156   *Fax:* (0503) 45187   **£60**
Open: lunch & dinner daily (closed 25 Dec)
Meals served: lunch 12.30-2.30, dinner 7-9.30

Reputedly the oldest inhabited castle in Ireland, Kilkea comes complete with ghost, and there are constant reminders of the history of the place—in the logo (which includes the date of origination, 1180); and in references to Hugh de Lacy (by whom it was built)—the dining room is named after him, so is the continental breakfast! Hospitality is paramount here—no request is too great or too small for them to accommodate, and Shana Cassidy instills this message into her young staff from Day One (the more mature staff members already know and adhere to her principles). Luxurious bedrooms each have a splendid view of gardens or countryside, and all are very well maintained. There are sports facilities galore, and a high standard of cooking to complement all other aspects of the Kilkea experience. Executive Chef George Smith offers well balanced menus with plenty of choice, using good local ingredients to their full potential. Try fresh Rossmore mussels steamed with garlic and shallots and finished with cream, loin of Wicklow venison pan-fried with garden herbs, carved over rösti potatoes and served with a poached pear, and chilled lemon parfait served with lime sauce and apple pearls. Some of the dessert combinations are frankly adventurous and ingenious—try for instance a duo of chocolate mousses set in a timbale and served with fresh English mustard; or home-made curry ice cream served with a shortbread biscuit! Even at breakfast you can be sure of something slightly different—roulade of smoked salmon with a hint of lemon placed on toasted muffins alongside the more traditional home-made potato scones with poached eggs. All in all, a gem of a place—see you there!

CASTLETOWNSHEND   Mary Ann's

Castletownshend, Nr Skibbereen, Co Cork
Tel: (028) 36146   *Fax:* (028) 36377   **£50**
Open: dinner Mon-Sat (closed Mon in winter)
Meals served: lunch winter Sun only 12.30-2.30, dinner 6.30-10,
    (light meals: bar open lunch & dinner daily)

Another of the oldest pubs in Ireland, this building dates from the early 17th century but celebrated 150 years in the hospitality business in 1994. A simple menu offers the likes of crab cocktail, chicken liver and herb pâté, scallops Mary Ann, chicken kiev, home-made puds, sandwiches and toasties.

CLIFDEN   O'Grady's Seafood Restaurant
Market Street, Clifden, Co Galway
Tel: (095) 21450   **£50**
Open: lunch & dinner daily (closed mid Nov-end Feb)
Meals served: lunch 12.30-2.30, dinner 6.30-10
Highly popular seafood restaurant specialising in bistro-style presentations, predominantly of good local seafood but with some meat dishes. In the same family for over 25 years.

COLLOONEY	Glebe House

Collooney, Co Sligo
Tel: (071) 67787 **£40**
Open: lunch by arrangment, dinner daily (closed 2 wks Jan)
Meals served: dinner 6.30-9.30

Marc and Brid Torrades rescued this country house from dereliction and are still refurbishing it. Brid takes charge in the kitchen, offering some excellent cooking based on local produce. Home-made soups and sorbets feature among starters with the likes of smoked salmon and dill in puff pastry; main courses offer various steaks, the day's Atlantic catch and dishes such as braised duck breast Grand Marnier or baked breast of chicken with smoked bacon and hollandaise sauce. Accommodation consists at present of four spacious rooms, all ensuite, two with baths.

CONG	Ashford Castle

Cong, Co Mayo
Tel: (092) 46003   *Fax:* (092) 46260 **£90**
Connaught Room:
Open: dinner daily
Meals served: dinner 7-9.30
George V Room:
Open: lunch & dinner daily
Meals served: lunch 1-2.15, dinner 7-9.30

Formal parkland—350 acres of it—on the shores of Lough Corrib form the setting for one of the country's grandest hotels, once the home of the Guinness family. The history of the castle dates back to the 13th century, and is well documented by photos and written material displayed throughout the hotel. The central building is a French-style chateau which incorporates the earlier  medieval castle. This is formal, traditional hospitality at its best. Rich panelling, intricate carving, fine antiques, chandeliers and suits of armour create a sense of grand exclusivity, and every luxury imaginable is on hand. The surrounding lakes offer plenty of choice to the angler, and 27,000 acres of shooting rights make this one of Europe's premier shoots. There's also a purpose-built equestrian centre 350 yards from the hotel. There are two restaurants: the dinner-only Connaught Room, serving a classic French repertoire; and the George V dining room where the emphasis is on Continental dishes and traditional specialities. The Connaught Room is part of the original Georgian house built by the Oranmore-Browne family in 1715. (The Oranmore-Brownes were the most powerful family in the county in their time and the house was built for entertainment purposes and sporting parties.) The larger George V Room offers a five-course set menu of imaginative, well-executed dishes. Excellent service throughout.

CORK   Arbutus Lodge

Montenotte, Cork, Co Cork
Tel: (021) 501237   *Fax:* (021) 502893   **£50**
Open: lunch & dinner Mon-Sat (closed 1 wk Xmas)
Meals served: lunch 1-2, dinner 7-9.30

Considered to be one of Ireland's finest establishments, Arbutus looks down over its terraced gardens to the city below. During the day, there are views of the River Lee and hills surrounding Cork; at night you can see the city lights. Arbutus, once the home of the Lord Mayor of Cork, gets its name from the Arbutus tree in the garden, which has won awards from the Irish Tourist Board for most outstanding hotel garden of the year. Indoors, it is a family affair, with the Ryans' private art collection a striking feature throughout. Declan Ryan, together with young Helen Ward, head the kitchen team to produce a mix of Irish and French cooking with imaginative use of local and home-grown produce from the garden. Galway oysters or grilled scallops with chervil or tarragon are typical starters; followed by the likes of salmis of roast pheasant, monkfish with mussels and saffron, or escalope of salmon with Japanese ginger and mangetout purée. Tempting desserts and excellent wines, including award-winning German section and some great old clarets and burgundies. Plenty of choice from a range of menus, including a seven-course tasting menu available to parties. 19 bedrooms, many of which have been considerably upgraded over the last year.

CORK   Bully's

40 Paul Street, Cork, Co Cork
Tel: (021) 273555   *Fax:* (021) 273427   **£45**
Open: all day daily (closed 25 & 26 Dec, Good Friday)
Meals served: 12-11.30

Pizzas with a difference are the mainstay here, the difference being that they are cooked in a special wood-burning stove which imparts a unique and delicious flavour. This almost certainly comes from the fuel—offcuts of (primarily) teak and beech provided by a local furniture maker. The toppings are slightly offbeat, too—try tomatoes, mozzarella, ham, sausage—and white and black pudding! Pasta is freshly made, steaks are charcoal-grilled, excellent local seafood is very reasonably priced, and the atmosphere is one of happy people having a fun time. Go and join them!

CORK   Clifford's

18 Dyke Parade, Cork, Co Cork
Tel: (021) 275333   **£65**
Open: lunch Tue-Fri, dinner Mon-Sat (closed Bank
    Holidays, 2 wks Aug)
Meals served: lunch 12.30-2.30, dinner 7.30-10.30

Housed in a former library building, now transformed with minimalist
decor and owners Michael and Deirdre Clifford's collection of Irish art,
this is one of the best restaurants in the city—first-class service and
creative cooking by Michael. Menus change regularly, using local
organic produce wherever possible. A typical menu might feature
tortellini of Irish smoked fish or Clonakilty black pudding in filo pastry
with Calvados-scented sauce among starters. Main courses might
include farmyard chicken filled with Irish milleens cheese mousse
flavoured with mushrooms; pan-fried monkfish with mussels; or tarragon and shallot-flavoured beef fillet served in a Beaujolais sauce.
Menus are set, both at lunch and dinner, offering a choice of four
options at each stage.

CORK   Crawford Gallery Café

Emmet Place, Cork, Co Cork
Tel: (021) 274415   **£45**
Open: lunch Mon-Sat, dinner Wed-Fri (closed Bank Holidays,
    2 wks Xmas)
Meals served: lunch 12-2.30, dinner 6.30-9.30

Renowned Ballymaloe House at Shanagarry has a strong hand in
affairs at this city gallery café next to the Opera House. The restaurant
uses fresh fish from Ballycotton (landed the previous night on the
pier), free-range meat and vegetables grown mostly on the Ballymaloe
farm. Lunchtime offers a select range of light snacks and hot meals.
Spinach and mushroom pancake, delicious little vegetable tarts and les
tartines, a selection of open brown and white sandwiches. Main
courses will feature the day's fish special, along with the likes of
casseroles and pies. Dinner is a little more sophisticated, with
bruschetta, Ballymaloe cheese fondue and Madhur Jaffrey's shish
kebabs or roast duck more typical. Open for breakfast, with free-range
eggs, Clonakilty black pudding, speciality sausages and crispy bacon
and maple pancakes among the early-morning offerings. Closes at
11pm prompt, when gallery security staff finish duty, hence the earlier
last orders time.

CORK — Flemings

Silver Grange House, Tivoli, Cork, Co Cork
Tel: (021) 821621   *Fax:* (021) 821800   **£45**
Open: lunch & dinner daily (closed 24-26 Dec, Good Friday)
Meals served: lunch 12.30-2.30, dinner 6.30-11

Large Georgian family house set in five acres of lovely gardens, which
include a kitchen garden that supplies chef Michael Fleming with all
the basics for his French culinary repertoire. The restaurant is on the
formal side, with smart, well-dressed waiters, upholstered chairs and
marble fireplaces providing a suitable setting. Pan-fried duck liver from
Riberac, lightly poached oysters, lobster bisque, rich venison stew,
seafood symphony with chive sauce and crème caramel en cage are
typical. Finish with coffee and petits fours. Spacious overnight accommodation is provided, with four ensuite room furnished in keeping with
the style of the house.

CORK — Isaacs

48 MacCurtain Street, Cork, Co Cork
Tel: (021) 503805   **£40**
Open: lunch Mon-Sat, dinner daily (closed 3 days Xmas)
Meals served: lunch 12-2.30, dinner 6.30-10.30 (Sun to 9)

Canice Sharkey offers simple, straightforward à la carte menus at this
handsome restaurant in a converted 18th-century warehouse. The
menus are eclectic, with lunchtime offerings including light snacks
(Mediterranean sandwich, char-grilled burger and fries) and tasty hot
dishes such as beef casserole or chicken and leek pie. Similar items
feature in the evening, along with more interesting fare: pheasant and
potato tart (served both as a main course or starter); Indian lamb curry;
salmon and potato cakes with sauce tartare; sirloin steak with rosemary
and garlic potatoes—good home cooking with flair. Interesting
desserts—Sauternes and olive oil cake with winter fruit salad,
caramelised oranges with Greek yoghurt, open French tart with crème
anglaise; and good vegetarian choices (black-eyed bean stew; home-
made fettucine with mushrooms, garlic and spinach). Daily blackboard
specials add further spice.

CORK   Ivory Tower Restaurant

35 Princes Street, Cork, Co Cork
Tel: (021) 274665   **£35**
Open: lunch Mon-Sat, dinner Wed-Sat
Meals served: lunch 12-4, dinner 6.30-11

Informal city-centre restaurant off one of the main shopping streets.
Bare floorboards, unclothed tables and the work of local artists on the
walls creates a simple rustic-style setting in this first-floor restaurant
housed in an old office building. The menu shows a keen eye on
modernity, with some unusual elements on a truly eclectic menu which
runs from sushi of the evening and goat's cheese fritters to braised
pheasant with chestnut mousse and peppered shark with ratatouille.
Chef-patron Seamus O'Connell's robust, individual style extends to vegetarian dishes on the menu: vermicelli tart baked in herb ricotta
cheese; sun-dried tomatoes stuffed with risotto and served on a yellow
pepper and cumin coulis. The "sweet things" are no less unusual:
banana stir-fry with Mexican rice pudding and mango, and saffron and
strawberry crème brûlée are typical. A no-choice set menu in the
evening (varying in price from as little as £13, rising to around £17)
offers good value, and lunchtime offers a less sophisticated choice
which might include risotto burgers, Irish stew, Swedish-style marinated herrings and osso buco.

CORK   Jacques

9 Phoenix Street, Cork, Co Cork
Tel: (021) 277387   *Fax:* (021) 270634   **£50**
Open: lunch Mon-Sat, dinner Tue-Sat
    (closed Bank Holidays, 10 days Xmas)
Meals served: lunch 12-4, dinner 6-10.30

Changes here in 1994—a new wooden floor for the downstairs room
which is now table service rather than self. Removal of the bar and
booths means more space, but happily the food remains the same—
and it's on the food that Eithne Barry has built up a good local reputation. Bistro-style dishes such as fishcakes with salsa verde, lamb's
kidneys dijonnaise, roast duck or monkfish in a beurre blanc sauce typify the range. White chocolate mousse with blackcurrant coulis is a
popular dessert. Modest wine list with good New World representation.

CORK   Michael's Bistro

4 Mardyke Street, Cork, Co Cork
Tel: (021) 276887   **£35**
Open: lunch & dinner Mon-Sat (closed Bank Holidays, 2 wks Aug)
Meals served: lunch 12-3.30, dinner 6-10.30

Michael Clifford's new venture, smaller sister to Clifford's main restaurant next door, has only been open a short time but is pulling the
crowds in to enjoy a concise menu of well cooked and presented
dishes. Try warm salad of Clonakilty black pudding with glazed apples,
potato and crab cakes served with garden greens and a parsley cream
sauce, and fresh fruit pastry tartlets to finish.

CORK	Morrisons Island Hotel

Morrisons Quay, Cork, Co Cork
Tel: (021) 275858   *Fax:* (021) 275833   **£50**
Open: lunch & dinner daily (closed 1 wk Xmas)
Meals served: lunch 12.30-2, dinner 6-9.30
Cork's first all-suite hotel (40 of them) at the heart of the business community, overlooking the River Lee. Stylish, with river and city views.

CORK   O'Keeffe's

23 Washington Street West, Cork, Co Cork
Tel: (021) 275645   **£55**
Open: dinner Mon-Sat (closed Bank Holidays, 10 days Xmas)
Meals served: lunch by arrangement, dinner 6.30-10.30

The menu at Tony and Marie O'Keeffe's welcoming little restaurant depends mainly on local seasonal produce; the cooking however looks further afield, with wide-ranging influences. Pig's trotter stuffed with a white pudding mousse, then rolled in breadcrumbs, or quenelles of sole with a Martini sauce might feature among starters. Main courses range from lemon chicken hollandaise or sirloin with Roquefort sauce, to tripe and onions with fried polenta or Chinese pancake with barbecued vegetables. The menu changes monthly and portions are generous.

CORK	Rochestown Park Hotel

Rochestown Road, Douglas, Cork, Co Cork
Tel: (021) 892233   *Fax:* (021) 892178   **£45**
Open: lunch & dinner daily (closed 25 Dec)
Meals served: lunch 12.30-2.30, dinner 7-10
63-bedroomed Georgian house close to the airport and ferry port, a former seminary and home to the Lord Mayors of Cork. Lovely gardens, good leisure and conference facilities.

DINGLE   Beginish Restaurant

Green Street, Dingle, Co Kerry
Tel: (066) 51588   *Fax:* (066) 51591   **£45**
Open: lunch & dinner Tue-Sun (closed mid Nov-Mar)
Meals served: lunch 12.30-2.15, dinner 6-9.30

Whatever is fresh and available at the time is the driving force behind Pat Moore's menu. The day's catch reveals all. Preparations vary, depending on her inspiration, and the results on the plate are more than a little skilful. Pat cooks with confidence and a keen eye on trends. Seafood is a major feature, with old-fashioned fish chowder appearing throughout the day. Start perhaps with half a dozen oysters au naturel or Dingle Bay prawns with spicy mayonnaise, before dishes such as black sole meunière, beef fillet with rösti, cognac and peppercorn sauce, or vegetarian pot-pourri in filo pastry. The restaurant—two lofty rooms with a small conservatory looking out on to the garden at the rear—takes its name from one of the Blasket islands.

DINGLE	Doyle's Seafood Bar

4 John Street, Dingle, Co Kerry
Tel: (066) 51174   *Fax:* (066) 51816   **£45**
Open: dinner Mon-Sat (closed mid Nov-mid Mar)
Meals served: dinner 6-9

The Dingle boats keep supplies ever-fresh at this unassuming, local restaurant, where flagstone floors and simple wooden tables and chairs create a homely, characterful setting. Lobster is the speciality, chosen

■ **Stella and John Doyle**

from the tank in the bar. Menus are made up on a daily basis depending on the local catch. Start perhaps with a millefeuille of warm oysters served with Guinness sauce or hot trout smokies, followed by lemon sole with scallop sauce, or a seafood quintet served with a light herb sauce. An early evening menu (6-7pm) offers excellent value, though limited choice. The cooking is straightforward, allowing natural flavours to come through as much as possible. Stay overnight in one of the eight stylish rooms to enjoy a wonderful breakfast, too.

DINGLE	Half Door

John Street, Dingle, Co Kerry
Tel: (066) 51600   *Fax:* (066) 51206   **£50**
Open: lunch & dinner Wed-Mon (closed Halloween-2nd wk Dec,
    early Jan-Easter)
Meals served: lunch 12.30-2.30, dinner 6-10

Seafood of course—given the location—is the thing to eat here, and it's as good as it has ever been. An extensive range of mussels, scallops, oysters, brill, salmon, plaice, John Dory, monkfish and crab—to name but a few—is available, cooked simply and presented with style. Irish farmhouse cheeses complete the picture. Good list of predominantly white wines.

DINGLE	Lord Baker's Bar & Restaurant

Main Street, Dingle, Co Kerry
Tel: (066) 51277   **£45**
Open: lunch & dinner daily (closed 25 Dec)
Meals served: lunch 12.30-2.30, dinner 6-10

Reputedly the oldest pub in Dingle, this place is atmospheric from the open log fires and pinewood floors through to displays of locally-made tapestries and pottery. Food is local and traditional—Dingle Bay prawn cocktail, wild Dingle Bay smoked salmon, seafood mornay, grilled salmon steak. As the menu says—in Gaelic—enjoy your meal.

DUBLIN   Blooms Hotel

Anglesea Street, Dublin, Co Dublin, 2
Tel: (01) 671 5622   *Fax:* (01) 671 5997   **£55**
Open: lunch Mon-Fri, dinner daily (closed 24-26 Dec)
Meals served: lunch 12.30-2, dinner 5-9.45

Leopold Bloom from James Joyce's Ulysses is the source of the name
of this 86-bedroomed hotel close to Trinity College and the Castle in
the trendy Temple Bar area of town. It's a modern, practical hotel, with
facilities which include a nightclub and pubby bar. Bedrooms are well-
kept and enjoy the benefits of triple-glazing and good bathrooms.
Complimentary wine and a newspaper are provided in the rooms. The
new restaurant offers dishes to suit the mood of the area: terrines,
char-grilled Irish heifer steaks, poached salmon.

DUBLIN   Chapter One

18/19 Parnell Square, Dublin, Co Dublin, 1
Tel: (01) 873 2266   *Fax:* (01) 873 2330   **£70**
Open: lunch Tue-Fri, dinner Tue-Sat
    (closed Bank Holidays, 1 wk Xmas)
Meals served: lunch 12-2.30, dinner 5.45-11

Situated in a basement cellar, beneath the
Dublin Writers' Museum, Chapter One offers
plenty of character with its vaults, arches, old
stone walls and scattered busts and paintings of
famous writers. For those who want more than
the all-day museum café fare, this is something
of a gem, given its location. A writer's dream:
write, work, take a few paces, turn the corner,
and bingo! Food, deliciously prepared and presented, enough to distract even the most preoc-
cupied of minds. Take a break from that *Ulysses*
research and enjoy a warm salad of calf's liver
with tender strips of bacon, poached quenelles of
fish, or blinis—the overall bias looks to the

North, to Scandinavia and Russia. Try poached rainbow trout with a
light cheesy sauce or tender slices of pork fillet served with potato cake
and a red wine and soy sauce. Grand-styled desserts.

DUBLIN   Commons Restaurant

Newman House, 85-86 St Stephen's Green, Dublin, Co Dublin, 2
Tel: (01) 475 2597   *Fax:* (01) 478 0551   **£70**
Open: lunch Mon-Fri, dinner Mon-Sat (closed Bank Holidays)
Meals served: lunch 12.30-2.15, dinner 7-10

The first home of University College Dublin, Newman House, forms
the setting for this elegant basement restaurant which opens out on to
a large courtyard at the rear, with some five acres of gardens spreading
out before it. Newman House (two of the city's finest town houses) represents the peak of Irish Palladian and Rococo design, and among the
distinguished writers who studied here were James Joyce, Flann
O'Brien and Gerard Manley Hopkins. Cooking is now in the hands of
former sous chef, Michael Bolster, who took over just as we went to
press.

DUBLIN   Hotel Conrad

Earlsfort Terrace, Dublin 8
Tel: (01) 676 5555   *Fax:* (01) 676 5424   **£80**
Open: lunch Mon-Fri, dinner Mon-Sat (closed Bank Holidays)
Meals served: lunch 12.30-3, dinner 6.30-11

The Hotel Conrad is ideally located to enjoy the best of what Dublin
has to offer – opposite the National Concert Hall, just around the corner from the beautiful gardens and fountains in St Stephen's Green and
a few minutes from the main commercial, shopping and cultural centres. Top-of-the-range business facilities, two well-appointed restaurants
(the more formal Alexandra and the brasserie-style Plurabelle) and its
own traditional pub (Alfie Byrne's) all help to make this modern,
191-bedroomed hotel a comfortable place to stay.

DUBLIN   Cooke's Café

14 South William Street, Dublin, Co Dublin, 2
Tel: (01) 679 0536   *Fax:* (01) 679 0546   **£50**
Open: lunch & dinner daily (closed Bank Holidays)
Meals served: lunch 12.30-4, dinner 6-11 (Fri & Sat to 11.30,
    Sun to 9.30), (light meals 8am-12 midnight May-Sep)

John Cooke's café-cum-restaurant is rather more elegant than the
name suggests. The style of cooking is modern, with a bias towards
Italian influences. Starters might include Beluga caviar, steamed mussels, Caesar salad, bruschetta and warm duck salad with tomato concassé and sherry vinaigrette; main courses include the likes of sautéed
veal liver, baked lobster with herb butter sauce, and Madeira-sauced
roast widgeon. Plenty of choice—about a dozen or so dishes at each
stage. The pre-theatre menu (£12.95) offers great value.

DUBLIN   Le Coq Hardi

35 Pembroke Road, Ballsbridge, Dublin, Co Dublin, 4
Tel: (01) 668 9070   *Fax:* (01) 668 9887   **£65**
Open: lunch Mon-Fri, dinner Mon-Sat (closed Bank Holidays,
    1 wk Xmas, 2 wks Aug)   ✿
Meals served: lunch 12-2.30, dinner 7-11

Long-established, classic French restaurant, with appropriately ornate
decor and immaculate settings. Chef-patron John Howard, pictured
with wife Catherine, makes the most of local produce on seasonal

menus in this end-of-terrace Georgian house. The
menu is based on classic French traditions, with
Irish and Mediterranean influences now coming
through quite strongly. Typical starters might
include a gateau of fresh white crabmeat with
lemon butter and fresh herb sauce; Clonakilty
black and white pudding, with colcannon potato
cake and apple; game soup with chestnuts and
port; or fresh Galway oysters. Main courses might include steamed
skate wing with nut-brown butter and hazelnuts, carved venison steak
Diane with braised red cabbage, or fresh Howth lobster with a tarragon
butter sauce. Good desserts followed by Irish farmhouse and French
cheeses. Connoisseur's wine list.

DUBLIN **Davenport HoteL**

Merrion Square, Dublin, Co Dublin, 2
Tel: (01) 661 6799   *Fax:* (01) 661 5663   **£45**
Open: lunch Sun-Fri, dinner daily
Meals served: lunch 12.30-2.30, dinner 5.30-10.45
City-centre hotel of graceful proportions with excellent leisure facilities.
Restaurants and suites are named after famous Irish architects.

DUBLIN L'Ecrivain

112 Lower Baggot Street, Dublin, Co Dublin, 2
Tel: (01) 661 1919   **£50**
Open: lunch Mon-Fri, dinner Mon-Sat
Meals served: lunch 12.30-2, dinner 6.30-11

Pictures of famous Irish writers, the work of local artist Liam O'Neill, adorn the terracotta-coloured walls of this little basement restaurant. Chef-patron Derry Clarke's French-inspired menus offer ample choice, with seasonal vegetarian and à la carte menus supplemented daily by set menus. At front of house, Sally Anne Clarke and her team welcome diners into a tiny reception lounge. Typical dishes range from starters such as gallantine of chicken with a citrus fruit glaze or warm smoked salmon blinis to prawn bisque with cognac or west coast mussel broth. Main-course selections might include rack of Wicklow lamb with onion marmalade and its own jus, steamed fillet of codling with prawn and saffron sauce, or salmon served with red peppers and pine nuts. Check out the Irish farmhouse cheeses, or opt for a classic flambée dessert.

DUBLIN Grey Door

22 Upper Pembroke Street, Dublin, Co Dublin, 2
Tel: (01) 676 3286   *Fax:* (01) 676 3287   **£40**
Open: lunch Mon-Fri, dinner Mon-Sat (closed Bank Holidays)
Meals served: lunch 12.30-2.15, dinner 7-11 (Bistro 6-11.30)

This well-established, cosy, pretty restaurant, decorated in classic grey and lemon, is housed in a Georgian terrace south of the city. Dinner is à la carte, with Russian-influenced dishes strong on the menu, and vodka also playing a part. Fish, shellfish and game are the mainstays. Simpler set menus take over at lunchtime and the basement bistro, Blushers, offers a lighter evening choice. There are also seven finely furnished bedrooms for overnight guests and an elegant drawing room for the use of residents.

DUBLIN Hibernian Hotel

Eastmoreland Place, Ballsbridge, Dublin, Co Dublin, 4
Tel: (01) 668 7666   *Fax:* (01) 660 2655   **£50**
Open: lunch Sun-Fri, dinner daily (closed Xmas, Good Friday)
Meals served: lunch 12.30-2.30, dinner 6.30-10.30 (Fri & Sat to 11)

City-centre, turn-of-the-century hotel in the townhouse style, with 30 individually designed bedrooms offering all modern amenities in an atmosphere of older-world charm. Both business and leisure needs are amply accommodated. Classic European dishes on a concise menu are in keeping with the overall ambience, just like the wine list.

DUBLIN	Kapriol

---

45 Lower Camden Street, Dublin, Co Dublin, 2
Tel: (01) 475 1235 **£55**
Open: dinner Mon-Sat (closed Bank Holidays, 2 wks Aug)
Meals served: dinner only 7.30-12

Long-standing Dublin restaurant where the prices have actually gone down slightly of late! Traditional Italian is the style here, with the menu reassuringly unchanged, to the relief of regulars. All pastas and desserts are home made. Stracciatella, bruschetta toscana, risotto alla calamari and pheasant alla cacciatora are all perennial favourites.

DUBLIN	Lobster Pot

---

9 Ballsbridge Terrace, Dublin, Co Dublin, 4
Tel: (01) 668 0025 **£55**
Open: lunch Mon-Fri, dinner Mon-Sat
(closed Bank Holidays, 1 wk Xmas)
Meals served: lunch 12.30-2.30, dinner 6.30-10.30

Longstanding, traditional restaurant specialising in fish. Cooking is straightforward and simple, with salmon and turbot offered grilled or poached, sole and plaice grilled on the bone, and many classic favourites featured. Dressed Kilmore crab, prawn bisque, Galway Bay oysters, goujons of sole and soused herring are amongst the starters. Main courses include lobster, monkfish Thermidor and plenty of choice for meat-eaters: from coq au vin or veal Holstein to roasts (duckling au Grand Marnier) and grills (lamb cutlets Nelson), with a wide choice of steak options. Simple, straightforward desserts follow. The restaurant is situated on the first-floor and has a cosy and relaxed ambience.

DUBLIN	Longfield's Hotel

Fitzwilliam Street Lower, Dublin, Co Dublin
Tel: (01) 676 1367   *Fax:* (01) 676 1542 **£40**
Open: lunch Mon-Fri, dinner daily (closed 24 Dec-3 Jan, lunch only Bank Holidays)
Meals served: lunch 12.30-2.30, dinner 6.30-10
A 28-bedroomed, Georgian-style hotel with traditional period furnishing. Irish breakfasts include potato cakes and brown and white pudding. The No. 10 Restaurant offers both à la carte and fixed-price lunch and dinner menus.

DUBLIN	Old Dublin Restaurant

90-91 Francis Street, Dublin, Co Dublin, 8
Tel: (01) 454 2028   *Fax:* (01) 454 1406 **£50**
Open: lunch Mon-Fri, dinner Mon-Sat (closed Bank Holidays)
Meals served: lunch 12.30-2.30, dinner 6-11

Table d'hôte lunch and set dinner menus form the basis of Eamonn Walsh and Nuala Dalton's success at this ground-floor restaurant comprising a series of inter-connecting rooms. The surprise, though, is in the number of Russian and Scandinavian dishes that crop up on Eamonn's menu—gravadlax, blinis, koulibiac, pelmeni, zakuski, piroshki, as well as Georgian lamb kebabs, darne of salmon with a mustard sauce, or warm smoked sea trout with essence of tomato and shallot and a basil-flavoured olive oil. Accompaniments like kasha and sticky pastries for dessert continue the theme. Dublin's answer to London's Gay Hussar?

DUBLIN — Patrick Guilbaud

46 James Place, Off Lower Baggot Street, Dublin, Co Dublin, 2
Tel: (01) 676 4192   *Fax:* (01) 660 1546   **£55**
Open: lunch & dinner Tue-Sat (closed Bank Holidays)
Meals served: lunch 12.30-2, dinner 7.30-10.15

Patrick Guilbaud's purpose-built restaurant has been the place to enjoy classic French cuisine since it opened here over a decade ago. Smart staff, lots of lush greenery and a plant-filled atrium provide an elegant setting for chef Guillaume Le Brun and his team's light, inspired approach. A number of menus (table d'hôte, à la carte and menu surprise) offer plenty of choice with starters which range from warm chicken wing salad with fresh basil or hot lobster tart to gigot-style boned quail perfumed with different spices. Main courses might provide casserole of sole and Dublin prawns, pan-fried turbot with Noilly Prat and tarragon sauce, fillet of beef in Syrah wine with marrow or grilled breast of chicken with raisins and couscous. All is just as it should be, down to the excellent French cheeseboard and wine list.

A delightful restaurant, well deserving of its long-standing success.

DUBLIN — Roly's Bistro

7 Ballsbridge Terrace, Dublin, Co Dublin, 4
Tel: (01) 668 2611   *Fax:* (01) 660 8535   **£35**
Open: lunch Sun-Fri, dinner daily   *A cut above the rest.*
   (closed 25 & 26 Dec, Good Friday)
Meals served: lunch 12-3, dinner 6-10 (Sun to 9)

An eclectic menu which takes its inspiration from just about anywhere and everywhere. Good breads supplied from the bakery next door (same ownership) give it an advantage over many in this class. Starters range from wild garlic mussels or carrot and caraway soup to Clonakilty black pudding and deep-fried brie. Main courses might include Cajun chicken breast with apple and raisin relish, rack of lamb with tarragon and mint sauce, grilled black sole on-the-bone with a crab and ginger sauce or grilled fillet of beef served with a cracked pepper Burgundy sauce. Lively and popular on both ground and first floors, with excellent value for money including the wine list.

■Colin O'Daly
Chef

DUBLIN Shelbourne Hotel

St Stephen's Green, Dublin, Co Dublin, 2
Tel: (01) 676 6471   *Fax:* (01) 661 6006   **£50**
Open: lunch & dinner daily
Meals served: lunch 12.30-2.30, dinner 6-10.30, Sun 6-10

Forte Grand's Shelbourne is certainly a brand leader. Steeped in history (the Irish Constitution was drafted here in 1922) and as famous in fiction (Joyce's Ulysses includes a reference) as in fact, its Georgian proportions have a timeless quality. Bedrooms and lounges maintain the atmosphere, whilst adding up-to-the minute technology and comforts. There's a good choice of eating, from full meals in the dining room to light meals in one of the bars, or—a Dublin tradition—afternoon tea in the Lord Mayor's Lounge.

DUBLIN La Stampa

35 Dawson Street, Dublin, Co Dublin, 2
Tel: (01) 677 8611   *Fax:* (01) 677 3336   **£40**
Open: lunch & dinner Mon-Fri
    (closed 2 days Xmas, Good Friday)
Meals served: lunch 12.30-2.30, dinner 6.30-11.30

Chef Paul Flynn spent several years working in top London restaurants, including a spell as head chef at Simply Nico, before coming to this lively, bustling, and highly stylish restaurant, complete with mirrors, pre-Raphaelite etchings, granite horse heads and large displays of fruit and flowers. The room is high and spacious, which lends a comfortable air amidst all the noise and bustle. Decent food at fair prices is the successful formula; this is hearty modern cooking which takes its lead from the sun: lots of Mediterranean ingredients and a well-planned menu with plenty of variety. Start perhaps with beef carpaccio with crispy leeks, French onion soup with Gruyère soufflé or bruschetta of wild mushroom and mozzarella; move on to dishes such as osso buco with rosemary-scented vegetables, spicy brill with creamed leeks, or Chinese-style chicken which has been coated in a blend of red peppers, pan-fried and served with noodles and oyster sauce. Lovely desserts—from tiramisu to strawberries and shortbread with marscapone cheese.

DUBLIN — Stephen's Hall Hotel

14-17 Lower Leeson Street, Dublin, Co Dublin, 2
Tel: (01) 661 0585   *Fax:* (01) 661 0606
The Terrace Bistro: **£35**
Open: lunch Mon-Fri, dinner Mon-Sat (closed 1 wk Xmas)
Meals served: lunch 12.15-2.30, dinner 6.15-9.30
The Terrace Restaurant: **£60**
Open: lunch Mon-Fri, dinner Mon-Sat (closed 1 wk Xmas)
Meals served: lunch 12.15-2.30, dinner 6.15-9.30

Dublin's first all-suite hotel is centrally located and thus popular with both business and leisure visitors. Well-maintained rooms are stylishly decorated and offer not only a full 24-hour room service but also a shopping service for guests who, taking advantage of having a kitchen, wish to cook for themselves. A third option, of course, is to eat in the airy Terrace Bistro where you can have an excellently priced menu of the day (only £14.50 for four courses plus coffee!) or choose from the carte, which is just as fairly priced. Try spinach and smoked bacon salad with avocado and sour cream, traditional braised rabbit with winter vegetables and thyme, and a selection of desserts or Irish cheeses. The Terrace Restaurant has slightly more sophisticated dishes at slightly higher prices.

DUBLIN — The Westbury

Off Grafton Street, Dublin, Co Dublin, 2
Tel: (01) 679 1122   Fax: (01) 679 7078   **£65**
Open: lunch & dinner daily
Meals served: lunch 12.30-2.30, dinner 6.30-10.30 (Sun to 9.30)

At the heart of Dublin's cosmopolitan centre, a short walk from many of the city's cultural landmarks, the 203-bedroomed Westbury is ideally placed for the visitor and offers excellent facilities, from leisure and shopping (its own mall) to boardroom and conference. The richly elegant interior includes a terrace bar and lively "Joycean" seafood bar decorated with stained glass and rich wood panelling. The Russell Room offers a more or less traditional repertoire, which includes grills and plenty of seafood, followed by soufflés and crepes Suzette flambées.

DUN LAOGHAIRE — De Selby's

17/18 Patrick Street, Dun Laoghaire, Co Dublin
Tel: (01) 284 1761   *Fax:* (01) 284 1762   **£30**
Open: dinner daily (closed 3 days Xmas, 3 days Easter)
Meals served: dinner 5.30-11, (all day Sun & Bank Holidays 12-10)

Popular with families, De Selby's is a no-nonsense, informal restaurant with an eclectic choice of dishes, which range from rack of lamb with mint sauce to Mexican tacos, beef stroganoff, burgers, steaks, and fresh fish—something of a speciality—fresh poached or grilled salmon, fish mixed grill, Dublin Bay scampi with tartare sauce. House specials feature traditional Irish stew and De Selby's boiled bacon and cabbage. The restaurant also has an outdoor dining area.

DUNDALK   Cellars Restaurant

Backhouse Centre, Clanbrassil Street, Dundalk, Co Louth
Tel: (042) 33745   **£15**
Open: lunch Mon-Fri (closed Bank Holidays)
Meals served: lunch 12.15-2

The menu changes daily at Alison and George O'Shea's little, lunch-only restaurant which features an extensive salad bar to complement the daily offerings. Roast leg of lamb, grilled mackerel in mustard sauce, pork-fried rice in a curry sauce, hamburger lyonnaise, smoked cod au gratin are typical. Desserts, which some say are to die for, are all home-made by Alison. Prices are exceptionally good-value and the atmosphere is relaxed and friendly.

DUNDERRY   Dunderry Lodge Restaurant

Dunderry, Navan, Co Meath
Tel: (046) 31671   **£35**
Open: lunch Sun, dinner Tue-Sat
    (closed Bank Holidays, 1 wk Jan, 1 wk Aug)
Meals served: lunch Sun 12.30-2.30 (other days by arr), dinner 7-9.30

Country restaurant of some renown, housed in a characterful stone building. Chef-patron Paul Groves keeps on top of current modes with a style of cooking which incorporates contemporary trends with a classic base. Grilled game sausage on sweet and sour red cabbage is served as a starter with a juniper jus, along with the likes of ravioli of oysters on a light thyme sauce or pan-fried squid in olive oil served with pesto sauce. Soups are interesting, with a chervil-flavoured broth of various mush-rooms, and lightly curried cream soup of cockles and mussels being typical. Main courses might feature char-grilled beef on crisp potato galette with tapenade jus, fried wild mallard with creamed celeriac and Madeira sauce, or fillet of John Dory with a light sauce flavoured with star anise and sun-dried tomatoes. The choice is plentiful, with around ten dishes at each stage. Excellent value on the Sunday and set menus. Leave room for Dunderry's famed dessert trolley.

DUNKINEELY   Castle Murray House

Dunkineely, Co Donegal
Tel: (073) 37022   *Fax:* (073) 37330   **£40**
Open: dinner daily (closed 24 & 25 Dec, Mon & Tue
    Nov-Easter, 2 wks Feb)
Meals served: dinner 7-9.30

The location—on a clifftop—of this 10-bedroomed hotel and restaurant is truly stunning. Overlooking the castle ruins (after which it is named), this small hotel to the west of Donegal offers panoramic views of the rugged coastline. The long, stone-floored conservatory-style lounge where aperitifs are served and large dining room take full advantage of the position. Chef Thierry Delcros produces some excellent French cooking to much acclaim, with dishes such as mushroom tart, fish quenelles gratinées and profiteroles of crab and shrimps followed by lobster casserole with pasta, grilled black sole with lime, beef bourguignonne or lamb in mustard sauce. Classic French desserts. The table d'hôte menu offers plenty of choice, with main-course pricing determining the cost. Seafood gets full exposure during the summer. The hotel has ten spacious rooms, which are stylish but simple following recent refurbishment.

DUNWORLEY   Dunworley Cottage

Butlerstown, Clonakilty, Dunworley, Co Cork
Tel: (023) 40314   **£40**
Open: lunch & dinner Wed-Sun (closed Nov, Jan & Feb)
Meals served: lunch 1-3, dinner 6.30-10

Katherine Noren's delightful little restaurant combines excellent Irish produce (organic when possible) with Swedish flair and simplicity to produce good value, interesting menus. Although there's an increasing bias towards fish, the specialities here will surely go on—nettle soup and Clonakilty black-and-white pudding being the perennial favourites. The immaculately-maintained cottage is deservedly popular.

DURRUS   Blairs Cove House

Blairs Cove, Durrus, Nr Bantry, Co Cork
Tel: (027) 61127   **£55**
Open: lunch & dinner Tue-Sat (closed Nov-Feb, Mon Sep-Jun)
Meals served: dinner 7.30-9.30

Philippe and Sabine de Mey's restaurant is housed in the converted outbuildings of a Georgian manor house overlooking Dunmanus Bay. Family portraits, contemporary artwork, lovely views across the bay (or into the garden) a pianist and the smell of woodsmoke from the wood-fired grill in the restaurant create plenty of character. An immense buffet of mousses, pâtés, smoked meats and fruits de mer kicks a meal off to an exciting start. Main courses are written up on a blackboard; fresh locally caught fish and the finest Irish beef and lamb are prepared by Philippe at the huge grill at the end of the room. Desserts, laid out along with some excellent local cheeses on the grand piano are no less rewarding. A small apartment above the restaurant, approached via an outside stone staircase, is available for overnight guests. Feast, sleep, then wake to some magnificent sea views.

ENNISKERRY — Enniscree Lodge

Glencree Valley, Enniskerry, Co Wicklow
Tel: (01) 286 3542 *Fax:* (01) 286 6037 **£50**
Open: lunch & dinner daily (Fri-Sun Jan & Feb)
Meals served: lunch 12.30-2.30, dinner 7.30-9.30 (Sat to 10, Sun to 9)

Set in the splendid Glencreee Valley Enniscree Lodge enjoys wonderful views over the exotically-named Sugarloaf, Djouce, Tonduff and Kippure Mountains. There are only ten bedrooms in the Lodge, all individually decorated with antique pine furnishings. In the warm and welcoming dining room, the dinner menus are seasonally sound and locally based: Wicklow lamb, Enniscree seafood, Irish cheeses. There's a warm welcome and a family atmosphere—a useful base from which to explore this attractive area just south of Dublin.

FOULKSMILLS — Horetown House

Foulksmills, Co Wexford
Tel: (051) 63771 *Fax:* (051) 63633 **£35**
Open: lunch Sun, dinner Tue-Sat (closed 1 wk Xmas)
Meals served: lunch 12.30-2.30, dinner 7-9

The Young family's residential equestrian centre and dairy farm attracts great local interest. First and foremost, this is a place for holidays with horses: the stables date back more than 300 years. Residents have the choice of a robust farmhouse dinner or the cosy, but more formal Cellar Restaurant which does a thriving non-resident business too. Here, you can't help but enjoy the peace of the countryside and all it offers. Pop in for afternoon tea if nothing else.

FURBO — Connemara Coast Hotel

Furbo, Nr Galway, Co Galway
Tel: (091) 92108 *Fax:* (091) 92065 **£45**
Open: dinner daily (closed 25 Dec)
Meals served: dinner 6-10

Overlooking Galway Bay and the Aran Islands, this 112-bedroomed hotel enjoys a superb location just six miles from Galway city, with grounds which sweep right down to the bay. Accommodation ranges from standard rooms to executive suites, and the hotel boasts extensive leisure and conference facilities. Lounges are elegant yet warm in outlook and the Gallery restaurant offers both à la carte and fixed-price menus, with the emphasis on fresh local produce, particularly fish—ragout of monkfish Indonesian style; the Connemara Kettle (fresh seafood in a white wine and dill velouté); plus plenty of choice for carnivores—roast Connemara lamb with a port wine sauce; minute steak provençale-style.

GALWAY   Casey's Westwood Restaurant

Dangan, Upper Newcastle, Galway, Co Galway
Tel: (091) 21442   **£50**
Open: lunch & dinner daily (closed 3 days Xmas, Good Friday)
Meals served: lunch 12.30-2.15, dinner 6.30-10

John Casey and family have been satisfying customers at their popular local restaurant for over a decade. With plenty of choice to suit your mood, from an array of bars and restaurant areas, this is well worth a visit. Lunchtime offers a good fixed menu with plenty of choice: deep-fried fillet of plaice tartare; baked cod on a tomato compote; chicken breast stuffed with cheese and mango, served with home-made noodles and bacon sauce; or the daily roast. Dinner takes on a fancier, more sophisticated approach along similar lines, beginning in the cocktail lounge where orders are taken. Delightful desserts might include hot plum tart with warm cinnamon sauce or blackberry and blackcurrant délice with home-made fig and port ice cream.

GOLEEN HARBOUR   Herons Cove

Goleen Harbour, Co Cork
Tel: (028) 35225   *Fax:* (028) 35422   **£35**
Open: lunch & dinner daily (closed Oct-May)
Meals served: lunch 12-5, dinner 6.30-9.45

A family-run restaurant on the picturesque shores of Goleen Harbour. By day, it's informal, with simple decor and a menu to match: robust home-made soups, open sandwiches, seafood specials, sirloin steak, and afternoon teas. In the evening it is transformed into a sophisti-cated candlelit operation. Sue Hill makes the most of local produce: lobster and oysters come from the restaurant's own seawater tank and local trawlers from the Goleen fleet supply her with other fish and shellfish. The carte offers a wide choice, and is supplemented by a concise set menu with choices such as chunky seafood soup, poached salmon fillet with herb butter, sirloin with hot pepper sauce and breast of chicken with fresh oregano cream sauce. The set dinner menu offers excellent value and changes frequently. Accommodation is available in three en-suite rooms.

GOREY   Marlfield House

Gorey, Co Wexford, Gorey
Tel: (055) 21124   *Fax:* (055) 21572   **£80**
Open: lunch & dinner daily (closed Dec & Jan)
Meals served: lunch 12.30-2, dinner 7-9.30

A civilised and elegant house from which to explore the delights of this lovely area of Ireland. Much of the produce used in the kitchen is home grown, and fish and game is of local origin. The conservatory dining room is a delight and bedrooms are superb.

GREENCASTLE — Kealy's Seafood Bar

The Harbour, Greencastle, Co Donegal
Tel: (077) 81010   **£35**
Open: lunch & dinner Tue-Sun (closed 1 wk Mar, 1 wk Oct, 25
     Dec, Good Friday)
Meals served: lunch 12.30-5, dinner 7-9.30

Walk into another world, from the busy commercial quayside into
James and Tricia Kealey's sophisticated seafood bar and restaurant. At
lunchtime, there's a bistro-style menu—eat as much or as little as you
desire: Inishowen oysters au gratin, seafood platter, chowder, poached
fillet of turbot with Stilton, pan-fried medallions of monkfish à la
Mediterranean, and a couple of steaks for the dedicated carnivore.
Evening brings a four-course fixed-price menu, with several choices.
An oasis of good food along the quay.

GREYSTONES — The Hungry Monk

Greystones, Co Wicklow
Tel: (01) 287 5759   **£50**
Open: lunch Sun, dinner Tue-Sat (closed 25 Dec, Good Friday)
Meals served: lunch 12-8, dinner 7-11 (Sat à la carte only)

Host Pat Keown's first-floor restaurant has a monastic theme to the
decor and menu design, and a monastic tradition of open-door hospitality, but there's no hint of abstemiousness here, for portions are generous, the wine cellar is extensive and value-for-money exceptional. The
menu, though written in French, covers Europe quite widely, offering
Irish oak-smoked salmon (with freshly baked brown bread), Galway
mussels served Normandy-style, pasta in starter or main course-sized
portions (angel hair a speciality, of course!) duck with cherries, lamb's
kidneys dijonnaise, and trencherman-sized steaks all claiming your
attention. The extensive wine list, with an amazing range of house
wines available by the glass, not only covers Europe comprehensively
but also includes Bulgaria, the Lebanon and the New World; and there
are even over 25 half-bottle selections. Oh, and the list is naturally
entitled The Thirsty Monk!

HOWTH — King Sitric

East Pier, Harbour Road, Howth, Co Dublin
Tel: (01) 832 6729   Fax: (01) 839 2442   **£50**
Open: (lunch Seafood Bar 12-3 May-Sep only), dinner Mon-Sat
     (closed Bank Holidays, 10 days Jan, 10 days Easter)
Meals served: (lunch 12-3), dinner 6.30-11

King Sitric III is said to have established the first Catholic church in
Howth—now, some 900 years later, the name is more familiar as a destination restaurant for dedicated fish eaters. The harbourside setting
sets the scene, chef/patron Aidan MacManus does the rest, serving
spanking-fresh seafood with just the right amount of additional
enhancements—fresh Howth prawn salad with plain mayonnaise or
aïoli, grilled queen scallops on a bed of aubergines and tomatoes or—a
speciality—monkfish King Sitric: tossed with a julienne of vegetables in
a pastry case with hollandaise. More simple, traditional choices like
black sole meunière or colbert, lobster thermidor or simply grilled
jostle alongside a few meat dishes for carnivores.

INISTIOGE   The Motte

Inistioge, Co Kilkenny
Tel: (056) 58655   **£45**
Open: dinner daily (closed Bank Holidays, 1 wk Xmas)
Meals served: dinner only 7-10 (Sun to 9)

Pronounced "moat", this is an artistically devised,
intimate little place in one of the prettiest villages in
the country. Candlelight works to great effect in a
room with great character, providing the perfect
scenario for an excellent meal. For starters, you
might find hare terrine with cranberry and orange
sauce or tomato and mozzarella crouton among a
choice of four or five options. Main courses might
offer plaice with a crispy herb and pine nut crust,
boned poussin stuffed with garlic and herbs and
served with a black cherry sauce or T-bone steak
with mushroom and olive sauce. Then come some
simple excellent desserts: baked white chocolate
cheesecake or coffee praline ice cream with butter-

scotch sauce, along with a more trendy, complicated concoction which
goes by the name of chocagansa.

KANTURK   Assolas Country House

Kanturk, Co Cork
Tel: (029) 50015   *Fax:* (029) 50795   **£60**
Open: dinner daily (closed Nov-Mar)
Meals served: dinner 7-8.30

Home to the Bourke family for generations, this 17th-century house,
with its creeper-clad façade, provides excellent accommodation in nine
rooms and a menu based on home-grown and regional produce delivered with skill and imagination by Hazel Bourke, who with husband
Joe has headed the family operation since 1984. The setting is picturesque, with award-winning gardens leading down to the river bank
and the house provides a perfect base from which to tour the south.
Dinner is a set four-course menu featuring the likes of devilled lamb's
kidneys in mustard sauce, twice-baked soufflé, or roast breast of duck
with glazed apples.

KENMARE   d'Arcy's

Main Street, Kenmare, Co Kerry
Tel: (064) 41589   *Fax:* (064) 41589   **£45**
Open: dinner daily (Wed-Sat in winter) (closed 2 wks Feb)
Meals served: dinner 7-9 (from 5 in summer)

Matthew and Aileen d'Arcy's converted bank with just five comfortable
bedrooms and restaurant is a good place to stop over and enjoy some
fine food whilst visiting Kerry. Good sauces are a feature of Matthew's
cooking, be it beurre blanc with a timbale of chicken and leeks, honey
and thyme with roast loin of lamb, cider sauce to accompany breast of
turkey or mild curry flavours to complement baked salmon. Small, reasonable wine list.

KENMARE   Packies

Henry Street, Kenmare, Co Kerry
Tel: (064) 41508   **£45**
Open: dinner Mon-Sat (closed Nov-Easter)
Meals served: dinner only 5.30-10

Maura Foley's popular local bistro explores the eating trends she enjoys most, so you find monkfish in garlic and ginger with a Thai dipping sauce alongside pig's trotters, boned and rolled in herb crumbs and served with mustard pickles. Desserts are similarly eclectic—compote of winter fruits with ice cream, tiramisu, Irish farmhouse cheeses.

KENMARE   Park Hotel Kenmare

Kenmare, Co Kerry
Tel: (064) 41200   *Fax:* (064) 41402   **£80**
Open: lunch & dinner daily (closed mid Nov-Xmas,
    4 wks Jan-Easter)
Meals served: lunch 1-1.45, dinner 7-8.45

Built in 1897 by the Great Southern and Western Railway Company, the hotel is set on the edge of town in 11 acres of beautifully unspoilt grounds on the shores of the bay, with views of the mountains beyond. The hotel has 40 rooms and is renowned for its unique collection of fine art and furnishings, and for the warm, relaxed service and attention to detail of Francis Brennan, pictured, and his young team. Relax

in front of a crackling log fire or go for a walk around the grounds to soak up the beauty. Ask for a picnic lunch and head off to explore the area before returning to dine in the quiet luxury of this elegant hotel and sample chef Brian Cleere's innovative style. "Modern trends in a progressive Irish manner" describes Brian's approach, which is partly formed by years of training in Australia. Lobster from Kenmare Bay—the head waiter will be delighted to help you choose how you would like it prepared; pan-fried fillet of beef with a char-

treuse of oxtail, onion confit and red wine glaze; sea trout in oriental spices with a light soy butter sauce; or pan-fried breast of duck with duck liver pancakes and a thyme sauce. There's plenty of choice to tempt you. The new 18-hole golf course adjoining the hotel boasts a superb location, where the Sheen and Roughty rivers meet the Atlantic waters of Kenmare Bay.

KENMARE   Sheen Falls Lodge

Kenmare, Co Kerry
Tel: (064) 41600   *Fax:* (064) 41386   **£80**
Open: lunch Sun, dinner daily (closed Dec-Feb, open Xmas)
Meals served: lunch 1-2, dinner 7.30-9.30

To one side of this remarkable hotel are the Sheen
Falls; on the other, woodland and lush gardens
overlooking Kenmare Bay. Facilities are excellent
throughout—this is a modern hotel in that it has
only been open a few years and much of the building is new, though extensions to the original 17th-
century house have been done so carefully that the
old and the new blend successfully. The distinctive
yellow-painted façade of the hotel high above the
bay is floodlit at night, as are the Falls which can be
seen from the restaurant where chef Fergus Moore
serves up some imaginative and sophisticated
dishes. Watch out for the local wild salmon from the
Atlantic, which is cured and smoked on the

premises. Elsewhere on the menu you'll find delights such as fresh
local scallops scented with lime and ginger, and meaty options such as
noisettes of lamb with glazed shallots and roasted chestnuts. Finish
with a warm compote of cherries with a brûlée of sweet rice. They take
a particular pride in the cellars here and the wine list is at the top of the
range.

KILKENNY   Kilkenny Kitchen
Kilkenny Design Centre, Castle Street, Kilkenny, Co Kilkenny
Tel: (056) 22118   **£20**
Open: lunch daily (closed Good Friday, Xmas, Sun Jan-Easter)
Meals served: lunch 12-4, (light meals 9-5 (Sun from 10))
Good home cooking a stone's throw from the Castle—soups, pâtés, terrines and
hot dishes (braised steak, baked cod), plus crusty home-made breads and cakes.

KILKENNY   Lacken House

Dublin Road, Kilkenny, Co Kilkenny
Tel: (056) 61085   *Fax:* (056) 62435   **£50**
Open: dinner Tue-Sat (closed 1 wk Xmas)
Meals served: dinner only 7-10.30

This restaurant and guesthouse was built as a Dower House in 1847 for
Viscount Montmorency. In the 1920s it became a nursing home and
remained as such until 1983 when Eugene and Breda McSweeney
acquired it and adapted the house to its current use. The scene is set
by the word "welcome" carved into the stained glass of the front door.
Eight ensuite bedrooms are comfortably equipped and breakfasts are
definitely worth getting up for! Eugene's dinner menus, which change
frequently, take full advantage of good local produce—Clonakilty black
pudding with onion confit and wholegrain mustard sauce, poached
salmon and hake in a dill cream (accompanied by a platter of organic
vegetables) and a selection of their desserts (the Lacken House Plate)
are the sort of thing you'll be offered. Concise, reasonably priced wine
list.

KILLARNEY	Aghadoe Heights Hotel

Aghadoe, Killarney, Co Kerry
Tel: (064) 31766   *Fax:* (064) 31345 **£70**
Open: lunch & dinner daily
Meals served: lunch 12.15-2, dinner 7-9.30

A stunning location for Aghadoe, looking down from its heights to panoramic views of the lovely lakes and mountains of Killarney. Elegance is the watchword once inside, with graceful proportions and well-maintained decor—although the hotel is modern, there is still a feeling of timelessness (as you often experience in the Emerald Isle). The restaurant, Fredrick's at the Heights, serves local seasonal produce in daily or weekly changing menus—fresh crab, langoustine and asparagus on a dill yoghurt dressing; fillet of lamb on fresh spinach and roast shallots; apple, banana and pineapple fritters. As you might guess from the restaurant's name, this is a sister establishment to Fredrick's in Maidenhead (see England section).

KILLARNEY	Dingles Restauraunt

40 New Street, Killarney, Co Kerry
Tel: (064) 31079 **£45**
Open: dinner Mon-Sat (Bank Holiday Sun) (closed Xmas-Feb)
Meals served: 6-10.30

Simplicity and congeniality are the hallmarks of the Cunninghams' all-day restaurant. Stone floors, pews and open fires, and the warmest of welcomes from Gerry (who clearly loves his trade) kicks things off to a good start. The cooking, simple but excellent, is the domain of wife Marion. Soups, sandwiches, BLTs, burgers, omelettes and steaks are joined later in the day by dishes such as garlic-stuffed mussels, beef stroganoff, Irish stew and monkfish in Creole sauce.

KILLARNEY	Gaby's Seafood Restaurant

27 High Street, Killarney, Co Kerry
Tel: (064) 32519   *Fax:* (064) 32747 **£55**
Open: lunch Tue-Sat, dinner Mon-Sat (closed Feb)
Meals served: lunch 12.30-2.30, dinner 6-10

Geert Maes has been a part of the Killarney culinary scene for almost 20 years. His new premises are larger and provide a lot more scope, with split-level eating, a little garden at the back and proper little diners' bar at the front, a feature increasingly common in this part of the world. Home-made soups, sandwiches, seafood specials and the popular Gaby's beef stew provide informal eating at lunchtime. Dinner brings on line the extensive carte, which opens with wild Atlantic mussels, prawn and monkfish cassoulet and seafood cream soup. Various seafood platters, grilled lobster picked from the tank, Atlantic rock oysters, oakwood-smoked trout and speciality dishes such as lobster Gaby, seafood mosaic and grilled wild salmon steak follow. For meat-eaters, there are one or two steaks and Gaby's rack of lamb. Good wine list, with worldwide representation.

KILLARNEY   Strawberry Tree

24 Plunkett Street, Killarney, Co Kerry
Tel & Fax: (064) 32688   **£60**
Open: dinner daily (closed Jan-Feb)
Meals served: lunch by arrangement, dinner 6.30-10.30

New standards were set at this first-floor restaurant in 1993, with a total commitment to wild, free-range, organic produce. The decor is appropriately informal, with open stone and whitewashed walls, low ceilings and open fire, but elegant settings create a sophisticated air. Here, you can look forward to organic vegetable soups with excellent home-made breads and home-smoked salmon (smoked over oak and apple wood). This is traditional Irish cooking at its best, with dishes such as terrine of Killarney venison with wild elderberry sauce and smoked haddock chowder to start, followed by winter game pie, baked hake (fresh from Dingle), fresh crab cake made entirely of fresh white crabmeat, and the daily beef dish, which comes free-range from a local farm—"beef like it used to taste!", announces the menu proudly. Excellent coffee and petits fours. Early diners might take advantage of the £14.95 Early Bird menu (6.30-8pm). Evan Doyle's wine list completes the enjoyable experience here.

KILLORGLIN   Nick's Restaurant

Lower Bridge Street, Killorglin, Co Kerry
Tel: (066) 61219   *Fax:* (066) 61233   **£60**
Open: dinner Wed-Sun (closed Nov-Easter)
Meals served: dinner 6-10

Nick Foley's steak and seafood restaurant continues to do a roaring trade, a success based on the sound principle of good fresh food, served simply in convivial surroundings. The menu sections are called Temptations, Sea Treasures, Gourmet's Choice and Encores. But although meat eaters are given equal billing in the restaurant's subtitle, its still the seafood that's the star turn, and the more local, the better. Fresh Cromane mussels, Kerry oysters from the tank, Dingle Bay prawns in a cocktail or a salad, Laune salmon, poached and served with salad, lobsters from the tank—or the simple but superb seafood platter. Local cheeses and fresh fruit are just as tempting as the dessert trolley. Charming service led by Anne Foley, good wine list—in all a great place for good food and good company.

KINSALE   Blue Haven Hotel

3 Pearse Street, Kinsale, Co Cork
Tel: (021) 772209   *Fax:* (021) 774268   **£50**
Open: dinner daily (closed 25 Dec, 2 days midwwek in winter)
Meals served: dinner 7-10.30,
    (light meals conservatory: 10.30am-9.30pm, teas 3-5)

A small cosy hotel in the historic sea-angling centre of Kinsale. The
hotel has its own ocean-going angling boat, the Peggy G, complete with
expert skipper and rods and tackle for hire. Brian and Anne Cronin
have created a country house feel to the house, with local artists' work
on display, plenty of wood panelling, natural stone and open log fire.
The Haven Bar, a popular local haunt, serves food throughout the day,
with the emphasis, naturally, on shellfish and seafood. The restaurant
overlooking the courtyard garden has a strong maritime theme, continued on the plate by chef Stanley Matthews with dishes such as fisherman's platter, brill and scallop bake, oriental seafood kashmiri or
simple Dover sole on the bone. Meaty options offer hot wood-smoked
salmon, steaks and Mitchelstown venison with spicy port wine sauce.
Brian and Anne were invited some years ago by Bloomingdale's in New
York to represent Ireland and its cuisine in their Ireland exhibition.

KINSALE   Chez Jean-Marc

Lower O'Connell Street, Kinsale, Co Cork
Tel: (021) 774625   Fax: (021) 774680   **£50**
Open: lunch daily, dinner Mon-Sat (closed Xmas, Feb
    (open weekends), all Mon in winter)
Meals served: lunch 12.30-3 (Sun only, in winter),
    dinner 6.45-10.30 (winter 7-10)

Jean-Marc Tsai's repertoire is faithful to his name: this is classically-
based French cuisine with Oriental influences. The setting is cheerful
and cosy, with a rustic-style, beamed interior. Starters include traditional French onion soup, home-made chicken liver parfait, local
Rossmore mussels, oysters and dishes such as raviolis of lobster and
scallops. Main courses might feature Thai stir-fry, spicy duck with
orange and honey sauce, organic lamb or salmon fillet in puff pastry
served with a mushroom duxelle, shallots and Vermouth. Plenty of
choice, and a good selection of house wines together with a Taste of
Ireland menu for the more traditionally minded.

KINSALE   Man Friday

Scilly, Kinsale, Co Cork
Tel: (021) 772260   **£60**
Open: lunch by arrangement, dinner daily
    (Mon-Sat in winter) (closed 24-26 Dec)
Meals served: dinner 7-10

With views over the harbour, it's not surprising that seafood is the
name of the game here, served in a series of small interconnecting
rooms. Irish oak-smoked salmon, hot oysters with a delicate beurre
blanc, seafood chowder, escalopes of monkfish served with a prawn
sauce and black sole Colbert are typical of the range.

KINSALE   Max's Wine Bar

Main Street, Kinsale, Co Cork
Tel: (021) 772443   **£40**
Open: lunch & dinner daily (closed Nov-Feb)
Meals served: lunch 1-3, dinner 7-10.30

Max's actually belongs to Wendy Tisdall, who operates a menu including an early-bird selection at a very reasonable reduced price. A full
range of dishes includes the likes of mussels grilled with garlic butter
and mushrooms, duck pâté with plum sauce, salads, pasta, monkfish in
cream and tarragon sauce, breast of chicken poached with lemon, and
puddings such as chocolate rum mousse and banoffi pie. Deservedly
popular.

KINSALE   Old Presbytery

Cork Street, Kinsale, Co Cork
Tel: (021) 772027   **£40**
Open: dinner Mon-Sat (closed 1 wk Xmas)
Meals served: dinner 7.30-8.30

Good home cooking at this quaint little restaurant
with rooms in the middle of a fishing village, but
note, you can only enjoy it if you're actually a resident. The menu changes daily, with fish leading
the way. Ken and Cathleen Buggy turned their old
kitchen into a small, rustic dining room with lots of
character. Ken does the cooking, producing short,
simple menus which offer a choice of three dishes
at each stage. Soups, salads and pâtés to start, with
some unusual combinations, followed perhaps by
pot-roast chicken, escalope of beef and freshly
caught fish (turbot, brill, John Dory). Six traditional-style bedrooms are available for overnight
guests—big beds and Irish linen promise a good
night's sleep. Nearby fishing, sailing and golf.

LARAGH   Mitchell's of Laragh

The Old Schoolhouse, Laragh, Co Wicklow
Tel & Fax: (0404) 45302   **£35**
Open: all day daily (closed dinner Sun-lunch Wed in
    winter, Bank Holidays, 4 wks in winter)
Meals served: 9am-10pm (Sun to 9)

Margaret Mitchell's good home cooking has given a new lease of life to
the old schoolhouse. This is a smashing little place, close to
Glendalough with its beautiful lakes and monastic ruins—a major
tourist attraction in the area. Check it out, then retire to the comfort of
the Mitchells' lovingly restored house, to eat as little or as much as you
like. Enjoy dishes such as roast lamb with home-made mint jelly or
steak and kidney pie. Great breads, lovely puds, and afternoon teas are
all well worth trying. There are five rooms for overnight guests; and a
sitting room was due for completion as we went to press.

LETTERFRACK   Rosleague Manor

Letterfrack, Connemara, Co Galway
Tel: (095) 41101   *Fax:* (095) 41168   **£55**
Open: lunch & dinner daily (closed Nov-Easter)
Meals served: lunch 1-2.30, dinner 8-9.30 (Sun to 9)

The Foyles (brother and sister) offer a warm welcome at this elegant 20-bedroomed Regency manor surrounded by 30 acres of gardens overlooking Ballinakill Bay. Take the little path from the hotel down to the ocean's edge before returning to enjoy brother-in-law Nigel Rush's four-course dinner menu served at round antique tables under chandeliers. Fresh seafood, much of it caught from the hotel's own boat, home-grown vegetables and herbs from the garden together with delicious Connemara lamb and beef are the sort of raw ingredients used. Typical dishes could include potato and walnut soup, sautéed lamb's kidneys in port, grilled wild salmon with scallion butter, ray wings with black butter and pork with grain mustard and cider sauce. A wealth of activities can be arranged from the hotel including wind surfing, sailing, mountaineering, horse riding, golf and fishing—the boats at nearby Cleggan harbour make daily trips and excursions to the island of Inisboffin.

LIMERICK   Castletroy Park Hotel

Dublin Road, Limerick, Co Limerick
Tel: (061) 335566   *Fax:* (061) 331117   **£50**
Open: lunch Sun-Fri, dinner Mon-Sat (closed 24 & 25 Dec)
Meals served: lunch 12.30-2, dinner 7-9.30

The new Castletroy Park Hotel offers state-of-the-art conference and leisure facilities, and is ideally located just outside the town on the Dublin Road, in 14 acres of beautifully landscaped gardens overlooking the Clare Hills and the River Shannon. Well-designed and purpose-built, it has 107 rooms and lies at the entrance to the 500-acre Plassey Park, home of the University of Limerick, Ireland's youngest. The atmosphere within is warm, lush and welcoming, with a pretty conservatory lounge and the Merry Pedlar Pub in which to while away the hours over a pint or light meal (smoked salmon platter, all-American beef burger, chicken stroganoff). The main dining room, McLaughlin's, offers international and local dishes, and is the setting for an excellent buffet breakfast.

LIMERICK   Restaurant de La Fontaine

12 Upper Gerald Griffin Street, Limerick, Co Limerick
Tel: (061) 414461   *Fax:* (061) 411337   **£45**
Open: lunch Mon-Fri, dinner Mon-Sat (closed Bank Holidays)
Meals served: lunch 12.30-2.30, dinner 7-10

Unusual, first-floor restaurant in an old part of town, reached via wide carpeted stairs. A modern foyer-bar, furnished with the owner's collection of bric-a-brac (toy cars, bottles, etc), makes an intriguing entrance to what continues to feel a somewhat extraordinary experience. It's as if you've walked into a traditional country restaurant in France and chef Bernard Brousse cooks in robust classic country fashion to bring the whole experience to a harmonious conclusion. Dishes such as poultry

consommé, venison terrine or spinach and smoked salmon bavarois
are followed by slices of Burren lamb with provençal herbs or escalope
of wild salmon with dill sauce. The restaurant is named after the famed
French fabler, Jean de la Fontaine.

MALAHIDE   Bon Appetit

9 St James Terrace, Malahide, Dublin, Co Dublin
Tel: (01) 845 0314   **£45**
Open: lunch Mon-Fri, dinner Mon-Sat
  (closed Bank Holidays, 1 wk Xmas)
Meals served: lunch 12.30-2, dinner 7-11

Cosy restaurant in a Georgian terrace overlooking the estuary. Chef-
patron Patsy McGuirk offers a wide choice of classically-based French
dishes, making much use of local produce. East coast mussels
provençale, sautéed lamb's kidneys dijonnaise, Dingle Bay scallops
with bacon and saffron rice; followed by the likes of Carlingford lobster
Thermidor, crispy duck on potato stuffing with Grand Marnier sauce,
or grilled sirloin served plain or with garlic butter. Good wine list,
strong on France. The restaurant is only 15 minutes from Dublin airport, and has built up a loyal patronage in the five years since Patsy
moved in.

MALAHIDE   Roches Bistro
12 New Street, Malahide, Co Dublin
Tel: (01) 845 2777   *Fax:* (01) 324147   **£45**
Open: lunch Mon-Sat (Tue-Sat Jan-Jun), dinner Wed-Sat
  (Thu-Sat in winter)
  (closed Bank Holidays, 2 wks Jan)
Meals served: lunch 12-2.30, dinner 6-10.30
Typically French-style restaurant, specialising in home-baked breads and good
Irish farmhouse cheeses. Loaves can be purchased to take home.

MALLOW   Longueville House

Mallow, Co Cork
Tel: (022) 47156   *Fax:* (022) 47459   **£55**
Open: lunch & dinner daily (closed 20 Dec-mid Mar)
Meals served: lunch 12.30-2, dinner 7-9

Longueville has a splendid setting—200
hectares of private wooded estate overlooking the glorious Blackwater
Estuary—and the gracious Georgian
house also lives up to the location.
Moulded ceilings and fine rugs set the
scene in the entrance hall and drawing
room. Sixteen individually decorated
rooms, many with antiques, enjoy the
same high standards. In the (non-smoking) Presidents Dining Room, portraits
of former presidents of the Republic
grace the walls, while fine linen, china
and glassware grace the tables. The
house has belonged to the O'Callaghan
family for over 300 years and the present
incumbent of the kitchen, William
O'Callaghan, pictured, carries on a fine

family tradition, producing simple sounding but excellent tasting menus that take full advantage of good local produce. So you might enjoy a winter meal of terrine of chicken and bacon with a garden salad, fish broth, rack of Longueville lamb with a herb sauce, charlotte of coconut mousse and biscuit wrapped in kiwi slices, and coffee with home-made petits fours to finish. There's also a Surprise Tasting Menu, which puts you totally in William's hands, and of course a carte. Well-balanced, well-priced wine list, and super service in all departments from the caring O'Callaghans.

MOYCULLEN   Drimcong House Restaurant

Moycullen, Co Galway
Tel: (091) 85115   **£40**
Open: dinner Tue-Sat (closed Jan & Feb)
Meals served: dinner only 7-10.30

It's ten years since Gerry and Marie Galvin opened the doors of their small Georgian country house to the public and it didn't take long for the word to spread. Gerry cooks from a classical base, bringing in influences from as far afield as the Orient. Menus depend on the best of what's available locally—game in season, free-range poultry, local lamb and seafood, including oysters from nearby Galway Bay. Straightforwardly presented dishes, which might include seafood stir-fry, game sausage or mussel soup among starters; and main-course choices such as pan-fried venison with onion marmalade and red vermouth sauce, or grilled breast of chicken with pesto and lemon aiöli. Home-made breads are baked daily.

NAVAN   Ardboyne Hotel

Dublin Road, Navan, Co Meath
Tel: (046) 23119   Fax: (046) 22355   **£40**
Open: lunch & dinner daily (closed 24-27 Dec)
Meals served: lunch 12.30-2.30, dinner 5.30-10 (Sun to 9)

Just outside the town, this modern, 27-bedroomed hotel offers simple, practical accommodation. Bright, cheerful public rooms include a lounge and bar where snacks are served throughout the day. The restaurant offers a wide range of mostly traditional menus, including an Early Bird option, Chef's Recommendations, a tourist menu and à la carte. Plenty of everything in straightforward familiar style, from breakfast grills to snails with garlic butter.

NEWBAY   Newbay Country House

Newbay, Nr Wexford, Co Wexford
Tel: (053) 42779   Fax: (053) 46318   **£50**
Open: dinner Tue-Sat (closed mid Nov-mid Mar)
Meals served: dinner at 7.30

The emphasis at this small but impressive, six-bedroomed house is on good food, a warm welcome and comfort. The house is situated in its own grounds and woodland, and is totally private. Built in 1822, it incorporates a 14th-century castle and 17th-century farmhouse. Dinner, the work of owner Paul Drum, is served at 7.30pm in the elegant Georgian dining room, where wife Mientje attends to service. Everyone eats around the table together before retiring to the drawing room for post-dinner drinks. The no-choice dinner menu changes daily, depending on availability of fresh produce. Home-made bread and farmhouse cheeses to finish.

NEWMARKET-ON-FERGUS Dromoland Castle

Newmarket-on-Fergus, Co Clare
Tel: (061) 368144   *Fax:* (061) 363355   **£80**
Open: lunch & dinner daily
Meals served: lunch 12.30-2, dinner 7-10.30

A magnificent castle in a picturesque setting where you can enjoy golf, fishing, shooting, tennis or archery. Jean-Baptiste Molinari is a talented chef whose classic style produces dishes such as medallions of veal sweetbreads and kidney served with vegetable confit and potato salad in sherry sauce, or breast of chicken roasted and served with a ragoût of lentils and barley, or fillets of John Dory with sautéed artichokes and black olives in tomato and olive oil jus. A serious wine list to please all tastes.

NEWPORT   Newport House

Newport, Co Mayo
Tel: (098) 41222   *Fax:* (098) 41613   **£65**
Open: dinner daily (closed 7 Oct-18 Mar)
Meals served: dinner 7.30-9.30

A beautiful, creeper-clad Georgian house on the edge of the town, over-looking the Newport River and quay, surrounded by mountains, streams and moor. Many of the guests come for fishing, returning home in the evening with the day's catch, which is traditionally weighed and displayed in the hall, before they retire to the fisherman's bar to compare stories over a pint of Guinness or two. Owners Kieran and Thelma Thompson have furnished their 20-bedroomed house with style: the hall, with its sweeping staircase and upper gallery is fitted with hand-woven Connemara-made carpet; the upstairs drawing room boasts Regency-style mirrors and chandelier. Dinner is a six-course affair, making use of home-grown organic produce from the kitchen garden and regional produce—home-smoked salmon, Clew Bay oysters, local game and fish. Typical dishes include onion tartlet with tossed salad, rack of lamb with red wine and shallot sauce, and char-coal-grilled salmon steak with wild sorrel sauce.

OUGHTERARD   Currarevagh House

Oughterard, Connemara, Co Galway
Tel: (091) 82312   *Fax:* (091) 82731   **£40**
Open: dinner daily (closed Nov-Mar)
Meals served: dinner only at 8

A lovely setting on the shores of Lough Corrib and a warm welcome from the Hodgsons, resident hosts for about 30 years, set you up when you arrive at this lovely Victorian manor house, complete with its own park, woods and gardens. Comfortable lounges and bedrooms (no intrusive TVs or phones!) enhance the feeling of wellbeing which is then completed by a splendid five-course dinner carefully prepared by June Hodgson. There's no choice but the whole event is well balanced so this should be no hardship! A typical menu might be game broth, then prawn and scallop mornay, roast rack of lamb served with potato loaves and stir-fry vegetables, a light lime soufflé, Irish farmhouse cheeses and finally, coffee. Lovely early morning lake views and a hearty breakfast see you on your way when you eventually decide to leave.

OYSTERHAVEN   The Oystercatcher

Oysterhaven, Nr Kinsale, Co Cork
Tel: (021) 770822   **£55**
Open: lunch by arrangement for parties of 7 or more,
     dinner daily
Meals served: dinner 7-9.30 (bookings only in winter)

The menus change with the seasons at the Pattersons' attractive, creekside, cottage restaurant, where the outside walls are clad with flowers. Menus show a modern mind at work, though the menu is classically-based. Oysters play a big role, appearing on their own, in sauces, and even in sausage form with saffron sauce. Elsewhere on the starter list, you might find tiger prawns in pastry with a nutty chili dip or poached free-range eggs topped with caviar and flambéed with vodka. Typical main courses include plenty of game, such as marinated wild boar with apples or roast partridge with wild mushrooms, chateaubriand with Madeira sauce or oven-baked sole. Puds are good and traditional with profiteroles, crème brûlée and pavlova typical of the range, but you might prefer a savoury at this stage: choose from the likes of angels or devils on horseback, garlic mushrooms on toast or Scotch woodcock.

RATHMULLAN   Rathmullan House

Rathmullan, Nr Letterkenny, Co Donegal
Tel: (074) 58188   *Fax:* (074) 58200   **£45**
Open: lunch Sun, dinner daily (closed Nov-mid Mar)
Meals served: lunch 1-1.45, dinner 7.30-8.45

Stylish Georgian house, with 23 bedrooms and lovely gardens which lead down to the beaches of Loch Swilly. In fact, deserted sandy beaches are in plentiful supply in this remote north-west corner of Ireland. For those who don't like sand, the hotel boasts a splendid pool complex, complete with Egyptian-style baths filled with ionised salt water. Bob and Robin Wheeler have been running the hotel for the past three decades, in friendly, informal style, offering a range of accommodation from suites and family rooms to budget standard. Liam McCormick's delightful tent-draped dining room overlooking the garden offers an excellent hors d'oeuvres buffet, plenty of seafood, and good vegetarian options. Great breakfasts too.

RATHNEW — Tinakilly House

Rathnew, Wicklow, Co Wicklow
Tel: (0404) 69274   *Fax:* (0404) 67806 **£65**
Open: lunch & dinner daily
Meals served: lunch 12.30-2, dinner 7.30-9

Thirty miles south of Dublin, this 29-bedroomed Victorian mansion is set in seven acres of gardens which sweep down to the Irish Sea. The Powers have lovingly restored and extended the house, with period furnishing throughout; some of the rooms boast four-posters, many have breathtaking coastal views, and ground-floor rooms have direct access to the garden. Chef John Moloney's daily-changing set menus offer limited choice but they are well-conceived and imaginative: cream of fennel and Pernod soup; farmed chicken with wild mushroom mousse; Barbary duck with cassis and lemon zest; fillets of brill with champagne and Sevruga caviar. Local produce plays a large part in what's on offer; fruit and vegetables come from the hotel garden; bread is homemade by owner Bee Power, and long may she continue to do so, for it is excellent. This country restaurant of some renown is well deserving of its reputation.

ROSSES POINT — The Moorings

Rosses Point, Co Sligo
Tel: (071) 77112 **£35**
Open: lunch Sun, dinner daily
   (Tue-Sun winter) (closed 1 wk winter)
Meals served: lunch Sun 12.30-2.30, dinner 5.30-9.30

With so much in its favour, it's no surprise that this cosy, beamed restaurant, in a seaside setting looking out over Sligo Bay, is popular. Seafood is central on a menu which features many traditional old favourites and prices are good. Galway Bay oysters, scallops, grilled trout with toasted almonds, deep-fried scampi, lobster mornay —these are just some of the familiar sights. Meat dishes follow like pattern, with beef stroganoff, chicken or prawn curry and various steaks (naturel, au poivre and served with parsley butter) among the list. Lighter appetites can be satisfied with a salad—smoked salmon, fresh salmon, prawn or chicken. Good straightforward, no-nonsense cooking with great appeal, particularly on Sundays at lunchtime.

ROUNDWOOD — Roundwood Inn

Roundwood, Co Wicklow
Tel: (01) 281 8107 **£50**
Open: lunch Tue-Sun, dinner Tue-Sat (closed 25 Dec, Good Friday)
Meals served: lunch 1-2.30, dinner 7.30-9.30 (Sat to 10)
17th-century inn furnished in traditional style, run by Jürgen and Aine Schwalm. Good range of Irish farmhouse cheeses.

SCOTSHOUSE   Hilton Park

Scotshouse, Nr Clones, Co Monaghan
Tel: (047) 56007   Fax: (047) 56033   **£55**
Open: dinner daily (closed Oct-Easter)
Meals served: dinner 8-9.30

The eighth generation of the Madden family are currently hosts at
Hilton Park, a 600-acre estate usefully located about two hours from
either Dublin or Belfast airports. The acreage includes no fewer than
three lakes, a nine-hole golf course, and plenty of natural woodland,
making it a popular destination for holiday makers who enjoy the outdoor life. There's a good level of hospitality offered by the Maddens,
and good county-house-style cooking on Lucy's five-course dinner
menus which make good use of local ingredients, some from the
estate, and specialise in an amazing range of Irish farmhouse cheeses.
Excellent breakfasts, too, with several freshly home baked breads to
set you up for the day.

SHANAGARRY   Ballymaloe House

Shanagarry, Co Cork
Tel: (021) 652531   *Fax:* (021) 652021   **£70**
Open: lunch & dinner daily (closed 24-26 Dec)
Meals served: lunch 12.30-2 (Sun at 1), dinner 7-9.30,
    Sun buffet only at 7.30

Ivan and Myrtle Allen and family are renowned for their hospitality.
This 30-bedroomed hotel in the middle of a 400-acre working farm
began life back in the 14th century (check out the surviving keep) as a
castle and was later adapted to a farmhouse. The farm is just 2 miles
from the coast, from the little fishing village of Ballycotton: the location
is superb. But the real charm here lies with the family and the relaxed
informal air that pervades throughout the house. Family and locals are
on hand to serve the meals, and Myrtle rules the roost in the kitchen,
and has inspired many a young chef on the road to success. Menus
change nightly, depending on what's best.
Vegetables and salads are picked fresh each day
and the farm supplies Myrtle with most of her
needs, though waiting for the boats to come in
to see what they have brought can result in a
number of surprises. The cooking is simple but
excellent. This is good honest Irish and French
country cooking. Breakfasts are excellent,
with locally smoked bacon and free-range
eggs, local honey, home-made marmalade
and breads. Lunchtime brings a buffet, or
you can take a tray-lunch out on to the
terrace or down to the pool. Packed
lunches are also provided on request.
This is a great place for children, who
can join Myrtle's grandchildren down by
the kiddies' pool, in the sandpit or for a
tour around the farm. Bedrooms are
divided between the main house, where
they're traditional, and converted outhouses
which provide pretty cottage-style rooms.

Biography

Myrtle Allen

Apart from attending a local technical school as a young girl Myrtle Allen is virtually self-taught. She's always devoured cookery books, and apart from looking after her growing family and giving friends dinner, her first move was a column in the Irish Farmer's Journal. Finally Myrtle opened her restaurant in Ballymaloe House and called it the Yeats Room. She has always adopted a very egalitarian approach, treating staff and family alike, avoiding hierarchies and making the house no hushed shrine to gastronomy but a living, thriving, healthy family enterprise. She almost single handedly put Irish food on the international map.

SPIDDAL   Boluisce Seafood Bar

Spiddal Village, Connemara, Co Galway
Tel: (091) 83286   *Fax:* (091) 83285   **£35**
Open: all day daily (closed lunch Sun, 24-26 Dec)
Meals served: 12-10

Family-run seafood bar and restaurant—in the hands of the same family for over 20 years. The ground-floor bar offers a wide range of seafood snacks and light meals; upstairs is more formal, though still altogether relaxed. Oysters come natural or baked in herb butter; alternatives include seafood chowder, lobster thermidor or the West Coast platter. Plenty of choice, with vegetarians and steak-eaters also well provided for. If you're wondering, Boluisce means a small patch of grazing beside water -how appropriate!

STRAFFAN   Kildare Hotel

Straffan, Co Kildare
Tel: (01) 6273333   *Fax:* (01) 6273312   **£80**
Open: lunch Sun-Fri, dinner daily
Meals served: lunch 12.30-2, dinner 7-10

The River Liffey runs through the grounds of this 45-bedroomed hotel and country club, known locally as the K Club. The original house has been carefully extended and furnished throughout in sumptuously opulent style, with fine period antiques and paintings, with several by Irish painter Jack B Yeats as well as a fine facsimile edition of the Book of Kells, published in co-operation with Trinity College, Dublin, where the original is closely guarded. Accommodation includes a number of self-contained apartments and a lodge, located in the more private setting of the courtyard annexe. The gardens are a horticulturist's dream, with splendid trees from all over the world. Two restaurants, one in the K Club, the other, the main hotel dining room, the Byerley Turk (named after the Arab stallion) offer plenty of choice. At the centre of the country club is the 18-hole golf course designed by Arnold Palmer; alternatively you can take advantage of the fishing rights on the Liffey, and nearby lakes.

| **SWORDS** | **Old Schoolhouse** |

Coolbanagher, Swords, Co Dublin
Tel: (01) 840 4160   *Fax:* (01) 840 5060   **£50**
Open: lunch Mon-Fri, dinner Mon-Sat (closed Bank Holidays)
Meals served: lunch 12.30-2.30, dinner 6.30-10.30
Bistro-style cooking in a friendly setting. Soups are all home made and desserts are a high point.

THOMASTOWN — Mount Juliet Hotel

Mount Juliet, Thomastown, Co Kilkenny
Tel: (056) 24455   *Fax:* (056) 24522   **£60**
Open: dinner daily
Meals served: dinner 7-10

An impressive 18th-century house surrounded by 1500 acres of formal landscaped gardens through which the Kings and Nore rivers flow. The hotel boasts a golf academy and superb course designed by Jack Nicklaus, an equestrian centre, new leisure complex and one of the country's oldest cricket clubs. There's all-day brasserie-style eating in the Hunter's Yard restaurant, which is very popular for Sunday lunch, or you can opt for the more sedate alternative in the Lady Helen dining room where chef Rory Morahan follows the art of traditional Celtic cuisine, based on adapting old recipes to modern ingredients and trends. Typical dishes from Rory's stable might include a saffron-scented minestrone of smoked salmon and seafood, followed by Irish coastal stew or Wicklow lamb with a light provençal jus. Various char-grilled steaks (salmon, black sole, lamb, beef and veal) are grilled over mesquite and apple. Good vegetarian options such as Oriental-style pancakes or layered pease pudding. Grand wine list.

TUAM — Cré na Cille

High Street, Tuam, Co Galway
Tel: (093) 28232   **£45**
Open: lunch & dinner Mon-Sat (closed Bank Holidays, 24-27 Dec)
Meals served: lunch 12.30-2.30, dinner 6-10

Bustling and businesslike at lunchtime, this attractive little restaurant on the high street takes on a softer, more sedate air in the evening. Cathal Reynolds uses local produce to good effect in uncomplicated, well-balanced menus. Smoked salmon and whisky pâté, grilled oysters, mussels and pan-fried Irish brie with vermouth sauce join seafood chowder (a house speciality) on the starters menu. Main courses offer a wide choice of fish, poultry and meat: black sole meunière, chicken supreme, grilled breast of Barbary duck with cherry and liqueur sauce, sauté of peppered beef fillet or stroganoff are typical of the range. Lunches are simpler, with chowder leading the way, followed by seafood salad, fried fillet of sole or roast lamb.

WATERFORD   Dwyer's Restaurant

8 Mary Street, Waterford, Co Waterford
Tel: (051) 77478   **£30**
Open: dinner Mon-Sat (closed 1 wk Xmas, Good Friday, 2 wks Jul)
Meals served: dinner 6-10 (set dinner 6-7.30)

A former barracks is the setting for some excellent cooking by Martin
Dwyer. Situated in a back street close to the bridge, this restaurant is
decorated in pastel shades, with background classical music setting the
tone. Martin provides a concise carte and well-planned set menus of
pan-European influences. Pork fillet stuffed with black pudding and
apple or roast cod with garlic crust and tomato coulis might feature
together on the set menu. The carte is more adventurous, with smoked
salmon soufflé en croute, mushroom and blue cheese pirozhki (little
Russian pies) and medallions of fillet steak with onion and thyme leaf
sauce, rounded off by walnut tart, three-chocolate marquise or Irish
coffee ice cream.

WATERFORD   Waterford Castle

The Island, Ballinakill, Waterford, Co Waterford
Tel: (051) 78203   *Fax:* (051) 79316   **£70**
Open: lunch & dinner
Meals served: lunch 12.30-2, dinner 7-10 (Sun to 9)

Surrounded by parkland on an island reached only by car ferry, this
splendidly restored 18th-century castle has 19 rooms. Inside, not surprisingly, all is grand, with stone carving, wood panelling, the
Fitzgerald coat of arms here and there (the castle was once home of
Edward Fitzgerald), Regency-style furnishing and crested plates in the
dining room. Some of the rooms have four-posters and most enjoy
lovely views of the park and water. Lunch and dinner menus offer
plenty of choice and menus change daily. Typical dishes from chef Paul
McCluskey include carrot soup with bacon, Dunmore East black sole
meunière, Atlantic scallops provençale and sirloin steak with honey
and green peppercorns. The golf and country club, which shares the
island (same owners), offers an extensive range of sporting activities,
and you may even be able to arrange a game of polo at nearby Whitby
estate.

All in all, a very special place to stay.

WICKLOW   Old Rectory

Wicklow, Co Wicklow
Tel: (0404) 67048   *Fax:* (0404) 69181   **£55**
Open: dinner daily (closed Nov-Easter)
Meals served: dinner at 8

Paul and Linda Saunders offer a warm welcome at their pink-washed early Victorian country house, lovingly restored, furnished with antiques and with six rooms individually tailored to guests' needs. Their idea of pampering even runs to a Champagne Swiss Breakfast in Bed! Linda's cooking is nothing if not inventive—themed dinners could be floral (flowers of plants and herbs starring in or at least featuring in every single dish), or gourmet (light quenelles of wild salmon trout with a Mediterranean tomato and herb sauce, pheasant en croute, chocolate and Cointreau mousse with candied oranges); but always take full advantage of good, local produce. Paul's wine list is a perfect foil to the cooking.

YOUGHAL   Aherne's Seafood Restaurant

163 North Main Street, Youghal, Co Cork
Tel: (024) 92424   *Fax:* (024) 93633   **£45**
Open: lunch & dinner daily (closed 5 dys Xmas)
Meals served: lunch 12.30-2.15 (Sun to 1.45),
    dinner 6.30-9.30, (bar food 11-10.30)

Pronounced "yawl", this historic walled port is home to one of the best seafood restaurants in the country. Owners the Fitzgibbons are now into their third generation at this renowned 50-seater bar and restaurant which specialises in the freshest of the local catch—lobster, prawns, turbot, sole, salmon, monkfish, crab, mussels and clams. Menus (both à la carte and set) are changed daily; lighter meals—native flat or rock oysters, seafood chowder, pasta and pies, sandwiches and salads—are served in the two bar areas. Ten stylishly-furnished rooms are available for overnight guests, and breakfasts are excellent. Open turf fires, lots of wood panelling and antiques about the place create a warm and cosy feel.

Hotel Groups

We have listed below, as useful numbers for the frequent traveller, some of the main hotel groups that we recommend.

Copthorne Hotels
Head Office: Victoria House, Victoria Road, Horley, Surrey RH6 7AF
Tel 01293 772288 Fax 01293 772345
Reservations: 0800 414741
12 UK hotels, primarily business but some suitable for family weekend breaks.

De Vere Hotels
Head Office: De Vere House, Chester Road, Daresbury, Warrington, Cheshire WA4 4BN
Reservations: Tel 01925 265050 Fax 01925 601264
Individual hotels ranging in style, with high standards of service, comfort and facilities.

Forte Hotels
Head Office: Forte Hotels (Exclusive, Grand, Heritage, Crest, Posthouse), 166 High Holborn London WC1V 6TT 0171-836 7744
Central Reservations (local call cost): 01345 404040 (leisure breaks) Fax 01296 81391. Business Guarantee Line: Freephone 0800 404040.
Inclusive packages: 01345 543555

Forte Exclusive, Grand & Heritage
Reservations: (local call cost) 01345 404040

World of Forte
Head Office: Great West House, Great West Road, Brentford, Middlesex TW8 9DF (World of Forte) Tel 0181-568 4540
Reservations: (local call cost) 01345 404040

Forte Crest
Reservations: (local call cost) 01345 404040

Forte Posthouse
Reservations: 0800 404040

Forte Travelodge
Head Office: Unit 2, Cartel Business Centre, Stroudley Road, Basingstoke, Hampshire RG24 8FW Tel 01256 812828
Travelodge Reservations: 0800 850950

Granada Lodges
Head Office: Toddington Service Area, M1 Service Area Southbound, Toddington, Near Dunstable, Bedfordshire LU5 6HR
Tel 01525 873881 Fax 01525 875358
Reservations: 0800 555 300 (24hr 7 days)
Located close to main routes, there are 26 hotels offering budget accommodation.

Hilton Hotels
Head Office: Hilton International Hotels (UK), Chancel House, Neasden Lane, London NW10 2XE Tel 0181-459 8031
Hilton National (UK), Millbuck House, Clarendon Road, Watford, Herts WD1 1DN Tel 01923 246464
Hilton UK Reservations, PO Box 137, Watford, Herts WD1 1DN
Reservations: Tel 01923 238877 Fax 01923 815594
Conference Reservations Tel 01923 250222
Now a combination of Hilton International (London-based), 25 Hilton National, and a further eight associate hotels around the country.

Holiday Inns
European Head Office Woluwe Office Park 1, Rue Neerveld 101, 1200
Brussels, Belgium
Tel 010 32 2 773 5511 Fax 010 32 2 772 0272
Holiday Inn Worldwide Reservations: Freephone Tel 0800 897 121 Fax: Guest
relations Tel 010 31 020 606 5456
UK: Area Director, c/o Holiday Inn Crowne Plaza, Stockley Road, West Drayton,
Middlesex UB7 9NA 01895 445555
Good leisure facilities, well-equipped conference rooms offered at both the top of the
range and standard Holiday Inns.

Jarvis Hotels
Head Office: Wye House, London Road, High Wycombe, Buckinghamshire
HP11 1LH
Tel 01494 473800 Fax 01494 471666
Linkline Reservations: (local call cost) Tel 01345 581 237 Fax 0171-589 8193
Conference Reservations: Tel 0171-581 3466 Fax 0171-589 8193
Fifth largest hotel operator in UK, offering nationwide hotels in the middle-range.

Marriott Hotels
Scott's Hotels Limited, Executive Office, Ditton Road, Langley,
Berkshire SL3 8PT
Tel 01753 544255 Fax 017153 585484
Worldwide Reservations: Freephone (UK) Tel 0800 221 222 Fax 0171-591 1128
Conferences & Groups Tel 0171-591 1100 Fax 0171-591 1128
Caters for the business market (during the week) and family business (weekends).

Mount Charlotte Thistle Hotels
Head Office: Mount Charlotte Thistle Hotels, 2 The Calls, Leeds, West Yorkshire
LS2 7JU
Tel 0113 2439111
Central Reservations: Tel 0171-937 8033 Fax 0171-938 3658
Highlife Shortbreaks Reservations: Freephone 0800 700 400
National Conference Sales: Tel 0171-938 1755 Fax 0171-938 3674
One of the most widespread in the UK, with 112 hotels ranging from the Tower Thistle
at Tower Bridge to the country house-style Cannizaro House in Wimbledon.

Novotel
Head Office: Novotel UK, 1 Shortlands, Hammersmith, London W6 8DR
Tel 0181-748 4580 Fax 0181-741 0672
Resinter Reservations: 0171-724 1000
18 hotels in the UK found close to motorway junctions and on the outskirts of cities.

Queens Moat Houses
Head Office: Queens Court, 9 Eastern Road, Romford, Essex RM1 3NG
Tel 01708 730522 Fax 01708 762691
Reservations: Tel Freephone 0800 289 330/331/332 Fax 01708 761033
Diverse range of 100 plus hotels.

Shire Inns
Head Office: Shire Inns Ltd, Colne Road, Reedley, Burnley,
Lancashire BB10 2NG
Tel 01282 414141 Fax 01282 415322
Elegant, small group of hotels catering to both business and leisure trade.

Stakis Hotels
Head Office: 3 Atlantic Quay, York Street, Glasgow G2 8GH
Tel 0141-221 0000 Fax 0141-204 1111
Hotel Reservations: Freephone 0800 262 626 Fax 0141-304 1111
Conference Call: Freephone 0800 833 900
Over 30 hotels throughout the UK, many found close to main business centres and
routes, some in country settings.

Swallow Hotels
Head Office: Swallow House, 19 Parsons Road, Washington,
Tyne & Wear NE37 1QS
Tel 0191-419 4545 Fax 0191-415 1888
Central Reservations: Tel 0191-419 4666 Fax 0191-415 1777
35 hotels in this northern-based chain, with some new hotels in the south.

Index